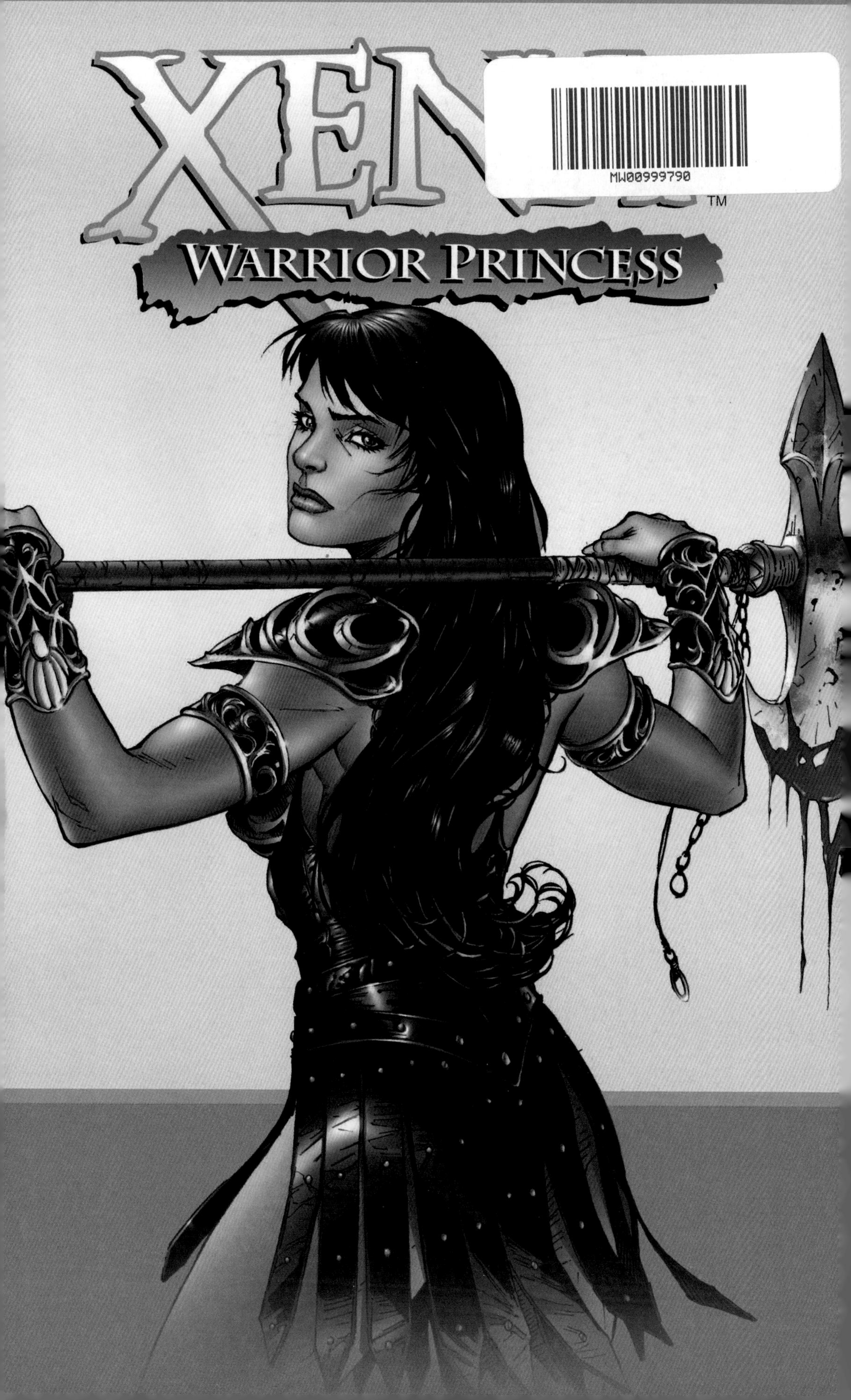
WARRIOR PRINCESS

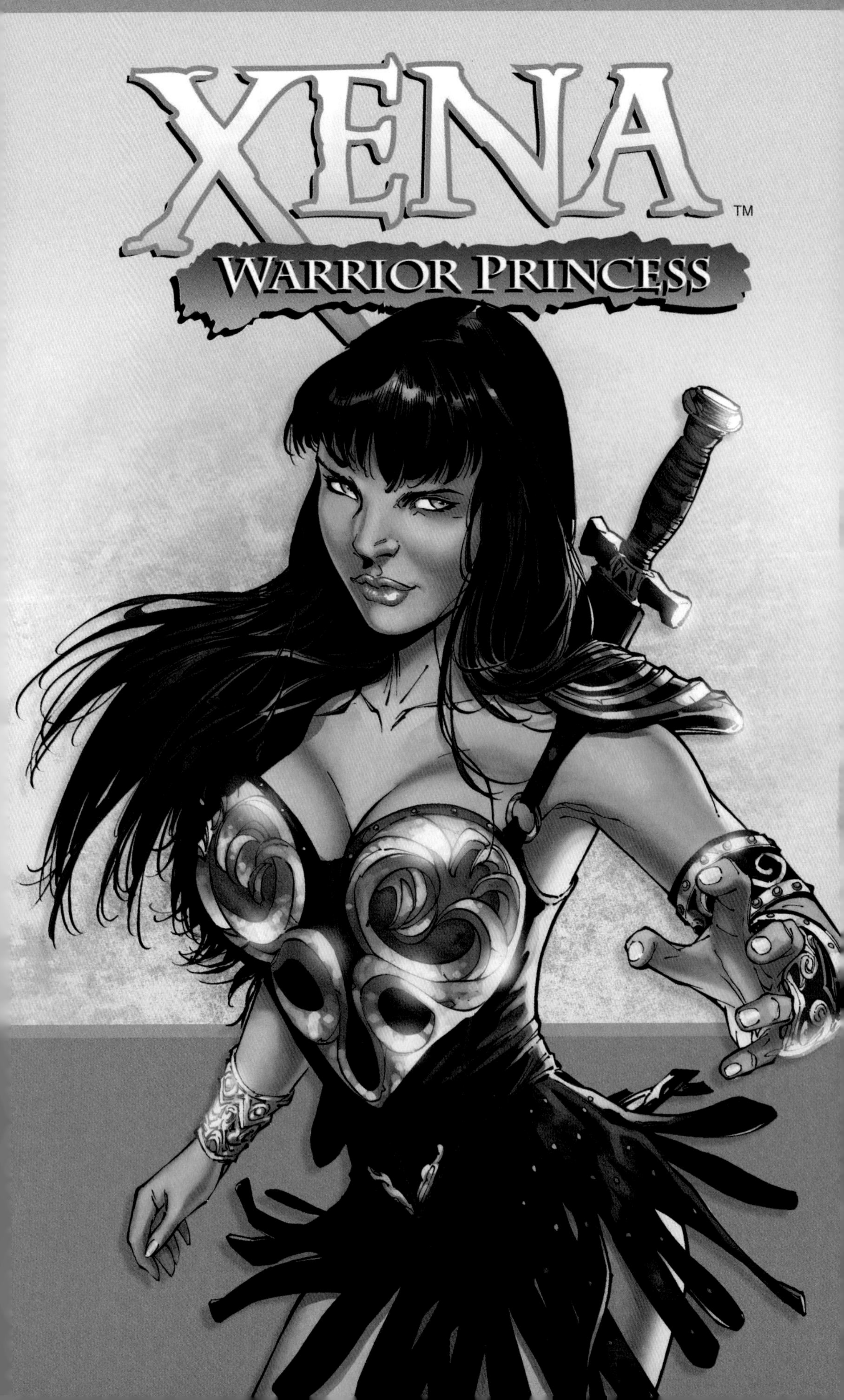
XENA™
WARRIOR PRINCESS

CONTEST OF PANTHEONS

WRITER: JOHN LAYMAN

ARTIST: FABIANO NEVES

COLORISTS: RICHARD ISANOVE (ISSUE #1),
CHRIS GARCIA (ISSUE #2-4)

LETTERER: SIMON BOWLAND

DARK XENA

WRITER: JOHN LAYMAN

ARTIST: NOAH SALONGA

COLORISTS: CHRIS GARCIA (ISSUE #1),
CARLOS HERNANDEZ OF INLIGHT STUDIO (ISSUE #2-4)

LETTERER: SIMON BOWLAND

STRANGE VISITOR

WRITER: KEITH CHAMPAGNE

ARTIST: NOAH SALONGA

COLORIST: CHRIS GARCIA

LETTERER: SIMON BOWLAND

COLLECTION COVER ARTIST: STJEPAN SEJIC

COLLECTION DESIGN BY: BILL TORTOLINI

SPECIAL THANKS TO:
JASON MCNAUGHTON AND LIZ UMEDA,
UNIVERSAL STUDIOS LICENSING

k Barrucci, CEO / Publisher
n Collado, President / COO

e Rybandt, Executive Editor
tt Idelson, Senior Editor
hony Marques, Associate Editor
in Ketner, Editorial Assistant

on Ullmeyer, Art Director
off Harkins, Senior Graphic Designer
hleen Heard, Graphic Designer
xis Persson, Production Artist

is Caniano, Digital Associate
hel Kilbury, Digital Assistant

ndon Dante Primavera, V.P. of IT and Operations
h Young, Director of Business Development

n Payne, V.P. of Sales and Marketing
th Davidsen, Marketing Director
O'Connell, Sales Manager

DYNAMITE f ⊙ t 𝕐 YouTube

Online at www.DYNAMITE.com | On Facebook /Dynamitecomics
On Instagram @Dynamitecomics | On Tumblr dynamitecomics.tumblr.com
On Twitter @dynamitecomics | On YouTube /Dynamitecomics

ISBN13: 978-1-5241-0251-7

For information regarding press, media rights, foreign rights, licensing, promotions, and advertising e-mail: marketing@dynamite.com

"IN A TIME OF ANCIENT GODS, WARLORDS, AND KINGS,
A LAND IN TURMOIL CRIED OUT FOR A HERO.
SHE WAS XENA, A MIGHTY PRINCESS FORGED IN BATTLE.
THE POWER, THE PASSION, THE DANGER...
HER COURAGE WOULD CHANGE THE WORLD!"

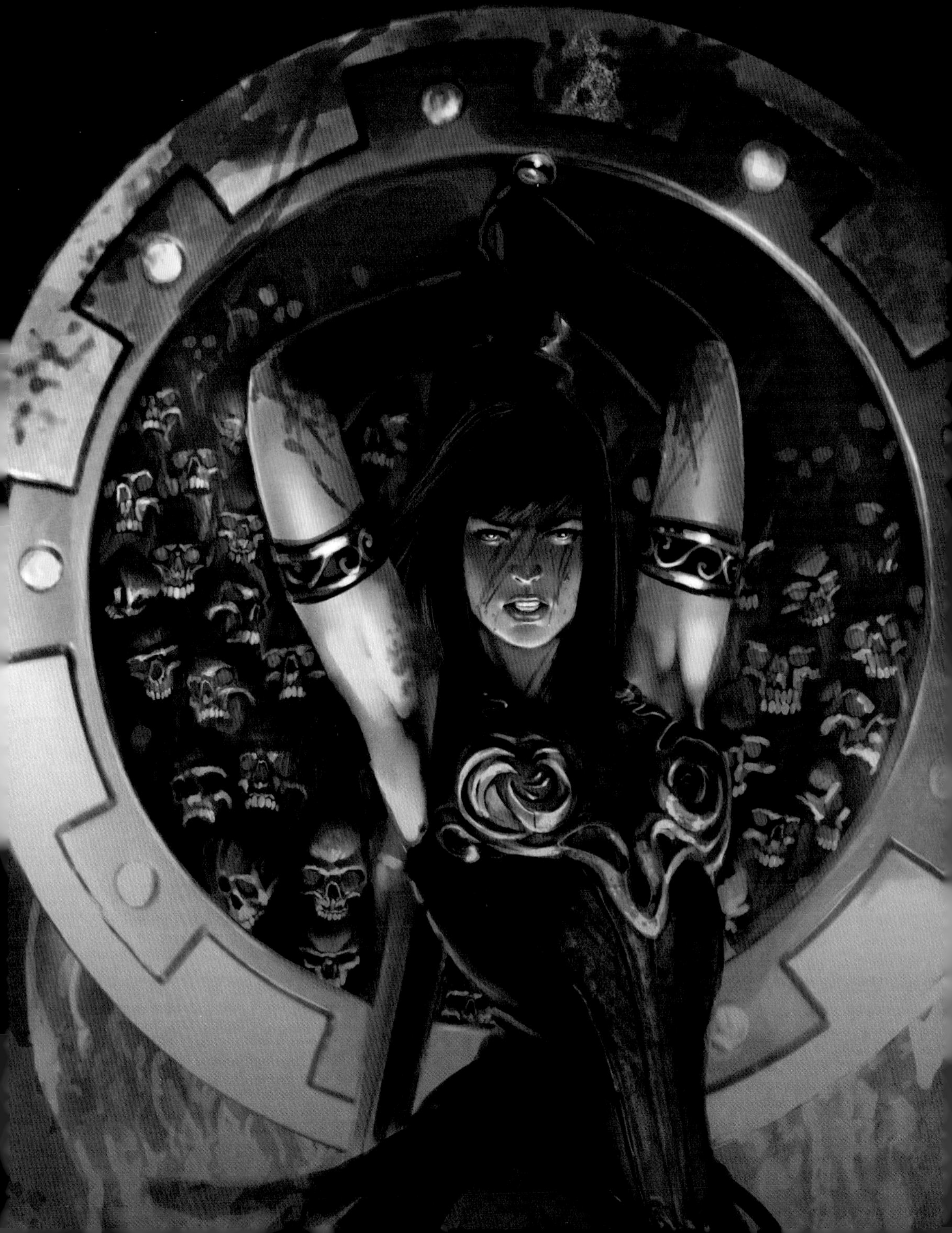

CONTEST OF PANTHEONS CHAPTER ONE

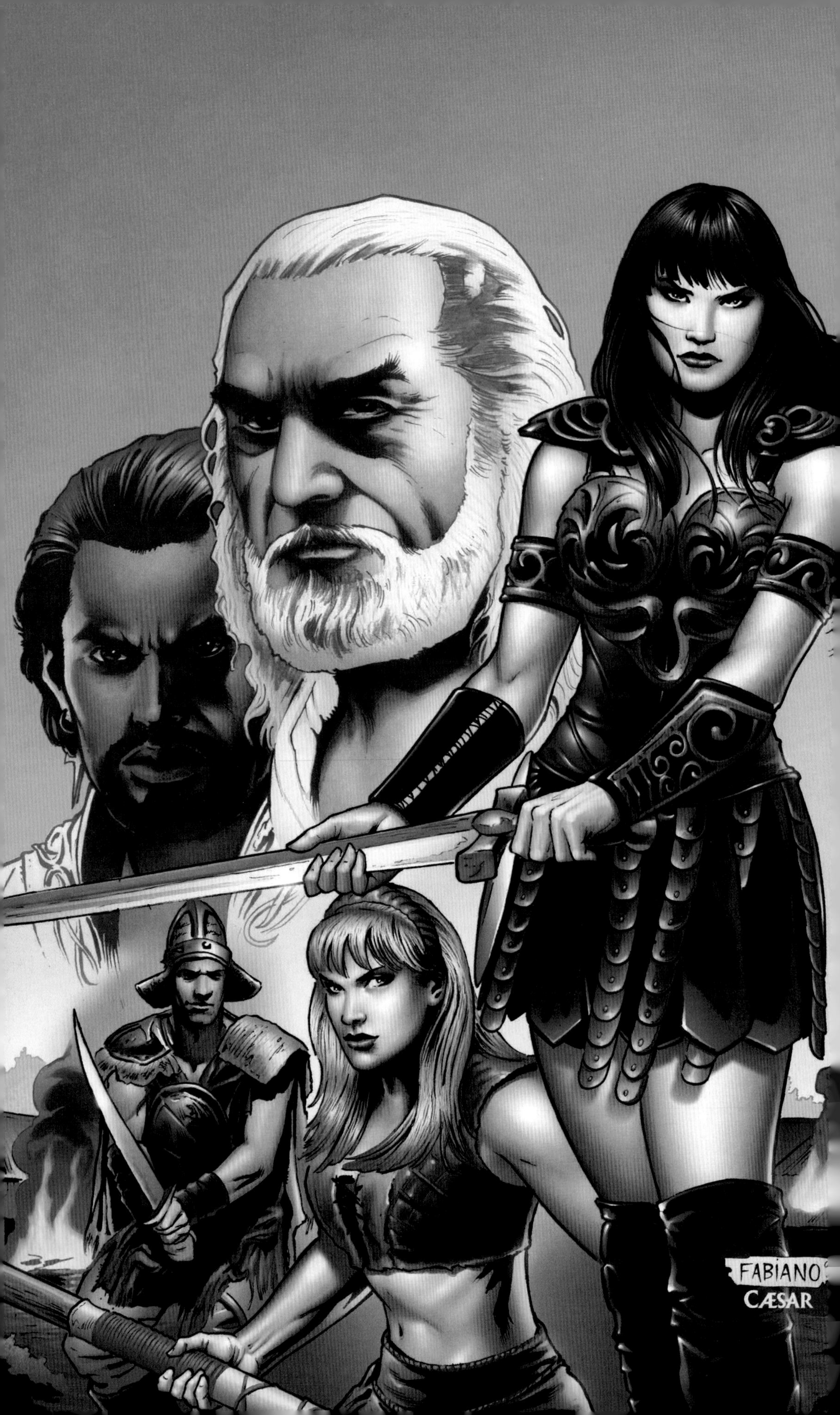
FABIANO
CÆSAR

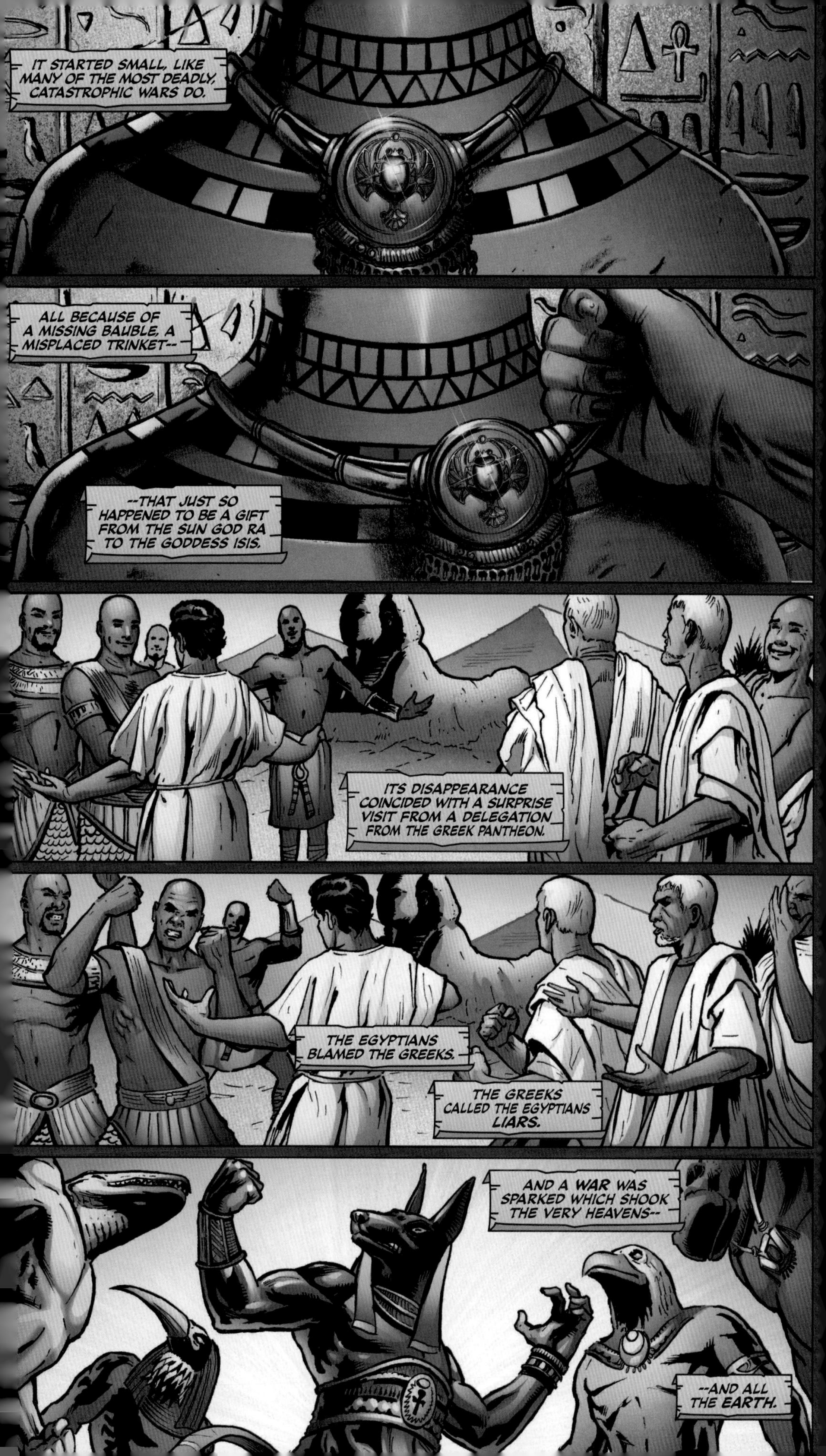
IT STARTED SMALL, LIKE MANY OF THE MOST DEADLY, CATASTROPHIC WARS DO.
ALL BECAUSE OF A MISSING BAUBLE, A MISPLACED TRINKET--
--THAT JUST SO HAPPENED TO BE A GIFT FROM THE SUN GOD RA TO THE GODDESS ISIS.
ITS DISAPPEARANCE COINCIDED WITH A SURPRISE VISIT FROM A DELEGATION FROM THE GREEK PANTHEON.
THE EGYPTIANS BLAMED THE GREEKS.
THE GREEKS CALLED THE EGYPTIANS LIARS.
AND A WAR WAS SPARKED WHICH SHOOK THE VERY HEAVENS--
--AND ALL THE EARTH.

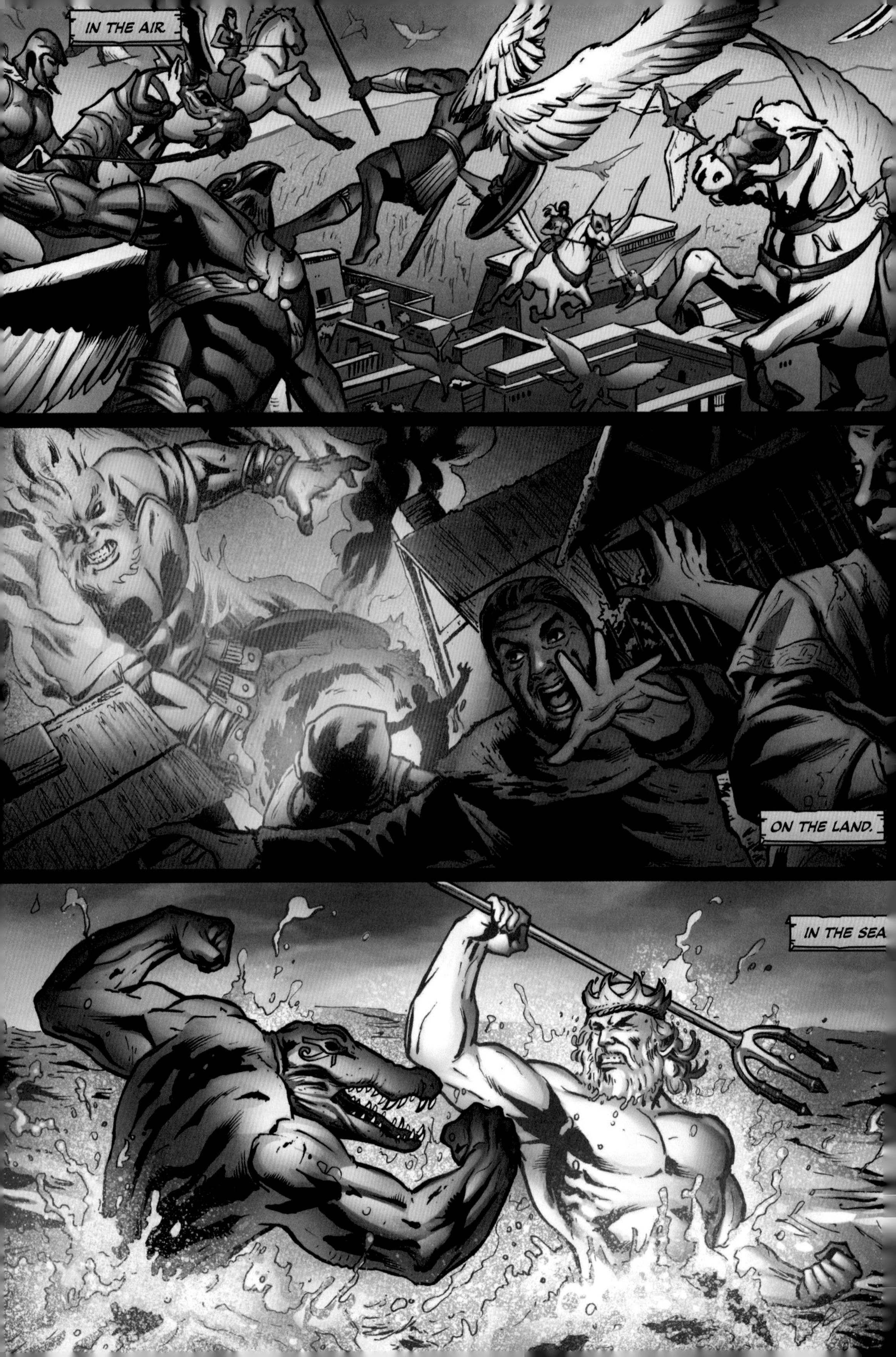
IN THE AIR
ON THE LAND.
IN THE SEA

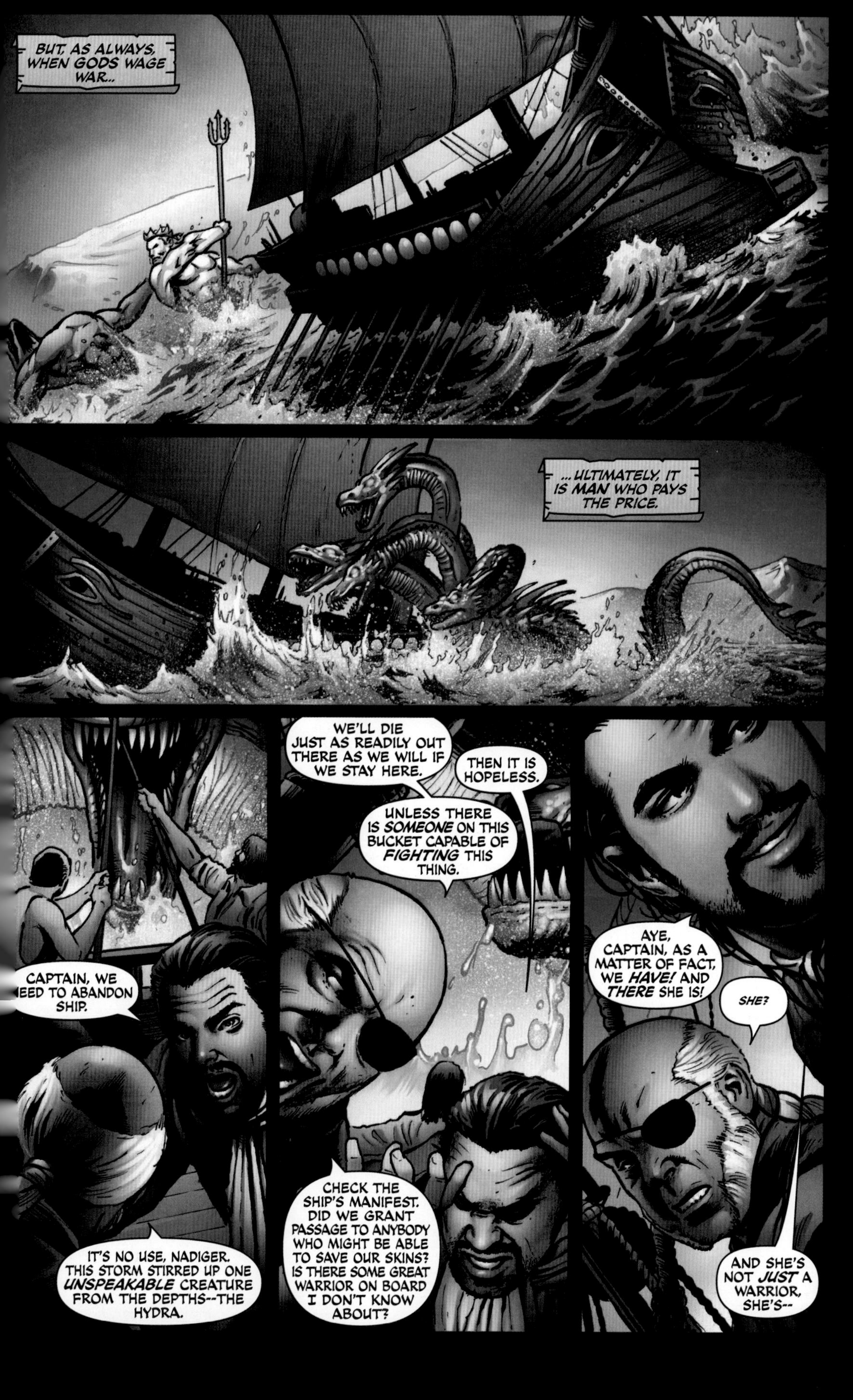

BUT, AS ALWAYS, WHEN GODS WAGE WAR...
...ULTIMATELY, IT IS MAN WHO PAYS THE PRICE.
CAPTAIN, WE NEED TO ABANDON SHIP.
IT'S NO USE, NADIGER. THIS STORM STIRRED UP ONE UNSPEAKABLE CREATURE FROM THE DEPTHS--THE HYDRA.
WE'LL DIE JUST AS READILY OUT THERE AS WE WILL IF WE STAY HERE.
THEN IT IS HOPELESS.
UNLESS THERE IS SOMEONE ON THIS BUCKET CAPABLE OF FIGHTING THIS THING.
CHECK THE SHIP'S MANIFEST. DID WE GRANT PASSAGE TO ANYBODY WHO MIGHT BE ABLE TO SAVE OUR SKINS? IS THERE SOME GREAT WARRIOR ON BOARD I DON'T KNOW ABOUT?
AYE, CAPTAIN, AS A MATTER OF FACT, WE HAVE! AND THERE SHE IS!
SHE?
AND SHE'S NOT JUST A WARRIOR, SHE'S--

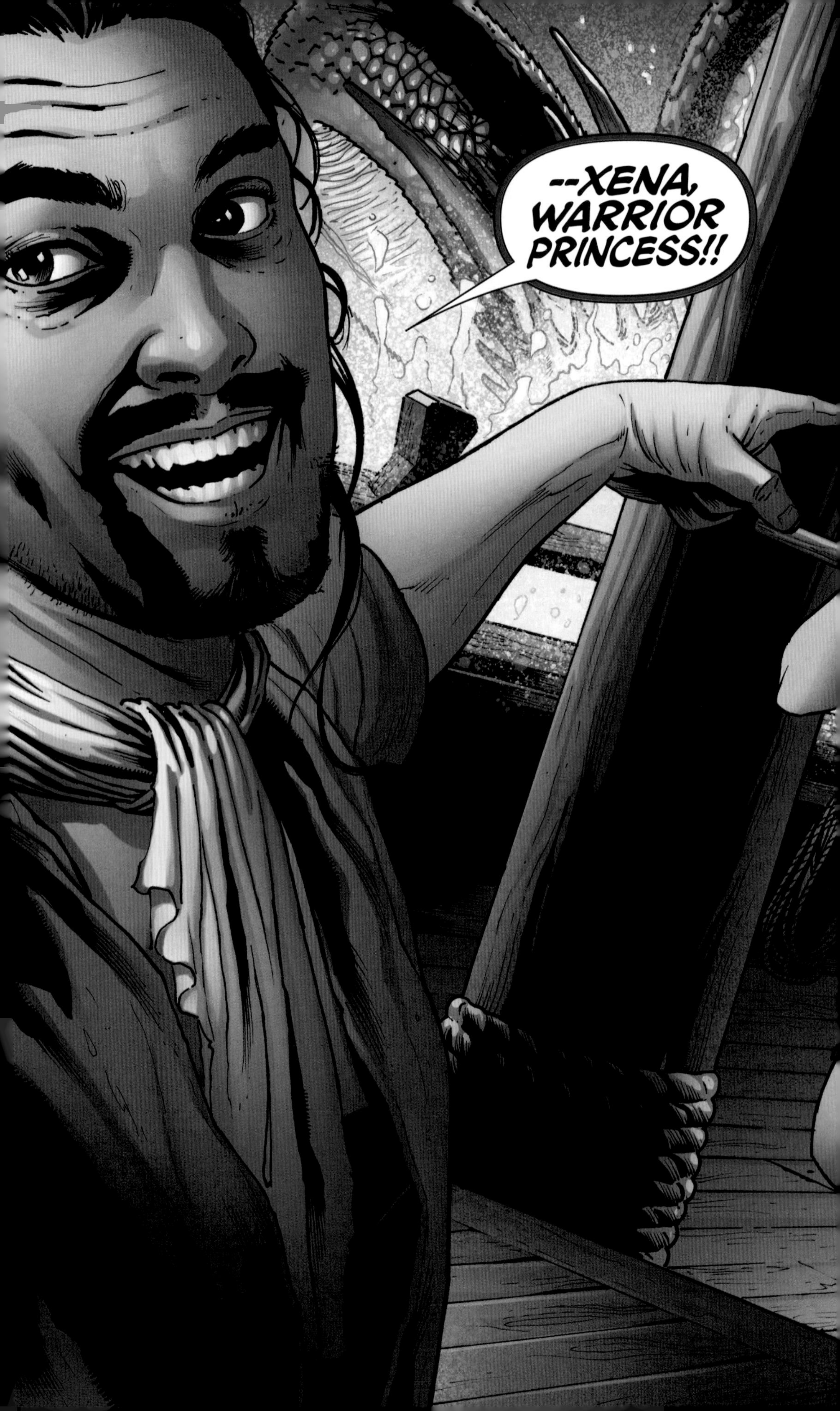
--XENA, WARRIOR PRINCESS!!

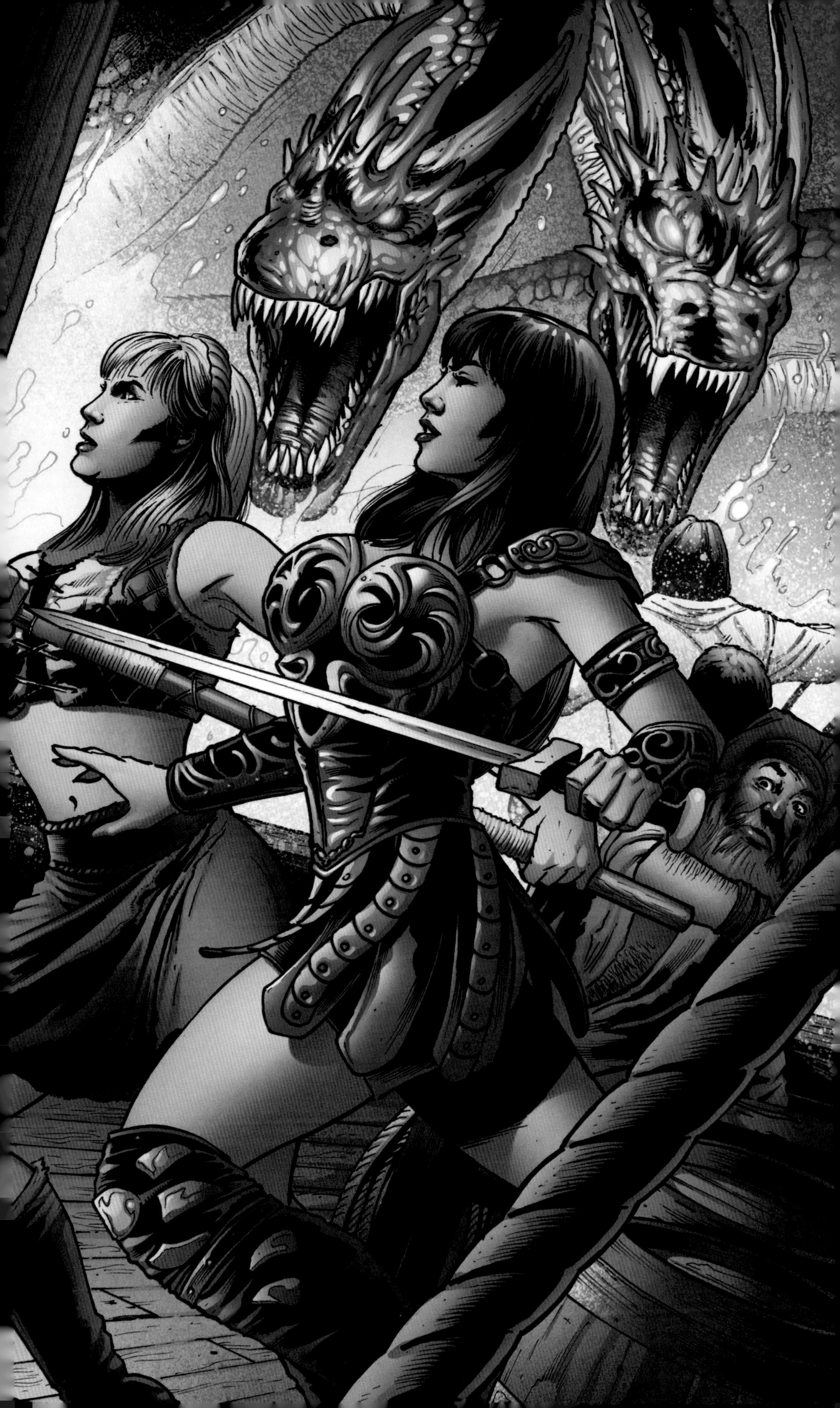

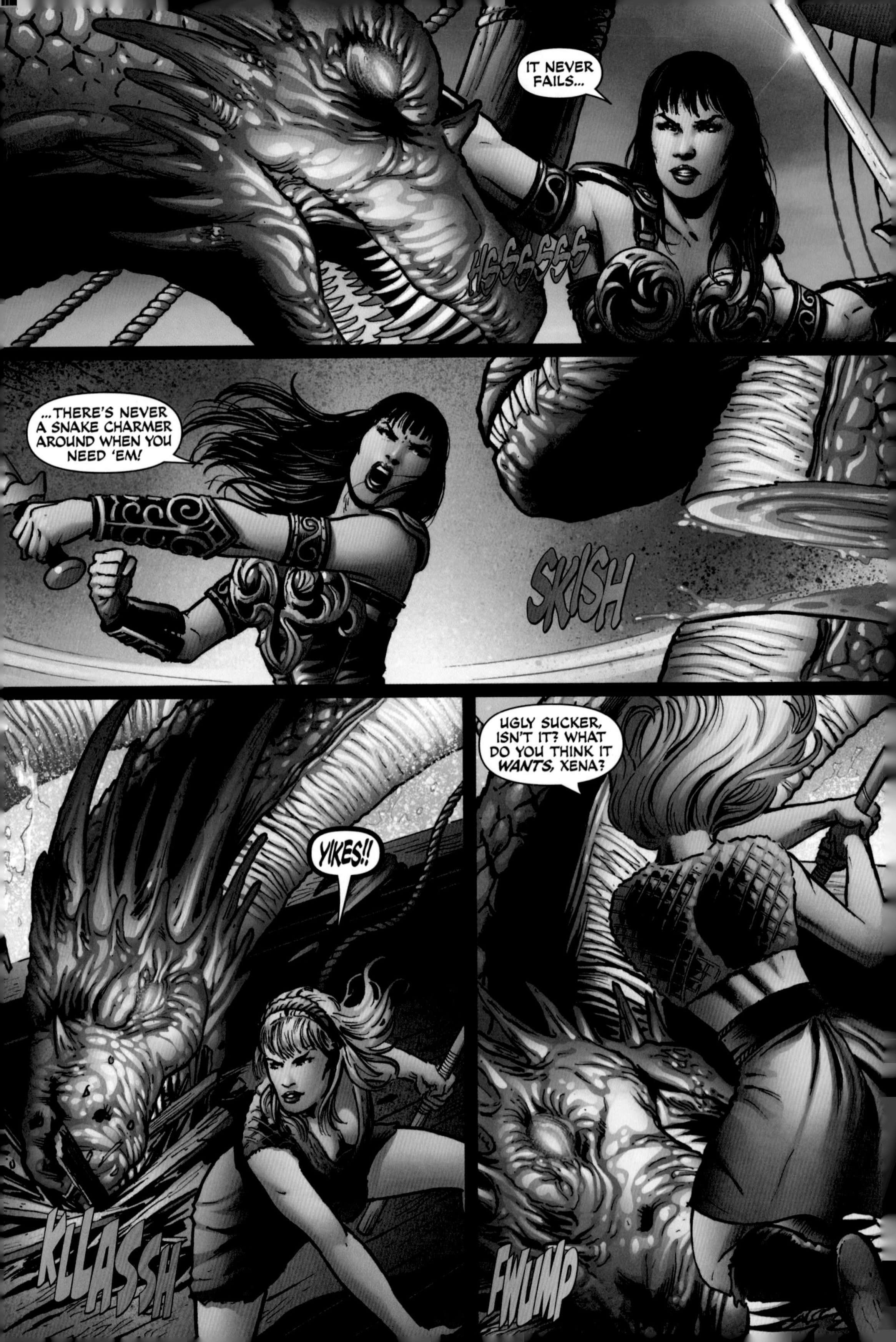

IT NEVER FAILS...
HSSSSSS
...THERE'S NEVER A SNAKE CHARMER AROUND WHEN YOU NEED 'EM!
SKISH
YIKES!!
KLLASSH
UGLY SUCKER, ISN'T IT? WHAT DO YOU THINK IT *WANTS*, XENA?
FWUMP

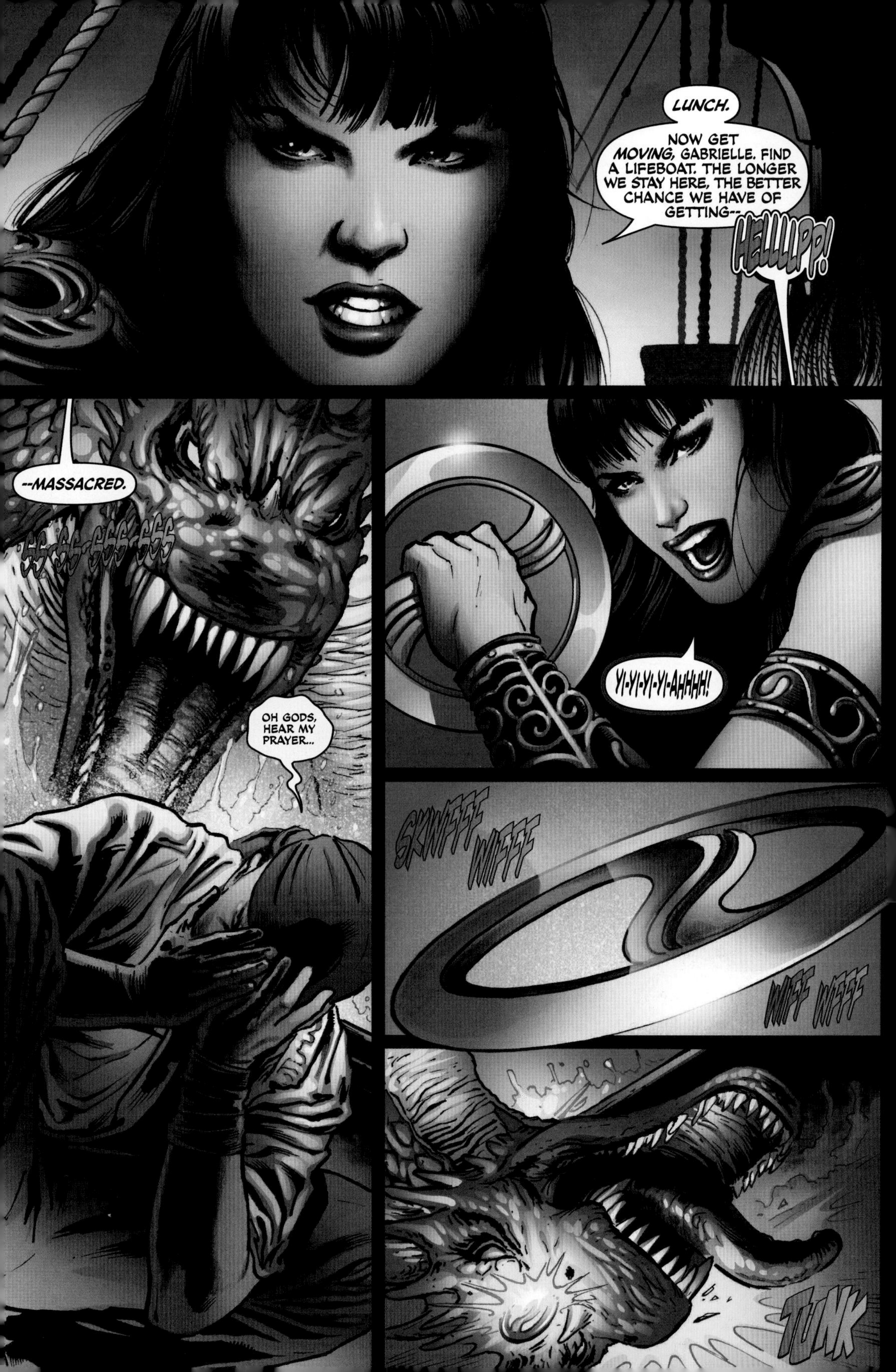
LUNCH.
NOW GET *MOVING*, GABRIELLE. FIND A LIFEBOAT. THE LONGER WE STAY HERE, THE BETTER CHANCE WE HAVE OF GETTING--
HELLLLPP!
--MASSACRED.
SS-SS-SSS-SSS
OH GODS, HEAR MY PRAYER...
YI-YI-YI-YI-AHHHH!
SKWFFF WIFFF
WIFF WIFFF
TUNK

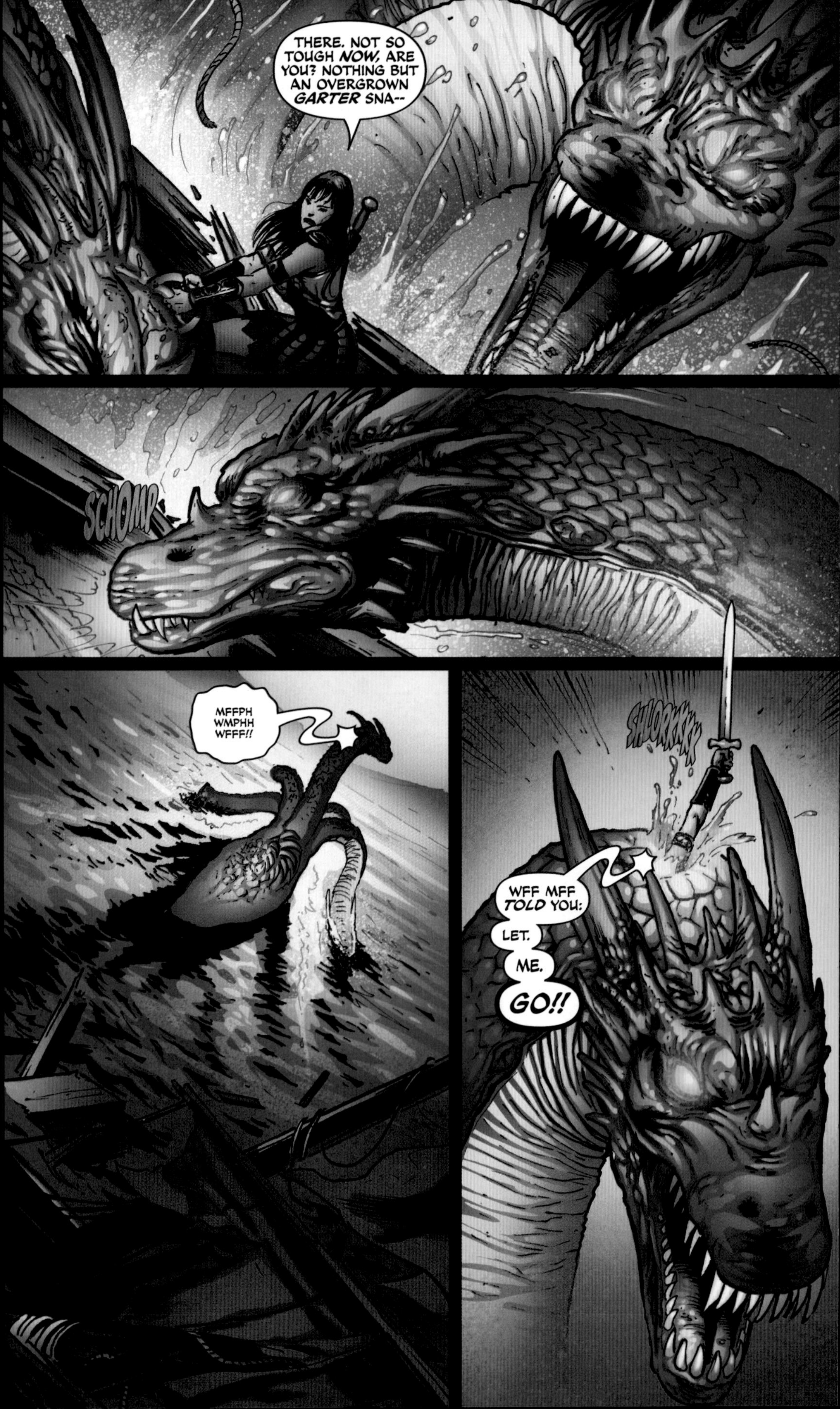
THERE. NOT SO TOUGH *NOW,* ARE YOU? NOTHING BUT AN OVERGROWN *GARTER* SNA--
SCHOMP
MFFPH WMPHH WFFF!!
SHLORKKK
WFF MFF *TOLD* YOU:
LET.
ME.
GO!!

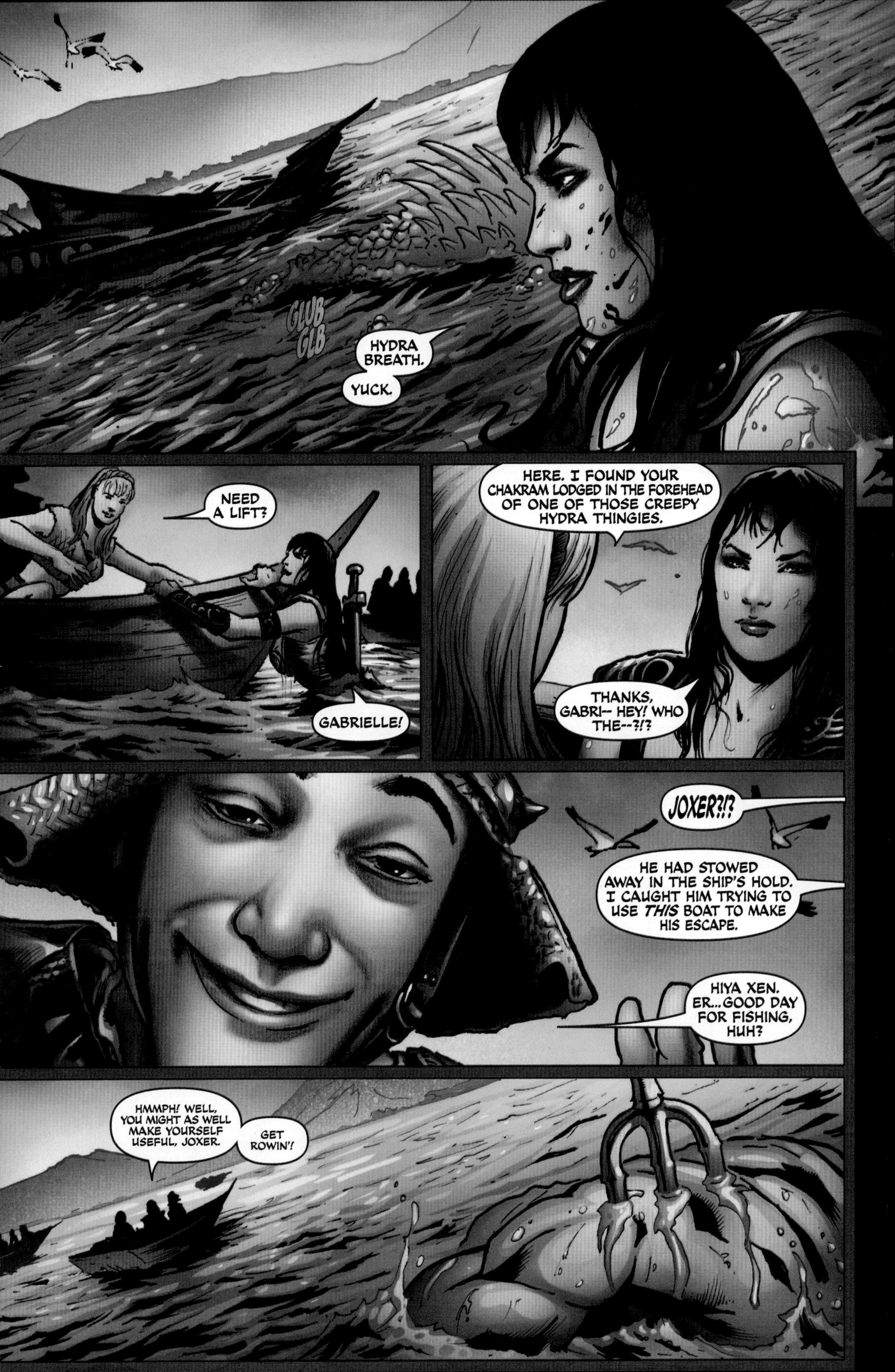
GLUB GLB
HYDRA BREATH.
YUCK.
NEED A LIFT?
GABRIELLE!
HERE. I FOUND YOUR CHAKRAM LODGED IN THE FOREHEAD OF ONE OF THOSE CREEPY HYDRA THINGIES.
THANKS, GABRI-- HEY! WHO THE--?!?
JOXER?!?
HE HAD STOWED AWAY IN THE SHIP'S HOLD. I CAUGHT HIM TRYING TO USE THIS BOAT TO MAKE HIS ESCAPE.
HIYA XEN. ER...GOOD DAY FOR FISHING, HUH?
HMMPH! WELL, YOU MIGHT AS WELL MAKE YOURSELF USEFUL, JOXER.
GET ROWIN'!

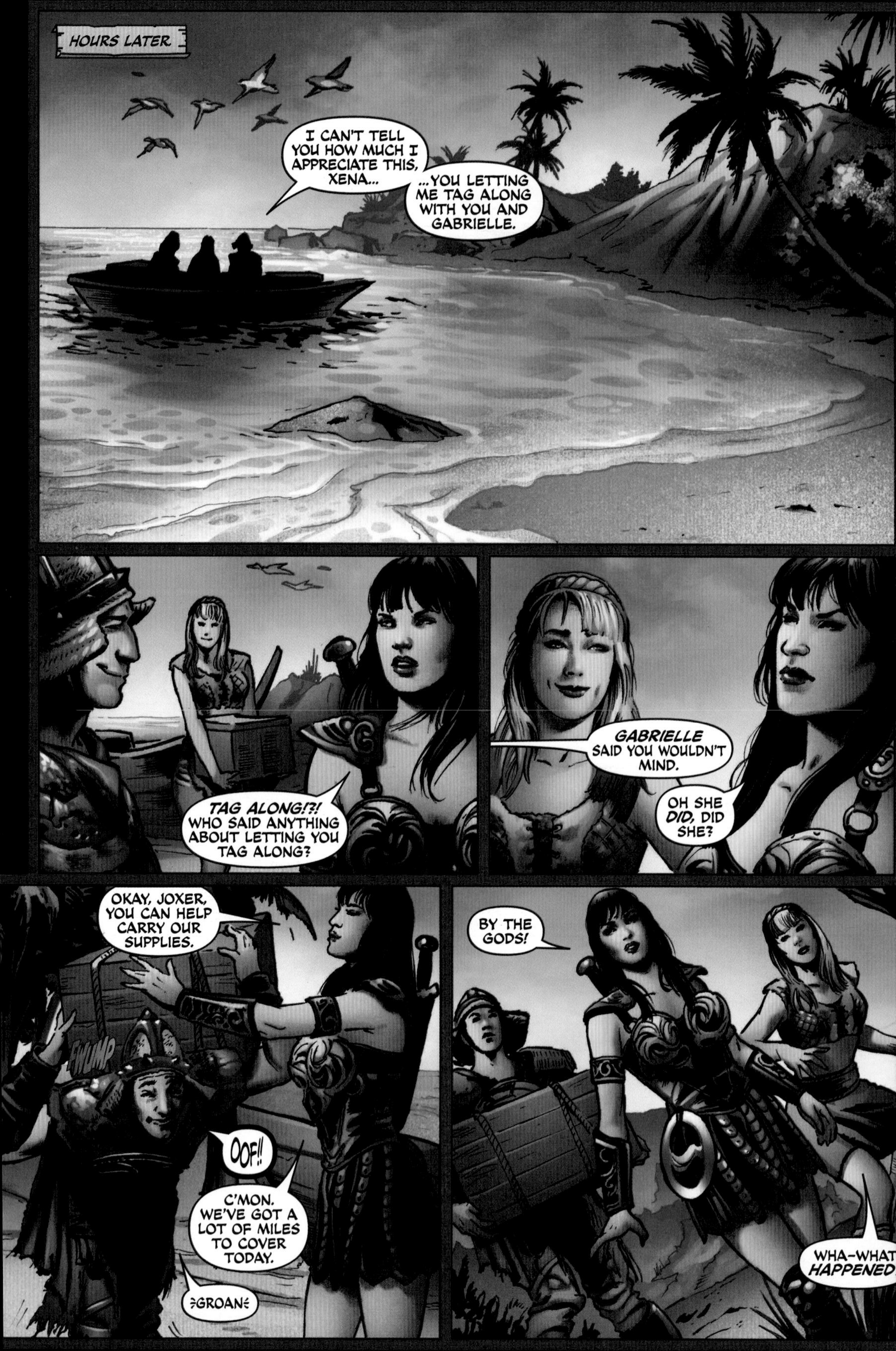
HOURS LATER
I CAN'T TELL YOU HOW MUCH I APPRECIATE THIS, XENA...
...YOU LETTING ME TAG ALONG WITH YOU AND GABRIELLE.
TAG ALONG!?! WHO SAID ANYTHING ABOUT LETTING YOU TAG ALONG?
GABRIELLE SAID YOU WOULDN'T MIND.
OH SHE DID, DID SHE?
OKAY, JOXER, YOU CAN HELP CARRY OUR SUPPLIES.
FWUMP
OOF!!
C'MON. WE'VE GOT A LOT OF MILES TO COVER TODAY.
GROAN
BY THE GODS!
WHA-WHAT HAPPENED

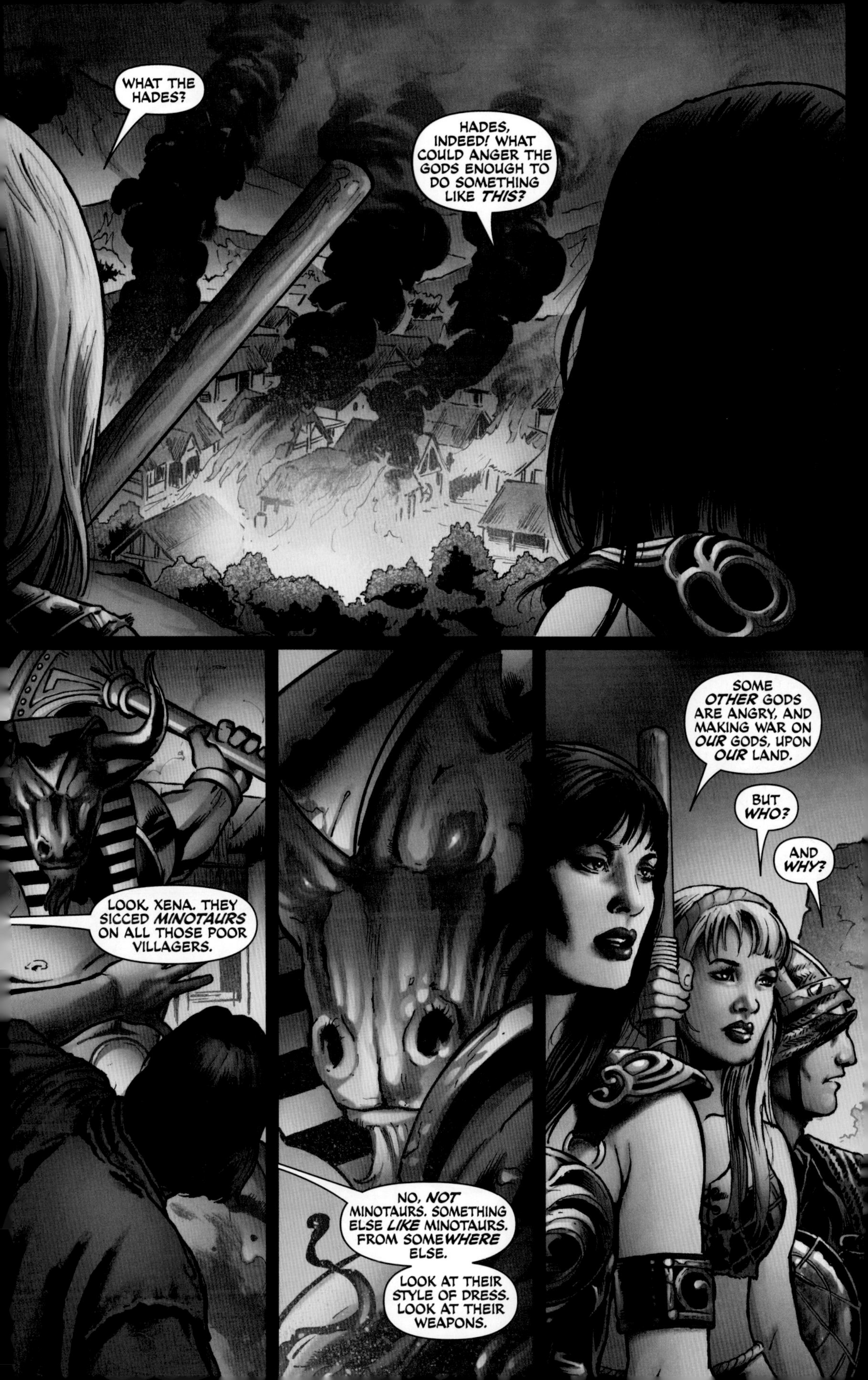
WHAT THE HADES?
HADES, INDEED! WHAT COULD ANGER THE GODS ENOUGH TO DO SOMETHING LIKE *THIS?*
LOOK, XENA. THEY SICCED *MINOTAURS* ON ALL THOSE POOR VILLAGERS.
NO, *NOT* MINOTAURS. SOMETHING ELSE *LIKE* MINOTAURS. FROM SOME*WHERE* ELSE.
LOOK AT THEIR STYLE OF DRESS. LOOK AT THEIR WEAPONS.
SOME *OTHER* GODS ARE ANGRY, AND MAKING WAR ON *OUR* GODS, UPON *OUR* LAND.
BUT *WHO?*
AND *WHY?*

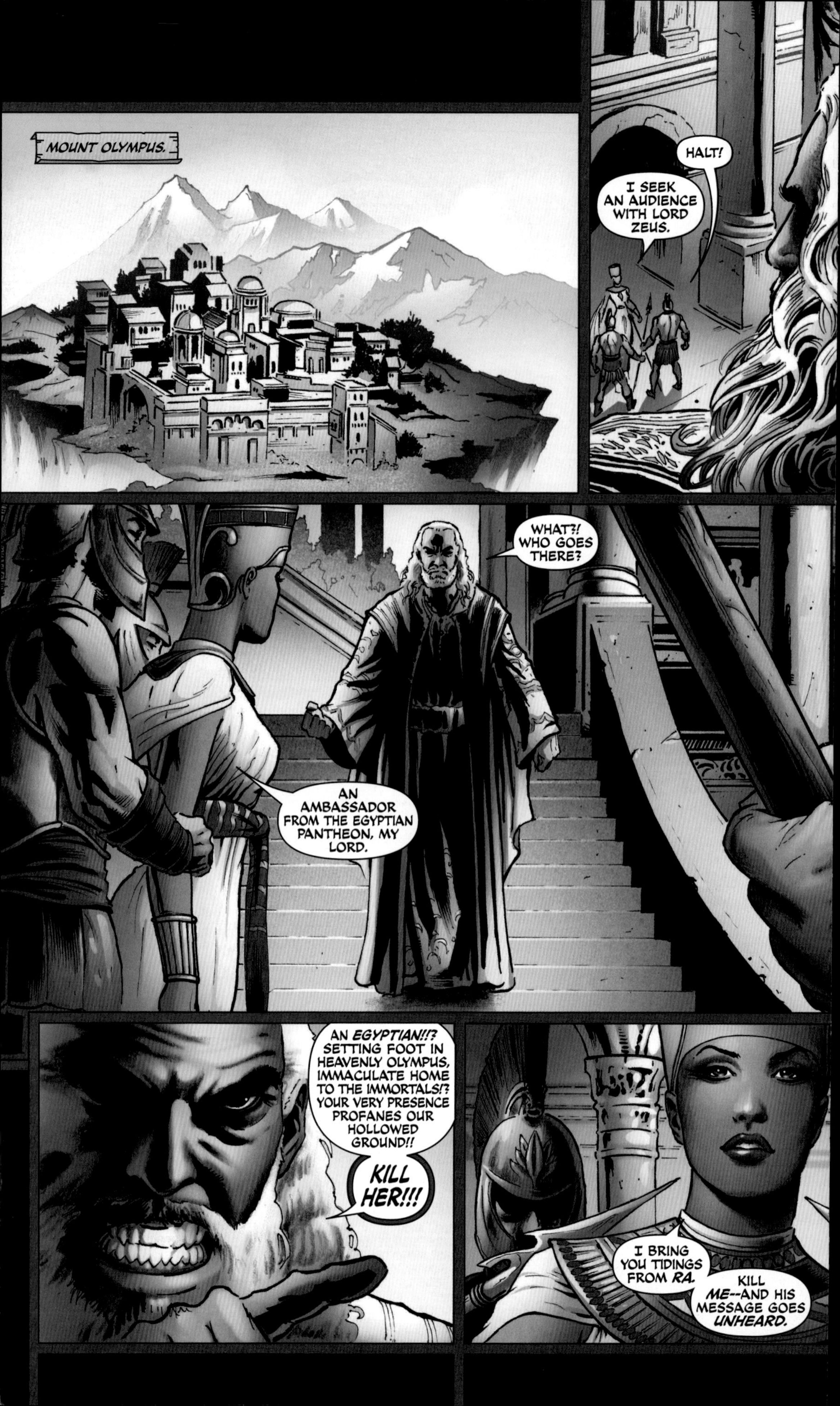
MOUNT OLYMPUS.
HALT!
I SEEK AN AUDIENCE WITH LORD ZEUS.
WHAT?! WHO GOES THERE?
AN AMBASSADOR FROM THE EGYPTIAN PANTHEON, MY LORD.
AN EGYPTIAN!!? SETTING FOOT IN HEAVENLY OLYMPUS, IMMACULATE HOME TO THE IMMORTALS!? YOUR VERY PRESENCE PROFANES OUR HOLLOWED GROUND!!
KILL HER!!!
I BRING YOU TIDINGS FROM RA.
KILL ME--AND HIS MESSAGE GOES UNHEARD.

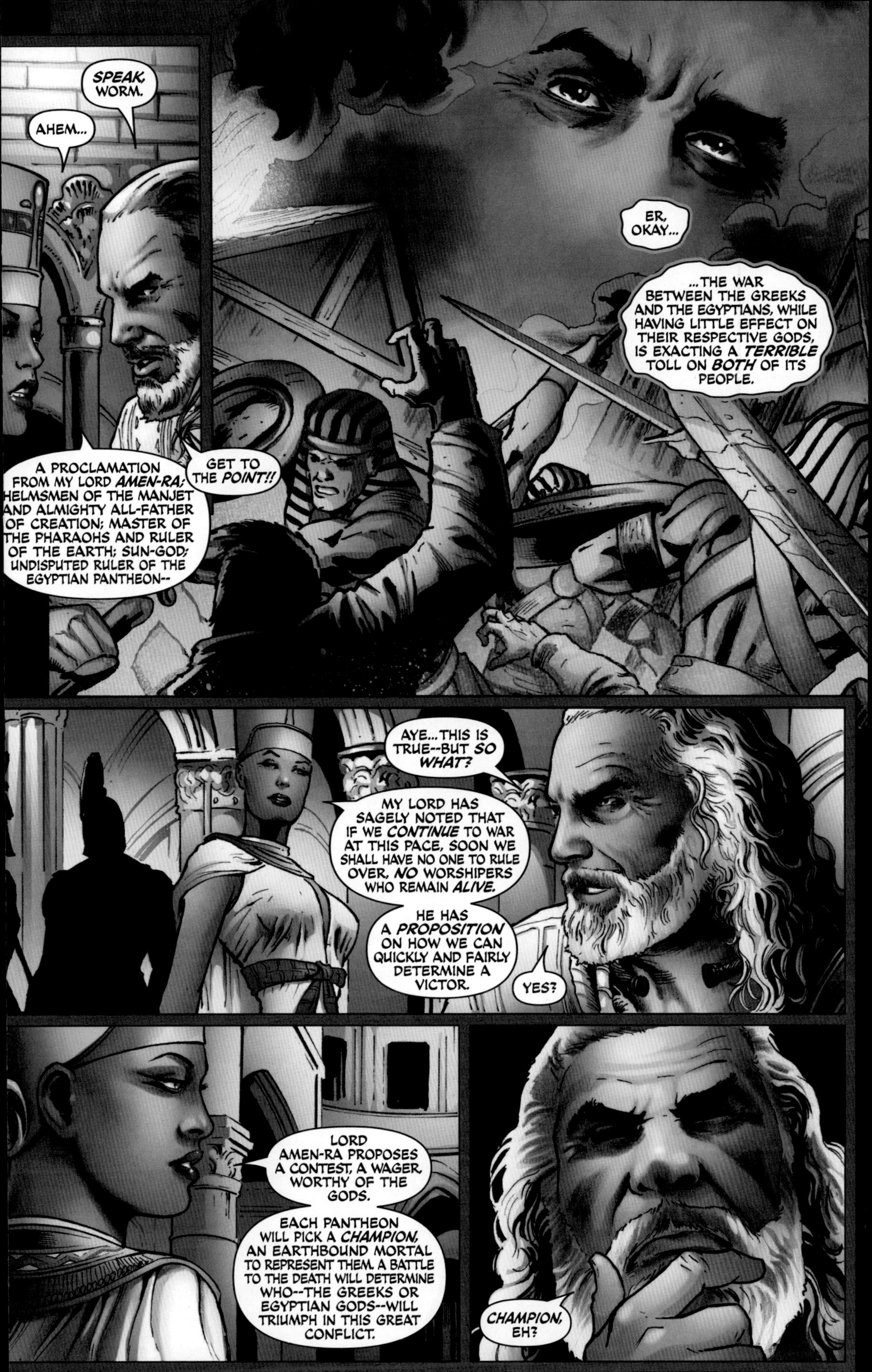
SPEAK, WORM.
AHEM...
ER, OKAY...
...THE WAR BETWEEN THE GREEKS AND THE EGYPTIANS, WHILE HAVING LITTLE EFFECT ON THEIR RESPECTIVE GODS, IS EXACTING A TERRIBLE TOLL ON BOTH OF ITS PEOPLE.
A PROCLAMATION FROM MY LORD AMEN-RA; HELMSMEN OF THE MANJET AND ALMIGHTY ALL-FATHER OF CREATION; MASTER OF THE PHARAOHS AND RULER OF THE EARTH; SUN-GOD; UNDISPUTED RULER OF THE EGYPTIAN PANTHEON--
GET TO THE POINT!!
AYE...THIS IS TRUE--BUT SO WHAT?
MY LORD HAS SAGELY NOTED THAT IF WE CONTINUE TO WAR AT THIS PACE, SOON WE SHALL HAVE NO ONE TO RULE OVER, NO WORSHIPERS WHO REMAIN ALIVE.
HE HAS A PROPOSITION ON HOW WE CAN QUICKLY AND FAIRLY DETERMINE A VICTOR.
YES?
LORD AMEN-RA PROPOSES A CONTEST, A WAGER, WORTHY OF THE GODS.
EACH PANTHEON WILL PICK A CHAMPION, AN EARTHBOUND MORTAL TO REPRESENT THEM. A BATTLE TO THE DEATH WILL DETERMINE WHO--THE GREEKS OR EGYPTIAN GODS--WILL TRIUMPH IN THIS GREAT CONFLICT.
CHAMPION, EH?

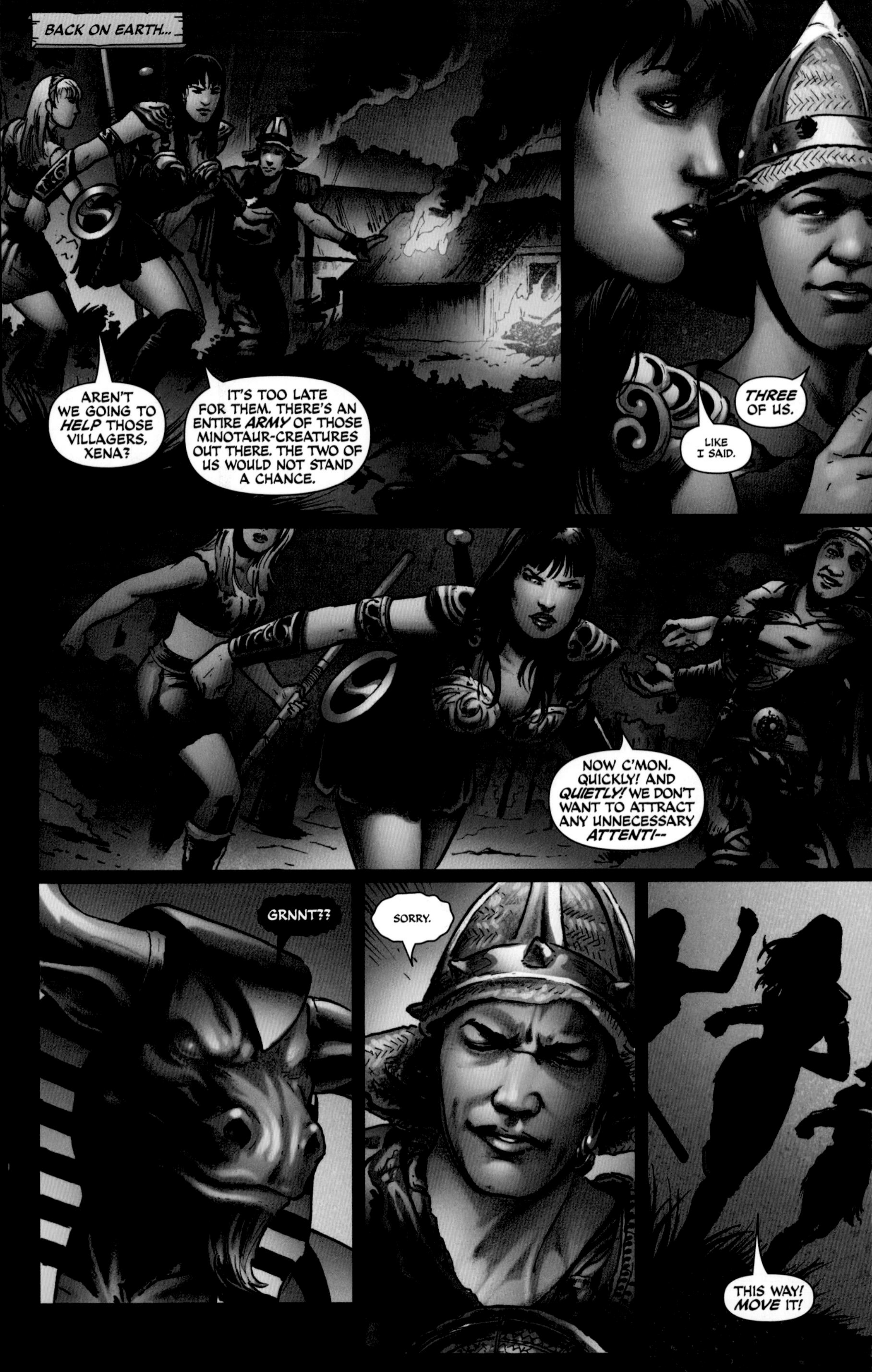
BACK ON EARTH...
AREN'T WE GOING TO *HELP* THOSE VILLAGERS, XENA?
IT'S TOO LATE FOR THEM. THERE'S AN ENTIRE *ARMY* OF THOSE MINOTAUR-CREATURES OUT THERE. THE TWO OF US WOULD NOT STAND A CHANCE.
LIKE I SAID.
THREE OF US.
NOW C'MON. QUICKLY! AND *QUIETLY!* WE DON'T WANT TO ATTRACT ANY UNNECESSARY *ATTENTI--*
GRNNT??
SORRY.
THIS WAY! *MOVE* IT!

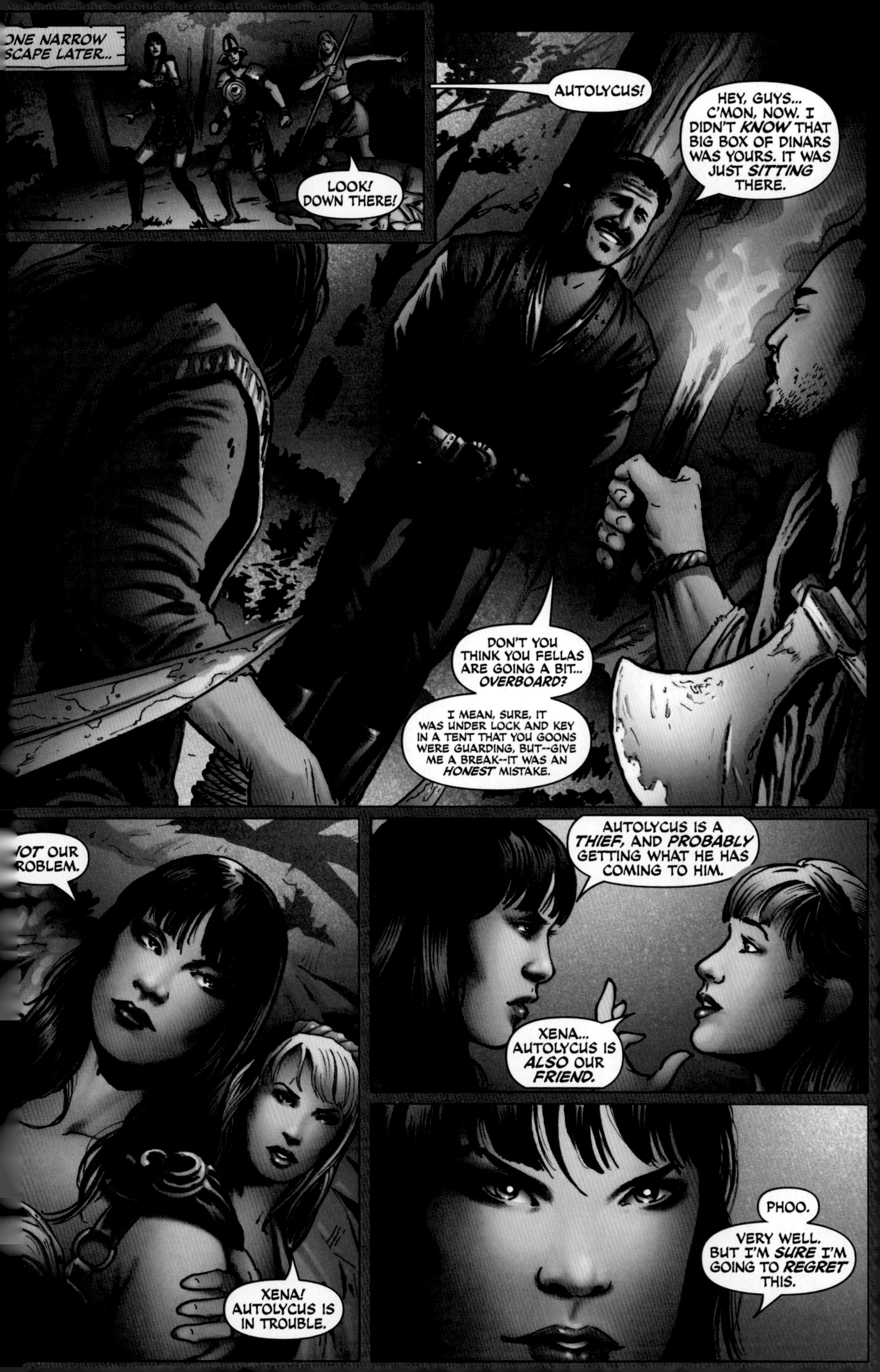

ONE NARROW ESCAPE LATER...
LOOK! DOWN THERE!
AUTOLYCUS!
HEY, GUYS... C'MON, NOW. I DIDN'T KNOW THAT BIG BOX OF DINARS WAS YOURS. IT WAS JUST SITTING THERE.
DON'T YOU THINK YOU FELLAS ARE GOING A BIT... OVERBOARD?
I MEAN, SURE, IT WAS UNDER LOCK AND KEY IN A TENT THAT YOU GOONS WERE GUARDING, BUT--GIVE ME A BREAK--IT WAS AN HONEST MISTAKE.
NOT OUR PROBLEM.
XENA! AUTOLYCUS IS IN TROUBLE.
AUTOLYCUS IS A THIEF, AND PROBABLY GETTING WHAT HE HAS COMING TO HIM.
XENA... AUTOLYCUS IS ALSO OUR FRIEND.
PHOO.
VERY WELL. BUT I'M SURE I'M GOING TO REGRET THIS.

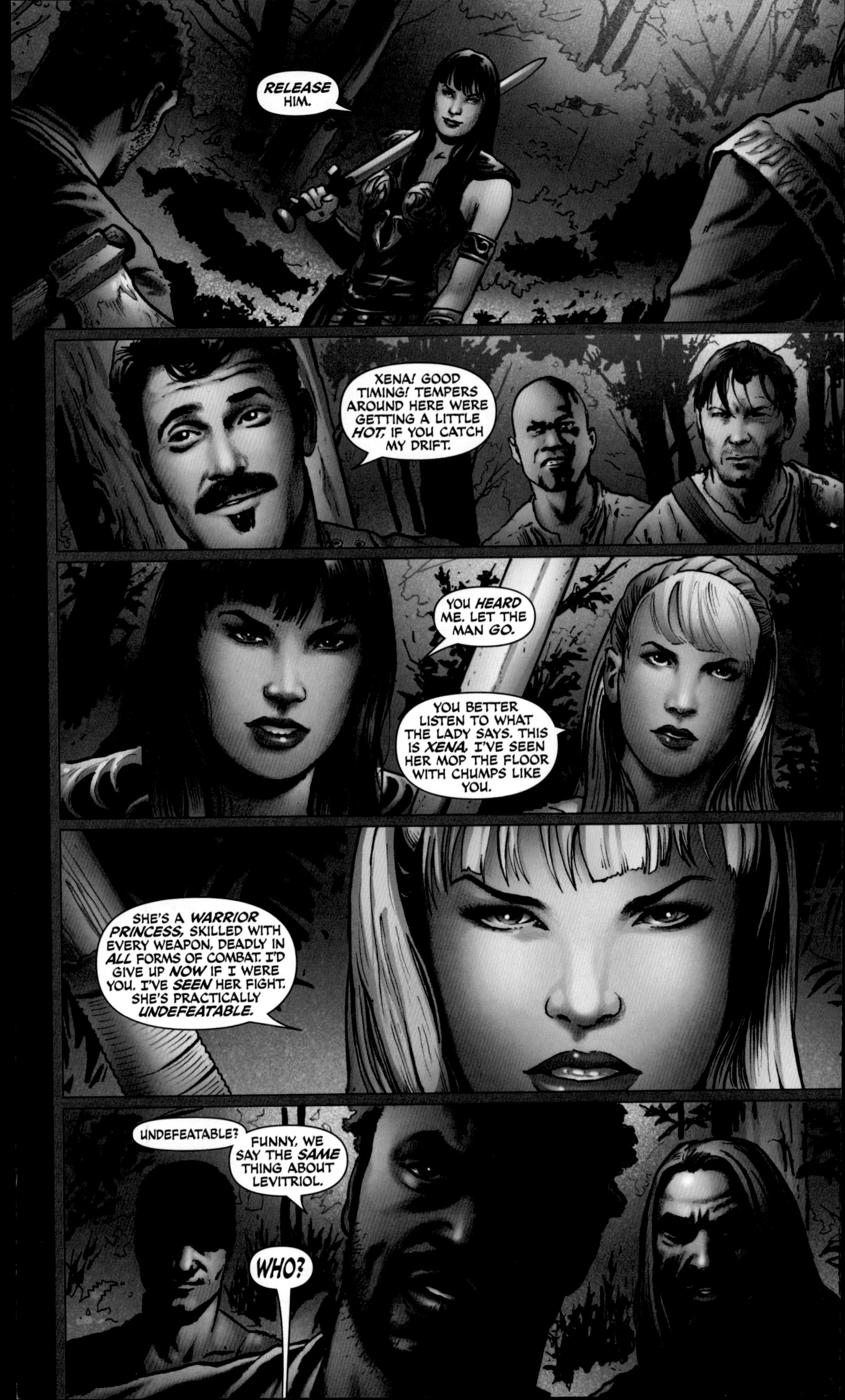
RELEASE HIM.
XENA! GOOD TIMING! TEMPERS AROUND HERE WERE GETTING A LITTLE HOT, IF YOU CATCH MY DRIFT.
YOU HEARD ME. LET THE MAN GO.
YOU BETTER LISTEN TO WHAT THE LADY SAYS. THIS IS XENA, I'VE SEEN HER MOP THE FLOOR WITH CHUMPS LIKE YOU.
SHE'S A WARRIOR PRINCESS, SKILLED WITH EVERY WEAPON, DEADLY IN ALL FORMS OF COMBAT. I'D GIVE UP NOW IF I WERE YOU. I'VE SEEN HER FIGHT. SHE'S PRACTICALLY UNDEFEATABLE.
UNDEFEATABLE?
FUNNY, WE SAY THE SAME THING ABOUT LEVITRIOL.
WHO?

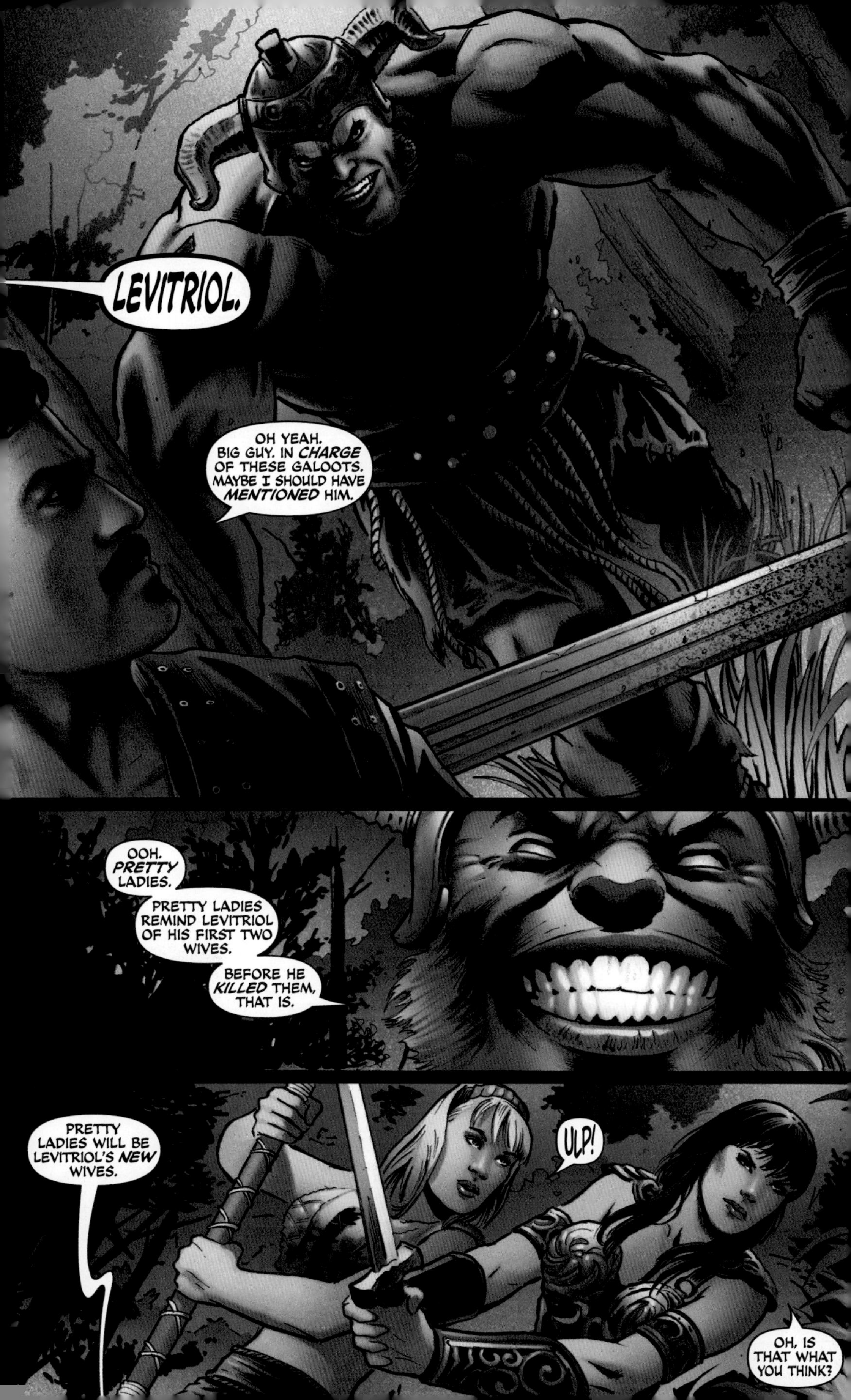
LEVITRIOL.
OH YEAH. BIG GUY. IN *CHARGE* OF THESE GALOOTS. MAYBE I SHOULD HAVE *MENTIONED* HIM.
OOH. *PRETTY* LADIES.
PRETTY LADIES REMIND LEVITRIOL OF HIS FIRST TWO WIVES.
BEFORE HE *KILLED* THEM, THAT IS.
PRETTY LADIES WILL BE LEVITRIOL'S *NEW* WIVES.
ULP!
OH, IS THAT WHAT YOU THINK?

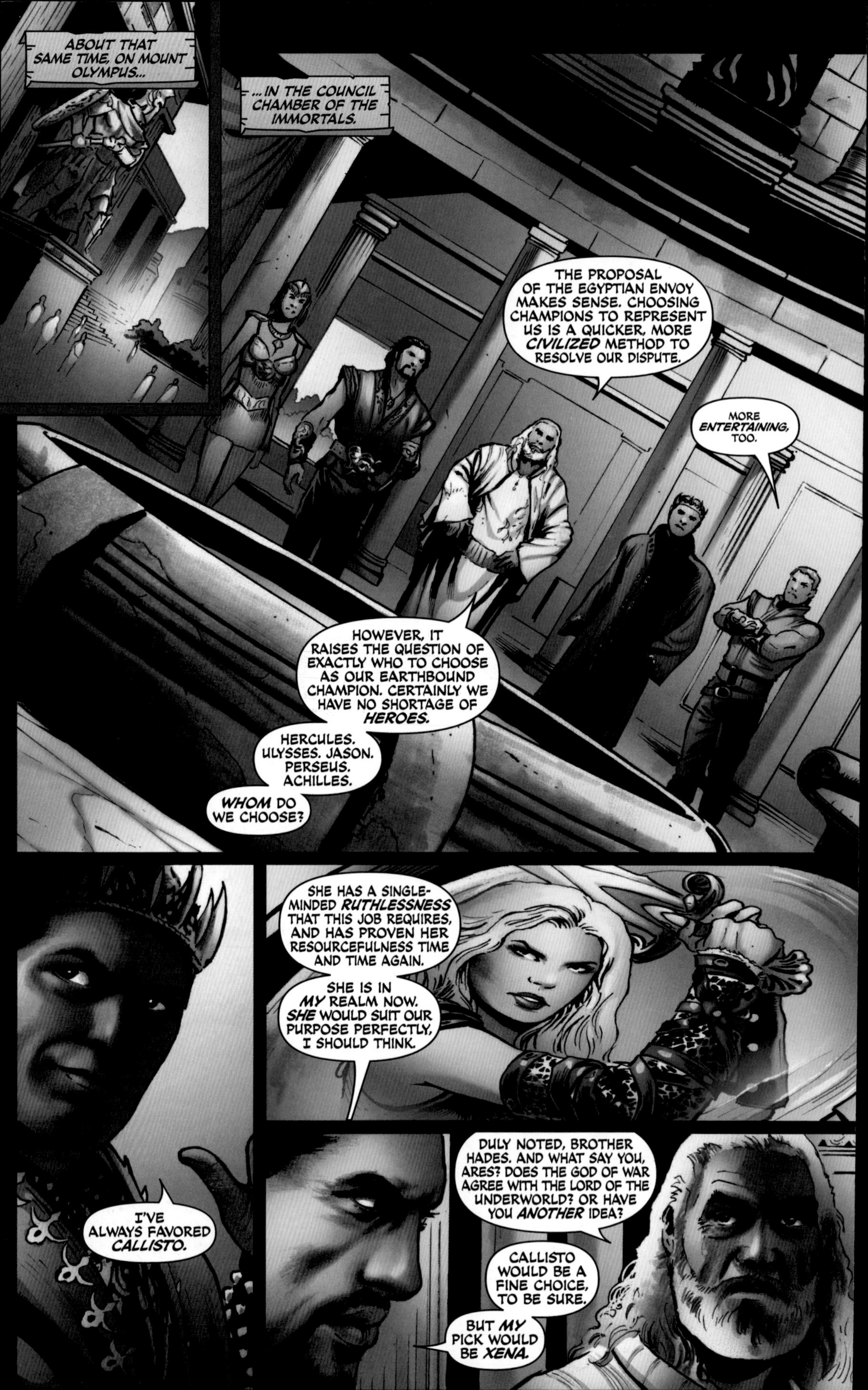
ABOUT THAT SAME TIME, ON MOUNT OLYMPUS...
...IN THE COUNCIL CHAMBER OF THE IMMORTALS.
THE PROPOSAL OF THE EGYPTIAN ENVOY MAKES SENSE. CHOOSING CHAMPIONS TO REPRESENT US IS A QUICKER, MORE *CIVILIZED* METHOD TO RESOLVE OUR DISPUTE.
MORE *ENTERTAINING,* TOO.
HOWEVER, IT RAISES THE QUESTION OF EXACTLY WHO TO CHOOSE AS OUR EARTHBOUND CHAMPION. CERTAINLY WE HAVE NO SHORTAGE OF *HEROES.*
HERCULES. ULYSSES. JASON. PERSEUS. ACHILLES.
WHOM DO WE CHOOSE?
I'VE ALWAYS FAVORED *CALLISTO.*
SHE HAS A SINGLE-MINDED *RUTHLESSNESS* THAT THIS JOB REQUIRES, AND HAS PROVEN HER RESOURCEFULNESS TIME AND TIME AGAIN.
SHE IS IN *MY* REALM NOW. *SHE* WOULD SUIT OUR PURPOSE PERFECTLY, I SHOULD THINK.
DULY NOTED, BROTHER HADES. AND WHAT SAY YOU, ARES? DOES THE GOD OF WAR AGREE WITH THE LORD OF THE UNDERWORLD? OR HAVE YOU *ANOTHER* IDEA?
CALLISTO WOULD BE A FINE CHOICE, TO BE SURE.
BUT *MY* PICK WOULD BE *XENA.*

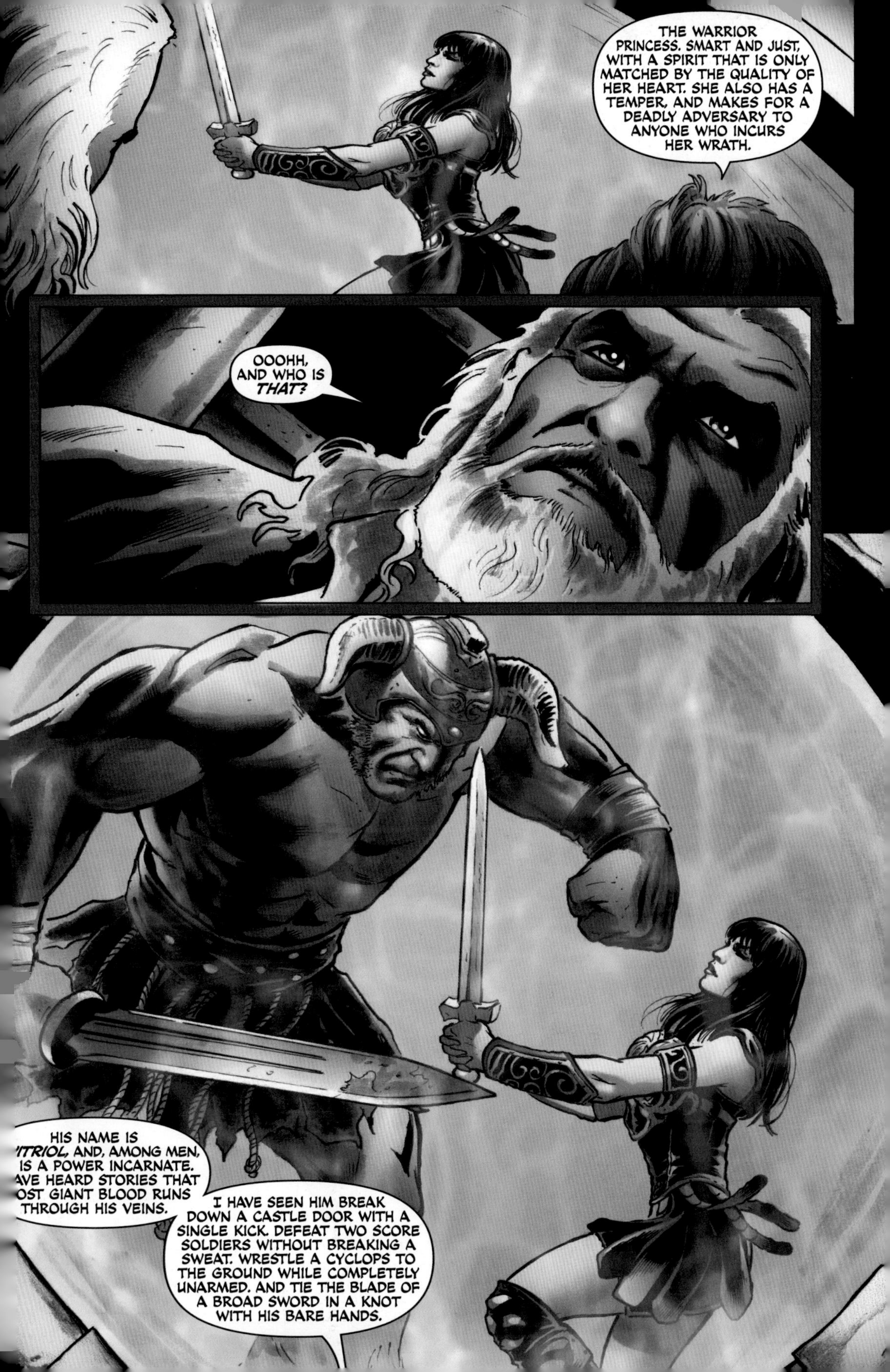
THE WARRIOR PRINCESS. SMART AND JUST, WITH A SPIRIT THAT IS ONLY MATCHED BY THE QUALITY OF HER HEART. SHE ALSO HAS A TEMPER, AND MAKES FOR A DEADLY ADVERSARY TO ANYONE WHO INCURS HER WRATH.
OOOHH, AND WHO IS *THAT?*
HIS NAME IS *ITRIOL,* AND, AMONG MEN, IS A POWER INCARNATE. AVE HEARD STORIES THAT OST GIANT BLOOD RUNS THROUGH HIS VEINS.
I HAVE SEEN HIM BREAK DOWN A CASTLE DOOR WITH A SINGLE KICK. DEFEAT TWO SCORE SOLDIERS WITHOUT BREAKING A SWEAT. WRESTLE A CYCLOPS TO THE GROUND WHILE COMPLETELY UNARMED. AND TIE THE BLADE OF A BROAD SWORD IN A KNOT WITH HIS BARE HANDS.

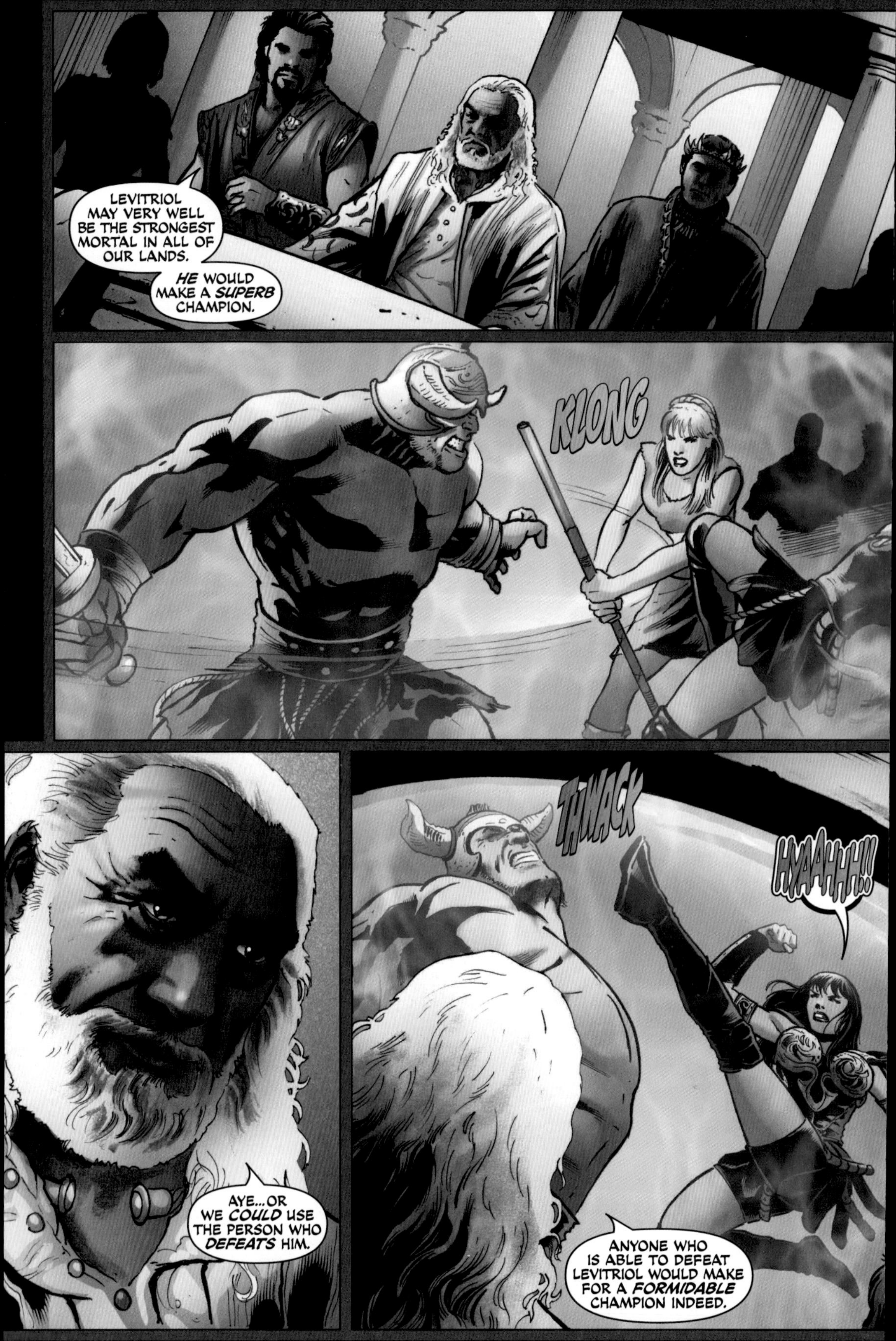
LEVITRIOL MAY VERY WELL BE THE STRONGEST MORTAL IN ALL OF OUR LANDS.
HE WOULD MAKE A SUPERB CHAMPION.
KLONG
AYE...OR WE COULD USE THE PERSON WHO DEFEATS HIM.
THWACK
HYAAHHH!!
ANYONE WHO IS ABLE TO DEFEAT LEVITRIOL WOULD MAKE FOR A FORMIDABLE CHAMPION INDEED.

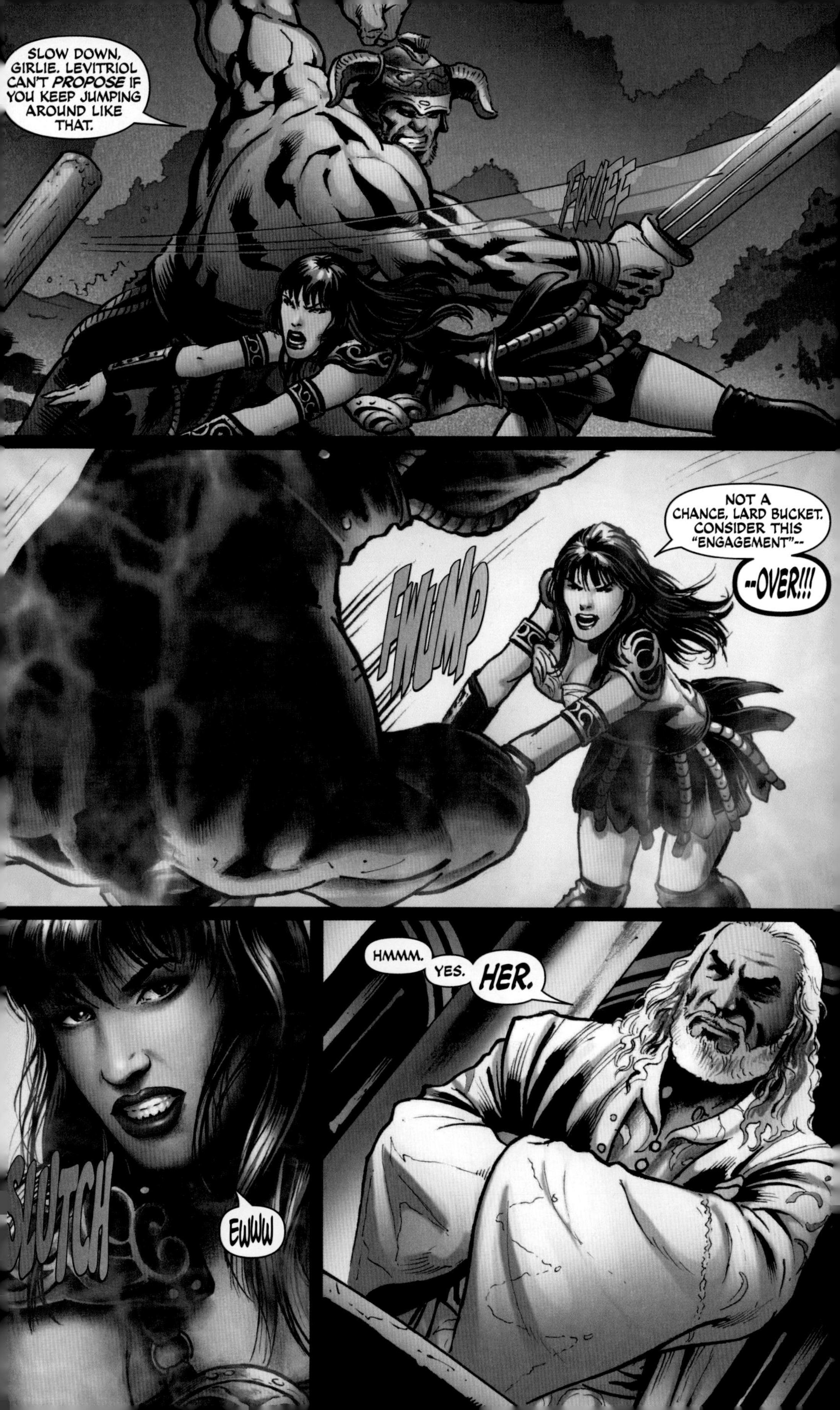

SLOW DOWN, GIRLIE. LEVITRIOL CAN'T *PROPOSE* IF YOU KEEP JUMPING AROUND LIKE THAT.
FWIFF
NOT A CHANCE, LARD BUCKET. CONSIDER THIS "ENGAGEMENT"--
--OVER!!!
FWUMP
SLUTCH
EWWW
HMMM.
YES.
HER.

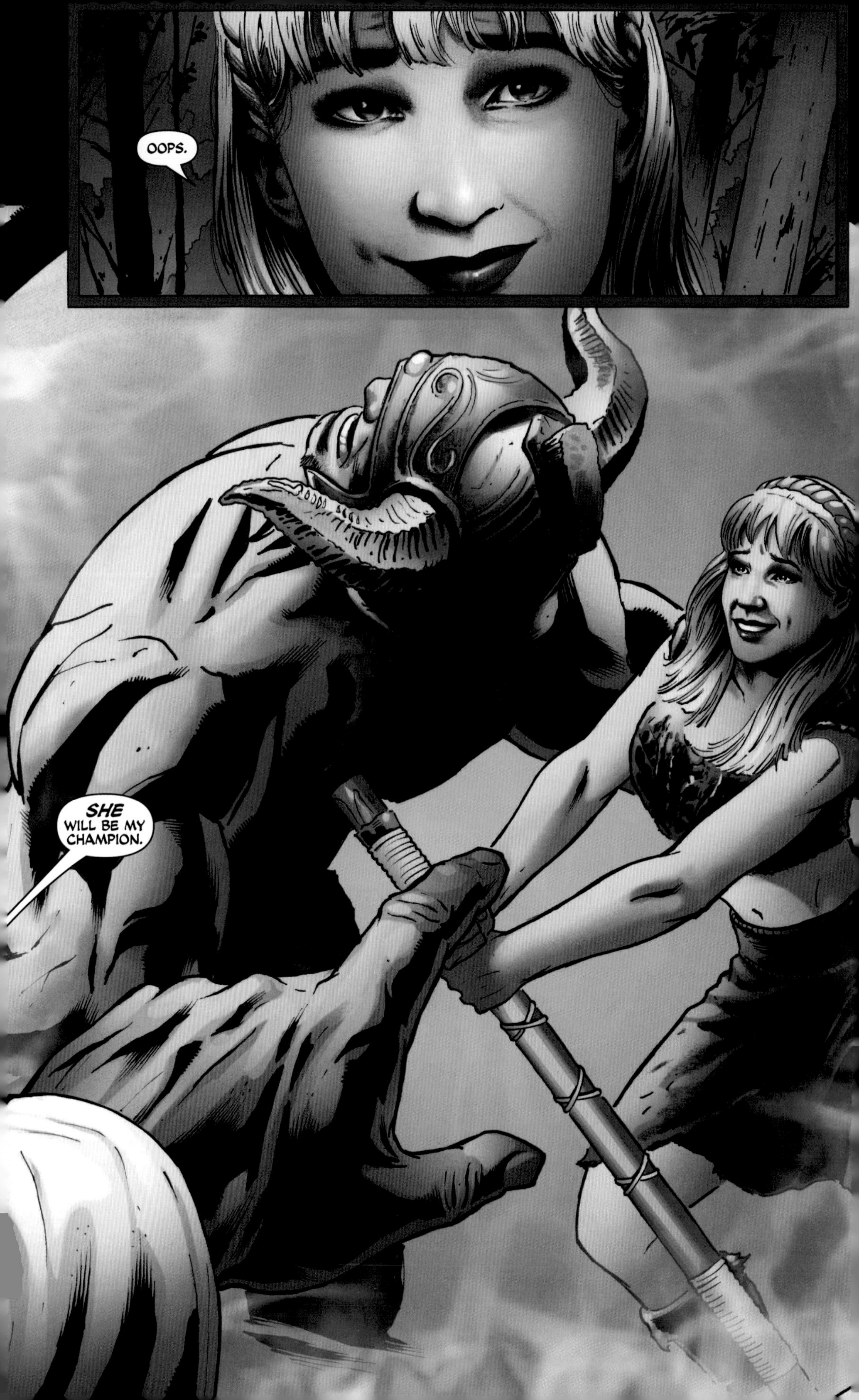
OOPS.
SHE WILL BE MY CHAMPION.

CONTEST OF PANTHEONS
CHAPTER TWO

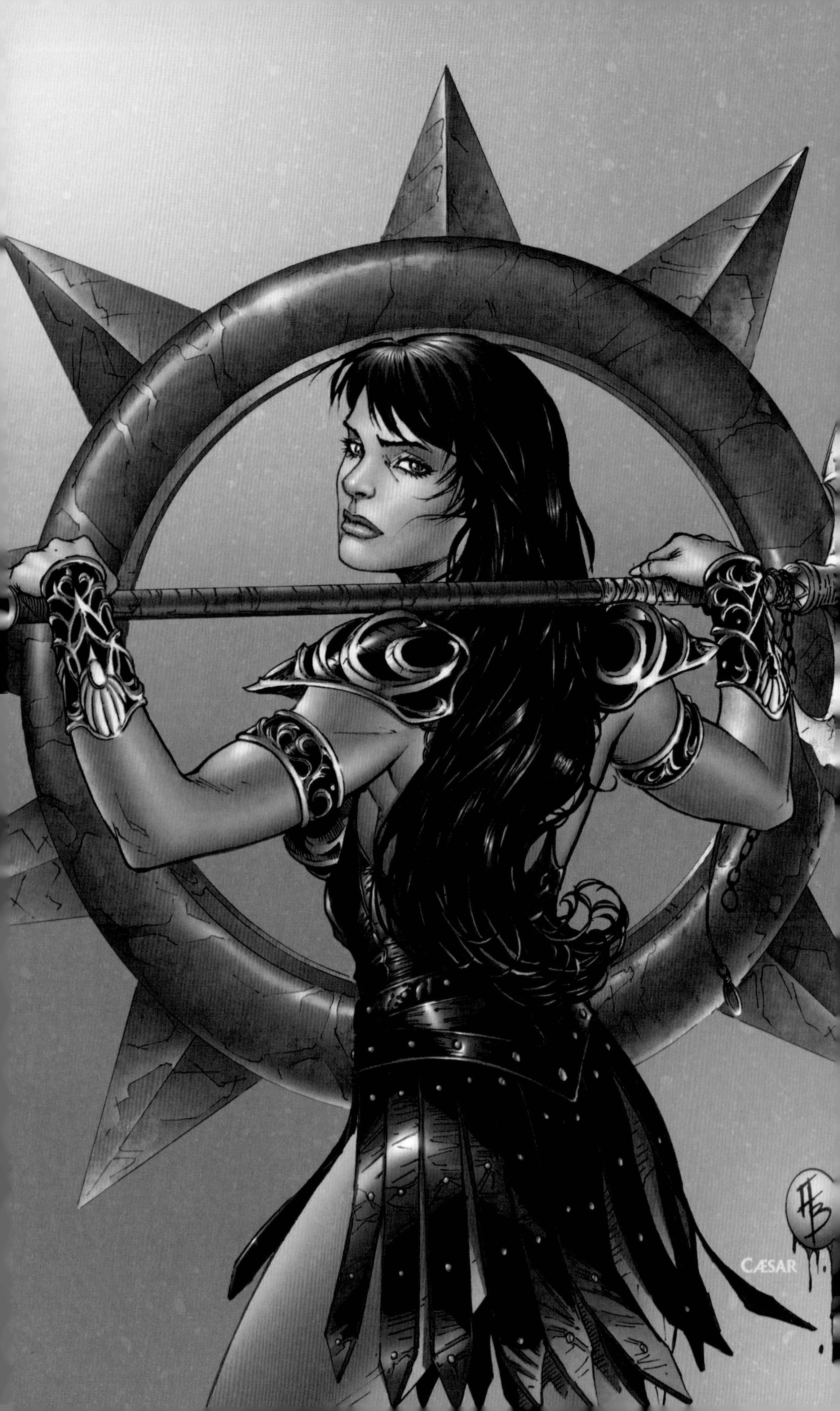
CÆSAR

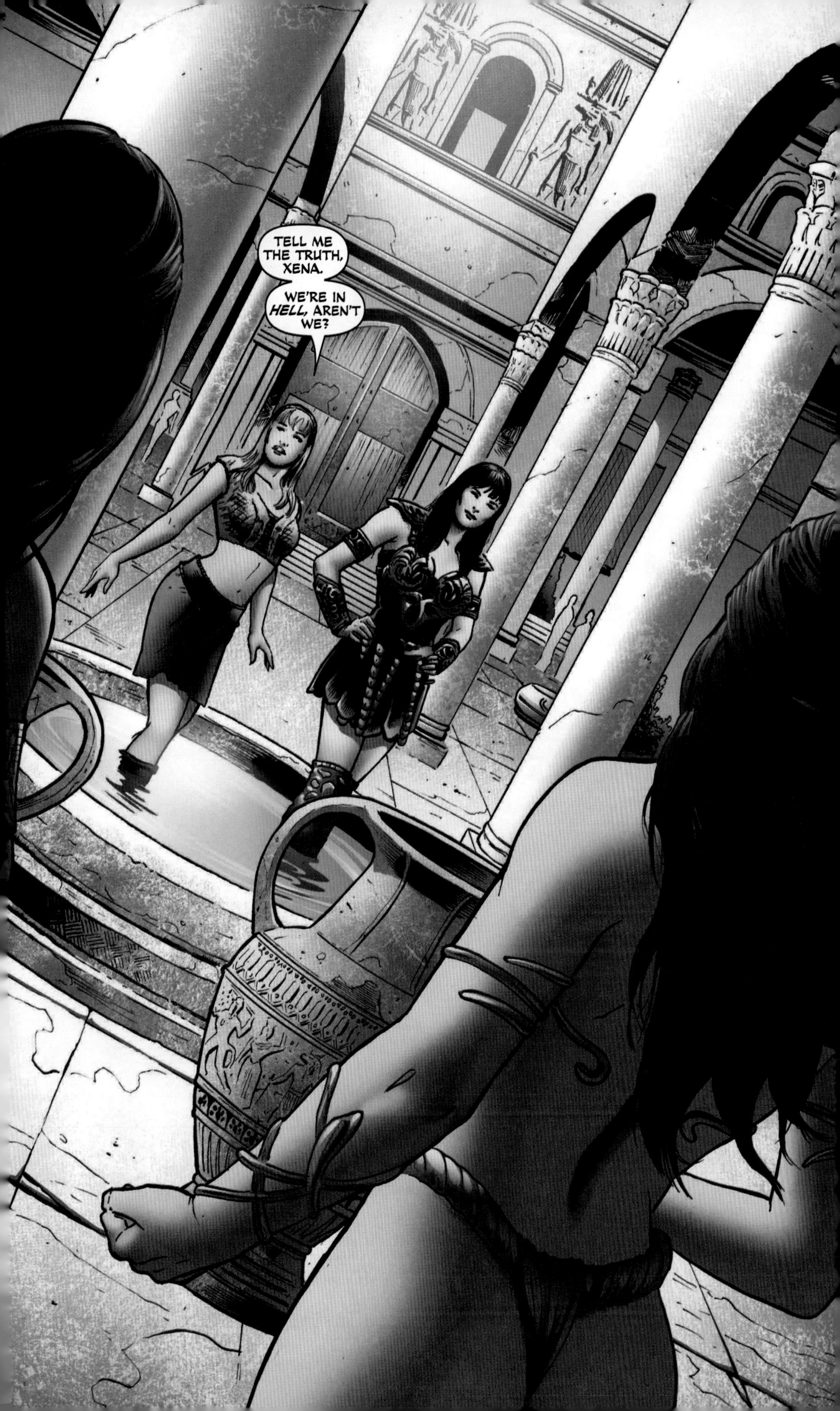
TELL ME THE TRUTH, XENA.
WE'RE IN *HELL*, AREN'T WE?

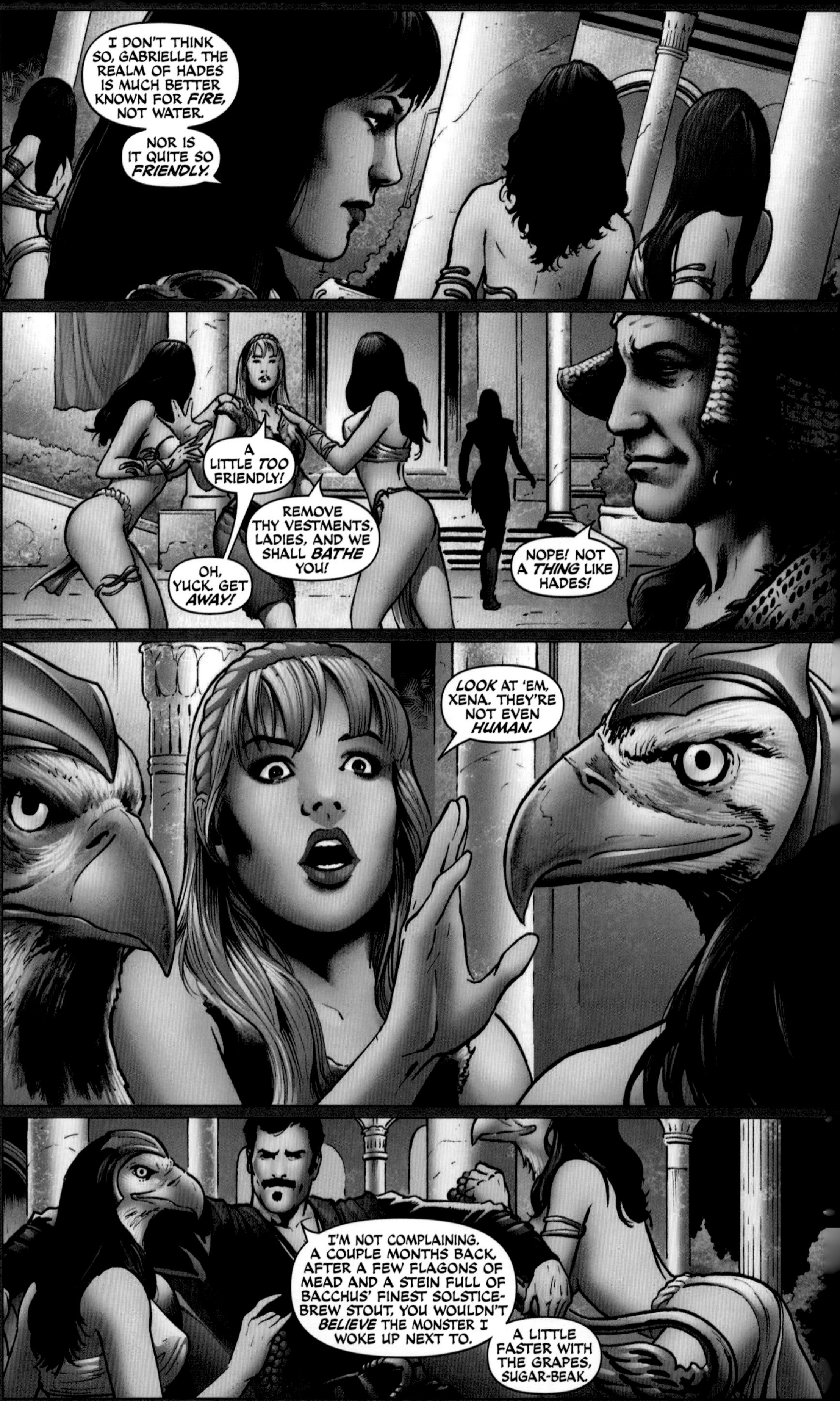
I DON'T THINK SO, GABRIELLE. THE REALM OF HADES IS MUCH BETTER KNOWN FOR *FIRE*, NOT WATER.
NOR IS IT QUITE SO *FRIENDLY.*
A LITTLE *TOO* FRIENDLY!
REMOVE THY VESTMENTS, LADIES, AND WE SHALL *BATHE* YOU!
OH, YUCK. GET *AWAY!*
NOPE! NOT A *THING* LIKE HADES!
LOOK AT 'EM, XENA. THEY'RE NOT EVEN *HUMAN.*
I'M NOT COMPLAINING. A COUPLE MONTHS BACK, AFTER A FEW FLAGONS OF MEAD AND A STEIN FULL OF BACCHUS' FINEST SOLSTICE-BREW STOUT, YOU WOULDN'T *BELIEVE* THE MONSTER I WOKE UP NEXT TO.
A LITTLE FASTER WITH THE GRAPES, SUGAR-BEAK.

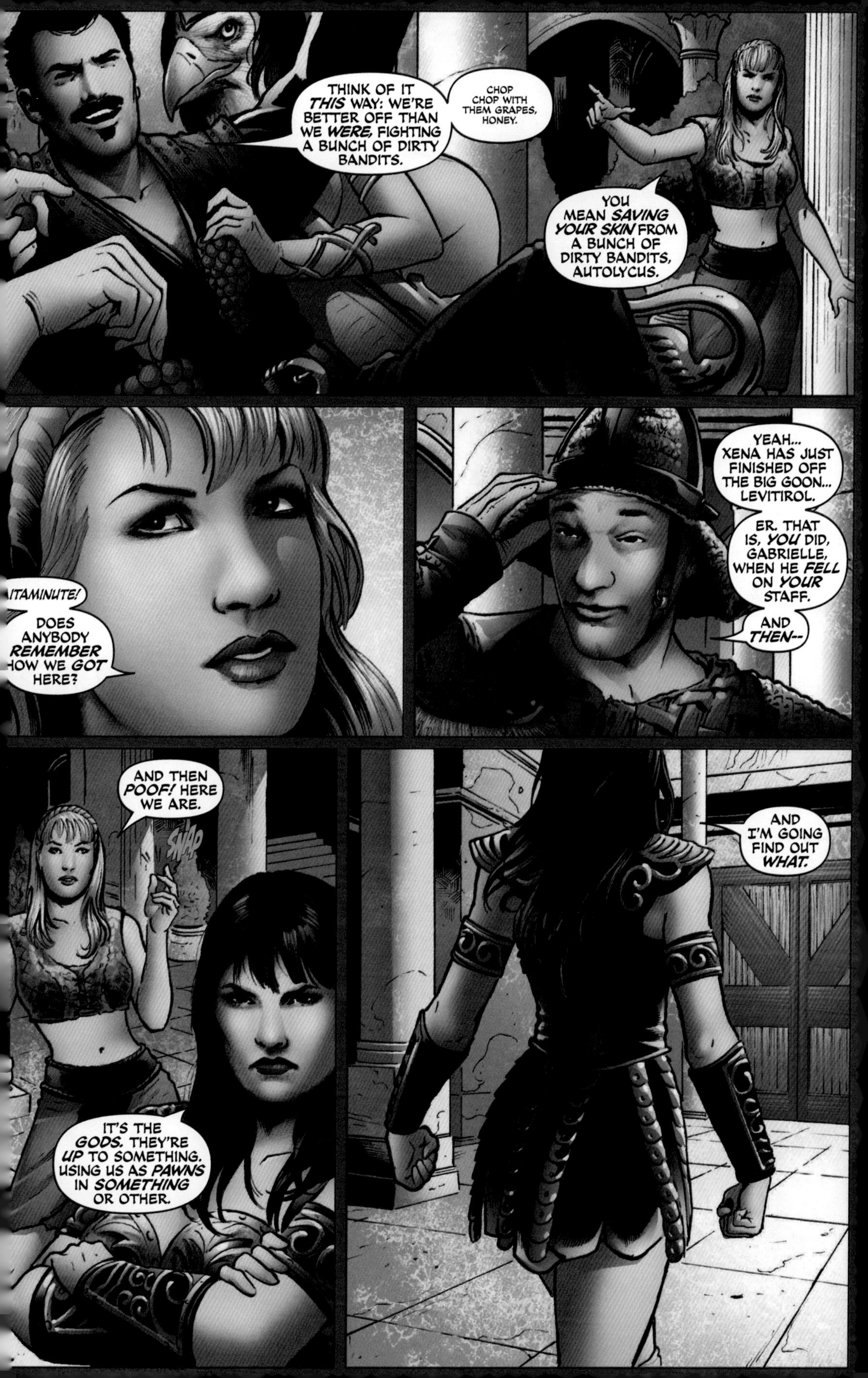
THINK OF IT THIS WAY: WE'RE BETTER OFF THAN WE WERE, FIGHTING A BUNCH OF DIRTY BANDITS.
CHOP CHOP WITH THEM GRAPES, HONEY.
YOU MEAN SAVING YOUR SKIN FROM A BUNCH OF DIRTY BANDITS, AUTOLYCUS.
ITAMINUTE!
DOES ANYBODY REMEMBER HOW WE GOT HERE?
YEAH... XENA HAS JUST FINISHED OFF THE BIG GOON... LEVITIROL.
ER. THAT IS, YOU DID, GABRIELLE, WHEN HE FELL ON YOUR STAFF.
AND THEN--
AND THEN POOF! HERE WE ARE.
SNAP
IT'S THE GODS. THEY'RE UP TO SOMETHING. USING US AS PAWNS IN SOMETHING OR OTHER.
AND I'M GOING FIND OUT WHAT.

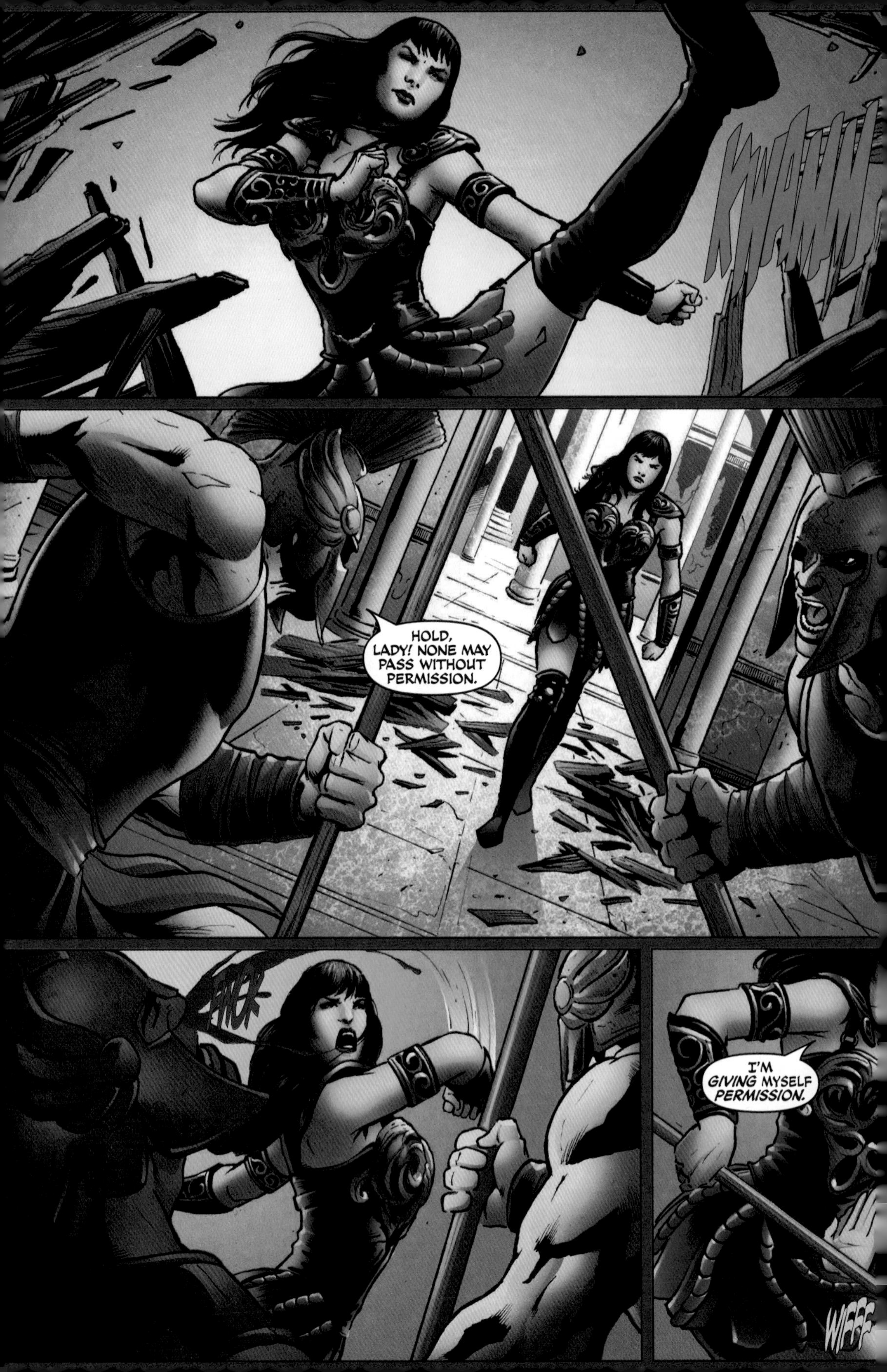
HOLD, LADY! NONE MAY PASS WITHOUT PERMISSION.
I'M *GIVING* MYSELF PERMISSION.
WIFFF

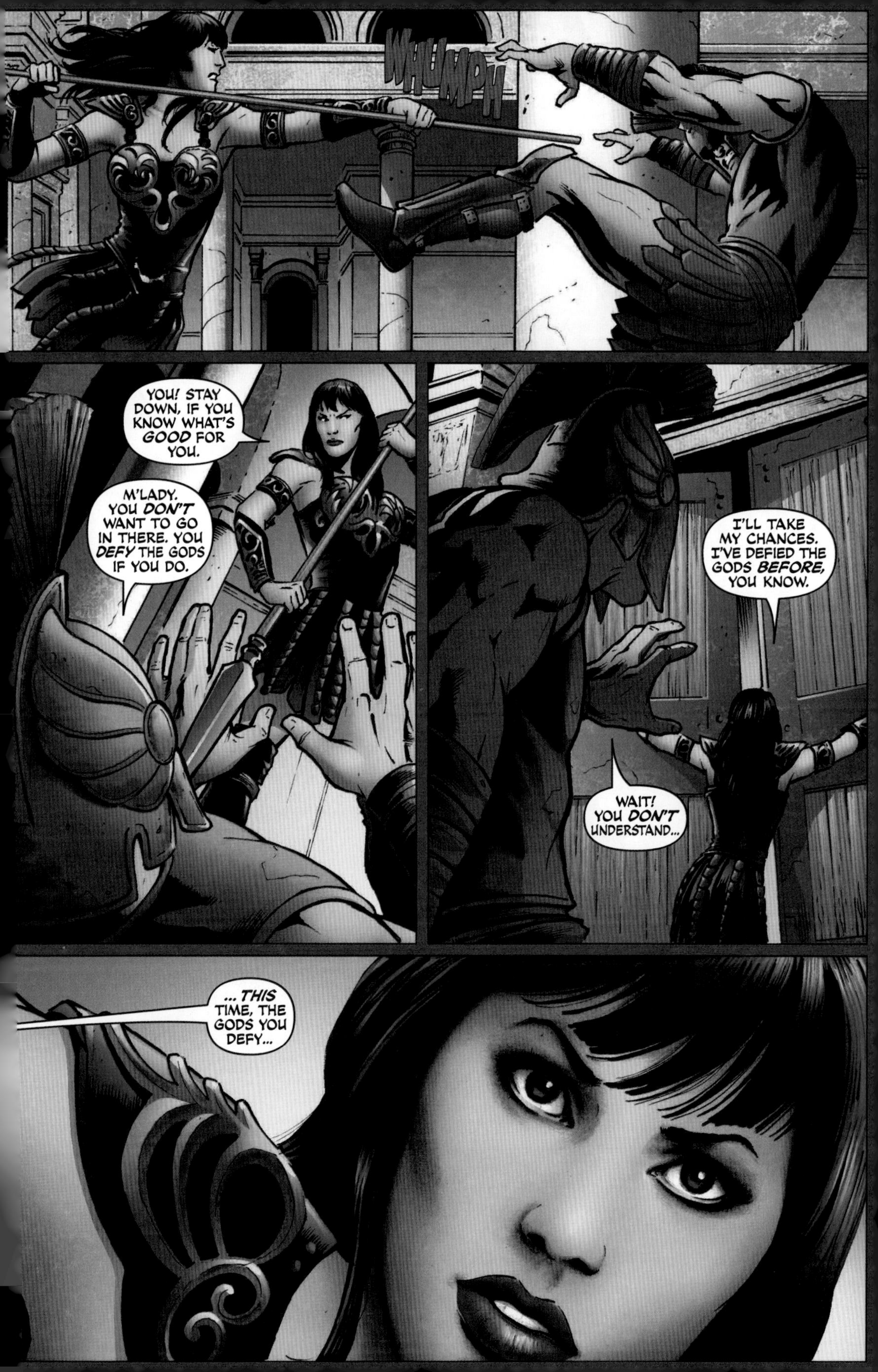
WHUMPH
YOU! STAY DOWN, IF YOU KNOW WHAT'S GOOD FOR YOU.
M'LADY. YOU DON'T WANT TO GO IN THERE. YOU DEFY THE GODS IF YOU DO.
I'LL TAKE MY CHANCES. I'VE DEFIED THE GODS BEFORE, YOU KNOW.
WAIT! YOU DON'T UNDERSTAND...
...THIS TIME, THE GODS YOU DEFY...

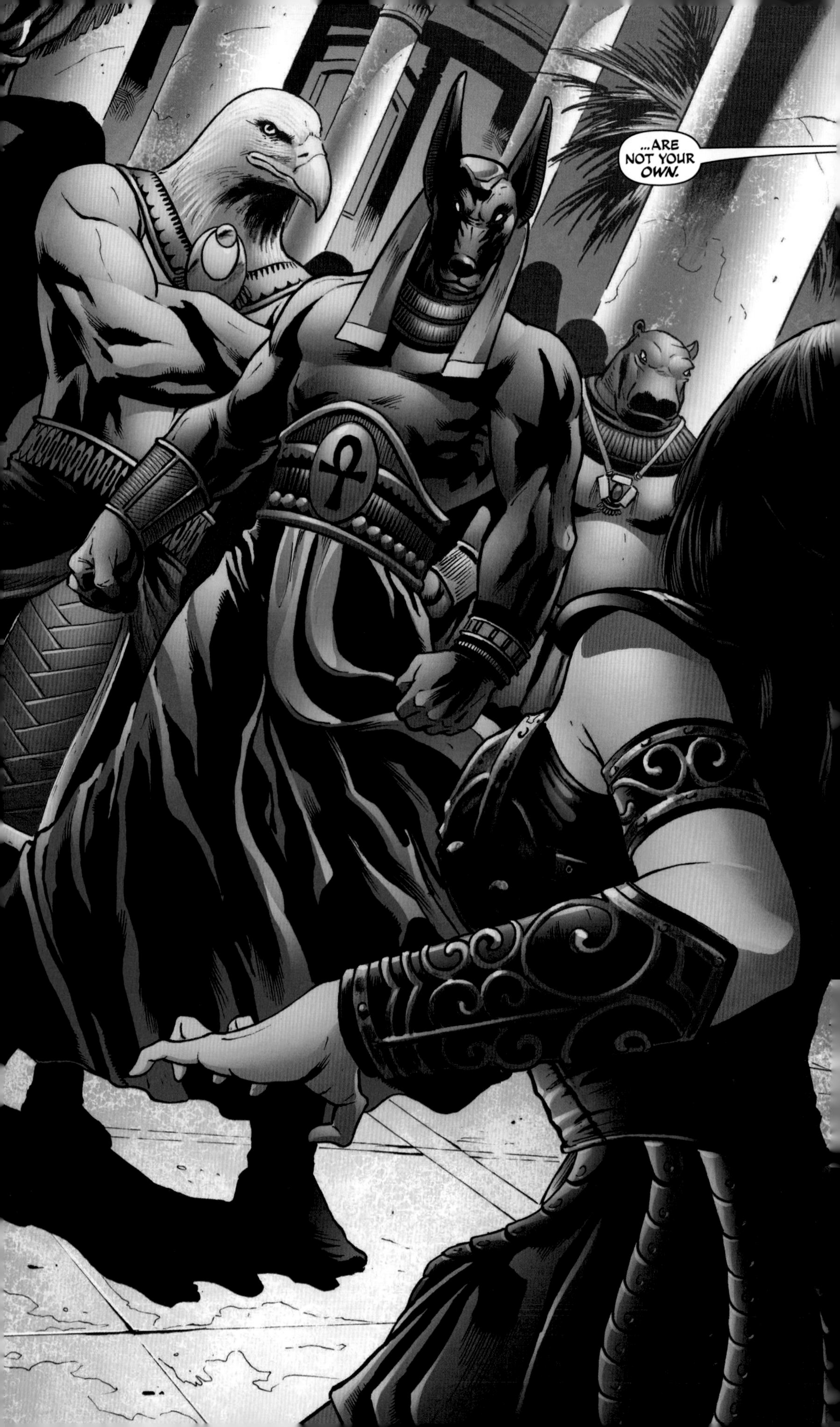
...ARE NOT YOUR OWN.

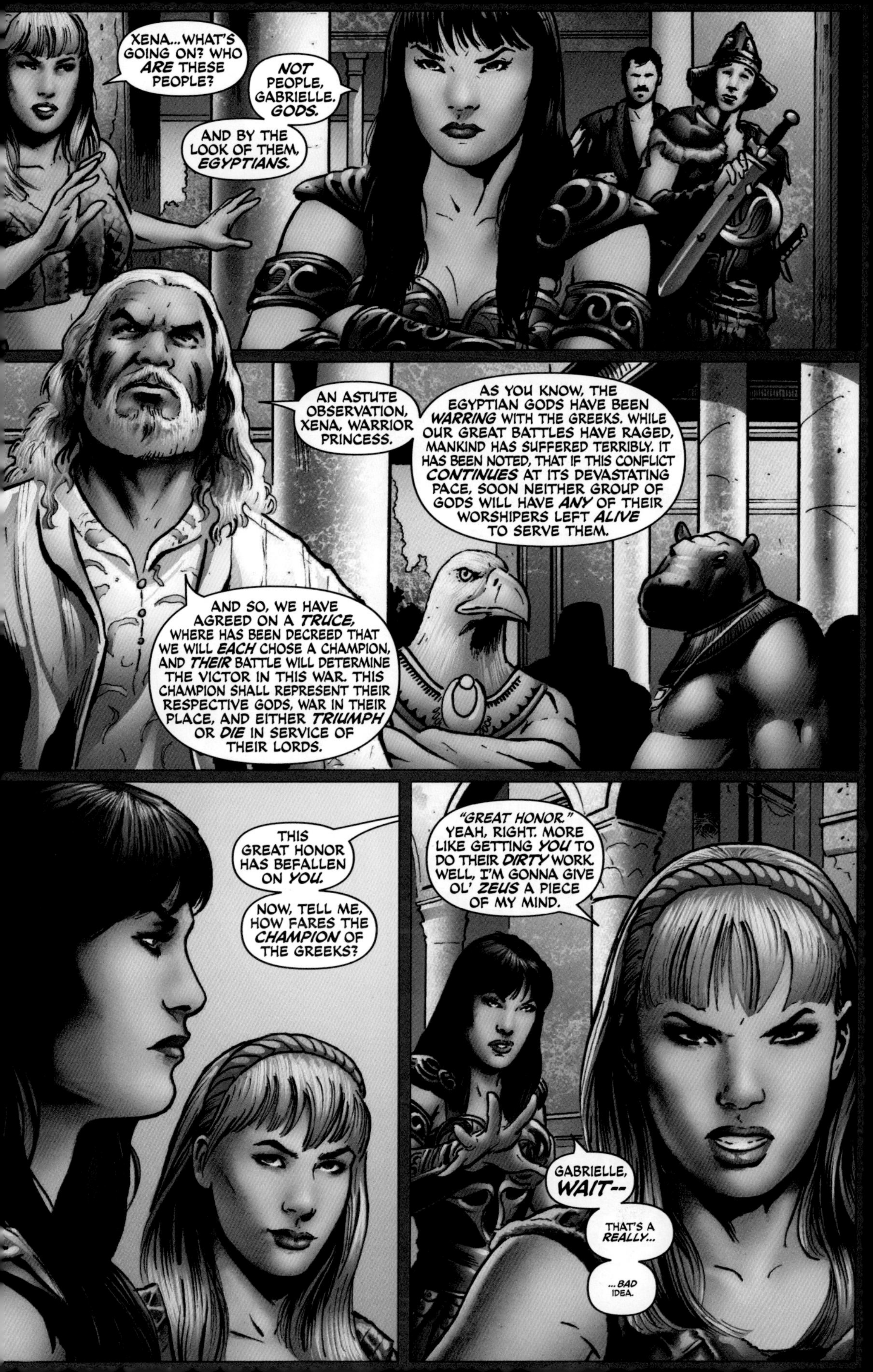
XENA...WHAT'S GOING ON? WHO ARE THESE PEOPLE?
NOT PEOPLE, GABRIELLE. GODS.
AND BY THE LOOK OF THEM, EGYPTIANS.
AN ASTUTE OBSERVATION, XENA, WARRIOR PRINCESS.
AS YOU KNOW, THE EGYPTIAN GODS HAVE BEEN WARRING WITH THE GREEKS. WHILE OUR GREAT BATTLES HAVE RAGED, MANKIND HAS SUFFERED TERRIBLY. IT HAS BEEN NOTED, THAT IF THIS CONFLICT CONTINUES AT ITS DEVASTATING PACE, SOON NEITHER GROUP OF GODS WILL HAVE ANY OF THEIR WORSHIPERS LEFT ALIVE TO SERVE THEM.
AND SO, WE HAVE AGREED ON A TRUCE, WHERE HAS BEEN DECREED THAT WE WILL EACH CHOSE A CHAMPION, AND THEIR BATTLE WILL DETERMINE THE VICTOR IN THIS WAR. THIS CHAMPION SHALL REPRESENT THEIR RESPECTIVE GODS, WAR IN THEIR PLACE, AND EITHER TRIUMPH OR DIE IN SERVICE OF THEIR LORDS.
THIS GREAT HONOR HAS BEFALLEN ON YOU.
NOW, TELL ME, HOW FARES THE CHAMPION OF THE GREEKS?
"GREAT HONOR." YEAH, RIGHT. MORE LIKE GETTING YOU TO DO THEIR DIRTY WORK. WELL, I'M GONNA GIVE OL' ZEUS A PIECE OF MY MIND.
GABRIELLE, WAIT--
THAT'S A REALLY...
...BAD IDEA.

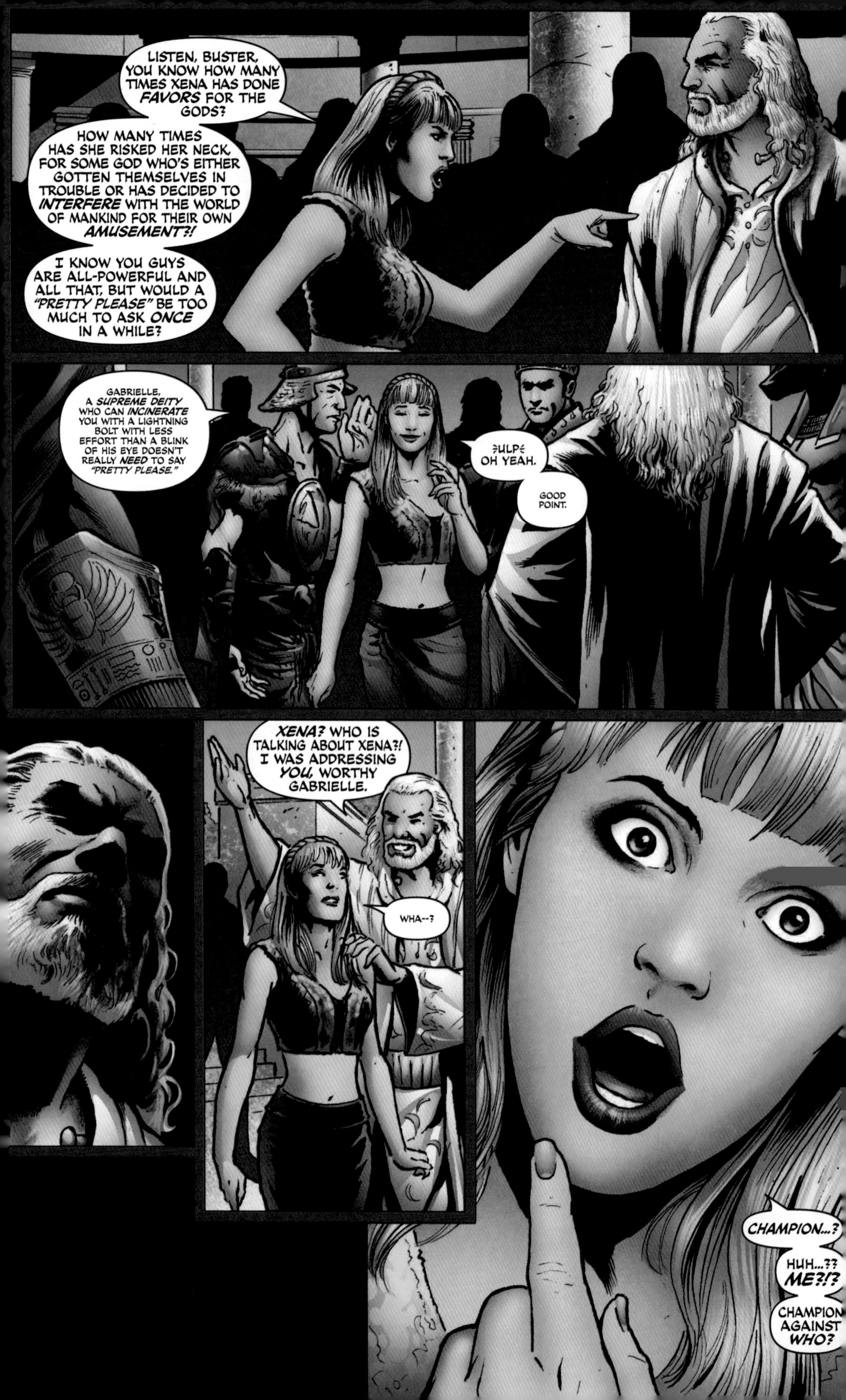
LISTEN, BUSTER, YOU KNOW HOW MANY TIMES XENA HAS DONE FAVORS FOR THE GODS?
HOW MANY TIMES HAS SHE RISKED HER NECK, FOR SOME GOD WHO'S EITHER GOTTEN THEMSELVES IN TROUBLE OR HAS DECIDED TO INTERFERE WITH THE WORLD OF MANKIND FOR THEIR OWN AMUSEMENT?!
I KNOW YOU GUYS ARE ALL-POWERFUL AND ALL THAT, BUT WOULD A "PRETTY PLEASE" BE TOO MUCH TO ASK ONCE IN A WHILE?
GABRIELLE, A SUPREME DEITY WHO CAN INCINERATE YOU WITH A LIGHTNING BOLT WITH LESS EFFORT THAN A BLINK OF HIS EYE DOESN'T REALLY NEED TO SAY "PRETTY PLEASE."
GULP OH YEAH.
GOOD POINT.
XENA? WHO IS TALKING ABOUT XENA?! I WAS ADDRESSING YOU, WORTHY GABRIELLE.
WHA--?
CHAMPION...?
HUH...?? ME?!?
CHAMPION AGAINST WHO?

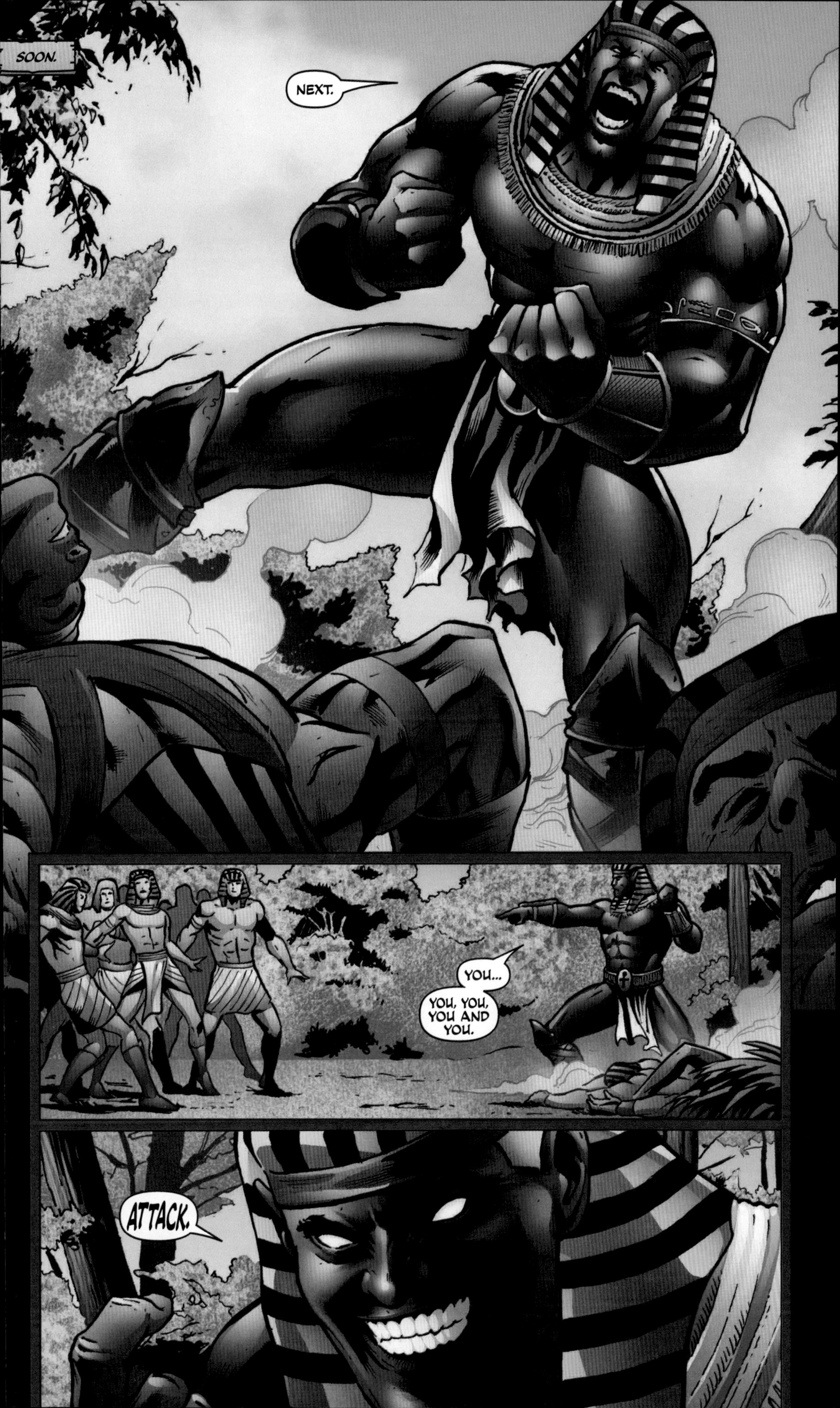
SOON.
NEXT.
YOU...
YOU, YOU, YOU AND YOU.
ATTACK.

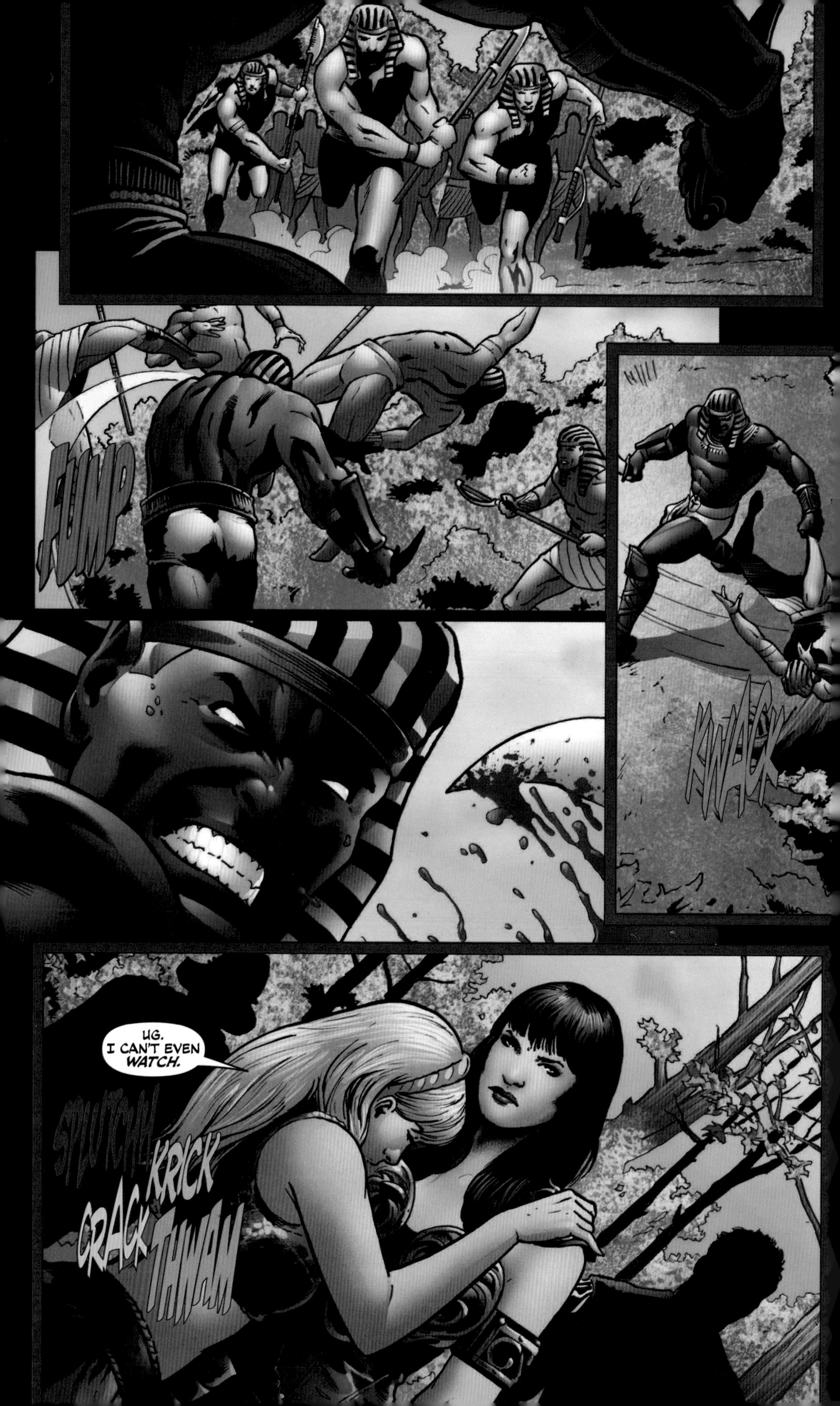
FUMP
KWACK
UG. I CAN'T EVEN *WATCH.*
SPLUTCHH
KRICK
CRACK
THWAM

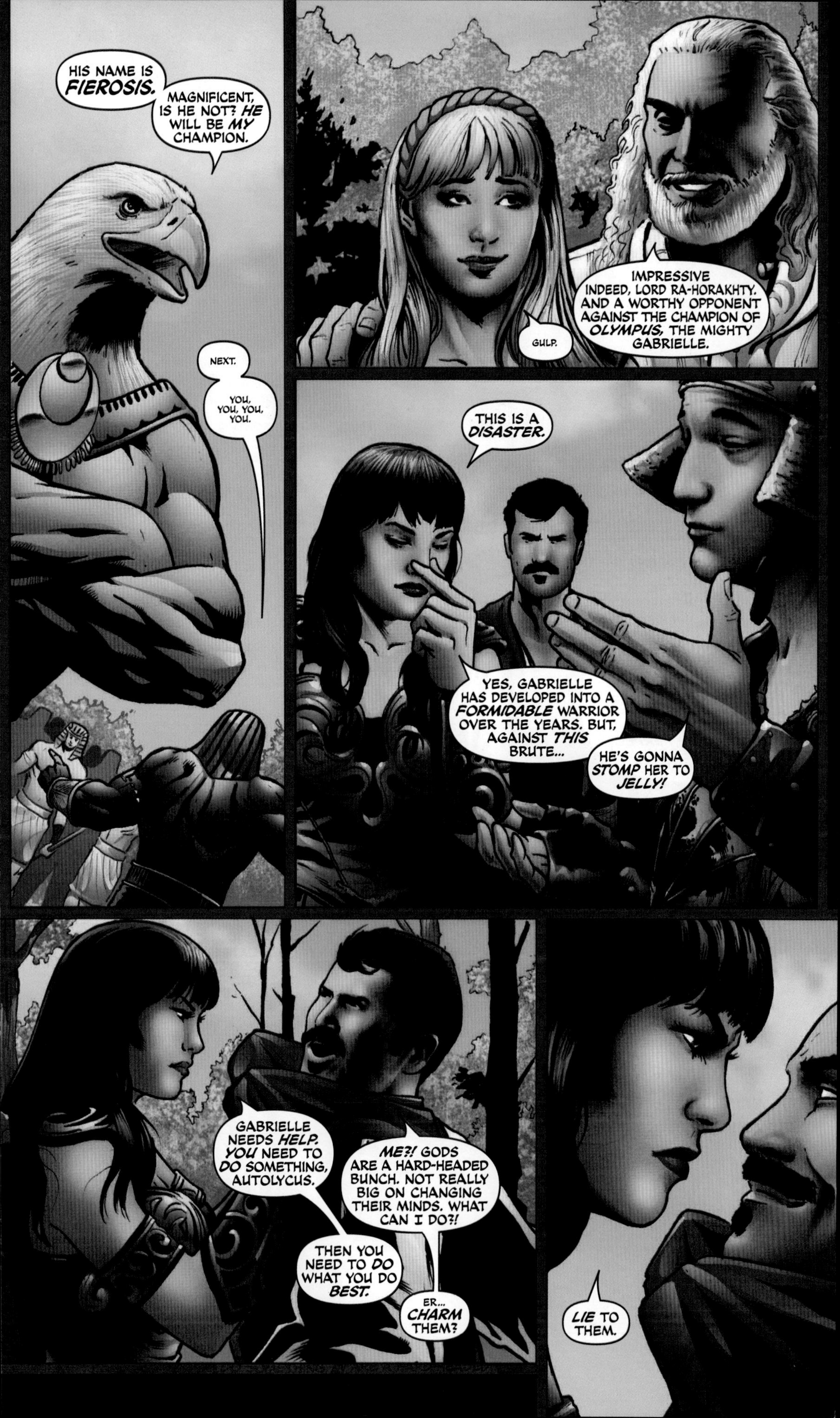

HIS NAME IS FIEROSIS.
MAGNIFICENT, IS HE NOT? HE WILL BE MY CHAMPION.
IMPRESSIVE INDEED, LORD RA-HORAKHTY. AND A WORTHY OPPONENT AGAINST THE CHAMPION OF OLYMPUS, THE MIGHTY GABRIELLE.
GULP.
NEXT.
YOU, YOU, YOU, YOU.
THIS IS A DISASTER.
YES, GABRIELLE HAS DEVELOPED INTO A FORMIDABLE WARRIOR OVER THE YEARS. BUT, AGAINST THIS BRUTE...
HE'S GONNA STOMP HER TO JELLY!
GABRIELLE NEEDS HELP. YOU NEED TO DO SOMETHING, AUTOLYCUS.
ME?! GODS ARE A HARD-HEADED BUNCH. NOT REALLY BIG ON CHANGING THEIR MINDS. WHAT CAN I DO?!
THEN YOU NEED TO DO WHAT YOU DO BEST.
ER... CHARM THEM?
LIE TO THEM.

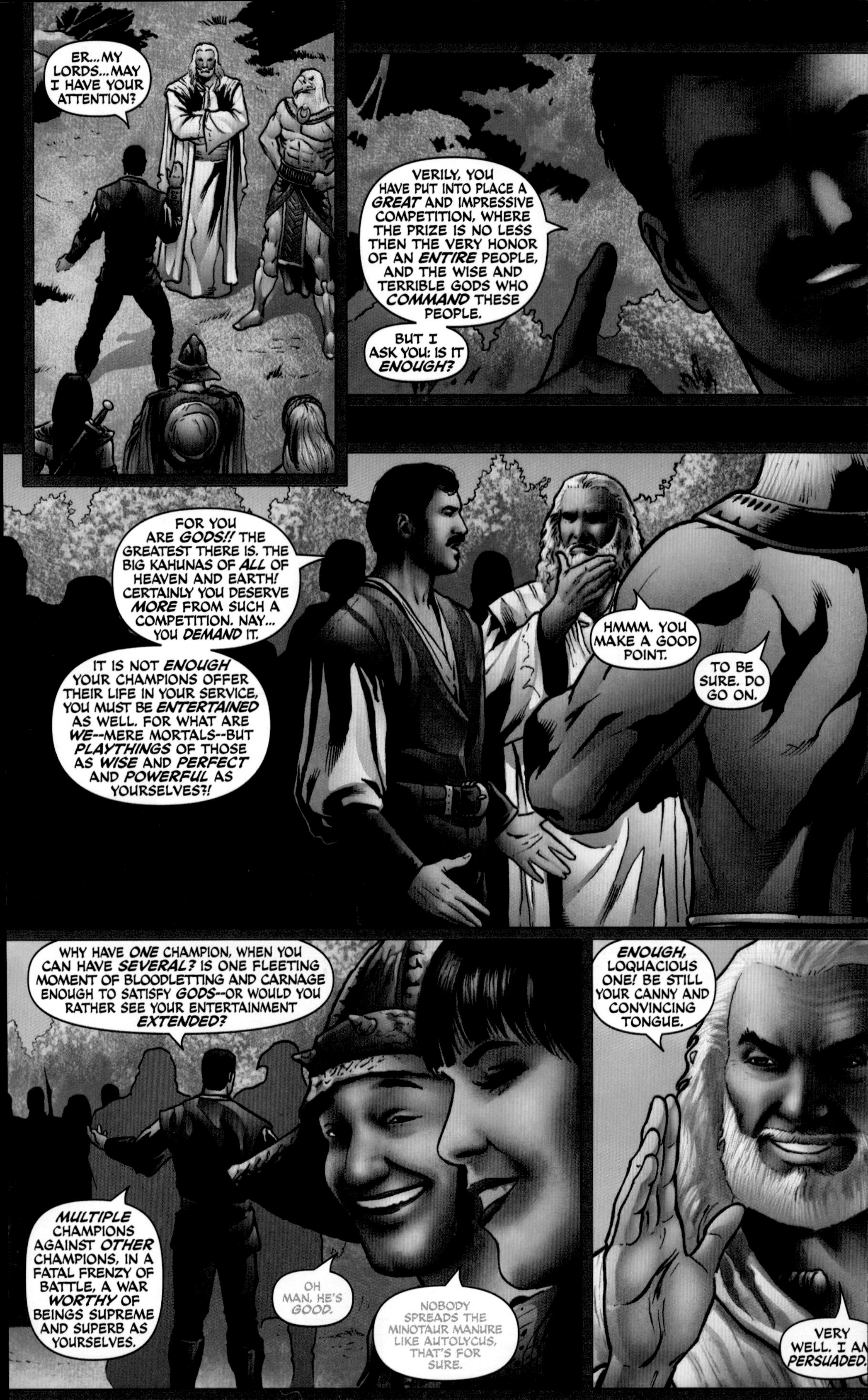
ER...MY LORDS...MAY I HAVE YOUR ATTENTION?
VERILY, YOU HAVE PUT INTO PLACE A GREAT AND IMPRESSIVE COMPETITION, WHERE THE PRIZE IS NO LESS THEN THE VERY HONOR OF AN ENTIRE PEOPLE, AND THE WISE AND TERRIBLE GODS WHO COMMAND THESE PEOPLE.
BUT I ASK YOU: IS IT ENOUGH?
FOR YOU ARE GODS!! THE GREATEST THERE IS. THE BIG KAHUNAS OF ALL OF HEAVEN AND EARTH! CERTAINLY YOU DESERVE MORE FROM SUCH A COMPETITION. NAY... YOU DEMAND IT.
IT IS NOT ENOUGH YOUR CHAMPIONS OFFER THEIR LIFE IN YOUR SERVICE, YOU MUST BE ENTERTAINED AS WELL. FOR WHAT ARE WE--MERE MORTALS--BUT PLAYTHINGS OF THOSE AS WISE AND PERFECT AND POWERFUL AS YOURSELVES?!
HMMM. YOU MAKE A GOOD POINT.
TO BE SURE. DO GO ON.
WHY HAVE ONE CHAMPION, WHEN YOU CAN HAVE SEVERAL? IS ONE FLEETING MOMENT OF BLOODLETTING AND CARNAGE ENOUGH TO SATISFY GODS--OR WOULD YOU RATHER SEE YOUR ENTERTAINMENT EXTENDED?
MULTIPLE CHAMPIONS AGAINST OTHER CHAMPIONS, IN A FATAL FRENZY OF BATTLE, A WAR WORTHY OF BEINGS SUPREME AND SUPERB AS YOURSELVES.
OH MAN, HE'S GOOD.
NOBODY SPREADS THE MINOTAUR MANURE LIKE AUTOLYCUS, THAT'S FOR SURE.
ENOUGH, LOQUACIOUS ONE! BE STILL YOUR CANNY AND CONVINCING TONGUE.
VERY WELL. I AM PERSUADED.

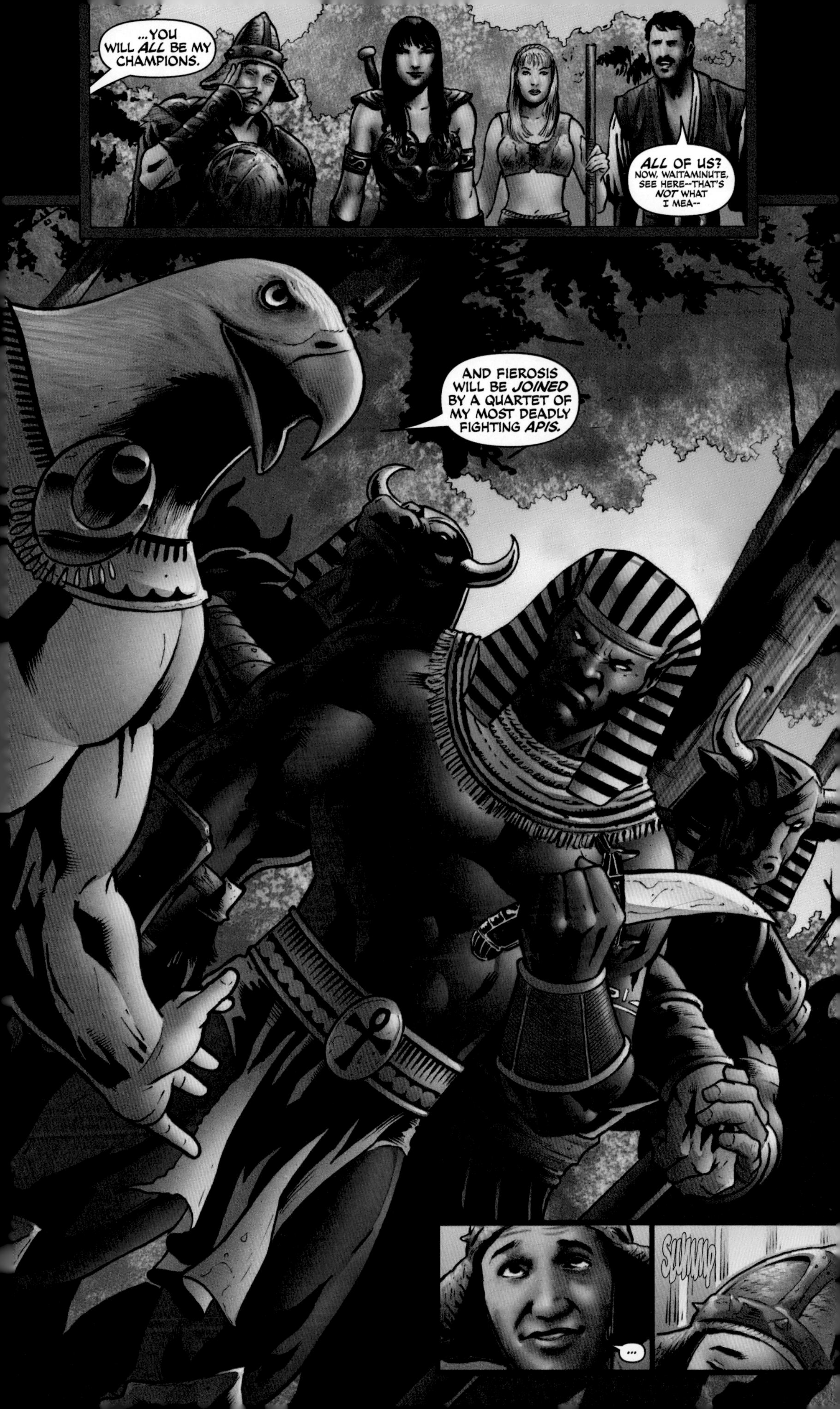

...YOU WILL ALL BE MY CHAMPIONS.
ALL OF US? NOW, WAITAMINUTE, SEE HERE--THAT'S NOT WHAT I MEA--
AND FIEROSIS WILL BE JOINED BY A QUARTET OF MY MOST DEADLY FIGHTING APIS.
...
SHHHNG

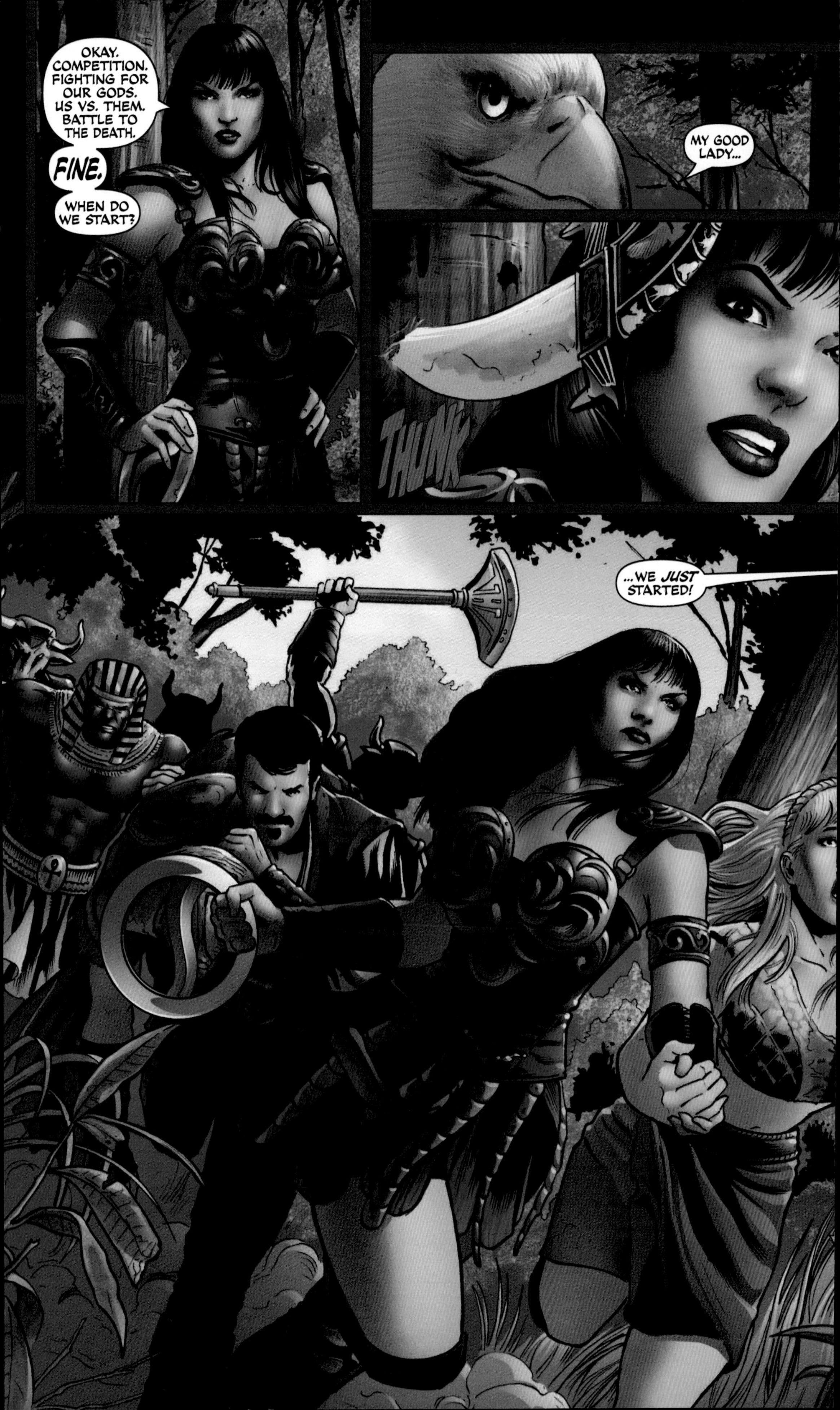
OKAY. COMPETITION. FIGHTING FOR OUR GODS. US VS. THEM. BATTLE TO THE DEATH.
FINE.
WHEN DO WE START?
MY GOOD LADY...
THUNK
...WE *JUST* STARTED!

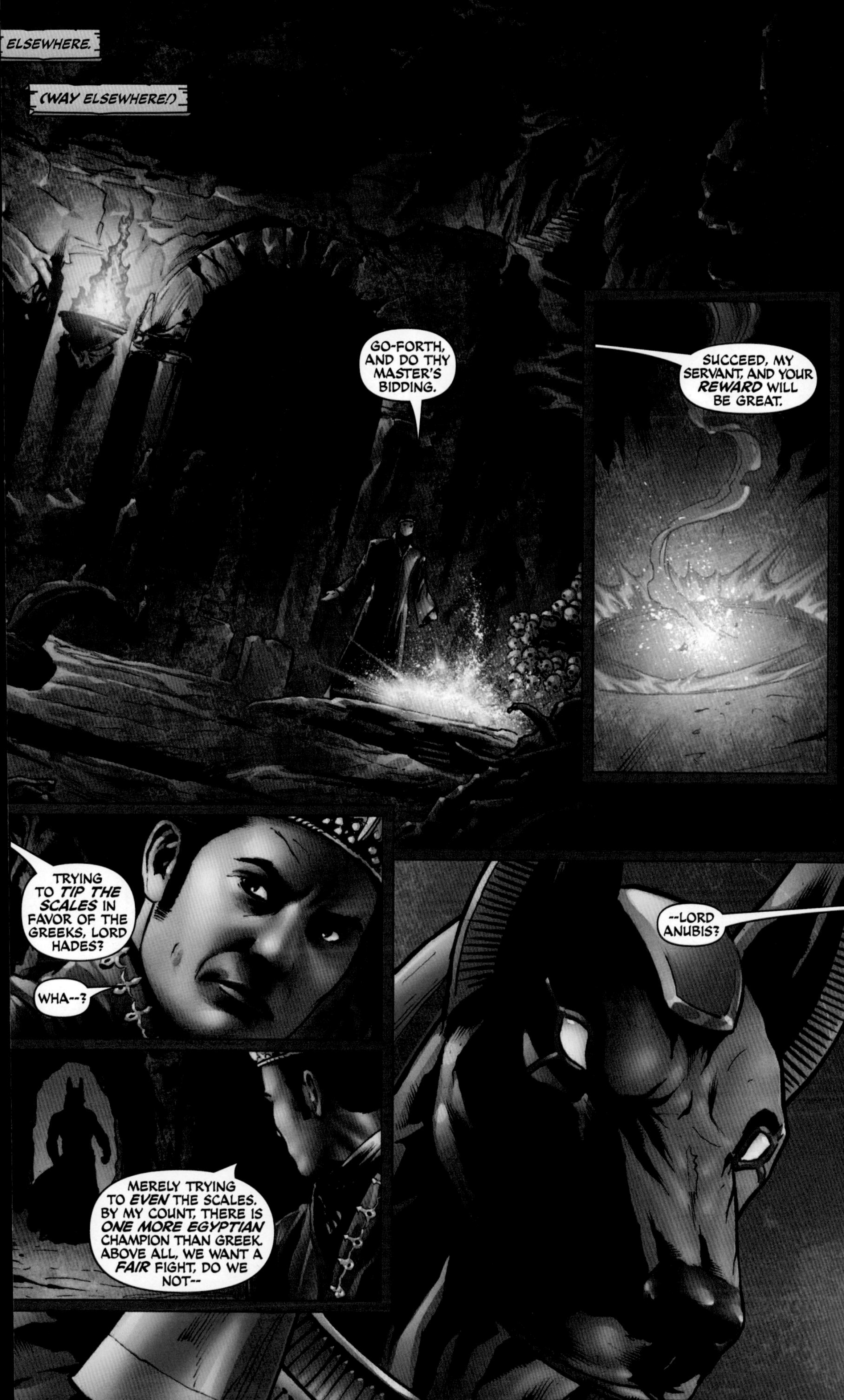
ELSEWHERE.
(WAY ELSEWHERE!)
GO-FORTH, AND DO THY MASTER'S BIDDING.
SUCCEED, MY SERVANT, AND YOUR REWARD WILL BE GREAT.
TRYING TO TIP THE SCALES IN FAVOR OF THE GREEKS, LORD HADES?
WHA--?
MERELY TRYING TO EVEN THE SCALES. BY MY COUNT, THERE IS ONE MORE EGYPTIAN CHAMPION THAN GREEK. ABOVE ALL, WE WANT A FAIR FIGHT, DO WE NOT--
--LORD ANUBIS?

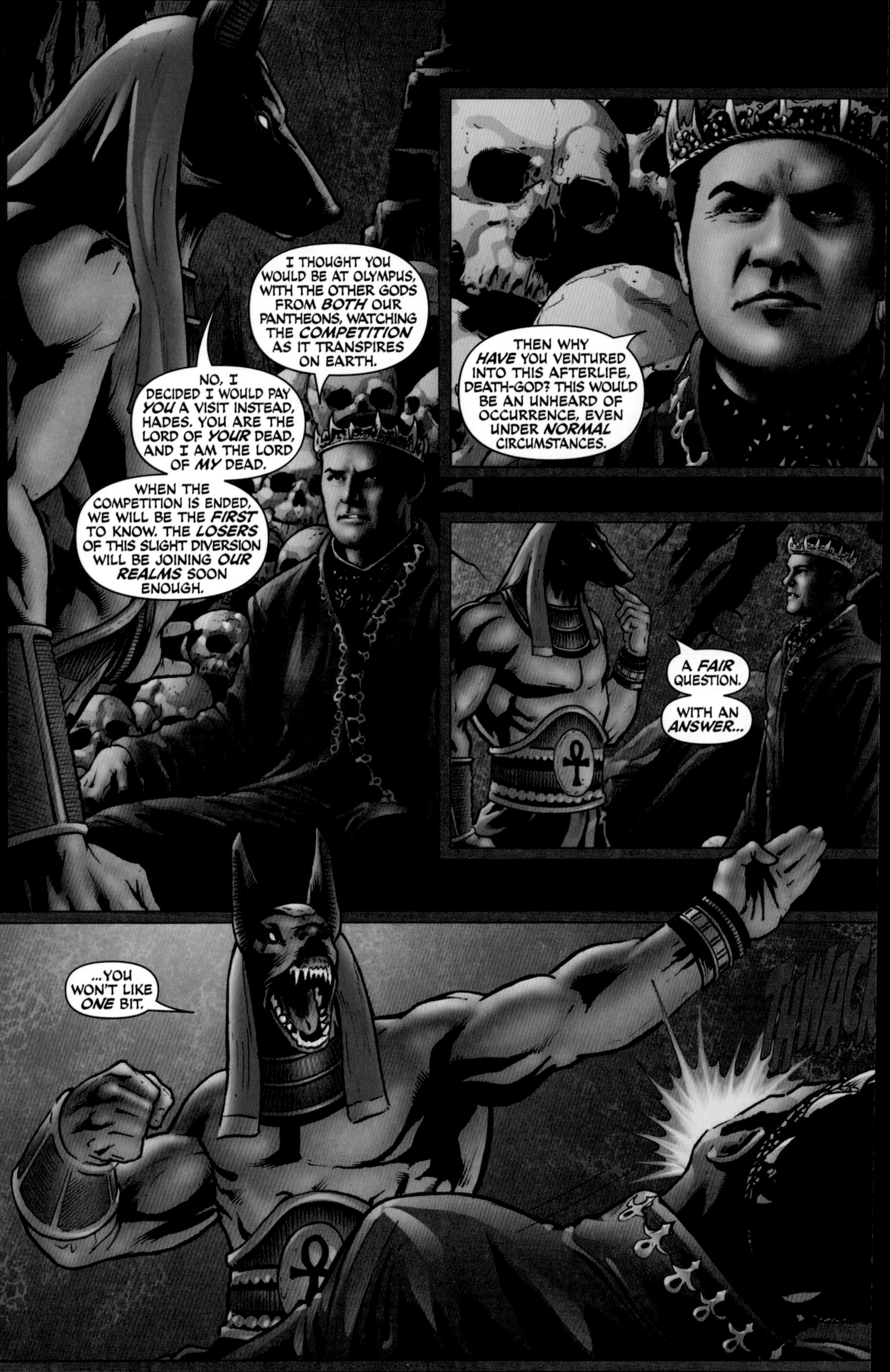
I THOUGHT YOU WOULD BE AT OLYMPUS, WITH THE OTHER GODS FROM *BOTH* OUR PANTHEONS, WATCHING THE *COMPETITION* AS IT TRANSPIRES ON EARTH.
NO, I DECIDED I WOULD PAY *YOU* A VISIT INSTEAD, HADES. YOU ARE THE LORD OF *YOUR* DEAD, AND I AM THE LORD OF *MY* DEAD.
WHEN THE COMPETITION IS ENDED, WE WILL BE THE *FIRST* TO KNOW. THE *LOSERS* OF THIS SLIGHT DIVERSION WILL BE JOINING *OUR REALMS* SOON ENOUGH.
THEN WHY *HAVE* YOU VENTURED INTO THIS AFTERLIFE, DEATH-GOD? THIS WOULD BE AN UNHEARD OF OCCURRENCE, EVEN UNDER *NORMAL* CIRCUMSTANCES.
A *FAIR* QUESTION.
WITH AN *ANSWER*...
...YOU WON'T LIKE *ONE* BIT.

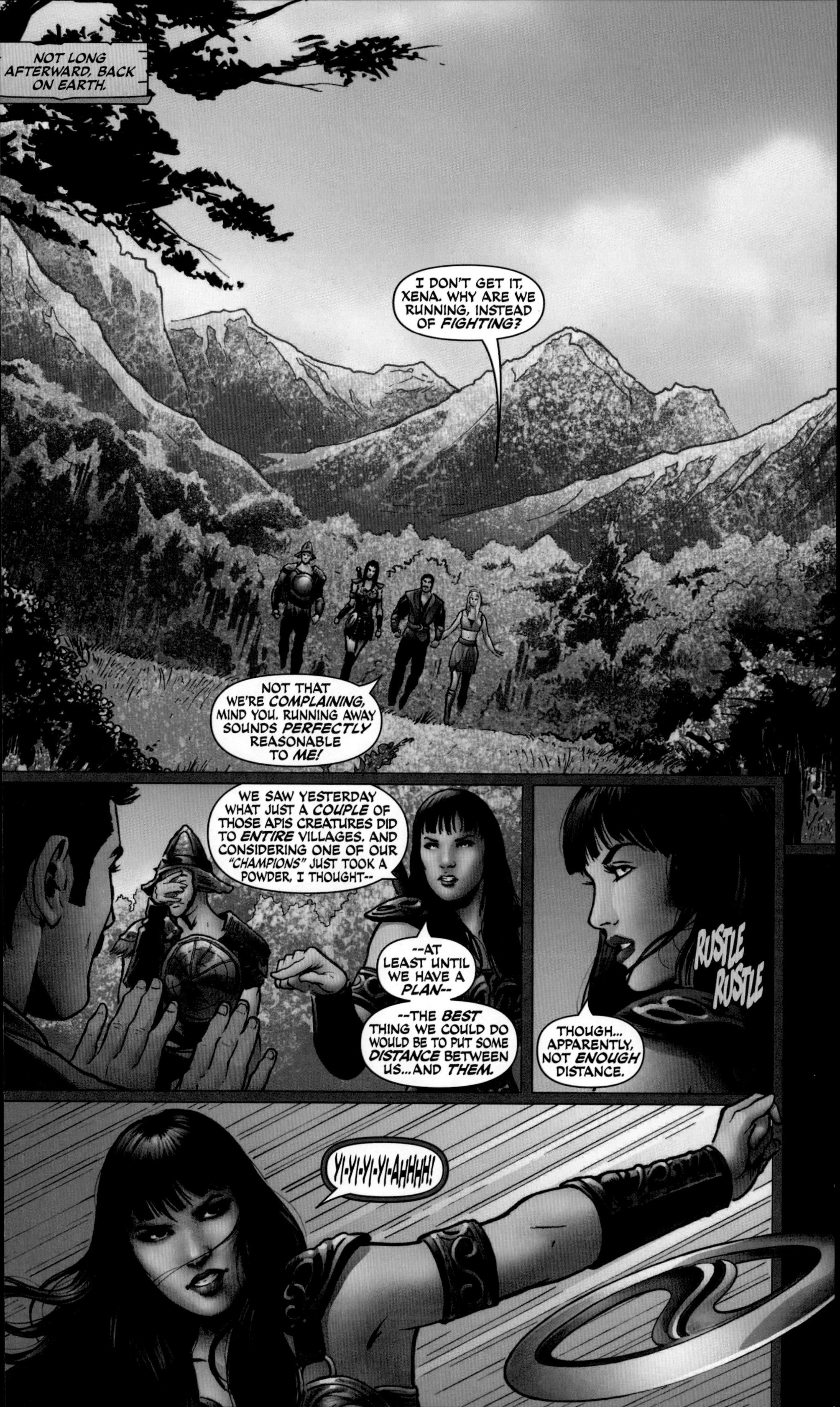
NOT LONG AFTERWARD, BACK ON EARTH.
I DON'T GET IT, XENA. WHY ARE WE RUNNING, INSTEAD OF FIGHTING?
NOT THAT WE'RE COMPLAINING, MIND YOU. RUNNING AWAY SOUNDS PERFECTLY REASONABLE TO ME!
WE SAW YESTERDAY WHAT JUST A COUPLE OF THOSE APIS CREATURES DID TO ENTIRE VILLAGES. AND CONSIDERING ONE OF OUR "CHAMPIONS" JUST TOOK A POWDER, I THOUGHT--
--AT LEAST UNTIL WE HAVE A PLAN--
--THE BEST THING WE COULD DO WOULD BE TO PUT SOME DISTANCE BETWEEN US...AND THEM.
RUSTLE RUSTLE
THOUGH... APPARENTLY, NOT ENOUGH DISTANCE.
YI-YI-YI-YI-AHHHH!

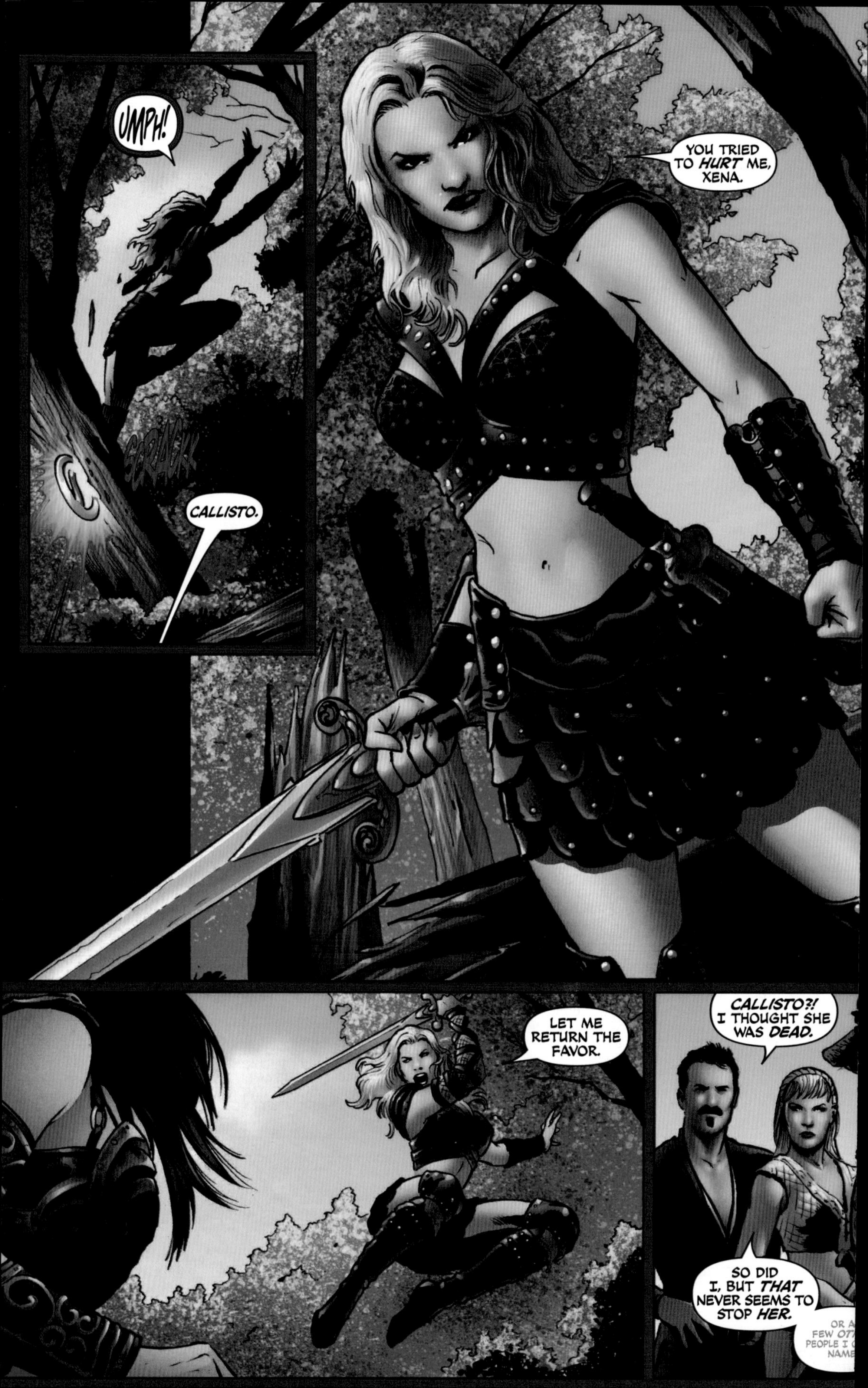
UMPH!
CALLISTO.
YOU TRIED TO *HURT* ME, XENA.
LET ME RETURN THE FAVOR.
CALLISTO?! I THOUGHT SHE WAS *DEAD.*
SO DID I, BUT *THAT* NEVER SEEMS TO STOP *HER.*

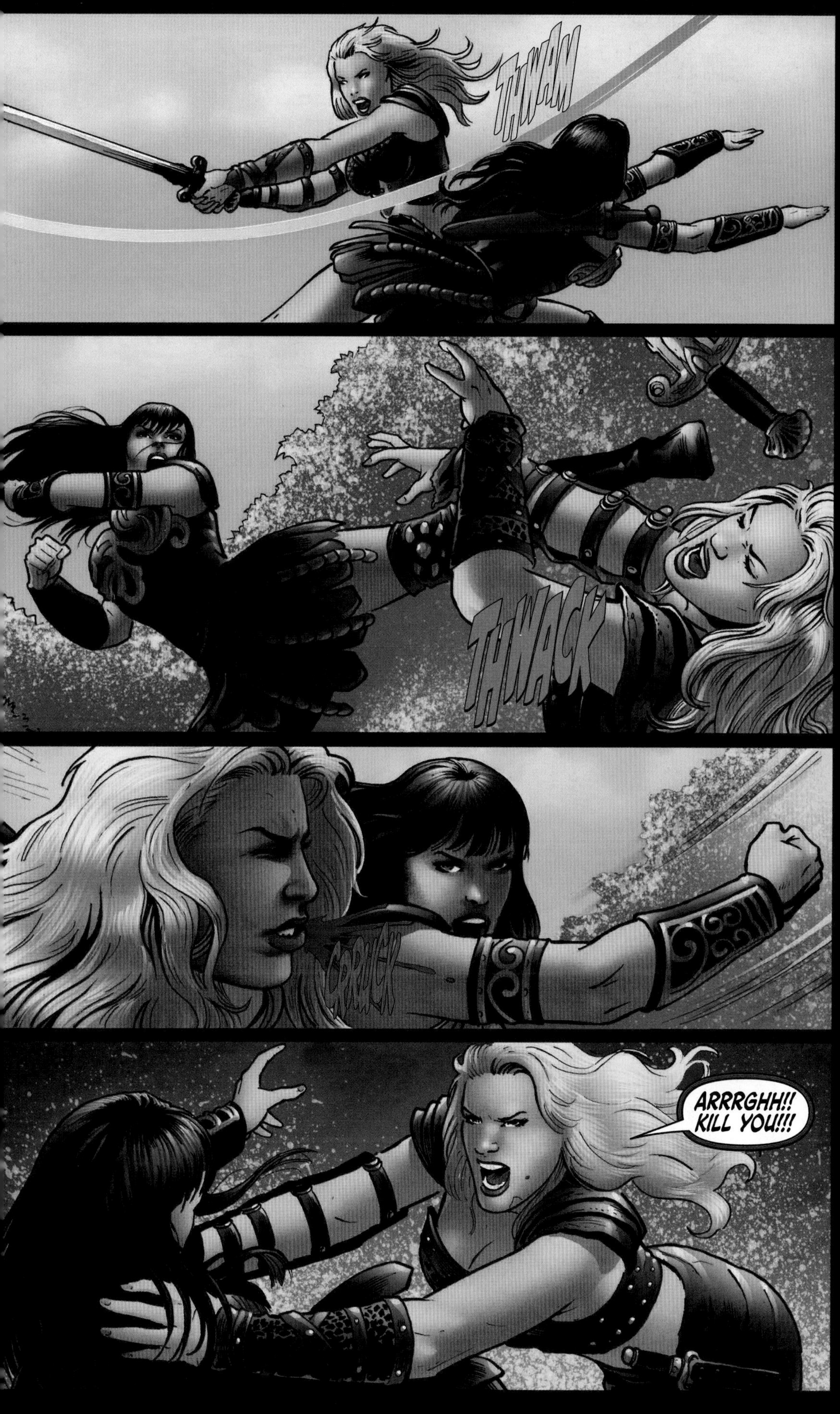

THWAM
THWACK
CRRUCK
ARRRGHH!! KILL YOU!!!

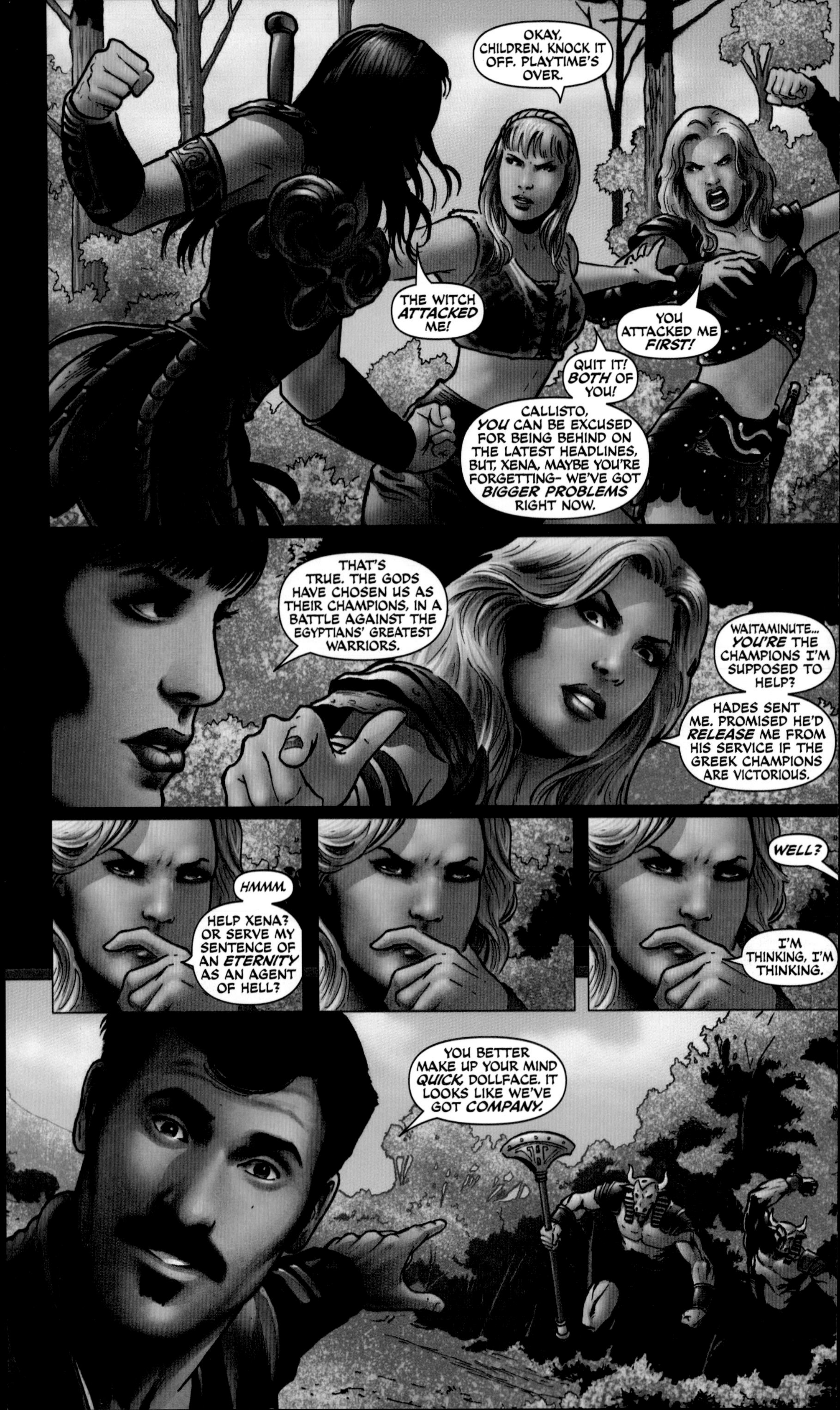
OKAY, CHILDREN. KNOCK IT OFF. PLAYTIME'S OVER.
THE WITCH ATTACKED ME!
YOU ATTACKED ME FIRST!
QUIT IT! BOTH OF YOU!
CALLISTO, YOU CAN BE EXCUSED FOR BEING BEHIND ON THE LATEST HEADLINES, BUT, XENA, MAYBE YOU'RE FORGETTING- WE'VE GOT BIGGER PROBLEMS RIGHT NOW.
THAT'S TRUE. THE GODS HAVE CHOSEN US AS THEIR CHAMPIONS, IN A BATTLE AGAINST THE EGYPTIANS' GREATEST WARRIORS.
WAITAMINUTE... YOU'RE THE CHAMPIONS I'M SUPPOSED TO HELP?
HADES SENT ME. PROMISED HE'D RELEASE ME FROM HIS SERVICE IF THE GREEK CHAMPIONS ARE VICTORIOUS.
HMMM.
HELP XENA? OR SERVE MY SENTENCE OF AN ETERNITY AS AN AGENT OF HELL?
WELL?
I'M THINKING, I'M THINKING.
YOU BETTER MAKE UP YOUR MIND QUICK, DOLLFACE. IT LOOKS LIKE WE'VE GOT COMPANY.

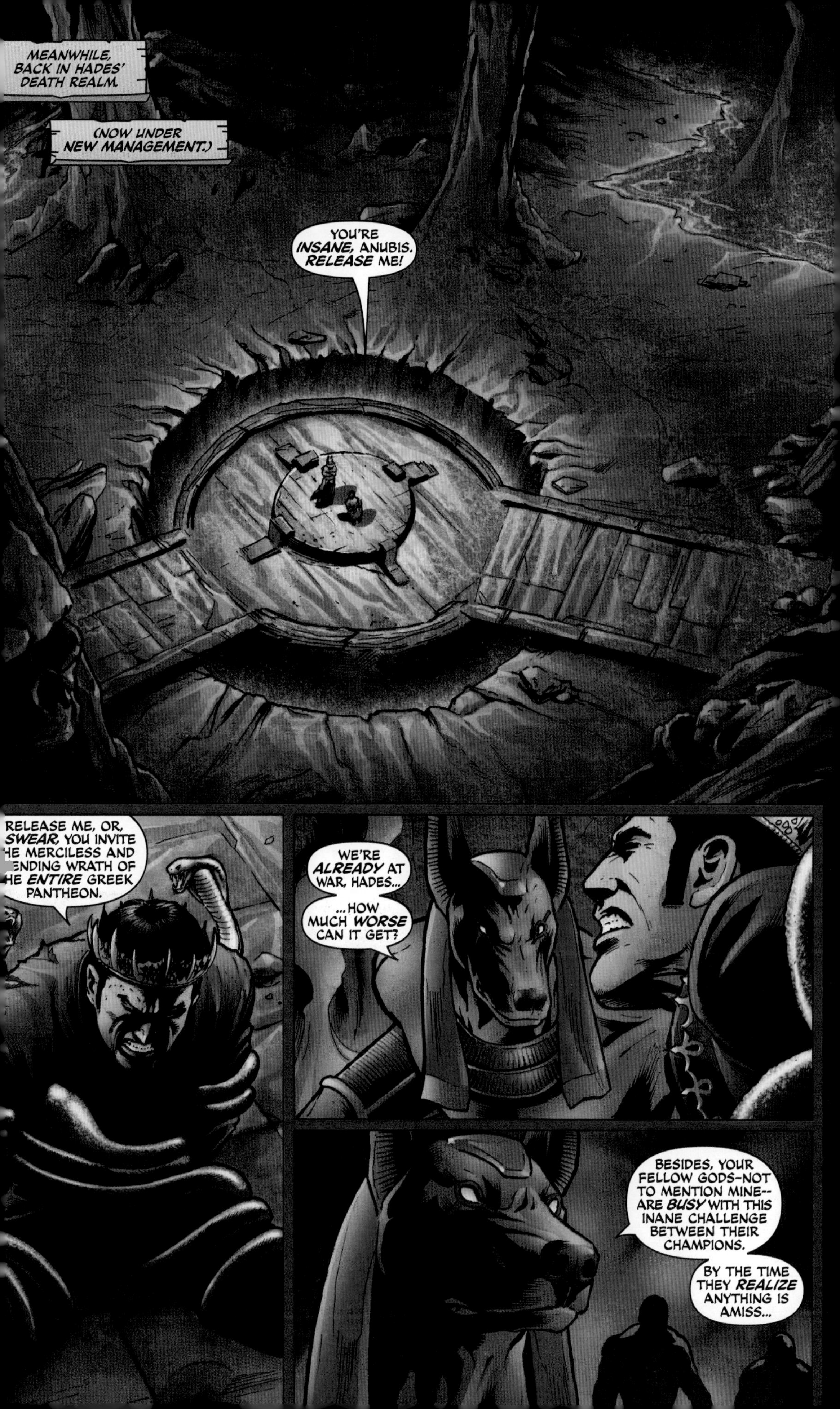

MEANWHILE, BACK IN HADES' DEATH REALM.
(NOW UNDER NEW MANAGEMENT.)
YOU'RE INSANE, ANUBIS. RELEASE ME!
RELEASE ME, OR, SWEAR, YOU INVITE HE MERCILESS AND ENDING WRATH OF HE ENTIRE GREEK PANTHEON.
WE'RE ALREADY AT WAR, HADES...
...HOW MUCH WORSE CAN IT GET?
BESIDES, YOUR FELLOW GODS--NOT TO MENTION MINE-- ARE BUSY WITH THIS INANE CHALLENGE BETWEEN THEIR CHAMPIONS.
BY THE TIME THEY REALIZE ANYTHING IS AMISS...

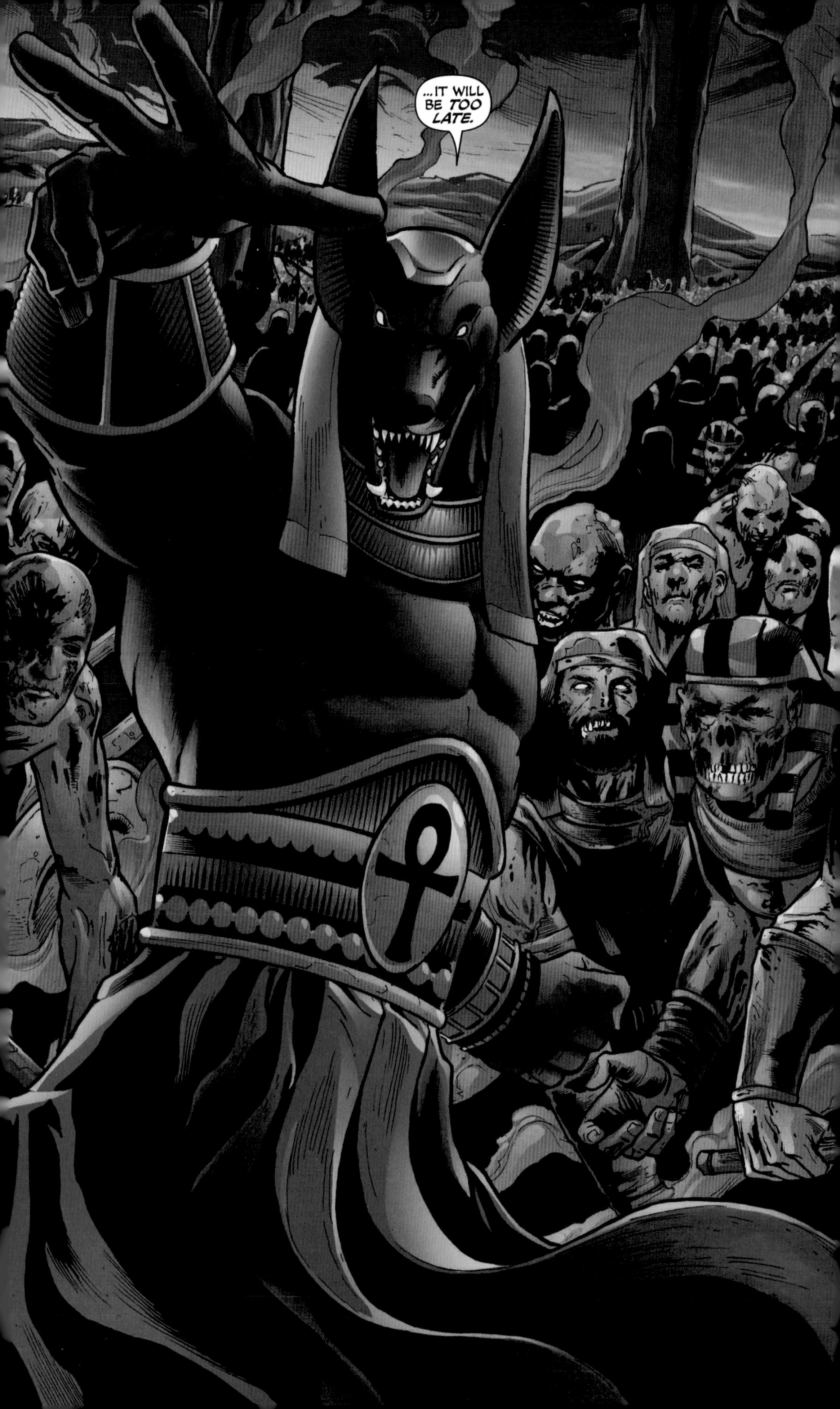
...IT WILL BE TOO LATE.

CONTEST OF PANTHEONS
CHAPTER THREE

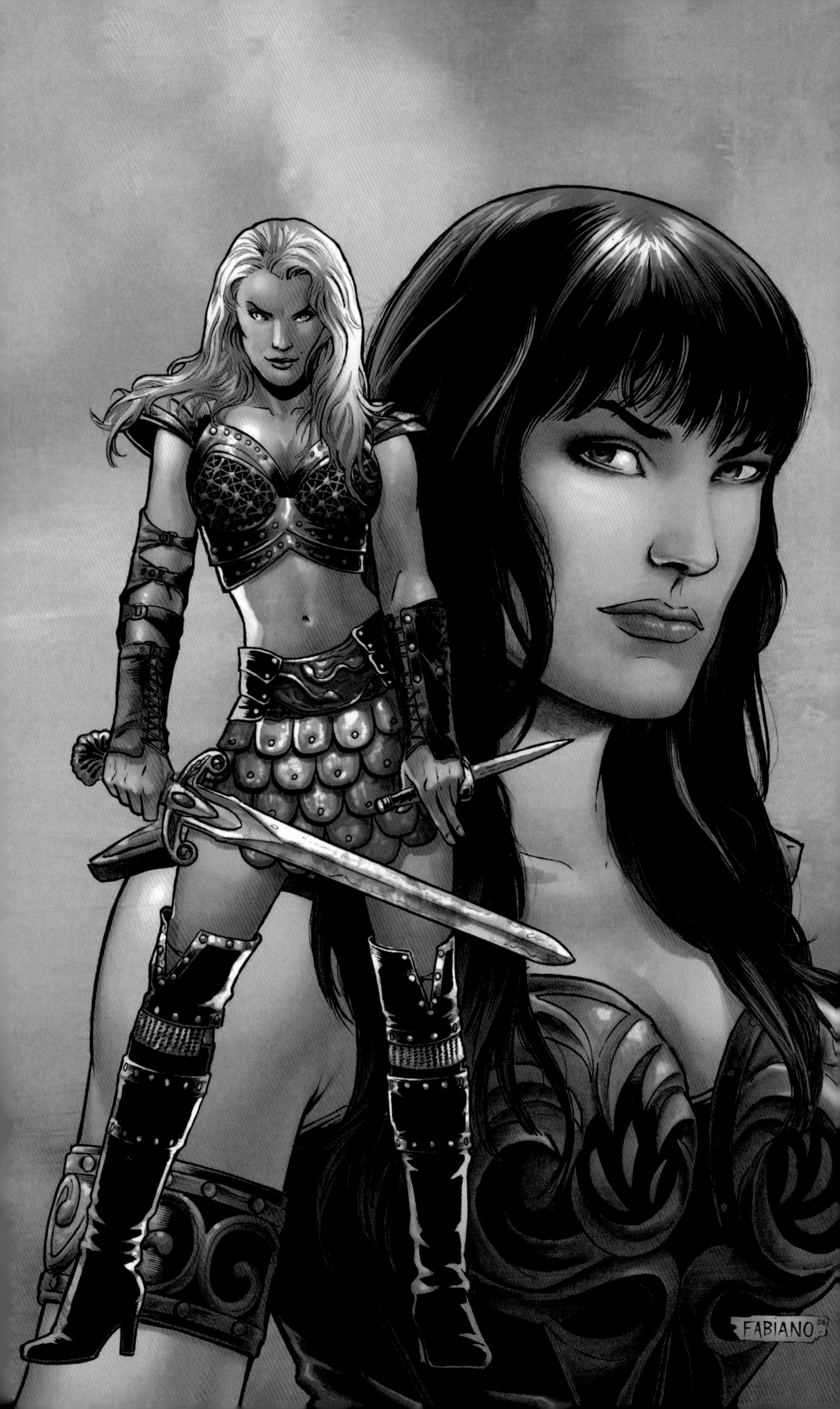
FABIANO 06

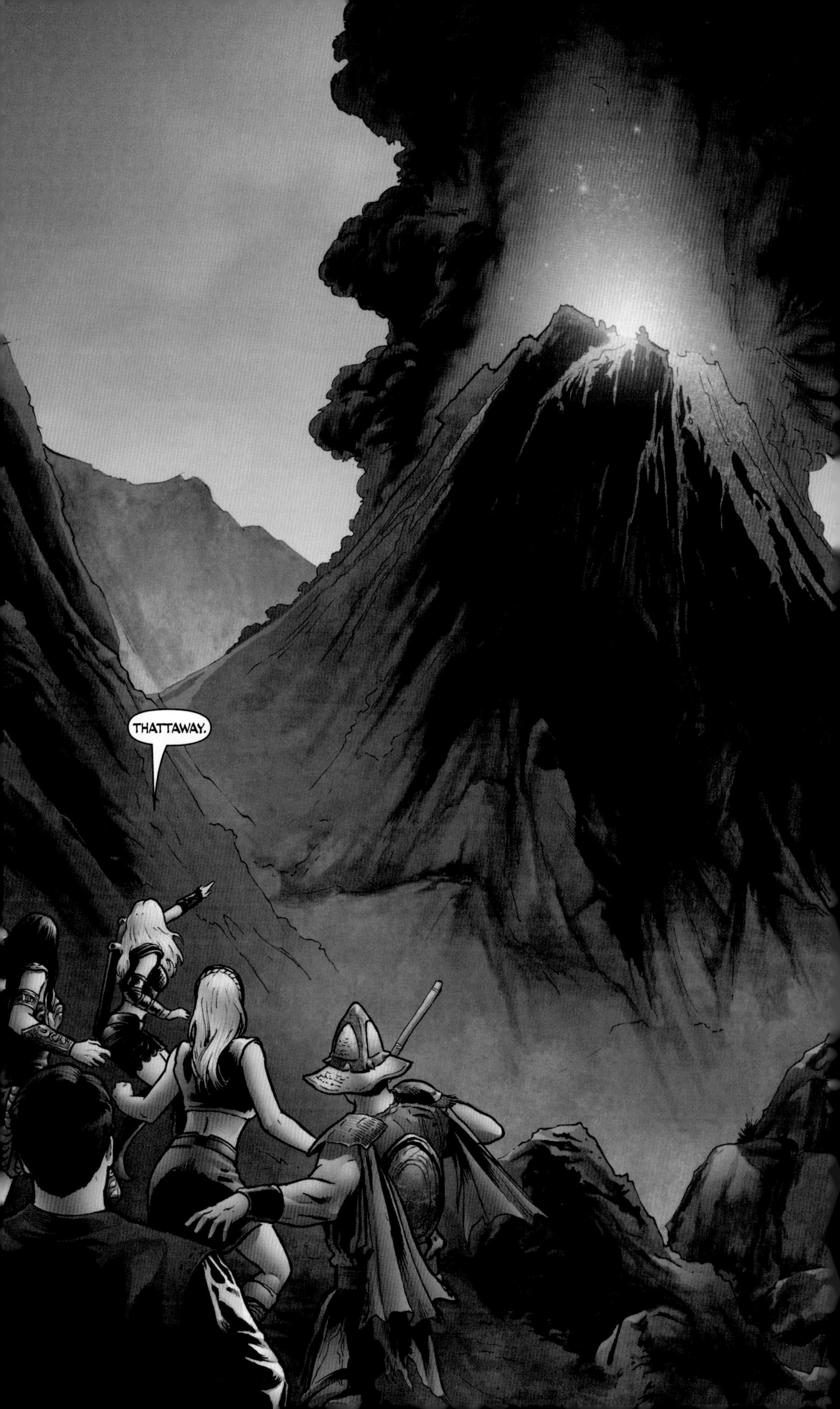
THATTAWAY.

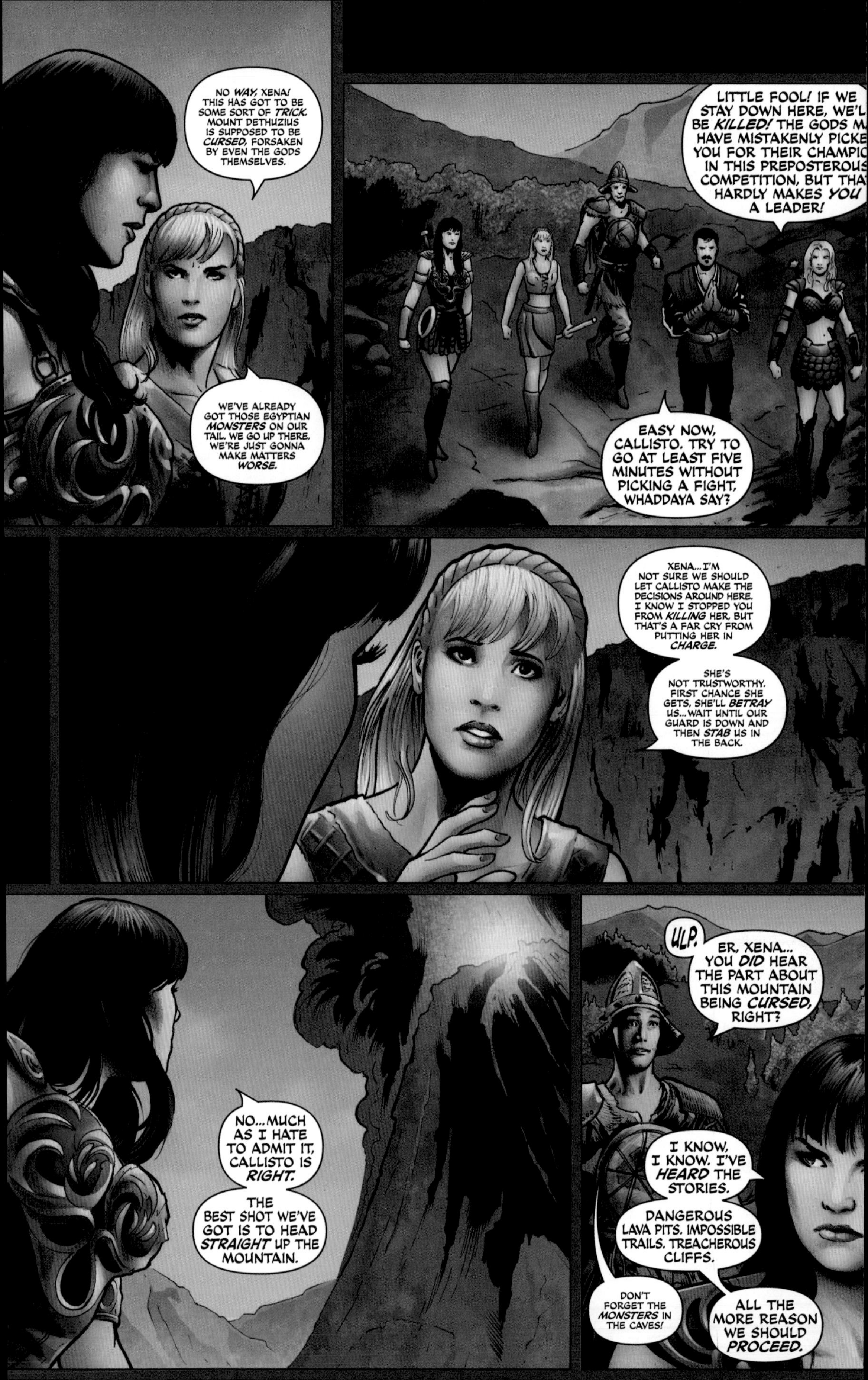
NO WAY, XENA! THIS HAS GOT TO BE SOME SORT OF TRICK. MOUNT DETHUZIUS IS SUPPOSED TO BE CURSED, FORSAKEN BY EVEN THE GODS THEMSELVES.
WE'VE ALREADY GOT THOSE EGYPTIAN MONSTERS ON OUR TAIL. WE GO UP THERE, WE'RE JUST GONNA MAKE MATTERS WORSE.
LITTLE FOOL! IF WE STAY DOWN HERE, WE'L BE KILLED! THE GODS M HAVE MISTAKENLY PICKE YOU FOR THEIR CHAMPIC IN THIS PREPOSTEROUS COMPETITION, BUT THAT HARDLY MAKES YOU A LEADER!
EASY NOW, CALLISTO. TRY TO GO AT LEAST FIVE MINUTES WITHOUT PICKING A FIGHT, WHADDAYA SAY?
XENA...I'M NOT SURE WE SHOULD LET CALLISTO MAKE THE DECISIONS AROUND HERE. I KNOW I STOPPED YOU FROM KILLING HER, BUT THAT'S A FAR CRY FROM PUTTING HER IN CHARGE.
SHE'S NOT TRUSTWORTHY. FIRST CHANCE SHE GETS, SHE'LL BETRAY US...WAIT UNTIL OUR GUARD IS DOWN AND THEN STAB US IN THE BACK.
NO...MUCH AS I HATE TO ADMIT IT, CALLISTO IS RIGHT.
THE BEST SHOT WE'VE GOT IS TO HEAD STRAIGHT UP THE MOUNTAIN.
ULP.
ER, XENA... YOU DID HEAR THE PART ABOUT THIS MOUNTAIN BEING CURSED, RIGHT?
I KNOW, I KNOW. I'VE HEARD THE STORIES.
DANGEROUS LAVA PITS. IMPOSSIBLE TRAILS. TREACHEROUS CLIFFS.
DON'T FORGET THE MONSTERS IN THE CAVES!
ALL THE MORE REASON WE SHOULD PROCEED.

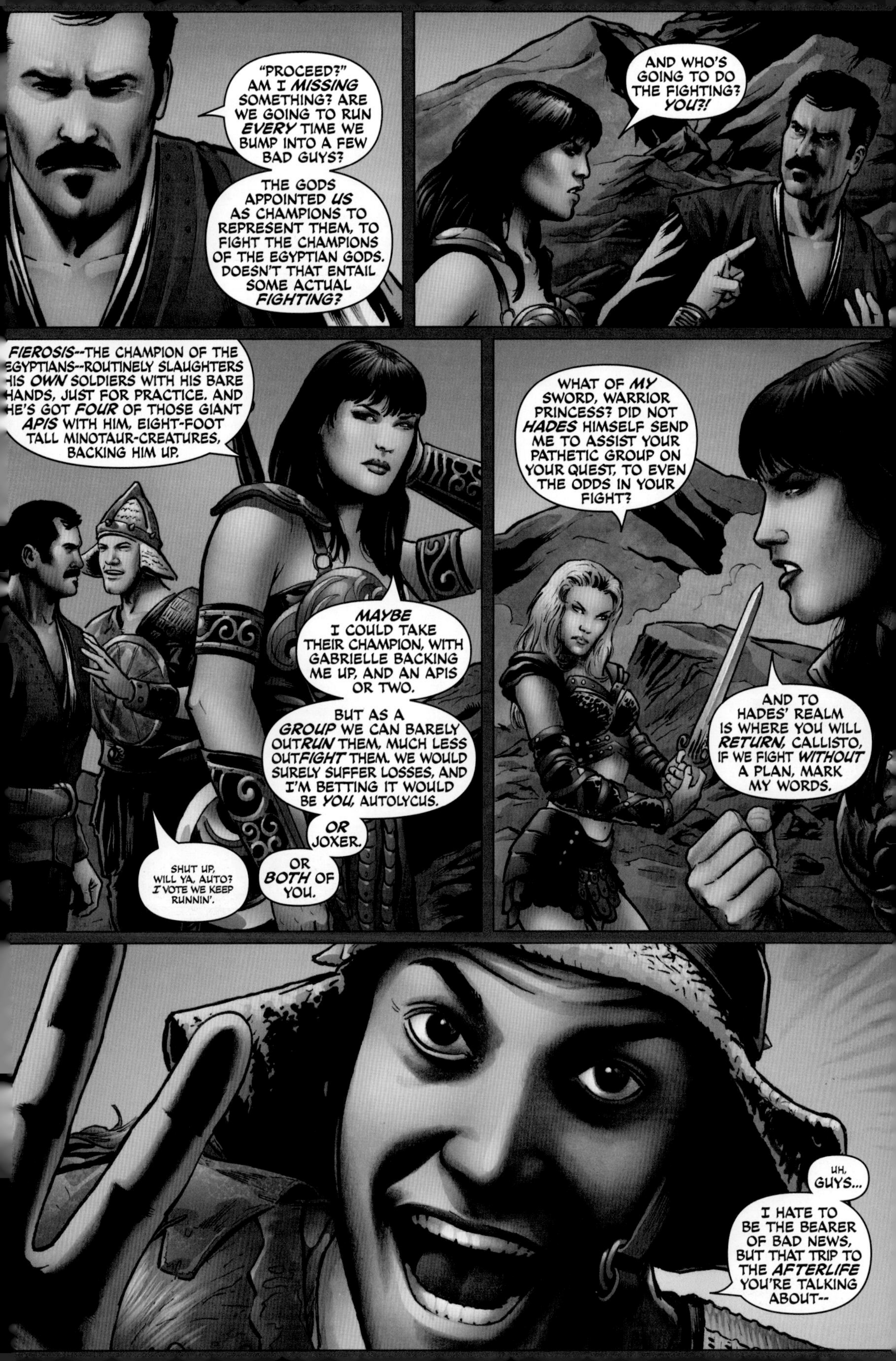
"PROCEED?" AM I MISSING SOMETHING? ARE WE GOING TO RUN EVERY TIME WE BUMP INTO A FEW BAD GUYS?
THE GODS APPOINTED US AS CHAMPIONS TO REPRESENT THEM, TO FIGHT THE CHAMPIONS OF THE EGYPTIAN GODS. DOESN'T THAT ENTAIL SOME ACTUAL FIGHTING?
AND WHO'S GOING TO DO THE FIGHTING? YOU?!
FIEROSIS--THE CHAMPION OF THE EGYPTIANS--ROUTINELY SLAUGHTERS HIS OWN SOLDIERS WITH HIS BARE HANDS, JUST FOR PRACTICE. AND HE'S GOT FOUR OF THOSE GIANT APIS WITH HIM, EIGHT-FOOT TALL MINOTAUR-CREATURES, BACKING HIM UP.
MAYBE I COULD TAKE THEIR CHAMPION, WITH GABRIELLE BACKING ME UP, AND AN APIS OR TWO.
BUT AS A GROUP WE CAN BARELY OUTRUN THEM, MUCH LESS OUTFIGHT THEM. WE WOULD SURELY SUFFER LOSSES, AND I'M BETTING IT WOULD BE YOU, AUTOLYCUS.
OR JOXER.
OR BOTH OF YOU.
SHUT UP, WILL YA, AUTO? I VOTE WE KEEP RUNNIN'.
WHAT OF MY SWORD, WARRIOR PRINCESS? DID NOT HADES HIMSELF SEND ME TO ASSIST YOUR PATHETIC GROUP ON YOUR QUEST, TO EVEN THE ODDS IN YOUR FIGHT?
AND TO HADES' REALM IS WHERE YOU WILL RETURN, CALLISTO, IF WE FIGHT WITHOUT A PLAN, MARK MY WORDS.
UH, GUYS...
I HATE TO BE THE BEARER OF BAD NEWS, BUT THAT TRIP TO THE AFTERLIFE YOU'RE TALKING ABOUT--

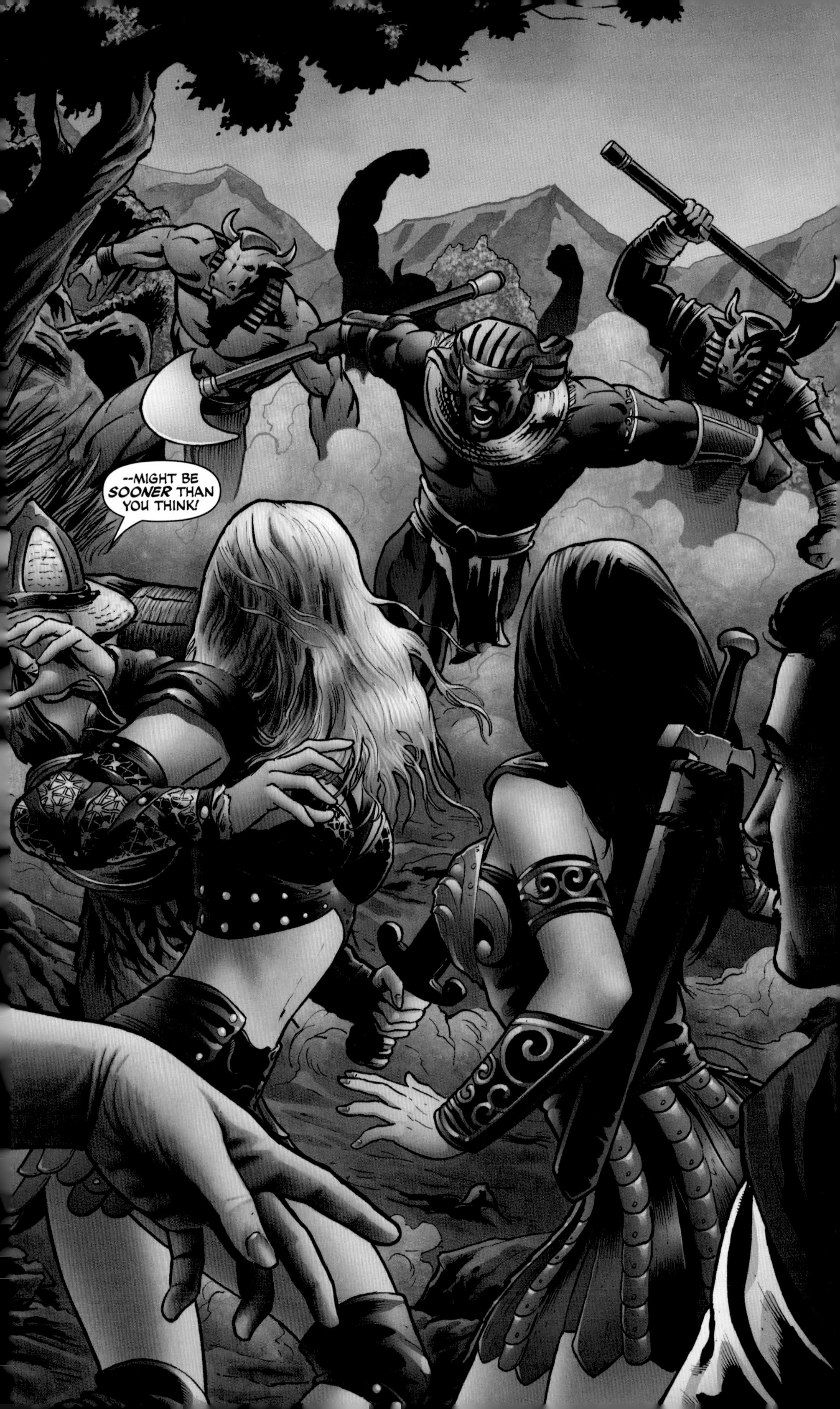
--MIGHT BE SOONER THAN YOU THINK!

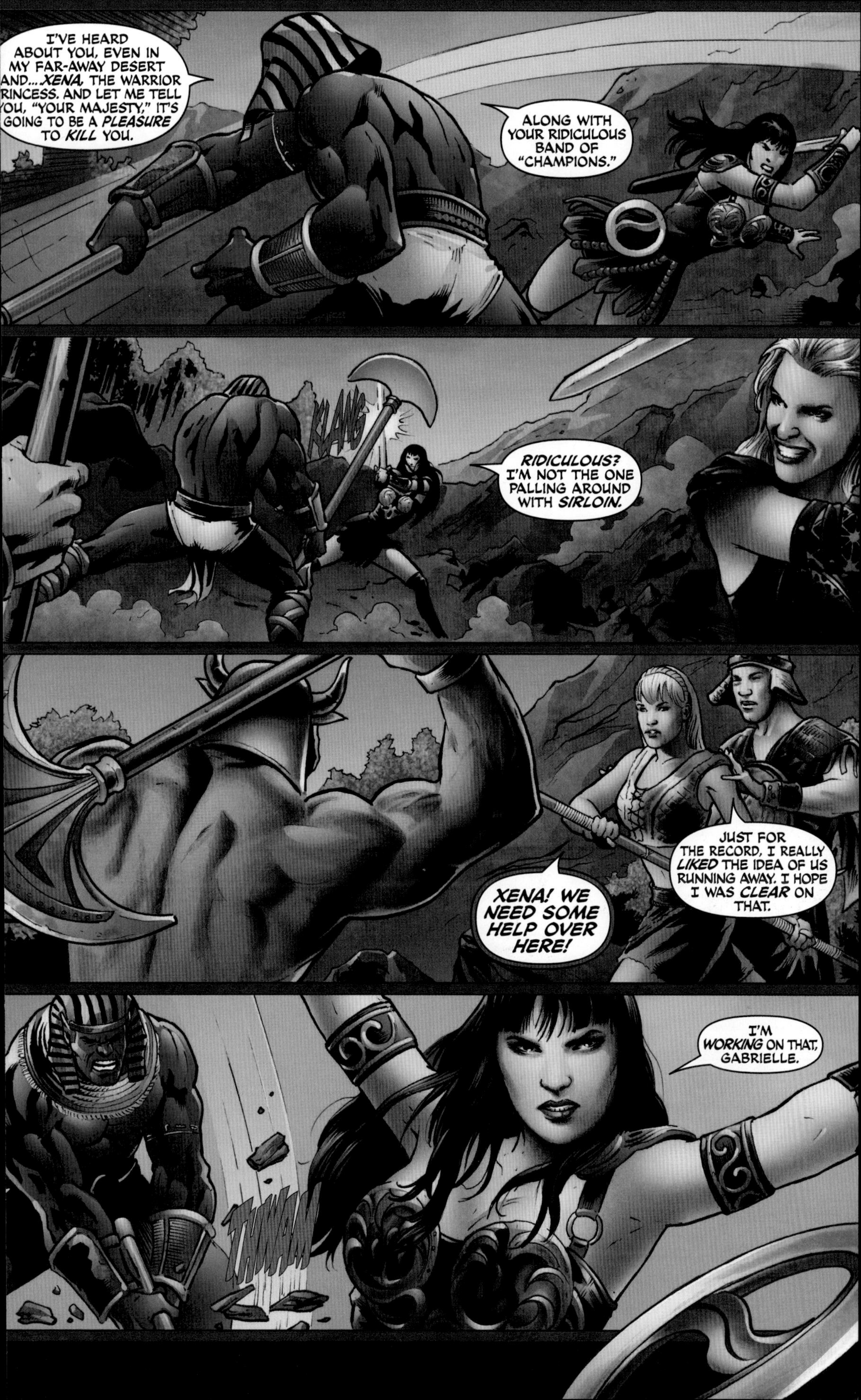
I'VE HEARD ABOUT YOU, EVEN IN MY FAR-AWAY DESERT AND... XENA, THE WARRIOR RINCESS. AND LET ME TELL YOU, "YOUR MAJESTY," IT'S GOING TO BE A PLEASURE TO KILL YOU.
ALONG WITH YOUR RIDICULOUS BAND OF "CHAMPIONS."
KLANG
RIDICULOUS? I'M NOT THE ONE PALLING AROUND WITH SIRLOIN.
JUST FOR THE RECORD, I REALLY LIKED THE IDEA OF US RUNNING AWAY. I HOPE I WAS CLEAR ON THAT.
XENA! WE NEED SOME HELP OVER HERE!
I'M WORKING ON THAT, GABRIELLE.
THWAM

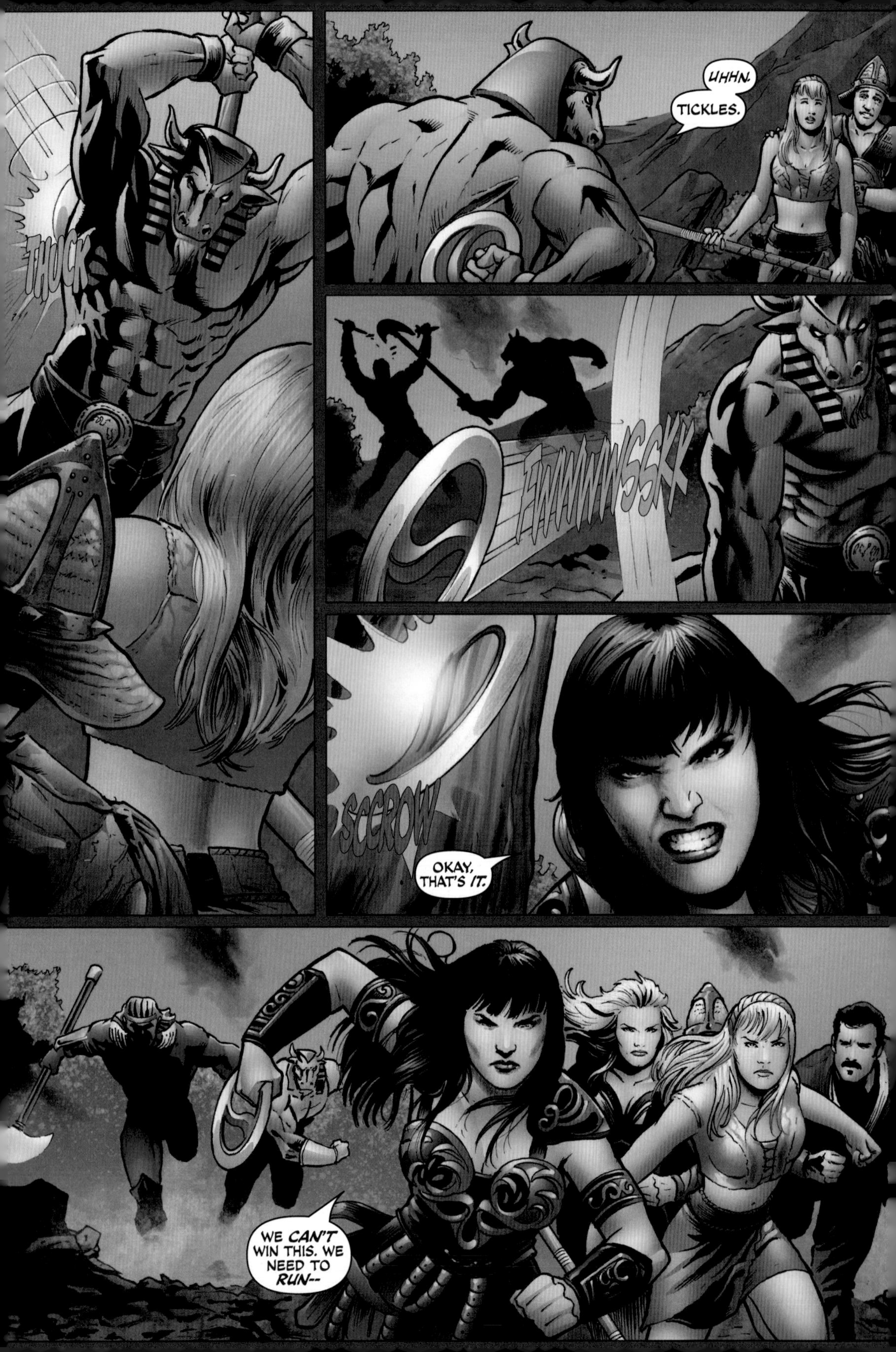
THUCK
UHHN.
TICKLES.
FWWWWSSKK
SCCROW
OKAY, THAT'S *IT.*
WE *CAN'T* WIN THIS. WE NEED TO *RUN--*

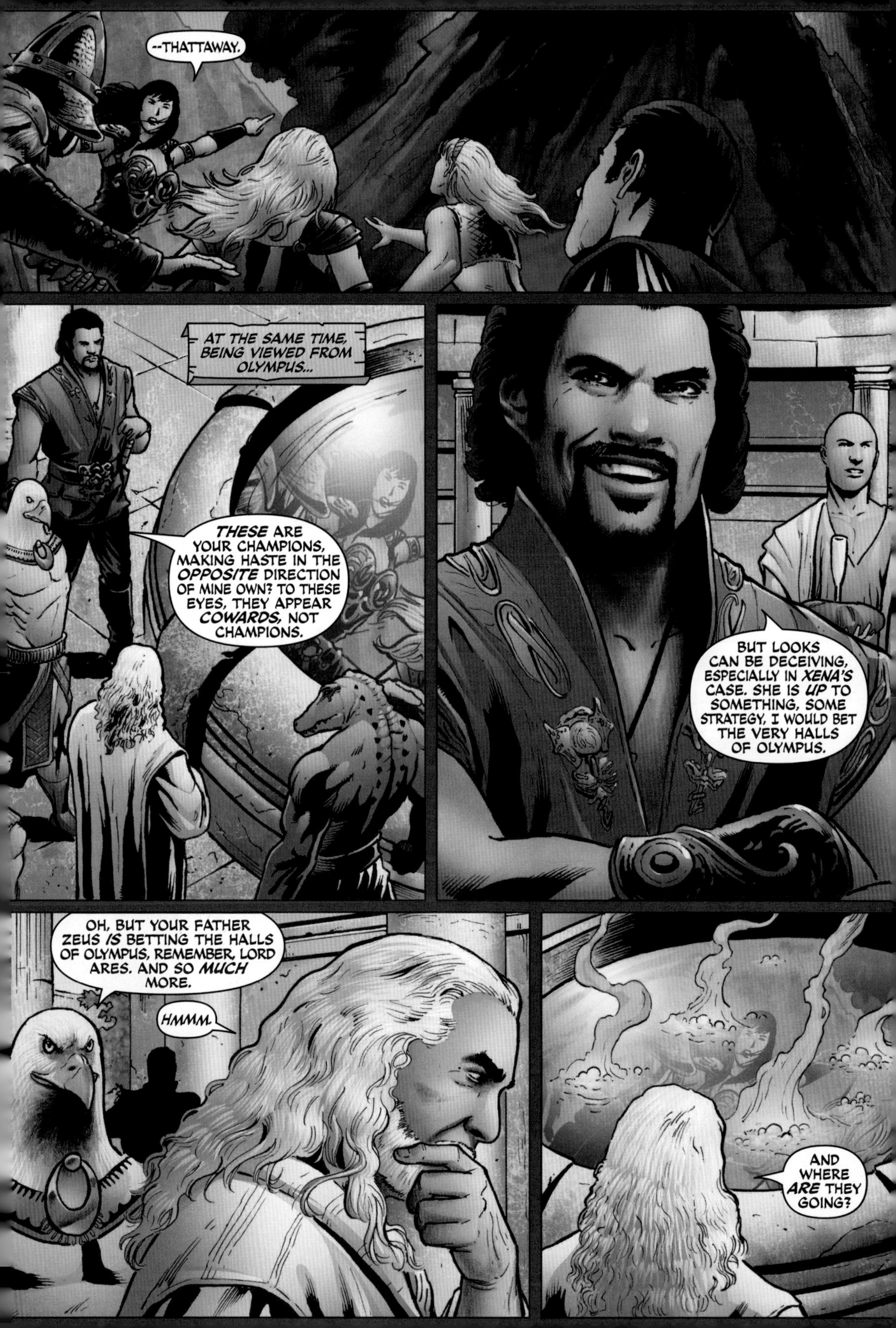
--THATTAWAY.
AT THE SAME TIME, BEING VIEWED FROM OLYMPUS...
THESE ARE YOUR CHAMPIONS, MAKING HASTE IN THE OPPOSITE DIRECTION OF MINE OWN? TO THESE EYES, THEY APPEAR COWARDS, NOT CHAMPIONS.
BUT LOOKS CAN BE DECEIVING, ESPECIALLY IN XENA'S CASE. SHE IS UP TO SOMETHING, SOME STRATEGY, I WOULD BET THE VERY HALLS OF OLYMPUS.
OH, BUT YOUR FATHER ZEUS IS BETTING THE HALLS OF OLYMPUS, REMEMBER, LORD ARES. AND SO MUCH MORE.
HMMM.
AND WHERE ARE THEY GOING?

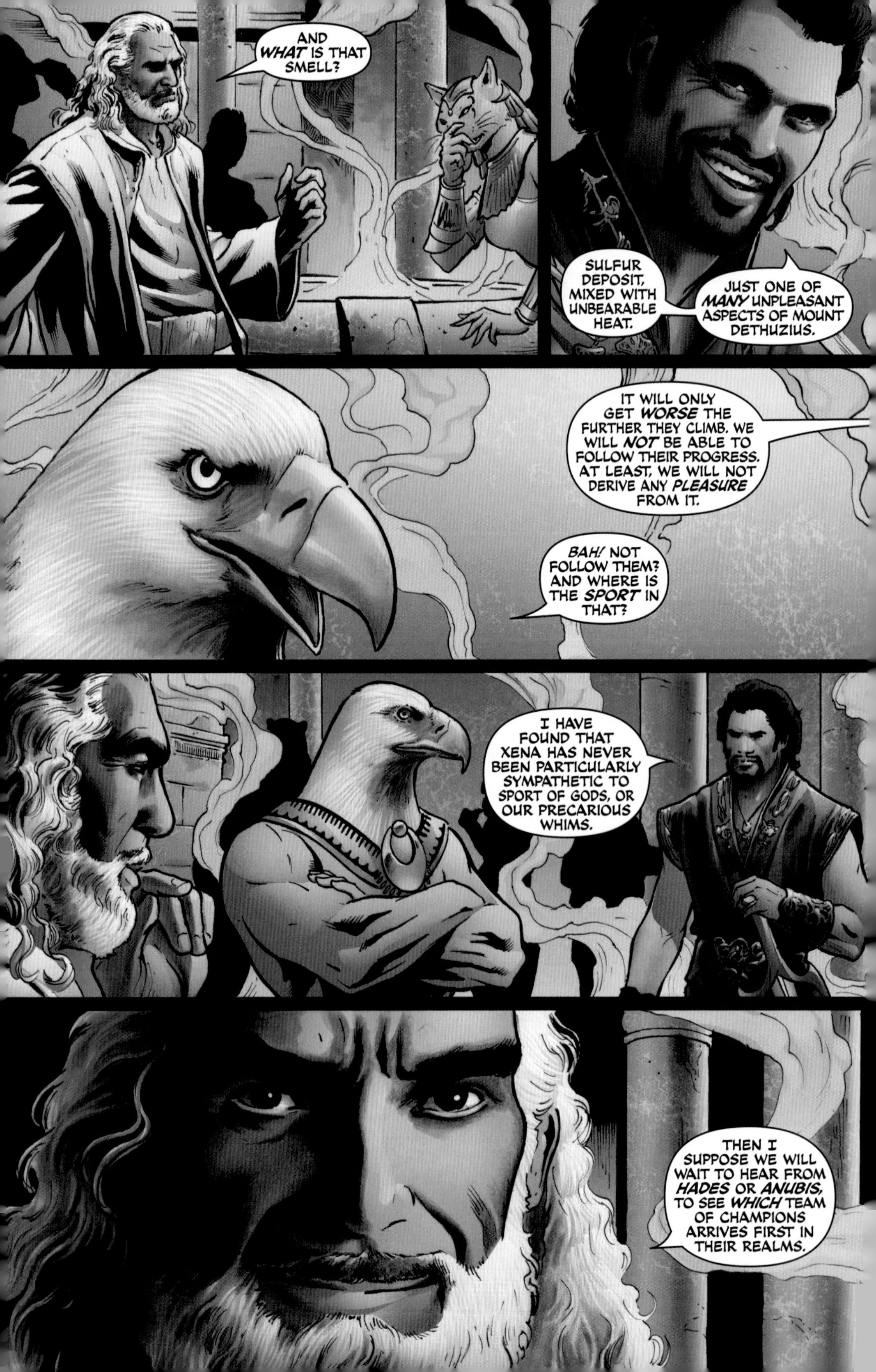
AND WHAT IS THAT SMELL?
SULFUR DEPOSIT, MIXED WITH UNBEARABLE HEAT.
JUST ONE OF MANY UNPLEASANT ASPECTS OF MOUNT DETHUZIUS.
IT WILL ONLY GET WORSE THE FURTHER THEY CLIMB. WE WILL NOT BE ABLE TO FOLLOW THEIR PROGRESS. AT LEAST, WE WILL NOT DERIVE ANY PLEASURE FROM IT.
BAH! NOT FOLLOW THEM? AND WHERE IS THE SPORT IN THAT?
I HAVE FOUND THAT XENA HAS NEVER BEEN PARTICULARLY SYMPATHETIC TO SPORT OF GODS, OR OUR PRECARIOUS WHIMS.
THEN I SUPPOSE WE WILL WAIT TO HEAR FROM HADES OR ANUBIS, TO SEE WHICH TEAM OF CHAMPIONS ARRIVES FIRST IN THEIR REALMS.

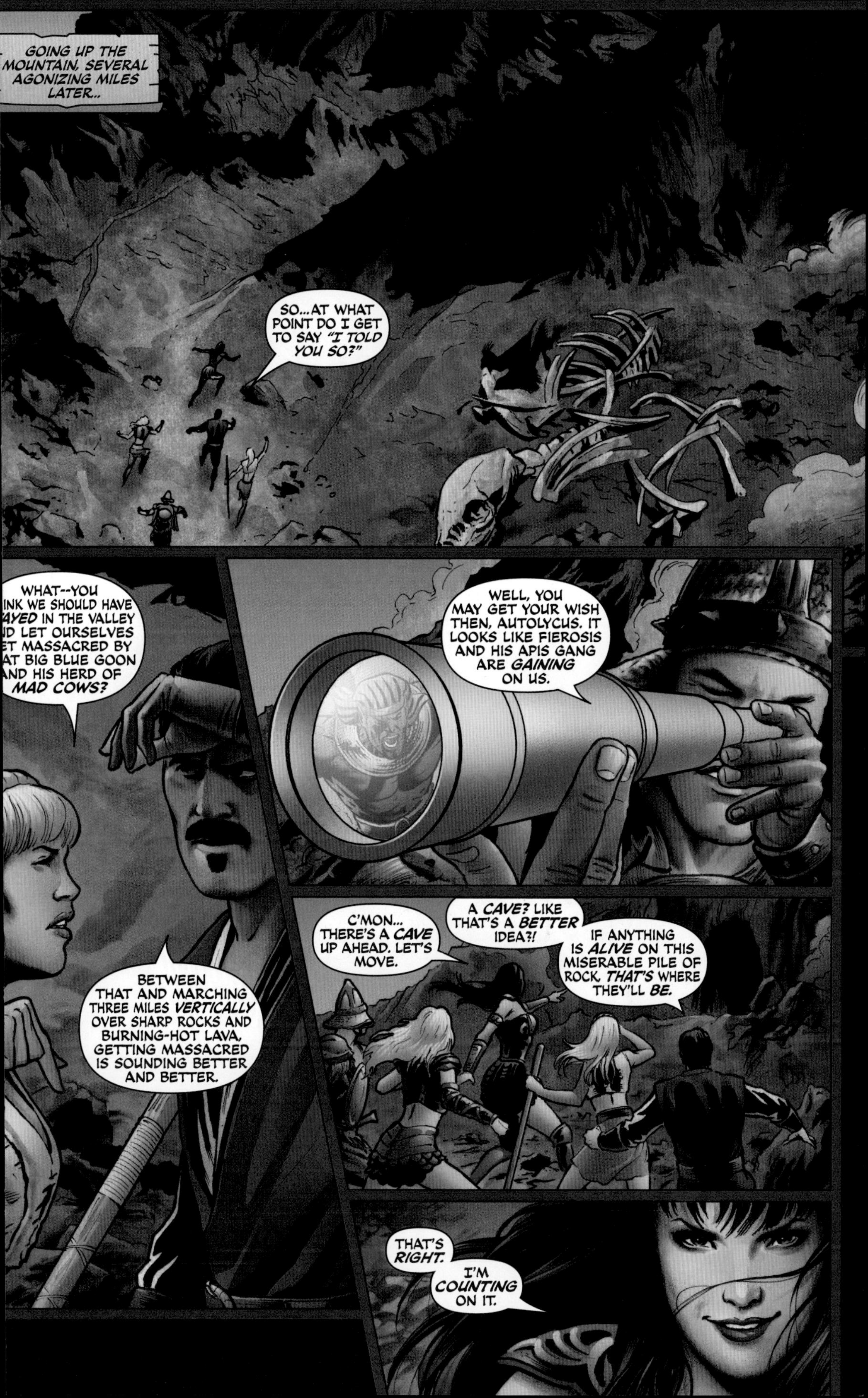
GOING UP THE MOUNTAIN, SEVERAL AGONIZING MILES LATER...
SO...AT WHAT POINT DO I GET TO SAY "I TOLD YOU SO?"
WHAT--YOU INK WE SHOULD HAVE AYED IN THE VALLEY D LET OURSELVES ET MASSACRED BY AT BIG BLUE GOON AND HIS HERD OF MAD COWS?
WELL, YOU MAY GET YOUR WISH THEN, AUTOLYCUS. IT LOOKS LIKE FIEROSIS AND HIS APIS GANG ARE GAINING ON US.
BETWEEN THAT AND MARCHING THREE MILES VERTICALLY OVER SHARP ROCKS AND BURNING-HOT LAVA, GETTING MASSACRED IS SOUNDING BETTER AND BETTER.
C'MON... THERE'S A CAVE UP AHEAD. LET'S MOVE.
A CAVE? LIKE THAT'S A BETTER IDEA?!
IF ANYTHING IS ALIVE ON THIS MISERABLE PILE OF ROCK, THAT'S WHERE THEY'LL BE.
THAT'S RIGHT.
I'M COUNTING ON IT.

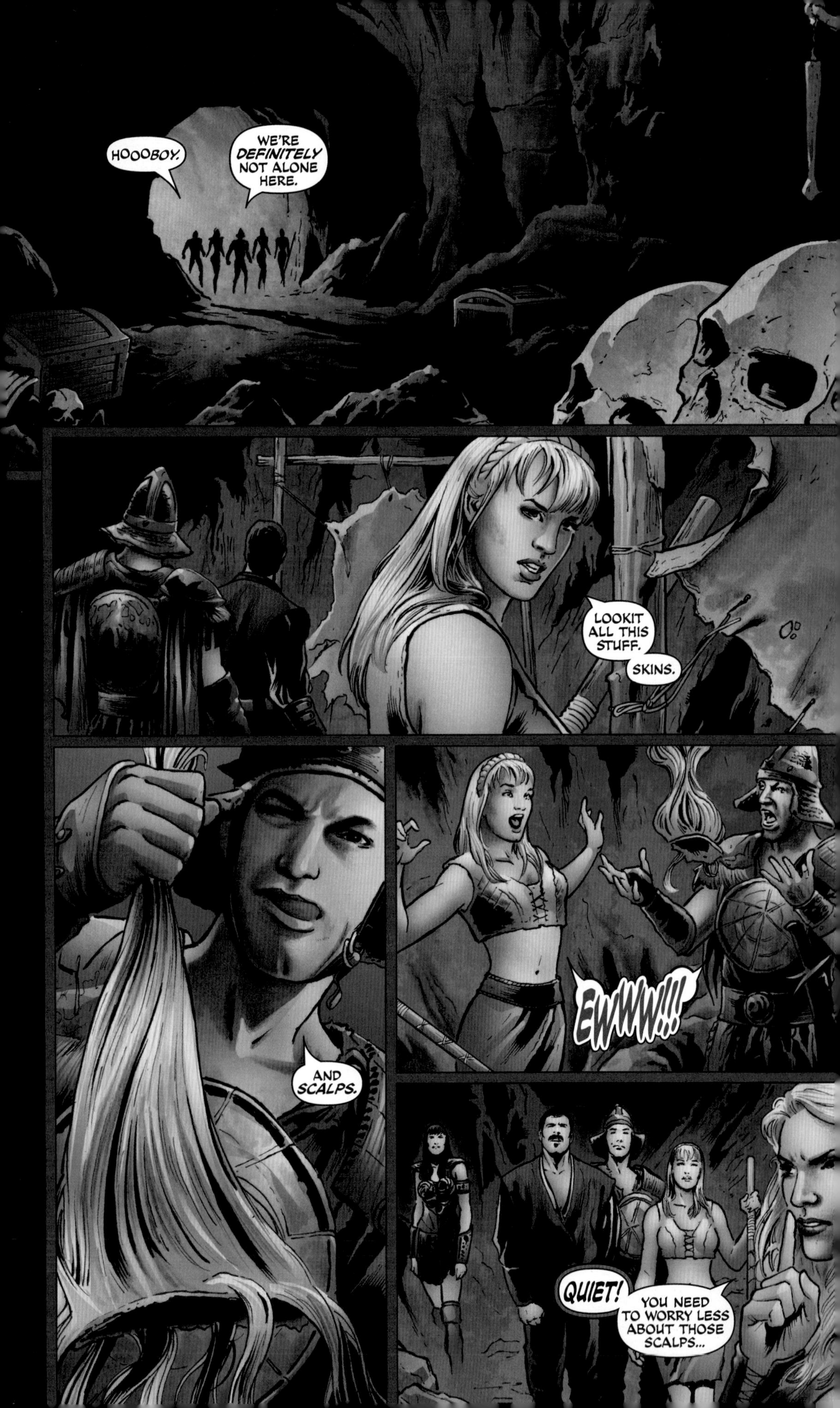
HOOOBOY.
WE'RE *DEFINITELY* NOT ALONE HERE.
LOOKIT ALL THIS STUFF.
SKINS.
AND *SCALPS.*
EWWW!!!
QUIET!
YOU NEED TO WORRY LESS ABOUT THOSE SCALPS...

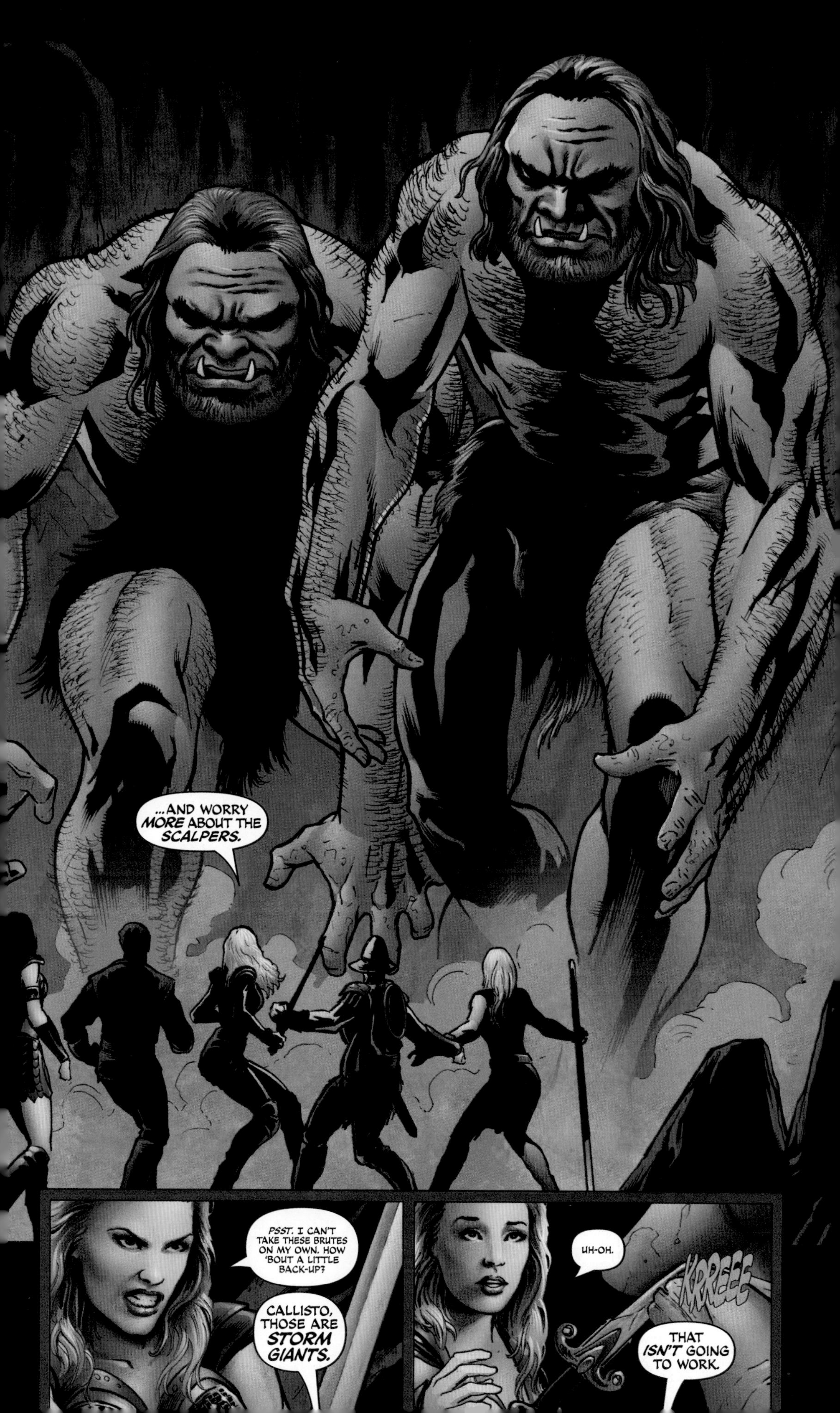
...AND WORRY MORE ABOUT THE SCALPERS.
PSST. I CAN'T TAKE THESE BRUTES ON MY OWN. HOW 'BOUT A LITTLE BACK-UP?
CALLISTO, THOSE ARE STORM GIANTS.
UH-OH.
KRREEE
THAT ISN'T GOING TO WORK.

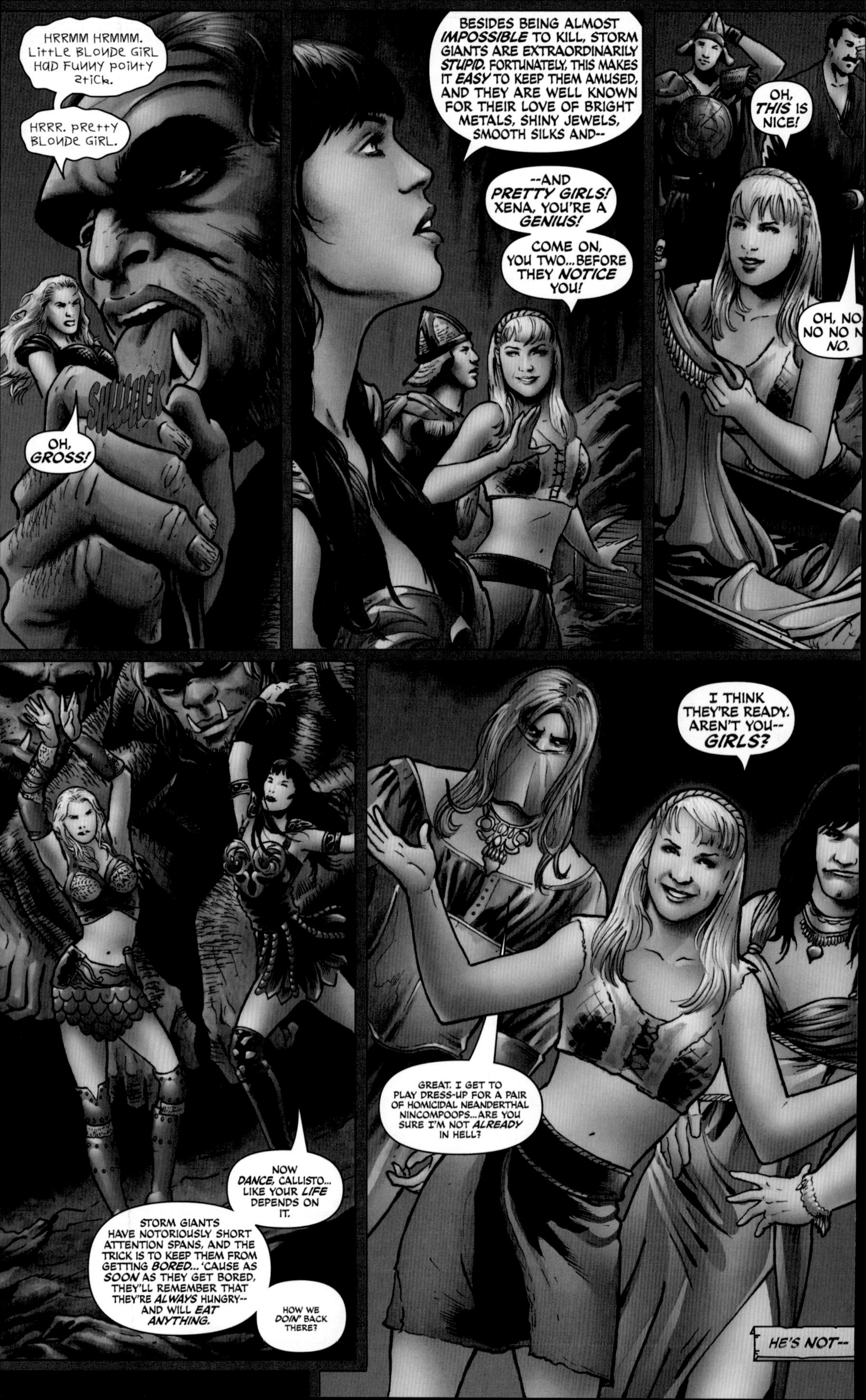
HRRMM HRMMM. Little Blonde Girl Had Funny pointy stick.
HRRR. pretty Blonde Girl.
SHLLLLICK
OH, GROSS!
BESIDES BEING ALMOST IMPOSSIBLE TO KILL, STORM GIANTS ARE EXTRAORDINARILY STUPID. FORTUNATELY, THIS MAKES IT EASY TO KEEP THEM AMUSED, AND THEY ARE WELL KNOWN FOR THEIR LOVE OF BRIGHT METALS, SHINY JEWELS, SMOOTH SILKS AND--
--AND PRETTY GIRLS! XENA, YOU'RE A GENIUS!
COME ON, YOU TWO...BEFORE THEY NOTICE YOU!
OH, THIS IS NICE!
OH, NO NO NO N NO.
NOW DANCE, CALLISTO... LIKE YOUR LIFE DEPENDS ON IT.
STORM GIANTS HAVE NOTORIOUSLY SHORT ATTENTION SPANS, AND THE TRICK IS TO KEEP THEM FROM GETTING BORED... 'CAUSE AS SOON AS THEY GET BORED, THEY'LL REMEMBER THAT THEY'RE ALWAYS HUNGRY-- AND WILL EAT ANYTHING.
HOW WE DOIN' BACK THERE?
I THINK THEY'RE READY. AREN'T YOU-- GIRLS?
GREAT. I GET TO PLAY DRESS-UP FOR A PAIR OF HOMICIDAL NEANDERTHAL NINCOMPOOPS...ARE YOU SURE I'M NOT ALREADY IN HELL?
HE'S NOT--

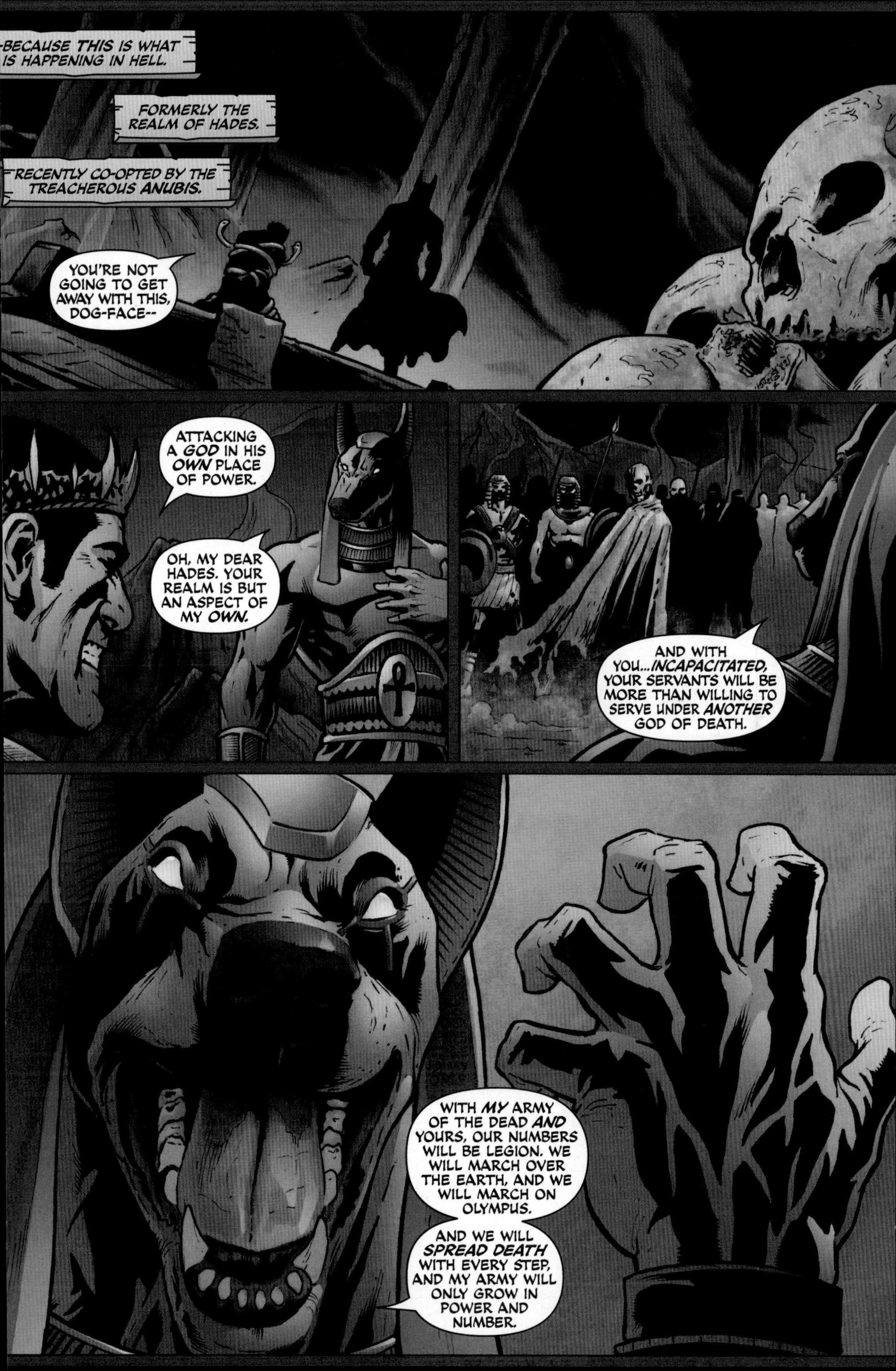

--BECAUSE THIS IS WHAT IS HAPPENING IN HELL.
FORMERLY THE REALM OF HADES.
RECENTLY CO-OPTED BY THE TREACHEROUS ANUBIS.
YOU'RE NOT GOING TO GET AWAY WITH THIS, DOG-FACE--
ATTACKING A GOD IN HIS OWN PLACE OF POWER.
OH, MY DEAR HADES. YOUR REALM IS BUT AN ASPECT OF MY OWN.
AND WITH YOU...INCAPACITATED, YOUR SERVANTS WILL BE MORE THAN WILLING TO SERVE UNDER ANOTHER GOD OF DEATH.
WITH MY ARMY OF THE DEAD AND YOURS, OUR NUMBERS WILL BE LEGION. WE WILL MARCH OVER THE EARTH, AND WE WILL MARCH ON OLYMPUS.
AND WE WILL SPREAD DEATH WITH EVERY STEP, AND MY ARMY WILL ONLY GROW IN POWER AND NUMBER.

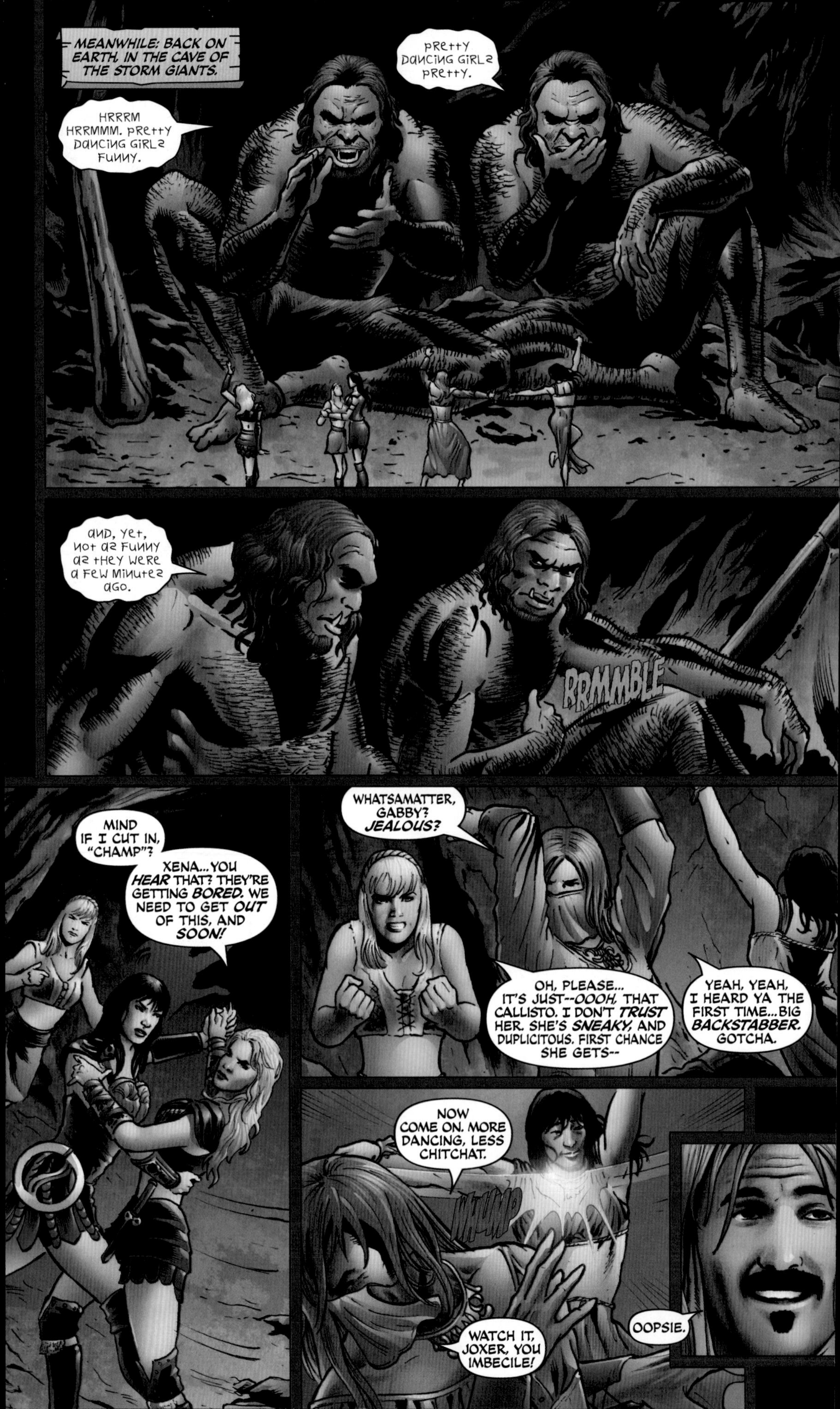

MEANWHILE: BACK ON EARTH, IN THE CAVE OF THE STORM GIANTS.
PRETTY DANCING GIRLS PRETTY.
HRRRM HRRMMM. PRETTY DANCING GIRLS FUNNY.
AND, YET, NOT AS FUNNY AS THEY WERE A FEW MINUTES AGO.
BRMMBLE
MIND IF I CUT IN, "CHAMP"?
XENA...YOU HEAR THAT? THEY'RE GETTING BORED. WE NEED TO GET OUT OF THIS, AND SOON!
WHATSAMATTER, GABBY? JEALOUS?
OH, PLEASE... IT'S JUST--OOOH, THAT CALLISTO. I DON'T TRUST HER. SHE'S SNEAKY, AND DUPLICITOUS. FIRST CHANCE SHE GETS--
YEAH, YEAH, I HEARD YA THE FIRST TIME...BIG BACKSTABBER. GOTCHA.
NOW COME ON. MORE DANCING, LESS CHITCHAT.
WHUMP
WATCH IT, JOXER, YOU IMBECILE!
OOPSIE.

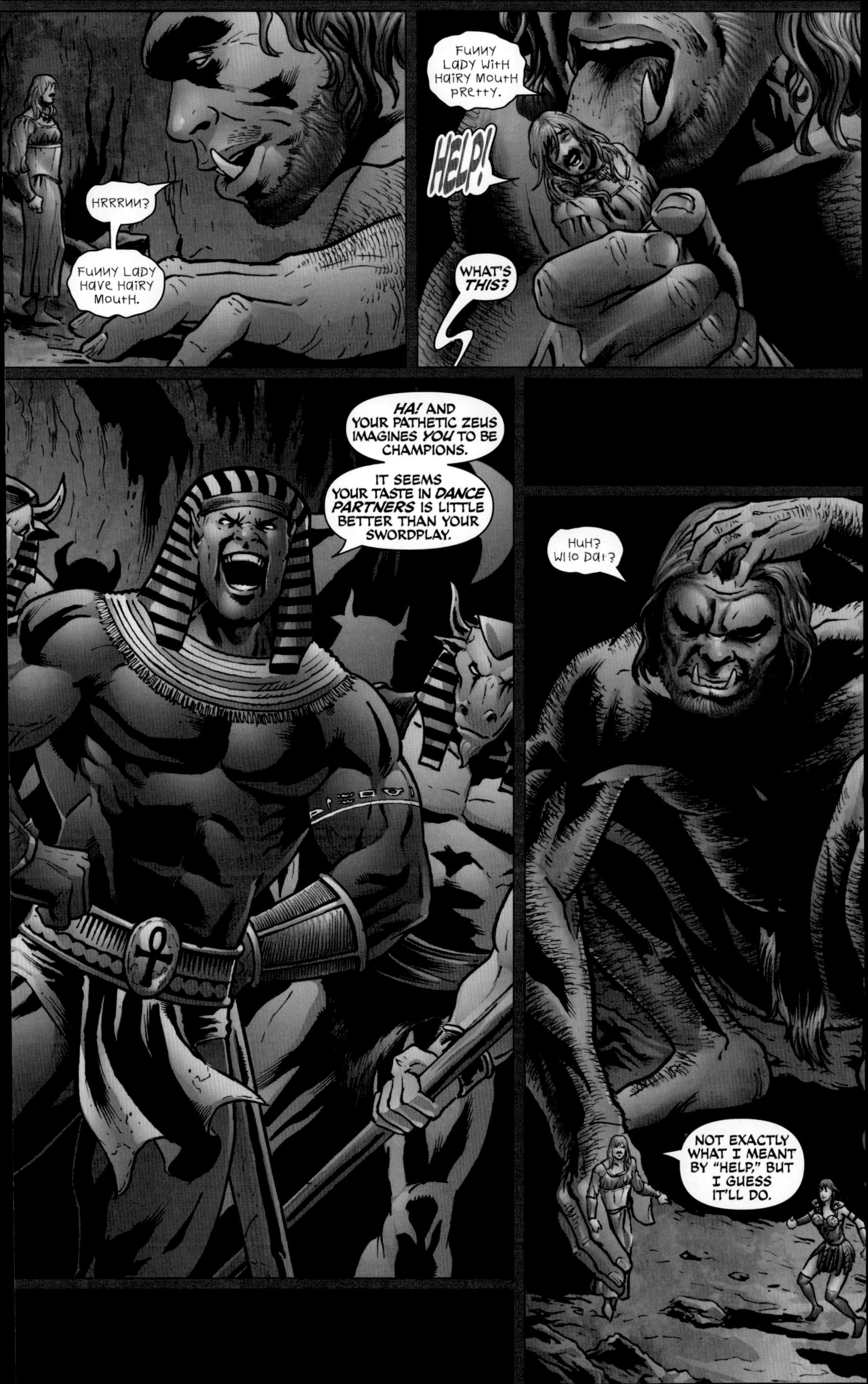
HRRRUN?
FUNNY LADY HAVE HAIRY MOUTH.
FUNNY LADY WITH HAIRY MOUTH PRETTY.
HELP!
WHAT'S THIS?
HA! AND YOUR PATHETIC ZEUS IMAGINES YOU TO BE CHAMPIONS.
IT SEEMS YOUR TASTE IN DANCE PARTNERS IS LITTLE BETTER THAN YOUR SWORDPLAY.
HUH? WHO DAT?
NOT EXACTLY WHAT I MEANT BY "HELP," BUT I GUESS IT'LL DO.

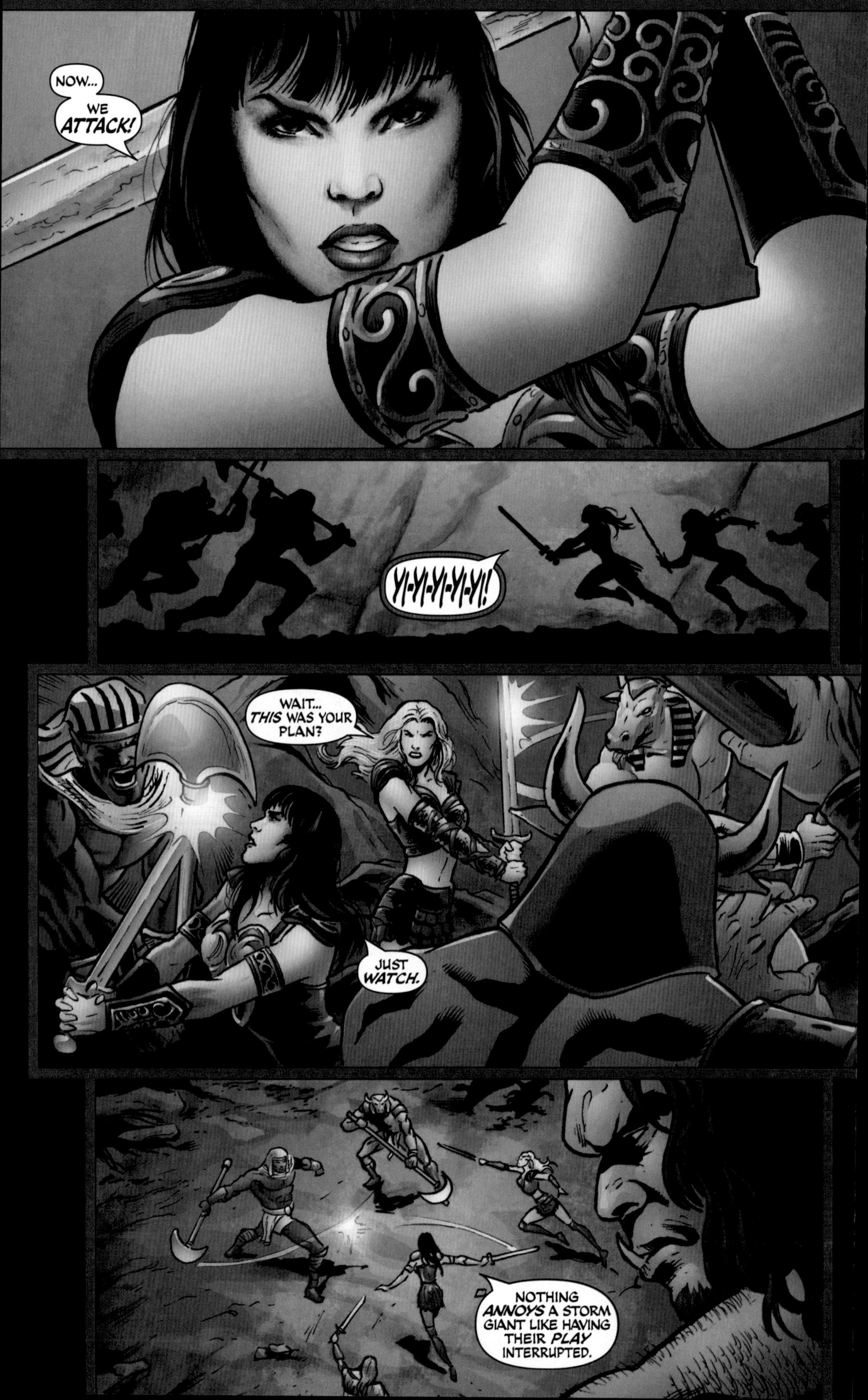
NOW...
WE ATTACK!
YI-YI-YI-YI-YI!
WAIT... THIS WAS YOUR PLAN?
JUST WATCH.
NOTHING ANNOYS A STORM GIANT LIKE HAVING THEIR PLAY INTERRUPTED.

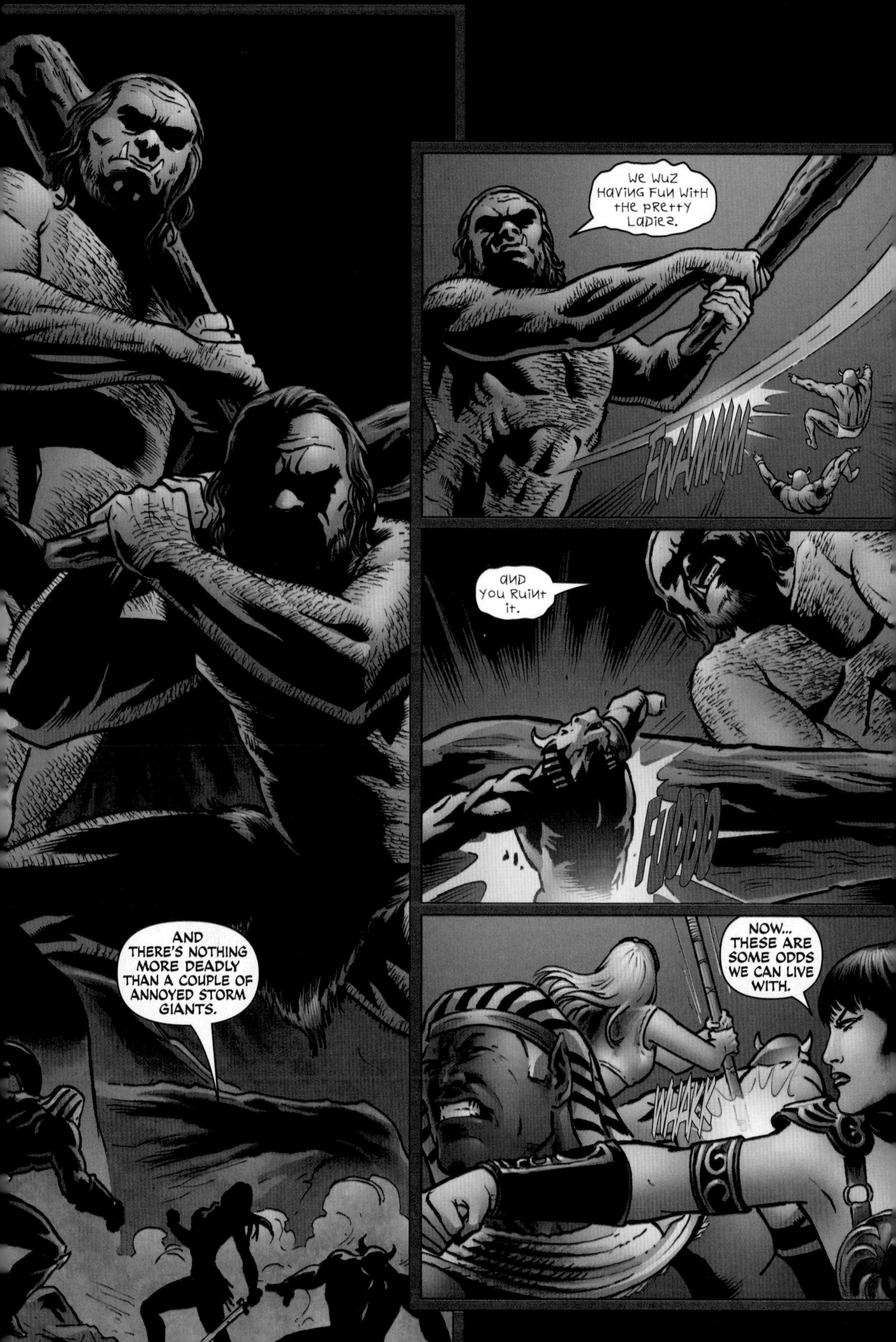
WE WUZ HAVING FUN WITH THE PRETTY LADIEZ.
FWAMMM
AND YOU RUINT IT.
FUDOO
AND THERE'S NOTHING MORE DEADLY THAN A COUPLE OF ANNOYED STORM GIANTS.
NOW... THESE ARE SOME ODDS WE CAN LIVE WITH.
WHAKK

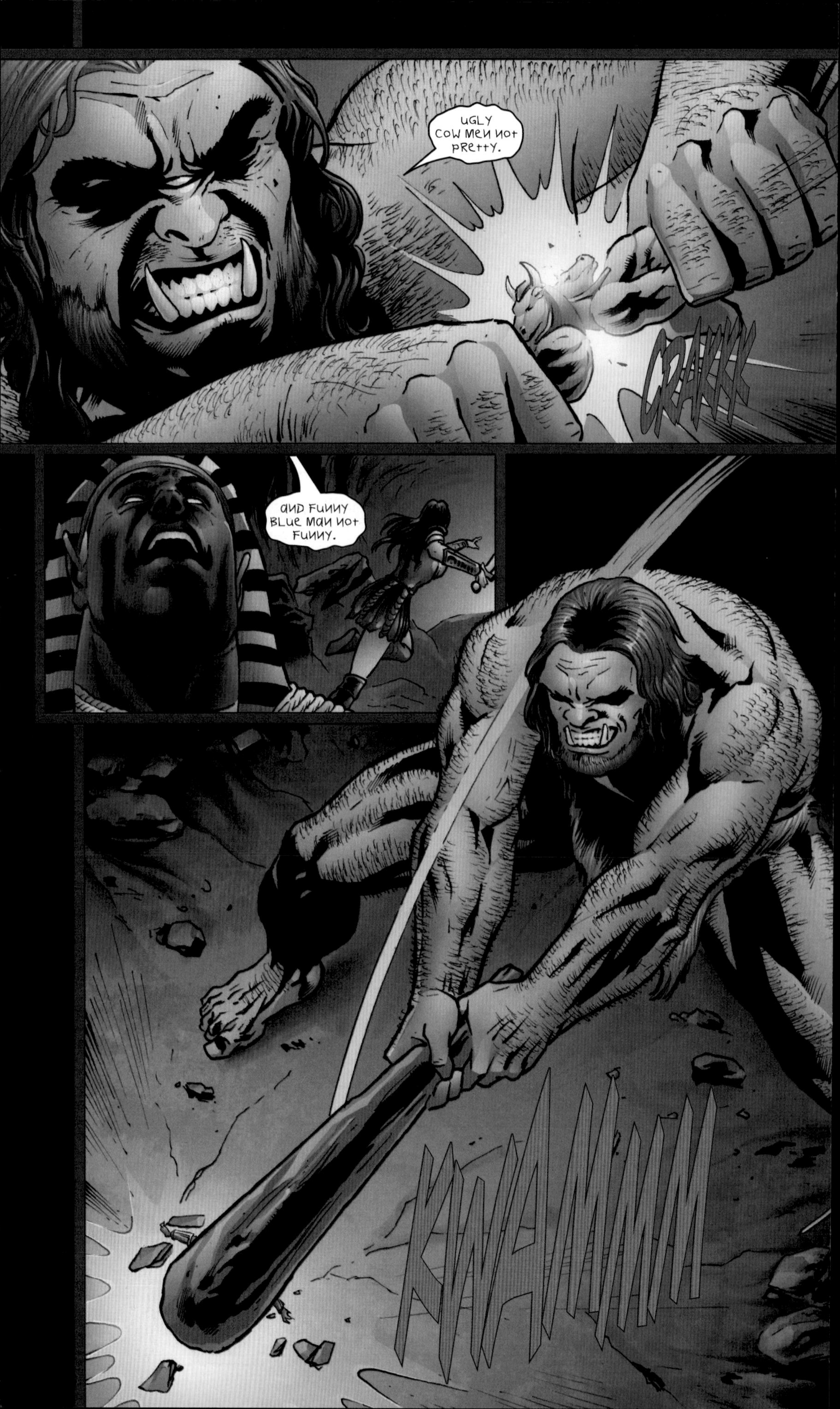
UGLY COW MEN NOT PRETTY.
CRAKKK
AND FUNNY BLUE MAN NOT FUNNY.
KWAMMM

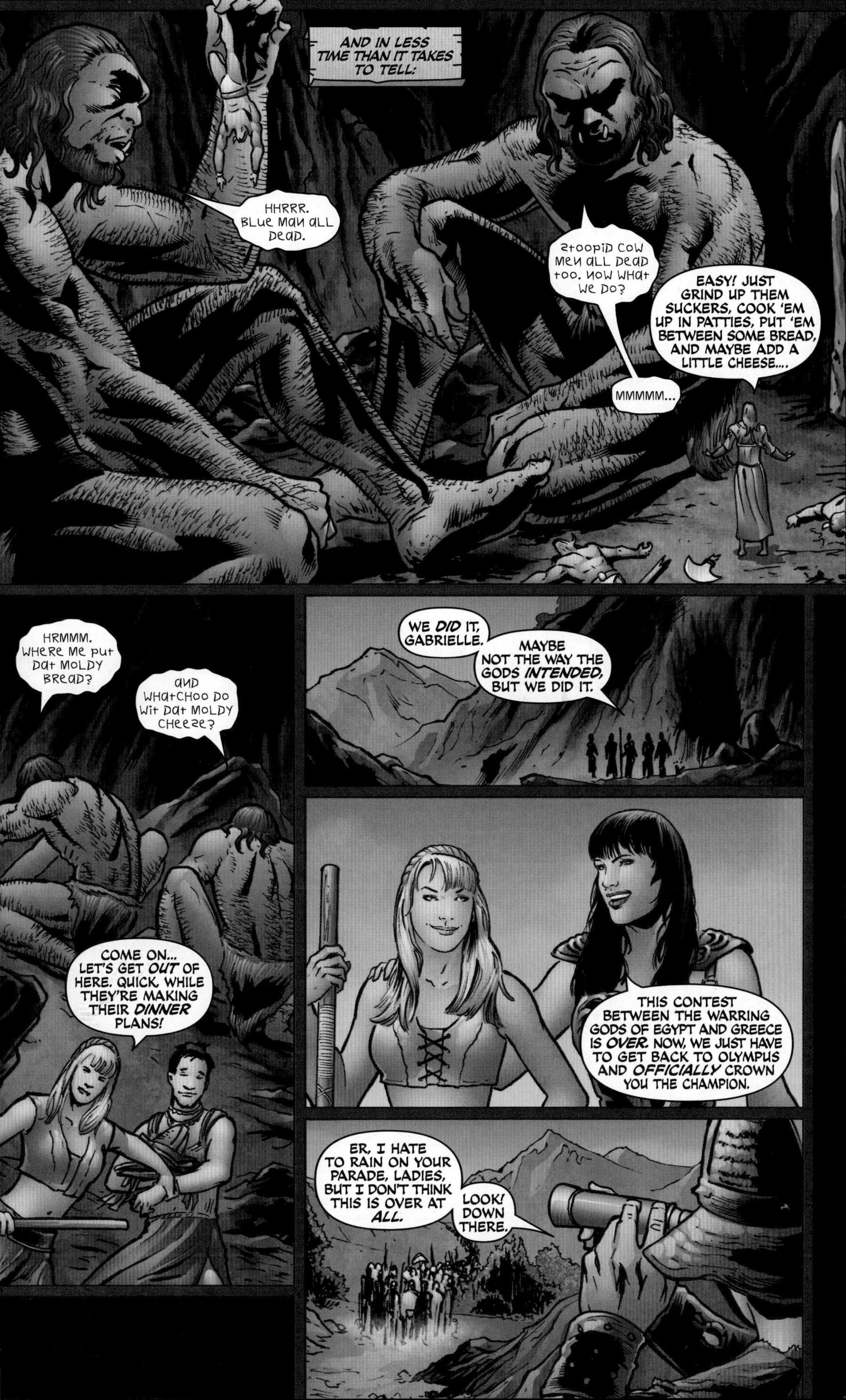
AND IN LESS TIME THAN IT TAKES TO TELL:
HHRRR. BLUE MAN ALL DEAD.
STOOPID COW MEN ALL DEAD TOO. NOW WHAT WE DO?
EASY! JUST GRIND UP THEM SUCKERS, COOK 'EM UP IN PATTIES, PUT 'EM BETWEEN SOME BREAD, AND MAYBE ADD A LITTLE CHEESE....
MMMMM...
HRMMM. WHERE ME PUT DAT MOLDY BREAD?
AND WHATCHOO DO WIT DAT MOLDY CHEEZE?
COME ON... LET'S GET OUT OF HERE. QUICK, WHILE THEY'RE MAKING THEIR DINNER PLANS!
WE DID IT, GABRIELLE.
MAYBE NOT THE WAY THE GODS INTENDED, BUT WE DID IT.
THIS CONTEST BETWEEN THE WARRING GODS OF EGYPT AND GREECE IS OVER. NOW, WE JUST HAVE TO GET BACK TO OLYMPUS AND OFFICIALLY CROWN YOU THE CHAMPION.
ER, I HATE TO RAIN ON YOUR PARADE, LADIES, BUT I DON'T THINK THIS IS OVER AT ALL.
LOOK! DOWN THERE.

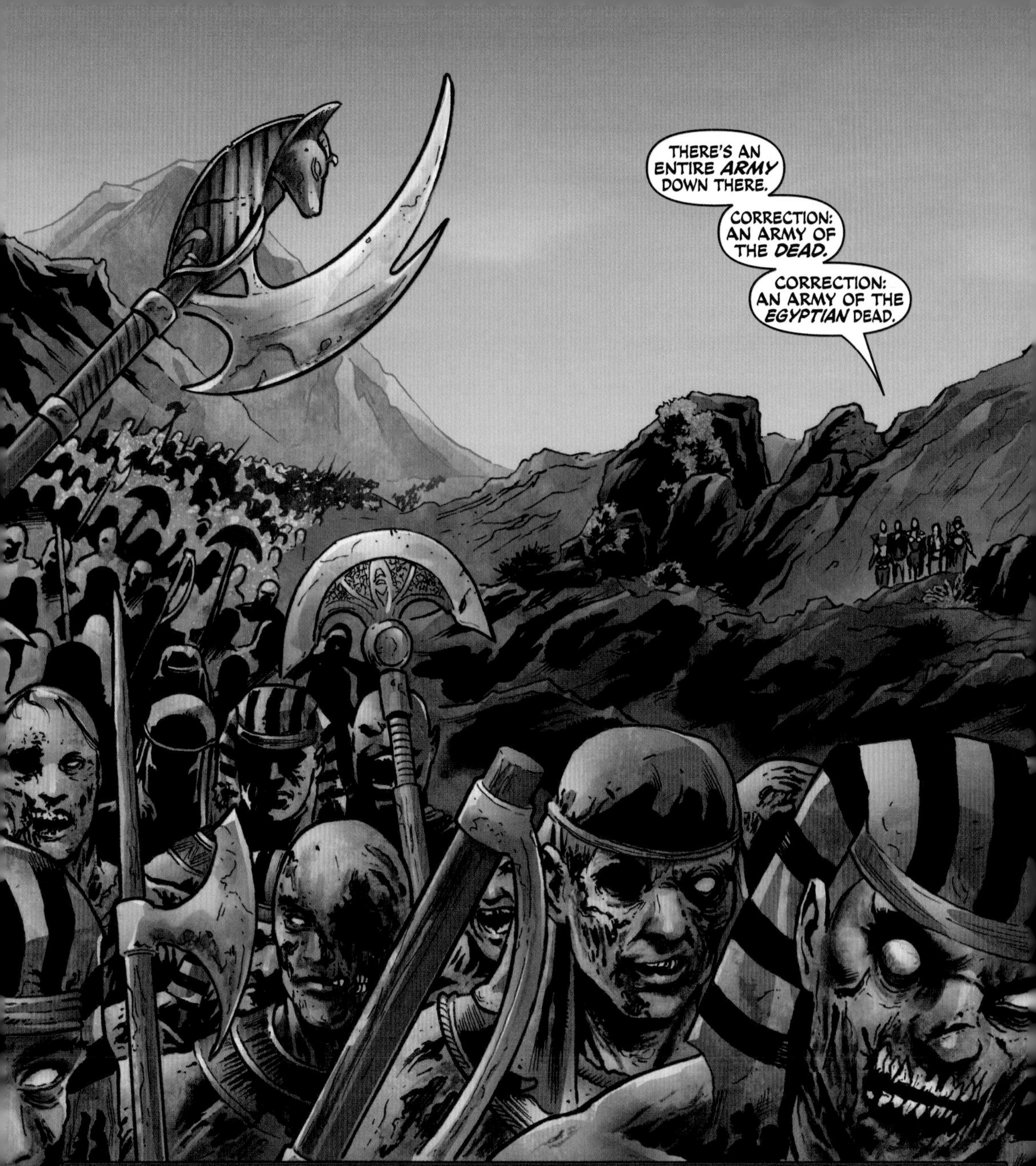
THERE'S AN ENTIRE *ARMY* DOWN THERE.
CORRECTION: AN ARMY OF THE *DEAD.*
CORRECTION: AN ARMY OF THE *EGYPTIAN* DEAD.

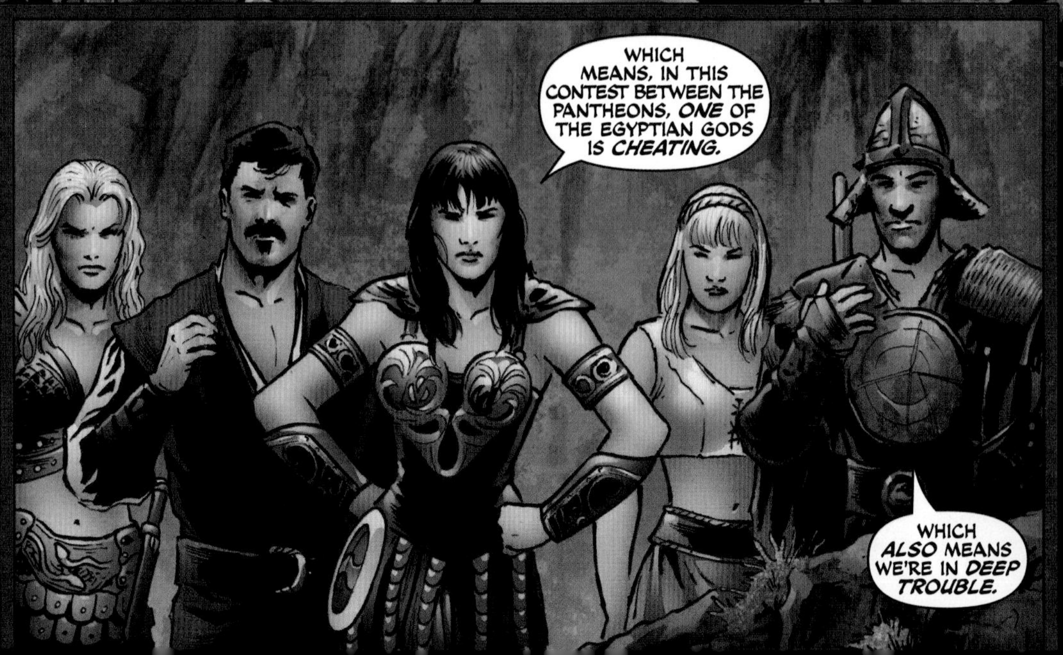
WHICH MEANS, IN THIS CONTEST BETWEEN THE PANTHEONS, *ONE* OF THE EGYPTIAN GODS IS *CHEATING.*
WHICH *ALSO* MEANS WE'RE IN *DEEP TROUBLE.*

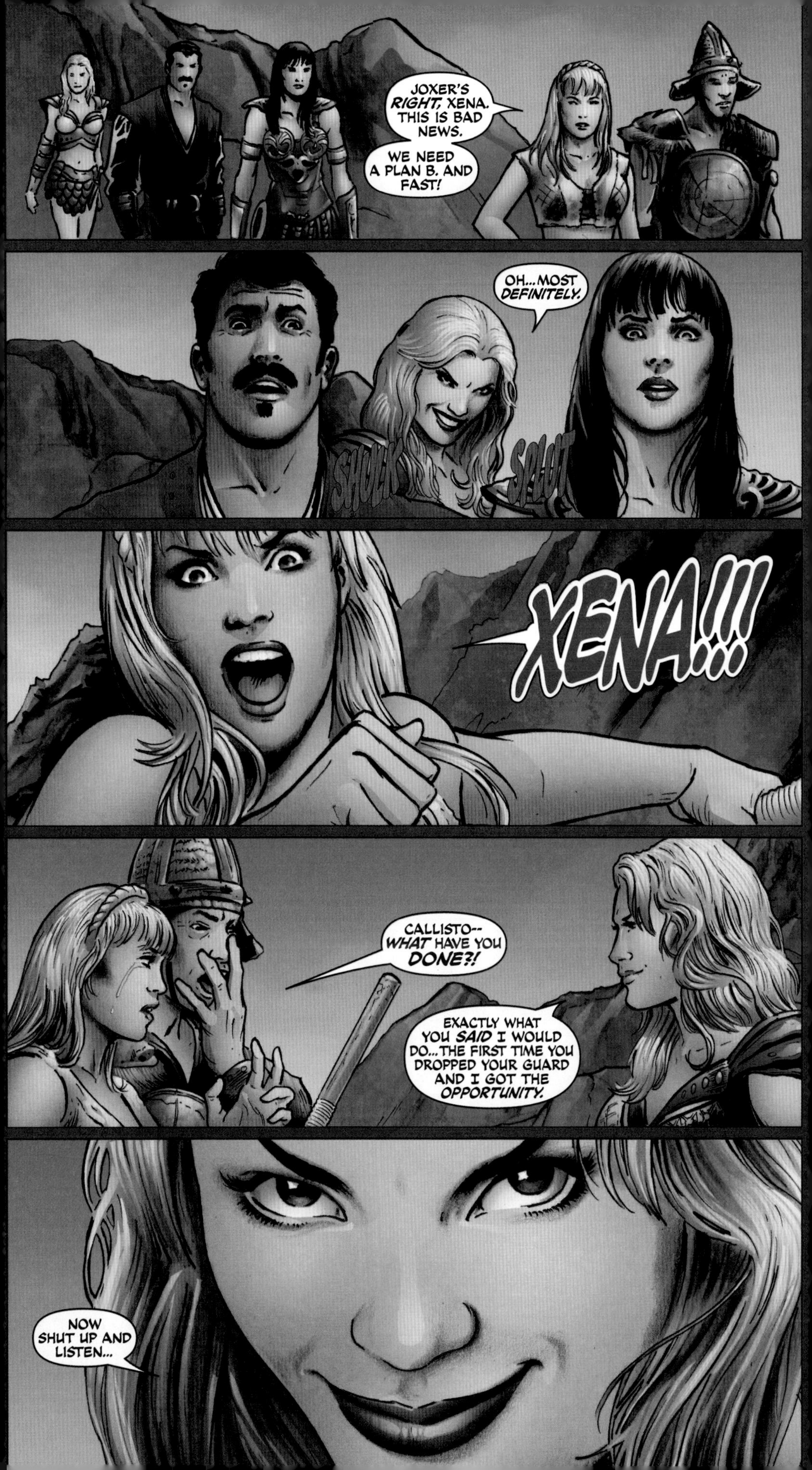
JOXER'S RIGHT, XENA. THIS IS BAD NEWS.
WE NEED A PLAN B. AND FAST!
OH...MOST DEFINITELY.
SHUNK
SPLUT
XENA!!!
CALLISTO-- WHAT HAVE YOU DONE?!
EXACTLY WHAT YOU SAID I WOULD DO...THE FIRST TIME YOU DROPPED YOUR GUARD AND I GOT THE OPPORTUNITY.
NOW SHUT UP AND LISTEN...

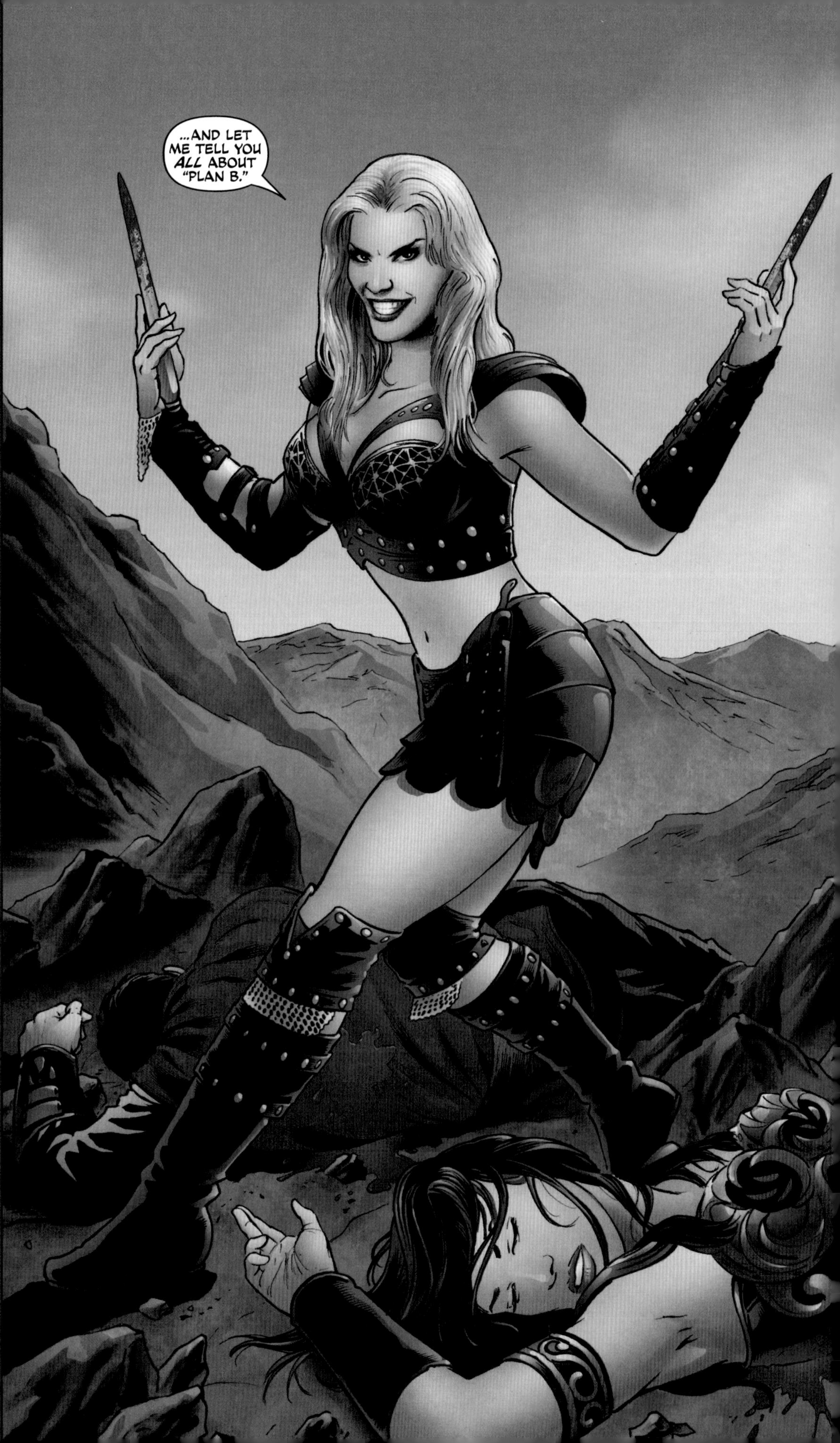
...AND LET ME TELL YOU ALL ABOUT "PLAN B."

CONTEST OF PANTHEONS
CHAPTER FOUR

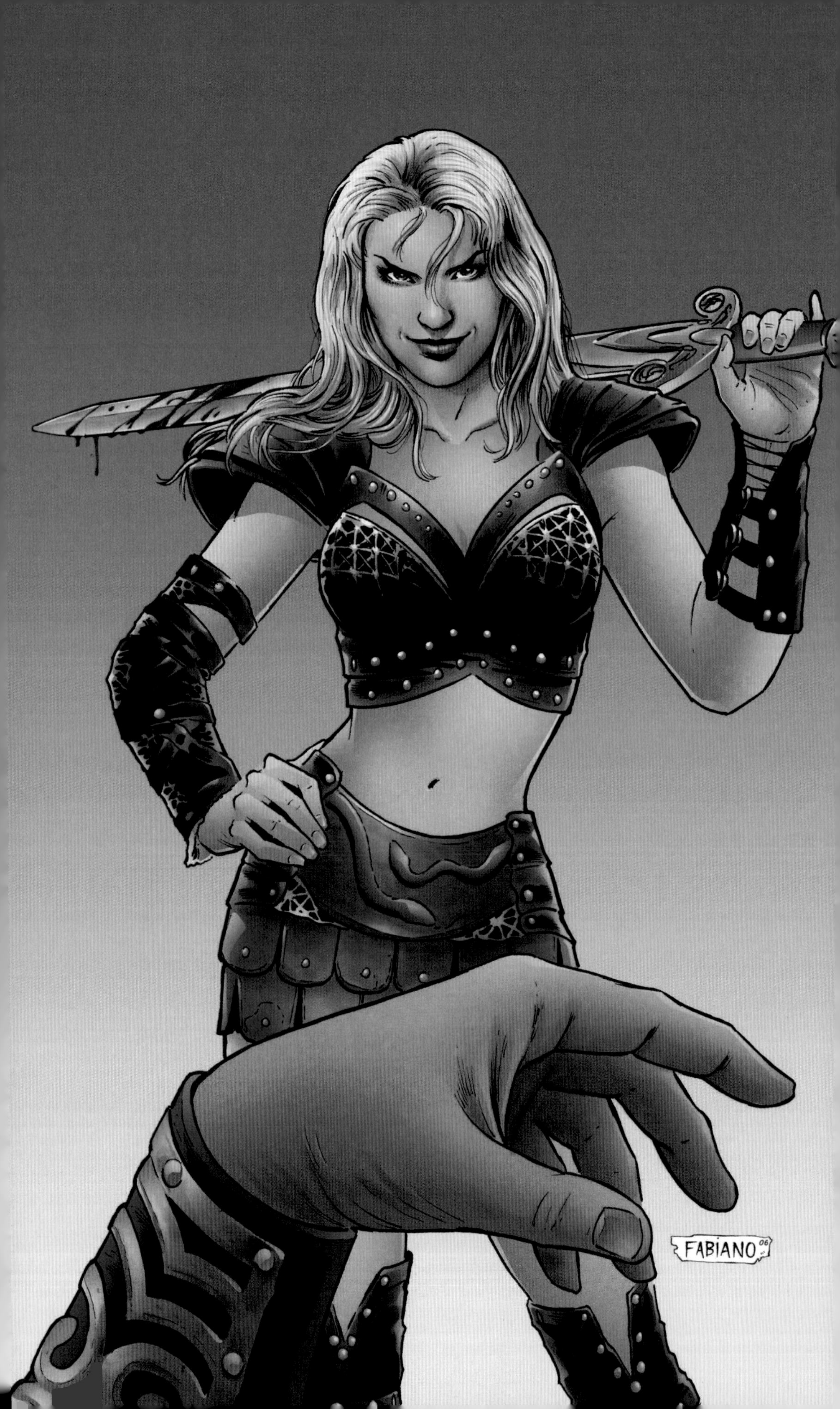
FABIANO 06

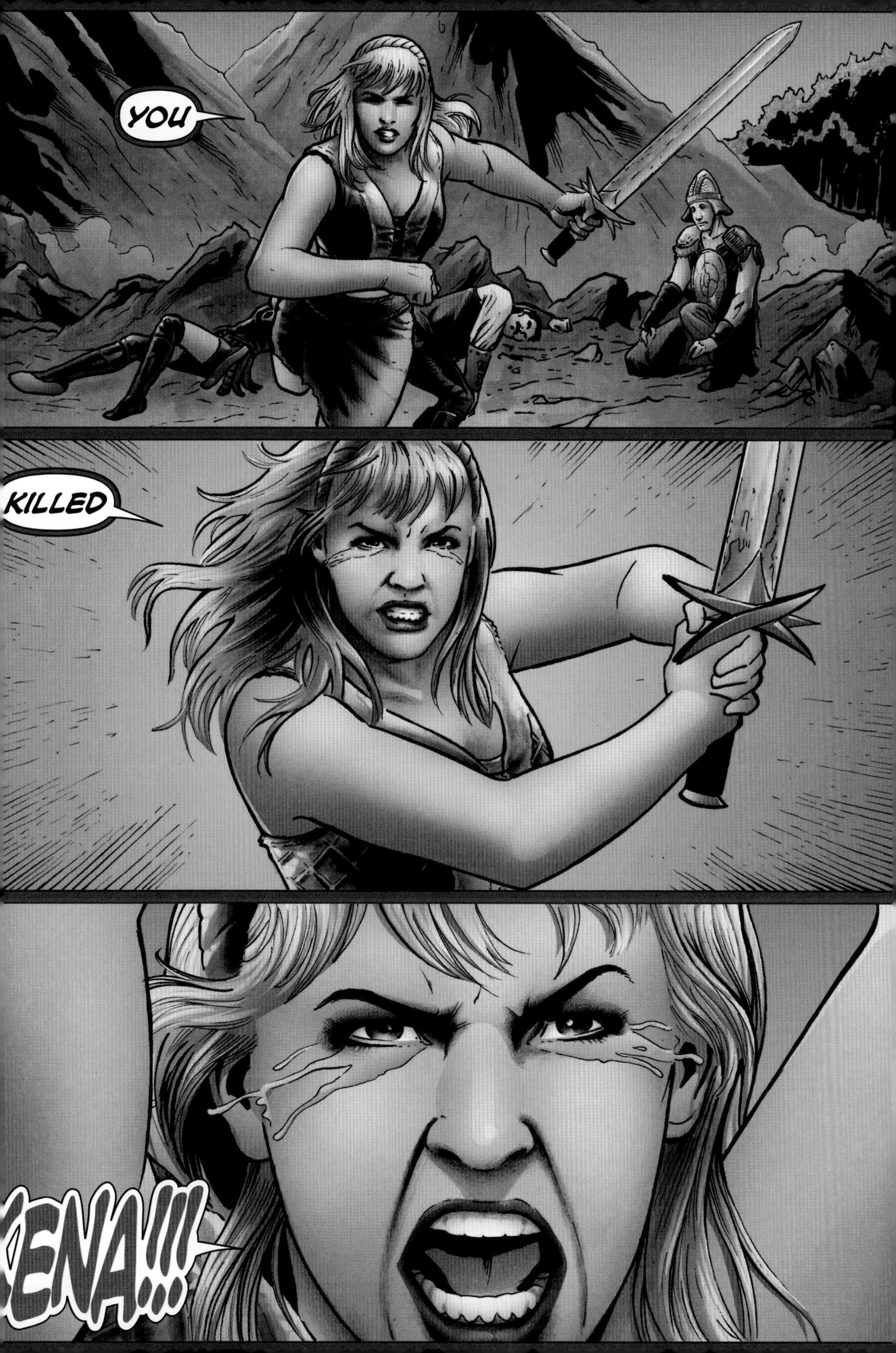
YOU
KILLED
ENA!!!

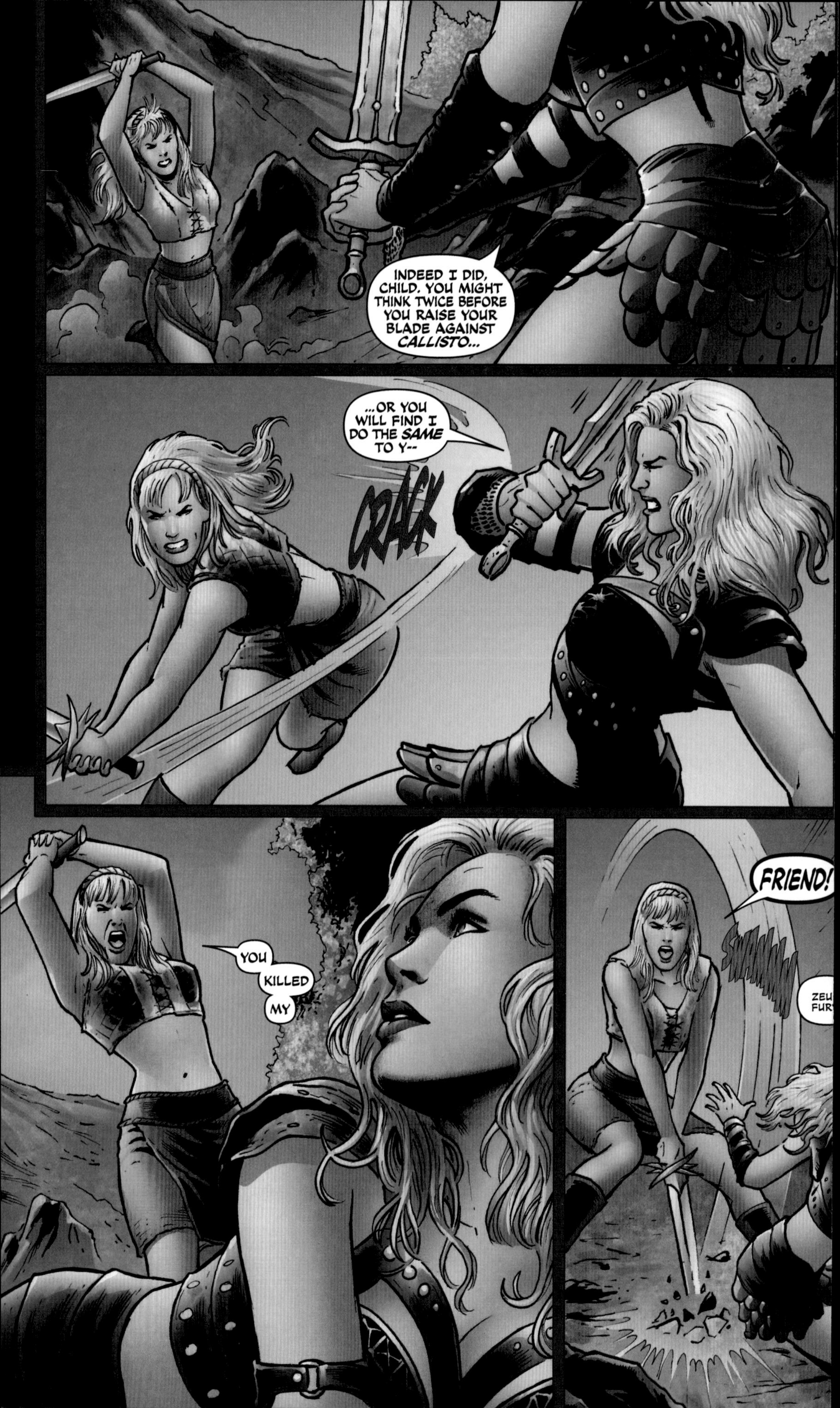
INDEED I DID, CHILD. YOU MIGHT THINK TWICE BEFORE YOU RAISE YOUR BLADE AGAINST CALLISTO...
...OR YOU WILL FIND I DO THE SAME TO Y--
CRACK
YOU
KILLED
MY
FRIEND!

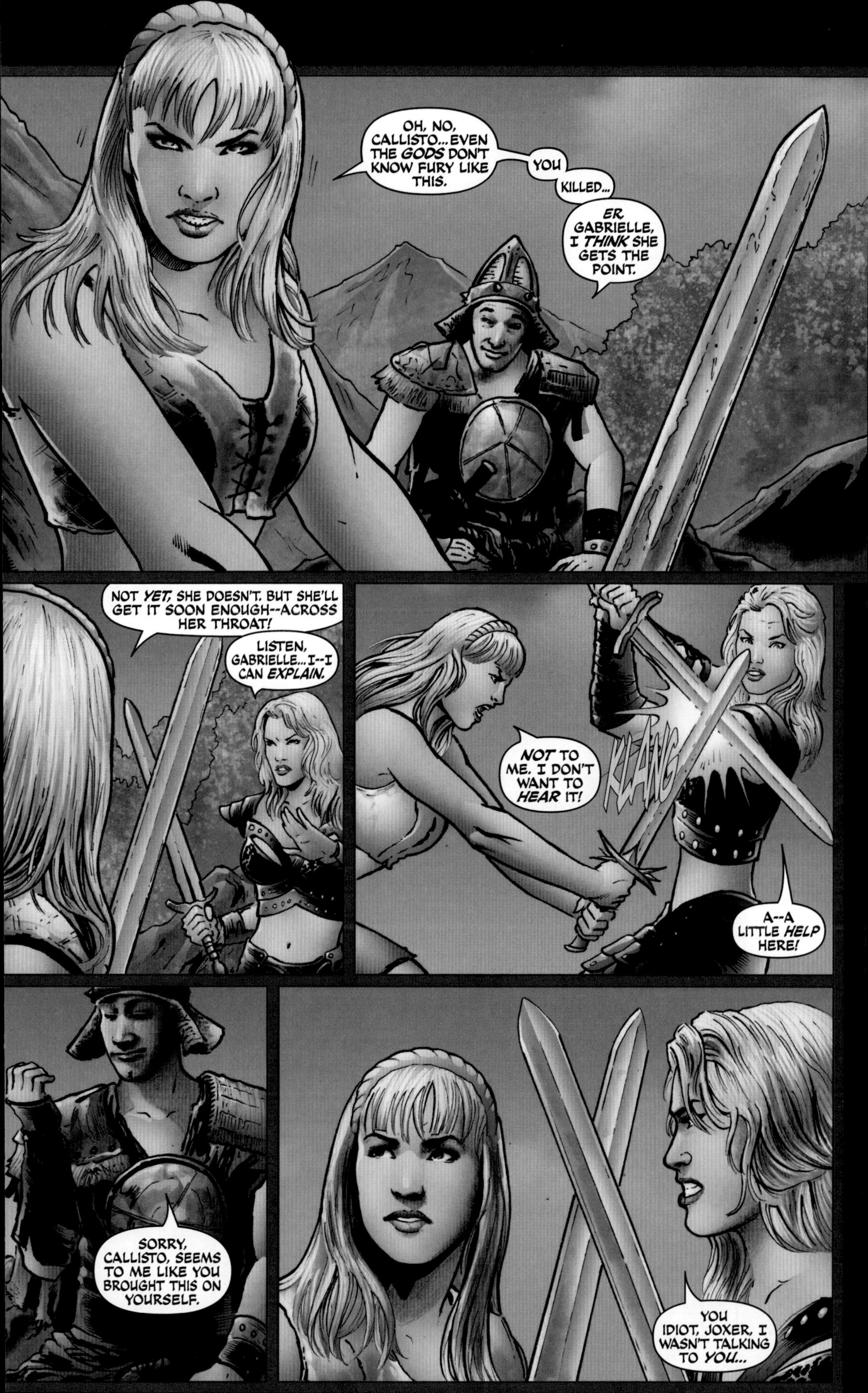

OH, NO, CALLISTO... EVEN THE GODS DON'T KNOW FURY LIKE THIS.
YOU
KILLED...
ER, GABRIELLE, I THINK SHE GETS THE POINT.
NOT YET, SHE DOESN'T. BUT SHE'LL GET IT SOON ENOUGH--ACROSS HER THROAT!
LISTEN, GABRIELLE... I--I CAN EXPLAIN.
NOT TO ME. I DON'T WANT TO HEAR IT!
KLANG
A--A LITTLE HELP HERE!
SORRY, CALLISTO, SEEMS TO ME LIKE YOU BROUGHT THIS ON YOURSELF.
YOU IDIOT, JOXER, I WASN'T TALKING TO YOU...

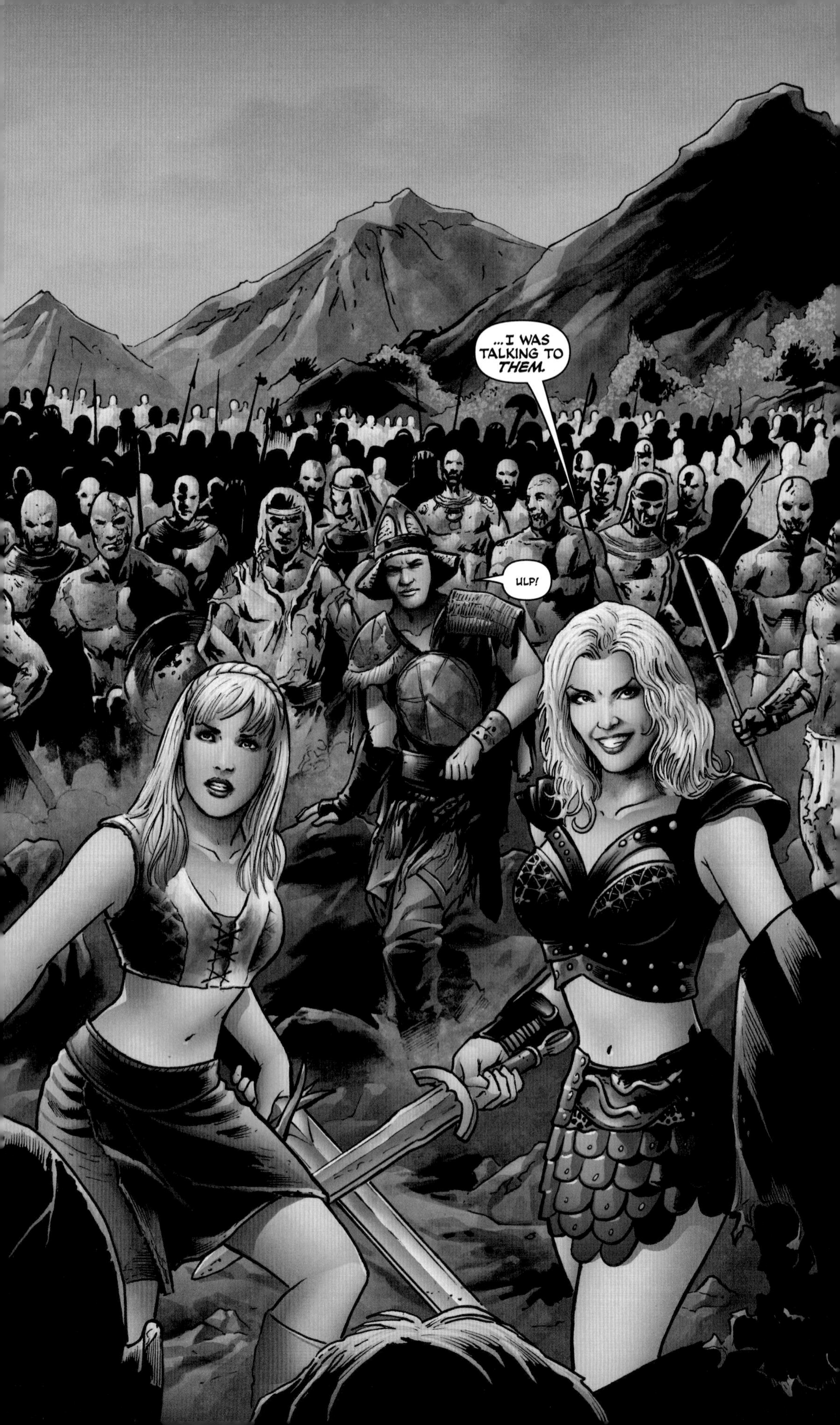

...I WAS TALKING TO *THEM.*
ULP!

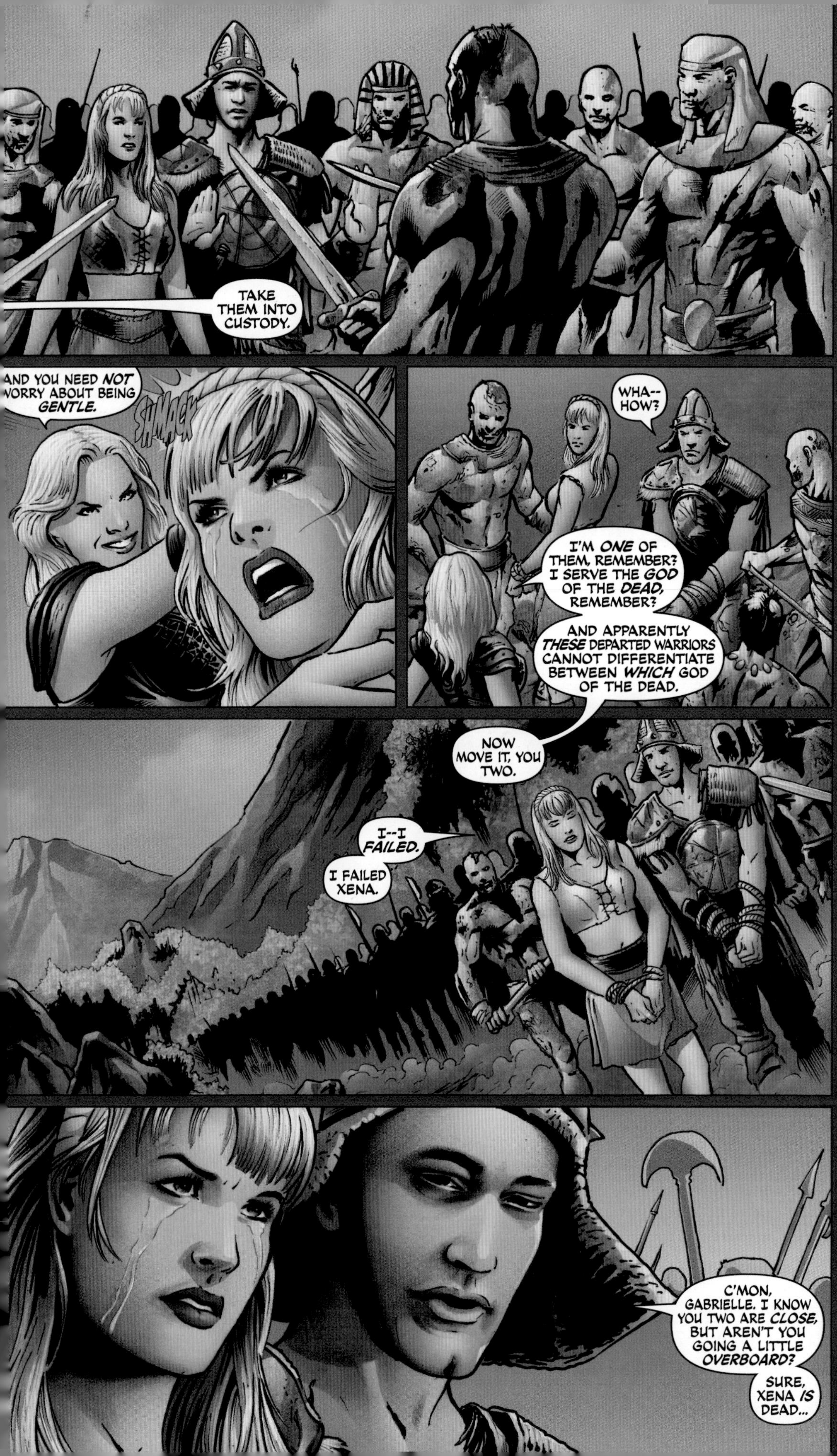
TAKE THEM INTO CUSTODY.
AND YOU NEED NOT WORRY ABOUT BEING GENTLE.
SHMACK
WHA-- HOW?
I'M ONE OF THEM, REMEMBER? I SERVE THE GOD OF THE DEAD, REMEMBER?
AND APPARENTLY THESE DEPARTED WARRIORS CANNOT DIFFERENTIATE BETWEEN WHICH GOD OF THE DEAD.
NOW MOVE IT, YOU TWO.
I--I FAILED.
I FAILED XENA.
C'MON, GABRIELLE. I KNOW YOU TWO ARE CLOSE, BUT AREN'T YOU GOING A LITTLE OVERBOARD?
SURE, XENA IS DEAD...

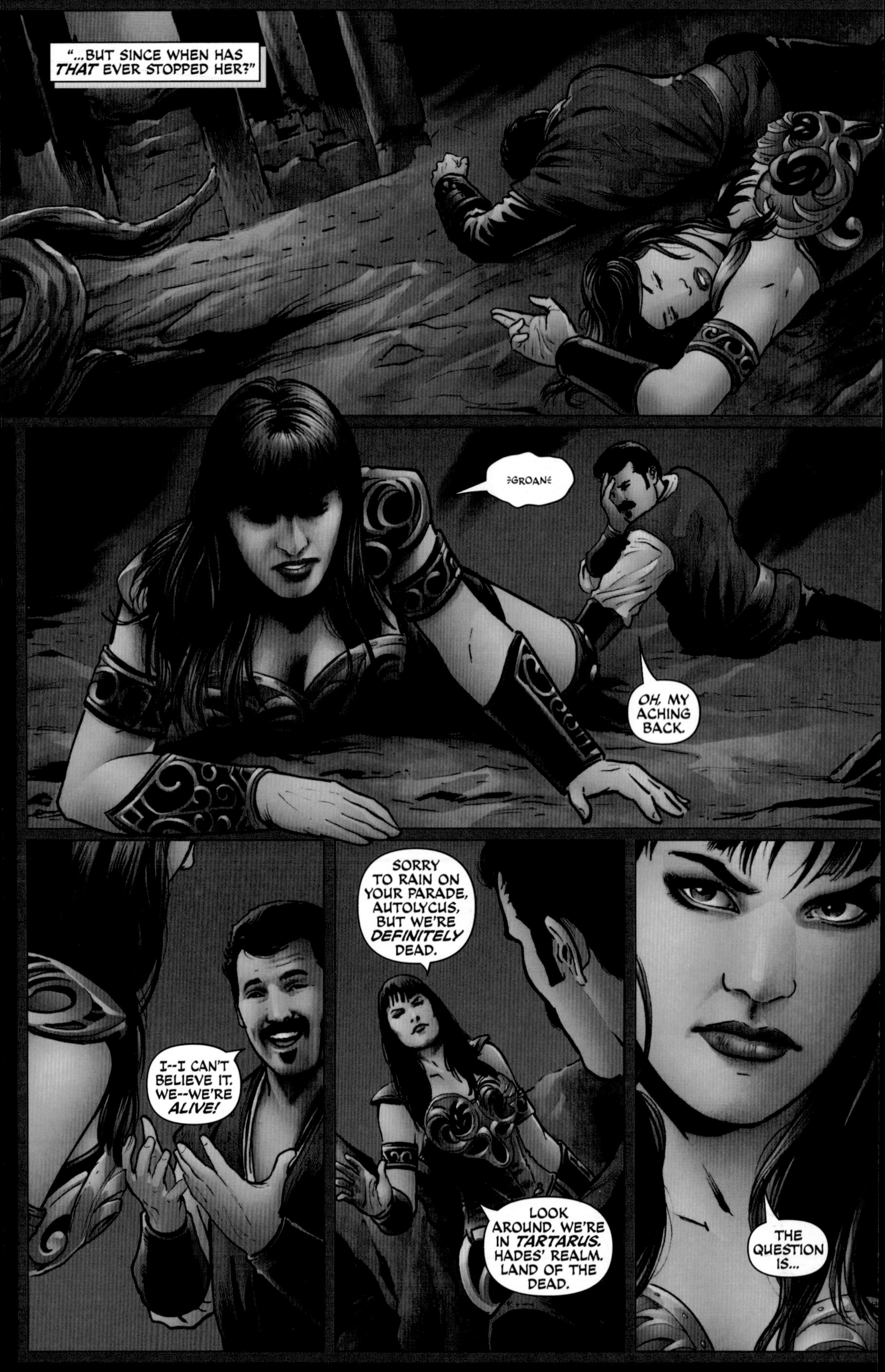
"...BUT SINCE WHEN HAS *THAT* EVER STOPPED HER?"
GROAN
OH, MY ACHING BACK.
I--I CAN'T BELIEVE IT. WE--WE'RE *ALIVE!*
SORRY TO RAIN ON YOUR PARADE, AUTOLYCUS, BUT WE'RE *DEFINITELY* DEAD.
LOOK AROUND. WE'RE IN *TARTARUS.* HADES' REALM. LAND OF THE DEAD.
THE QUESTION IS...

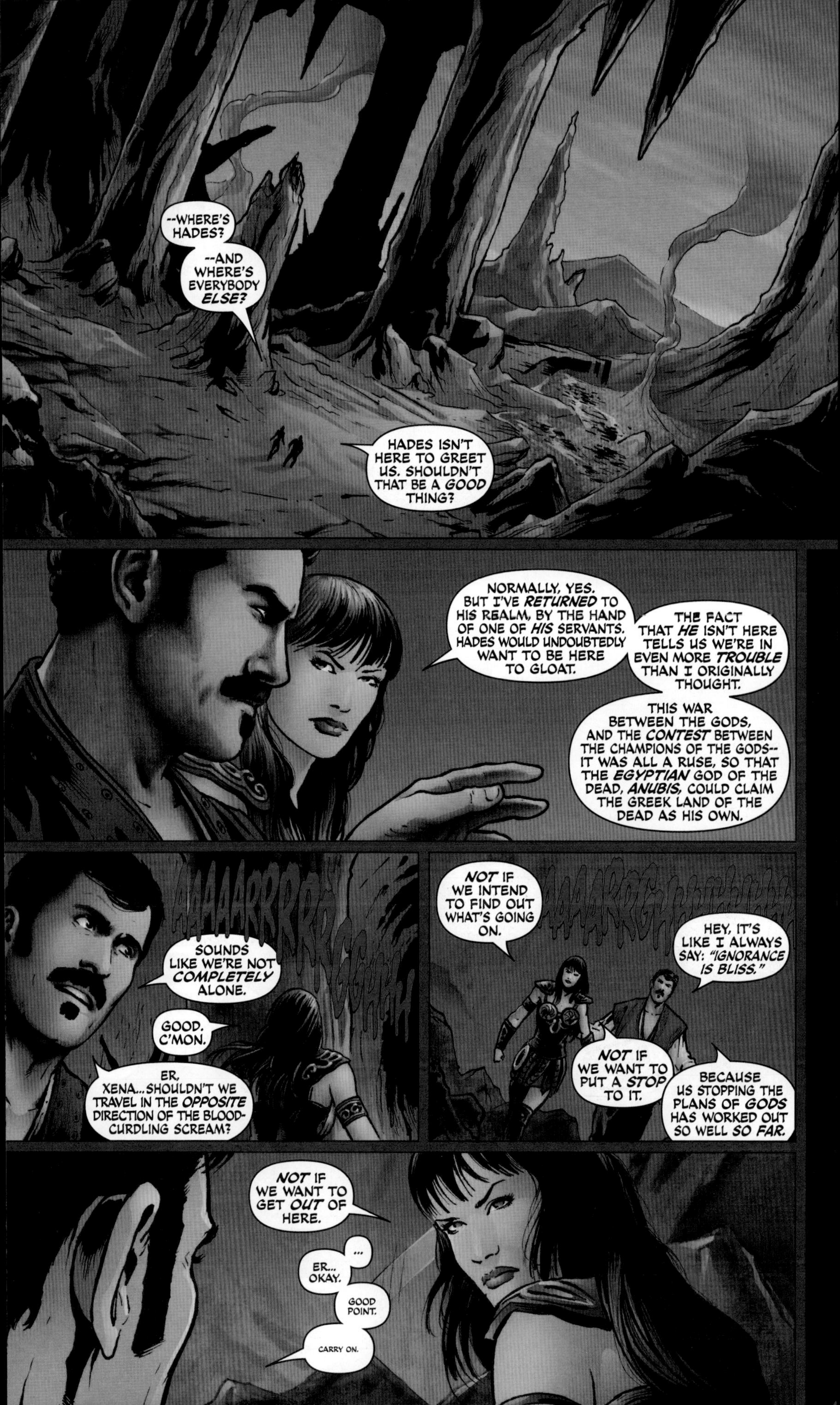
--WHERE'S HADES?
--AND WHERE'S EVERYBODY ELSE?
HADES ISN'T HERE TO GREET US. SHOULDN'T THAT BE A GOOD THING?
NORMALLY, YES. BUT I'VE RETURNED TO HIS REALM, BY THE HAND OF ONE OF HIS SERVANTS. HADES WOULD UNDOUBTEDLY WANT TO BE HERE TO GLOAT.
THE FACT THAT HE ISN'T HERE TELLS US WE'RE IN EVEN MORE TROUBLE THAN I ORIGINALLY THOUGHT.
THIS WAR BETWEEN THE GODS, AND THE CONTEST BETWEEN THE CHAMPIONS OF THE GODS-- IT WAS ALL A RUSE, SO THAT THE EGYPTIAN GOD OF THE DEAD, ANUBIS, COULD CLAIM THE GREEK LAND OF THE DEAD AS HIS OWN.
SOUNDS LIKE WE'RE NOT COMPLETELY ALONE.
GOOD. C'MON.
ER, XENA...SHOULDN'T WE TRAVEL IN THE OPPOSITE DIRECTION OF THE BLOOD-CURDLING SCREAM?
NOT IF WE INTEND TO FIND OUT WHAT'S GOING ON.
HEY, IT'S LIKE I ALWAYS SAY: "IGNORANCE IS BLISS."
NOT IF WE WANT TO PUT A STOP TO IT.
BECAUSE US STOPPING THE PLANS OF GODS HAS WORKED OUT SO WELL SO FAR.
NOT IF WE WANT TO GET OUT OF HERE.
...
ER... OKAY.
GOOD POINT.
CARRY ON.

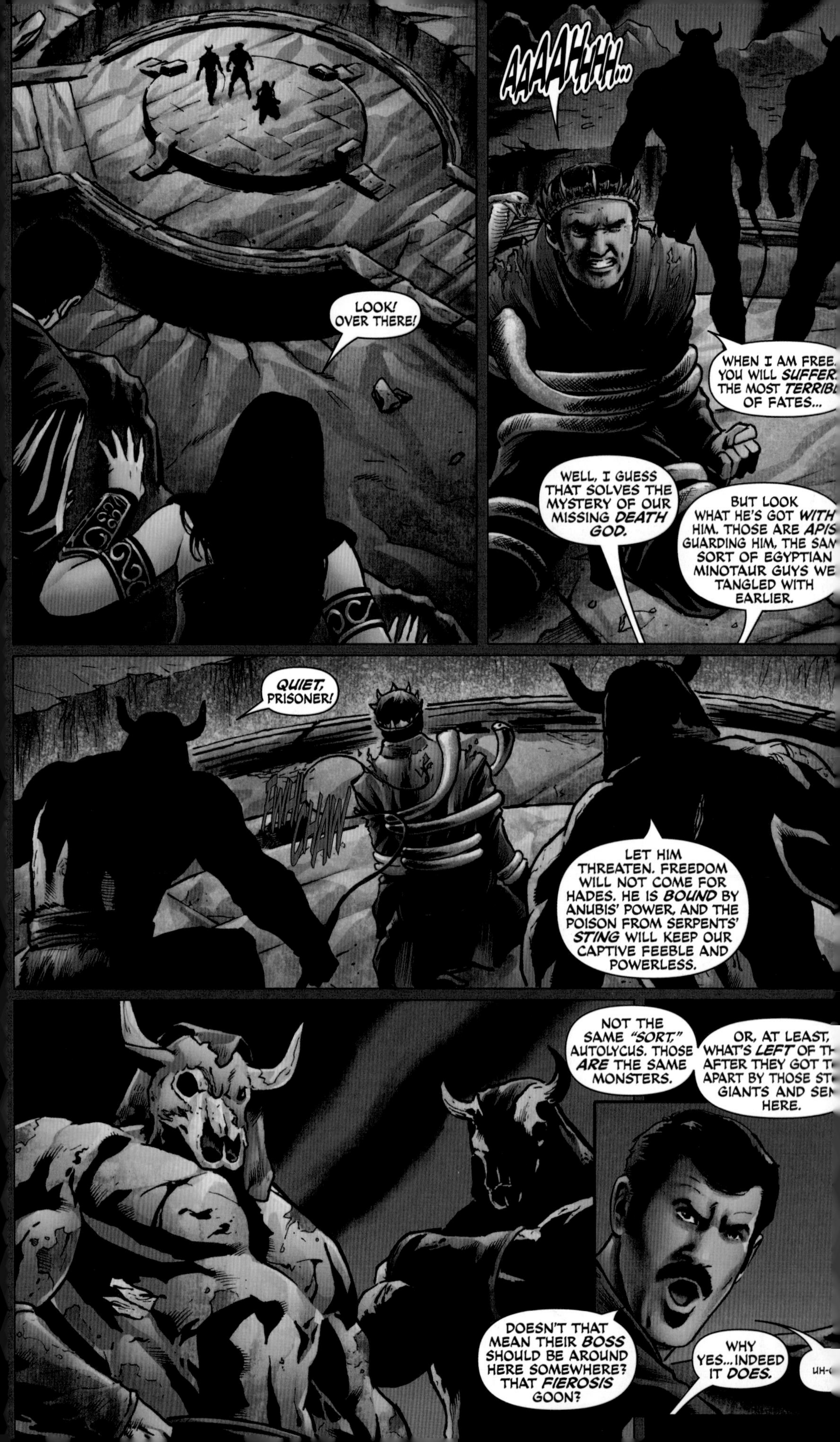
LOOK! OVER THERE!
AAAAHHH...
WHEN I AM FREE. YOU WILL SUFFER. THE MOST TERRIBL OF FATES...
WELL, I GUESS THAT SOLVES THE MYSTERY OF OUR MISSING DEATH GOD.
BUT LOOK WHAT HE'S GOT WITH HIM. THOSE ARE APIS GUARDING HIM, THE SAM SORT OF EGYPTIAN MINOTAUR GUYS WE TANGLED WITH EARLIER.
QUIET, PRISONER!
FWHE-CHAW
LET HIM THREATEN. FREEDOM WILL NOT COME FOR HADES. HE IS BOUND BY ANUBIS' POWER, AND THE POISON FROM SERPENTS' STING WILL KEEP OUR CAPTIVE FEEBLE AND POWERLESS.
NOT THE SAME "SORT," AUTOLYCUS. THOSE ARE THE SAME MONSTERS.
OR, AT LEAST, WHAT'S LEFT OF TH AFTER THEY GOT T APART BY THOSE ST GIANTS AND SEN HERE.
DOESN'T THAT MEAN THEIR BOSS SHOULD BE AROUND HERE SOMEWHERE? THAT FIEROSIS GOON?
WHY YES...INDEED IT DOES.
UH-

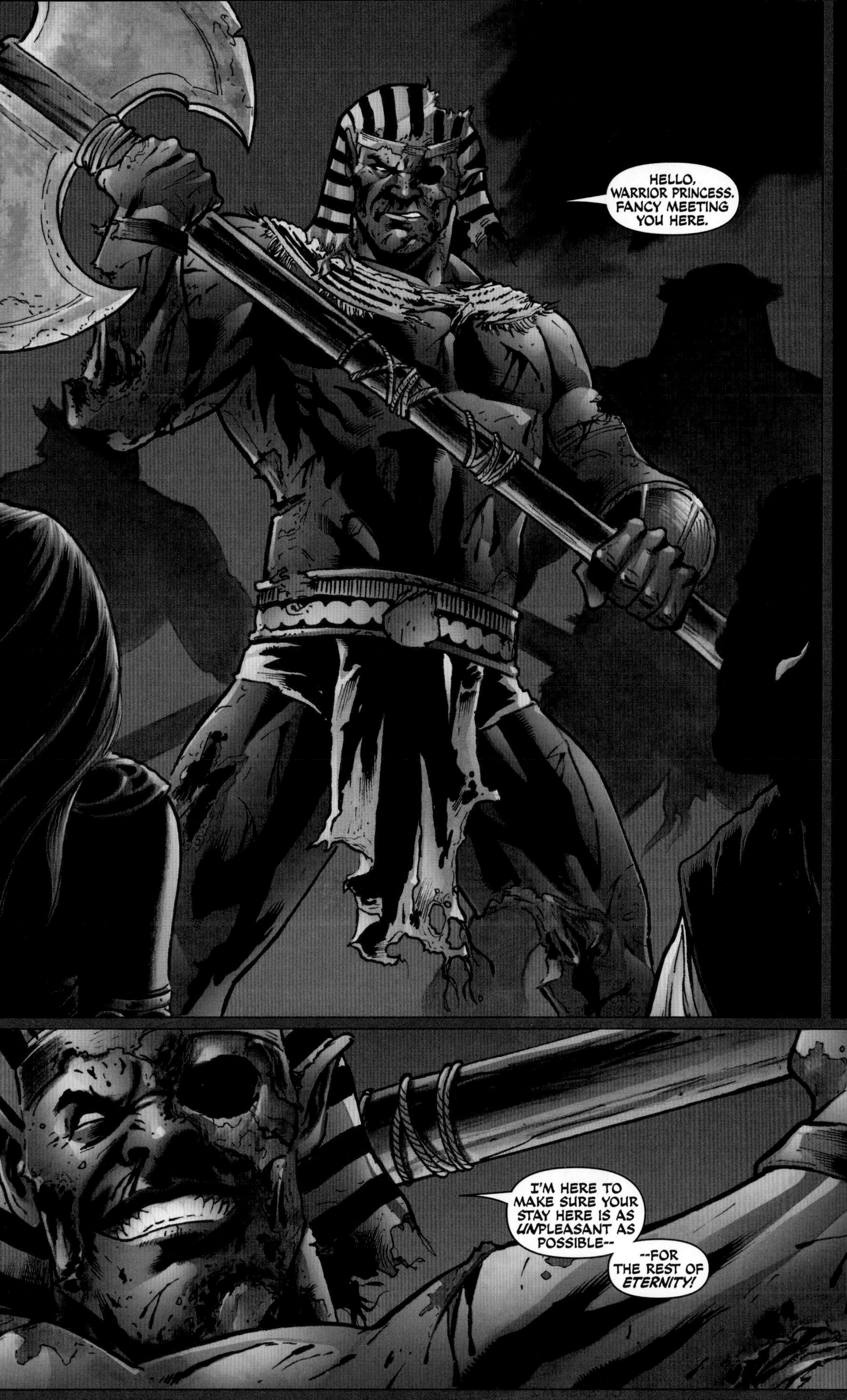
HELLO, WARRIOR PRINCESS. FANCY MEETING YOU HERE.
I'M HERE TO MAKE SURE YOUR STAY HERE IS AS *UN*PLEASANT AS POSSIBLE--
--FOR THE REST OF *ETERNITY!*

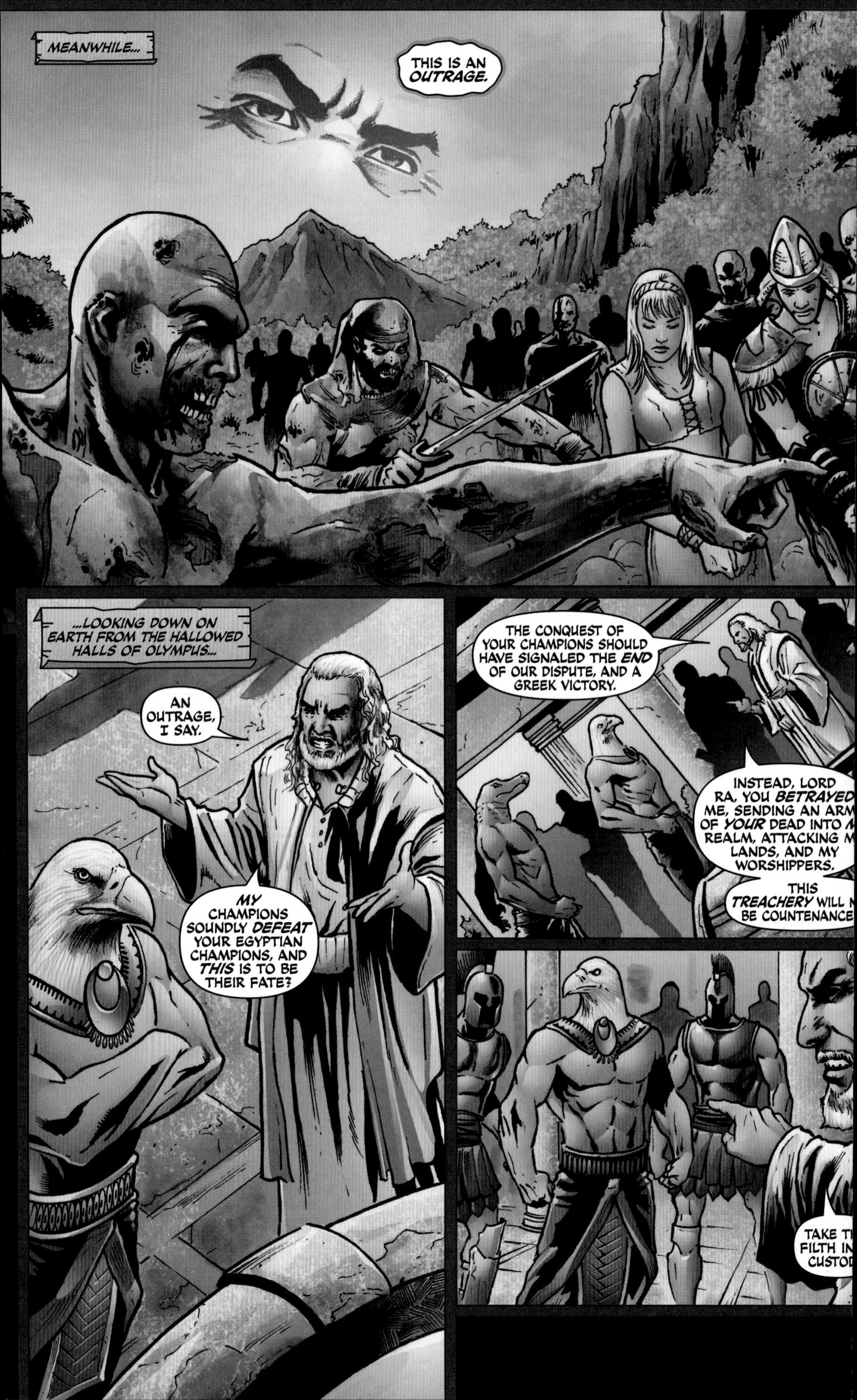
MEANWHILE...
THIS IS AN OUTRAGE.
...LOOKING DOWN ON EARTH FROM THE HALLOWED HALLS OF OLYMPUS...
AN OUTRAGE, I SAY.
MY CHAMPIONS SOUNDLY DEFEAT YOUR EGYPTIAN CHAMPIONS, AND THIS IS TO BE THEIR FATE?
THE CONQUEST OF YOUR CHAMPIONS SHOULD HAVE SIGNALED THE END OF OUR DISPUTE, AND A GREEK VICTORY.
INSTEAD, LORD RA, YOU BETRAYED ME, SENDING AN ARM OF YOUR DEAD INTO M REALM, ATTACKING M LANDS, AND MY WORSHIPPERS.
THIS TREACHERY WILL N BE COUNTENANCE
TAKE T FILTH IN CUSTOD

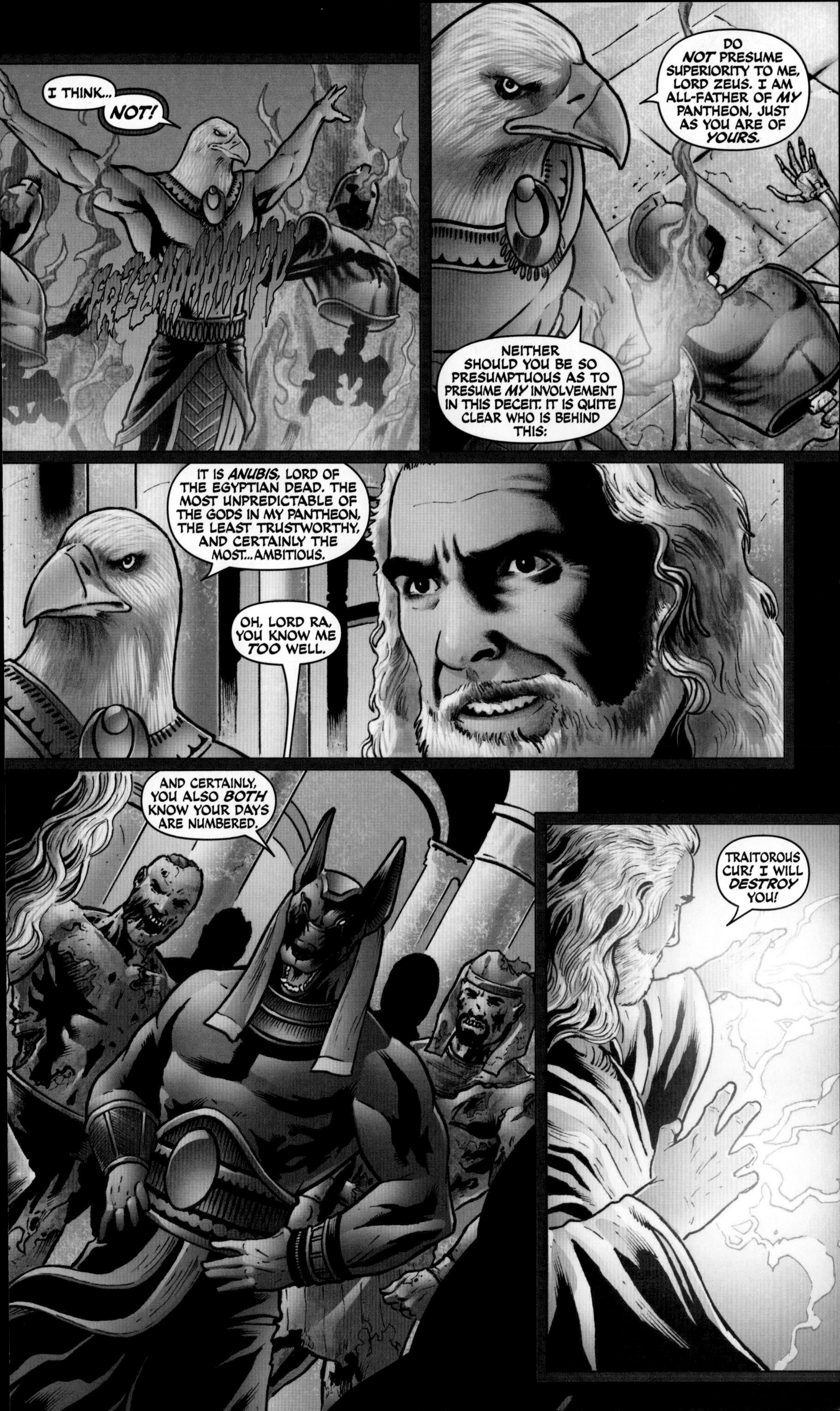
I THINK... NOT!
FRZZAAHHHHPPP
DO NOT PRESUME SUPERIORITY TO ME, LORD ZEUS. I AM ALL-FATHER OF MY PANTHEON, JUST AS YOU ARE OF YOURS.
NEITHER SHOULD YOU BE SO PRESUMPTUOUS AS TO PRESUME MY INVOLVEMENT IN THIS DECEIT. IT IS QUITE CLEAR WHO IS BEHIND THIS:
IT IS ANUBIS, LORD OF THE EGYPTIAN DEAD. THE MOST UNPREDICTABLE OF THE GODS IN MY PANTHEON, THE LEAST TRUSTWORTHY, AND CERTAINLY THE MOST...AMBITIOUS.
OH, LORD RA, YOU KNOW ME TOO WELL.
AND CERTAINLY, YOU ALSO BOTH KNOW YOUR DAYS ARE NUMBERED.
TRAITOROUS CUR! I WILL DESTROY YOU!

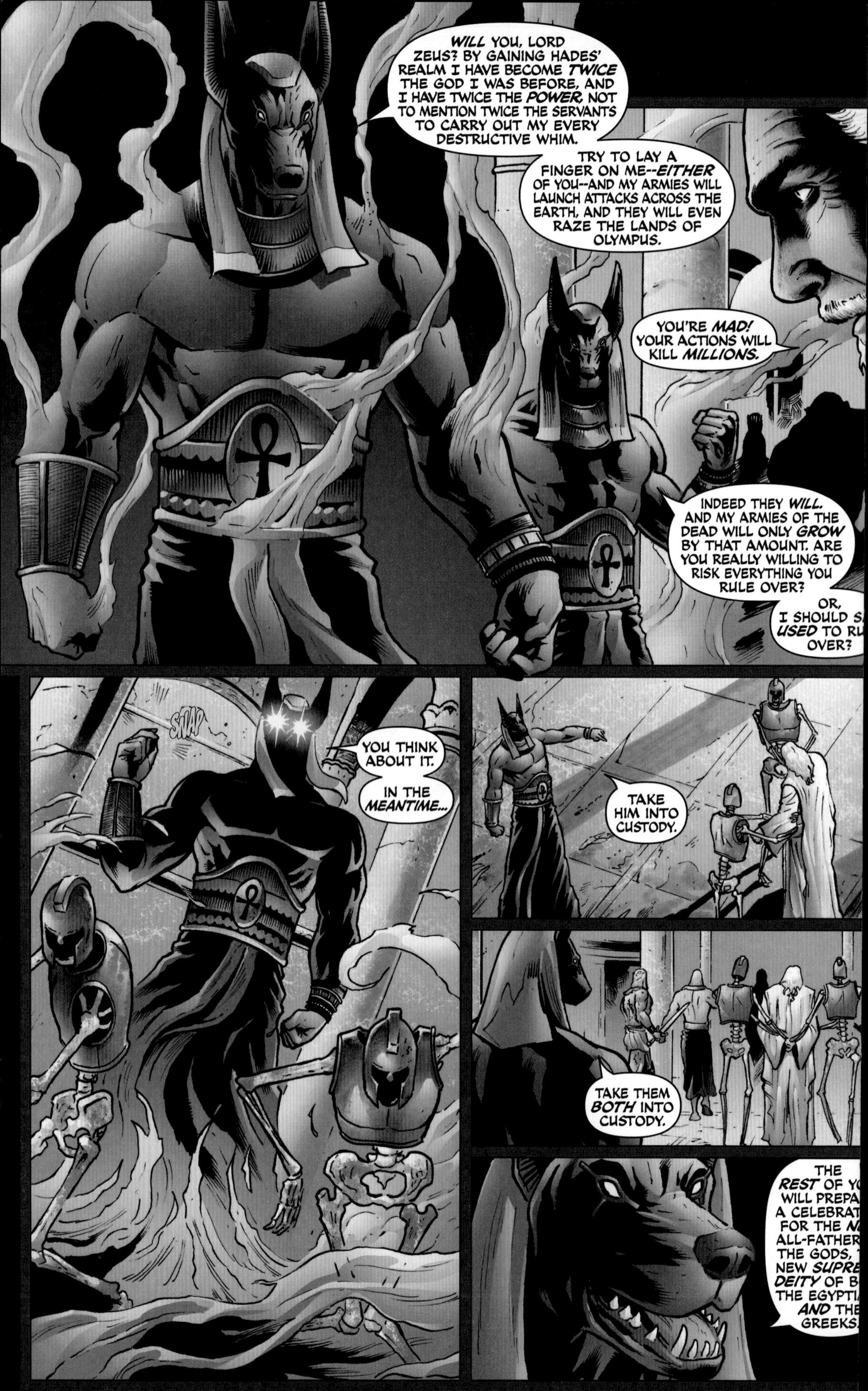
WILL YOU, LORD ZEUS? BY GAINING HADES' REALM I HAVE BECOME TWICE THE GOD I WAS BEFORE, AND I HAVE TWICE THE POWER, NOT TO MENTION TWICE THE SERVANTS TO CARRY OUT MY EVERY DESTRUCTIVE WHIM.
TRY TO LAY A FINGER ON ME--EITHER OF YOU--AND MY ARMIES WILL LAUNCH ATTACKS ACROSS THE EARTH, AND THEY WILL EVEN RAZE THE LANDS OF OLYMPUS.
YOU'RE MAD! YOUR ACTIONS WILL KILL MILLIONS.
INDEED THEY WILL. AND MY ARMIES OF THE DEAD WILL ONLY GROW BY THAT AMOUNT. ARE YOU REALLY WILLING TO RISK EVERYTHING YOU RULE OVER?
OR, I SHOULD S USED TO RU OVER?
SNAP
YOU THINK ABOUT IT.
IN THE MEANTIME...
TAKE HIM INTO CUSTODY.
TAKE THEM BOTH INTO CUSTODY.
THE REST OF YO WILL PREPA A CELEBRAT FOR THE N ALL-FATHER THE GODS, NEW SUPRE DEITY OF B THE EGYPTI AND THE GREEKS.

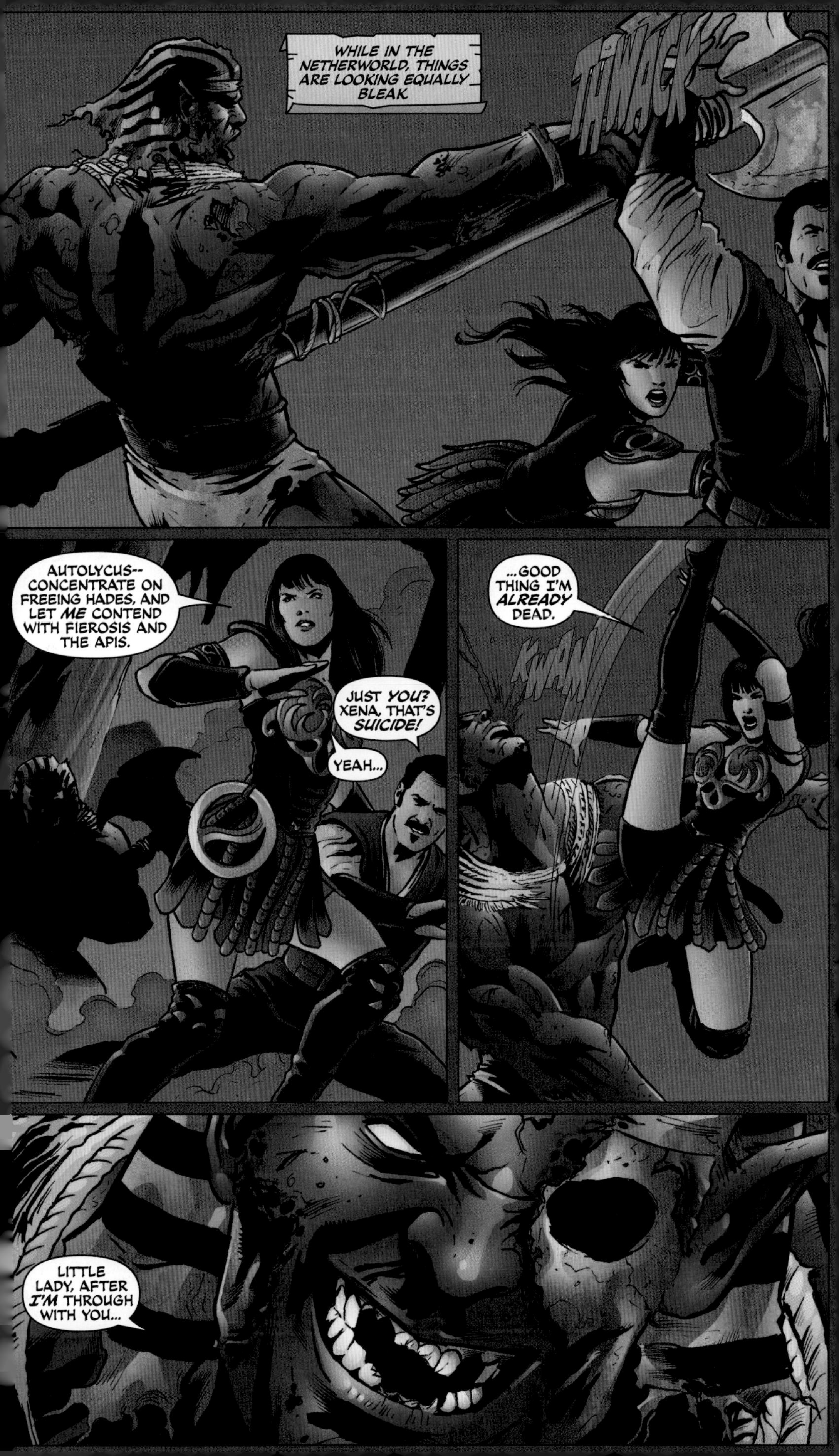
WHILE IN THE NETHERWORLD, THINGS ARE LOOKING EQUALLY BLEAK.
THWACK
AUTOLYCUS--CONCENTRATE ON FREEING HADES, AND LET *ME* CONTEND WITH FIEROSIS AND THE APIS.
JUST *YOU*? XENA, THAT'S *SUICIDE!*
YEAH...
...GOOD THING I'M *ALREADY* DEAD.
KWAM
LITTLE LADY, AFTER *I'M* THROUGH WITH YOU...

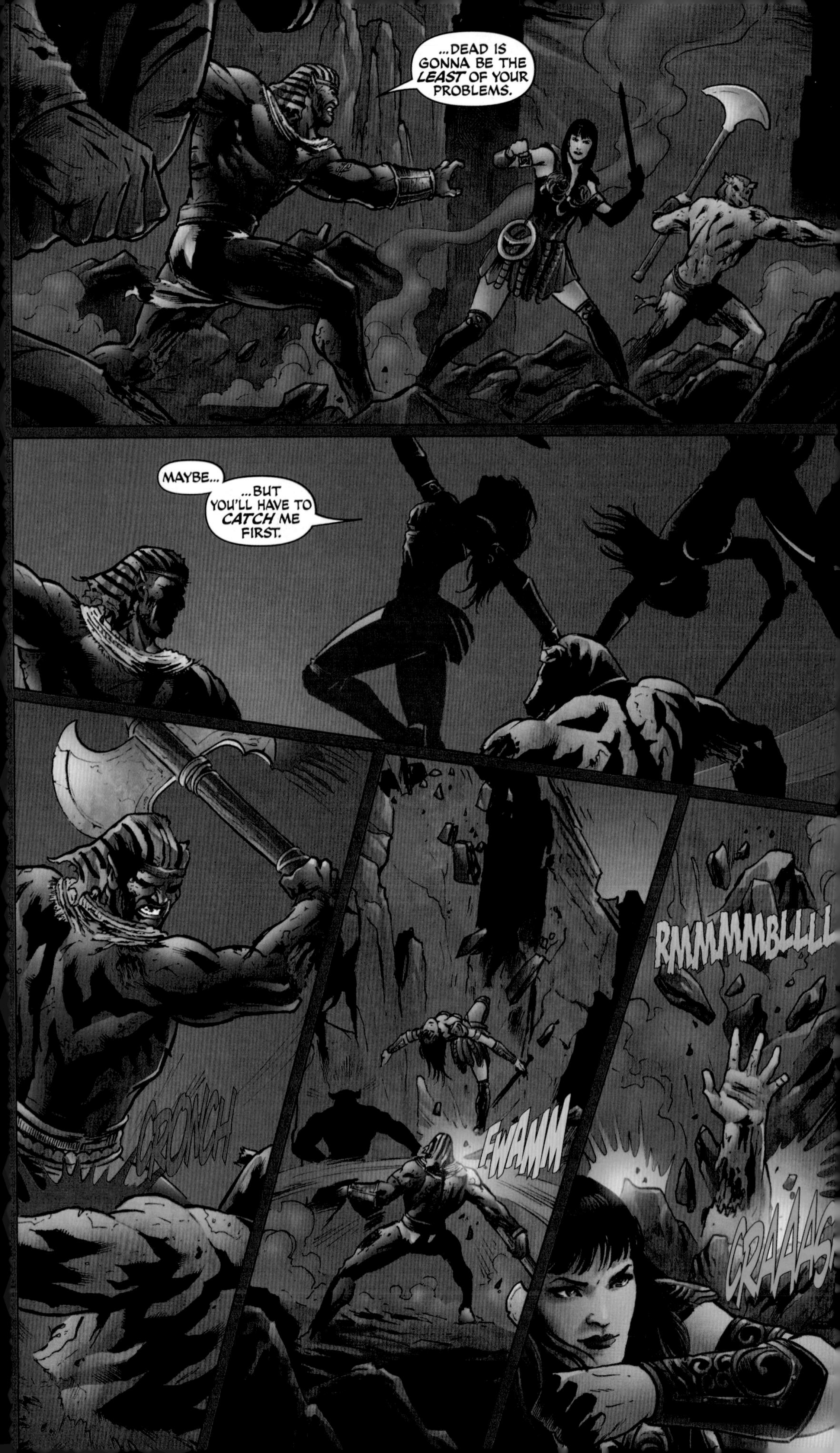
...DEAD IS GONNA BE THE LEAST OF YOUR PROBLEMS.
MAYBE...
...BUT YOU'LL HAVE TO CATCH ME FIRST.
CRONCH
FWAMM
RMMMMBLLLL
CRAAAS

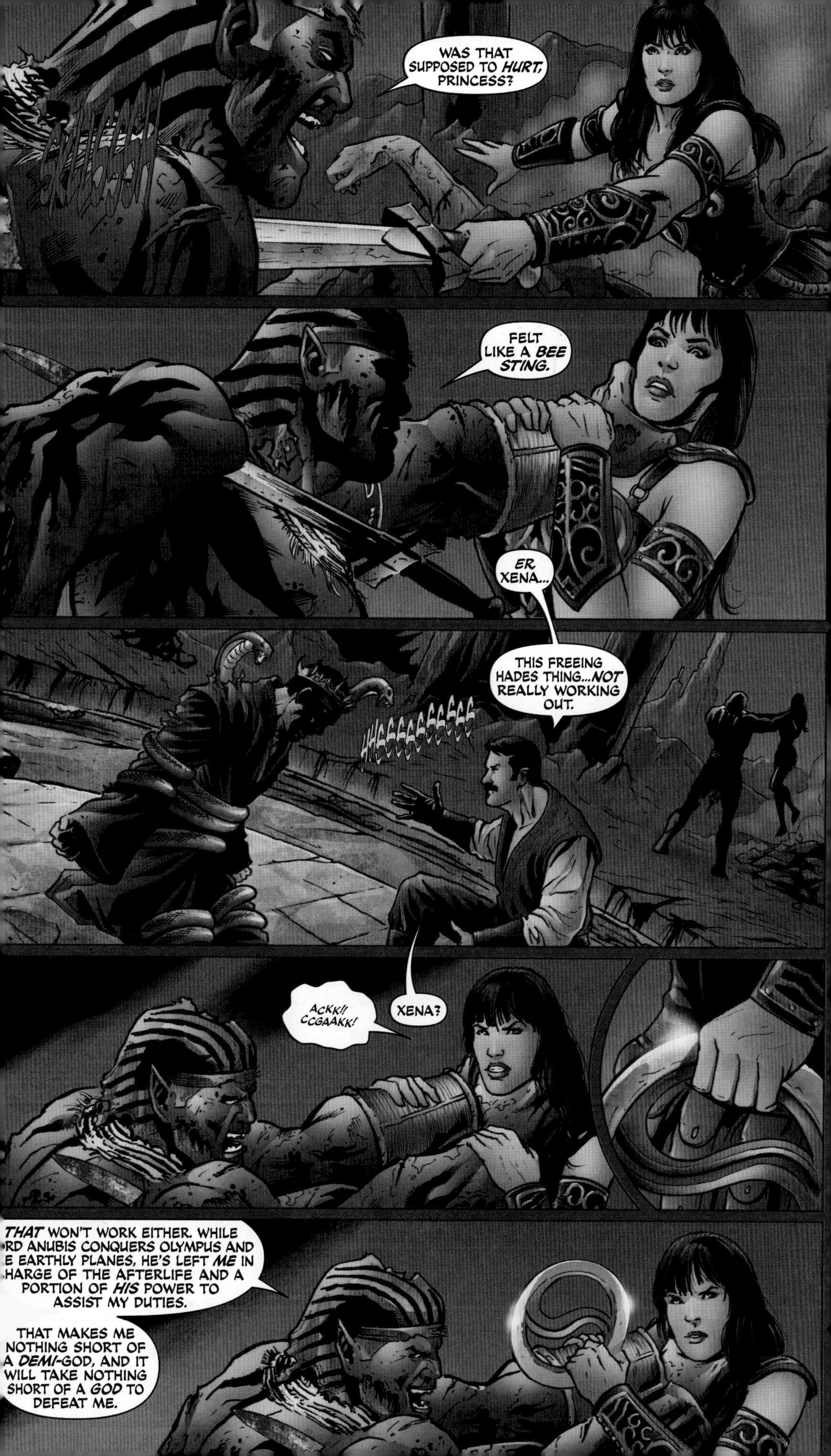
SKLUSSH
WAS THAT SUPPOSED TO *HURT,* PRINCESS?
FELT LIKE A *BEE STING.*
ER, XENA...
THIS FREEING HADES THING...*NOT* REALLY WORKING OUT.
HHSSSSSSSSSSS
XENA?
ACKK!! CCGAAKK!
THAT WON'T WORK EITHER. WHILE RD ANUBIS CONQUERS OLYMPUS AND E EARTHLY PLANES, HE'S LEFT *ME* IN HARGE OF THE AFTERLIFE AND A PORTION OF *HIS* POWER TO ASSIST MY DUTIES.
THAT MAKES ME NOTHING SHORT OF A *DEMI*-GOD, AND IT WILL TAKE NOTHING SHORT OF A *GOD* TO DEFEAT ME.

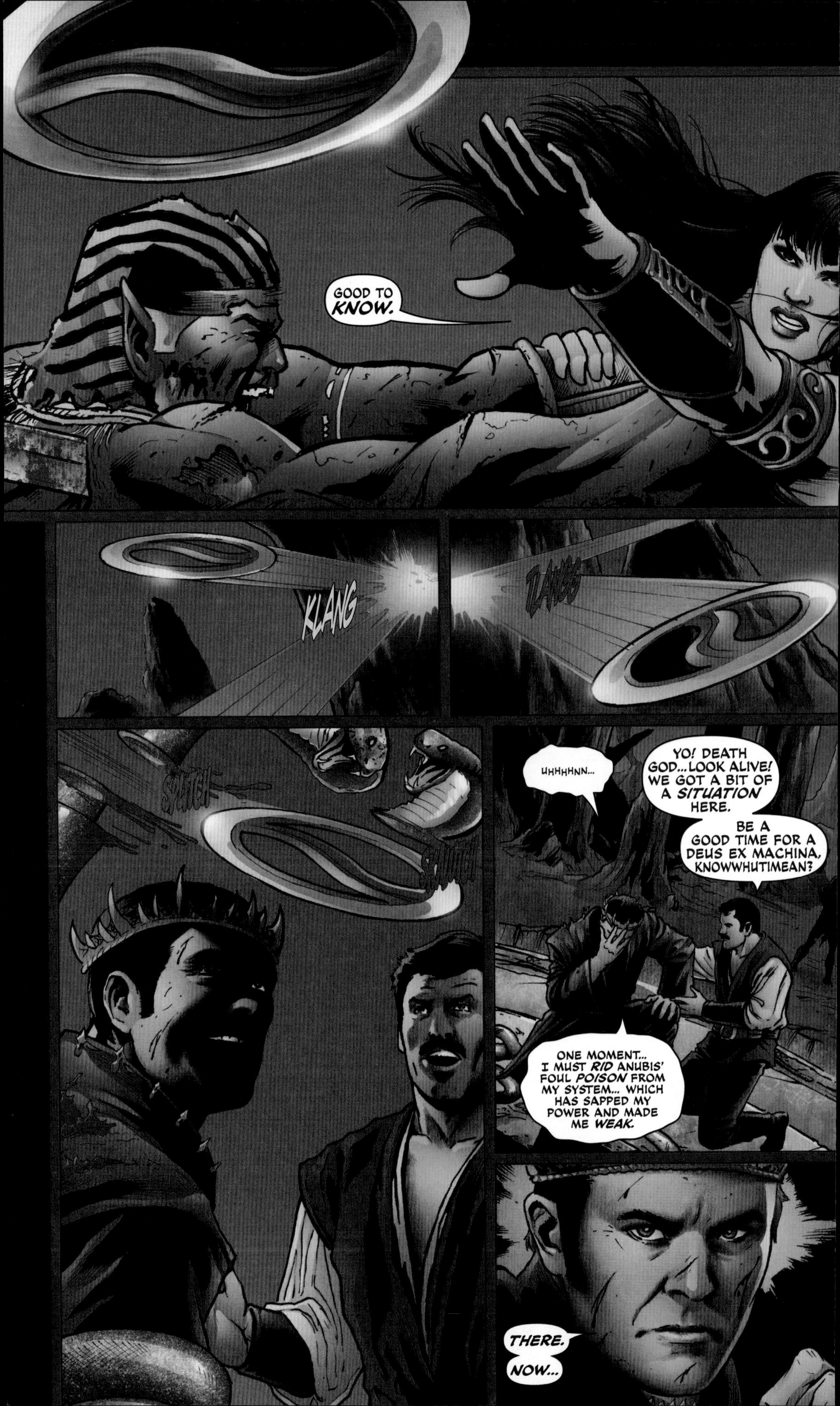
GOOD TO KNOW.
KLANG
TLANGG
SPLATCH
SPLATCH
UHHHHHNN...
YO! DEATH GOD...LOOK ALIVE! WE GOT A BIT OF A SITUATION HERE.
BE A GOOD TIME FOR A DEUS EX MACHINA, KNOWWHUTIMEAN?
ONE MOMENT... I MUST RID ANUBIS' FOUL POISON FROM MY SYSTEM... WHICH HAS SAPPED MY POWER AND MADE ME WEAK.
THERE.
NOW...

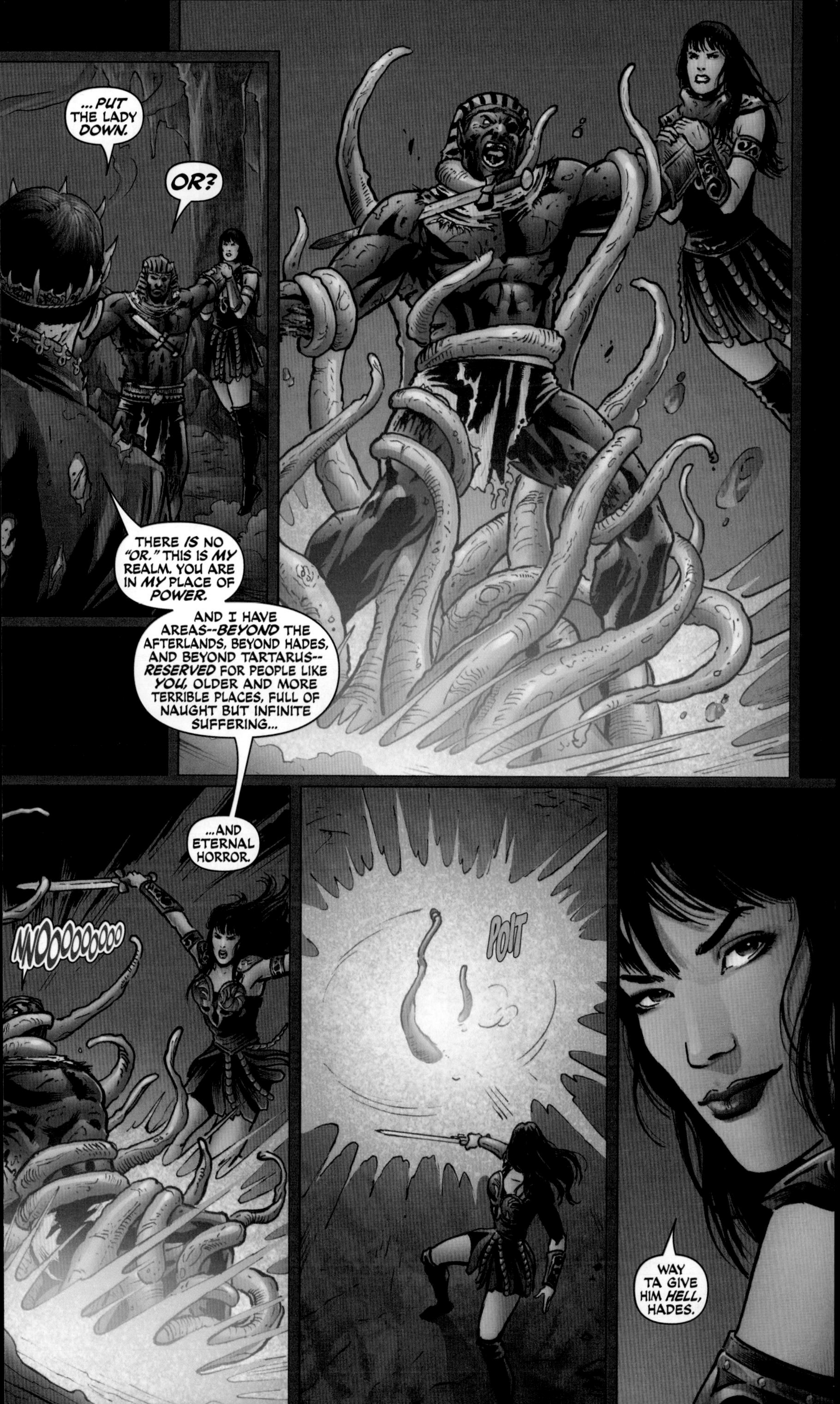
...PUT THE LADY DOWN.
OR?
THERE IS NO "OR." THIS IS MY REALM. YOU ARE IN MY PLACE OF POWER.
AND I HAVE AREAS--BEYOND THE AFTERLANDS, BEYOND HADES, AND BEYOND TARTARUS--RESERVED FOR PEOPLE LIKE YOU, OLDER AND MORE TERRIBLE PLACES, FULL OF NAUGHT BUT INFINITE SUFFERING...
...AND ETERNAL HORROR.
NNOOOOOOOOO
POIT
WAY TA GIVE HIM HELL, HADES.

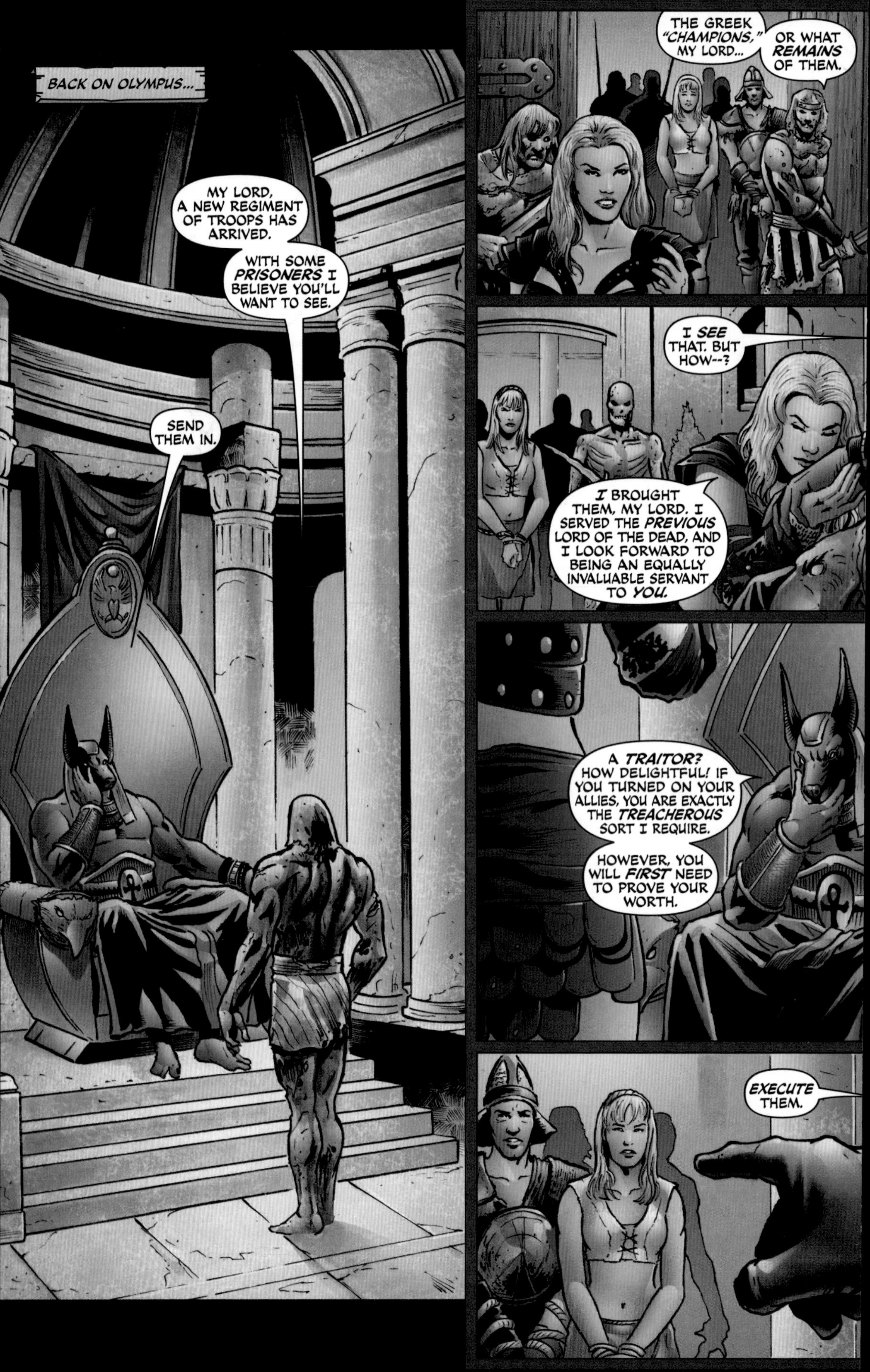
BACK ON OLYMPUS...
MY LORD, A NEW REGIMENT OF TROOPS HAS ARRIVED.
WITH SOME PRISONERS I BELIEVE YOU'LL WANT TO SEE.
SEND THEM IN.
THE GREEK "CHAMPIONS," MY LORD...
OR WHAT REMAINS OF THEM.
I SEE THAT. BUT HOW--?
I BROUGHT THEM, MY LORD. I SERVED THE PREVIOUS LORD OF THE DEAD, AND I LOOK FORWARD TO BEING AN EQUALLY INVALUABLE SERVANT TO YOU.
A TRAITOR? HOW DELIGHTFUL! IF YOU TURNED ON YOUR ALLIES, YOU ARE EXACTLY THE TREACHEROUS SORT I REQUIRE.
HOWEVER, YOU WILL FIRST NEED TO PROVE YOUR WORTH.
EXECUTE THEM.

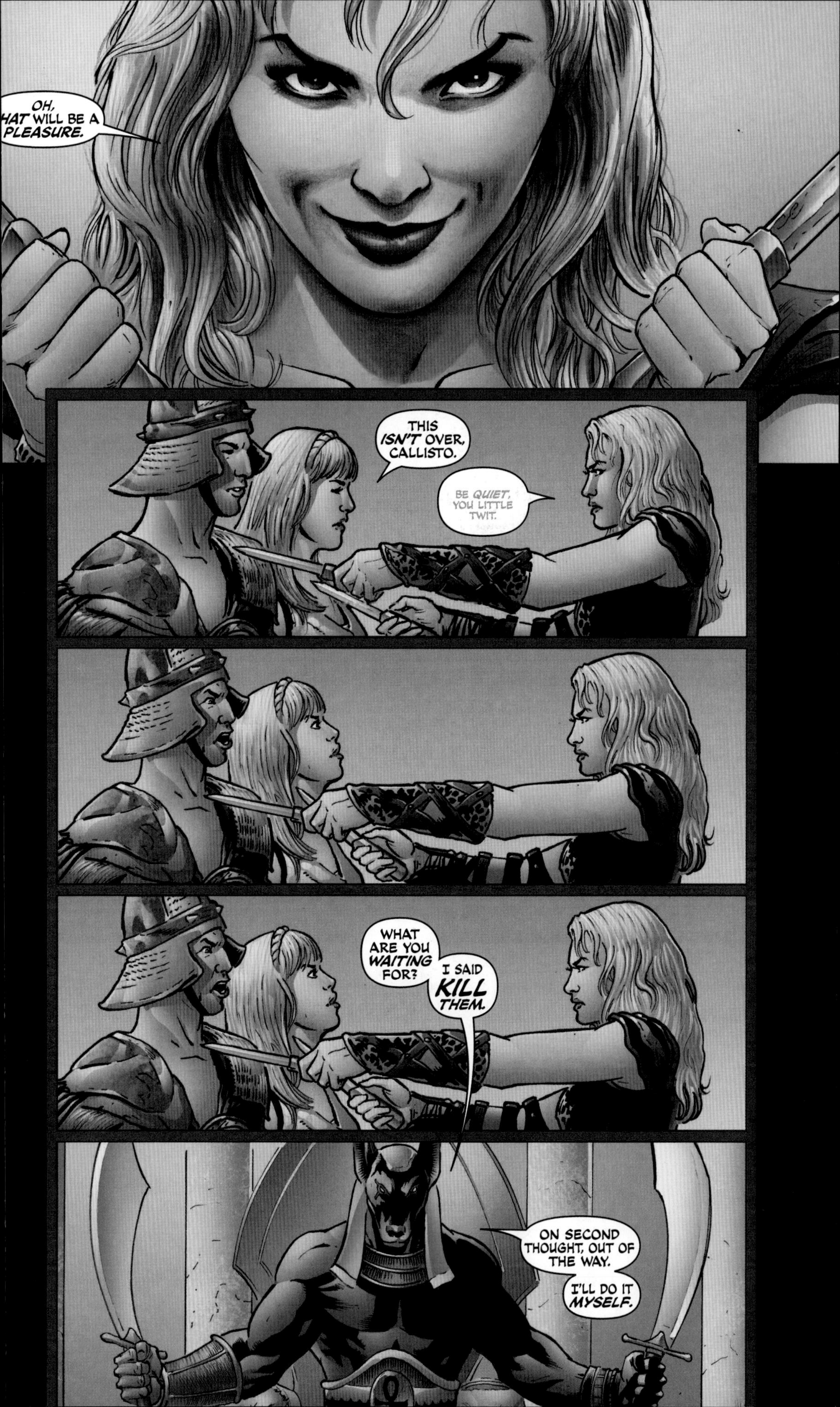

OH, HAT WILL BE A PLEASURE.
THIS ISN'T OVER, CALLISTO.
BE QUIET, YOU LITTLE TWIT.
WHAT ARE YOU WAITING FOR?
I SAID KILL THEM.
ON SECOND THOUGHT, OUT OF THE WAY.
I'LL DO IT MYSELF.

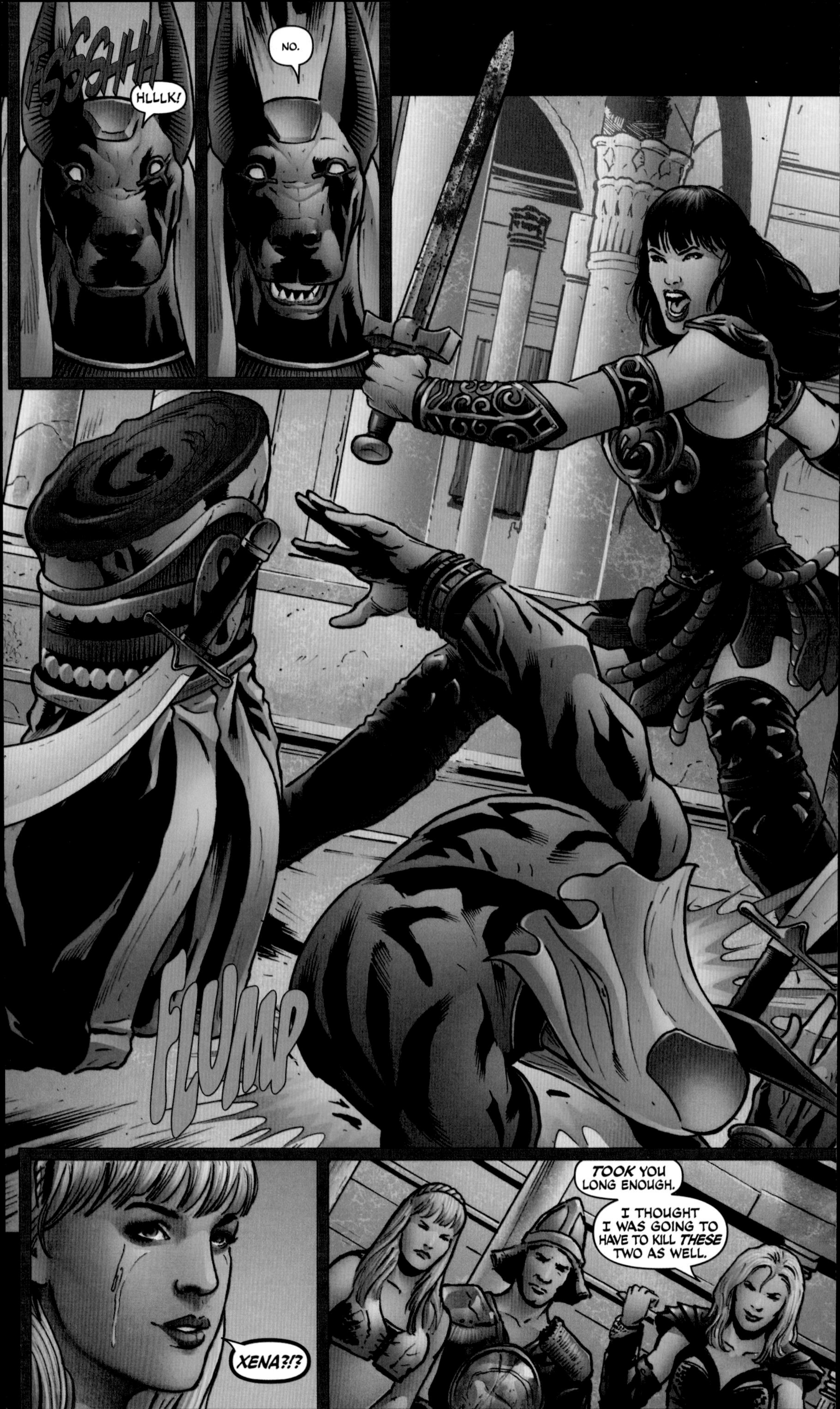
FSSSHHH
HLLLK!
NO.
FLUMP
XENA?!?
TOOK YOU LONG ENOUGH.
I THOUGHT I WAS GOING TO HAVE TO KILL THESE TWO AS WELL.

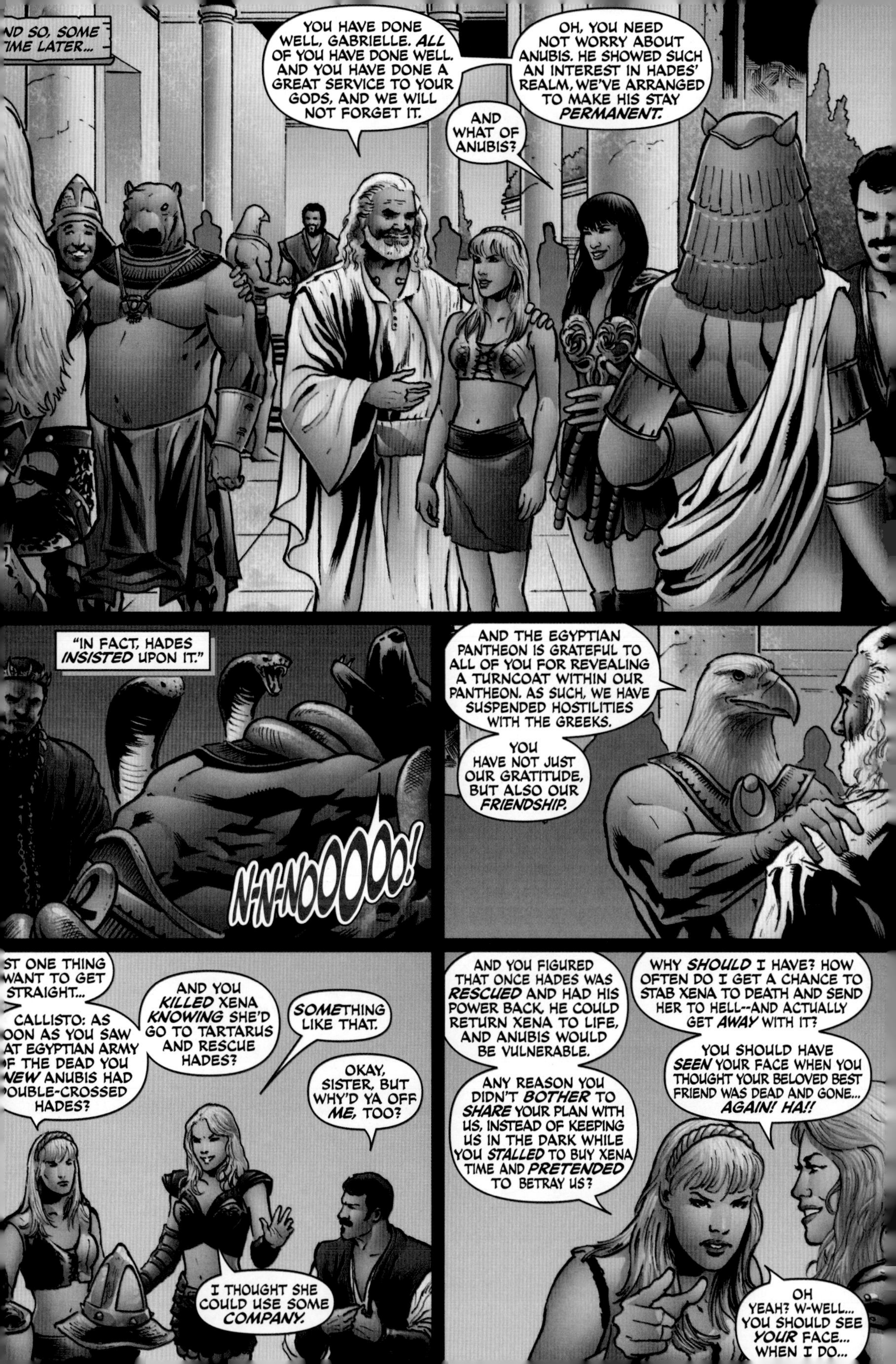
ND SO, SOME
TIME LATER...
YOU HAVE DONE WELL, GABRIELLE. ALL OF YOU HAVE DONE WELL. AND YOU HAVE DONE A GREAT SERVICE TO YOUR GODS, AND WE WILL NOT FORGET IT.
AND WHAT OF ANUBIS?
OH, YOU NEED NOT WORRY ABOUT ANUBIS. HE SHOWED SUCH AN INTEREST IN HADES' REALM, WE'VE ARRANGED TO MAKE HIS STAY PERMANENT.
"IN FACT, HADES INSISTED UPON IT."
N-N-NOOOOO!
AND THE EGYPTIAN PANTHEON IS GRATEFUL TO ALL OF YOU FOR REVEALING A TURNCOAT WITHIN OUR PANTHEON. AS SUCH, WE HAVE SUSPENDED HOSTILITIES WITH THE GREEKS.
YOU HAVE NOT JUST OUR GRATITUDE, BUT ALSO OUR FRIENDSHIP.
ST ONE THING WANT TO GET STRAIGHT...
CALLISTO: AS OON AS YOU SAW AT EGYPTIAN ARMY F THE DEAD YOU NEW ANUBIS HAD OUBLE-CROSSED HADES?
AND YOU KILLED XENA KNOWING SHE'D GO TO TARTARUS AND RESCUE HADES?
SOMETHING LIKE THAT.
OKAY, SISTER, BUT WHY'D YA OFF ME, TOO?
I THOUGHT SHE COULD USE SOME COMPANY.
AND YOU FIGURED THAT ONCE HADES WAS RESCUED AND HAD HIS POWER BACK, HE COULD RETURN XENA TO LIFE, AND ANUBIS WOULD BE VULNERABLE.
ANY REASON YOU DIDN'T BOTHER TO SHARE YOUR PLAN WITH US, INSTEAD OF KEEPING US IN THE DARK WHILE YOU STALLED TO BUY XENA TIME AND PRETENDED TO BETRAY US?
WHY SHOULD I HAVE? HOW OFTEN DO I GET A CHANCE TO STAB XENA TO DEATH AND SEND HER TO HELL--AND ACTUALLY GET AWAY WITH IT?
YOU SHOULD HAVE SEEN YOUR FACE WHEN YOU THOUGHT YOUR BELOVED BEST FRIEND WAS DEAD AND GONE... AGAIN! HA!!
OH YEAH? W-WELL... YOU SHOULD SEE YOUR FACE... WHEN I DO...

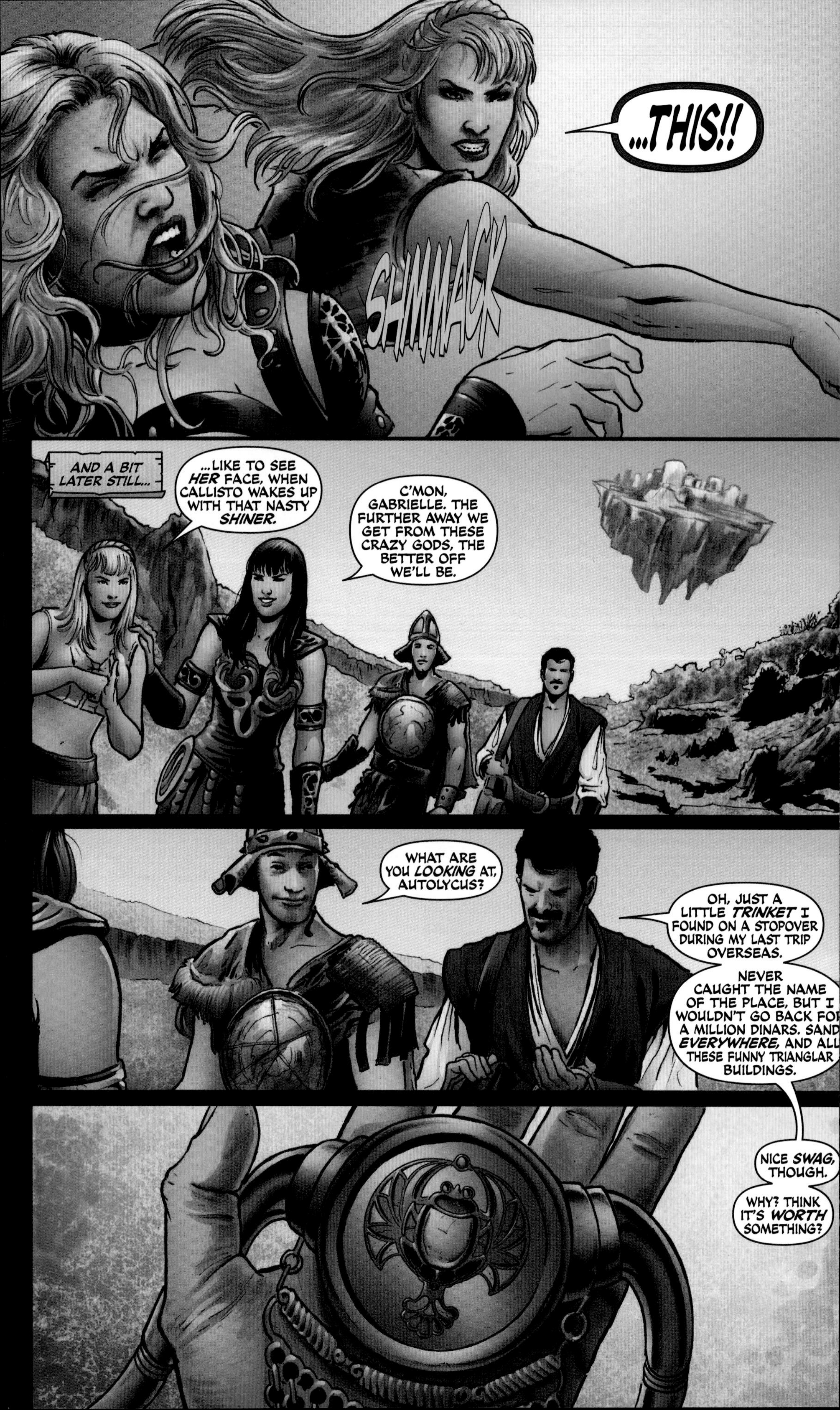

...THIS!!
SHMMACK
AND A BIT LATER STILL...
...LIKE TO SEE HER FACE, WHEN CALLISTO WAKES UP WITH THAT NASTY SHINER.
C'MON, GABRIELLE. THE FURTHER AWAY WE GET FROM THESE CRAZY GODS, THE BETTER OFF WE'LL BE.
WHAT ARE YOU LOOKING AT, AUTOLYCUS?
OH, JUST A LITTLE TRINKET I FOUND ON A STOPOVER DURING MY LAST TRIP OVERSEAS.
NEVER CAUGHT THE NAME OF THE PLACE, BUT I WOULDN'T GO BACK FOR A MILLION DINARS. SAND EVERYWHERE, AND ALL THESE FUNNY TRIANGLAR BUILDINGS.
NICE SWAG, THOUGH.
WHY? THINK IT'S WORTH SOMETHING?

DARK XENA
CHAPTER ONE

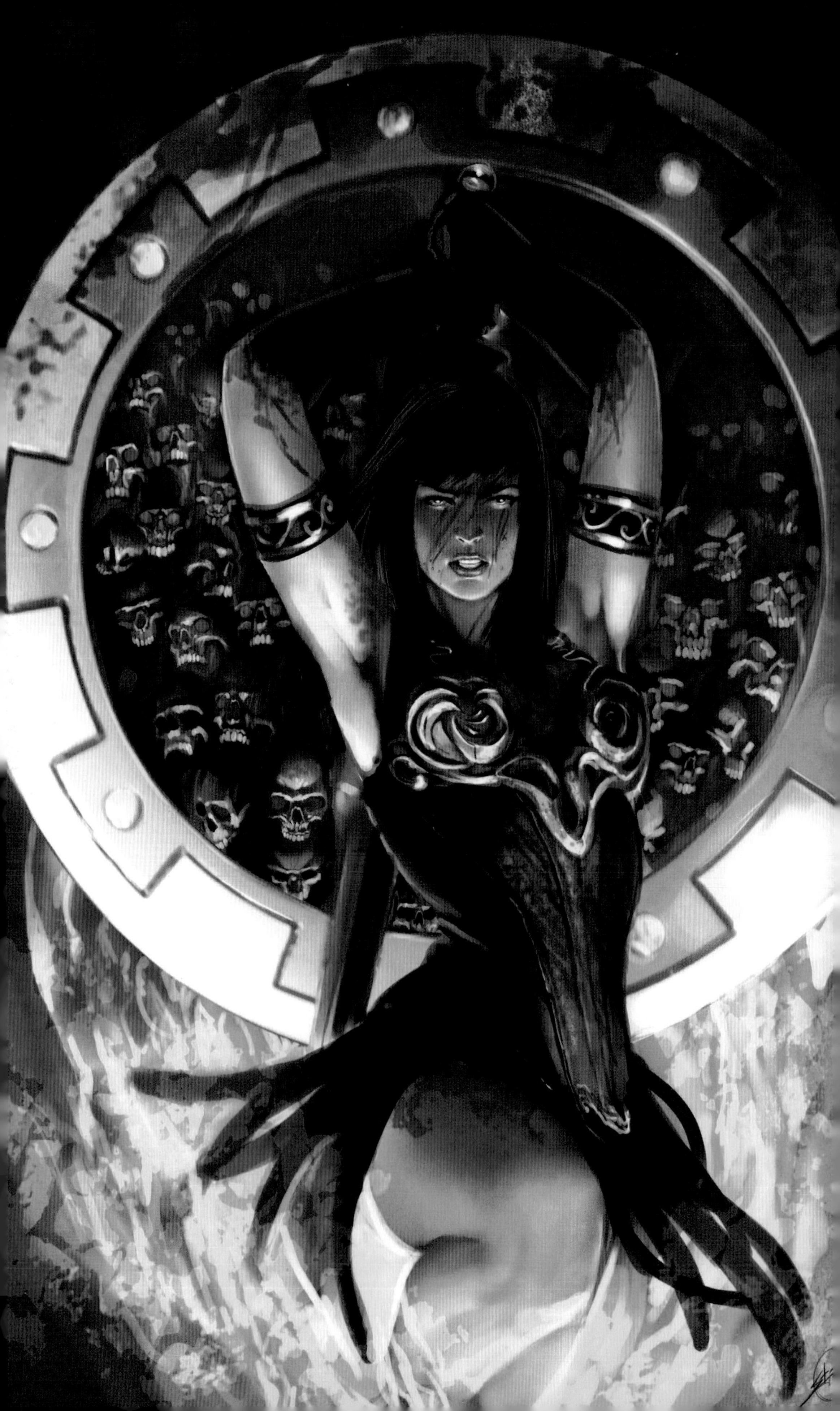

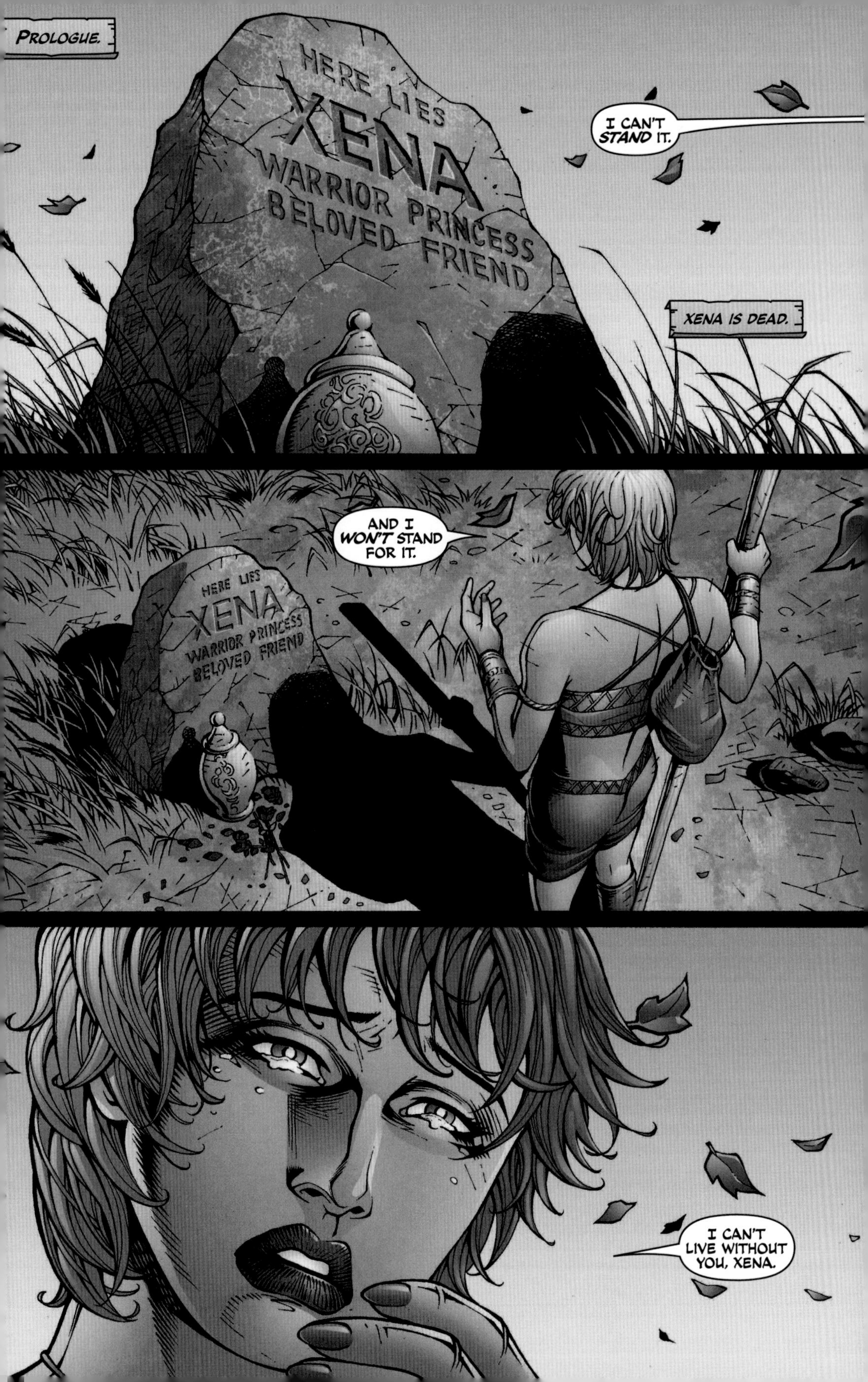
PROLOGUE.
HERE LIES XENA WARRIOR PRINCESS BELOVED FRIEND
I CAN'T STAND IT.
XENA IS DEAD.
AND I WON'T STAND FOR IT.
HERE LIES XENA WARRIOR PRINCESS BELOVED FRIEND
I CAN'T LIVE WITHOUT YOU, XENA.

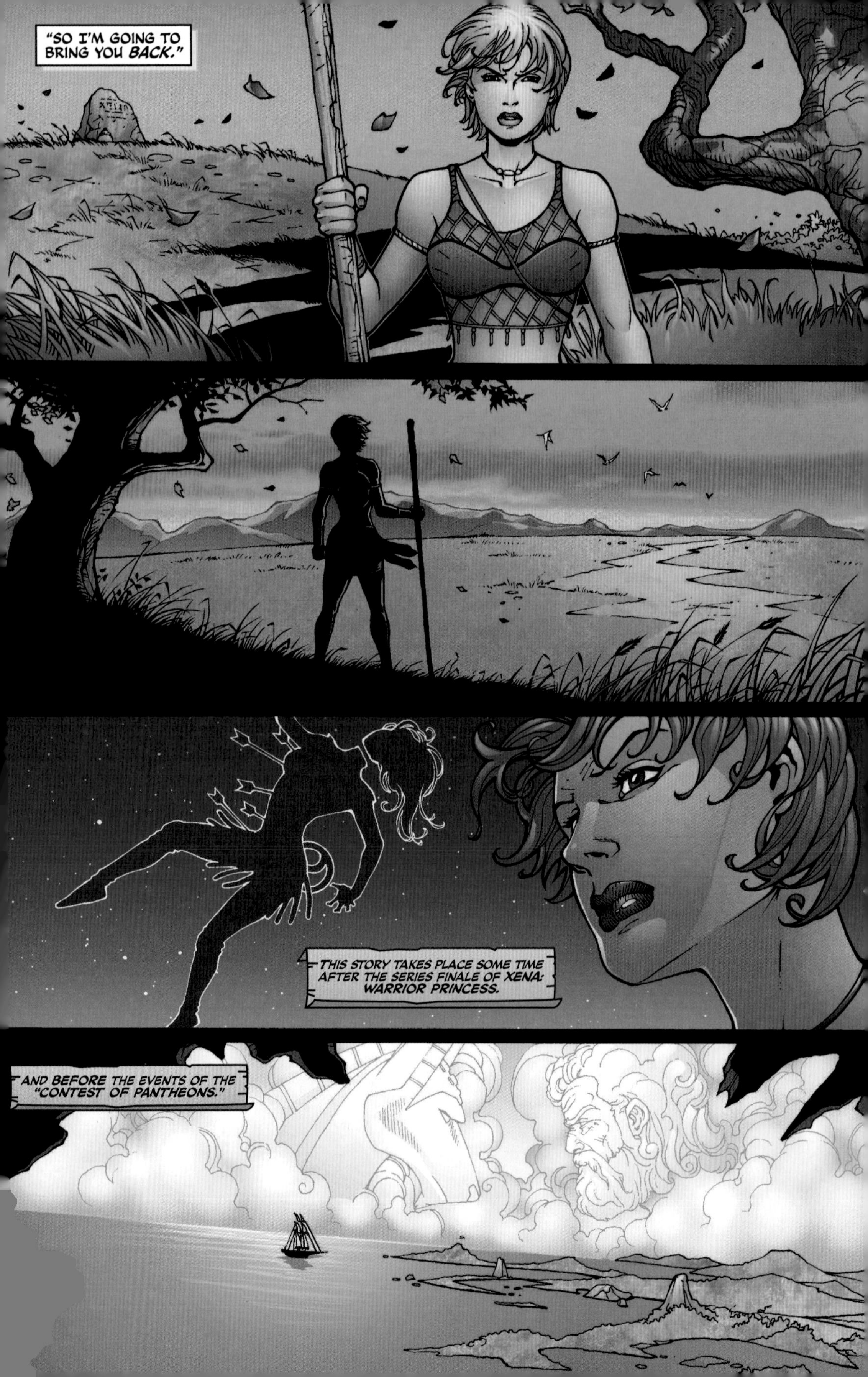
"SO I'M GOING TO BRING YOU *BACK.*"
THIS STORY TAKES PLACE SOME TIME AFTER THE SERIES FINALE OF XENA: WARRIOR PRINCESS.
AND BEFORE THE EVENTS OF THE "CONTEST OF PANTHEONS."

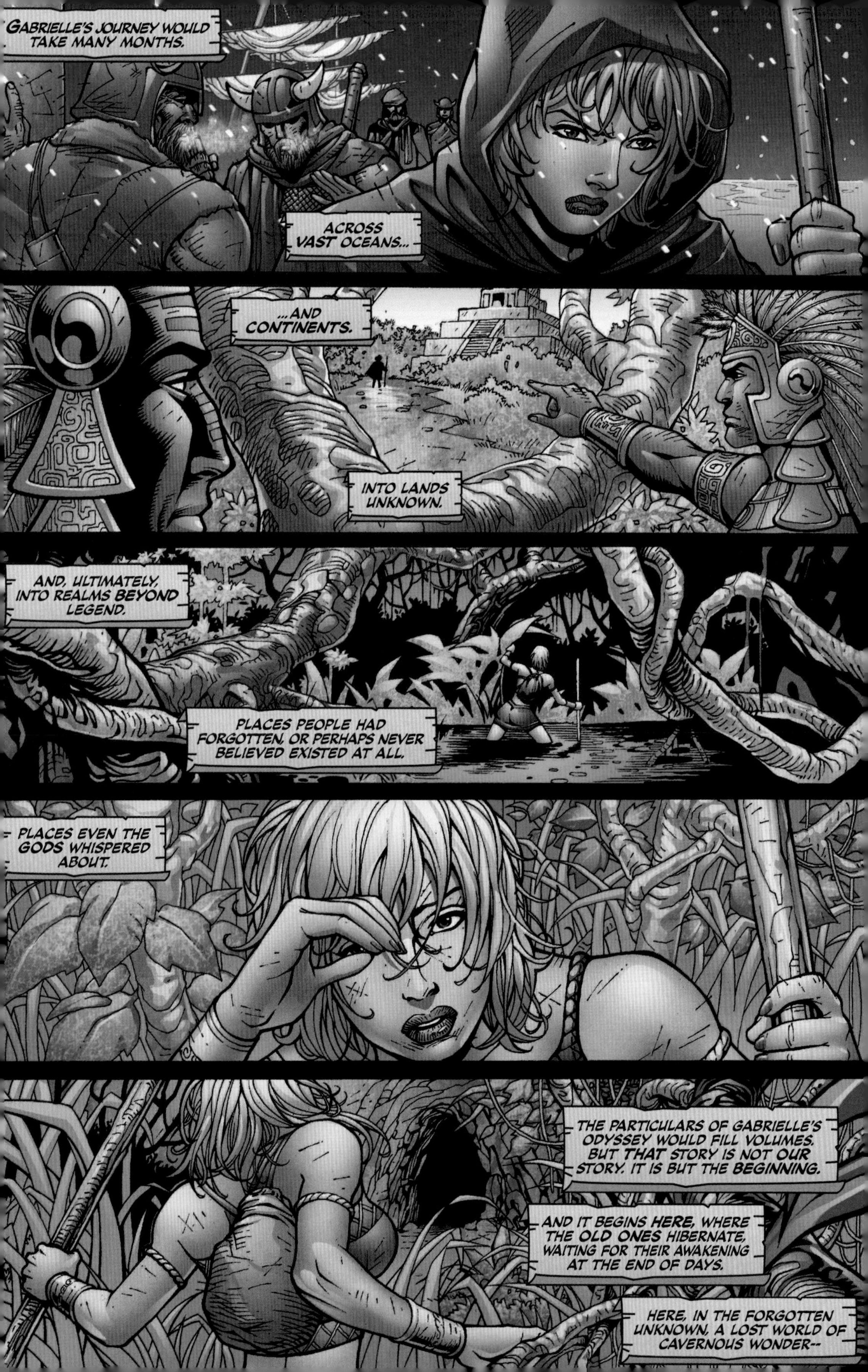
GABRIELLE'S JOURNEY WOULD TAKE MANY MONTHS.
ACROSS VAST OCEANS...
...AND CONTINENTS.
INTO LANDS UNKNOWN.
AND, ULTIMATELY, INTO REALMS BEYOND LEGEND.
PLACES PEOPLE HAD FORGOTTEN, OR PERHAPS NEVER BELIEVED EXISTED AT ALL.
PLACES EVEN THE GODS WHISPERED ABOUT.
THE PARTICULARS OF GABRIELLE'S ODYSSEY WOULD FILL VOLUMES. BUT THAT STORY IS NOT OUR STORY. IT IS BUT THE BEGINNING.
AND IT BEGINS HERE, WHERE THE OLD ONES HIBERNATE, WAITING FOR THEIR AWAKENING AT THE END OF DAYS.
HERE, IN THE FORGOTTEN UNKNOWN, A LOST WORLD OF CAVERNOUS WONDER--

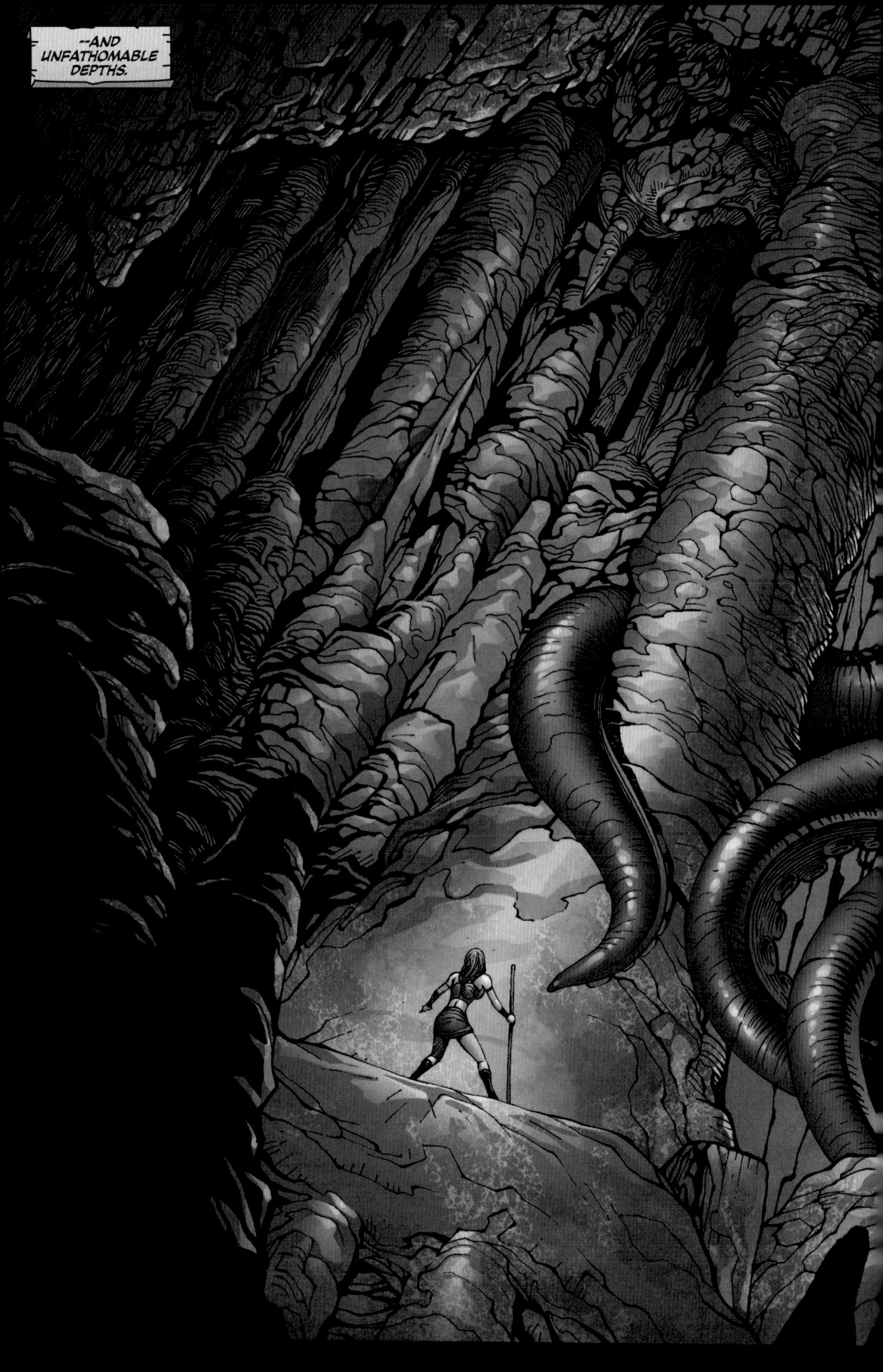
--AND UNFATHOMABLE DEPTHS.

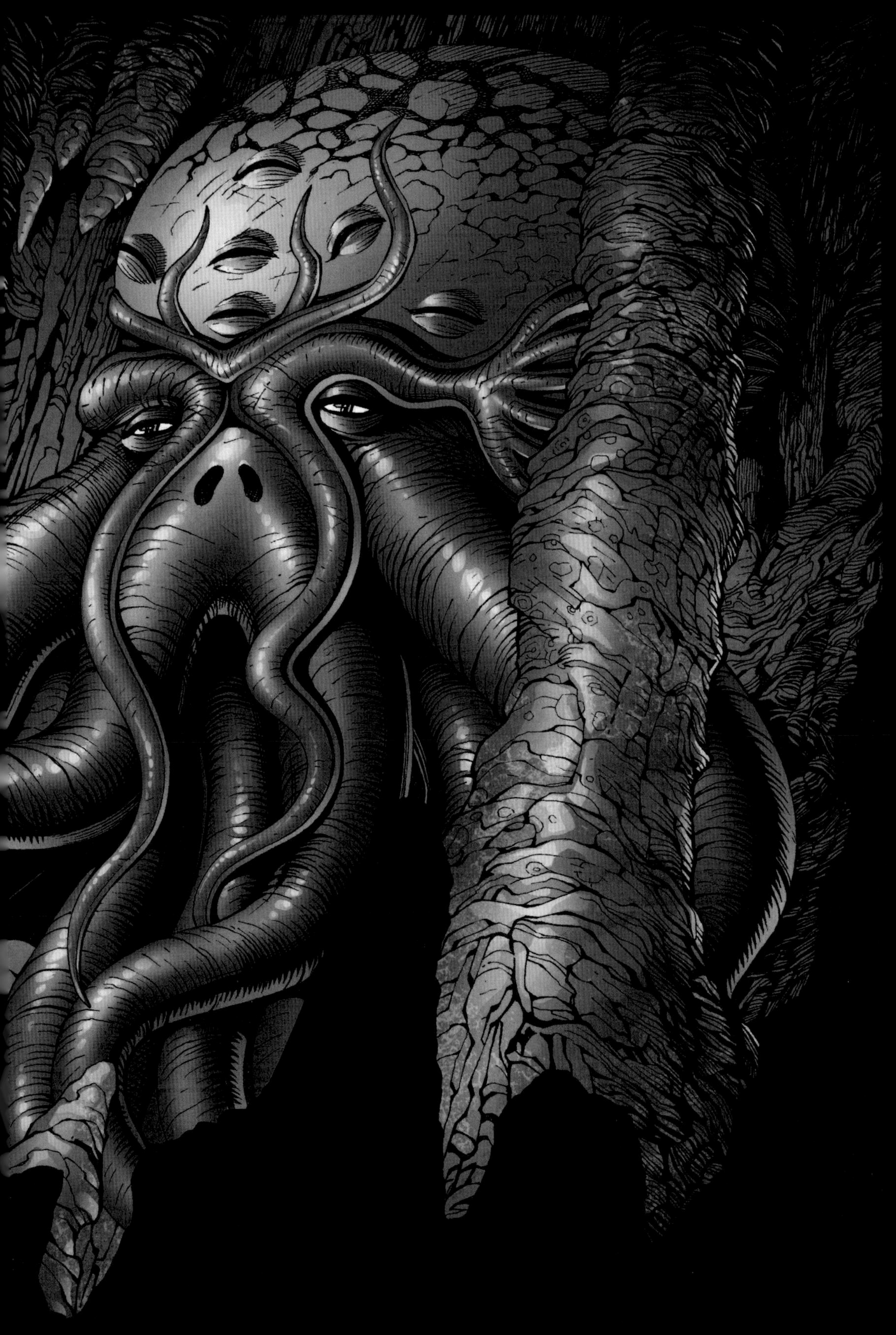

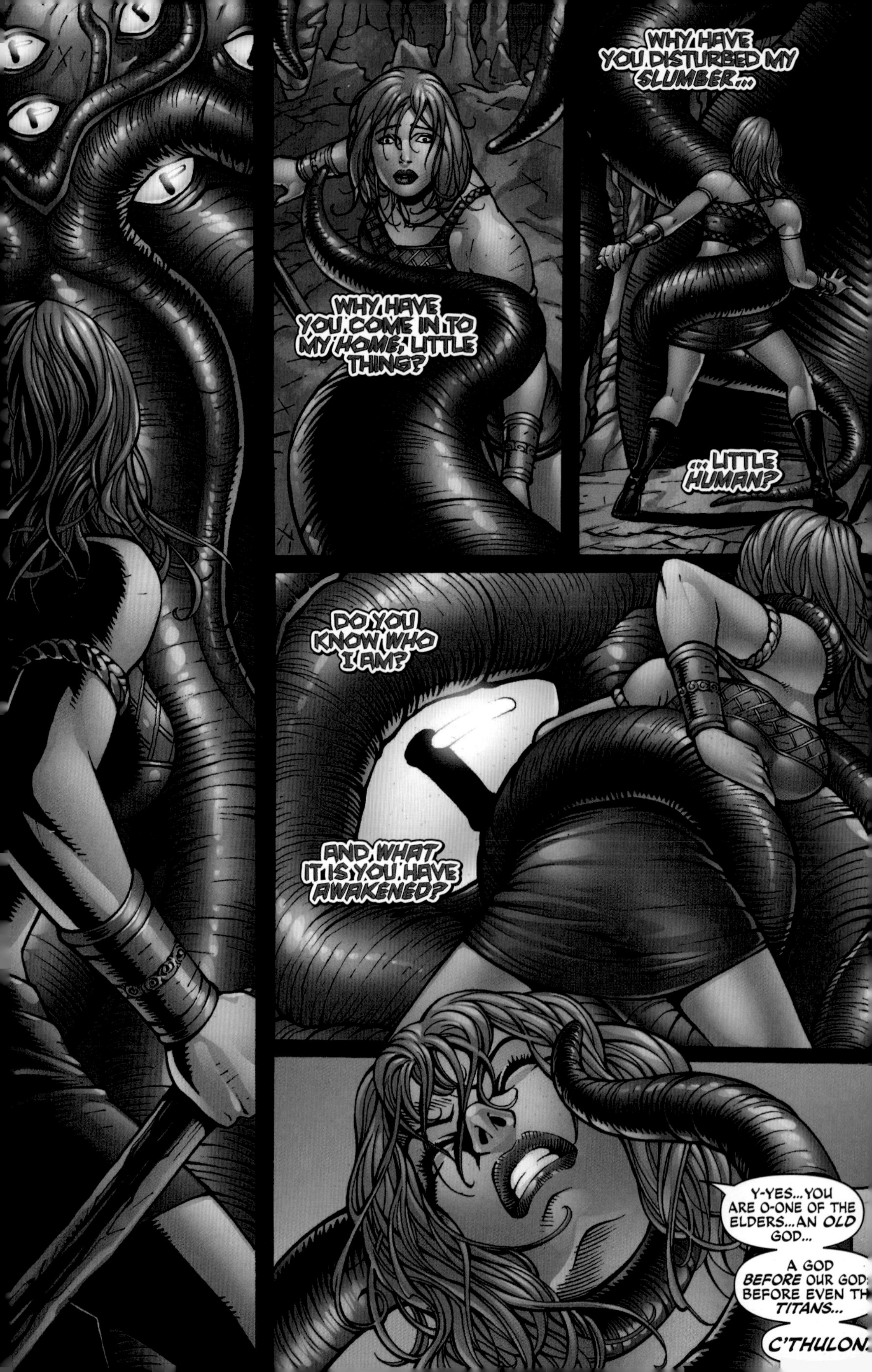
WHY HAVE YOU COME IN TO MY HOME, LITTLE THING?
WHY HAVE YOU DISTURBED MY SLUMBER...
...LITTLE HUMAN?
DO YOU KNOW WHO I AM?
AND WHAT IT IS YOU HAVE AWAKENED?
Y-YES... YOU ARE O-ONE OF THE ELDERS... AN OLD GOD...
A GOD BEFORE OUR GODS BEFORE EVEN THE TITANS...
C'THULON.

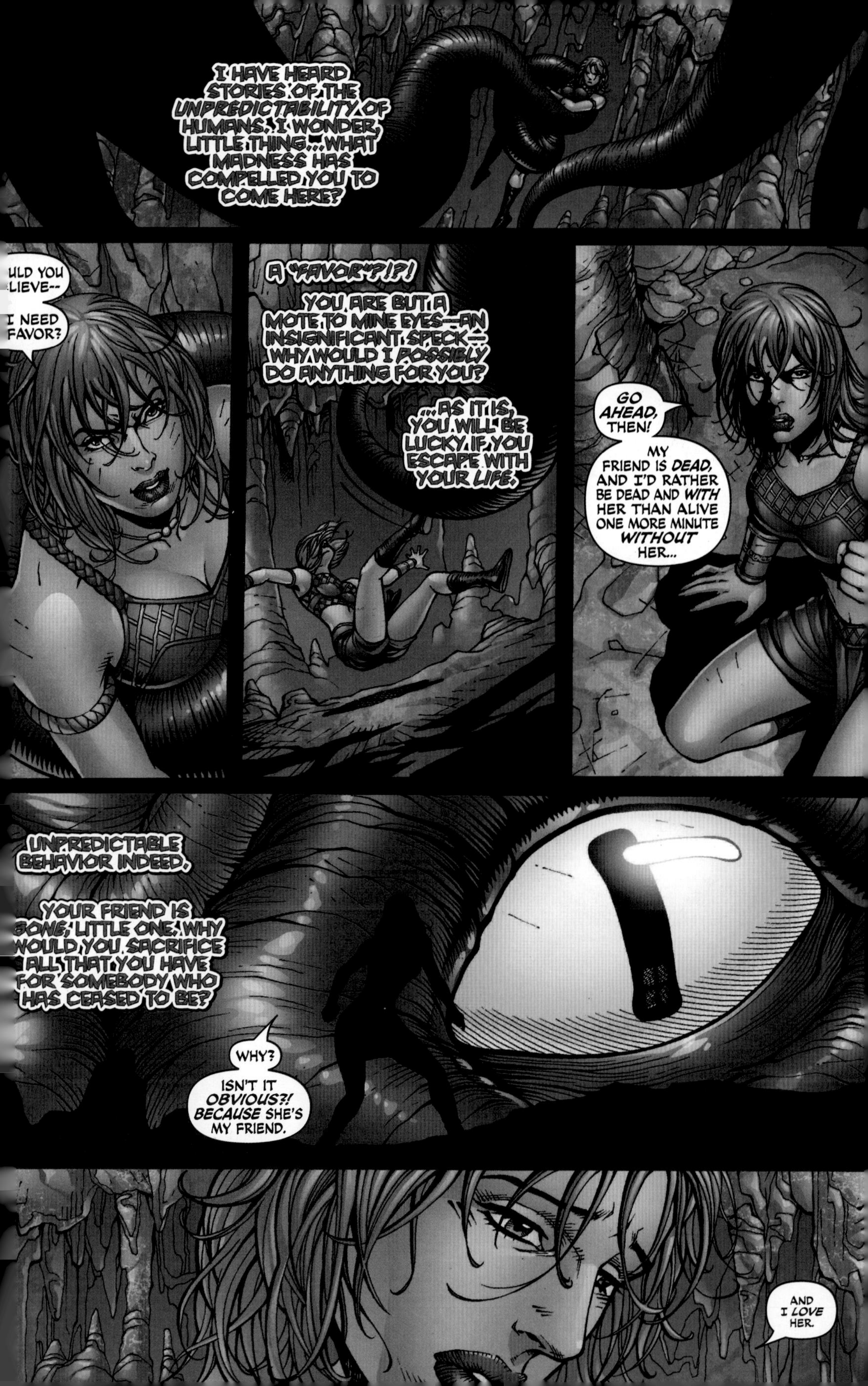

I HAVE HEARD STORIES OF THE UNPREDICTABILITY OF HUMANS. I WONDER, LITTLE THING... WHAT MADNESS HAS COMPELLED YOU TO COME HERE?
ULD YOU LIEVE--
I NEED FAVOR?
A "FAVOR"?!?!
YOU ARE BUT A MOTE TO MINE EYES--AN INSIGNIFICANT SPECK--WHY WOULD I POSSIBLY DO ANYTHING FOR YOU?
...AS IT IS, YOU WILL BE LUCKY IF YOU ESCAPE WITH YOUR LIFE.
GO AHEAD, THEN!
MY FRIEND IS DEAD, AND I'D RATHER BE DEAD AND WITH HER THAN ALIVE ONE MORE MINUTE WITHOUT HER...
UNPREDICTABLE BEHAVIOR INDEED.
YOUR FRIEND IS GONE, LITTLE ONE. WHY WOULD YOU SACRIFICE ALL THAT YOU HAVE FOR SOMEBODY WHO HAS CEASED TO BE?
WHY?
ISN'T IT OBVIOUS?! BECAUSE SHE'S MY FRIEND.
AND I LOVE HER.

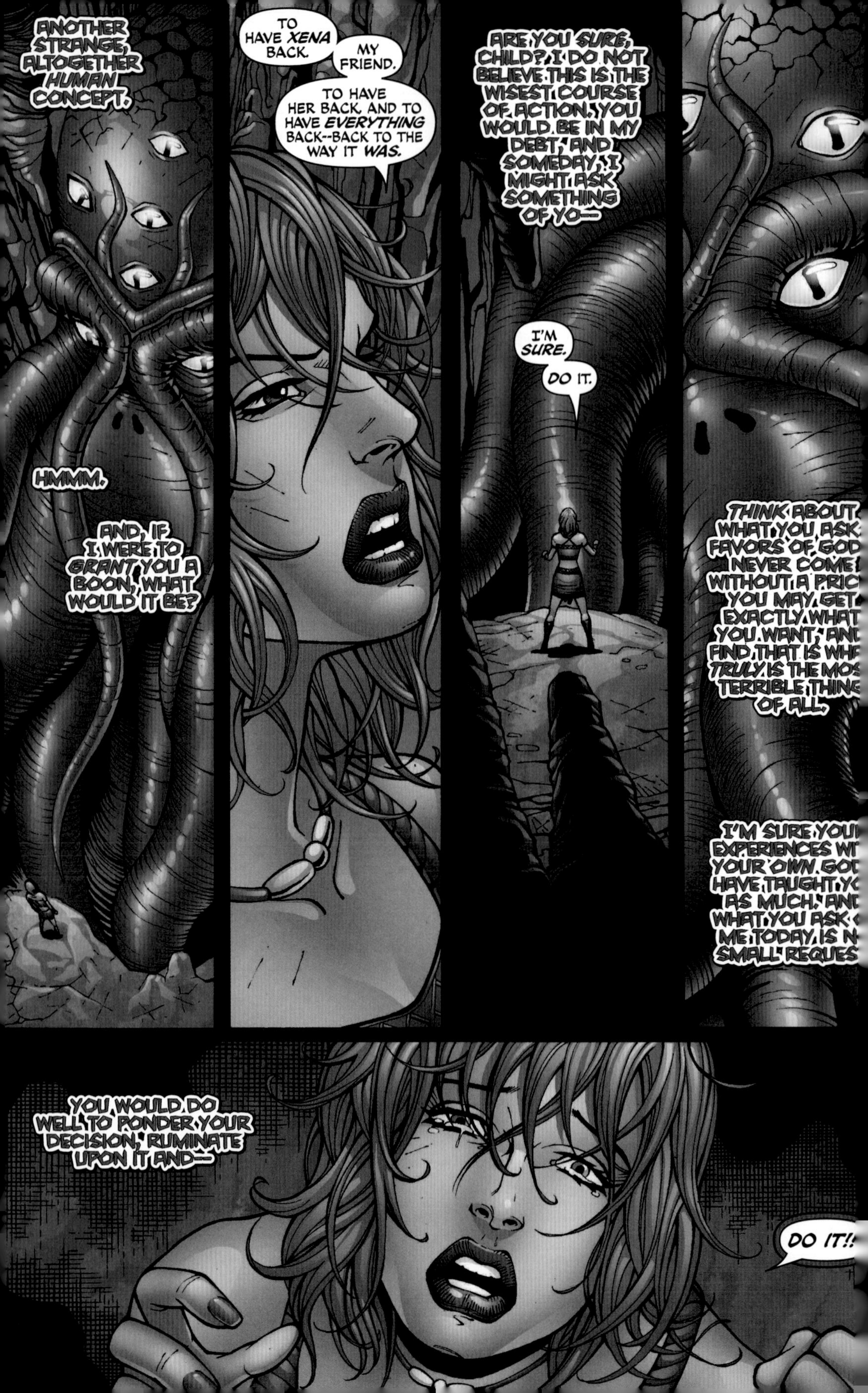
ANOTHER STRANGE, ALTOGETHER HUMAN CONCEPT.
HMMM.
AND, IF I WERE TO GRANT YOU A BOON, WHAT WOULD IT BE?
TO HAVE XENA BACK.
MY FRIEND.
TO HAVE HER BACK, AND TO HAVE EVERYTHING BACK--BACK TO THE WAY IT WAS.
ARE YOU SURE, CHILD? I DO NOT BELIEVE THIS IS THE WISEST COURSE OF ACTION. YOU WOULD BE IN MY DEBT, AND SOMEDAY, I MIGHT ASK SOMETHING OF YO--
I'M SURE.
DO IT.
THINK ABOUT WHAT YOU ASK. FAVORS OF GOD NEVER COME WITHOUT A PRIC YOU MAY GET EXACTLY WHAT YOU WANT, AND FIND THAT IS WH TRULY IS THE MOS TERRIBLE THING OF ALL.
I'M SURE YOU EXPERIENCES W YOUR OWN GOD HAVE TAUGHT Y AS MUCH. AND WHAT YOU ASK ME TODAY IS N SMALL REQUES
YOU WOULD DO WELL TO PONDER YOUR DECISION, RUMINATE UPON IT AND--
DO IT!!

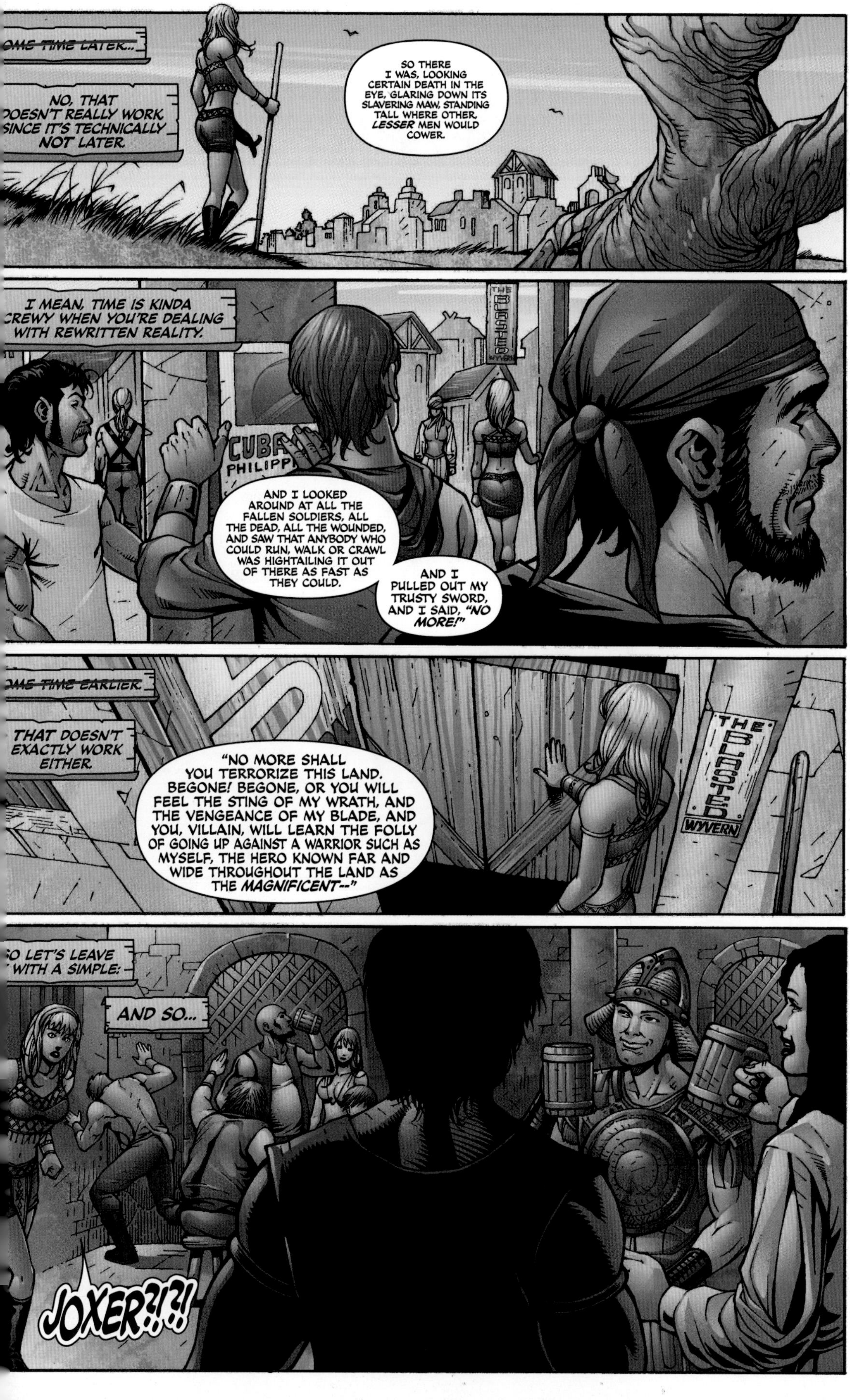

OME TIME LATER...
NO, THAT DOESN'T REALLY WORK, SINCE IT'S TECHNICALLY NOT LATER.
SO THERE I WAS, LOOKING CERTAIN DEATH IN THE EYE, GLARING DOWN ITS SLAVERING MAW, STANDING TALL WHERE OTHER, LESSER MEN WOULD COWER.
I MEAN, TIME IS KINDA CREWY WHEN YOU'RE DEALING WITH REWRITTEN REALITY.
THE BLASTED WYVERN
CUBA PHILIPP
AND I LOOKED AROUND AT ALL THE FALLEN SOLDIERS, ALL THE DEAD, ALL THE WOUNDED, AND SAW THAT ANYBODY WHO COULD RUN, WALK OR CRAWL WAS HIGHTAILING IT OUT OF THERE AS FAST AS THEY COULD.
AND I PULLED OUT MY TRUSTY SWORD, AND I SAID, "NO MORE!"
OME TIME EARLIER.
THAT DOESN'T EXACTLY WORK EITHER.
"NO MORE SHALL YOU TERRORIZE THIS LAND. BEGONE! BEGONE, OR YOU WILL FEEL THE STING OF MY WRATH, AND THE VENGEANCE OF MY BLADE, AND YOU, VILLAIN, WILL LEARN THE FOLLY OF GOING UP AGAINST A WARRIOR SUCH AS MYSELF, THE HERO KNOWN FAR AND WIDE THROUGHOUT THE LAND AS THE MAGNIFICENT--"
THE BLASTED WYVERN
O LET'S LEAVE WITH A SIMPLE:
AND SO...
JOXER?!?!

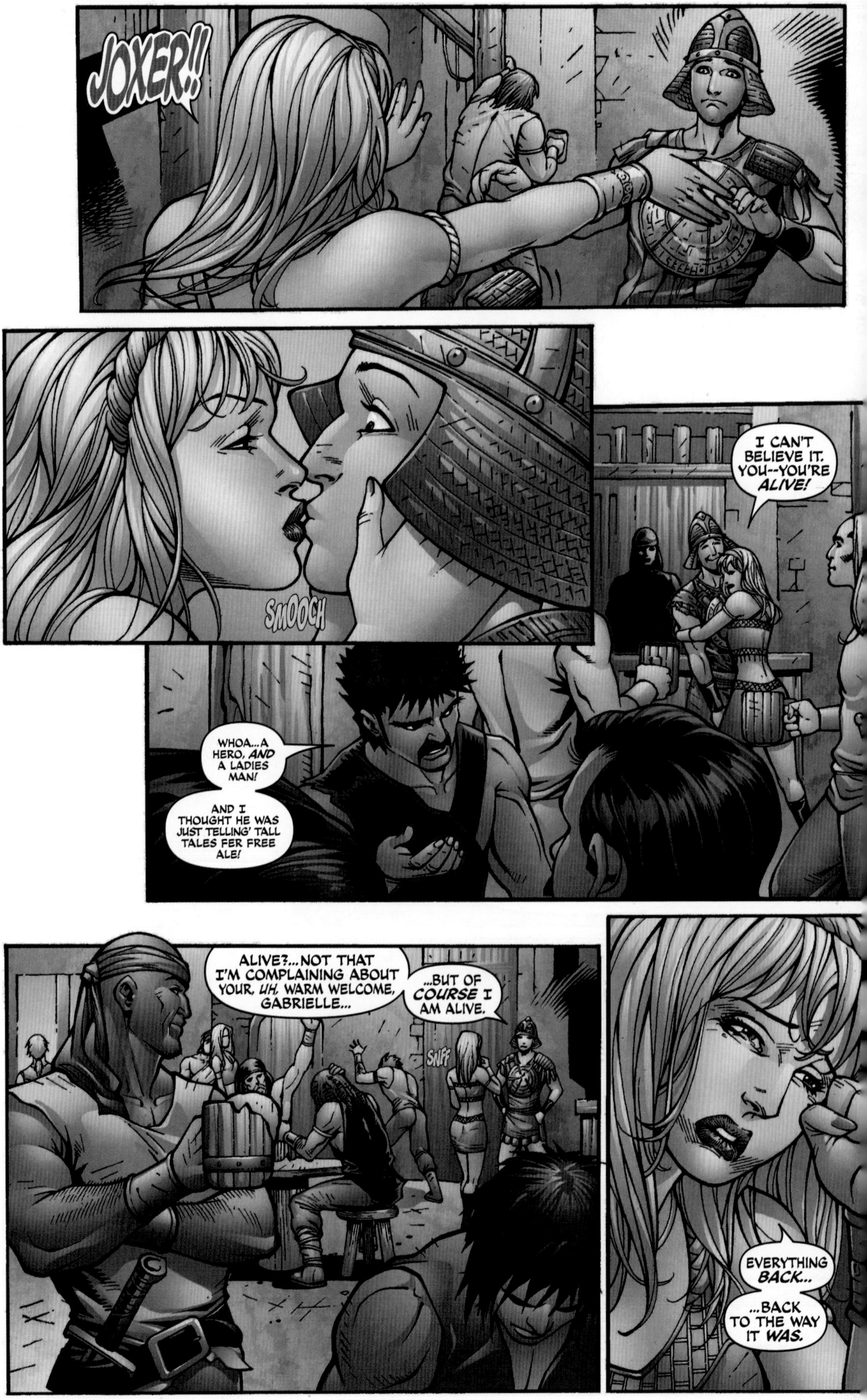
JOXER!!
SMOOCH
I CAN'T BELIEVE IT. YOU--YOU'RE ALIVE!
WHOA...A HERO, AND A LADIES MAN!
AND I THOUGHT HE WAS JUST TELLING' TALL TALES FER FREE ALE!
ALIVE?...NOT THAT I'M COMPLAINING ABOUT YOUR, UH, WARM WELCOME, GABRIELLE...
...BUT OF COURSE I AM ALIVE.
SNIFF
EVERYTHING BACK...
...BACK TO THE WAY IT WAS.

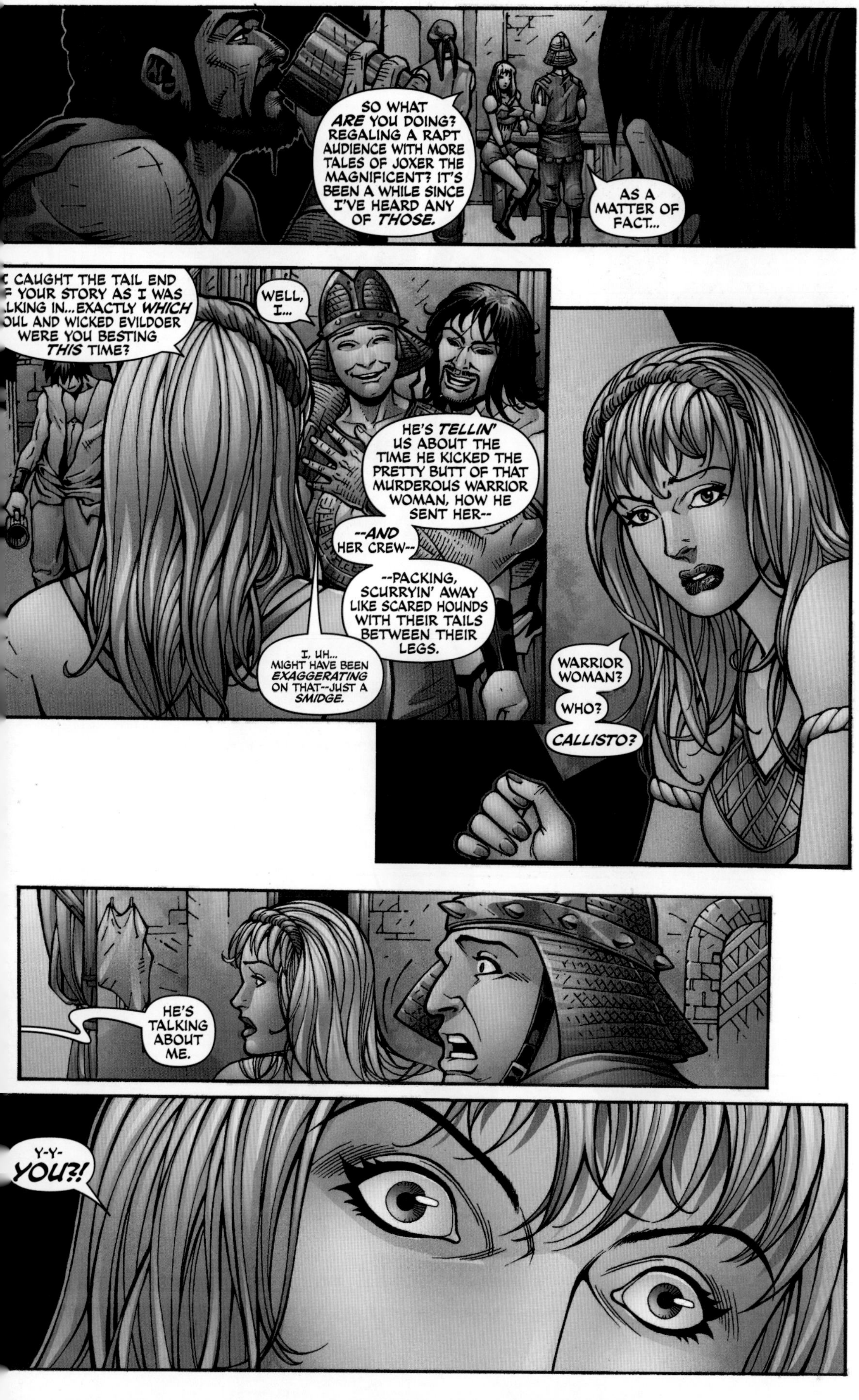
SO WHAT ARE YOU DOING? REGALING A RAPT AUDIENCE WITH MORE TALES OF JOXER THE MAGNIFICENT? IT'S BEEN A WHILE SINCE I'VE HEARD ANY OF THOSE.
AS A MATTER OF FACT...
CAUGHT THE TAIL END F YOUR STORY AS I WAS LKING IN...EXACTLY WHICH OUL AND WICKED EVILDOER WERE YOU BESTING THIS TIME?
WELL, I...
HE'S TELLIN' US ABOUT THE TIME HE KICKED THE PRETTY BUTT OF THAT MURDEROUS WARRIOR WOMAN, HOW HE SENT HER--
--AND HER CREW--
--PACKING, SCURRYIN' AWAY LIKE SCARED HOUNDS WITH THEIR TAILS BETWEEN THEIR LEGS.
I, UH... MIGHT HAVE BEEN EXAGGERATING ON THAT--JUST A SMIDGE.
WARRIOR WOMAN?
WHO?
CALLISTO?
HE'S TALKING ABOUT ME.
Y-Y- YOU?!

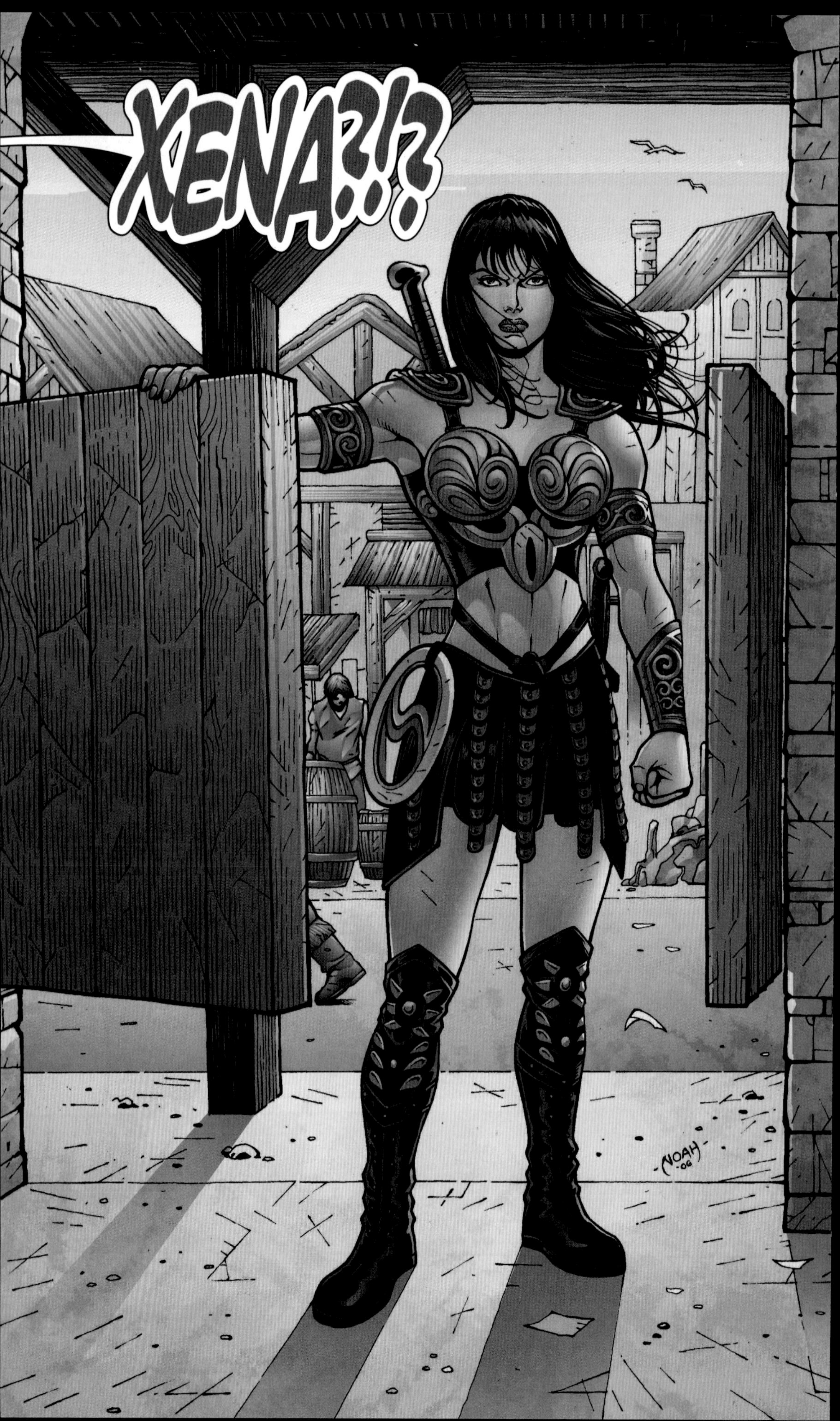
XENA?!?
NOAH
06

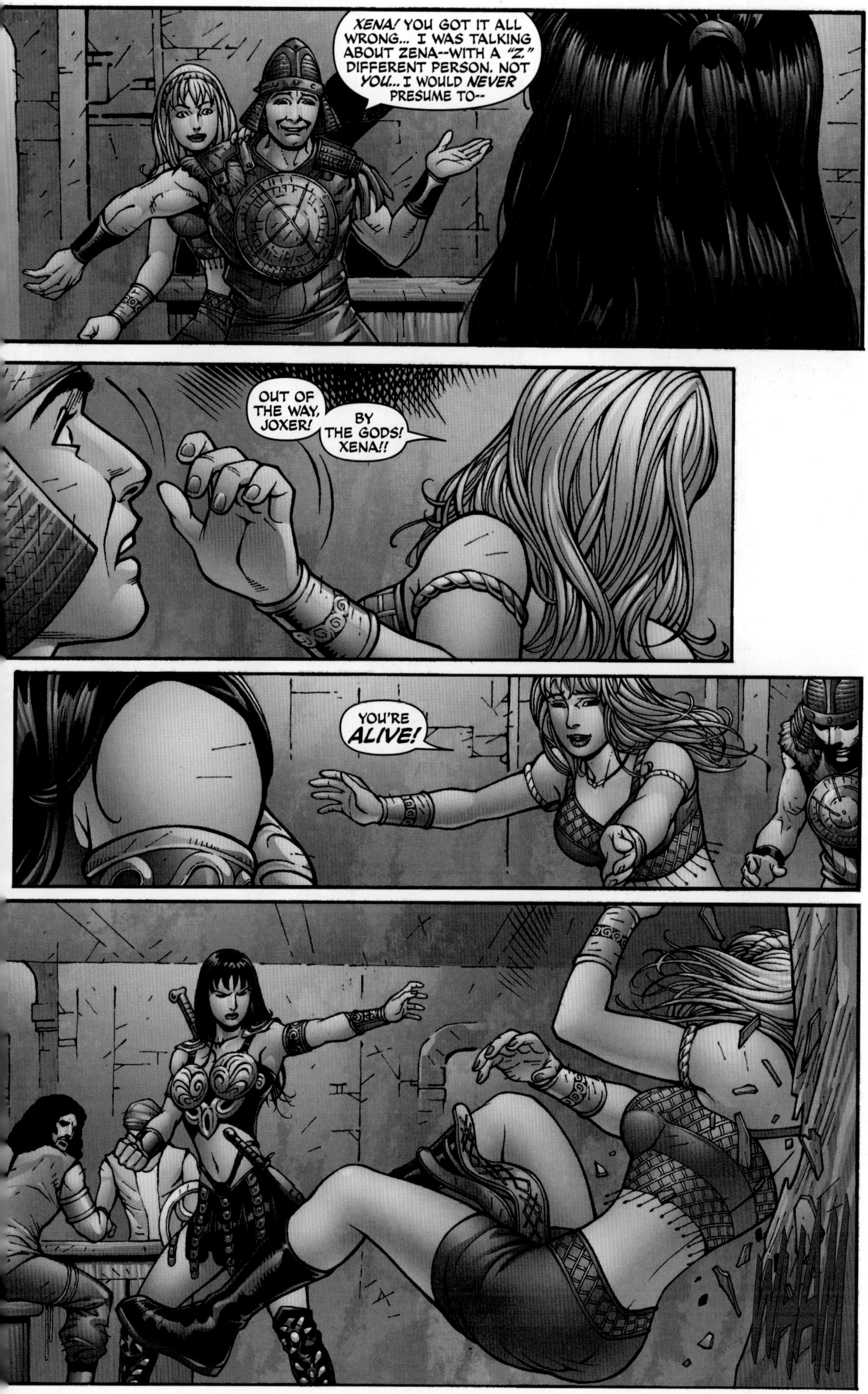

XENA! YOU GOT IT ALL WRONG... I WAS TALKING ABOUT ZENA--WITH A "Z." DIFFERENT PERSON. NOT YOU... I WOULD NEVER PRESUME TO--
OUT OF THE WAY, JOXER!
BY THE GODS! XENA!!
YOU'RE ALIVE!

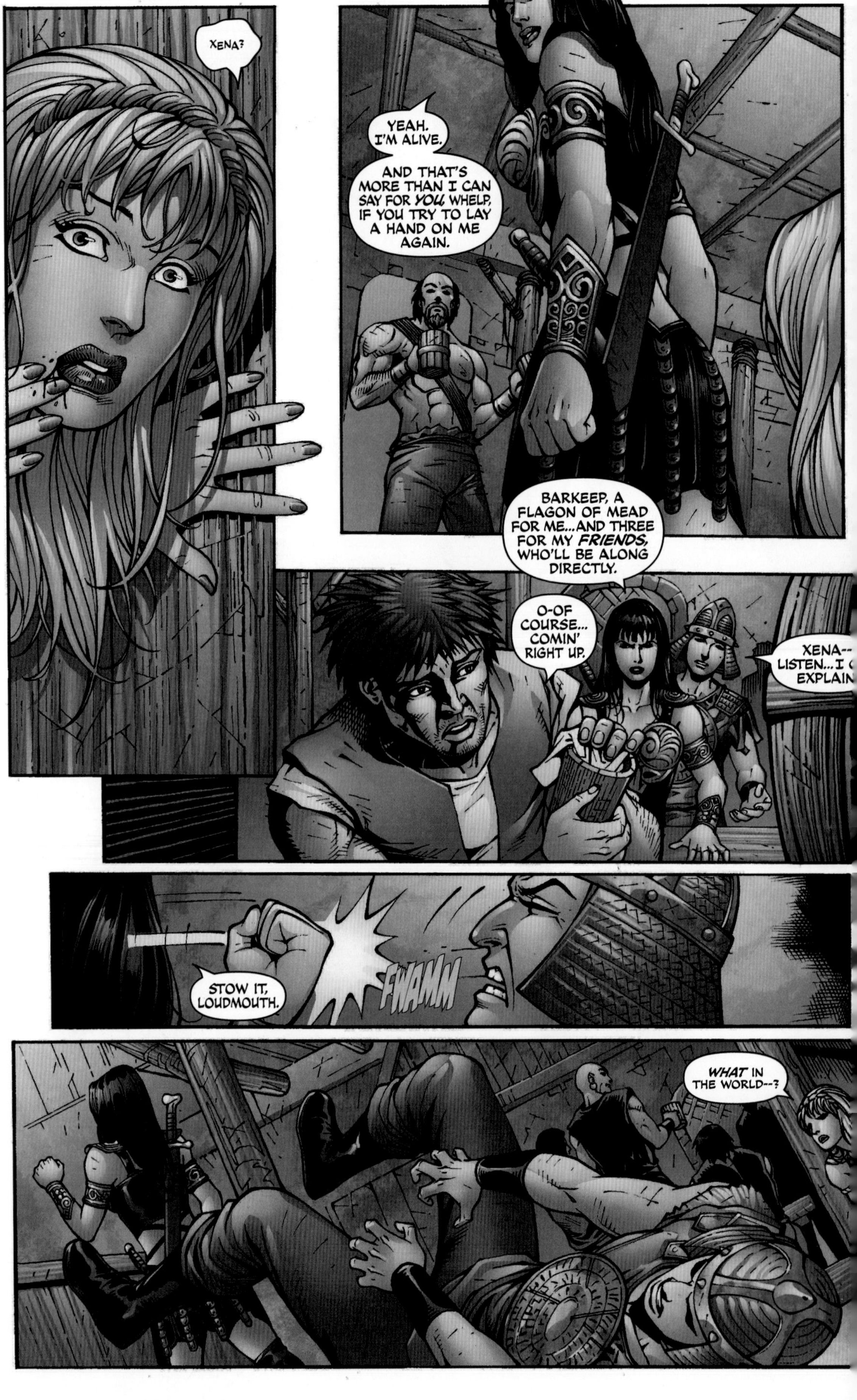

XENA?
YEAH. I'M ALIVE.
AND THAT'S MORE THAN I CAN SAY FOR *YOU*, WHELP, IF YOU TRY TO LAY A HAND ON ME AGAIN.
BARKEEP, A FLAGON OF MEAD FOR ME...AND THREE FOR MY *FRIENDS*, WHO'LL BE ALONG DIRECTLY.
O-OF COURSE... COMIN' RIGHT UP.
XENA-- LISTEN...I
STOW IT, LOUDMOUTH.
FWAMM
WHAT IN THE WORLD--?

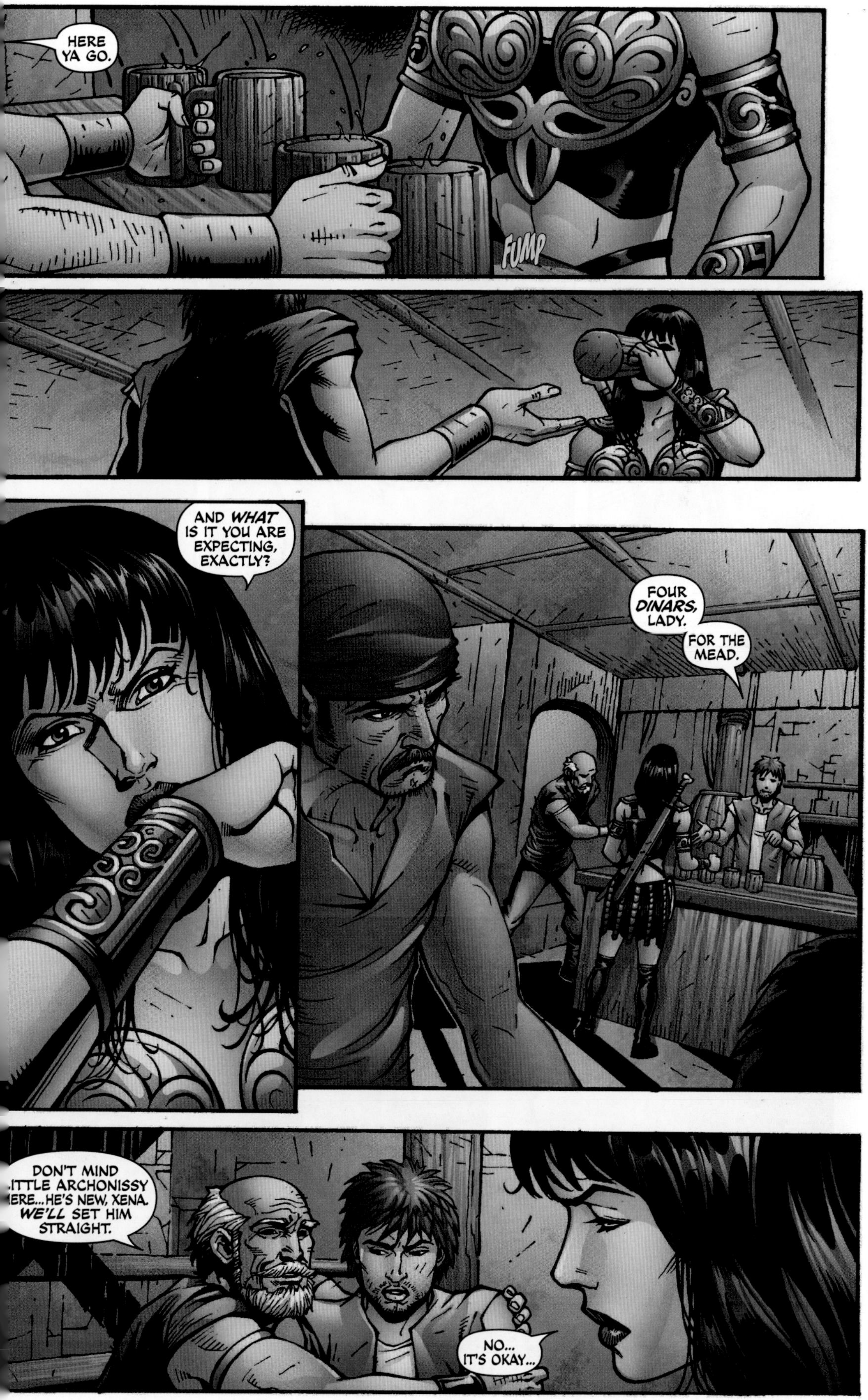

HERE YA GO.
FUMP
AND WHAT IS IT YOU ARE EXPECTING, EXACTLY?
FOUR DINARS, LADY.
FOR THE MEAD.
DON'T MIND LITTLE ARCHONISSY HERE...HE'S NEW, XENA. WE'LL SET HIM STRAIGHT.
NO... IT'S OKAY...

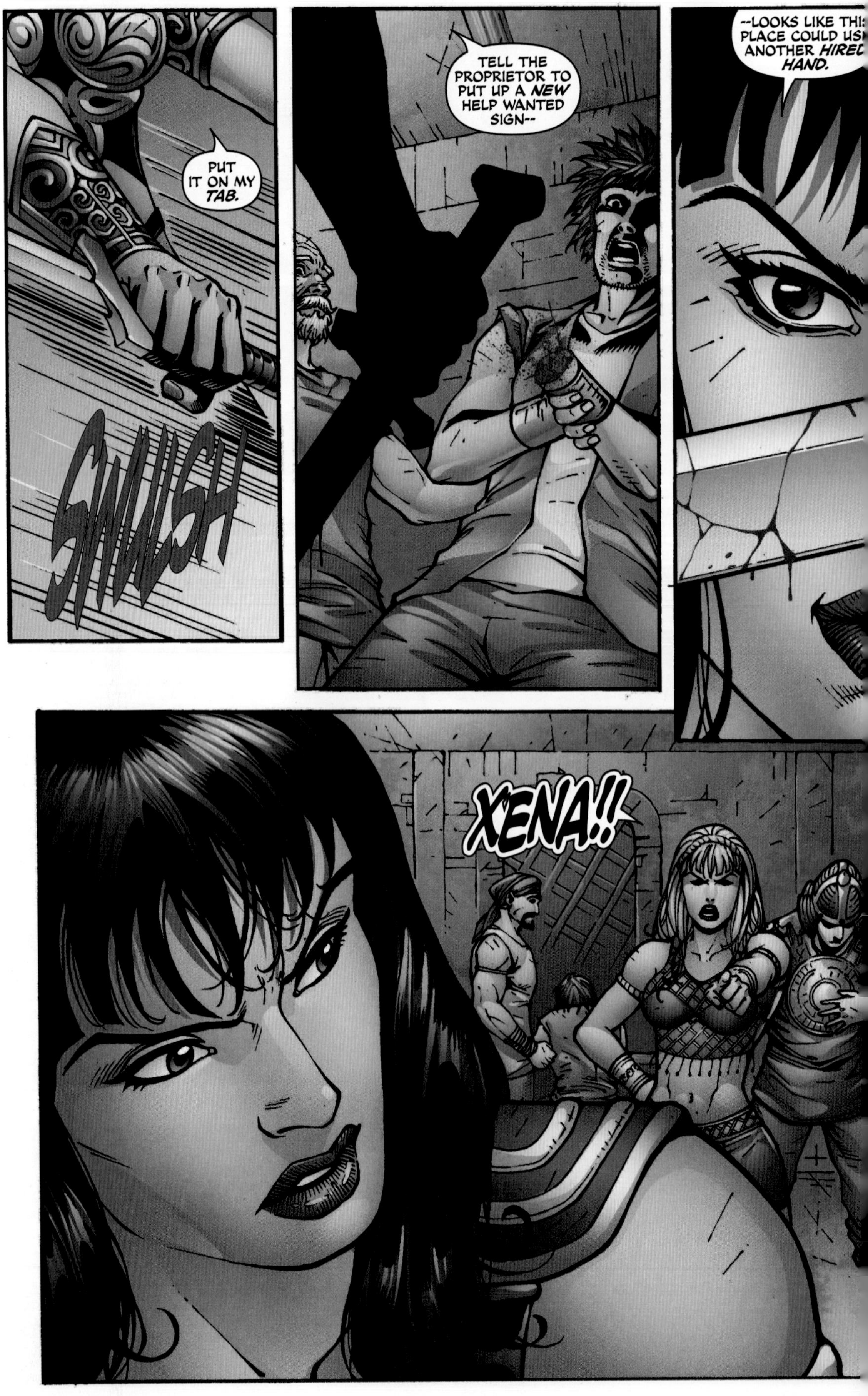
PUT IT ON MY TAB.
SWUSH
TELL THE PROPRIETOR TO PUT UP A NEW HELP WANTED SIGN--
--LOOKS LIKE THIS PLACE COULD USE ANOTHER HIRED HAND.
XENA!!

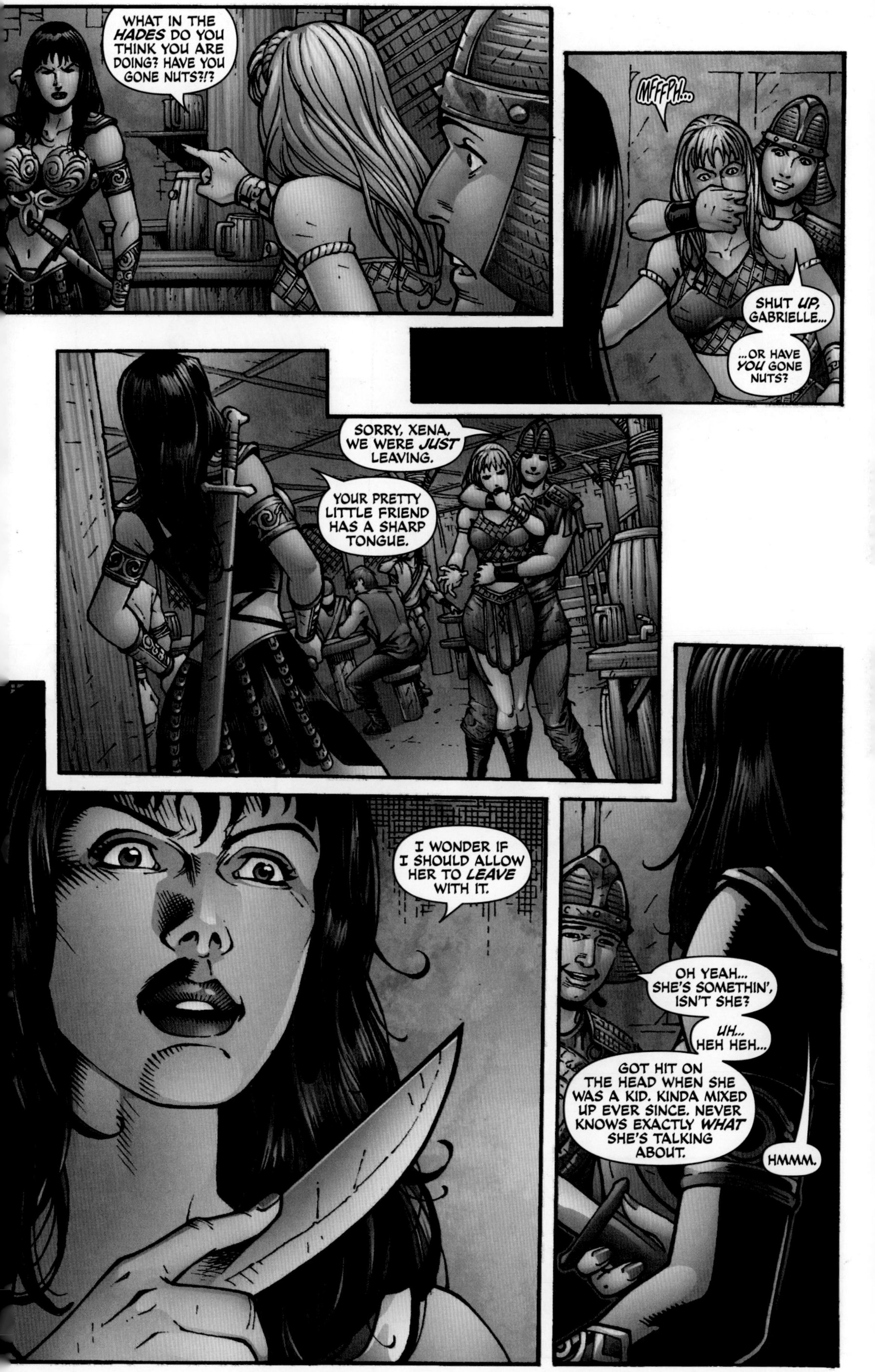

WHAT IN THE HADES DO YOU THINK YOU ARE DOING? HAVE YOU GONE NUTS?!?
MFFFPH...
SHUT UP, GABRIELLE...
...OR HAVE YOU GONE NUTS?
SORRY, XENA, WE WERE JUST LEAVING.
YOUR PRETTY LITTLE FRIEND HAS A SHARP TONGUE.
I WONDER IF I SHOULD ALLOW HER TO LEAVE WITH IT.
OH YEAH... SHE'S SOMETHIN', ISN'T SHE?
UH... HEH HEH...
GOT HIT ON THE HEAD WHEN SHE WAS A KID. KINDA MIXED UP EVER SINCE. NEVER KNOWS EXACTLY WHAT SHE'S TALKING ABOUT.
HMMM.

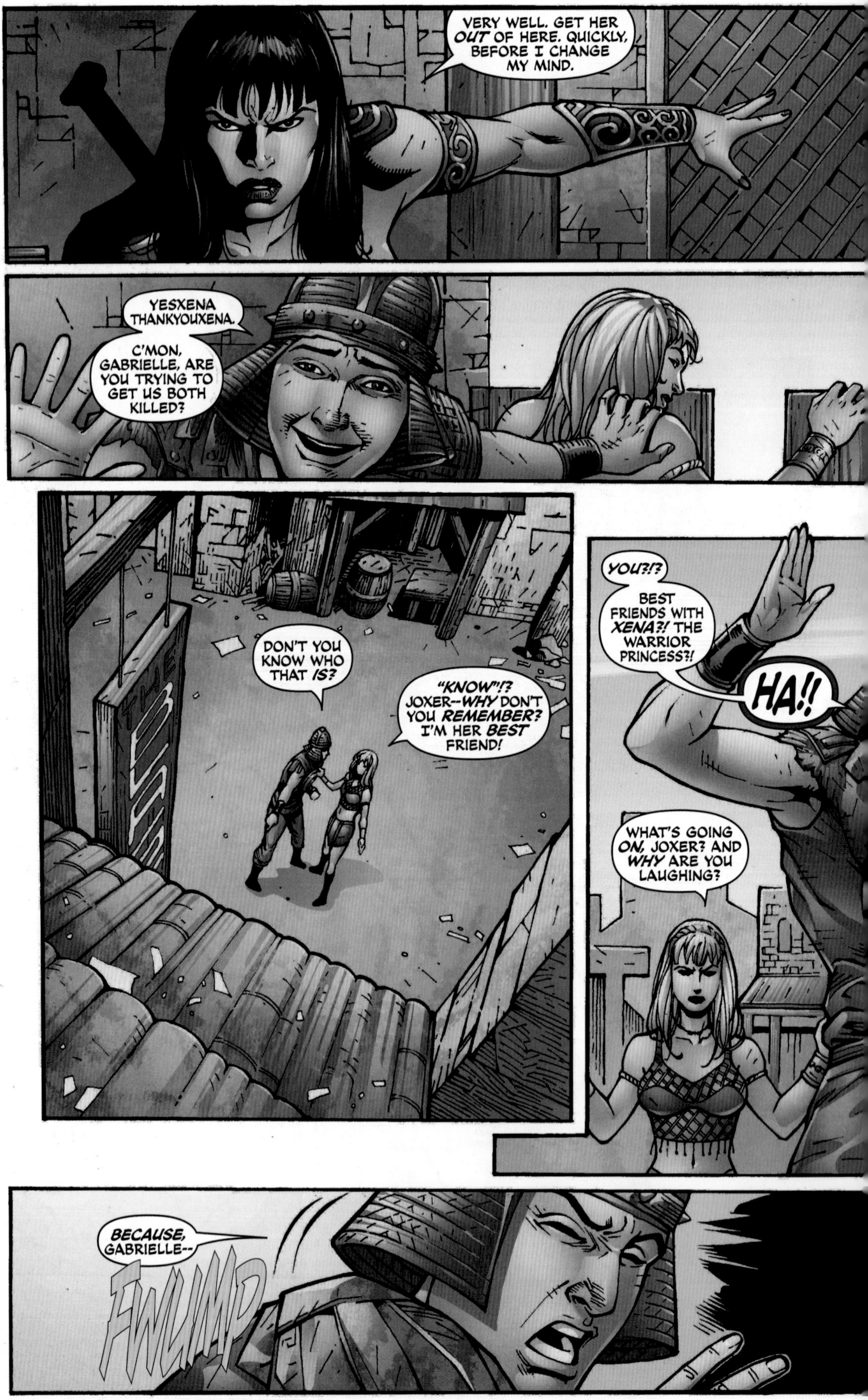
VERY WELL. GET HER OUT OF HERE. QUICKLY, BEFORE I CHANGE MY MIND.
YESXENA THANKYOUXENA.
C'MON, GABRIELLE, ARE YOU TRYING TO GET US BOTH KILLED?
DON'T YOU KNOW WHO THAT IS?
"KNOW"!? JOXER--WHY DON'T YOU REMEMBER? I'M HER BEST FRIEND!
YOU?!?
BEST FRIENDS WITH XENA?! THE WARRIOR PRINCESS?!
HA!!
WHAT'S GOING ON, JOXER? AND WHY ARE YOU LAUGHING?
BECAUSE, GABRIELLE--
FWUMP

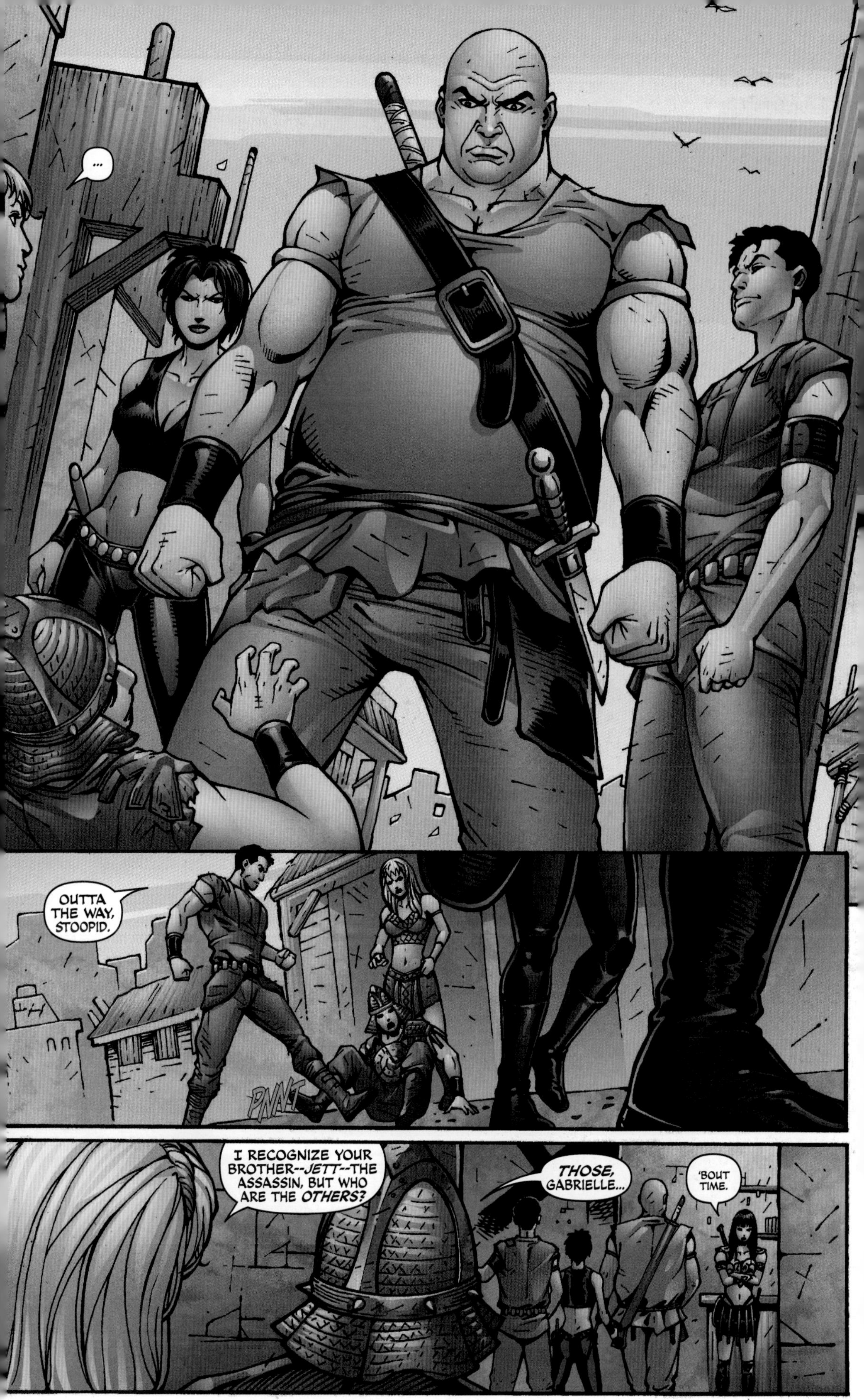
...
OUTTA THE WAY, STOOPID.
PNNT
I RECOGNIZE YOUR BROTHER--JETT--THE ASSASSIN, BUT WHO ARE THE OTHERS?
THOSE, GABRIELLE...
'BOUT TIME.

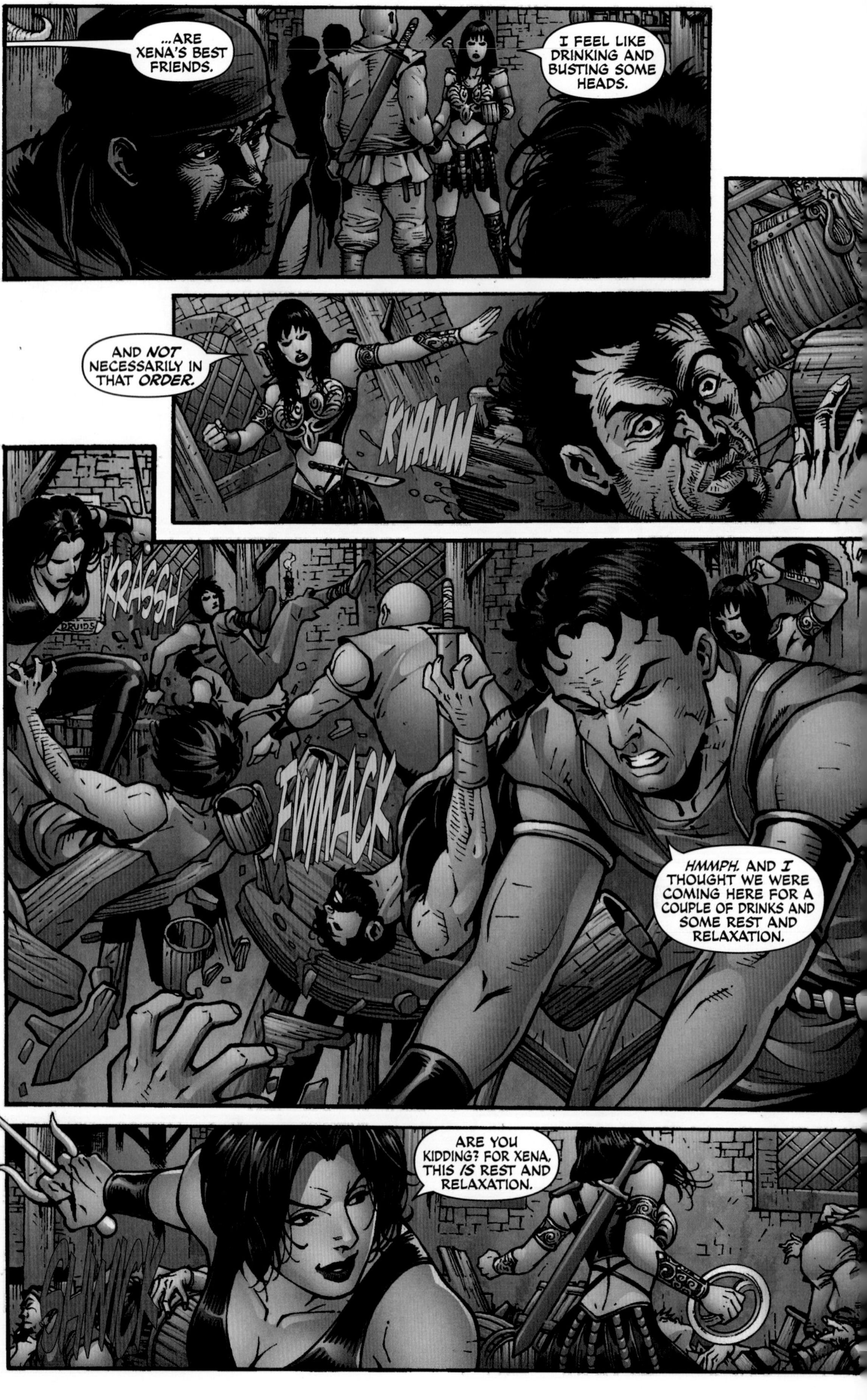
...ARE XENA'S BEST FRIENDS.
I FEEL LIKE DRINKING AND BUSTING SOME HEADS.
AND NOT NECESSARILY IN THAT ORDER.
KWAMM
KRASSH
DRUIDS
FWMACK
HMMPH. AND I THOUGHT WE WERE COMING HERE FOR A COUPLE OF DRINKS AND SOME REST AND RELAXATION.
ARE YOU KIDDING? FOR XENA, THIS IS REST AND RELAXATION.

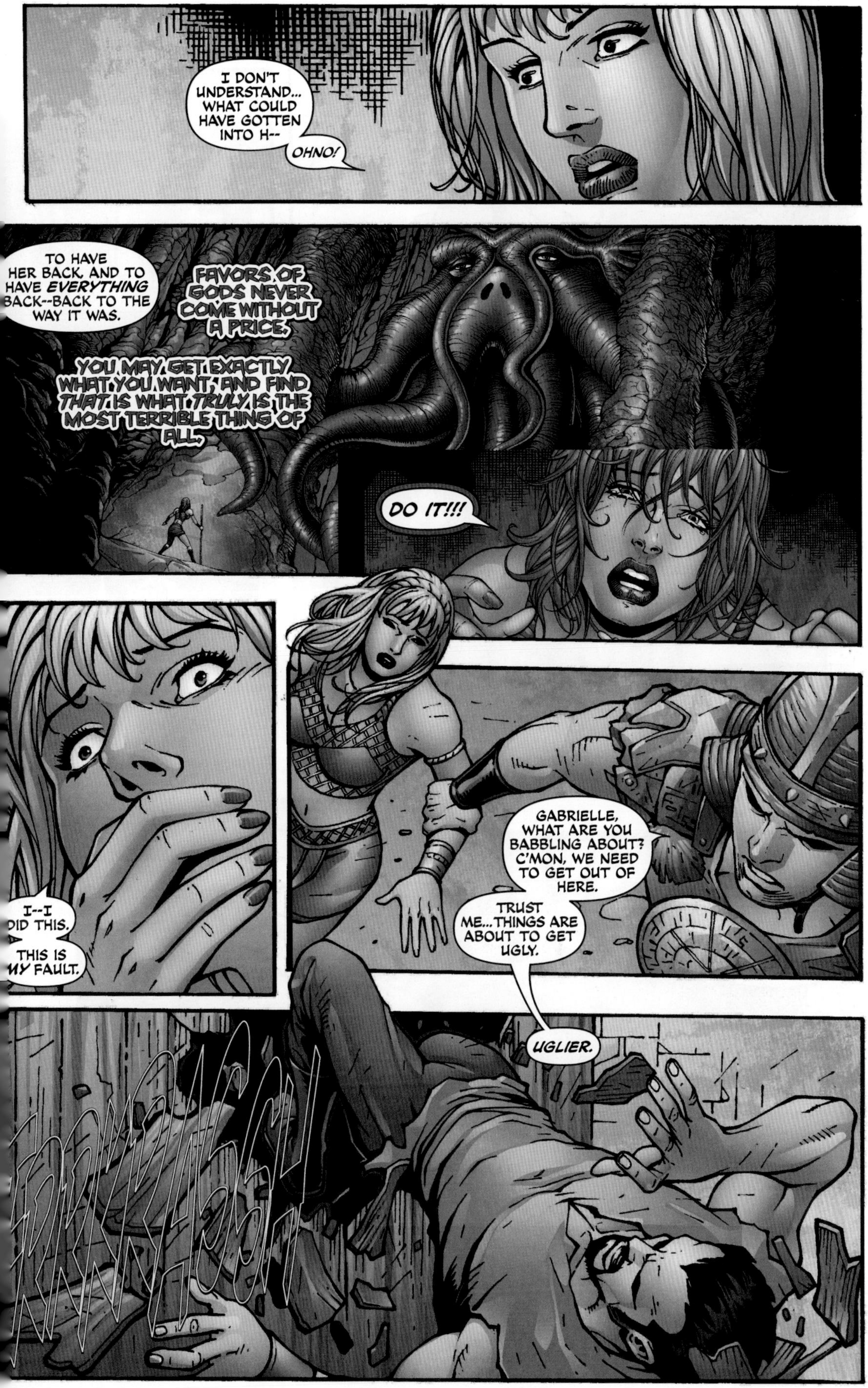
I DON'T UNDERSTAND... WHAT COULD HAVE GOTTEN INTO H--
OHNO!
TO HAVE HER BACK, AND TO HAVE EVERYTHING BACK--BACK TO THE WAY IT WAS.
FAVORS OF GODS NEVER COME WITHOUT A PRICE.
YOU MAY GET EXACTLY WHAT YOU WANT, AND FIND THAT IS WHAT TRULY IS THE MOST TERRIBLE THING OF ALL.
DO IT!!!
I--I DID THIS.
THIS IS MY FAULT.
GABRIELLE, WHAT ARE YOU BABBLING ABOUT? C'MON, WE NEED TO GET OUT OF HERE.
TRUST ME...THINGS ARE ABOUT TO GET UGLY.
UGLIER.
KRAKKASH!

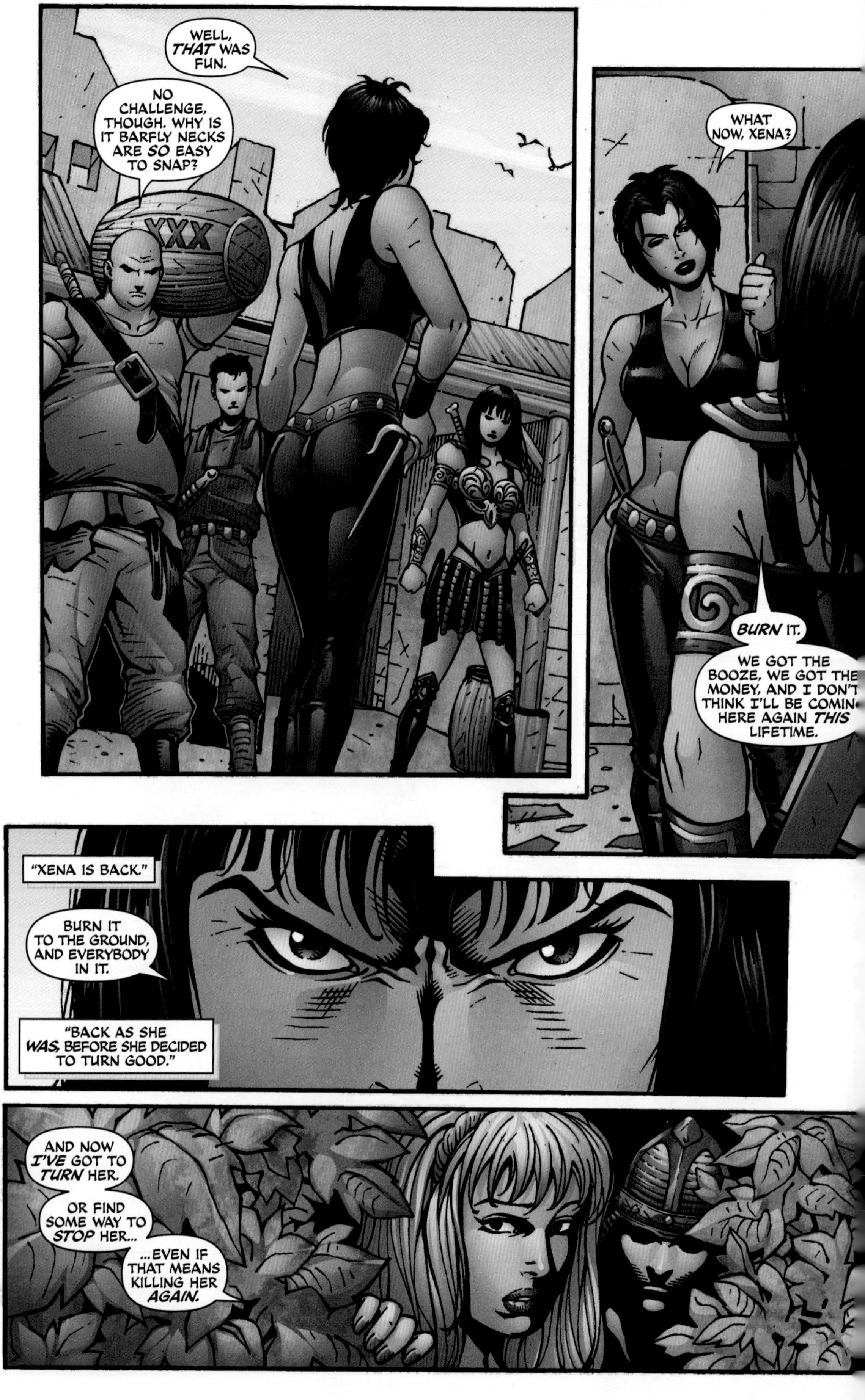
WELL, THAT WAS FUN.
NO CHALLENGE, THOUGH. WHY IS IT BARFLY NECKS ARE SO EASY TO SNAP?
XXX
WHAT NOW, XENA?
BURN IT.
WE GOT THE BOOZE, WE GOT THE MONEY, AND I DON'T THINK I'LL BE COMING HERE AGAIN THIS LIFETIME.
"XENA IS BACK."
BURN IT TO THE GROUND, AND EVERYBODY IN IT.
"BACK AS SHE WAS, BEFORE SHE DECIDED TO TURN GOOD."
AND NOW I'VE GOT TO TURN HER.
OR FIND SOME WAY TO STOP HER...
...EVEN IF THAT MEANS KILLING HER AGAIN.

DARK XENA
CHAPTER TWO

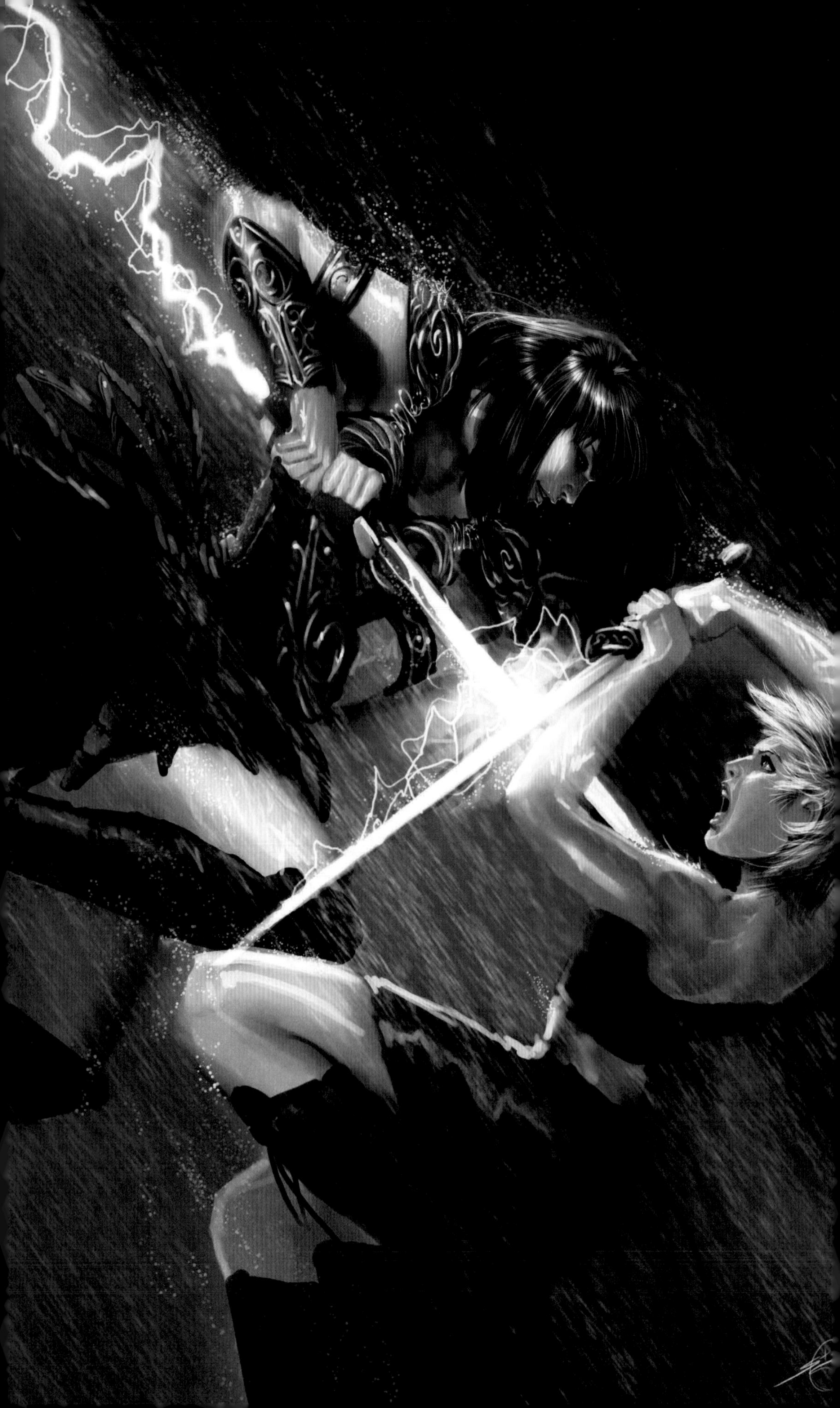

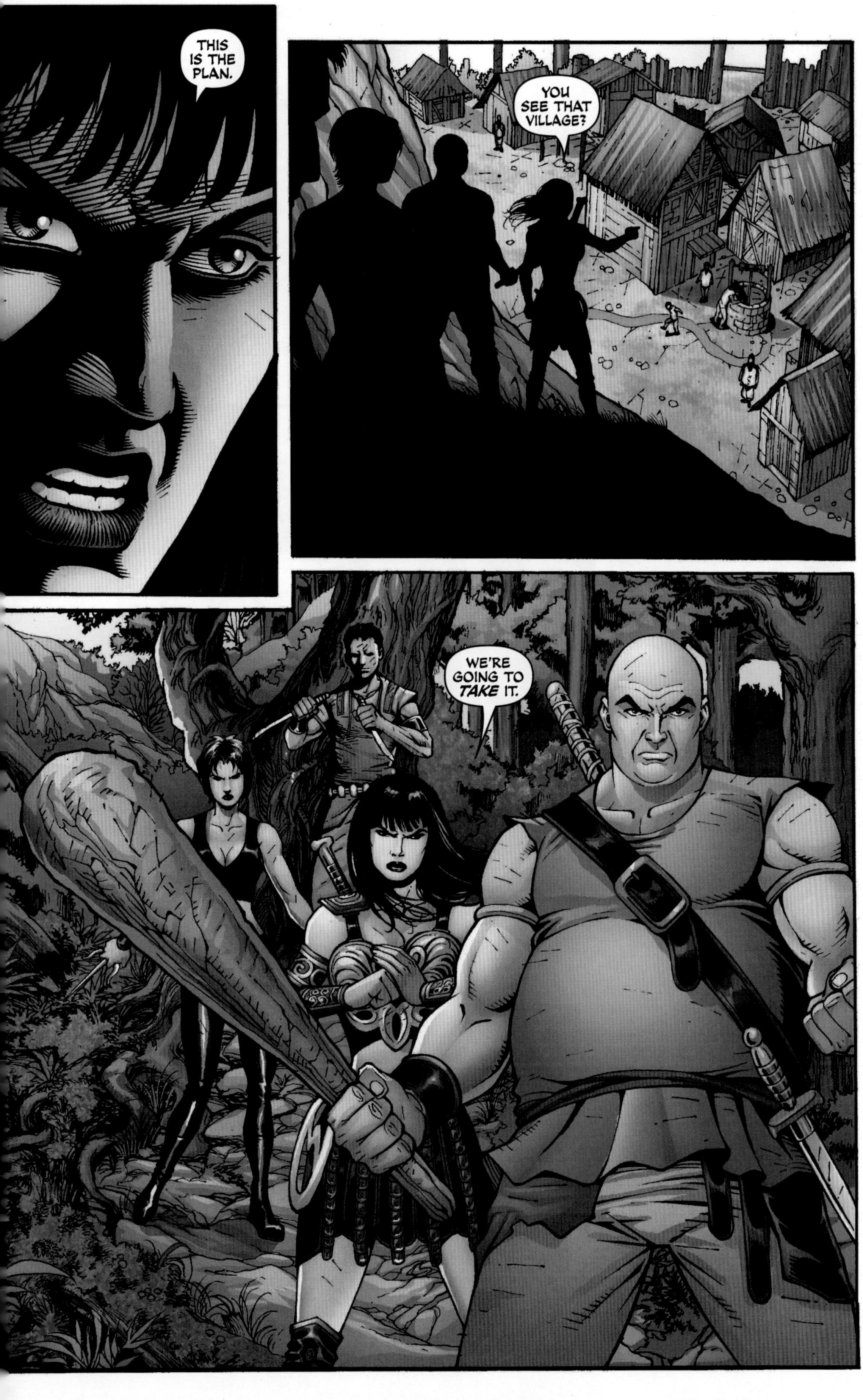
THIS IS THE PLAN.
YOU SEE THAT VILLAGE?
WE'RE GOING TO *TAKE* IT.

WE'RE GOING TO *SACK* IT. RUN THE PEASANTS OUT OF TOWN, KILL ANYBODY WHO DEFIES US, TAKE WHATEVER WE LIKE, AND *BURN* WHATEVER WE FEEL LIKE.

GAR, YOU'RE THE MUSCLE.

JA.

"GO IN FIRST, AND MAKE AN *IMPRESSION.* GO IN HARD, AND SEND 'EM RUNNING.

"*JETT,* YOU'RE ON *FIRE* DUTY.

CAN DO!

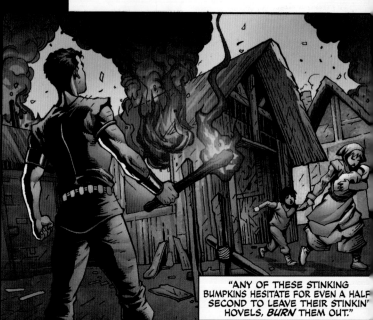

"ANY OF THESE STINKING BUMPKINS HESITATE FOR EVEN A HALF SECOND TO LEAVE THEIR STINKIN' HOVELS, *BURN* THEM OUT."

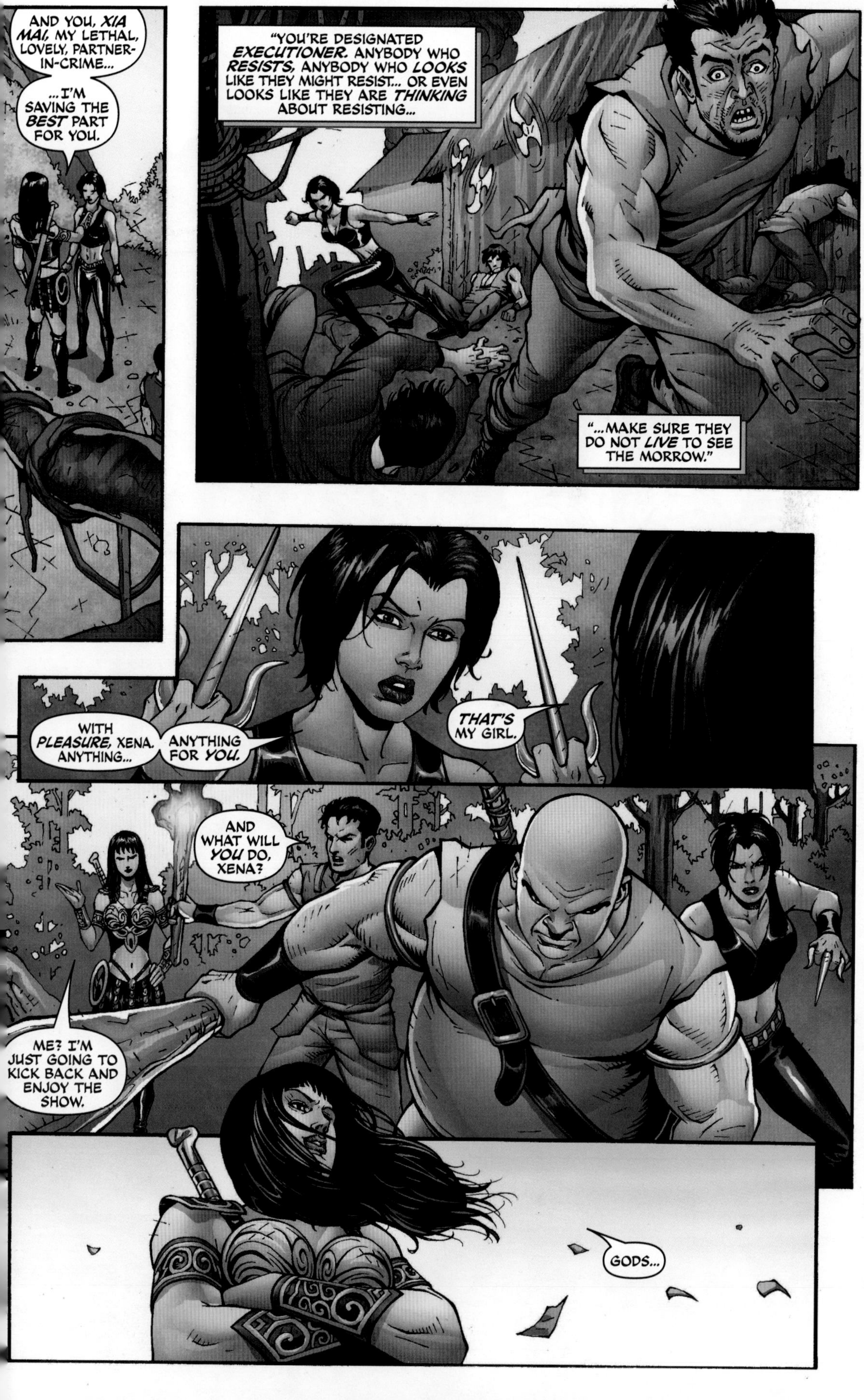
AND YOU, XIA MAI, MY LETHAL, LOVELY, PARTNER-IN-CRIME...
...I'M SAVING THE BEST PART FOR YOU.
"YOU'RE DESIGNATED EXECUTIONER. ANYBODY WHO RESISTS, ANYBODY WHO LOOKS LIKE THEY MIGHT RESIST... OR EVEN LOOKS LIKE THEY ARE THINKING ABOUT RESISTING...
"...MAKE SURE THEY DO NOT LIVE TO SEE THE MORROW."
WITH PLEASURE, XENA. ANYTHING...
ANYTHING FOR YOU.
THAT'S MY GIRL.
AND WHAT WILL YOU DO, XENA?
ME? I'M JUST GOING TO KICK BACK AND ENJOY THE SHOW.
GODS...

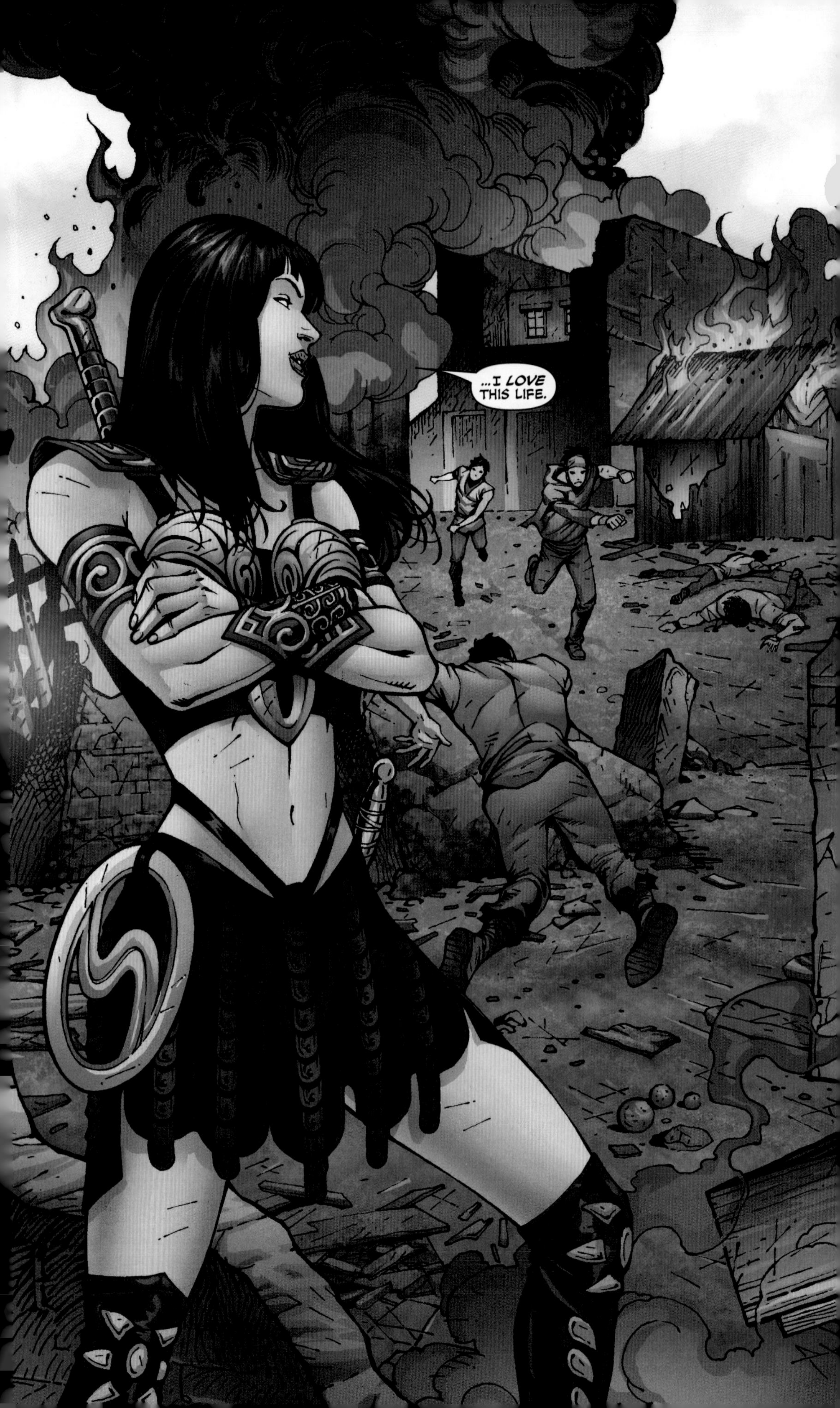
...I *LOVE* THIS LIFE.

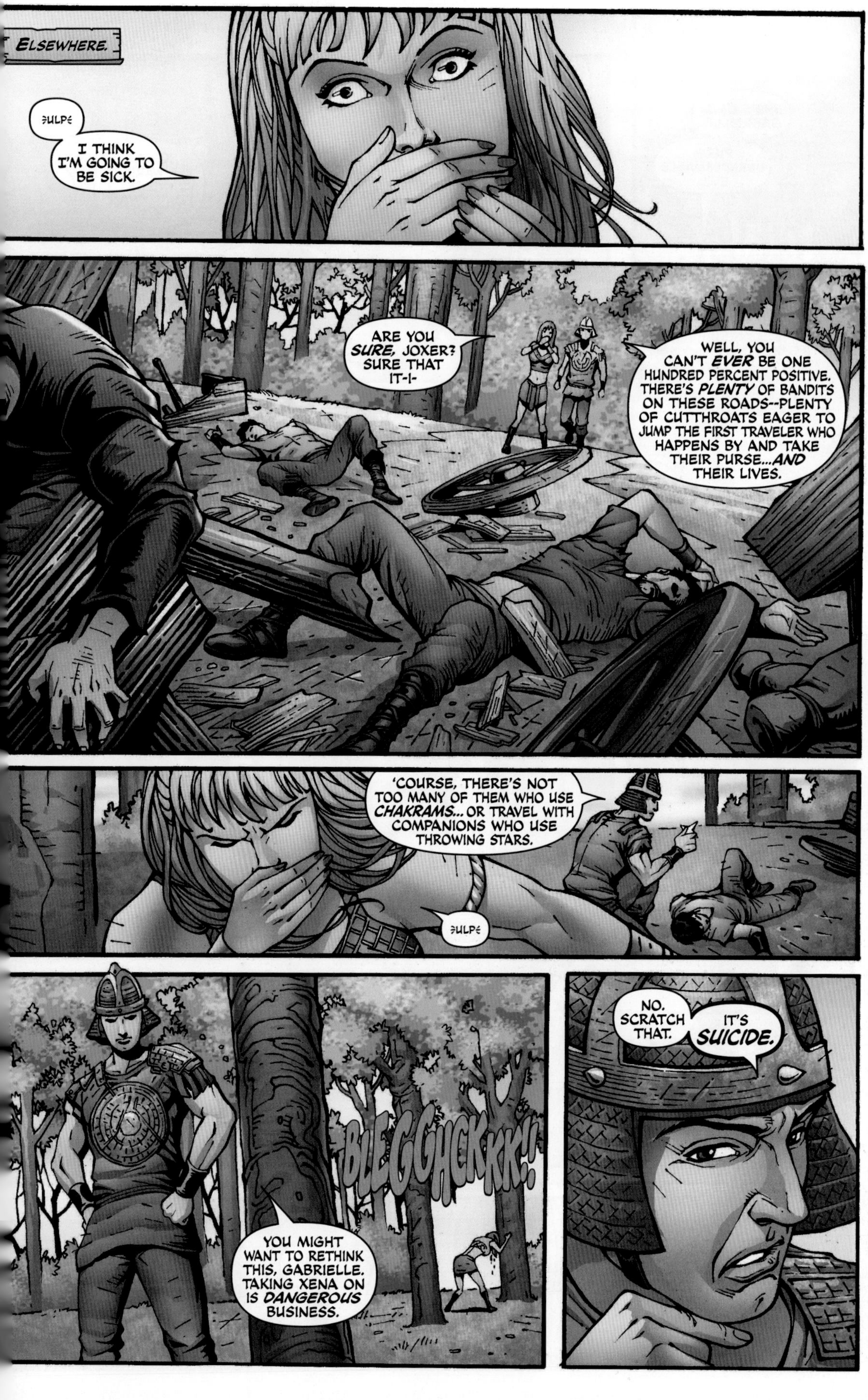

ELSEWHERE.
≡ULP≡
I THINK I'M GOING TO BE SICK.
ARE YOU *SURE,* JOXER? SURE THAT IT-I-
WELL, YOU CAN'T *EVER* BE ONE HUNDRED PERCENT POSITIVE. THERE'S *PLENTY* OF BANDITS ON THESE ROADS--PLENTY OF CUTTHROATS EAGER TO JUMP THE FIRST TRAVELER WHO HAPPENS BY AND TAKE THEIR PURSE...*AND* THEIR LIVES.
'COURSE, THERE'S NOT TOO MANY OF THEM WHO USE *CHAKRAMS*... OR TRAVEL WITH COMPANIONS WHO USE THROWING STARS.
≡ULP≡
BLEGGHCKKK!!
YOU MIGHT WANT TO RETHINK THIS, GABRIELLE. TAKING XENA ON IS *DANGEROUS* BUSINESS.
NO. SCRATCH THAT.
IT'S *SUICIDE.*

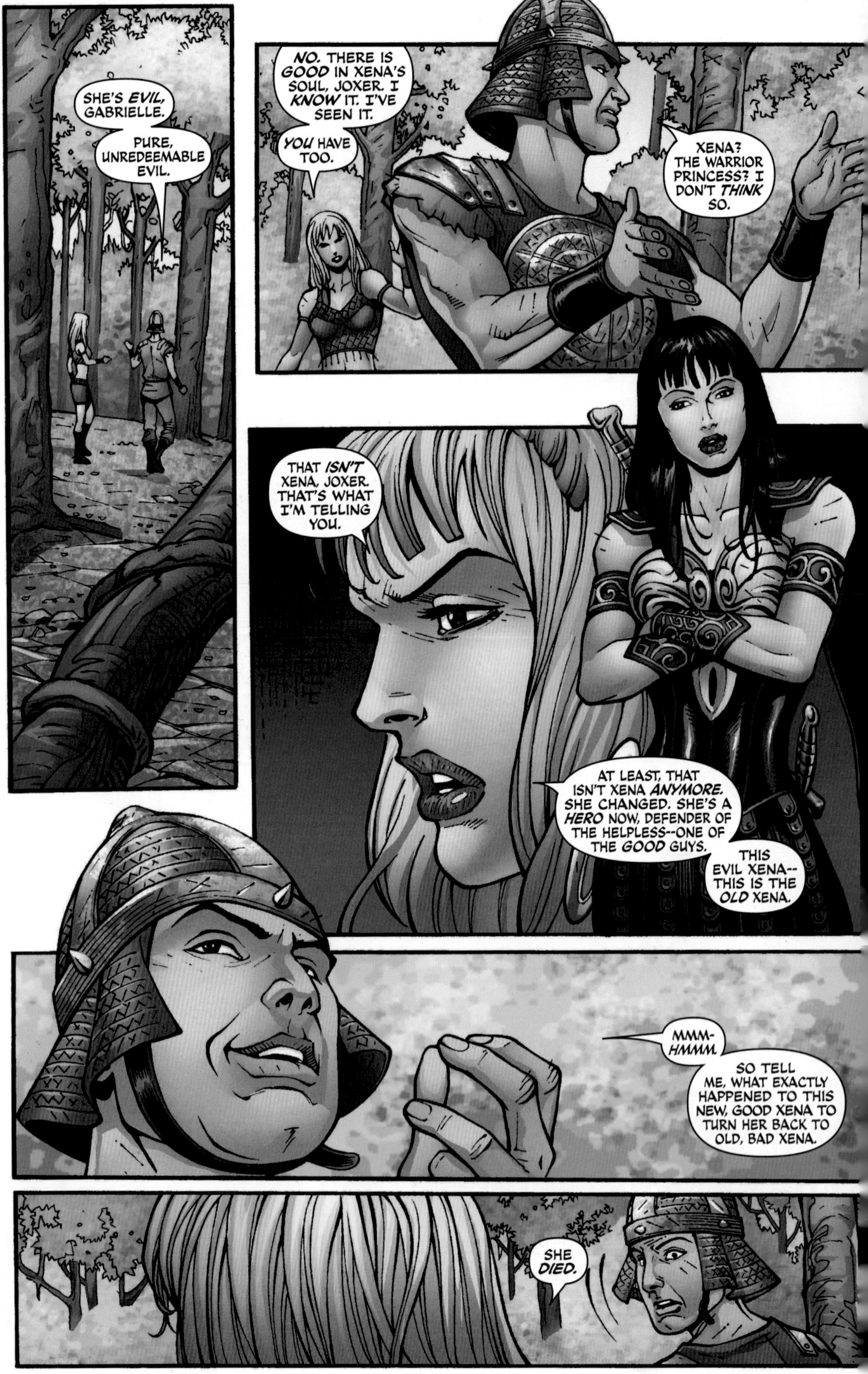
SHE'S *EVIL,* GABRIELLE.
PURE, UNREDEEMABLE EVIL.
NO. THERE IS *GOOD* IN XENA'S SOUL, JOXER. I *KNOW* IT. I'VE SEEN IT.
YOU HAVE TOO.
XENA? THE WARRIOR PRINCESS? I DON'T *THINK* SO.
THAT *ISN'T* XENA, JOXER. THAT'S WHAT I'M TELLING YOU.
AT LEAST, THAT ISN'T XENA *ANYMORE.* SHE CHANGED. SHE'S A *HERO* NOW, DEFENDER OF THE HELPLESS--ONE OF THE *GOOD* GUYS.
THIS EVIL XENA-- THIS IS THE *OLD* XENA.
MMM-*HMMM.*
SO TELL ME, WHAT EXACTLY HAPPENED TO THIS NEW, GOOD XENA TO TURN HER BACK TO OLD, BAD XENA.
SHE *DIED.*

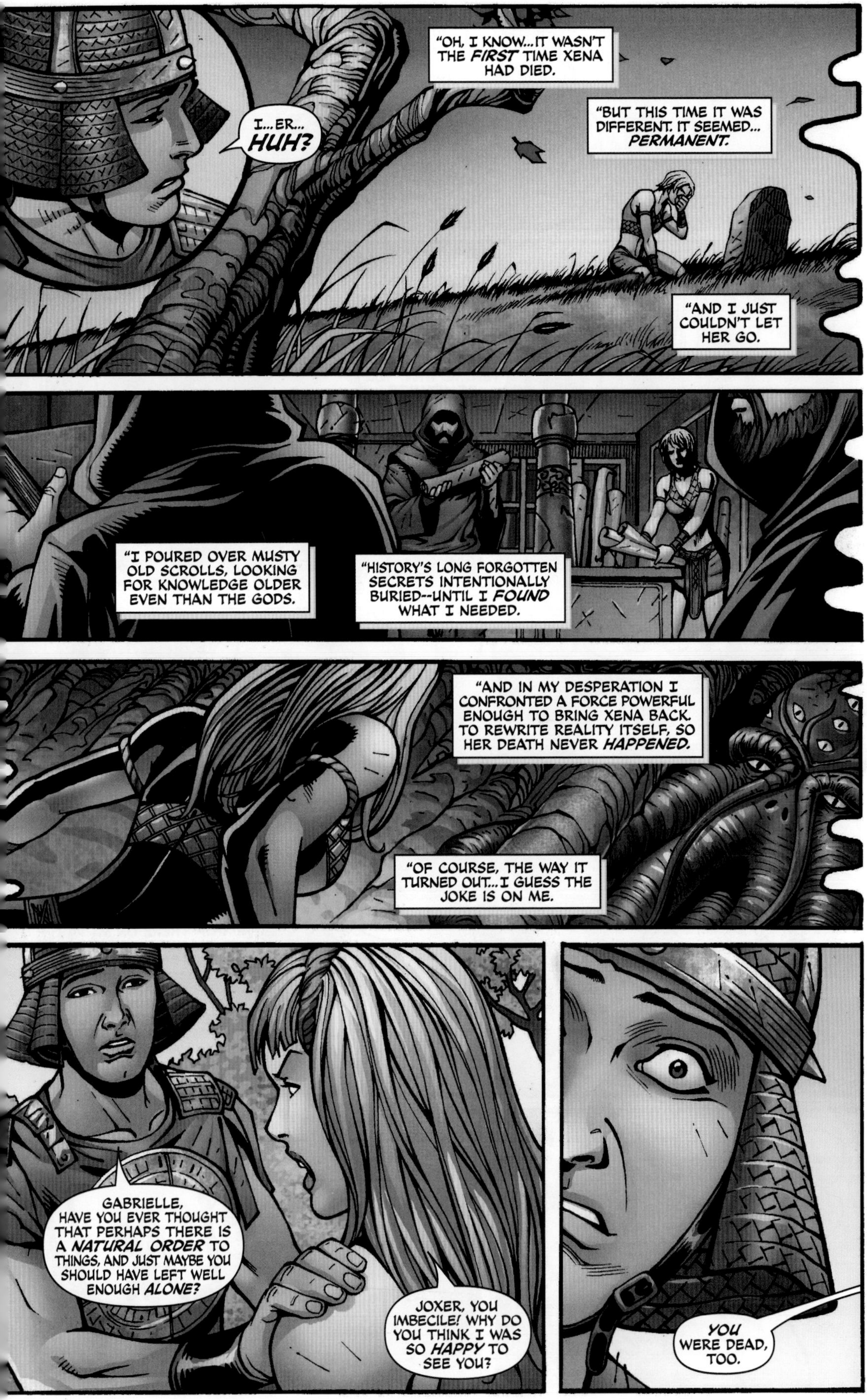
I...ER... HUH?
"OH, I KNOW...IT WASN'T THE FIRST TIME XENA HAD DIED.
"BUT THIS TIME IT WAS DIFFERENT. IT SEEMED... PERMANENT.
"AND I JUST COULDN'T LET HER GO.
"I POURED OVER MUSTY OLD SCROLLS, LOOKING FOR KNOWLEDGE OLDER EVEN THAN THE GODS.
"HISTORY'S LONG FORGOTTEN SECRETS INTENTIONALLY BURIED--UNTIL I FOUND WHAT I NEEDED.
"AND IN MY DESPERATION I CONFRONTED A FORCE POWERFUL ENOUGH TO BRING XENA BACK. TO REWRITE REALITY ITSELF, SO HER DEATH NEVER HAPPENED.
"OF COURSE, THE WAY IT TURNED OUT...I GUESS THE JOKE IS ON ME.
GABRIELLE, HAVE YOU EVER THOUGHT THAT PERHAPS THERE IS A NATURAL ORDER TO THINGS, AND JUST MAYBE YOU SHOULD HAVE LEFT WELL ENOUGH ALONE?
JOXER, YOU IMBECILE! WHY DO YOU THINK I WAS SO HAPPY TO SEE YOU?
YOU WERE DEAD, TOO.

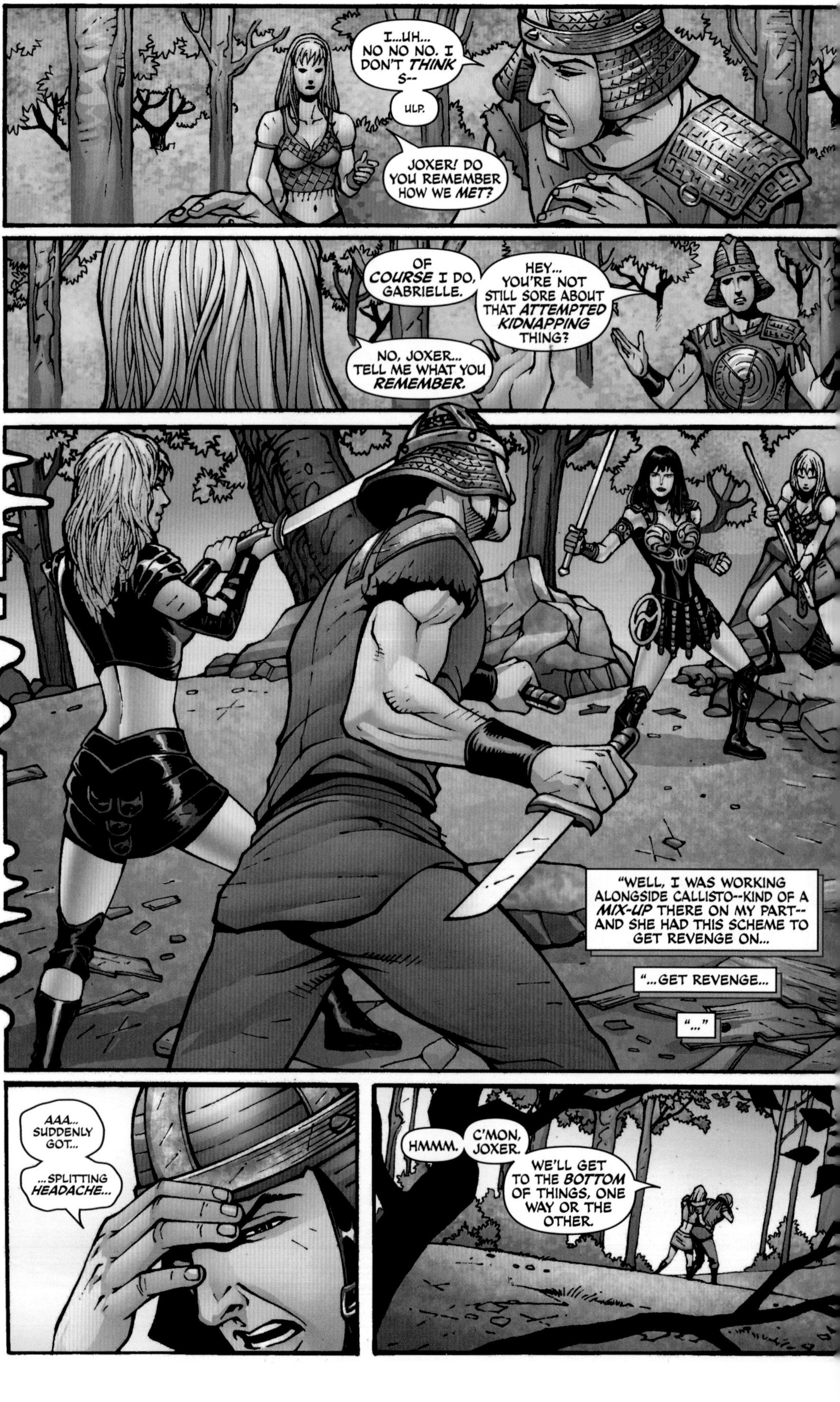

I...UH... NO NO NO. I DON'T THINK S--
ULP.
JOXER! DO YOU REMEMBER HOW WE MET?
OF COURSE I DO, GABRIELLE.
HEY... YOU'RE NOT STILL SORE ABOUT THAT ATTEMPTED KIDNAPPING THING?
NO, JOXER... TELL ME WHAT YOU REMEMBER.
"WELL, I WAS WORKING ALONGSIDE CALLISTO--KIND OF A MIX-UP THERE ON MY PART--AND SHE HAD THIS SCHEME TO GET REVENGE ON...
"...GET REVENGE...
"..."
AAA... SUDDENLY GOT...
...SPLITTING HEADACHE...
HMMM.
C'MON, JOXER.
WE'LL GET TO THE BOTTOM OF THINGS, ONE WAY OR THE OTHER.

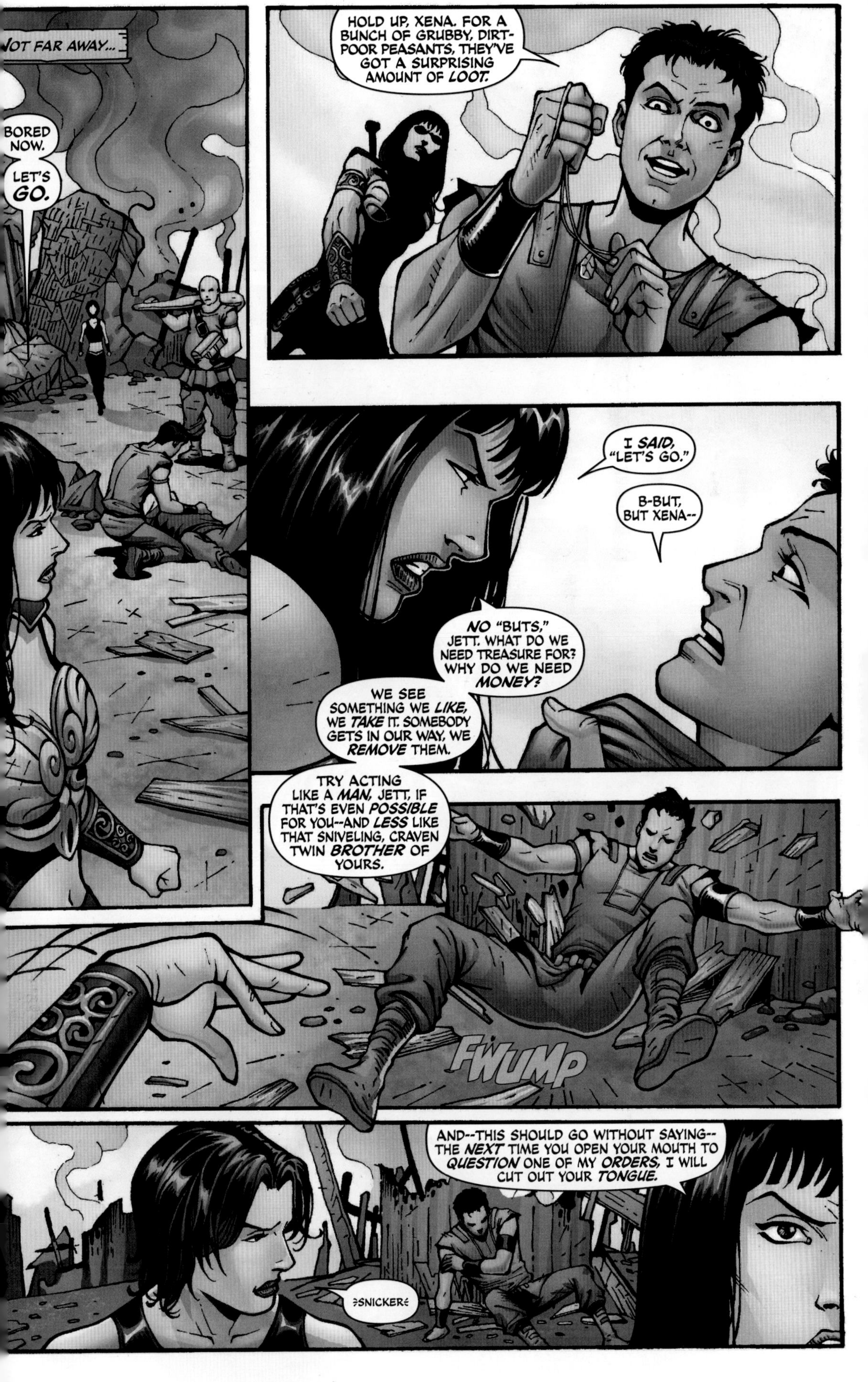
NOT FAR AWAY...
BORED NOW.
LET'S GO.
HOLD UP, XENA. FOR A BUNCH OF GRUBBY, DIRT-POOR PEASANTS, THEY'VE GOT A SURPRISING AMOUNT OF LOOT.
I SAID, "LET'S GO."
B-BUT, BUT XENA--
NO "BUTS," JETT. WHAT DO WE NEED TREASURE FOR? WHY DO WE NEED MONEY?
WE SEE SOMETHING WE LIKE, WE TAKE IT. SOMEBODY GETS IN OUR WAY, WE REMOVE THEM.
TRY ACTING LIKE A MAN, JETT, IF THAT'S EVEN POSSIBLE FOR YOU--AND LESS LIKE THAT SNIVELING, CRAVEN TWIN BROTHER OF YOURS.
FWUMP
AND--THIS SHOULD GO WITHOUT SAYING--THE NEXT TIME YOU OPEN YOUR MOUTH TO QUESTION ONE OF MY ORDERS, I WILL CUT OUT YOUR TONGUE.
≈SNICKER≈

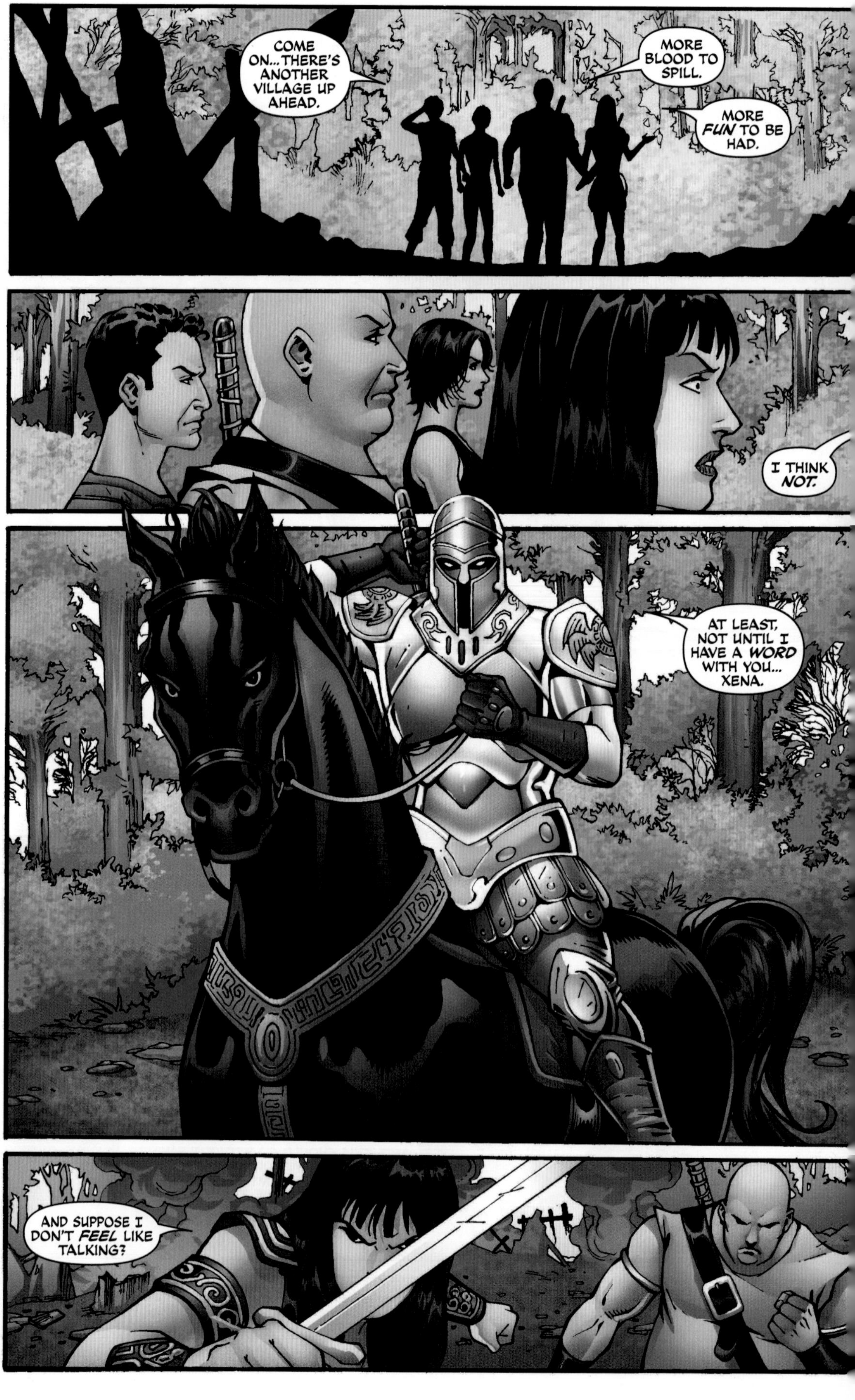
COME ON... THERE'S ANOTHER VILLAGE UP AHEAD.
MORE BLOOD TO SPILL.
MORE *FUN* TO BE HAD.
I THINK *NOT.*
AT LEAST, NOT UNTIL I HAVE A *WORD* WITH YOU... XENA.
AND SUPPOSE I DON'T *FEEL* LIKE TALKING?

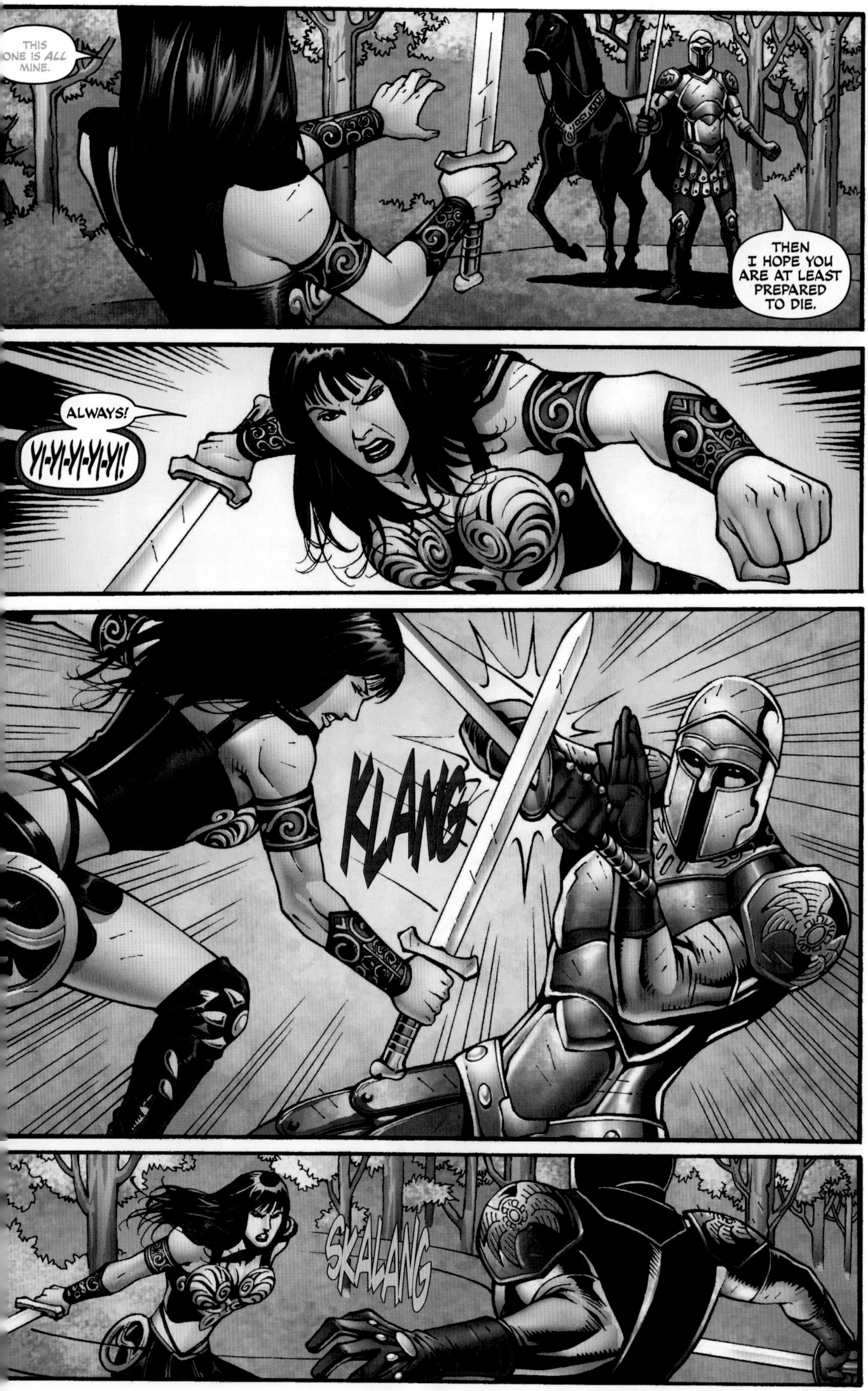
THIS ONE IS ALL MINE.
THEN I HOPE YOU ARE AT LEAST PREPARED TO DIE.
ALWAYS!
YI-YI-YI-YI-YI-YI!
KLANG
SKALANG

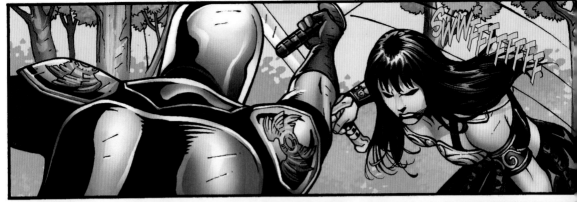

THINK WE SHOULD HELP, GAR?

SHE *SAID* "THIS ONE IS HERS."

SWWFFEEEEEE

KAWHAMM

ENOUGH! HOLD, WOMAN!

"*HOLD?*" YOU ARE QUITE MISTAKEN IF YOU THINK I WILL TAKE THE *ORDER* OF SOME NO-CONSEQUENCE WAYFARER WITH A SHARP TONGUE.

BUT WHAT OF... A GOD?

ARES!!

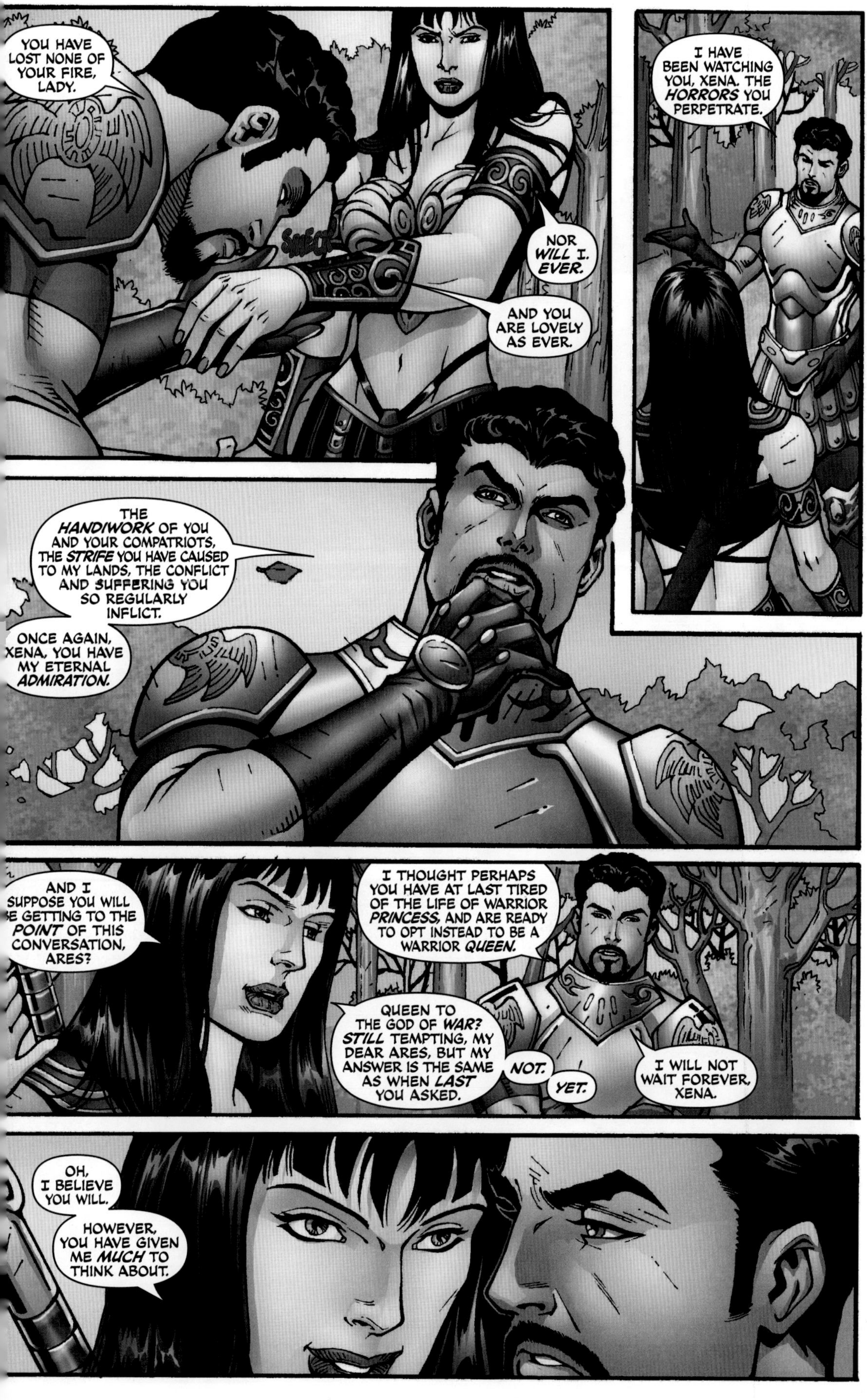

YOU HAVE LOST NONE OF YOUR FIRE, LADY.
SMECK
NOR WILL I. EVER.
AND YOU ARE LOVELY AS EVER.
I HAVE BEEN WATCHING YOU, XENA. THE HORRORS YOU PERPETRATE.
THE HANDIWORK OF YOU AND YOUR COMPATRIOTS, THE STRIFE YOU HAVE CAUSED TO MY LANDS, THE CONFLICT AND SUFFERING YOU SO REGULARLY INFLICT.
ONCE AGAIN, XENA, YOU HAVE MY ETERNAL ADMIRATION.
AND I SUPPOSE YOU WILL BE GETTING TO THE POINT OF THIS CONVERSATION, ARES?
I THOUGHT PERHAPS YOU HAVE AT LAST TIRED OF THE LIFE OF WARRIOR PRINCESS, AND ARE READY TO OPT INSTEAD TO BE A WARRIOR QUEEN.
QUEEN TO THE GOD OF WAR? STILL TEMPTING, MY DEAR ARES, BUT MY ANSWER IS THE SAME AS WHEN LAST YOU ASKED.
NOT.
YET.
I WILL NOT WAIT FOREVER, XENA.
OH, I BELIEVE YOU WILL.
HOWEVER, YOU HAVE GIVEN ME MUCH TO THINK ABOUT.

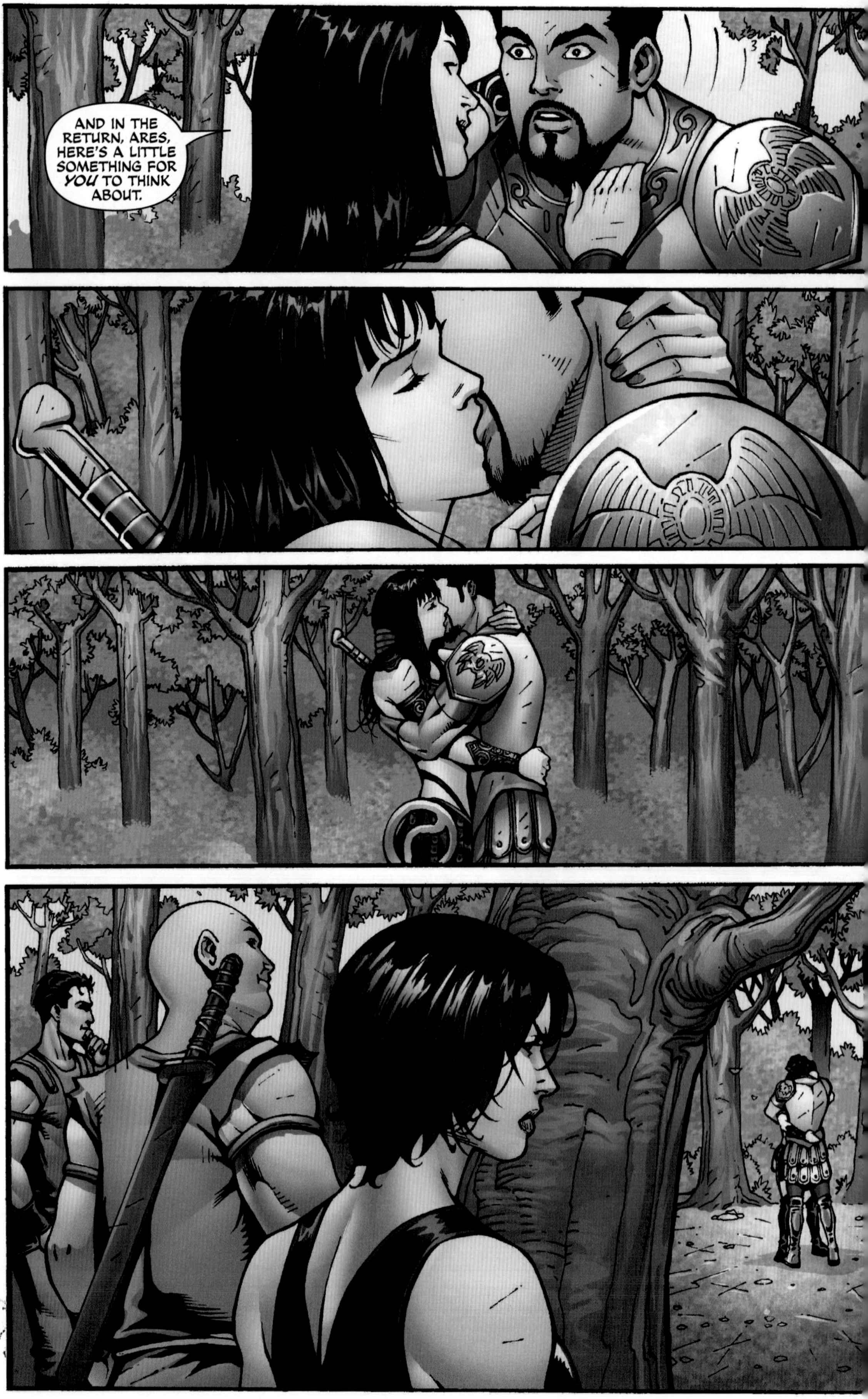
AND IN THE RETURN, ARES, HERE'S A LITTLE SOMETHING FOR *YOU* TO THINK ABOUT.

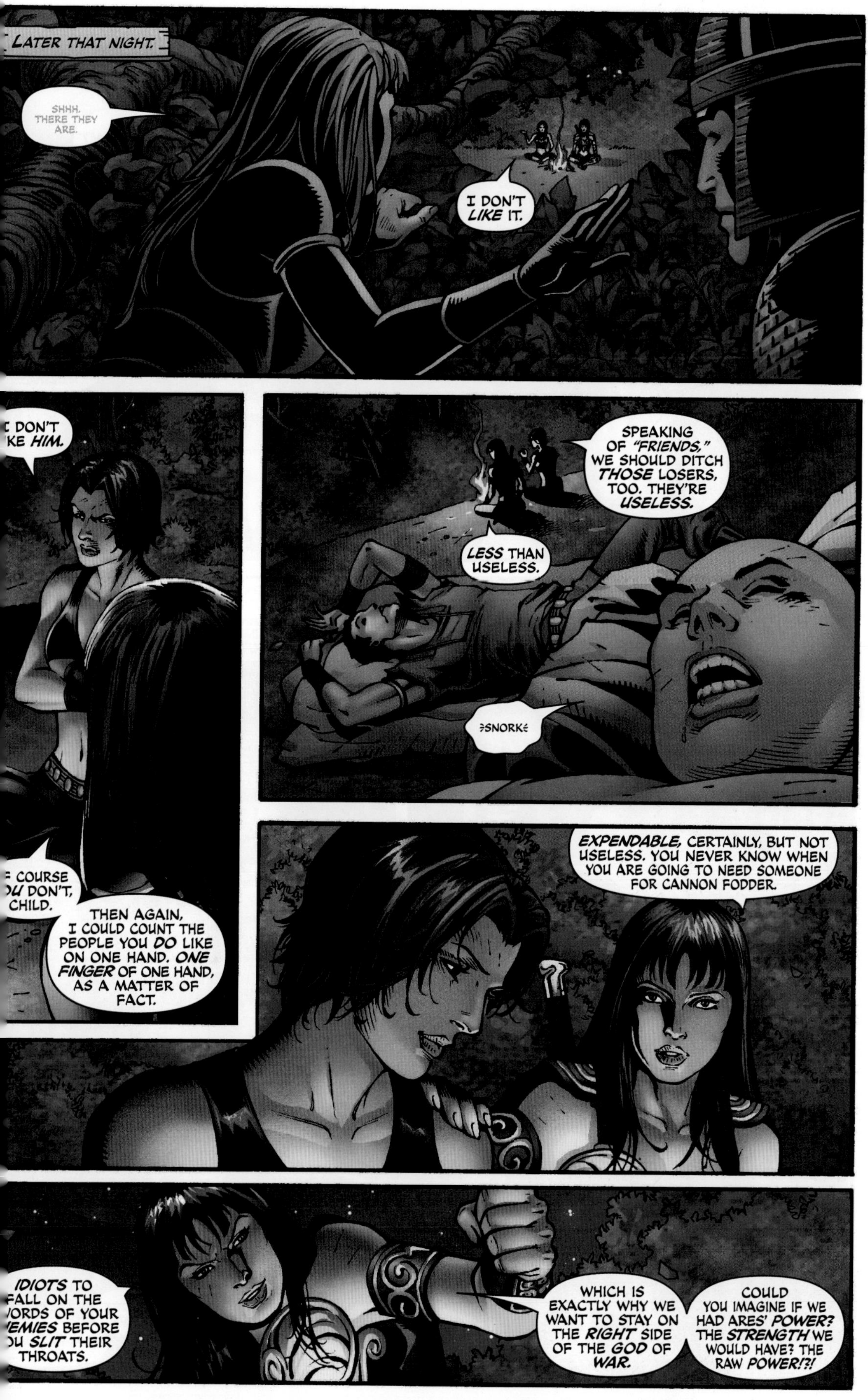

LATER THAT NIGHT.
SHHH. THERE THEY ARE.
I DON'T LIKE IT.
I DON'T LIKE HIM.
SPEAKING OF "FRIENDS," WE SHOULD DITCH THOSE LOSERS, TOO. THEY'RE USELESS.
LESS THAN USELESS.
SNORK
OF COURSE YOU DON'T, CHILD.
THEN AGAIN, I COULD COUNT THE PEOPLE YOU DO LIKE ON ONE HAND. ONE FINGER OF ONE HAND, AS A MATTER OF FACT.
EXPENDABLE, CERTAINLY, BUT NOT USELESS. YOU NEVER KNOW WHEN YOU ARE GOING TO NEED SOMEONE FOR CANNON FODDER.
IDIOTS TO FALL ON THE SWORDS OF YOUR ENEMIES BEFORE YOU SLIT THEIR THROATS.
WHICH IS EXACTLY WHY WE WANT TO STAY ON THE RIGHT SIDE OF THE GOD OF WAR.
COULD YOU IMAGINE IF WE HAD ARES' POWER? THE STRENGTH WE WOULD HAVE? THE RAW POWER!?!

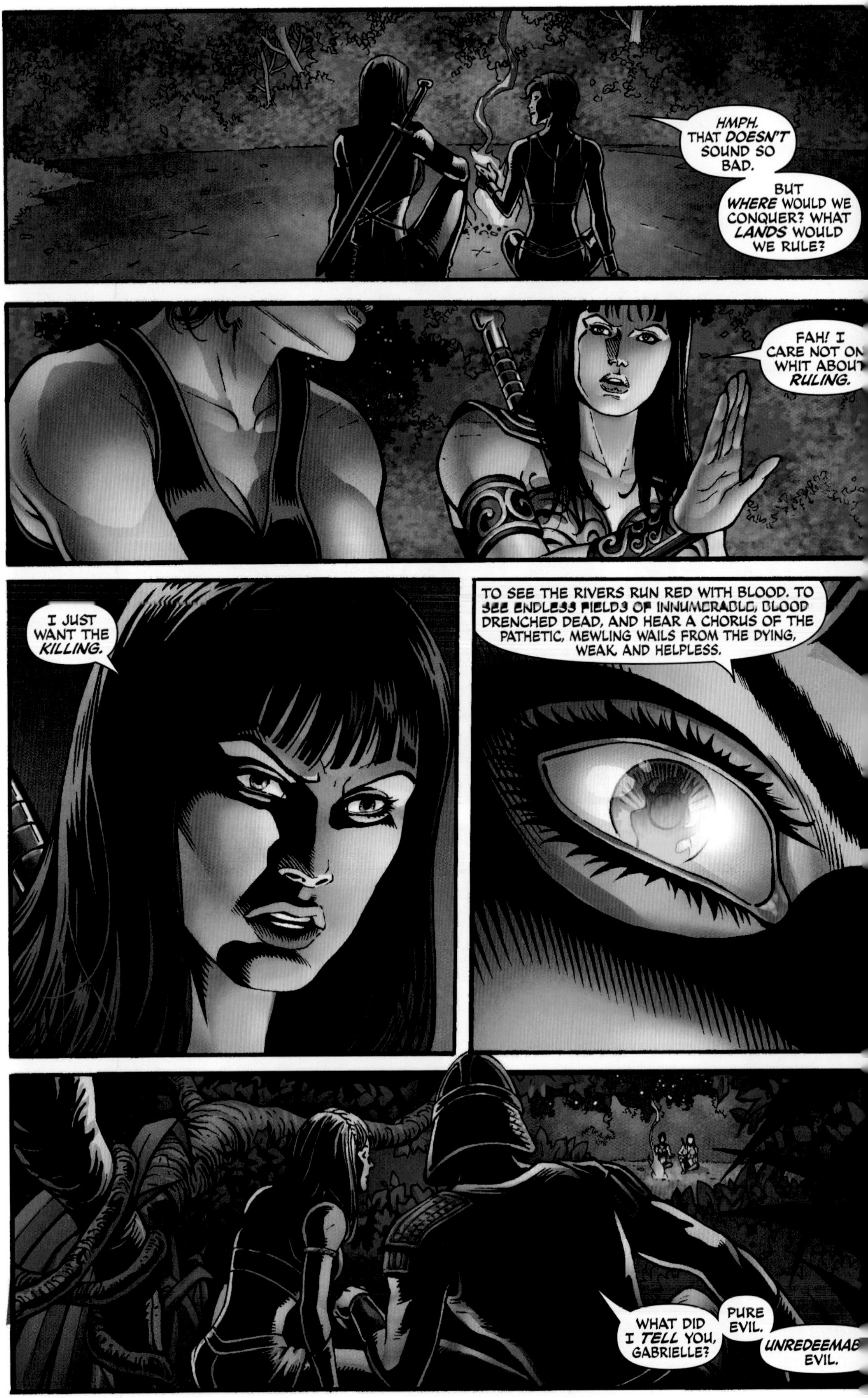
HMPH. THAT DOESN'T SOUND SO BAD.
BUT WHERE WOULD WE CONQUER? WHAT LANDS WOULD WE RULE?
FAH! I CARE NOT ON WHIT ABOUT RULING.
I JUST WANT THE KILLING.
TO SEE THE RIVERS RUN RED WITH BLOOD. TO SEE ENDLESS FIELDS OF INNUMERABLE, BLOOD DRENCHED DEAD, AND HEAR A CHORUS OF THE PATHETIC, MEWLING WAILS FROM THE DYING, WEAK, AND HELPLESS.
WHAT DID I TELL YOU, GABRIELLE?
PURE EVIL.
UNREDEEMAB EVIL.

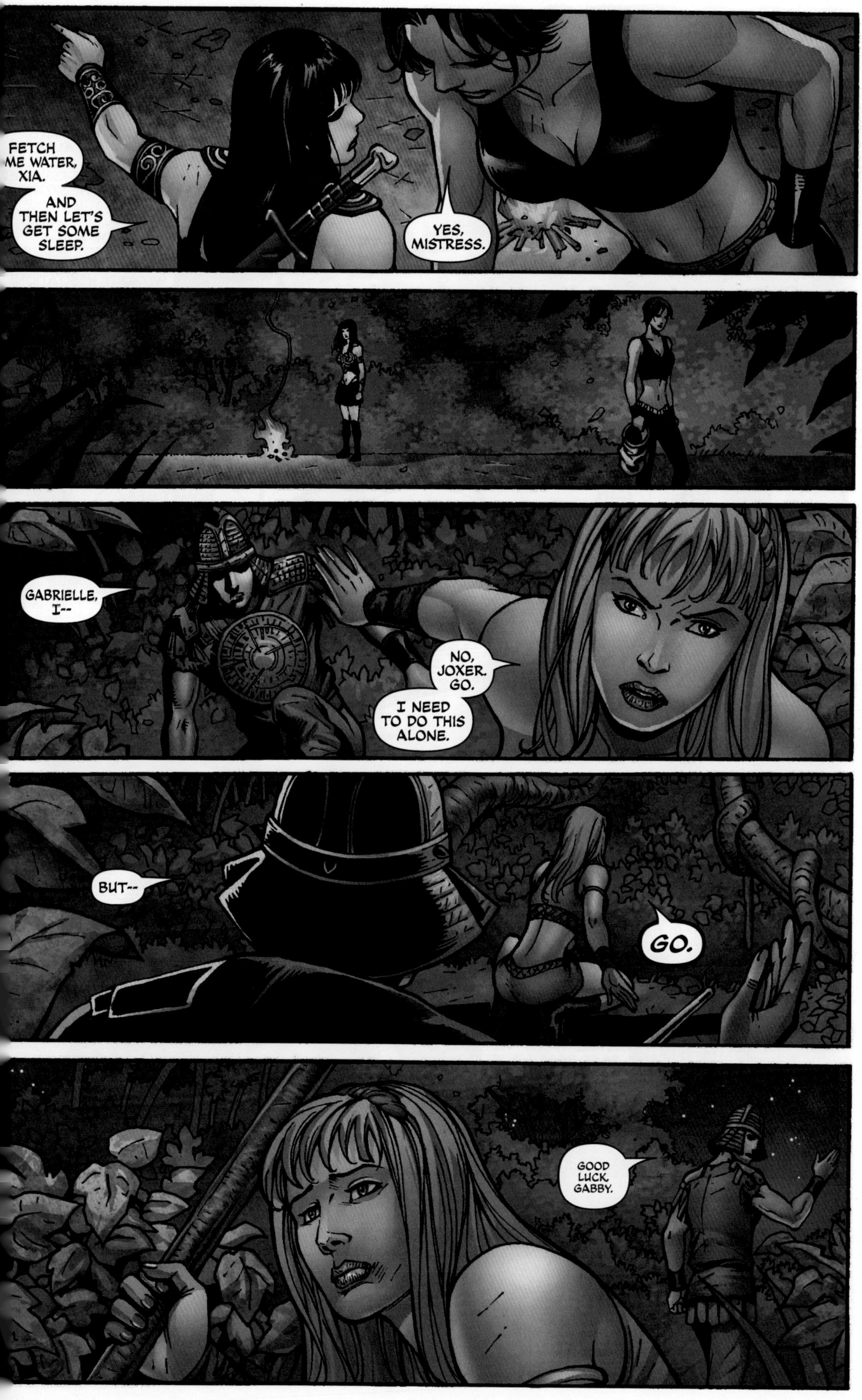
FETCH ME WATER, XIA.
AND THEN LET'S GET SOME SLEEP.
YES, MISTRESS.
GABRIELLE, I--
NO, JOXER. GO.
I NEED TO DO THIS ALONE.
BUT--
GO.
GOOD LUCK, GABBY.

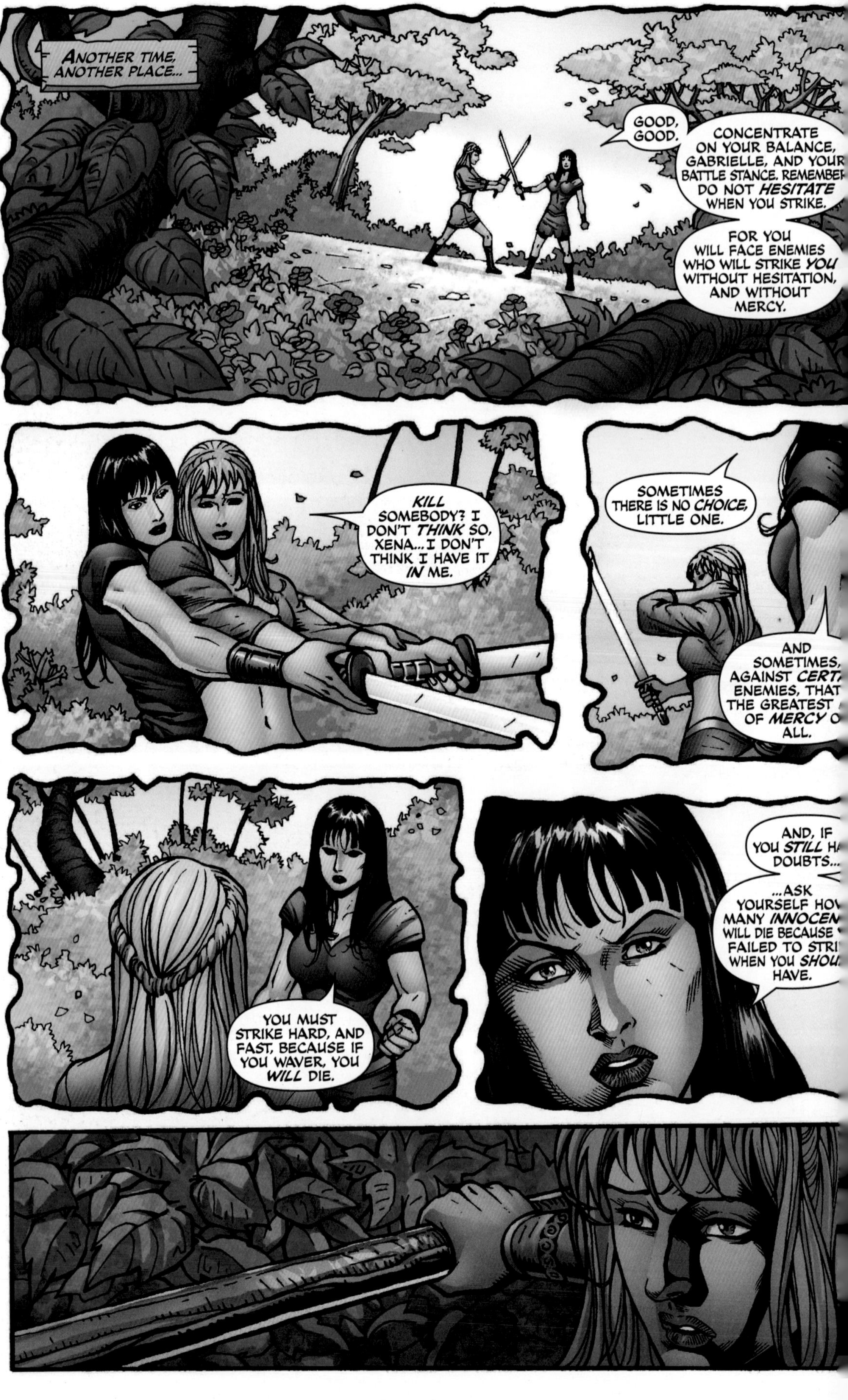
ANOTHER TIME, ANOTHER PLACE...
GOOD, GOOD.
CONCENTRATE ON YOUR BALANCE, GABRIELLE, AND YOUR BATTLE STANCE. REMEMBER DO NOT HESITATE WHEN YOU STRIKE.
FOR YOU WILL FACE ENEMIES WHO WILL STRIKE YOU WITHOUT HESITATION, AND WITHOUT MERCY.
KILL SOMEBODY? I DON'T THINK SO, XENA...I DON'T THINK I HAVE IT IN ME.
SOMETIMES THERE IS NO CHOICE, LITTLE ONE.
AND SOMETIMES, AGAINST CERT ENEMIES, THAT THE GREATEST OF MERCY O ALL.
YOU MUST STRIKE HARD, AND FAST, BECAUSE IF YOU WAVER, YOU WILL DIE.
AND, IF YOU STILL HA DOUBTS...
...ASK YOURSELF HOW MANY INNOCEN WILL DIE BECAUSE FAILED TO STRI WHEN YOU SHOU HAVE.

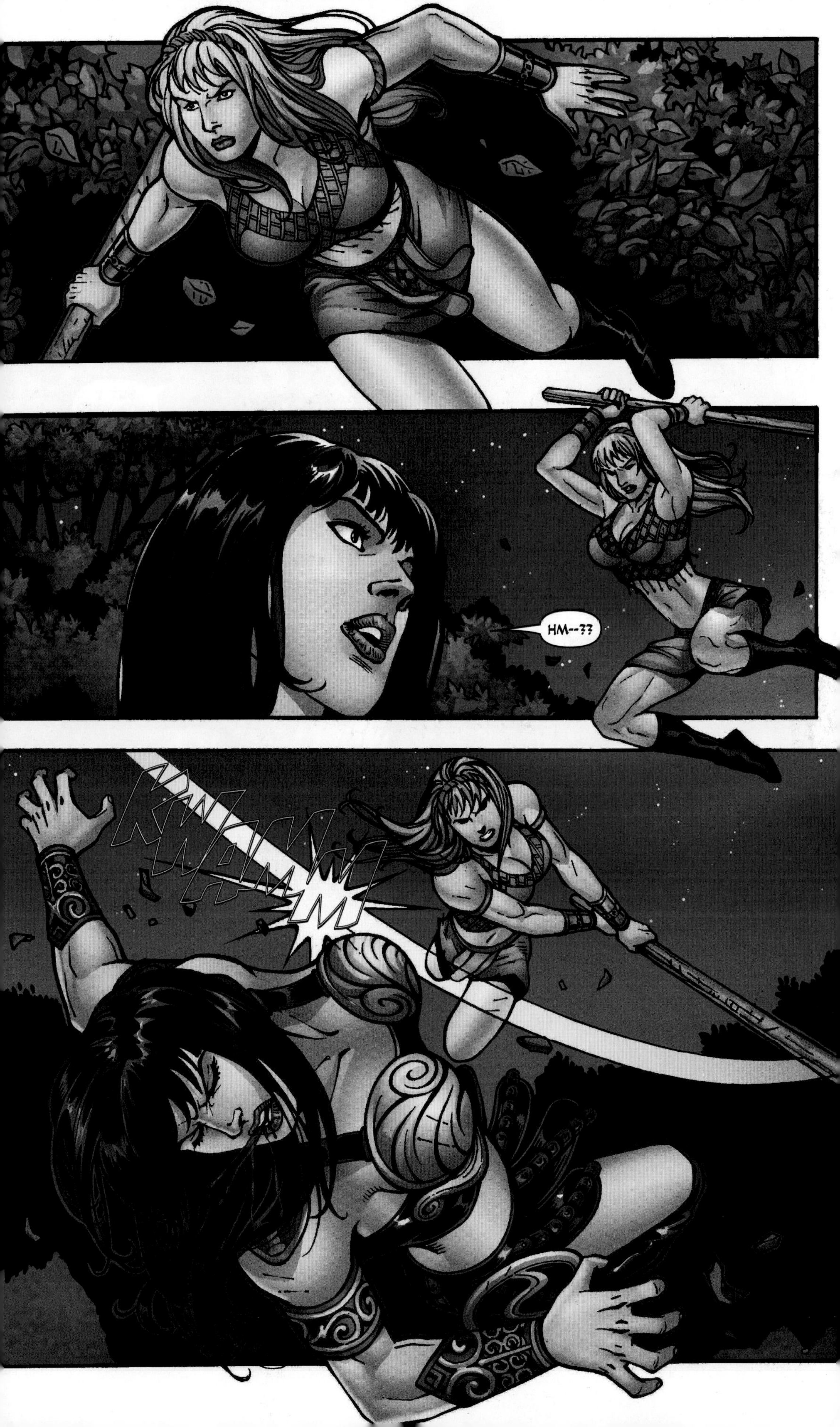
HM--??

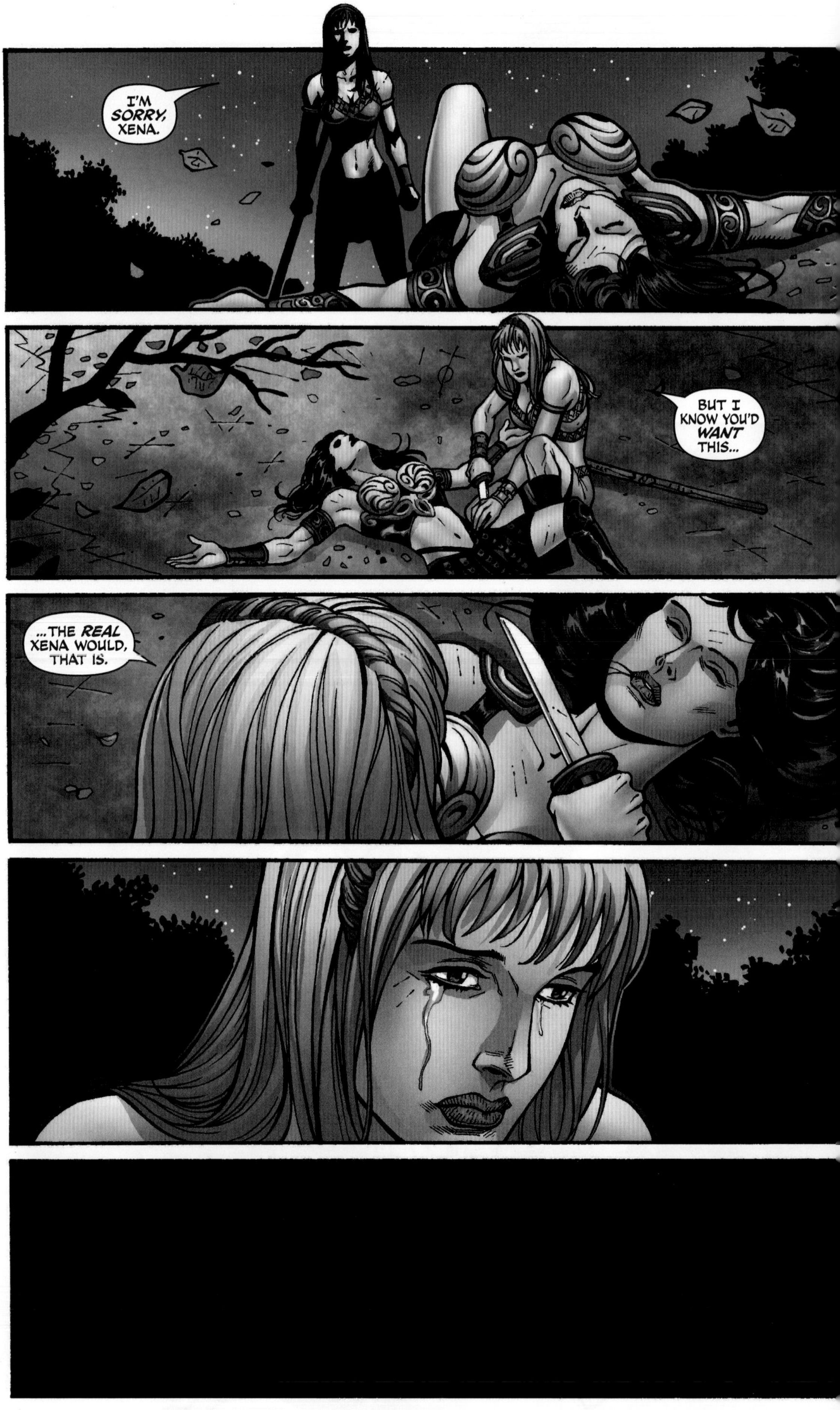
I'M SORRY, XENA.
BUT I KNOW YOU'D WANT THIS...
...THE REAL XENA WOULD, THAT IS.

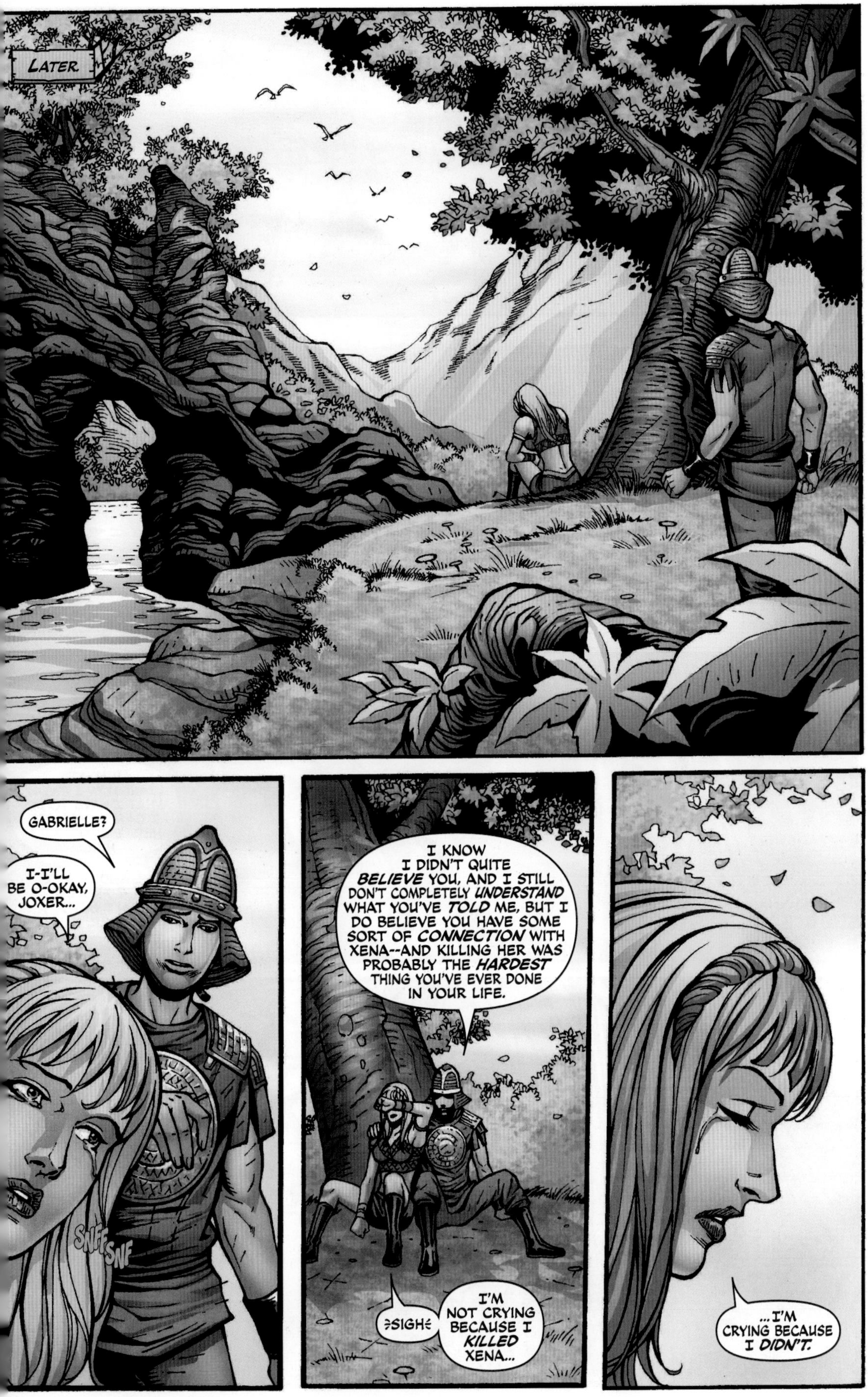
LATER
GABRIELLE?
I-I'LL BE O-OKAY, JOXER...
SNIF SNIF
I KNOW I DIDN'T QUITE BELIEVE YOU, AND I STILL DON'T COMPLETELY UNDERSTAND WHAT YOU'VE TOLD ME, BUT I DO BELIEVE YOU HAVE SOME SORT OF CONNECTION WITH XENA--AND KILLING HER WAS PROBABLY THE HARDEST THING YOU'VE EVER DONE IN YOUR LIFE.
SIGH
I'M NOT CRYING BECAUSE I KILLED XENA...
...I'M CRYING BECAUSE I DIDN'T.

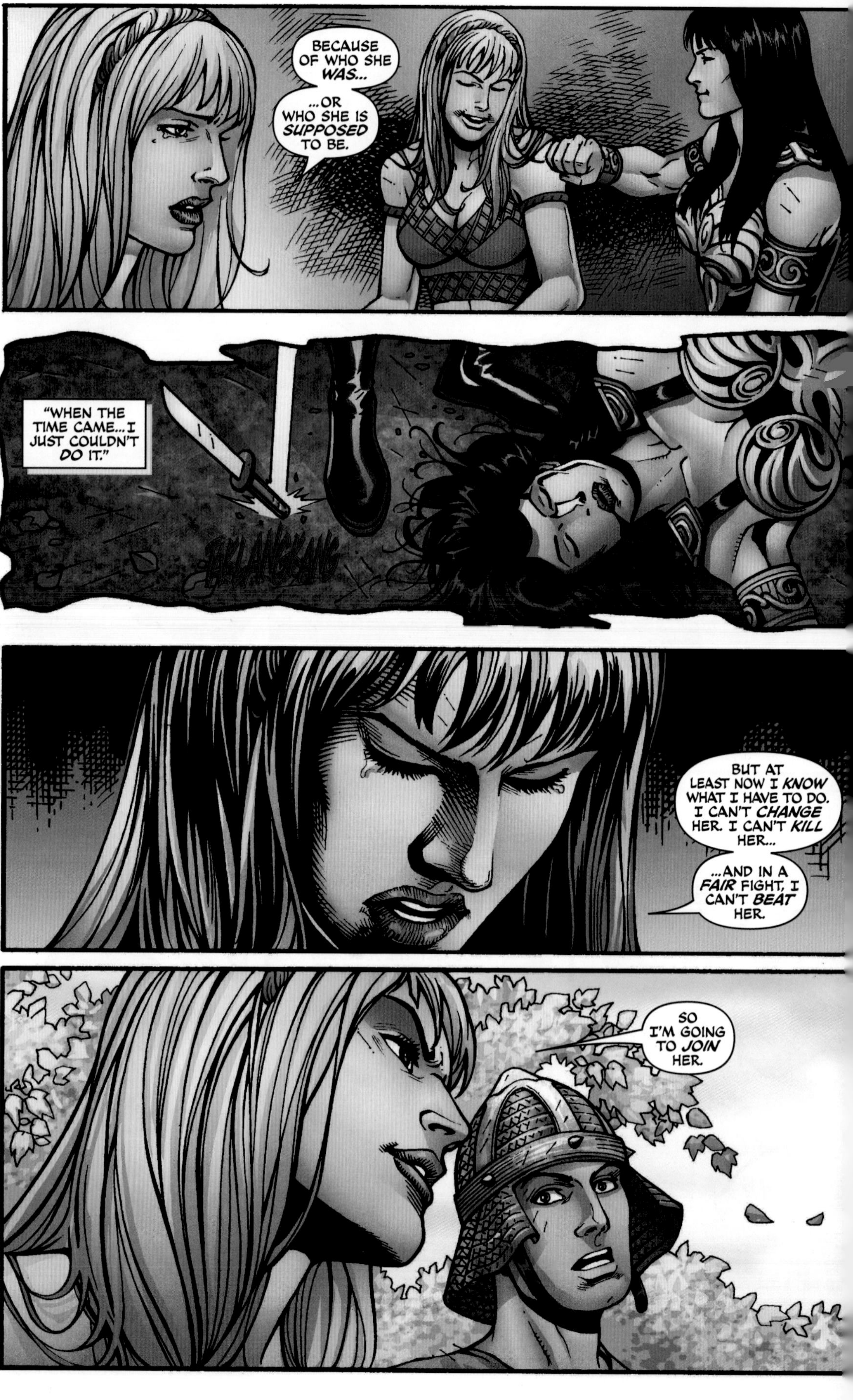
BECAUSE OF WHO SHE WAS...
...OR WHO SHE IS SUPPOSED TO BE.
"WHEN THE TIME CAME... I JUST COULDN'T DO IT."
BUT AT LEAST NOW I KNOW WHAT I HAVE TO DO. I CAN'T CHANGE HER. I CAN'T KILL HER...
...AND IN A FAIR FIGHT, I CAN'T BEAT HER.
SO I'M GOING TO JOIN HER.

DARK XENA
CHAPTER THREE

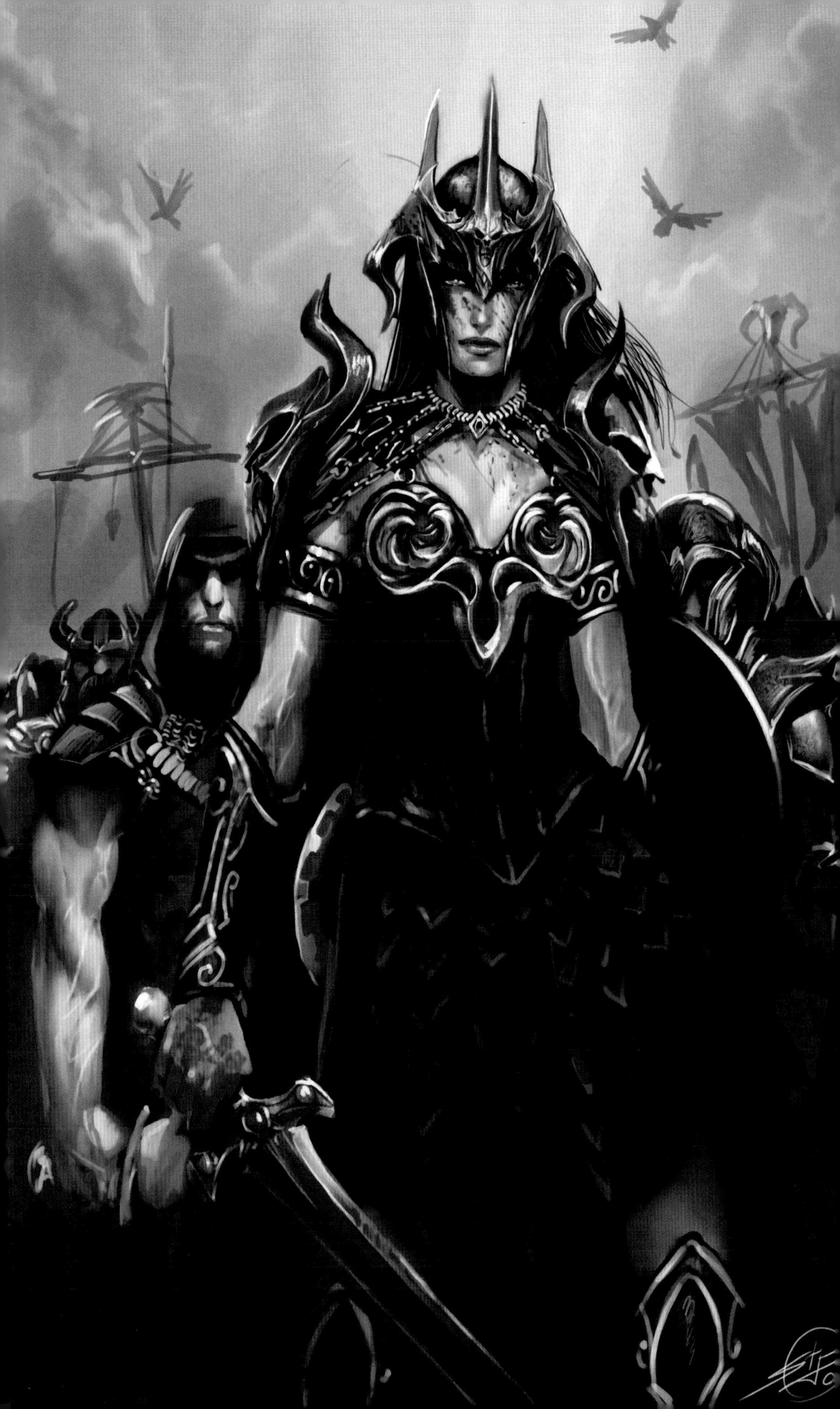

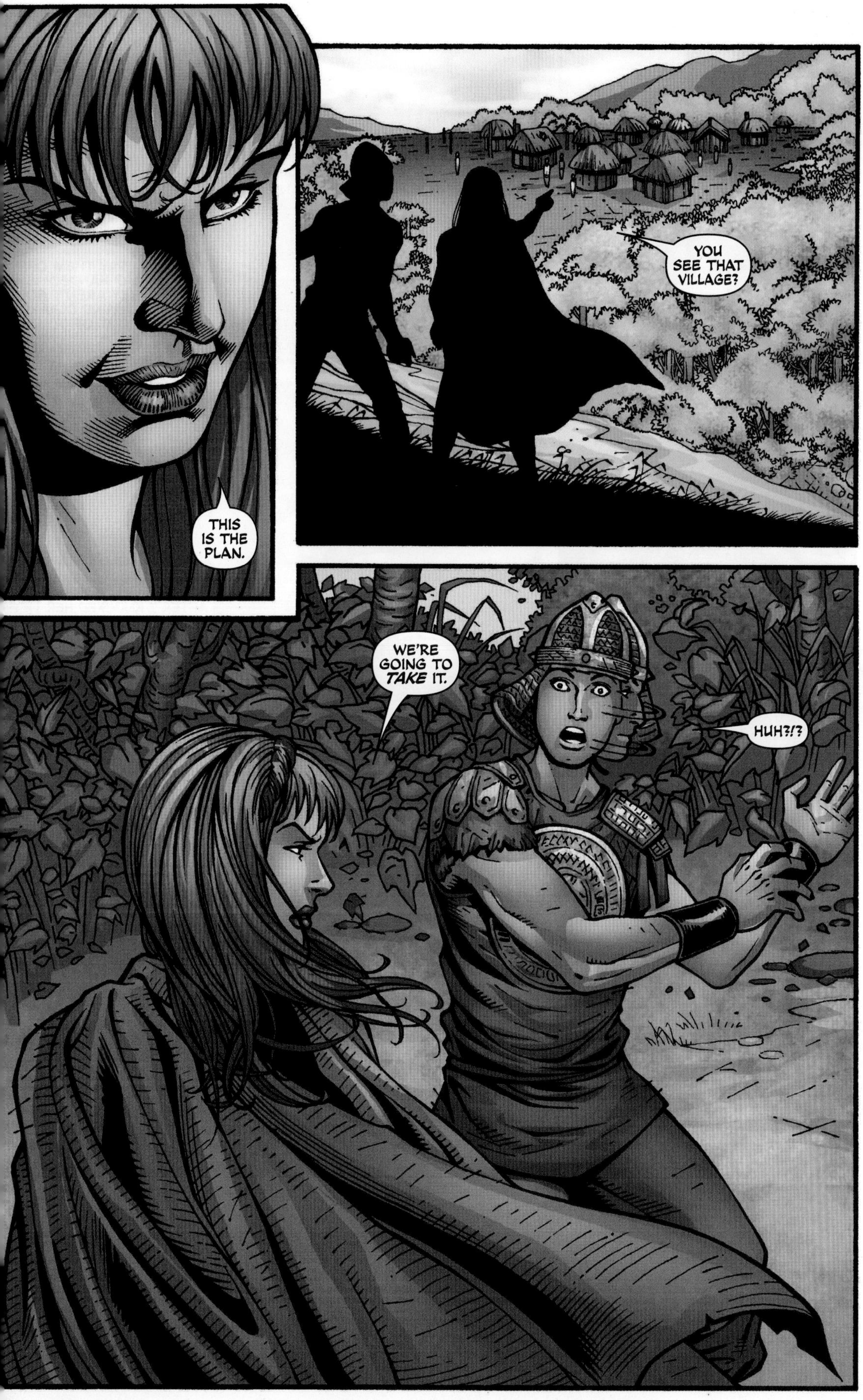
THIS IS THE PLAN.
YOU SEE THAT VILLAGE?
WE'RE GOING TO *TAKE* IT.
HUH?!?

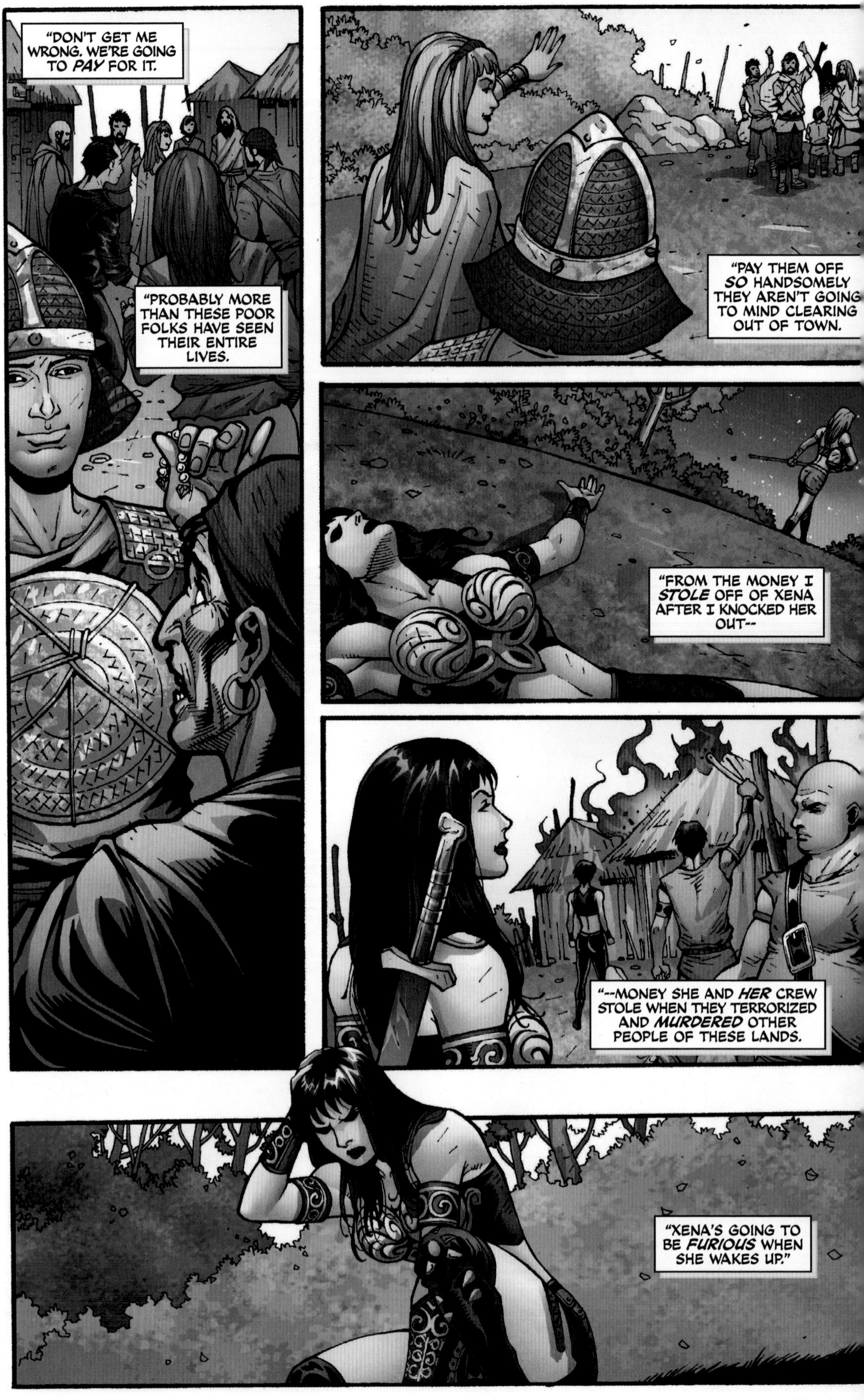
"DON'T GET ME WRONG. WE'RE GOING TO *PAY* FOR IT.
"PROBABLY MORE THAN THESE POOR FOLKS HAVE SEEN THEIR ENTIRE LIVES.
"PAY THEM OFF *SO* HANDSOMELY THEY AREN'T GOING TO MIND CLEARING OUT OF TOWN.
"FROM THE MONEY I *STOLE* OFF OF XENA AFTER I KNOCKED HER OUT--
"--MONEY SHE AND *HER* CREW STOLE WHEN THEY TERRORIZED AND *MURDERED* OTHER PEOPLE OF THESE LANDS.
"XENA'S GOING TO BE *FURIOUS* WHEN SHE WAKES UP."

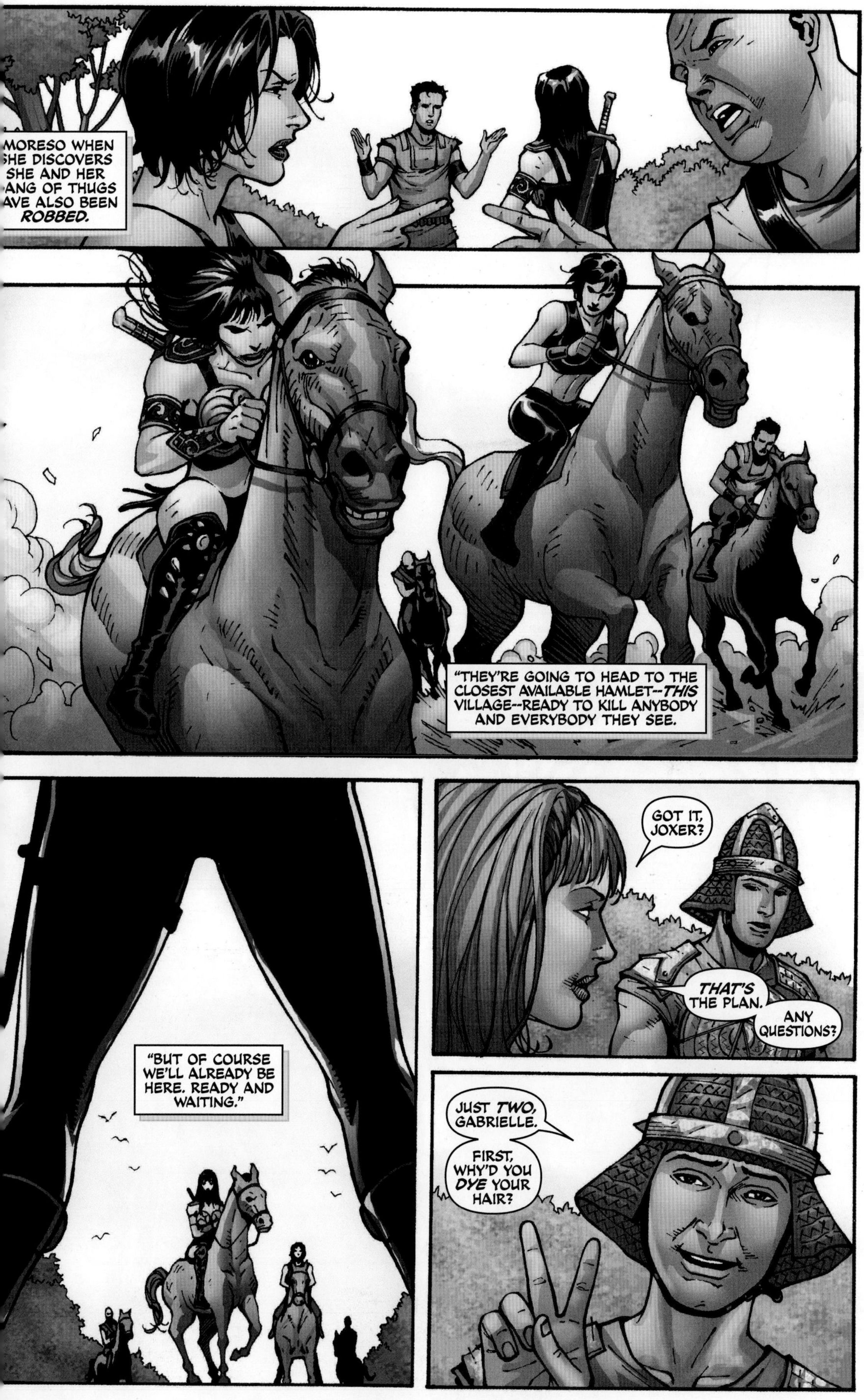
MORESO WHEN SHE DISCOVERS SHE AND HER GANG OF THUGS HAVE ALSO BEEN *ROBBED.*
"THEY'RE GOING TO HEAD TO THE CLOSEST AVAILABLE HAMLET--*THIS* VILLAGE--READY TO KILL ANYBODY AND EVERYBODY THEY SEE.
"BUT OF COURSE WE'LL ALREADY BE HERE. READY AND WAITING."
GOT IT, JOXER?
THAT'S THE PLAN.
ANY QUESTIONS?
JUST *TWO*, GABRIELLE.
FIRST, WHY'D YOU *DYE* YOUR HAIR?

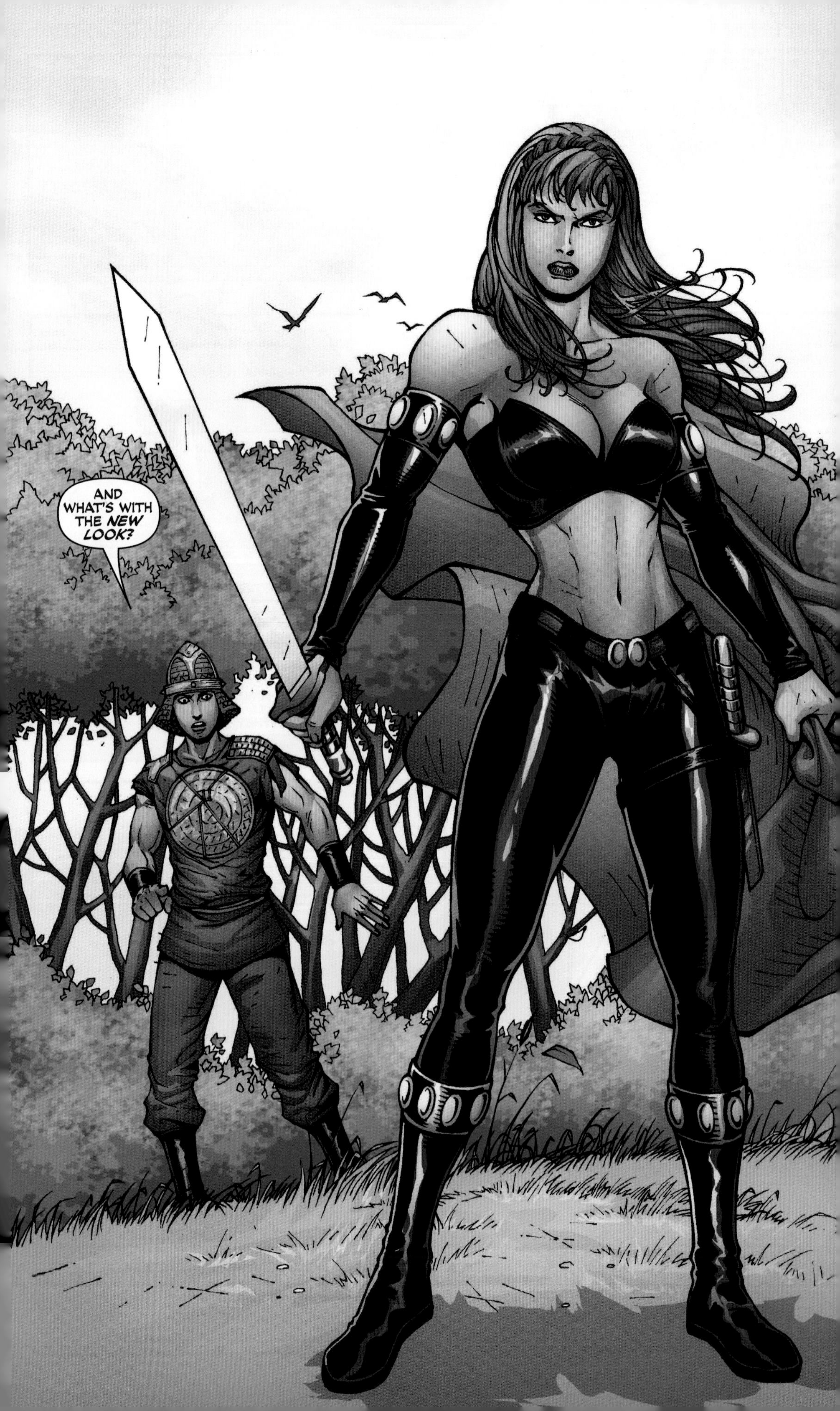
AND WHAT'S WITH THE NEW LOOK?

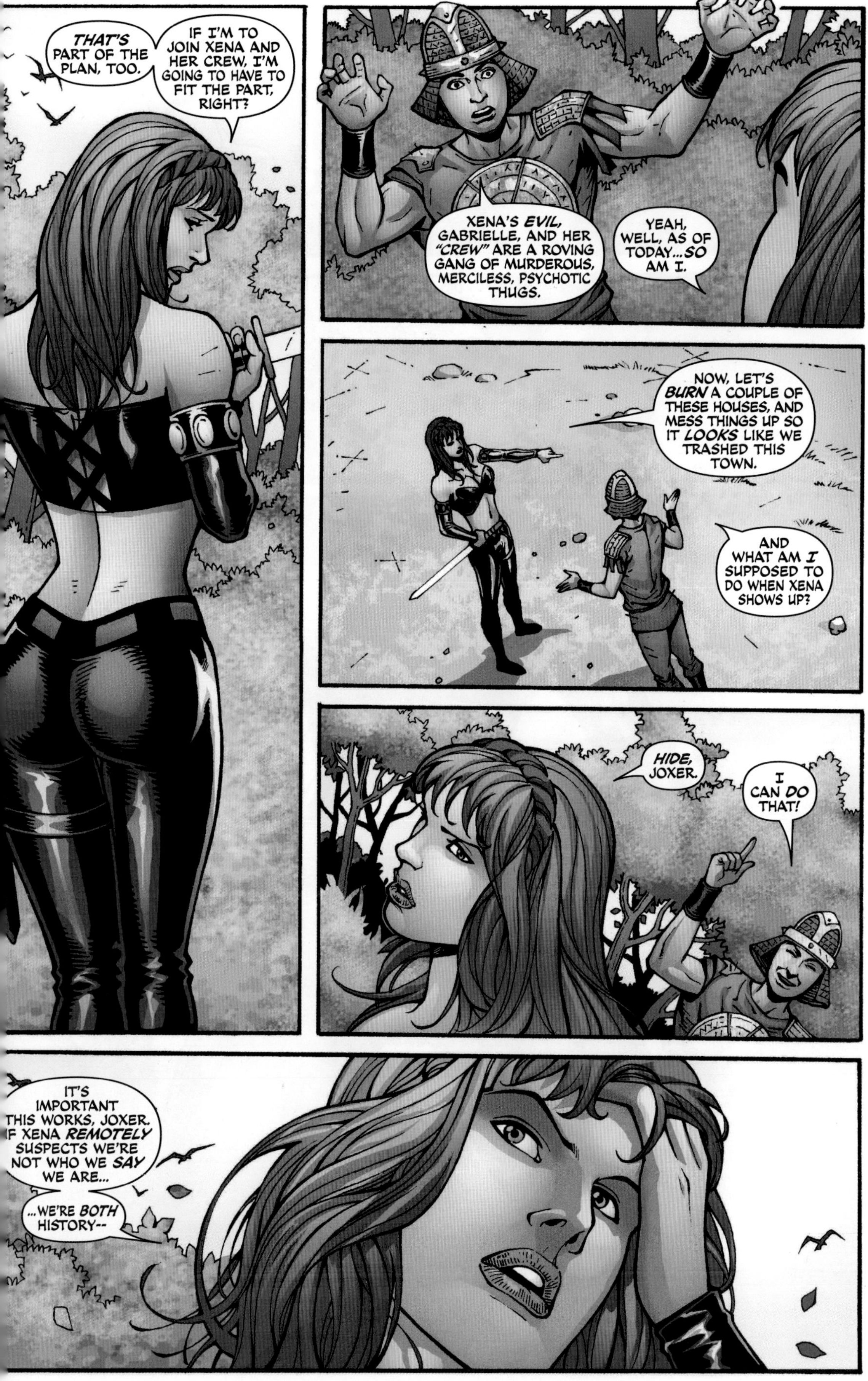
THAT'S PART OF THE PLAN, TOO.
IF I'M TO JOIN XENA AND HER CREW, I'M GOING TO HAVE TO FIT THE PART, RIGHT?
XENA'S EVIL, GABRIELLE, AND HER "CREW" ARE A ROVING GANG OF MURDEROUS, MERCILESS, PSYCHOTIC THUGS.
YEAH, WELL, AS OF TODAY...SO AM I.
NOW, LET'S BURN A COUPLE OF THESE HOUSES, AND MESS THINGS UP SO IT LOOKS LIKE WE TRASHED THIS TOWN.
AND WHAT AM I SUPPOSED TO DO WHEN XENA SHOWS UP?
HIDE, JOXER.
I CAN DO THAT!
IT'S IMPORTANT THIS WORKS, JOXER. IF XENA REMOTELY SUSPECTS WE'RE NOT WHO WE SAY WE ARE...
...WE'RE BOTH HISTORY--

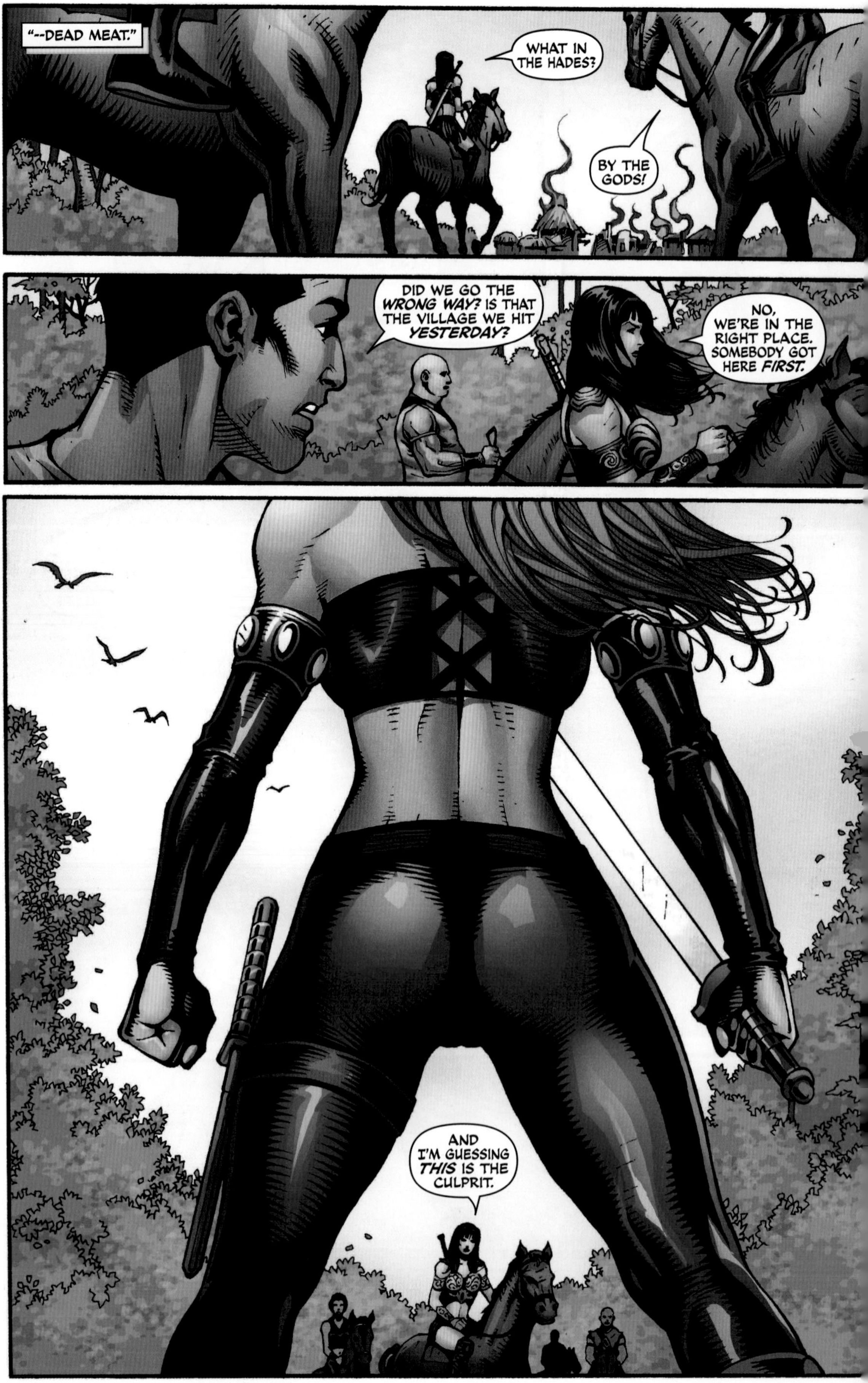
"--DEAD MEAT."
WHAT IN THE HADES?
BY THE GODS!
DID WE GO THE *WRONG WAY?* IS THAT THE VILLAGE WE HIT *YESTERDAY?*
NO, WE'RE IN THE RIGHT PLACE. SOMEBODY GOT HERE *FIRST.*
AND I'M GUESSING *THIS* IS THE CULPRIT.

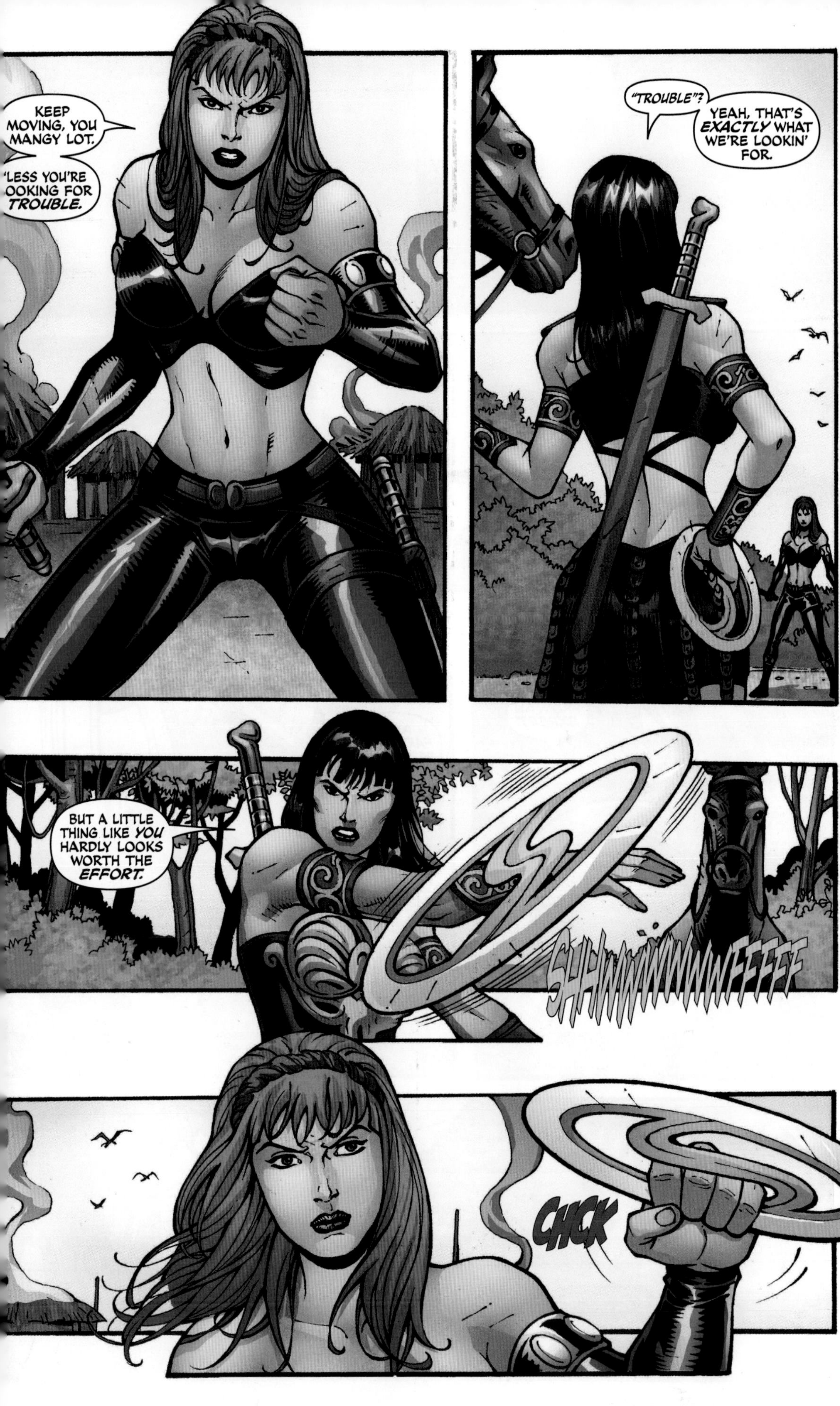
KEEP MOVING, YOU MANGY LOT.
'LESS YOU'RE LOOKING FOR *TROUBLE.*
"TROUBLE"?
YEAH, THAT'S *EXACTLY* WHAT WE'RE LOOKIN' FOR.
BUT A LITTLE THING LIKE *YOU* HARDLY LOOKS WORTH THE *EFFORT.*
SHHWWWWWWWFFFFF
CHCK

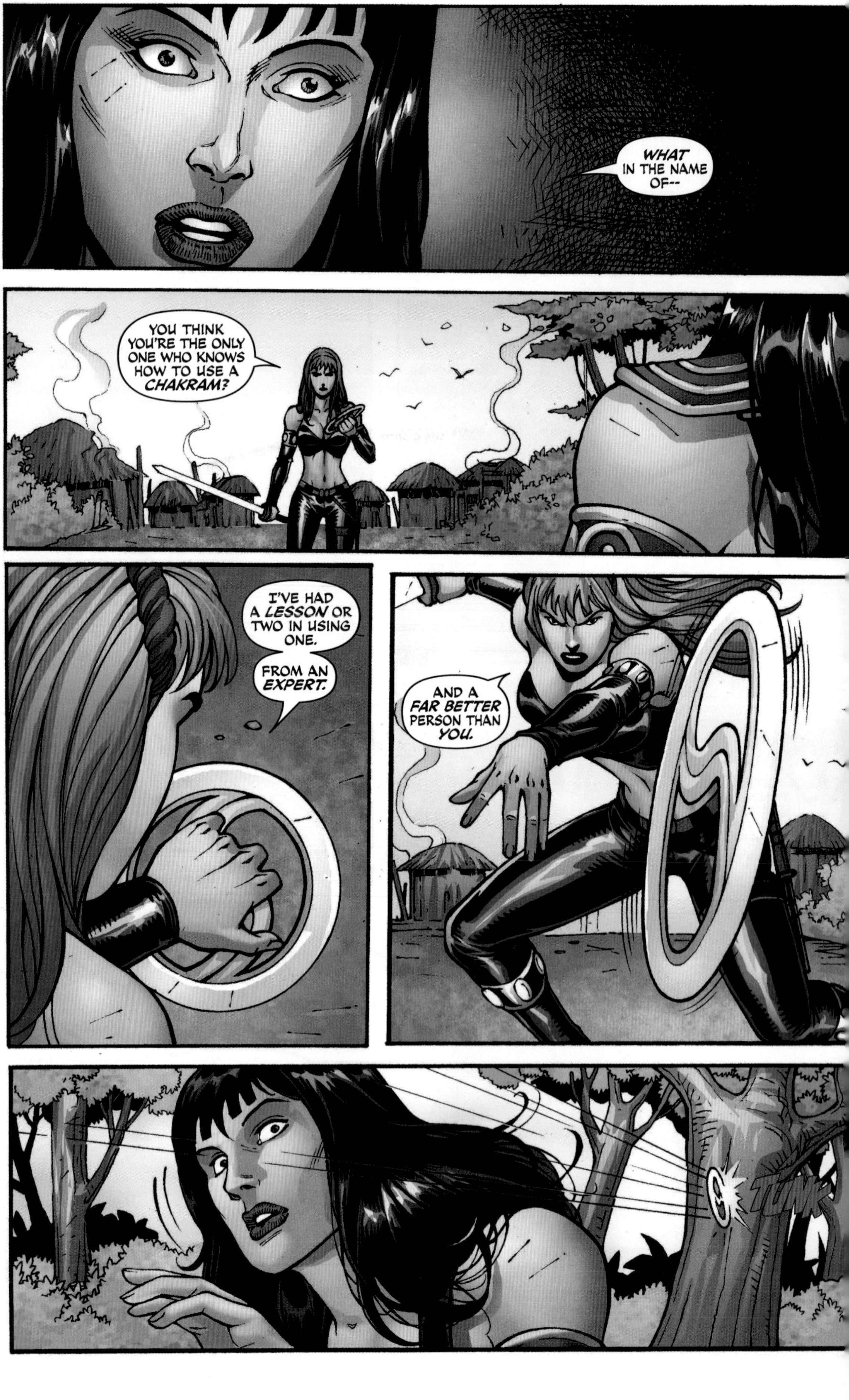
WHAT IN THE NAME OF--
YOU THINK YOU'RE THE ONLY ONE WHO KNOWS HOW TO USE A CHAKRAM?
I'VE HAD A LESSON OR TWO IN USING ONE.
FROM AN EXPERT.
AND A FAR BETTER PERSON THAN YOU.
TUNK

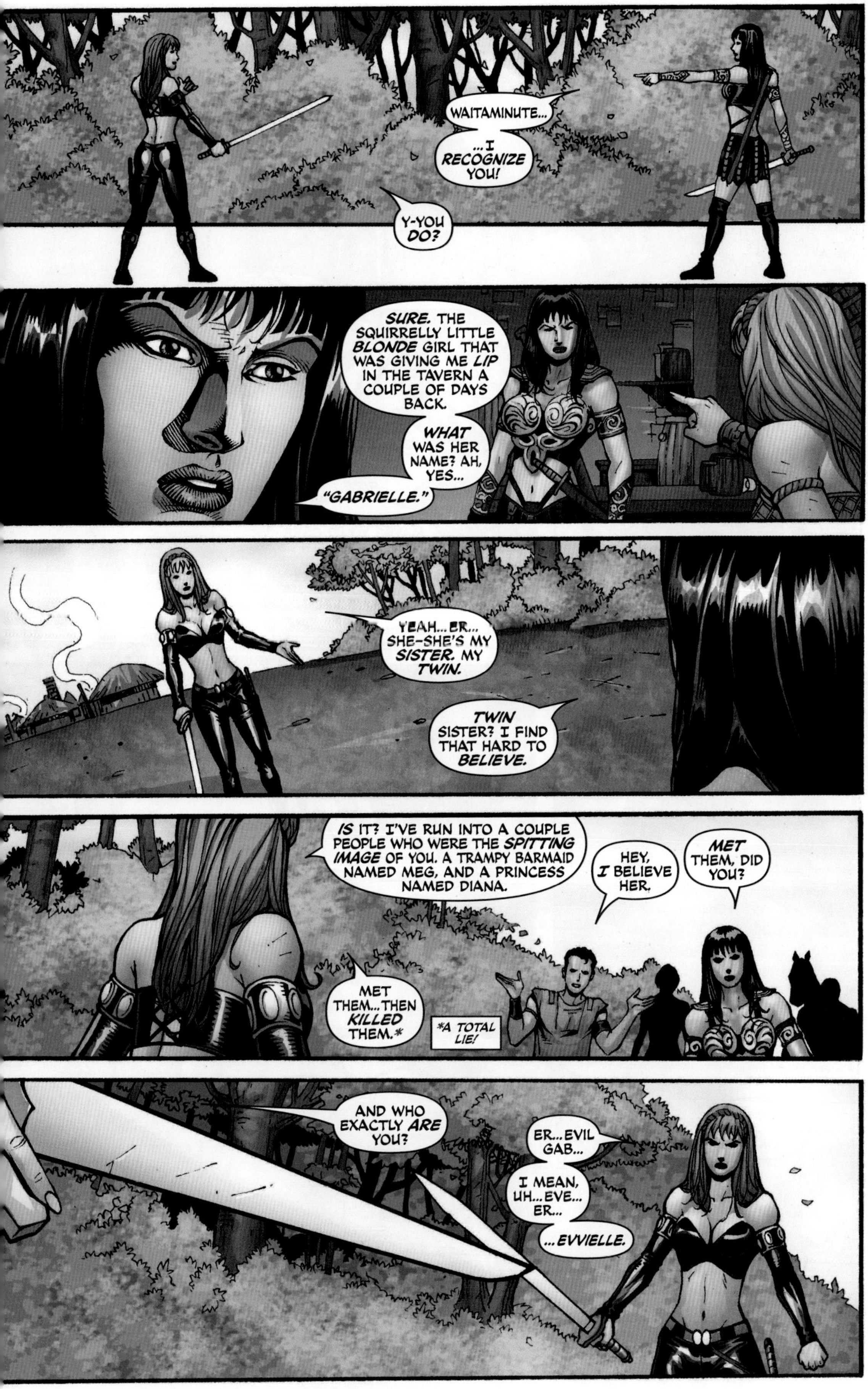

WAITAMINUTE...
...I RECOGNIZE YOU!
Y-YOU DO?
SURE. THE SQUIRRELLY LITTLE BLONDE GIRL THAT WAS GIVING ME LIP IN THE TAVERN A COUPLE OF DAYS BACK.
WHAT WAS HER NAME? AH, YES...
"GABRIELLE."
YEAH...ER... SHE-SHE'S MY SISTER. MY TWIN.
TWIN SISTER? I FIND THAT HARD TO BELIEVE.
IS IT? I'VE RUN INTO A COUPLE PEOPLE WHO WERE THE SPITTING IMAGE OF YOU. A TRAMPY BARMAID NAMED MEG, AND A PRINCESS NAMED DIANA.
HEY, I BELIEVE HER.
MET THEM, DID YOU?
MET THEM...THEN KILLED THEM.*
*A TOTAL LIE!
AND WHO EXACTLY ARE YOU?
ER...EVIL GAB...
I MEAN, UH...EVE... ER...
...EVVIELLE.

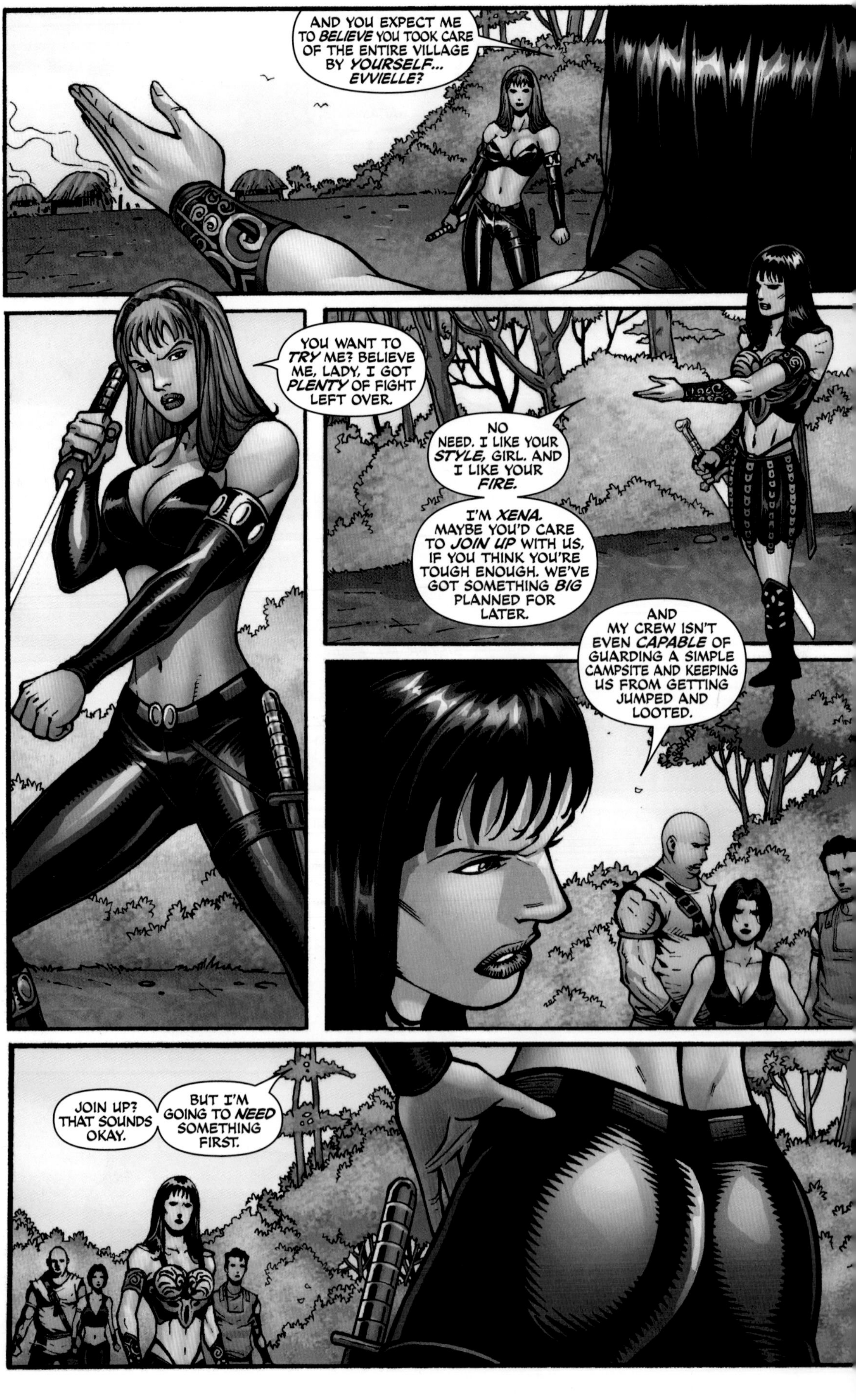
AND YOU EXPECT ME TO BELIEVE YOU TOOK CARE OF THE ENTIRE VILLAGE BY YOURSELF... EVVIELLE?
YOU WANT TO TRY ME? BELIEVE ME, LADY, I GOT PLENTY OF FIGHT LEFT OVER.
NO NEED. I LIKE YOUR STYLE, GIRL. AND I LIKE YOUR FIRE.
I'M XENA. MAYBE YOU'D CARE TO JOIN UP WITH US, IF YOU THINK YOU'RE TOUGH ENOUGH. WE'VE GOT SOMETHING BIG PLANNED FOR LATER.
AND MY CREW ISN'T EVEN CAPABLE OF GUARDING A SIMPLE CAMPSITE AND KEEPING US FROM GETTING JUMPED AND LOOTED.
JOIN UP? THAT SOUNDS OKAY.
BUT I'M GOING TO NEED SOMETHING FIRST.

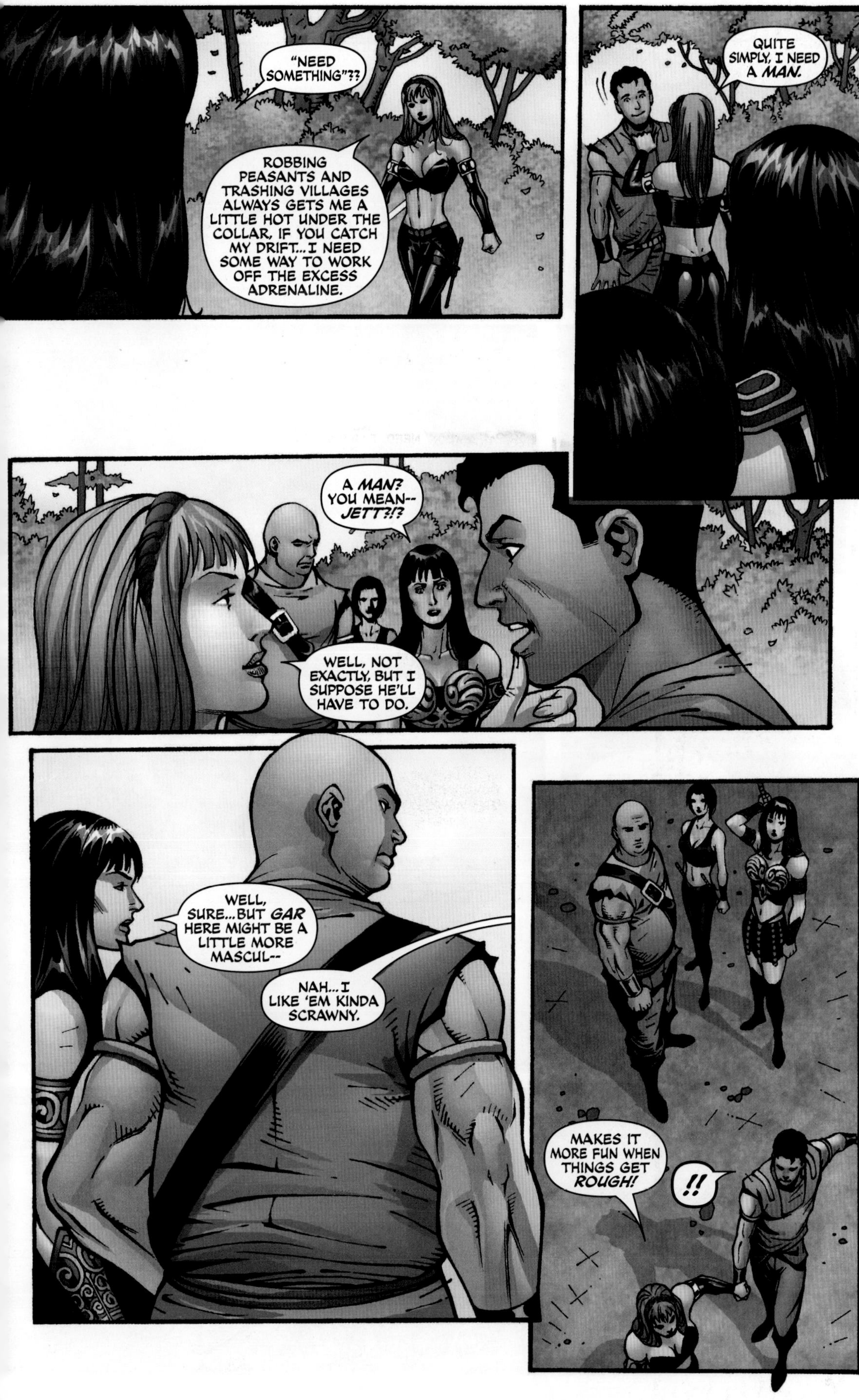
"NEED SOMETHING"??
ROBBING PEASANTS AND TRASHING VILLAGES ALWAYS GETS ME A LITTLE HOT UNDER THE COLLAR, IF YOU CATCH MY DRIFT...I NEED SOME WAY TO WORK OFF THE EXCESS ADRENALINE.
QUITE SIMPLY, I NEED A *MAN.*
A *MAN?* YOU MEAN-- *JETT?!?*
WELL, NOT EXACTLY, BUT I SUPPOSE HE'LL HAVE TO DO.
WELL, SURE...BUT *GAR* HERE MIGHT BE A LITTLE MORE MASCUL--
NAH...I LIKE 'EM KINDA SCRAWNY.
MAKES IT MORE FUN WHEN THINGS GET *ROUGH!*
!!

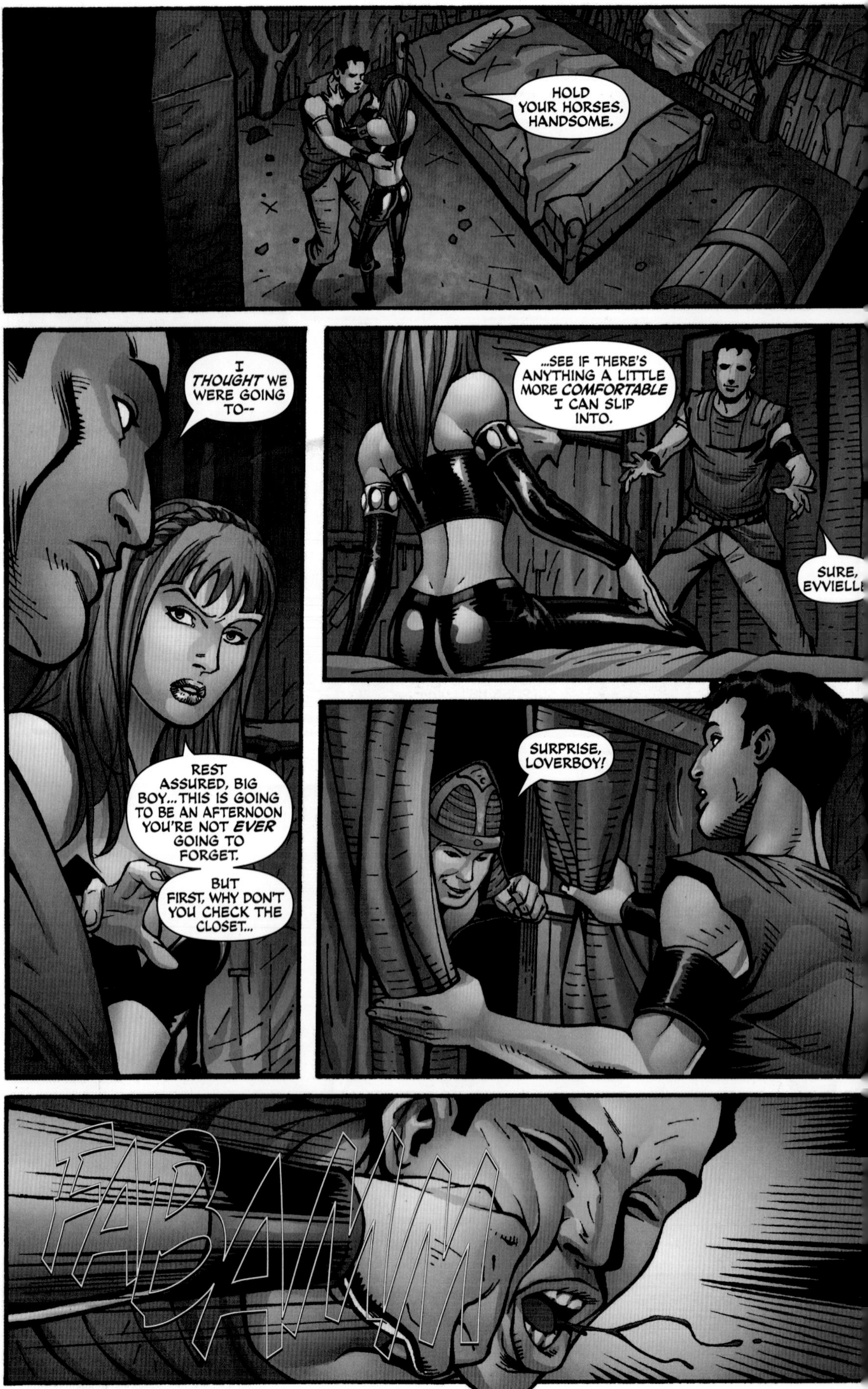
HOLD YOUR HORSES, HANDSOME.
I THOUGHT WE WERE GOING TO--
REST ASSURED, BIG BOY...THIS IS GOING TO BE AN AFTERNOON YOU'RE NOT EVER GOING TO FORGET.
BUT FIRST, WHY DON'T YOU CHECK THE CLOSET...
...SEE IF THERE'S ANYTHING A LITTLE MORE COMFORTABLE I CAN SLIP INTO.
SURE, EVVIELLE
SURPRISE, LOVERBOY!
FABAMM

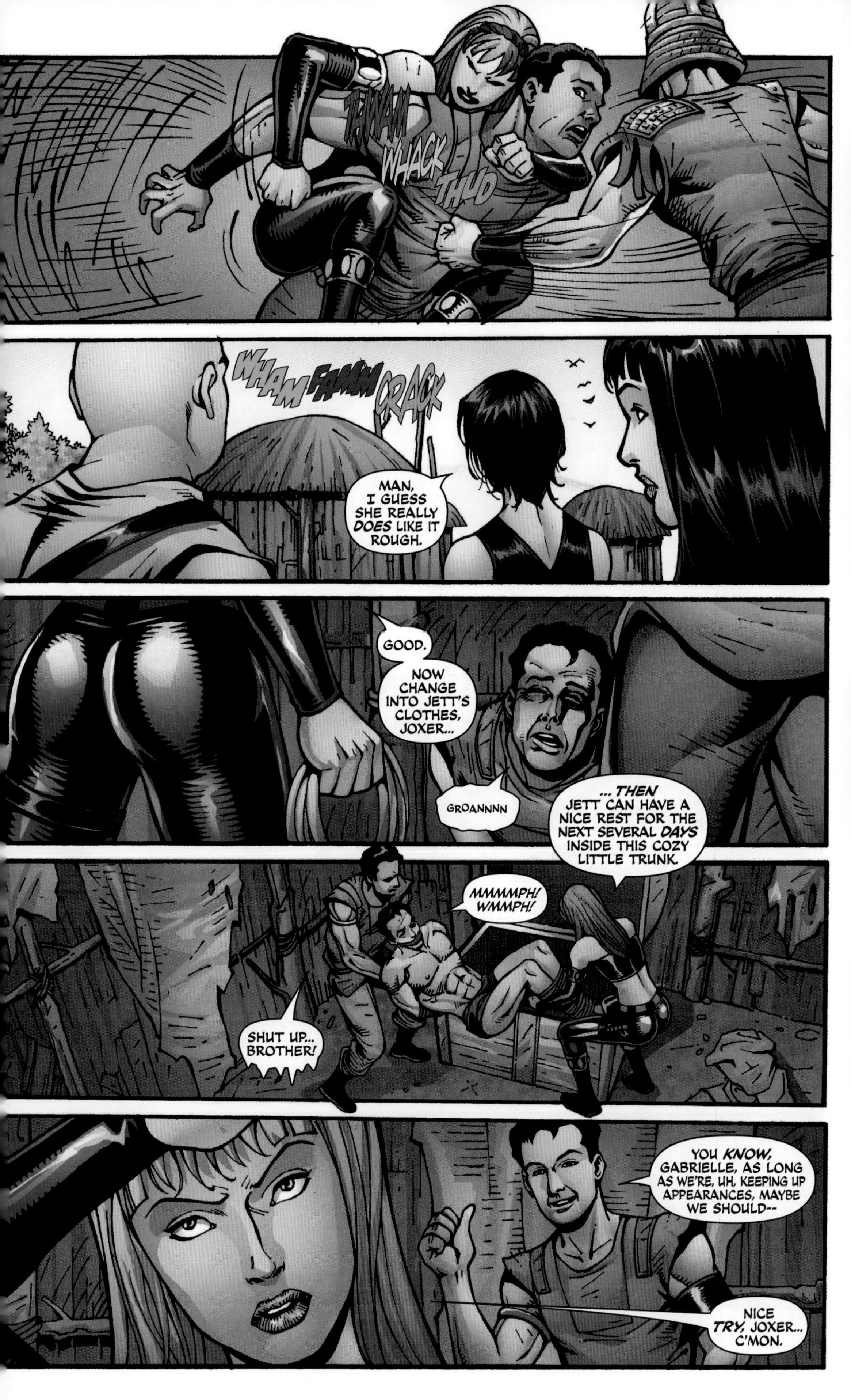
THWAM
WHACK
THUD
WHAM
FAMM
CRACK
MAN, I GUESS SHE REALLY *DOES* LIKE IT ROUGH.
GOOD.
NOW CHANGE INTO JETT'S CLOTHES, JOXER...
GROANNNN
...*THEN* JETT CAN HAVE A NICE REST FOR THE NEXT SEVERAL *DAYS* INSIDE THIS COZY LITTLE TRUNK.
MMMMPH! WMMPH!
SHUT UP... BROTHER!
YOU *KNOW,* GABRIELLE, AS LONG AS WE'RE, UH, KEEPING UP APPEARANCES, MAYBE WE SHOULD--
NICE *TRY,* JOXER... C'MON.

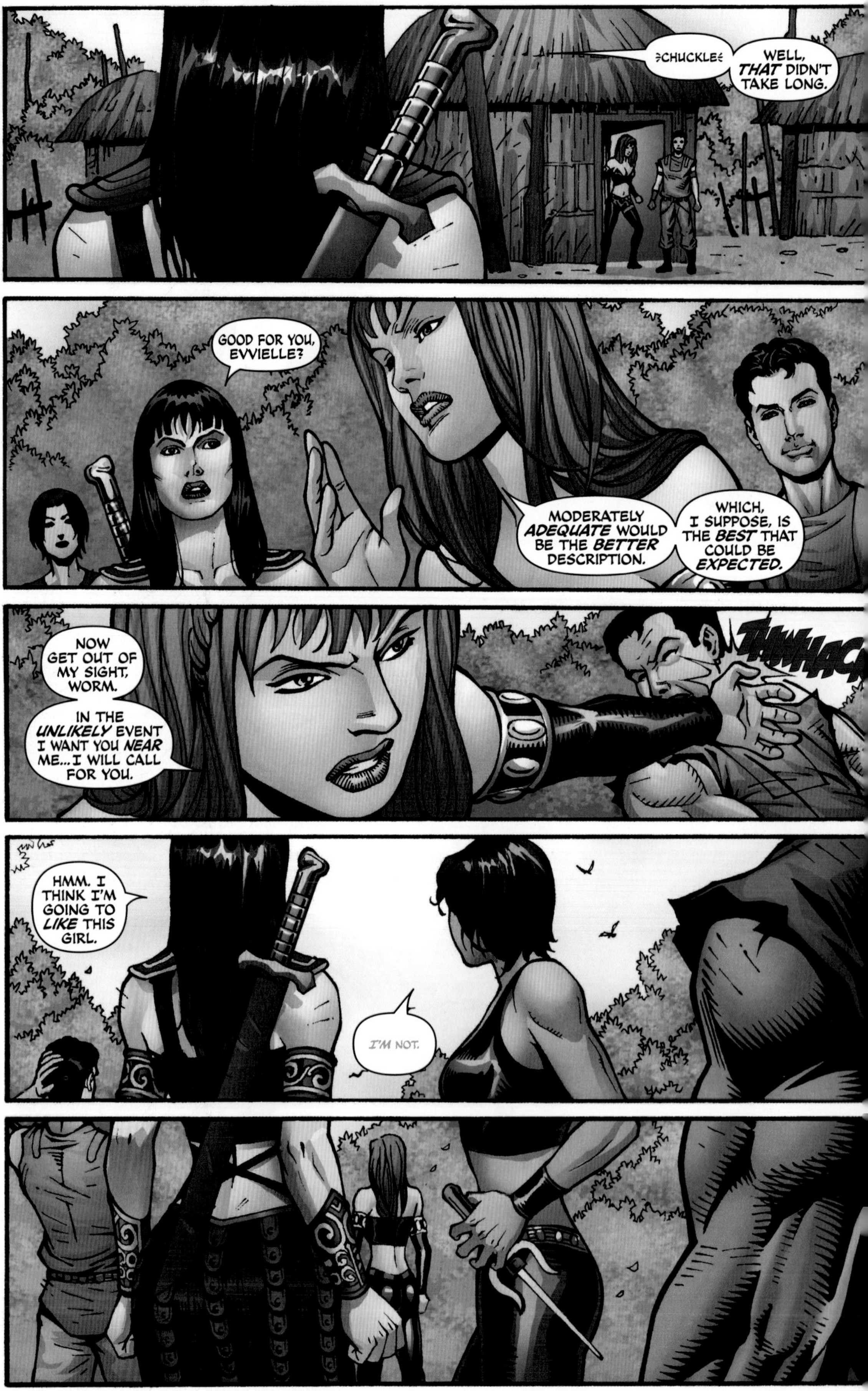

CHUCKLE
WELL, THAT DIDN'T TAKE LONG.
GOOD FOR YOU, EVVIELLE?
MODERATELY ADEQUATE WOULD BE THE BETTER DESCRIPTION.
WHICH, I SUPPOSE, IS THE BEST THAT COULD BE EXPECTED.
NOW GET OUT OF MY SIGHT, WORM.
IN THE UNLIKELY EVENT I WANT YOU NEAR ME...I WILL CALL FOR YOU.
HMM. I THINK I'M GOING TO LIKE THIS GIRL.
I'M NOT.

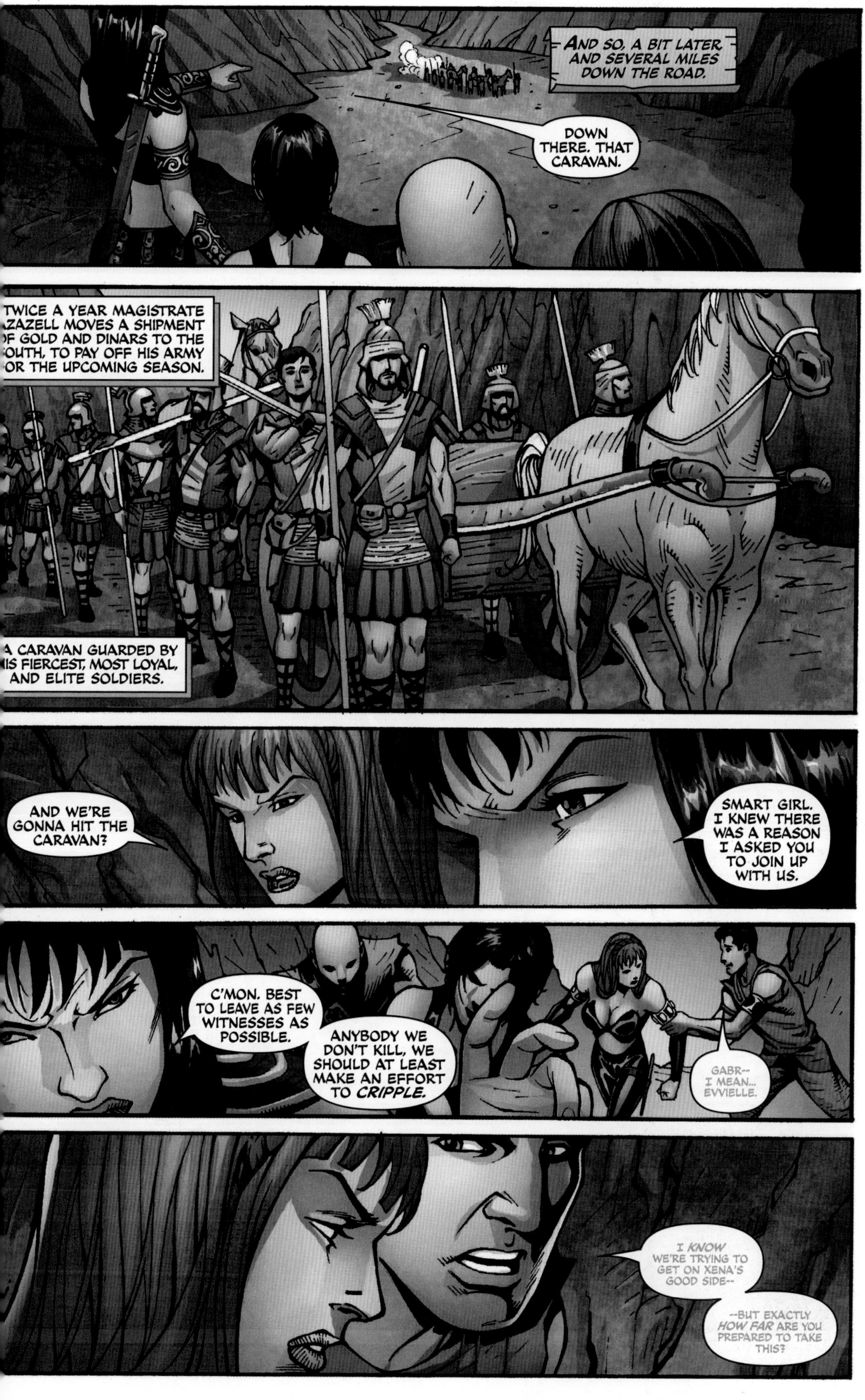
AND SO, A BIT LATER AND SEVERAL MILES DOWN THE ROAD.
DOWN THERE. THAT CARAVAN.
TWICE A YEAR MAGISTRATE AZAZELL MOVES A SHIPMENT OF GOLD AND DINARS TO THE SOUTH, TO PAY OFF HIS ARMY FOR THE UPCOMING SEASON.
A CARAVAN GUARDED BY HIS FIERCEST, MOST LOYAL, AND ELITE SOLDIERS.
AND WE'RE GONNA HIT THE CARAVAN?
SMART GIRL. I KNEW THERE WAS A REASON I ASKED YOU TO JOIN UP WITH US.
C'MON. BEST TO LEAVE AS FEW WITNESSES AS POSSIBLE.
ANYBODY WE DON'T KILL, WE SHOULD AT LEAST MAKE AN EFFORT TO *CRIPPLE.*
GABR-- I MEAN... EVVIELLE.
I *KNOW* WE'RE TRYING TO GET ON XENA'S GOOD SIDE--
--BUT EXACTLY *HOW FAR* ARE YOU PREPARED TO TAKE THIS?

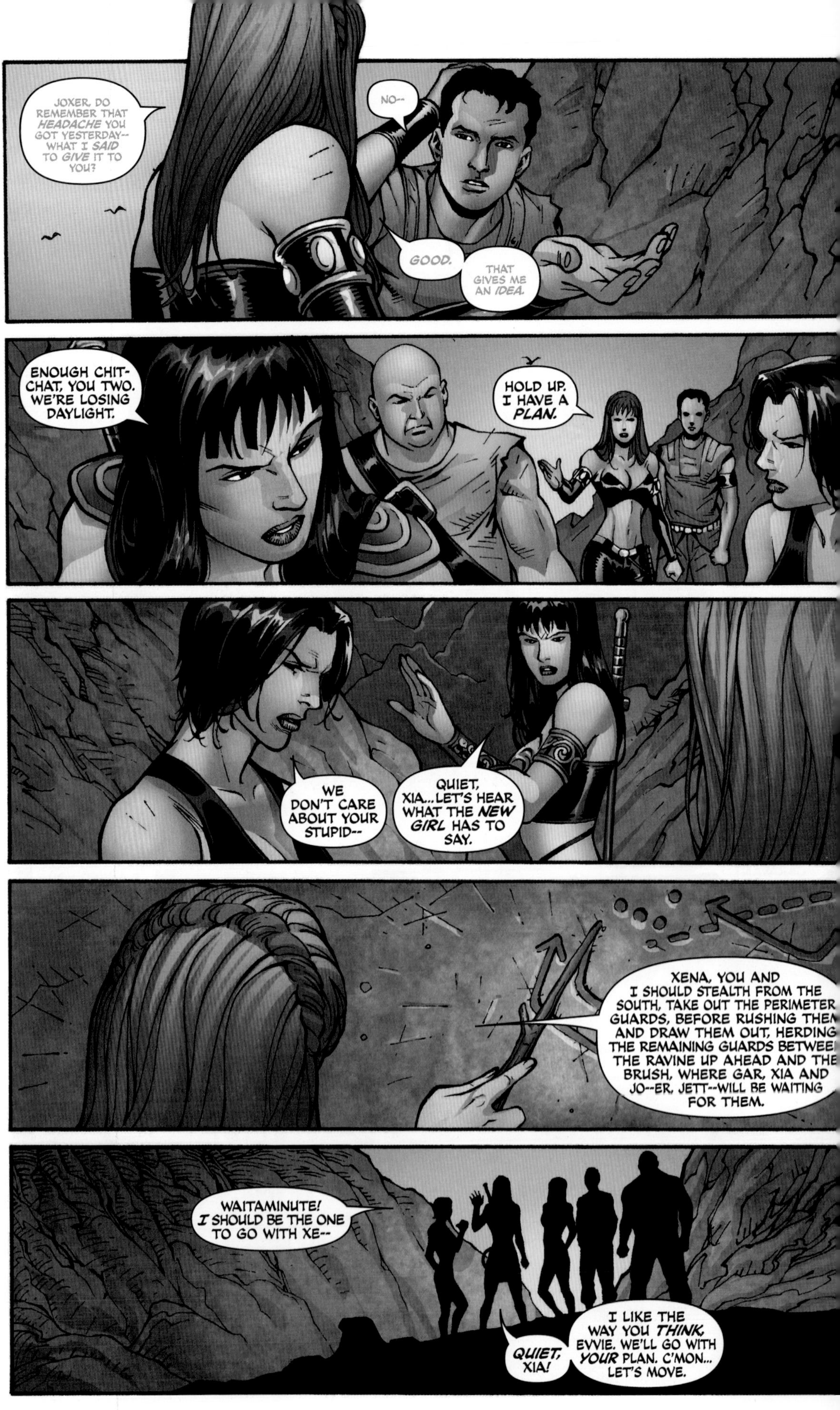
JOXER, DO REMEMBER THAT HEADACHE YOU GOT YESTERDAY-- WHAT I SAID TO GIVE IT TO YOU?
NO--
GOOD.
THAT GIVES ME AN IDEA.
ENOUGH CHIT-CHAT, YOU TWO. WE'RE LOSING DAYLIGHT.
HOLD UP. I HAVE A PLAN.
WE DON'T CARE ABOUT YOUR STUPID--
QUIET, XIA...LET'S HEAR WHAT THE NEW GIRL HAS TO SAY.
XENA, YOU AND I SHOULD STEALTH FROM THE SOUTH, TAKE OUT THE PERIMETER GUARDS, BEFORE RUSHING THEM AND DRAW THEM OUT, HERDING THE REMAINING GUARDS BETWEEN THE RAVINE UP AHEAD AND THE BRUSH, WHERE GAR, XIA AND JO--ER, JETT--WILL BE WAITING FOR THEM.
WAITAMINUTE! I SHOULD BE THE ONE TO GO WITH XE--
QUIET, XIA!
I LIKE THE WAY YOU THINK, EVVIE. WE'LL GO WITH YOUR PLAN. C'MON... LET'S MOVE.

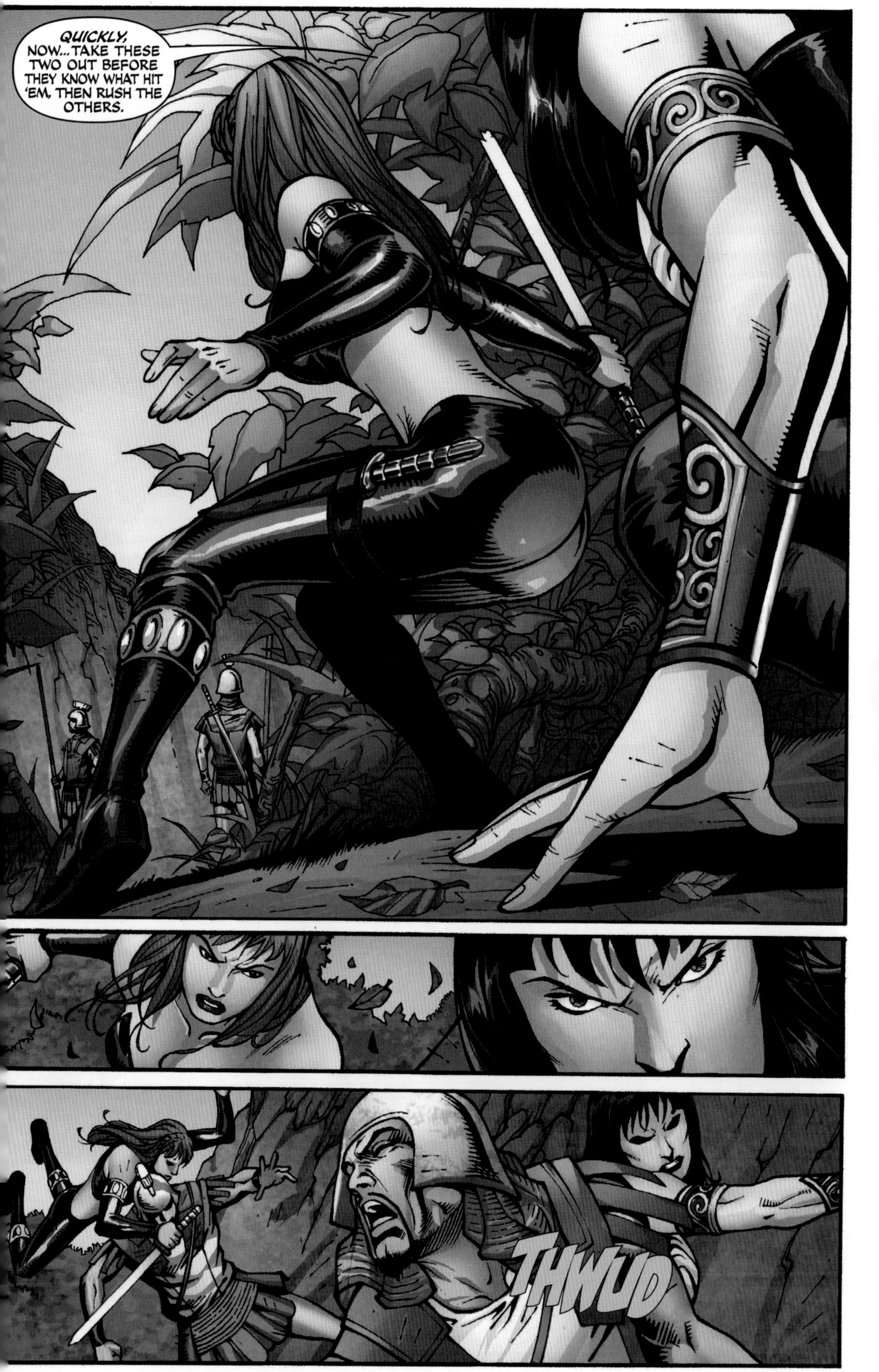
QUICKLY. NOW...TAKE THESE TWO OUT BEFORE THEY KNOW WHAT HIT 'EM, THEN RUSH THE OTHERS.
THWUD

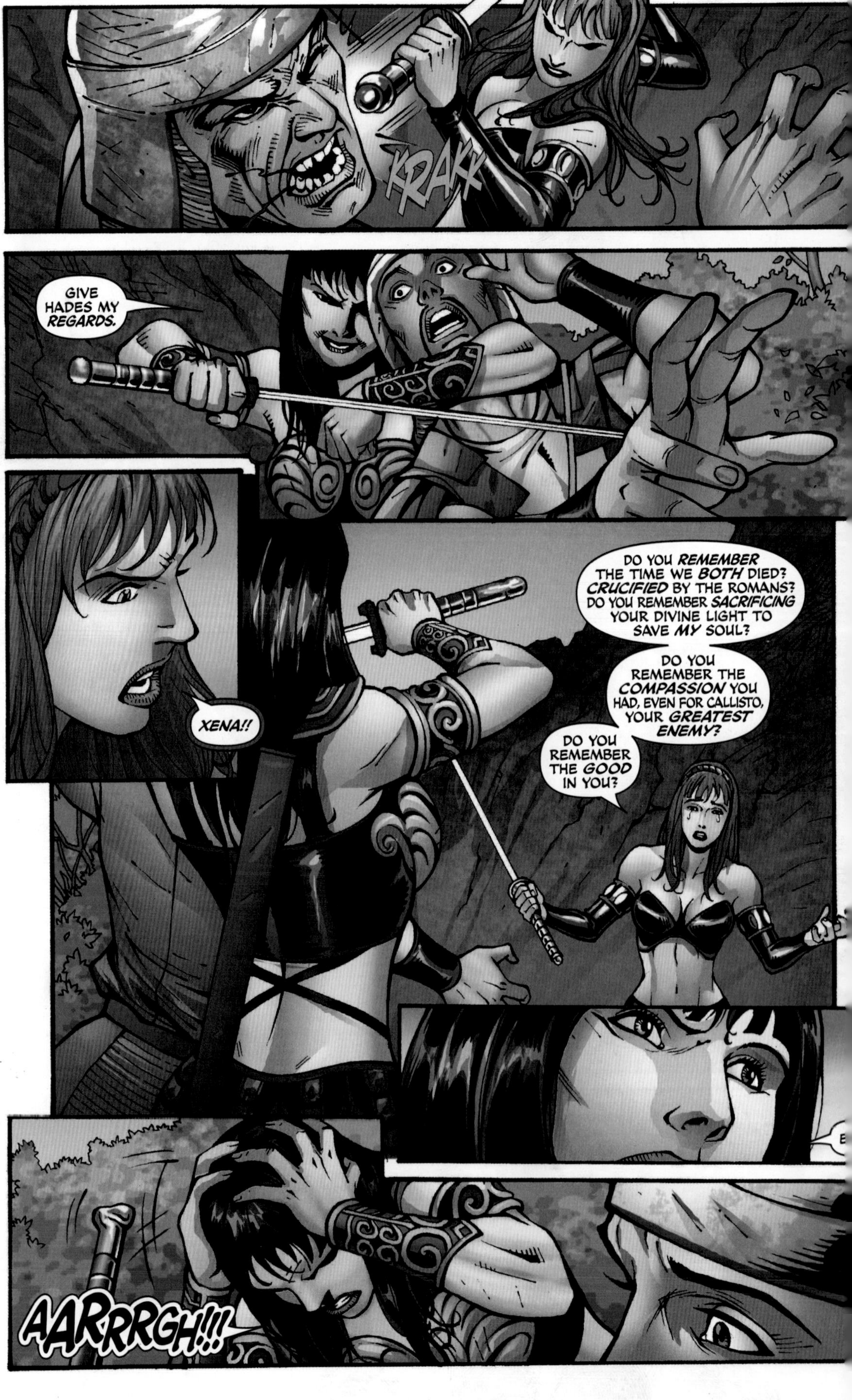

KRAKK
GIVE HADES MY REGARDS.
XENA!!
DO YOU REMEMBER THE TIME WE BOTH DIED? CRUCIFIED BY THE ROMANS? DO YOU REMEMBER SACRIFICING YOUR DIVINE LIGHT TO SAVE MY SOUL?
DO YOU REMEMBER THE COMPASSION YOU HAD, EVEN FOR CALLISTO, YOUR GREATEST ENEMY?
DO YOU REMEMBER THE GOOD IN YOU?
AARRRGH!!!

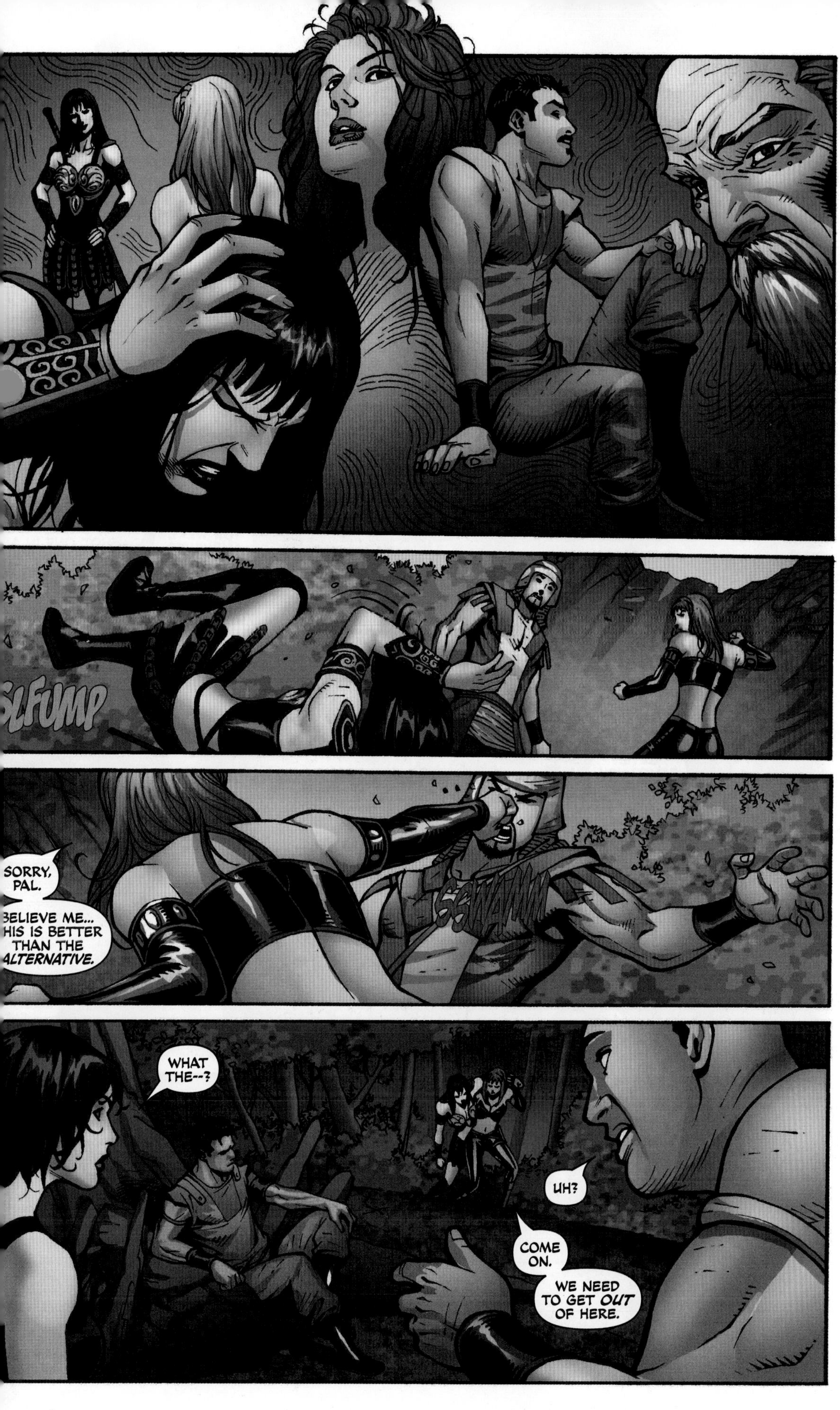
SLFUMP
SORRY, PAL.
BELIEVE ME... HIS IS BETTER THAN THE ALTERNATIVE.
SCWAMM
WHAT THE--?
UH?
COME ON.
WE NEED TO GET OUT OF HERE.

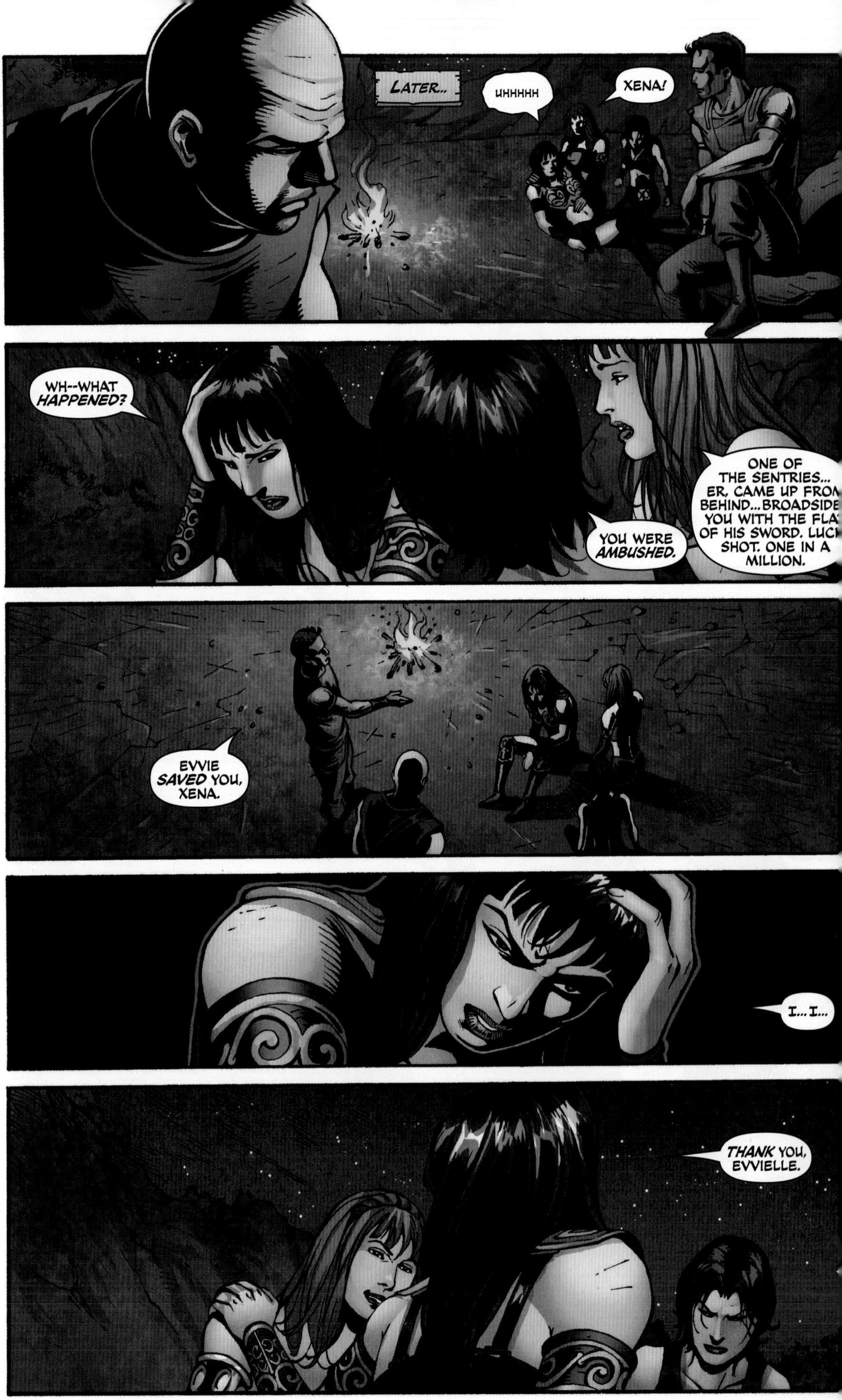
LATER...
UHHHHH
XENA!
WH--WHAT HAPPENED?
YOU WERE AMBUSHED.
ONE OF THE SENTRIES... ER, CAME UP FROM BEHIND...BROADSIDE YOU WITH THE FLA OF HIS SWORD. LUC SHOT. ONE IN A MILLION.
EVVIE SAVED YOU, XENA.
I... I...
THANK YOU, EVVIELLE.

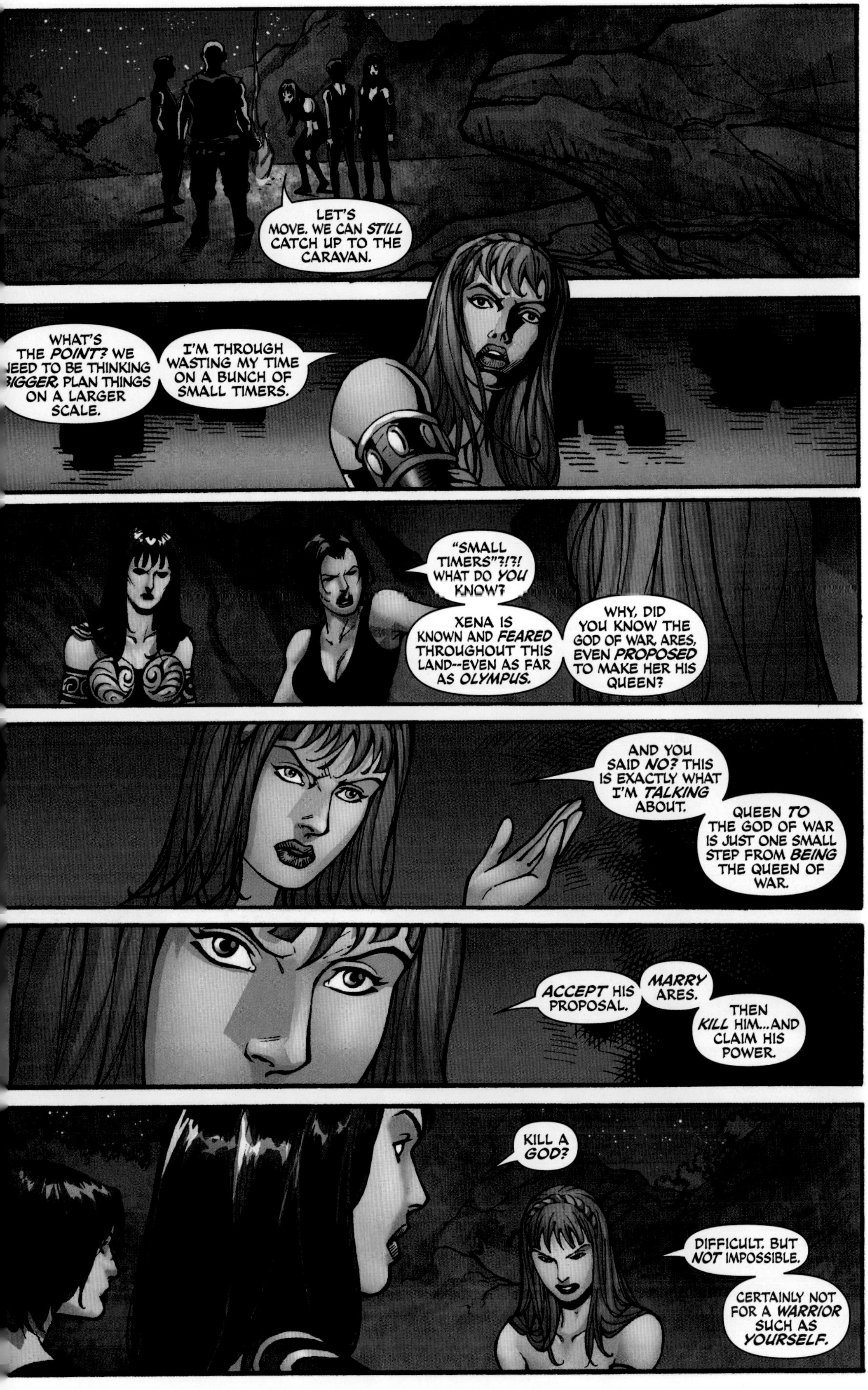
LET'S MOVE. WE CAN STILL CATCH UP TO THE CARAVAN.
WHAT'S THE POINT? WE NEED TO BE THINKING BIGGER, PLAN THINGS ON A LARGER SCALE.
I'M THROUGH WASTING MY TIME ON A BUNCH OF SMALL TIMERS.
"SMALL TIMERS"?!?! WHAT DO YOU KNOW?
XENA IS KNOWN AND FEARED THROUGHOUT THIS LAND--EVEN AS FAR AS OLYMPUS.
WHY, DID YOU KNOW THE GOD OF WAR, ARES, EVEN PROPOSED TO MAKE HER HIS QUEEN?
AND YOU SAID NO? THIS IS EXACTLY WHAT I'M TALKING ABOUT.
QUEEN TO THE GOD OF WAR IS JUST ONE SMALL STEP FROM BEING THE QUEEN OF WAR.
ACCEPT HIS PROPOSAL.
MARRY ARES.
THEN KILL HIM...AND CLAIM HIS POWER.
KILL A GOD?
DIFFICULT. BUT NOT IMPOSSIBLE.
CERTAINLY NOT FOR A WARRIOR SUCH AS YOURSELF.

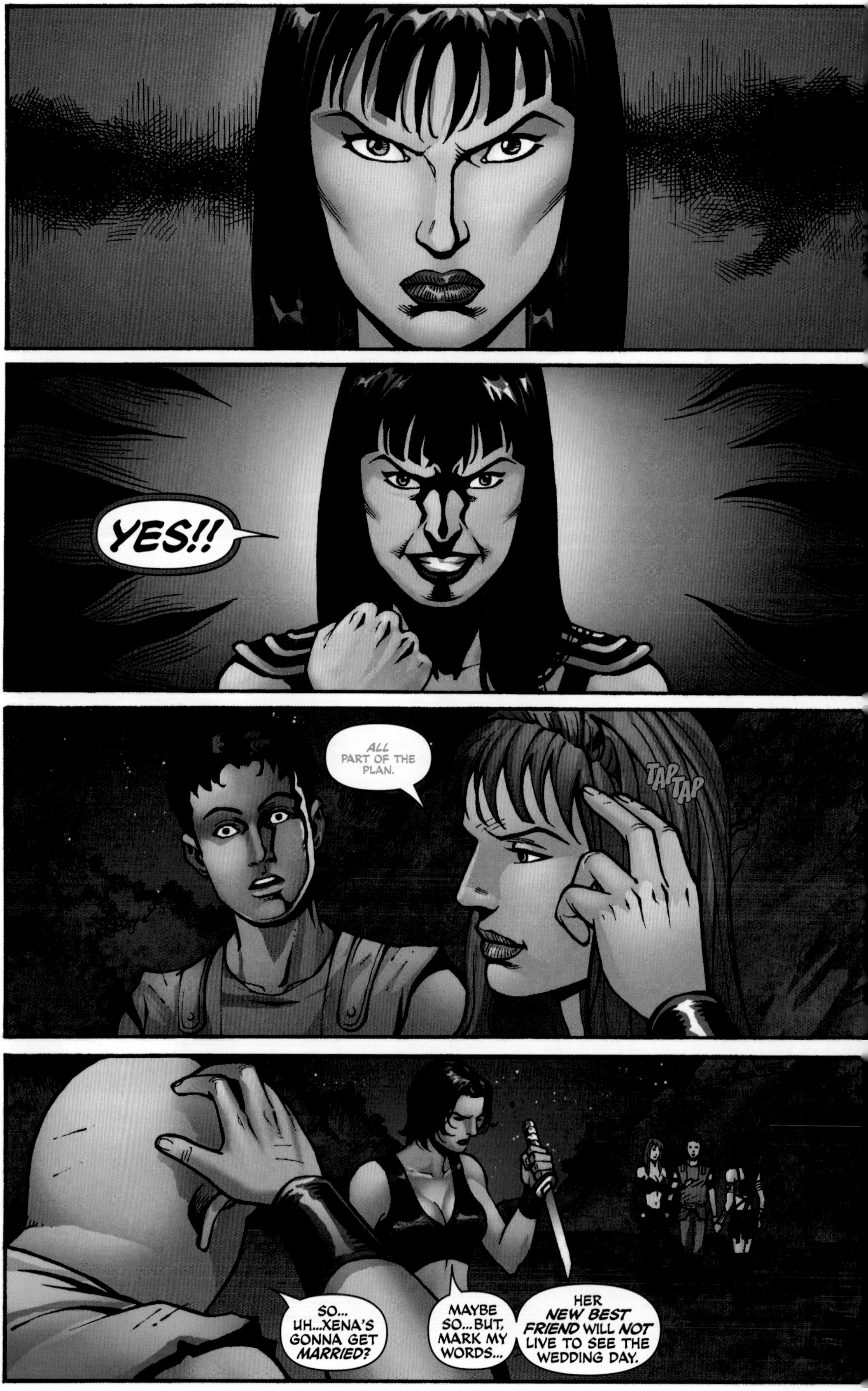
YES!!
ALL PART OF THE PLAN.
TAP TAP
SO... UH...XENA'S GONNA GET *MARRIED?*
MAYBE SO...BUT, MARK MY WORDS...
HER *NEW BEST FRIEND* WILL *NOT* LIVE TO SEE THE WEDDING DAY.

DARK XENA
CHAPTER FOUR

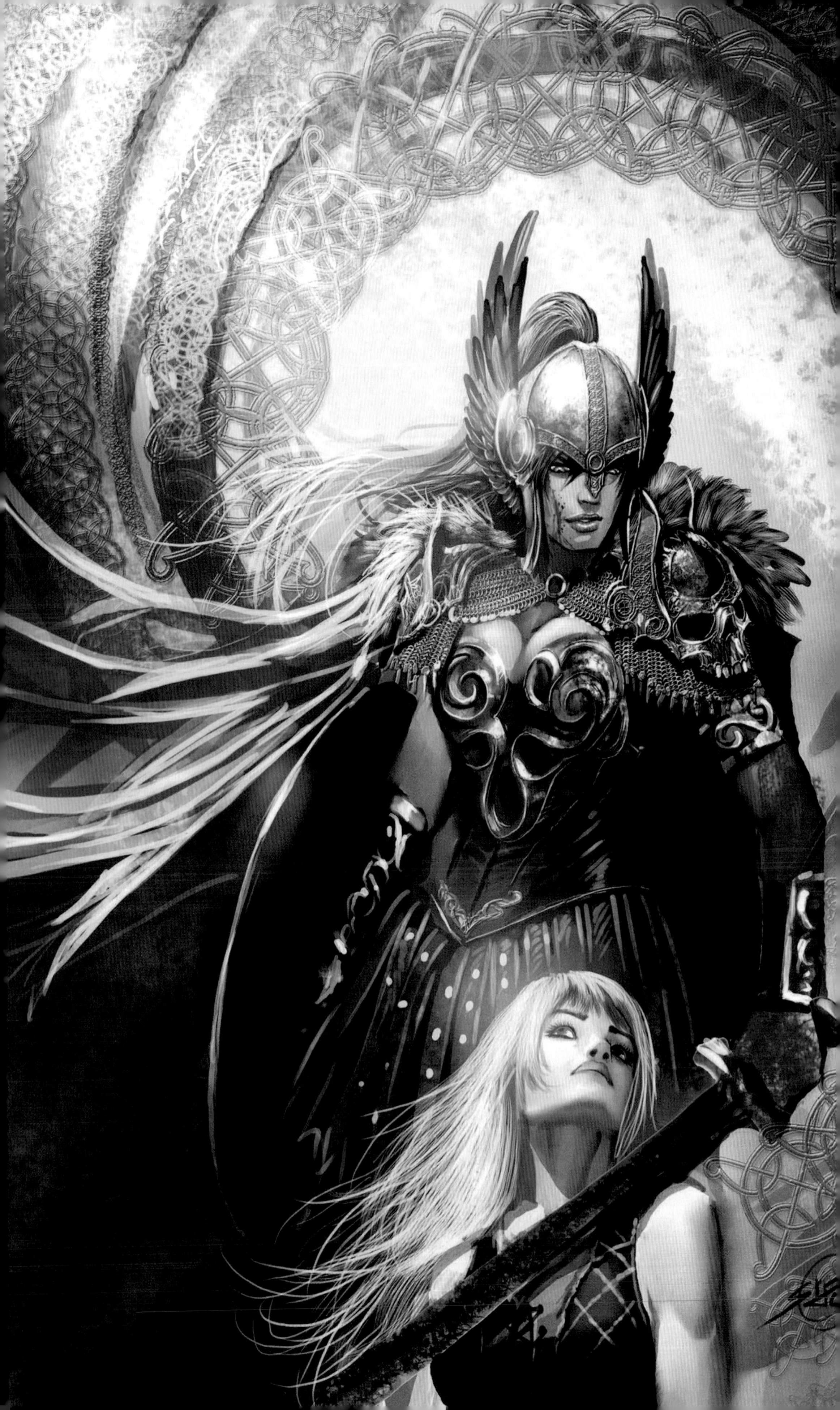

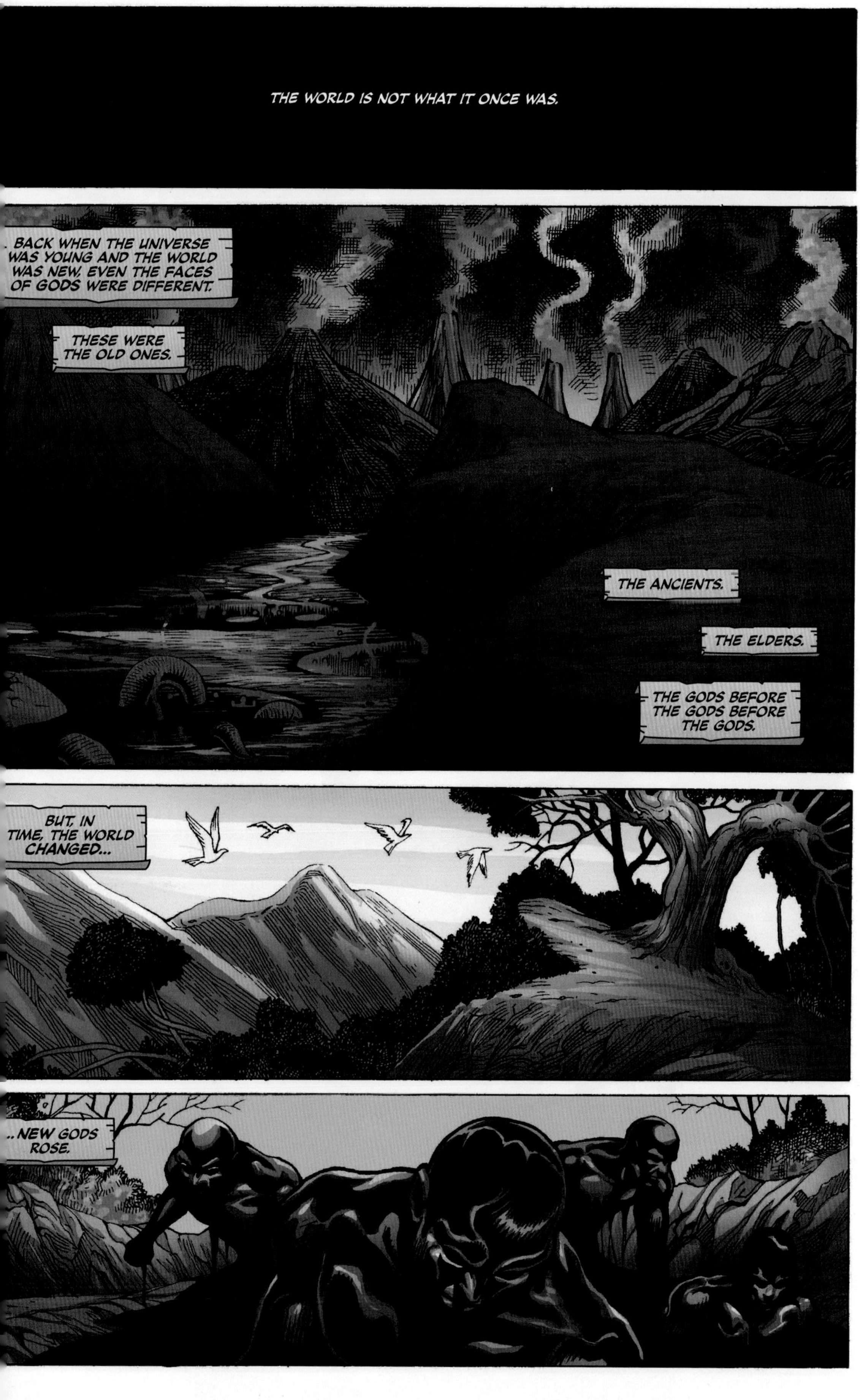
THE WORLD IS NOT WHAT IT ONCE WAS.
BACK WHEN THE UNIVERSE WAS YOUNG AND THE WORLD WAS NEW, EVEN THE FACES OF GODS WERE DIFFERENT.
THESE WERE THE OLD ONES.
THE ANCIENTS.
THE ELDERS.
THE GODS BEFORE THE GODS BEFORE THE GODS.
BUT, IN TIME, THE WORLD CHANGED...
...NEW GODS ROSE.

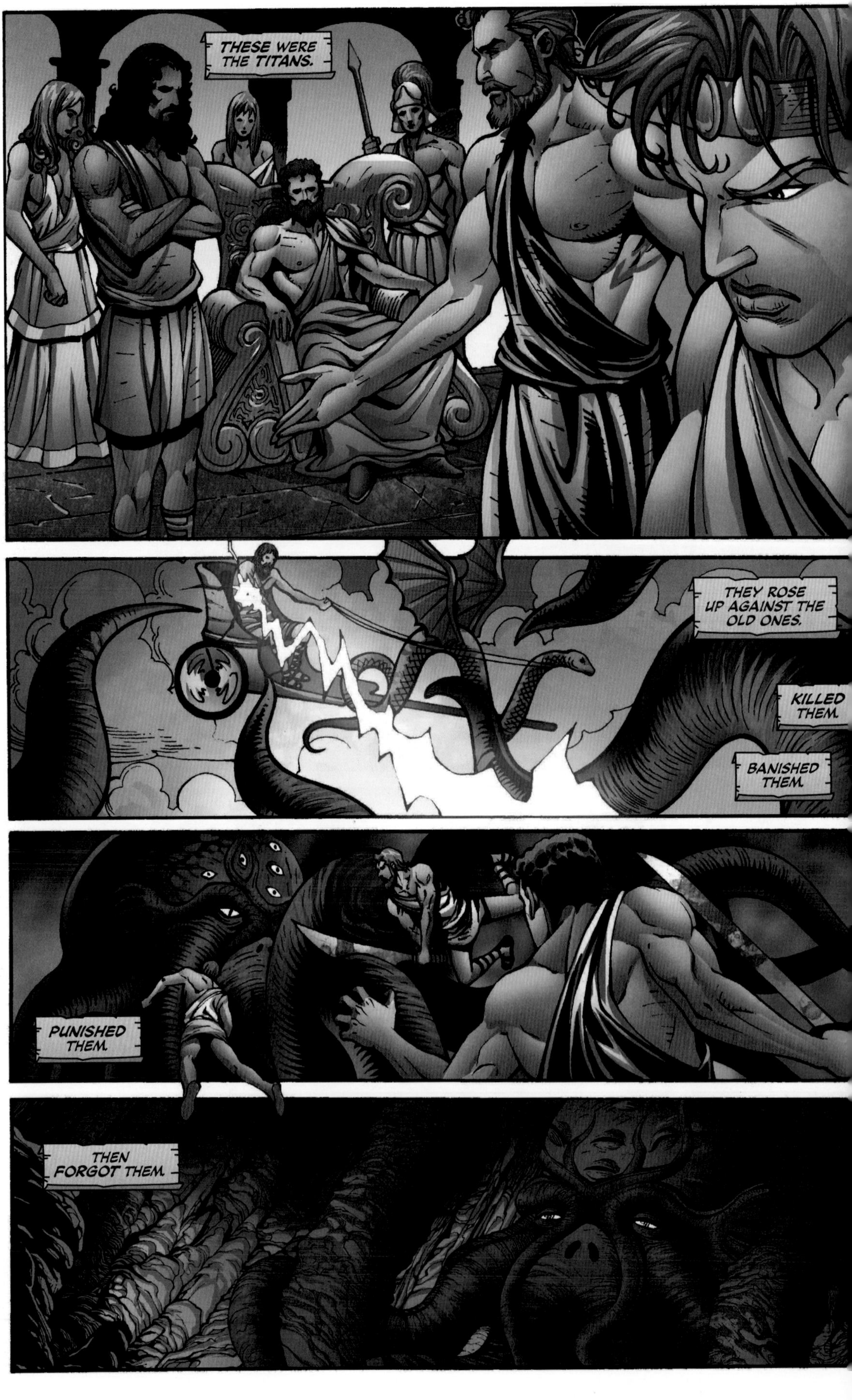
THESE WERE THE TITANS.
THEY ROSE UP AGAINST THE OLD ONES.
KILLED THEM.
BANISHED THEM.
PUNISHED THEM.
THEN FORGOT THEM.

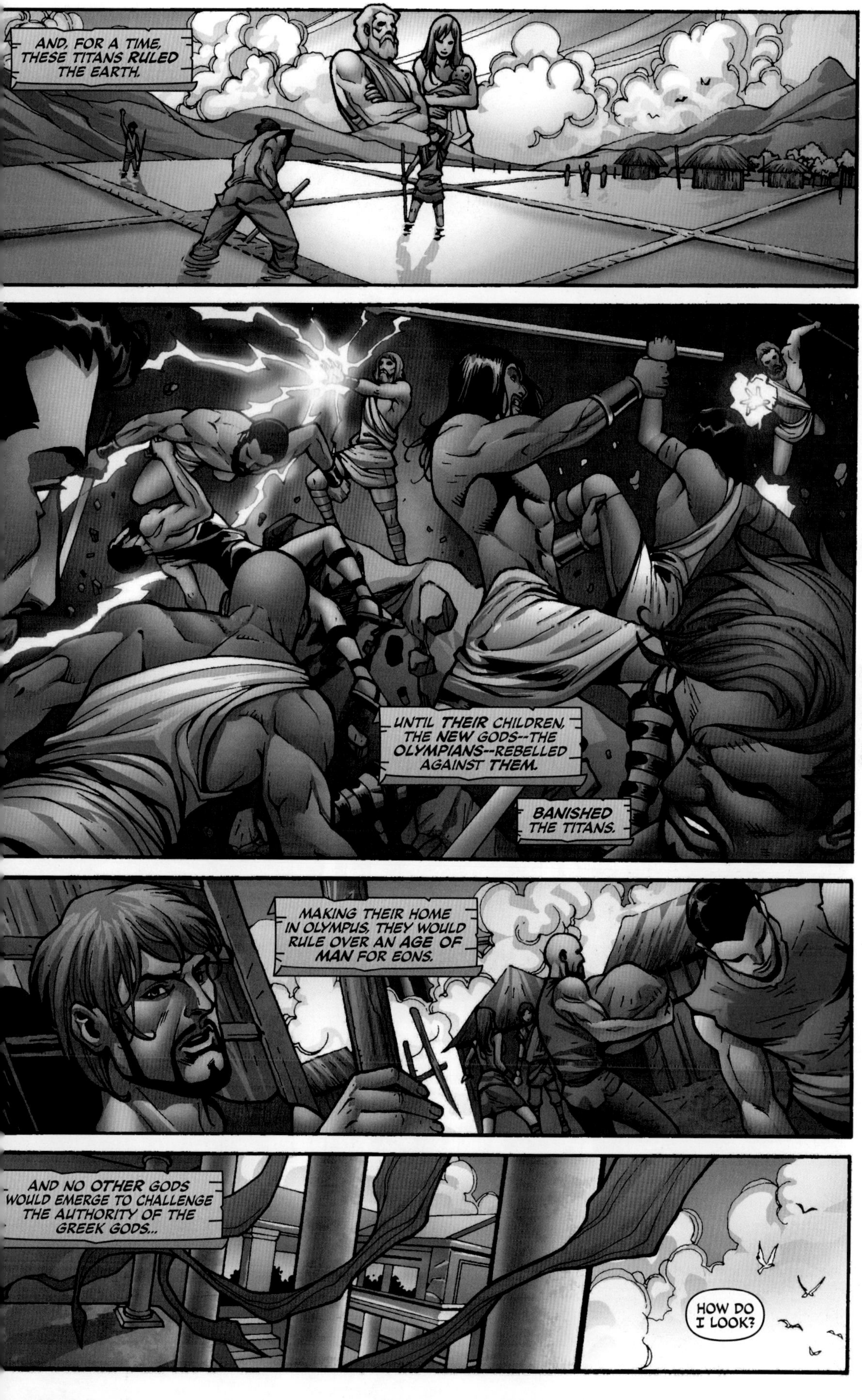

AND, FOR A TIME, THESE TITANS RULED THE EARTH.
UNTIL THEIR CHILDREN, THE NEW GODS--THE OLYMPIANS--REBELLED AGAINST THEM.
BANISHED THE TITANS.
MAKING THEIR HOME IN OLYMPUS, THEY WOULD RULE OVER AN AGE OF MAN FOR EONS.
AND NO OTHER GODS WOULD EMERGE TO CHALLENGE THE AUTHORITY OF THE GREEK GODS...
HOW DO I LOOK?

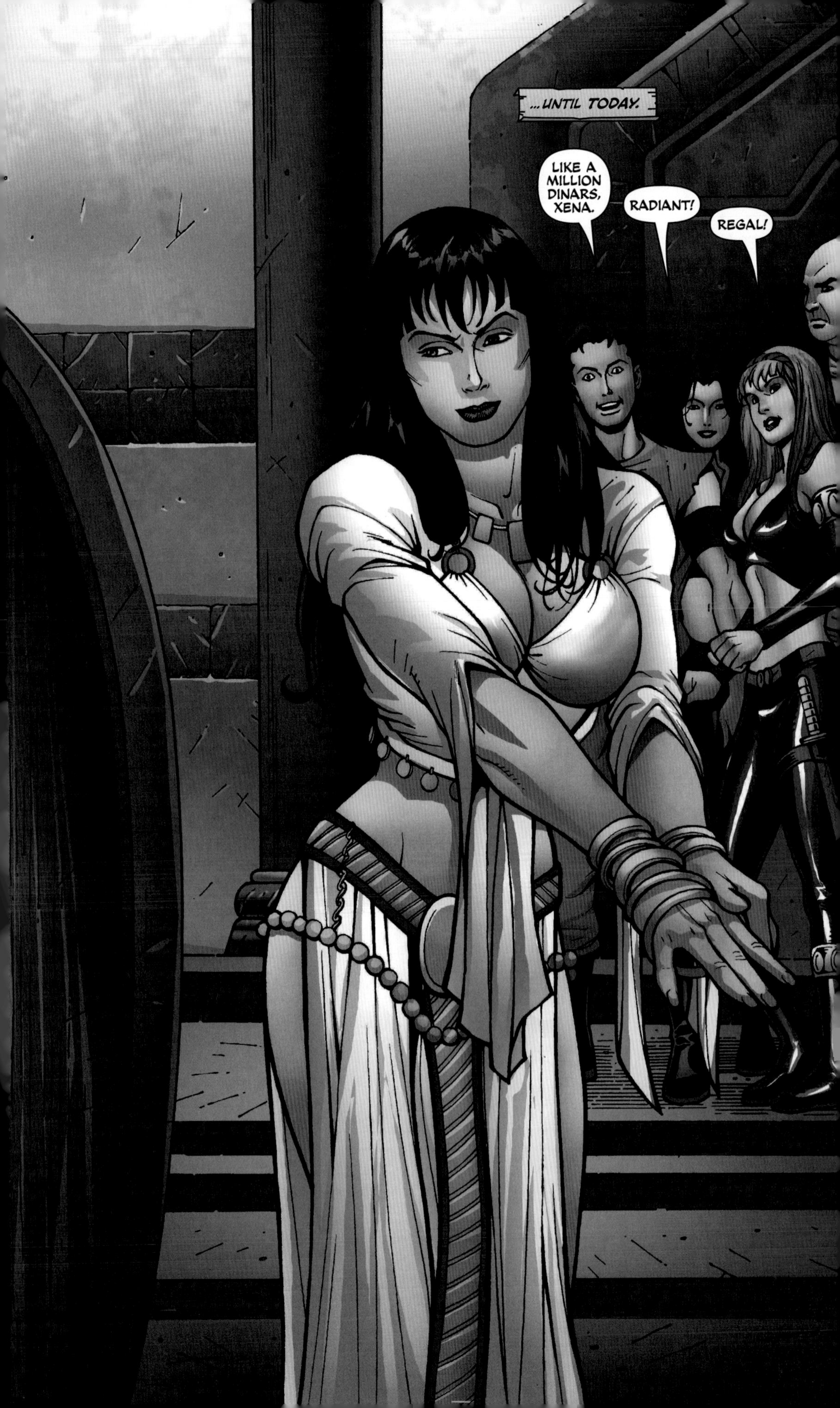
...UNTIL TODAY.
LIKE A MILLION DINARS, XENA.
RADIANT!
REGAL!

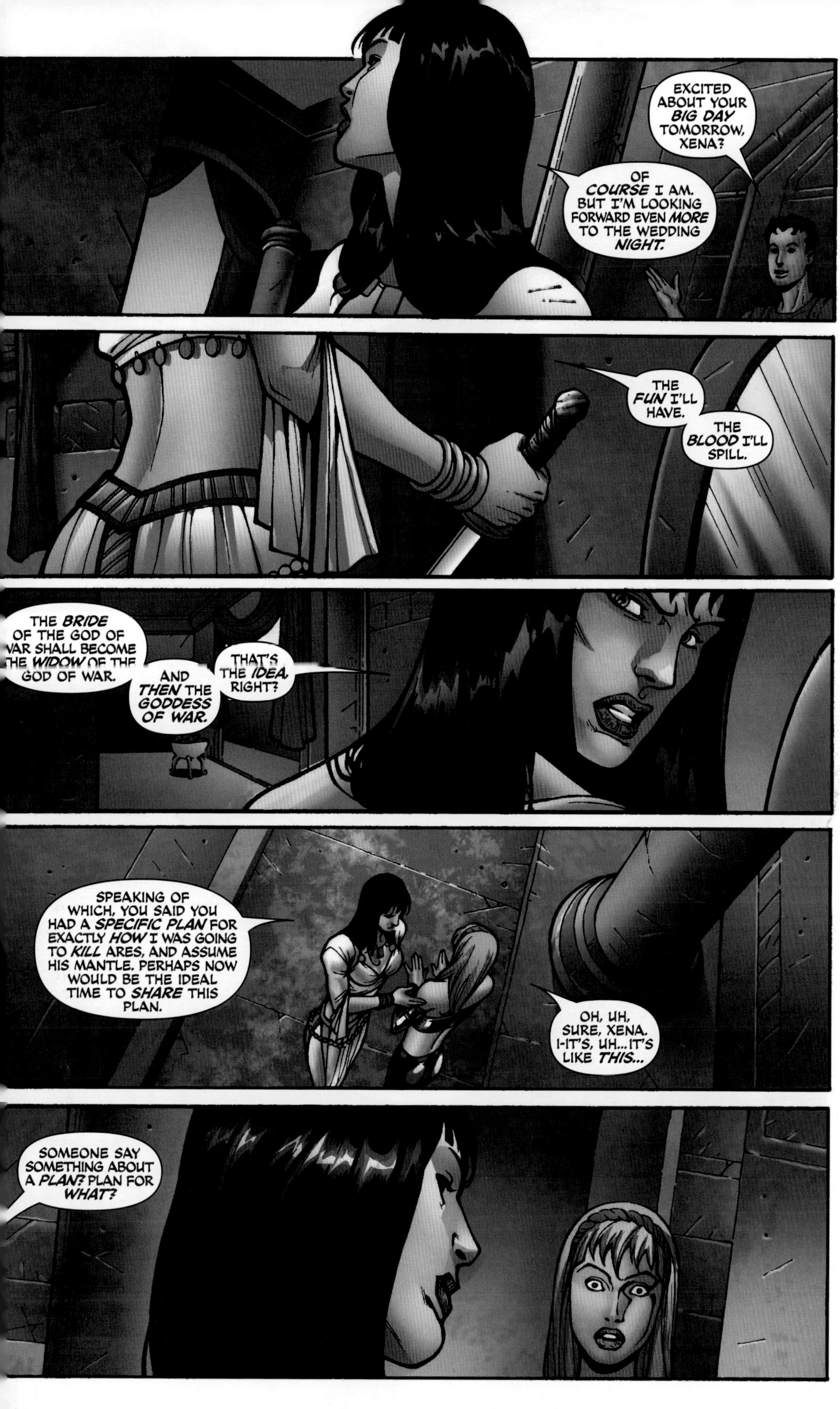

EXCITED ABOUT YOUR BIG DAY TOMORROW, XENA?
OF COURSE I AM. BUT I'M LOOKING FORWARD EVEN MORE TO THE WEDDING NIGHT.
THE FUN I'LL HAVE.
THE BLOOD I'LL SPILL.
THE BRIDE OF THE GOD OF WAR SHALL BECOME THE WIDOW OF THE GOD OF WAR.
AND THEN THE GODDESS OF WAR.
THAT'S THE IDEA, RIGHT?
SPEAKING OF WHICH, YOU SAID YOU HAD A SPECIFIC PLAN FOR EXACTLY HOW I WAS GOING TO KILL ARES, AND ASSUME HIS MANTLE. PERHAPS NOW WOULD BE THE IDEAL TIME TO SHARE THIS PLAN.
OH, UH, SURE, XENA. I-IT'S, UH...IT'S LIKE THIS...
SOMEONE SAY SOMETHING ABOUT A PLAN? PLAN FOR WHAT?

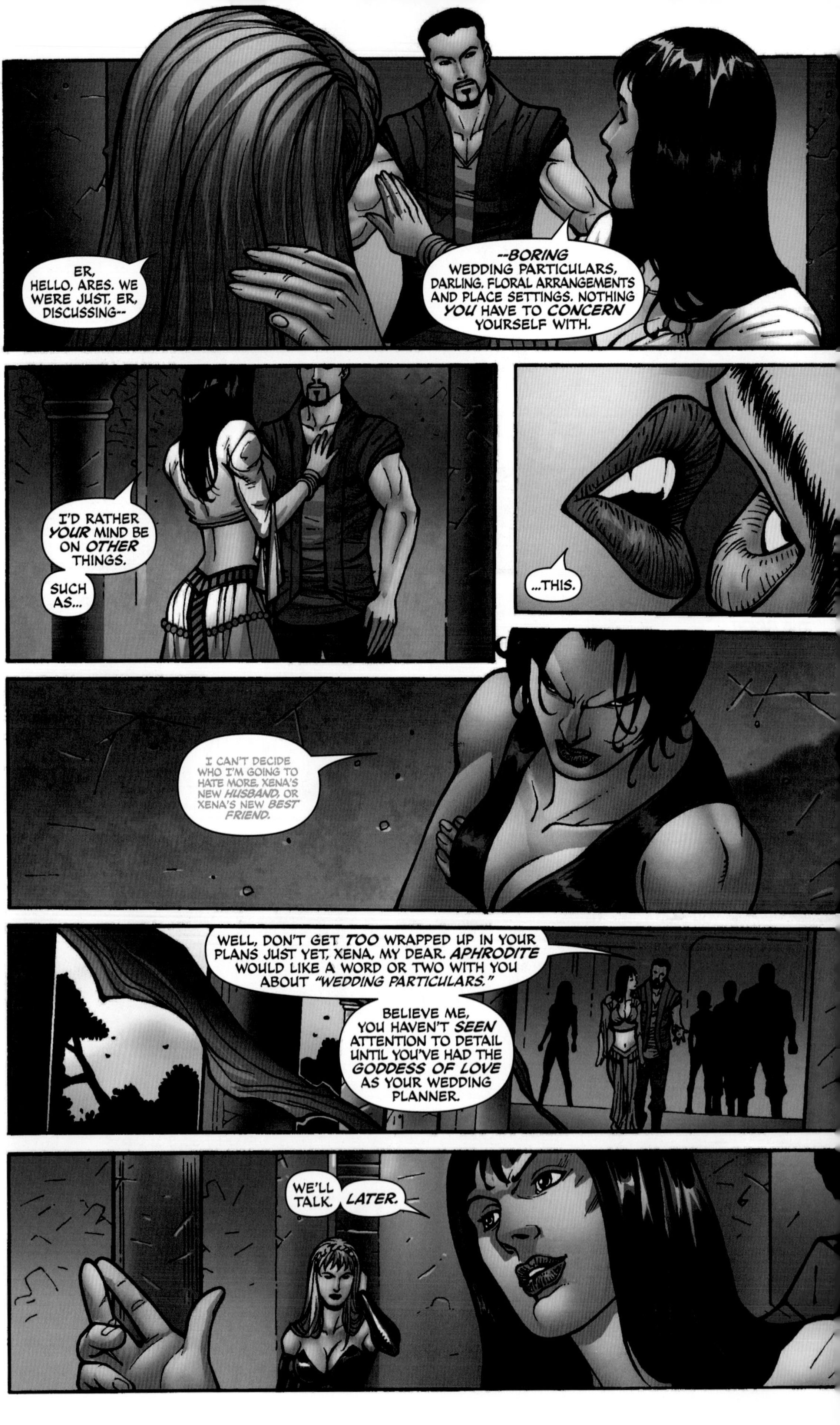

ER, HELLO, ARES. WE WERE JUST, ER, DISCUSSING--
--BORING WEDDING PARTICULARS, DARLING. FLORAL ARRANGEMENTS AND PLACE SETTINGS. NOTHING YOU HAVE TO CONCERN YOURSELF WITH.
I'D RATHER YOUR MIND BE ON OTHER THINGS.
SUCH AS...
...THIS.
I CAN'T DECIDE WHO I'M GOING TO HATE MORE, XENA'S NEW HUSBAND, OR XENA'S NEW BEST FRIEND.
WELL, DON'T GET TOO WRAPPED UP IN YOUR PLANS JUST YET, XENA, MY DEAR. APHRODITE WOULD LIKE A WORD OR TWO WITH YOU ABOUT "WEDDING PARTICULARS."
BELIEVE ME, YOU HAVEN'T SEEN ATTENTION TO DETAIL UNTIL YOU'VE HAD THE GODDESS OF LOVE AS YOUR WEDDING PLANNER.
WE'LL TALK.
LATER.

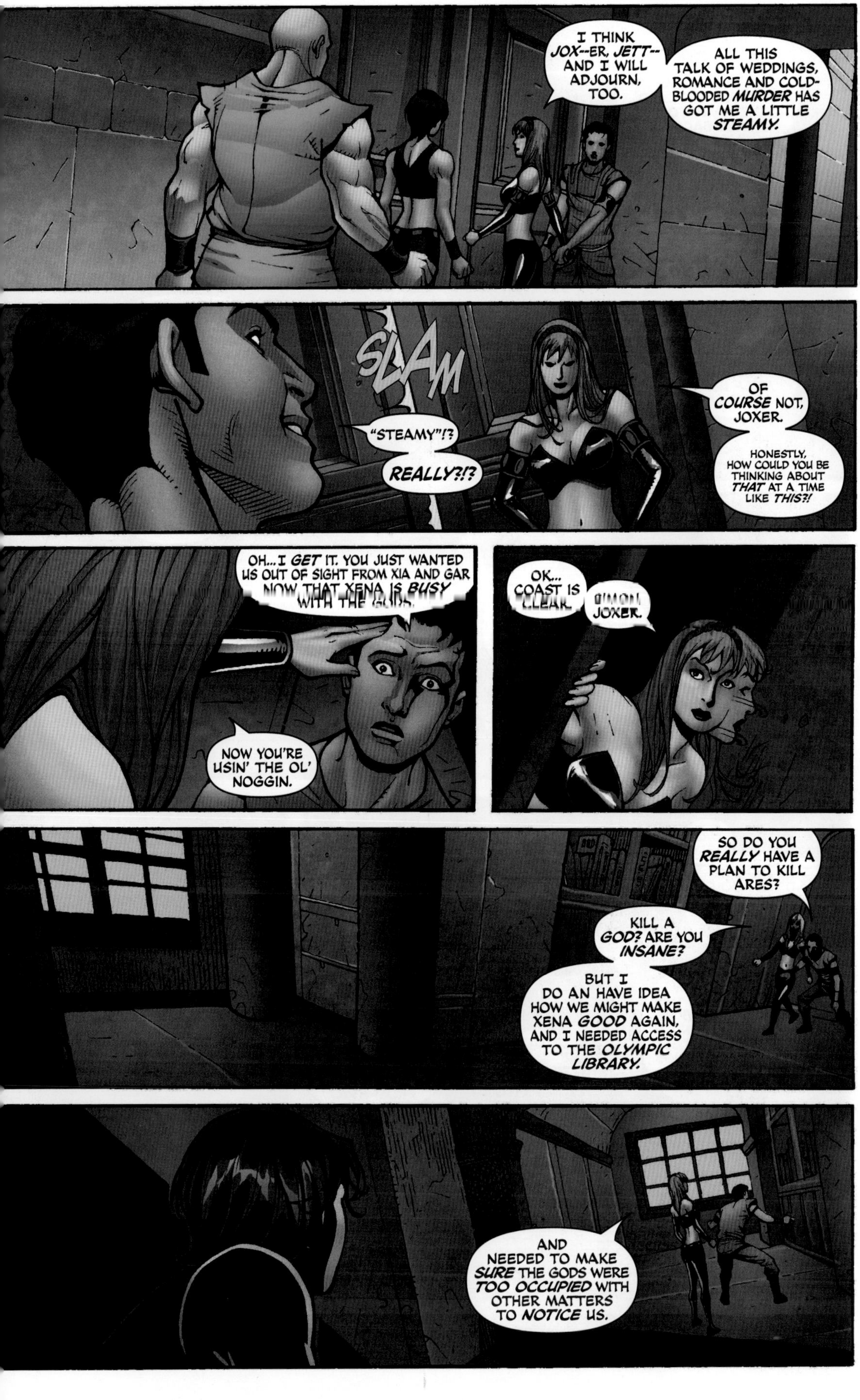
I THINK JOX--ER, JETT-- AND I WILL ADJOURN, TOO.
ALL THIS TALK OF WEDDINGS, ROMANCE AND COLD-BLOODED MURDER HAS GOT ME A LITTLE STEAMY.
SLAM
"STEAMY"!?
REALLY?!?
OF COURSE NOT, JOXER.
HONESTLY, HOW COULD YOU BE THINKING ABOUT THAT AT A TIME LIKE THIS?!
OH...I GET IT. YOU JUST WANTED US OUT OF SIGHT FROM XIA AND GAR NOW THAT XENA IS BUSY WITH THE GODS.
NOW YOU'RE USIN' THE OL' NOGGIN.
OK... COAST IS CLEAR.
JOXER.
SO DO YOU REALLY HAVE A PLAN TO KILL ARES?
KILL A GOD? ARE YOU INSANE?
BUT I DO AN HAVE IDEA HOW WE MIGHT MAKE XENA GOOD AGAIN, AND I NEEDED ACCESS TO THE OLYMPIC LIBRARY.
AND NEEDED TO MAKE SURE THE GODS WERE TOO OCCUPIED WITH OTHER MATTERS TO NOTICE US.

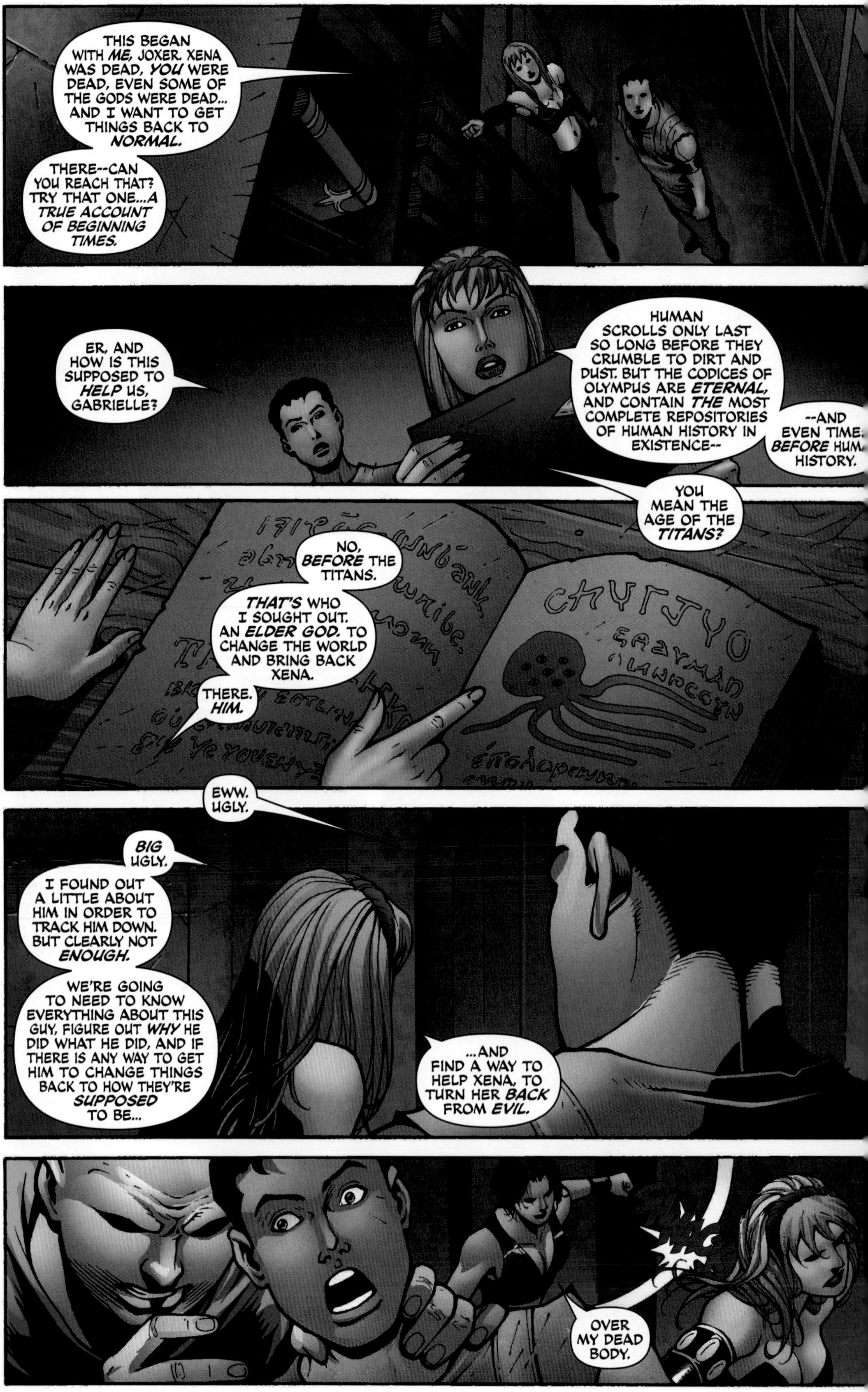
THIS BEGAN WITH ME, JOXER. XENA WAS DEAD, YOU WERE DEAD, EVEN SOME OF THE GODS WERE DEAD... AND I WANT TO GET THINGS BACK TO NORMAL.
THERE--CAN YOU REACH THAT? TRY THAT ONE...A TRUE ACCOUNT OF BEGINNING TIMES.
ER, AND HOW IS THIS SUPPOSED TO HELP US, GABRIELLE?
HUMAN SCROLLS ONLY LAST SO LONG BEFORE THEY CRUMBLE TO DIRT AND DUST. BUT THE CODICES OF OLYMPUS ARE ETERNAL, AND CONTAIN THE MOST COMPLETE REPOSITORIES OF HUMAN HISTORY IN EXISTENCE--
--AND EVEN TIME BEFORE HUM HISTORY.
YOU MEAN THE AGE OF THE TITANS?
NO, BEFORE THE TITANS.
THAT'S WHO I SOUGHT OUT. AN ELDER GOD. TO CHANGE THE WORLD AND BRING BACK XENA.
THERE. HIM.
EWW. UGLY.
BIG UGLY.
I FOUND OUT A LITTLE ABOUT HIM IN ORDER TO TRACK HIM DOWN. BUT CLEARLY NOT ENOUGH.
WE'RE GOING TO NEED TO KNOW EVERYTHING ABOUT THIS GUY, FIGURE OUT WHY HE DID WHAT HE DID, AND IF THERE IS ANY WAY TO GET HIM TO CHANGE THINGS BACK TO HOW THEY'RE SUPPOSED TO BE...
...AND FIND A WAY TO HELP XENA, TO TURN HER BACK FROM EVIL.
OVER MY DEAD BODY.

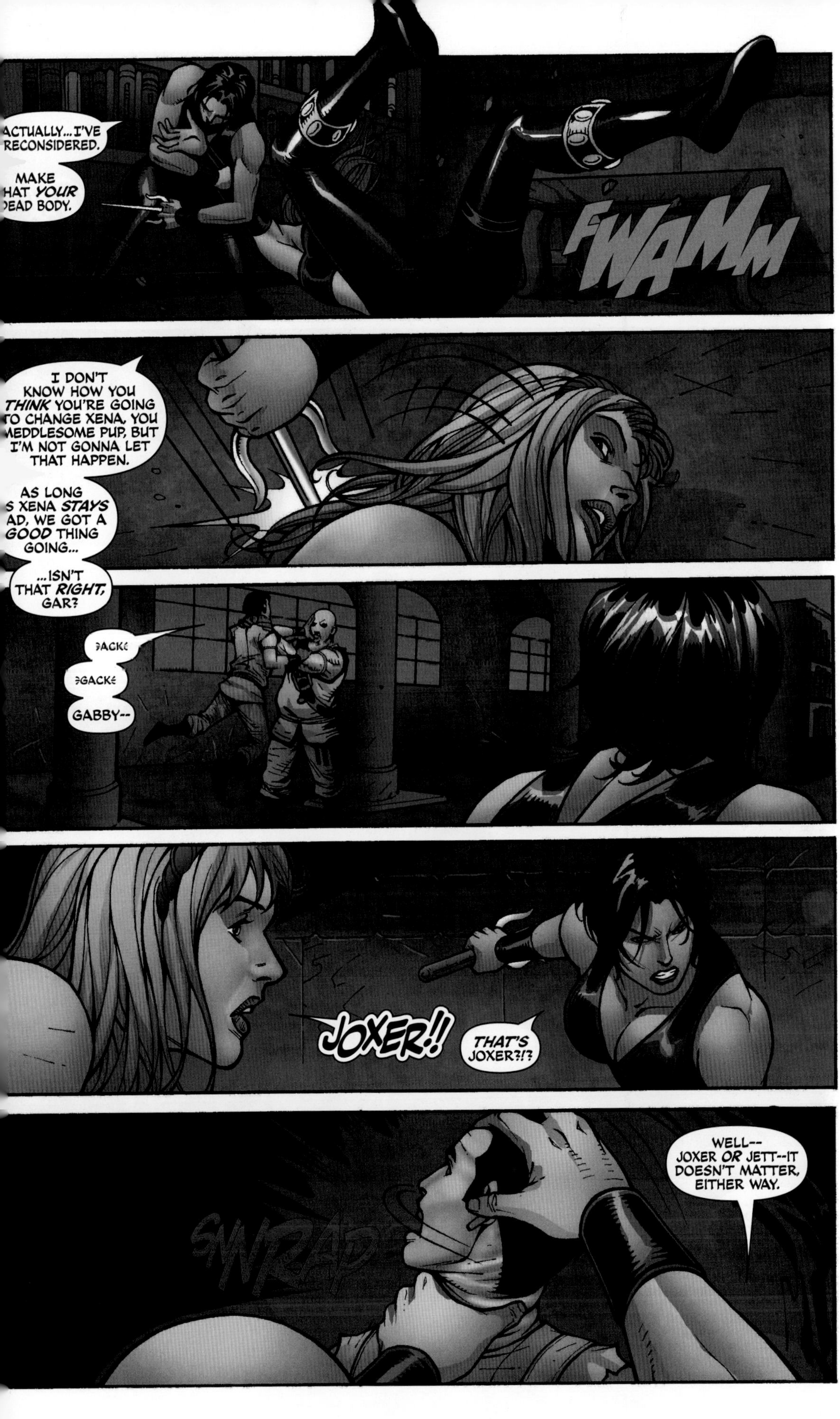

ACTUALLY... I'VE RECONSIDERED.
MAKE HAT YOUR EAD BODY.
FWAMM
I DON'T KNOW HOW YOU THINK YOU'RE GOING TO CHANGE XENA, YOU MEDDLESOME PUP, BUT I'M NOT GONNA LET THAT HAPPEN.
AS LONG S XENA STAYS AD, WE GOT A GOOD THING GOING...
...ISN'T THAT RIGHT, GAR?
GACK
GACK
GABBY--
JOXER!!
THAT'S JOXER?!?
WELL-- JOXER OR JETT--IT DOESN'T MATTER, EITHER WAY.

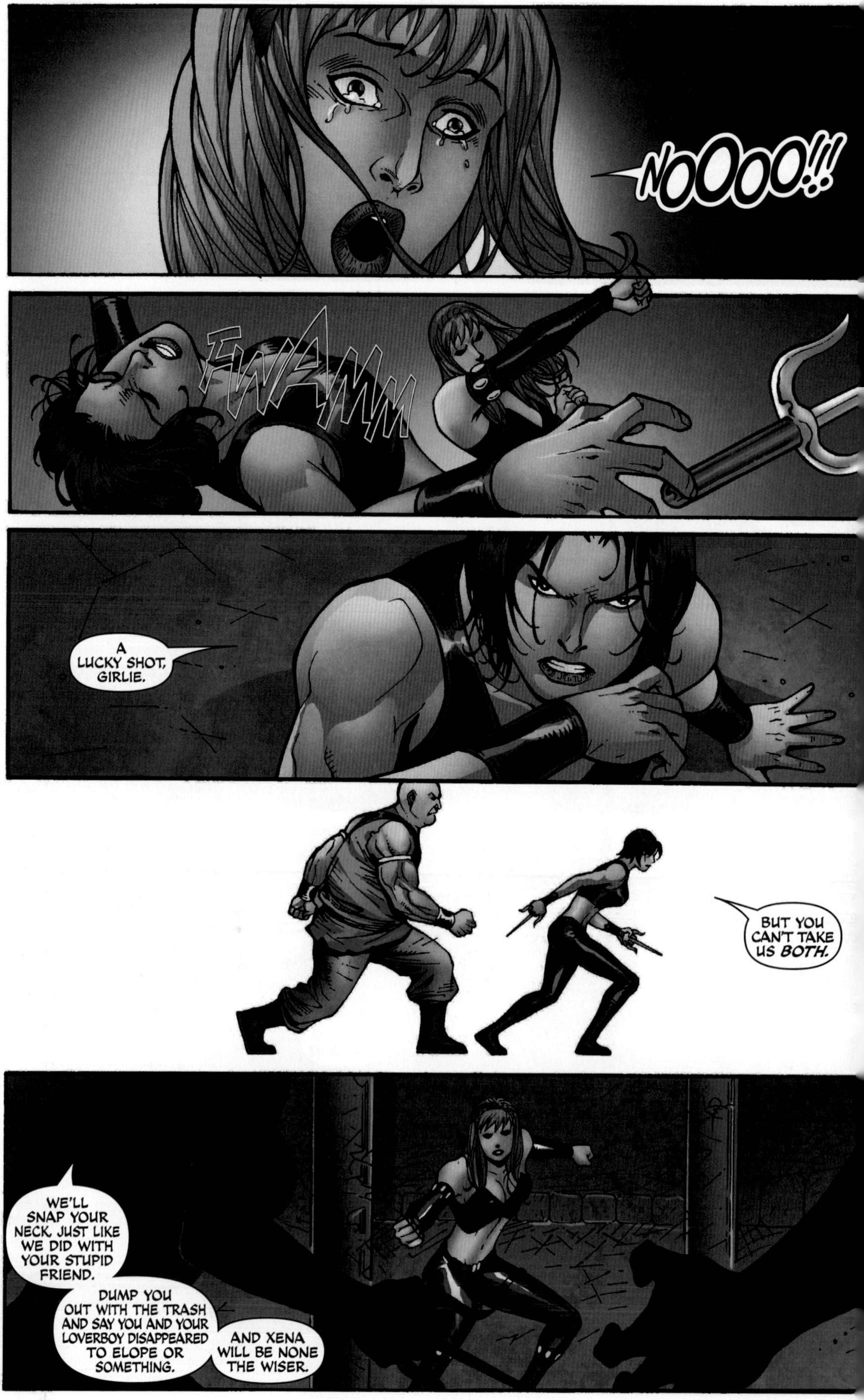
NOOOO!!!
FWAMM
A LUCKY SHOT, GIRLIE.
BUT YOU CAN'T TAKE US *BOTH.*
WE'LL SNAP YOUR NECK, JUST LIKE WE DID WITH YOUR STUPID FRIEND.
DUMP YOU OUT WITH THE TRASH AND SAY YOU AND YOUR LOVERBOY DISAPPEARED TO ELOPE OR SOMETHING.
AND XENA WILL BE NONE THE WISER.

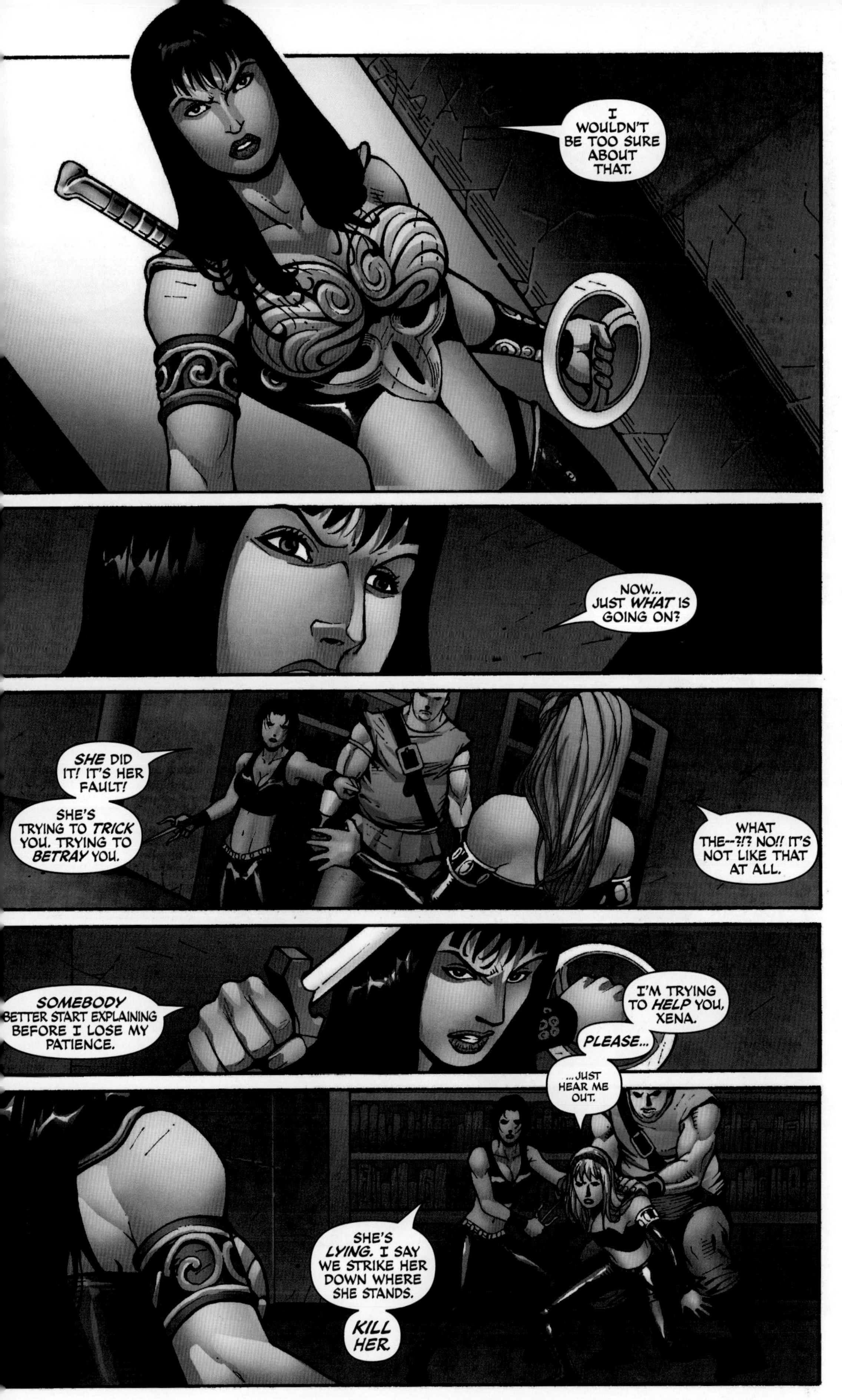
I WOULDN'T BE TOO SURE ABOUT THAT.
NOW... JUST *WHAT* IS GOING ON?
SHE DID IT! IT'S HER FAULT!
SHE'S TRYING TO *TRICK* YOU. TRYING TO *BETRAY* YOU.
WHAT THE--?!? NO!! IT'S NOT LIKE THAT AT ALL.
SOMEBODY BETTER START EXPLAINING BEFORE I LOSE MY PATIENCE.
I'M TRYING TO *HELP* YOU, XENA.
PLEASE...
...JUST HEAR ME OUT.
SHE'S *LYING*. I SAY WE STRIKE HER DOWN WHERE SHE STANDS.
KILL HER.

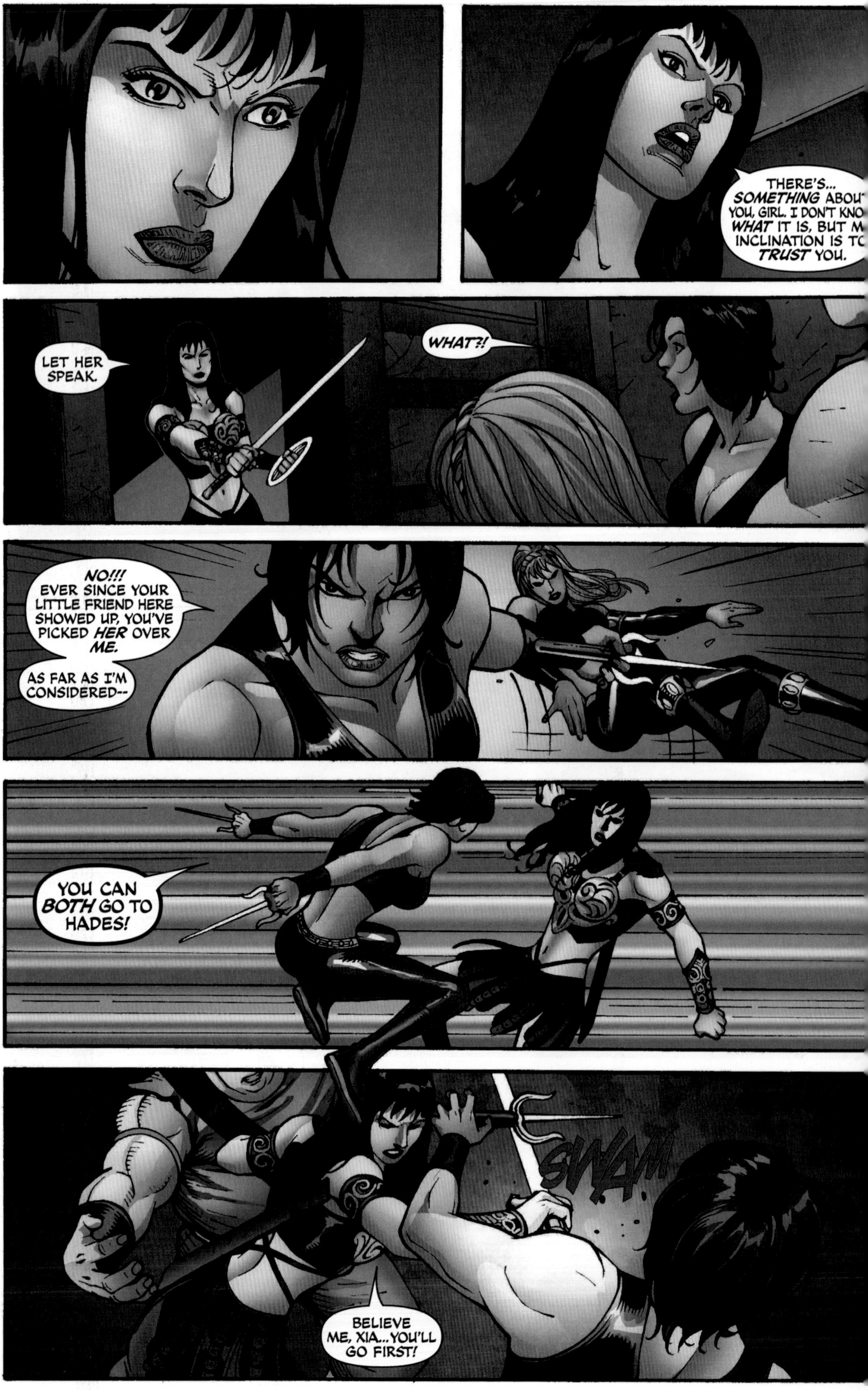

THERE'S... SOMETHING ABOU YOU, GIRL. I DON'T KNO WHAT IT IS, BUT M INCLINATION IS TO TRUST YOU.
LET HER SPEAK.
WHAT?!
NO!!! EVER SINCE YOUR LITTLE FRIEND HERE SHOWED UP, YOU'VE PICKED HER OVER ME.
AS FAR AS I'M CONSIDERED--
YOU CAN BOTH GO TO HADES!
SWAM
BELIEVE ME, XIA...YOU'LL GO FIRST!

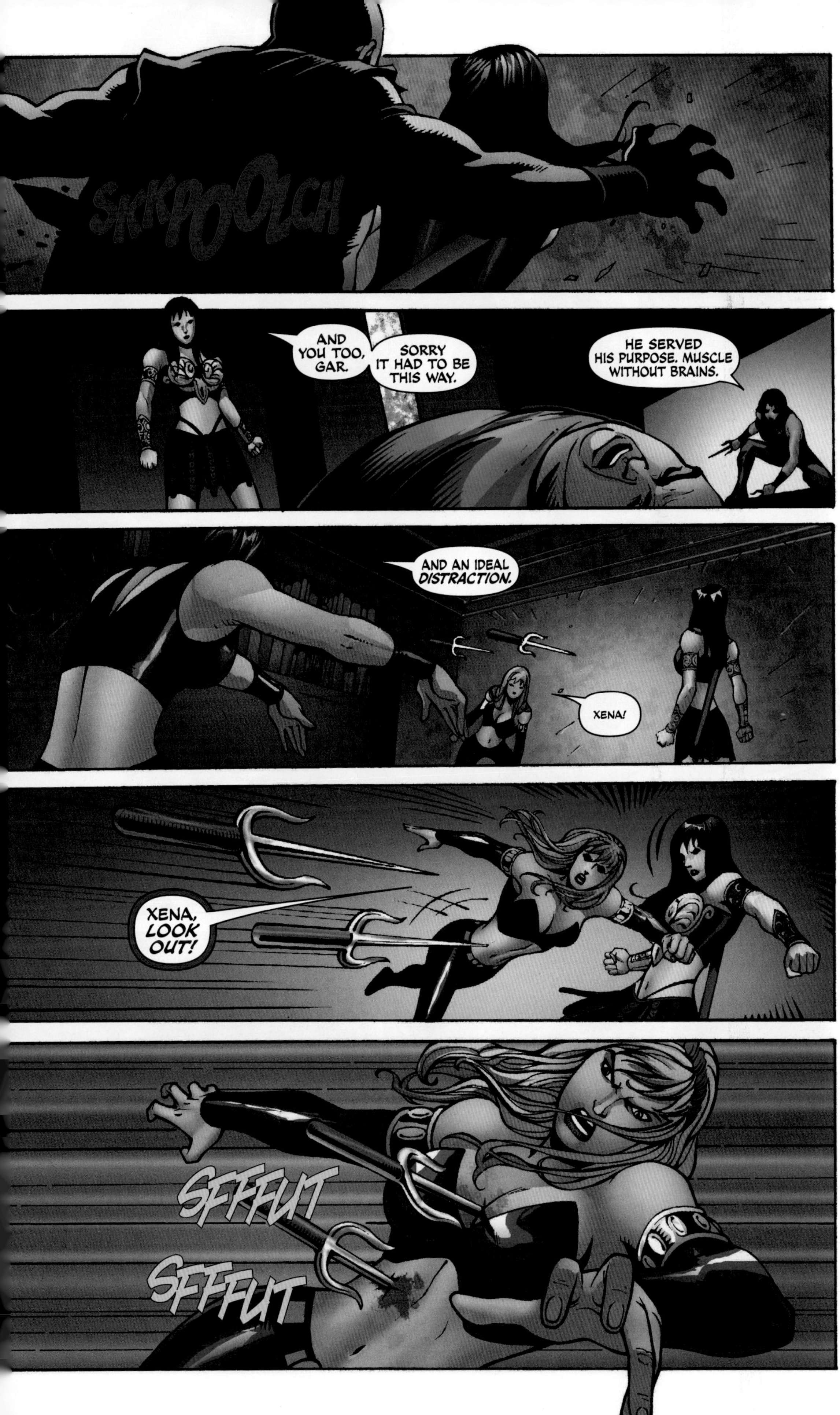
SKKPOOLCH
AND YOU TOO, GAR.
SORRY IT HAD TO BE THIS WAY.
HE SERVED HIS PURPOSE. MUSCLE WITHOUT BRAINS.
AND AN IDEAL *DISTRACTION.*
XENA!
XENA, *LOOK OUT!*
SFFFUT
SFFFUT

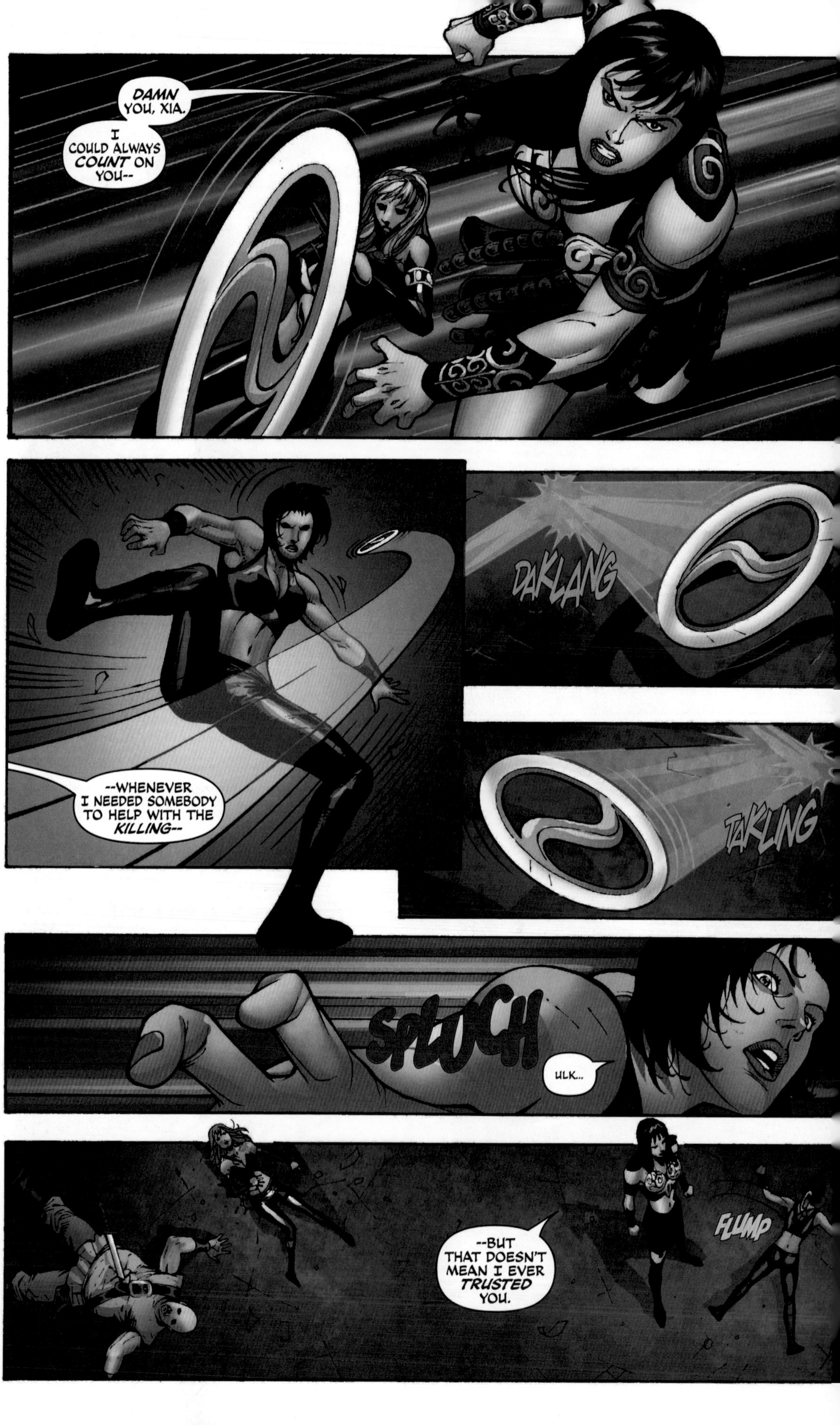
DAMN YOU, XIA.
I COULD ALWAYS COUNT ON YOU--
--WHENEVER I NEEDED SOMEBODY TO HELP WITH THE KILLING--
DAKLANG
TAKLING
SPLOTCH
ULK...
FLUMP
--BUT THAT DOESN'T MEAN I EVER TRUSTED YOU.

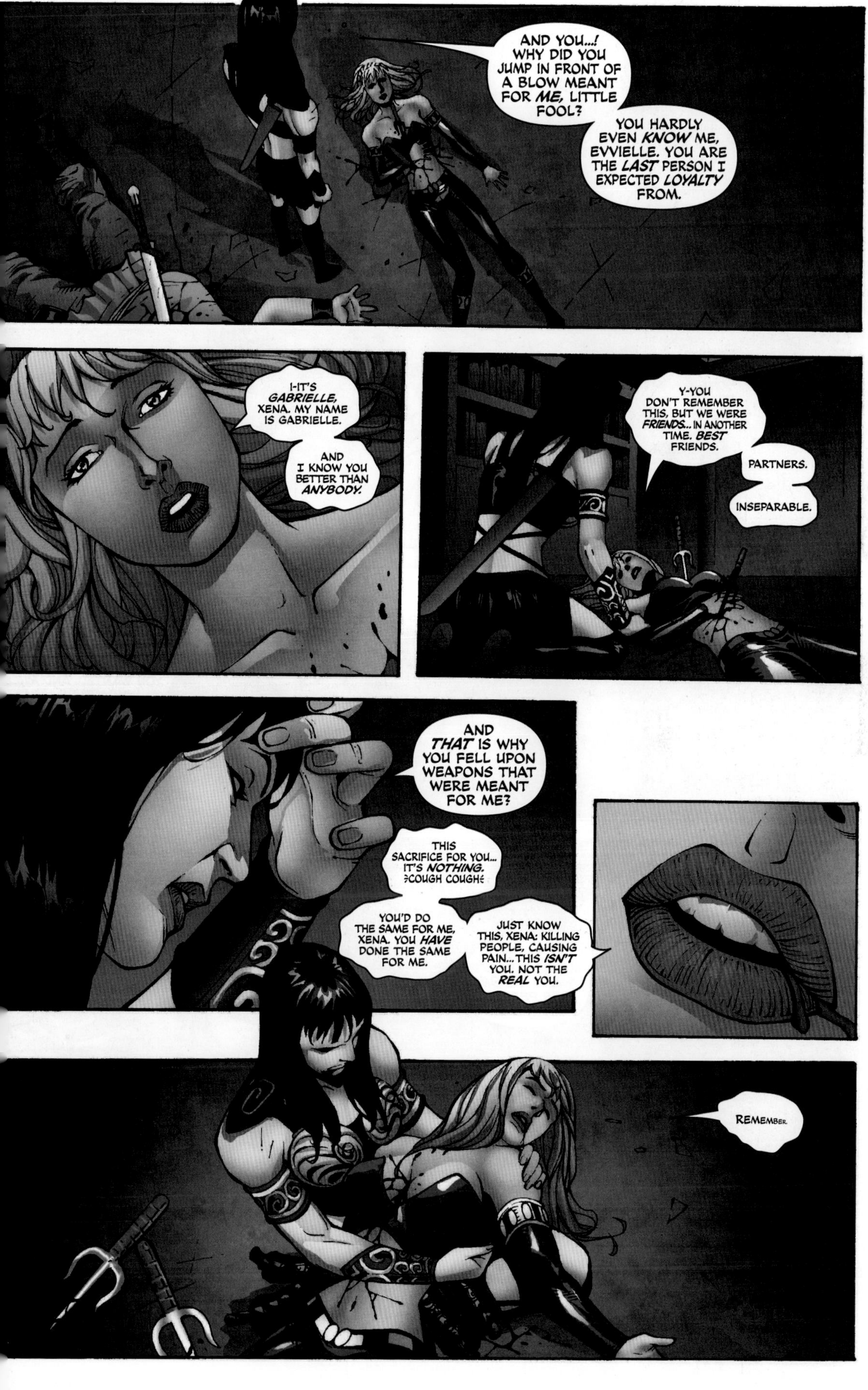
AND YOU...! WHY DID YOU JUMP IN FRONT OF A BLOW MEANT FOR ME, LITTLE FOOL?
YOU HARDLY EVEN KNOW ME, EVVIELLE. YOU ARE THE LAST PERSON I EXPECTED LOYALTY FROM.
I-IT'S GABRIELLE, XENA. MY NAME IS GABRIELLE.
AND I KNOW YOU BETTER THAN ANYBODY.
Y-YOU DON'T REMEMBER THIS, BUT WE WERE FRIENDS... IN ANOTHER TIME. BEST FRIENDS.
PARTNERS.
INSEPARABLE.
AND THAT IS WHY YOU FELL UPON WEAPONS THAT WERE MEANT FOR ME?
THIS SACRIFICE FOR YOU... IT'S NOTHING. ≷COUGH COUGH≶
YOU'D DO THE SAME FOR ME, XENA. YOU HAVE DONE THE SAME FOR ME.
JUST KNOW THIS, XENA: KILLING PEOPLE, CAUSING PAIN... THIS ISN'T YOU. NOT THE REAL YOU.
REMEMBER.

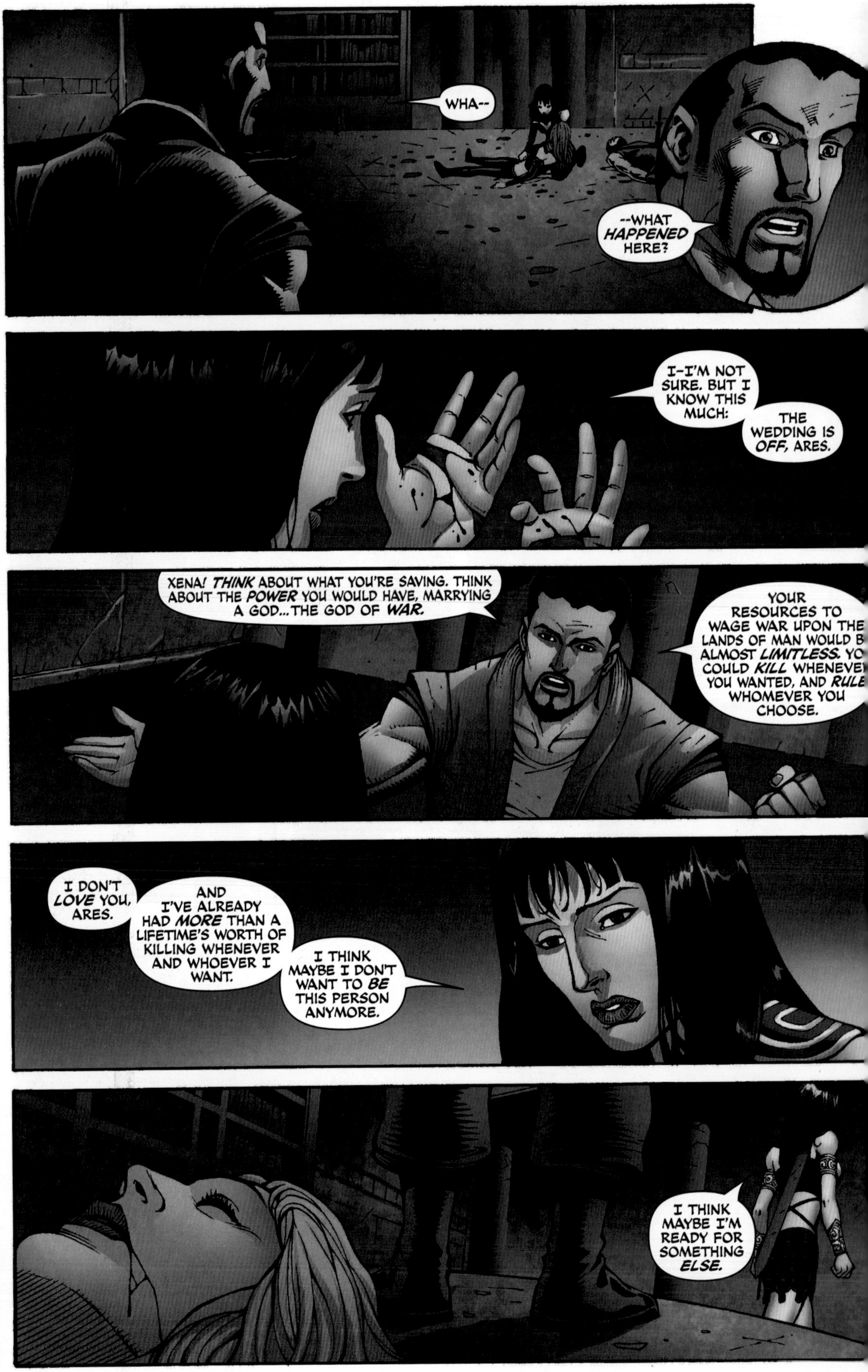
WHA--
--WHAT HAPPENED HERE?
I-I'M NOT SURE. BUT I KNOW THIS MUCH:
THE WEDDING IS OFF, ARES.
XENA! THINK ABOUT WHAT YOU'RE SAVING. THINK ABOUT THE POWER YOU WOULD HAVE, MARRYING A GOD...THE GOD OF WAR.
YOUR RESOURCES TO WAGE WAR UPON THE LANDS OF MAN WOULD B ALMOST LIMITLESS. YO COULD KILL WHENEVE YOU WANTED, AND RULE WHOMEVER YOU CHOOSE.
I DON'T LOVE YOU, ARES.
AND I'VE ALREADY HAD MORE THAN A LIFETIME'S WORTH OF KILLING WHENEVER AND WHOEVER I WANT.
I THINK MAYBE I DON'T WANT TO BE THIS PERSON ANYMORE.
I THINK MAYBE I'M READY FOR SOMETHING ELSE.

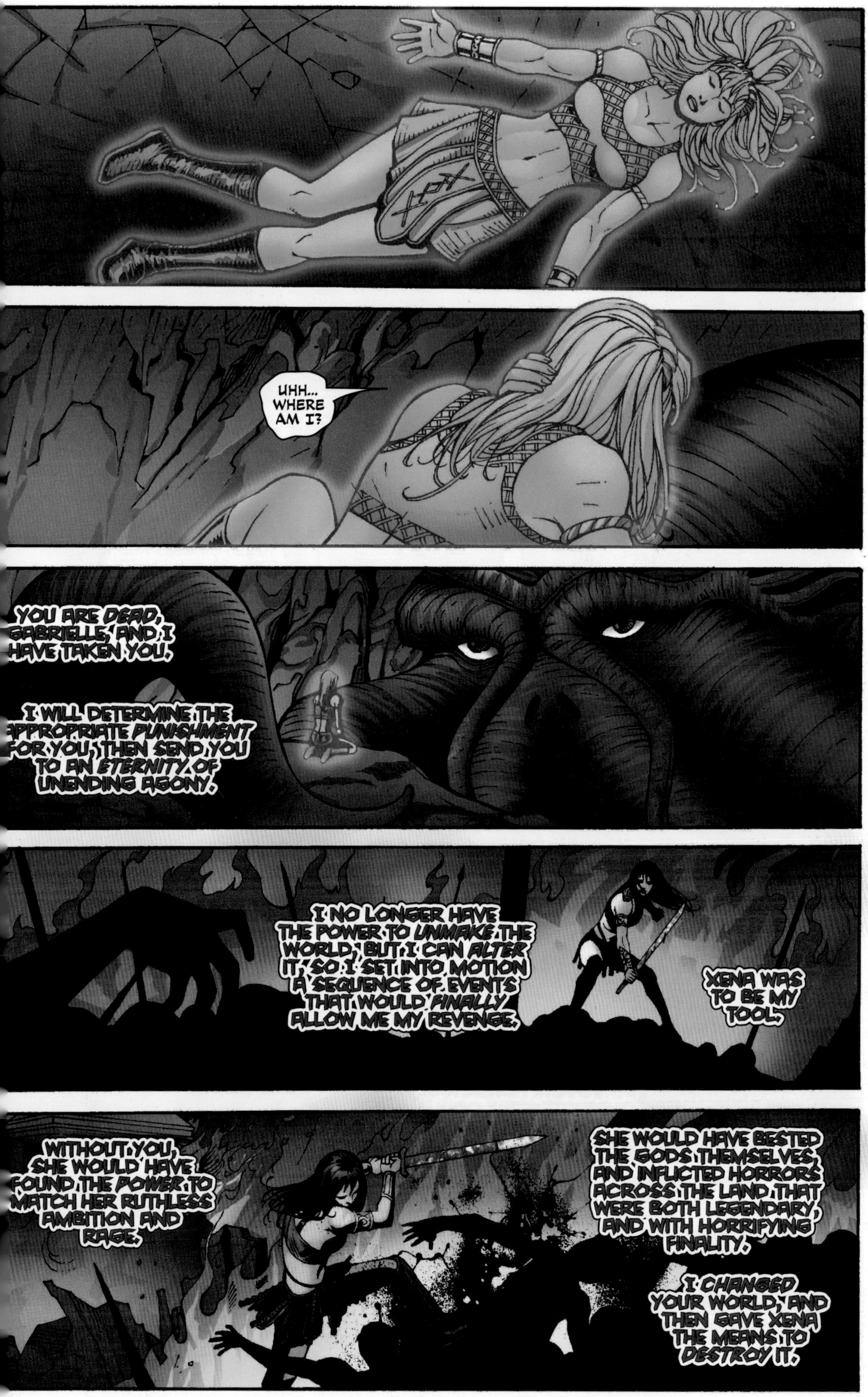
UHH... WHERE AM I?
YOU ARE DEAD, GABRIELLE, AND I HAVE TAKEN YOU.
I WILL DETERMINE THE APPROPRIATE PUNISHMENT FOR YOU, THEN SEND YOU TO AN ETERNITY OF UNENDING AGONY.
I NO LONGER HAVE THE POWER TO UNMAKE THE WORLD, BUT I CAN ALTER IT, SO I SET INTO MOTION A SEQUENCE OF EVENTS THAT WOULD FINALLY ALLOW ME MY REVENGE.
XENA WAS TO BE MY TOOL.
WITHOUT YOU, SHE WOULD HAVE FOUND THE POWER TO MATCH HER RUTHLESS AMBITION AND RAGE.
SHE WOULD HAVE BESTED THE GODS THEMSELVES, AND INFLICTED HORRORS ACROSS THE LAND THAT WERE BOTH LEGENDARY, AND WITH HORRIFYING FINALITY.
I CHANGED YOUR WORLD, AND THEN GAVE XENA THE MEANS TO DESTROY IT.

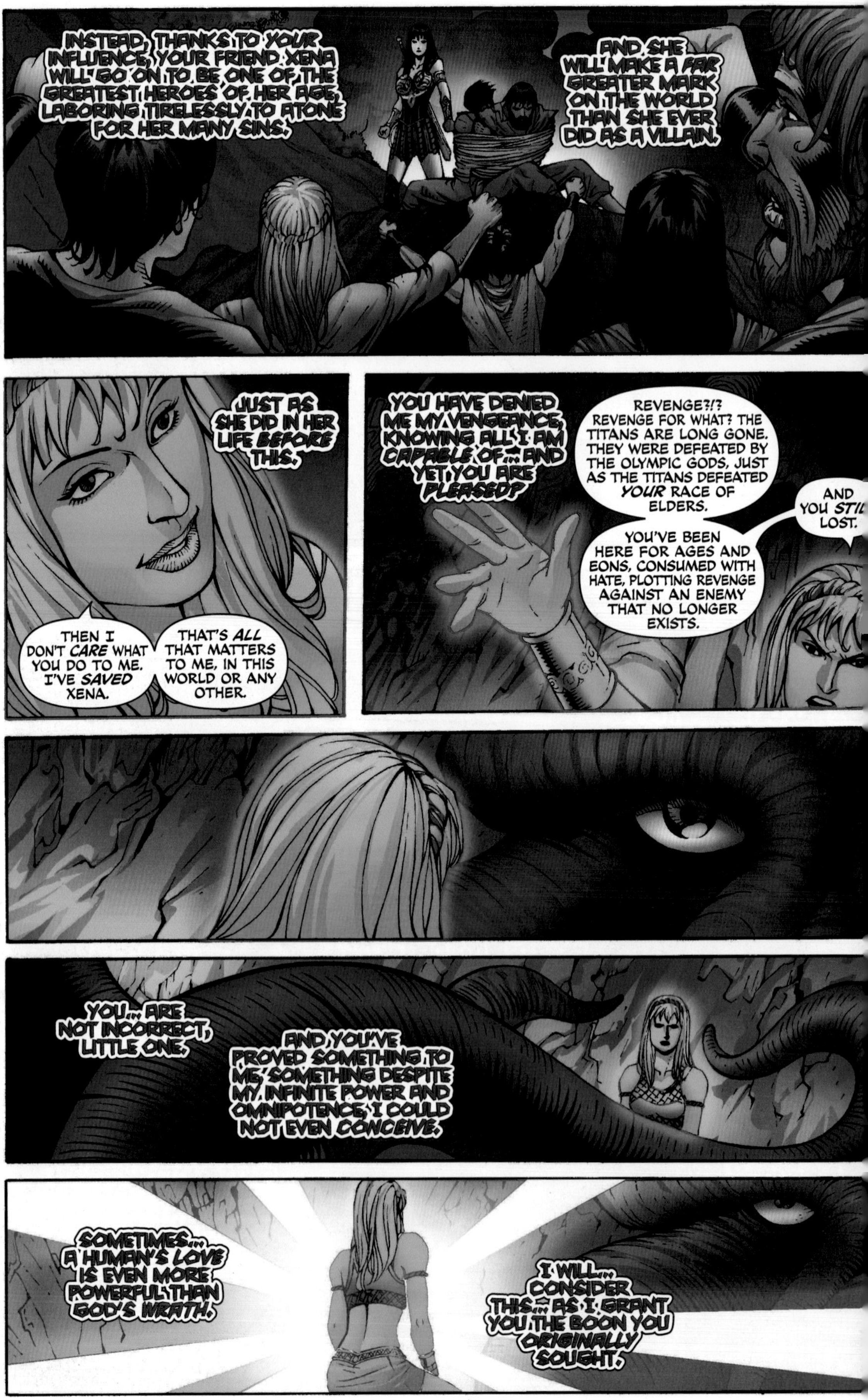
INSTEAD, THANKS TO YOUR INFLUENCE, YOUR FRIEND XENA WILL GO ON TO BE ONE OF THE GREATEST HEROES OF HER AGE, LABORING TIRELESSLY TO ATONE FOR HER MANY SINS.
AND SHE WILL MAKE A FAR GREATER MARK ON THE WORLD THAN SHE EVER DID AS A VILLAIN.
JUST AS SHE DID IN HER LIFE BEFORE THIS.
THEN I DON'T CARE WHAT YOU DO TO ME. I'VE SAVED XENA.
THAT'S ALL THAT MATTERS TO ME, IN THIS WORLD OR ANY OTHER.
YOU HAVE DENIED ME MY VENGEANCE, KNOWING ALL I AM CAPABLE OF... AND YET YOU ARE PLEASED?
REVENGE?!? REVENGE FOR WHAT? THE TITANS ARE LONG GONE. THEY WERE DEFEATED BY THE OLYMPIC GODS, JUST AS THE TITANS DEFEATED YOUR RACE OF ELDERS.
YOU'VE BEEN HERE FOR AGES AND EONS, CONSUMED WITH HATE, PLOTTING REVENGE AGAINST AN ENEMY THAT NO LONGER EXISTS.
YOU... ARE NOT INCORRECT, LITTLE ONE.
AND YOU'VE PROVED SOMETHING TO ME, SOMETHING DESPITE MY INFINITE POWER AND OMNIPOTENCE, I COULD NOT EVEN CONCEIVE.
SOMETIMES... A HUMAN'S LOVE IS EVEN MORE POWERFUL THAN GOD'S WRATH.
I WILL... CONSIDER THIS... AS I GRANT YOU THE BOON YOU ORIGINALLY SOUGHT.

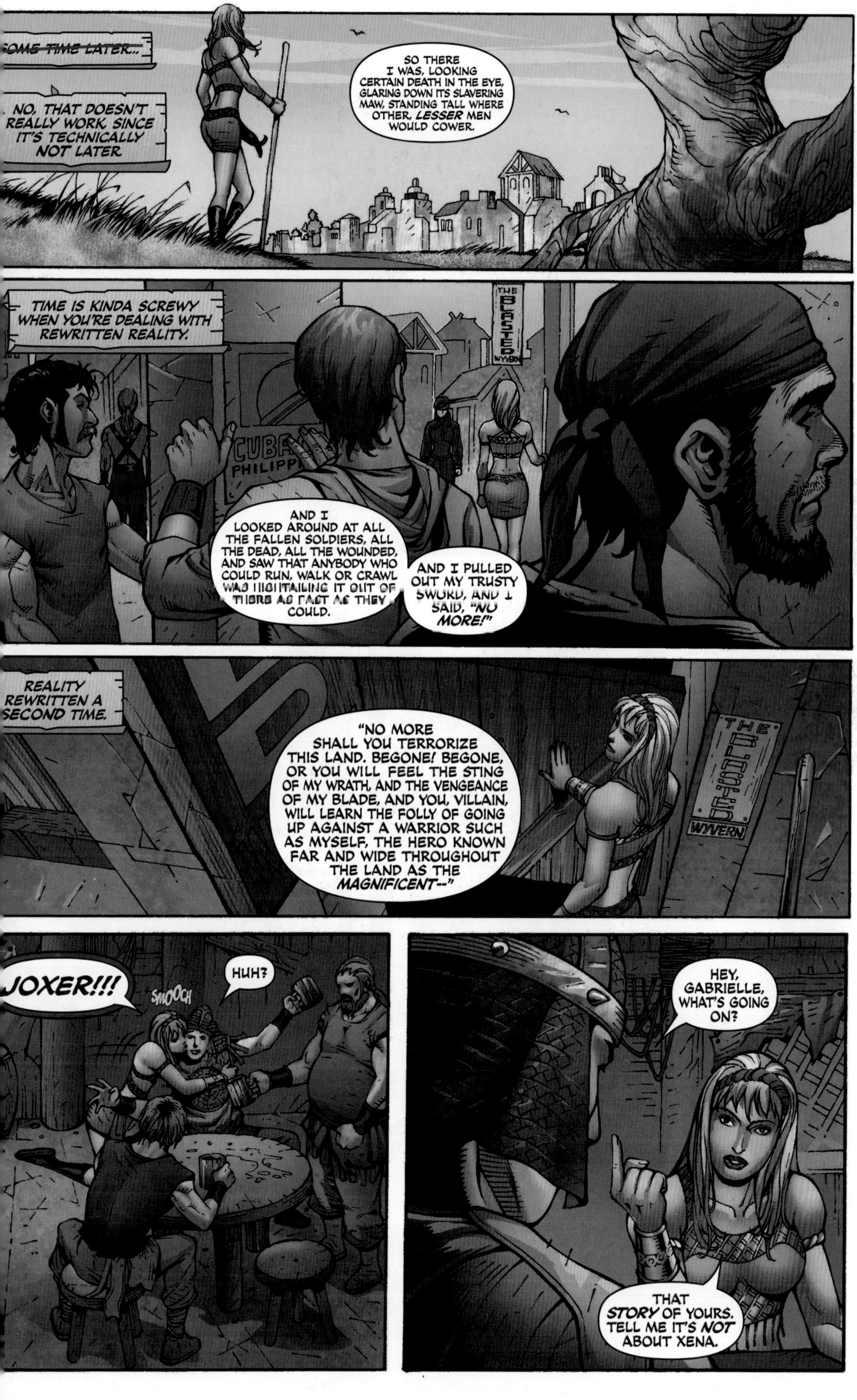
SOME TIME LATER...
NO, THAT DOESN'T REALLY WORK SINCE IT'S TECHNICALLY NOT LATER.
SO THERE I WAS, LOOKING CERTAIN DEATH IN THE EYE, GLARING DOWN ITS SLAVERING MAW, STANDING TALL WHERE OTHER, LESSER MEN WOULD COWER.
TIME IS KINDA SCREWY WHEN YOU'RE DEALING WITH REWRITTEN REALITY.
THE BLASTED WYVERN
CUBA
PHILIPP
AND I LOOKED AROUND AT ALL THE FALLEN SOLDIERS, ALL THE DEAD, ALL THE WOUNDED, AND SAW THAT ANYBODY WHO COULD RUN, WALK OR CRAWL WAS HIGHTAILING IT OUT OF THERE AS FAST AS THEY COULD.
AND I PULLED OUT MY TRUSTY SWORD, AND I SAID, "NO MORE!"
REALITY REWRITTEN A SECOND TIME.
"NO MORE SHALL YOU TERRORIZE THIS LAND. BEGONE! BEGONE, OR YOU WILL FEEL THE STING OF MY WRATH, AND THE VENGEANCE OF MY BLADE, AND YOU, VILLAIN, WILL LEARN THE FOLLY OF GOING UP AGAINST A WARRIOR SUCH AS MYSELF, THE HERO KNOWN FAR AND WIDE THROUGHOUT THE LAND AS THE MAGNIFICENT--"
THE BLASTED WYVERN
JOXER!!!
SMOOCH
HUH?
HEY, GABRIELLE, WHAT'S GOING ON?
THAT STORY OF YOURS. TELL ME IT'S NOT ABOUT XENA.

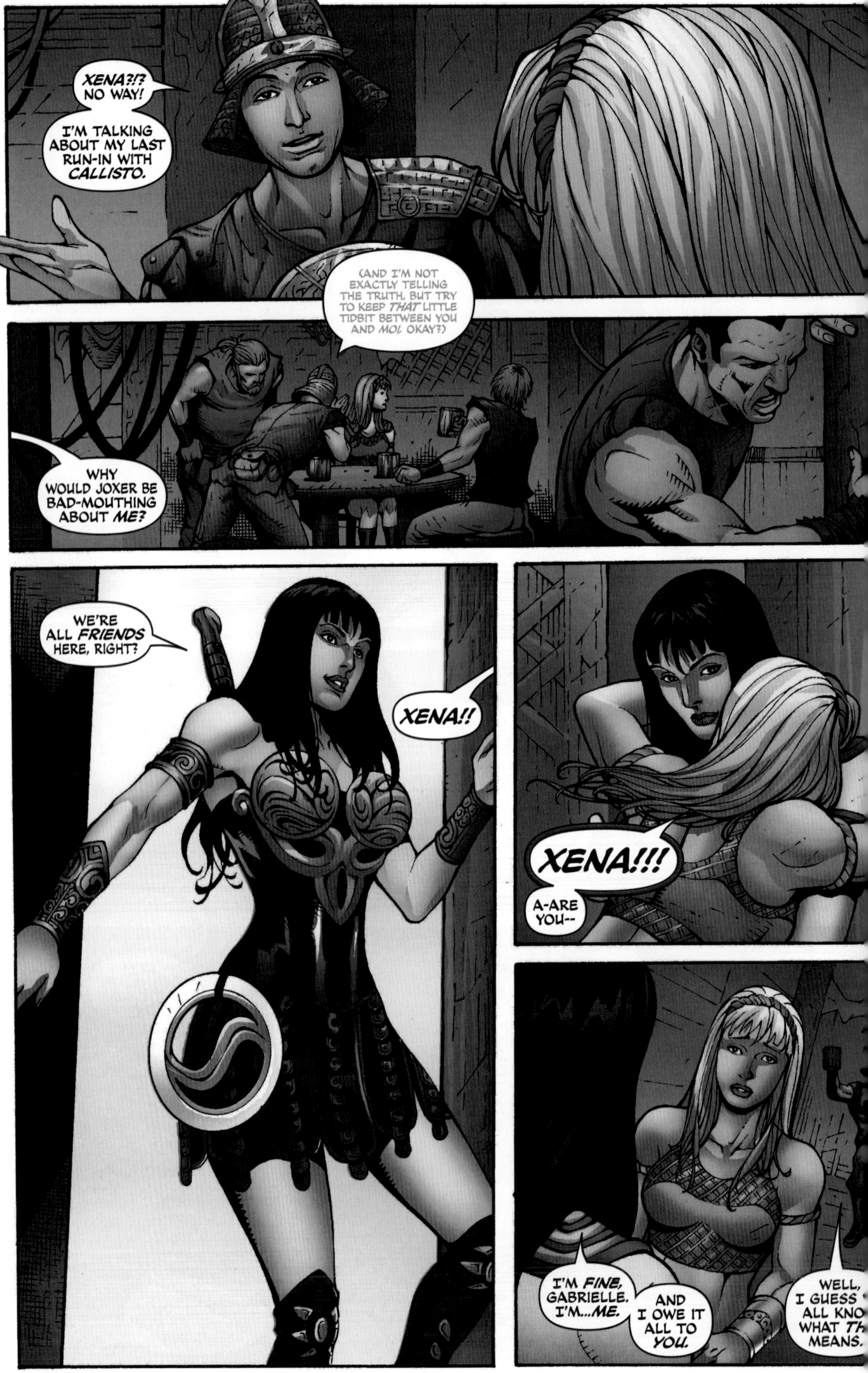
XENA?!? NO WAY!
I'M TALKING ABOUT MY LAST RUN-IN WITH CALLISTO.
(AND I'M NOT EXACTLY TELLING THE TRUTH, BUT TRY TO KEEP THAT LITTLE TIDBIT BETWEEN YOU AND MOI, OKAY?)
WHY WOULD JOXER BE BAD-MOUTHING ABOUT ME?
WE'RE ALL FRIENDS HERE, RIGHT?
XENA!!
XENA!!!
A-ARE YOU--
I'M FINE, GABRIELLE. I'M...ME.
AND I OWE IT ALL TO YOU.
WELL, I GUESS
ALL KNO
WHAT
MEANS.

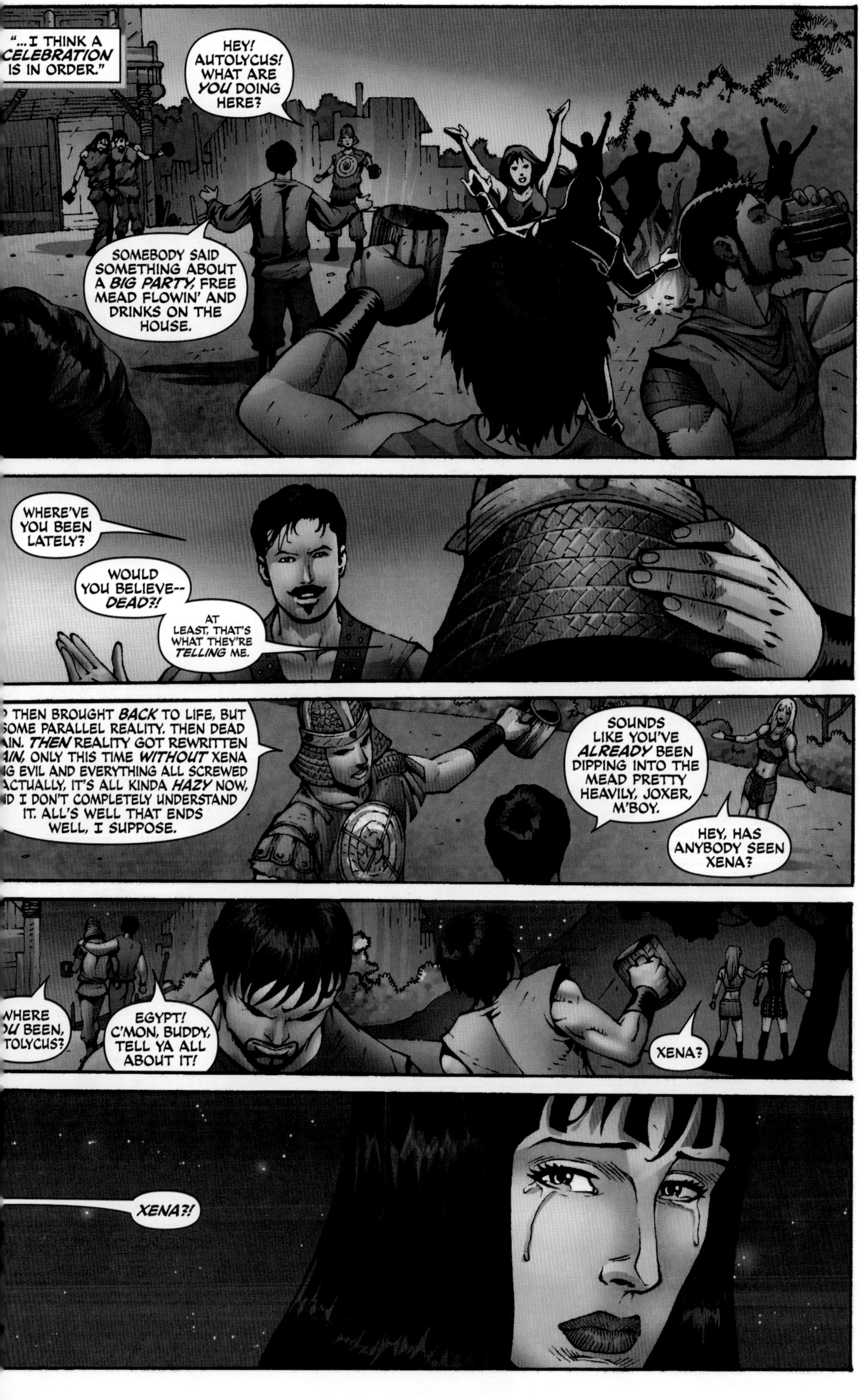
"...I THINK A CELEBRATION IS IN ORDER."
HEY! AUTOLYCUS! WHAT ARE YOU DOING HERE?
SOMEBODY SAID SOMETHING ABOUT A BIG PARTY, FREE MEAD FLOWIN' AND DRINKS ON THE HOUSE.
WHERE'VE YOU BEEN LATELY?
WOULD YOU BELIEVE-- DEAD?!
AT LEAST, THAT'S WHAT THEY'RE TELLING ME.
THEN BROUGHT BACK TO LIFE, BUT SOME PARALLEL REALITY. THEN DEAD AIN. THEN REALITY GOT REWRITTEN AIN, ONLY THIS TIME WITHOUT XENA IG EVIL AND EVERYTHING ALL SCREWED ACTUALLY, IT'S ALL KINDA HAZY NOW, D I DON'T COMPLETELY UNDERSTAND IT. ALL'S WELL THAT ENDS WELL, I SUPPOSE.
SOUNDS LIKE YOU'VE ALREADY BEEN DIPPING INTO THE MEAD PRETTY HEAVILY, JOXER, M'BOY.
HEY, HAS ANYBODY SEEN XENA?
WHERE U BEEN, TOLYCUS?
EGYPT! C'MON, BUDDY, TELL YA ALL ABOUT IT!
XENA?
XENA?!

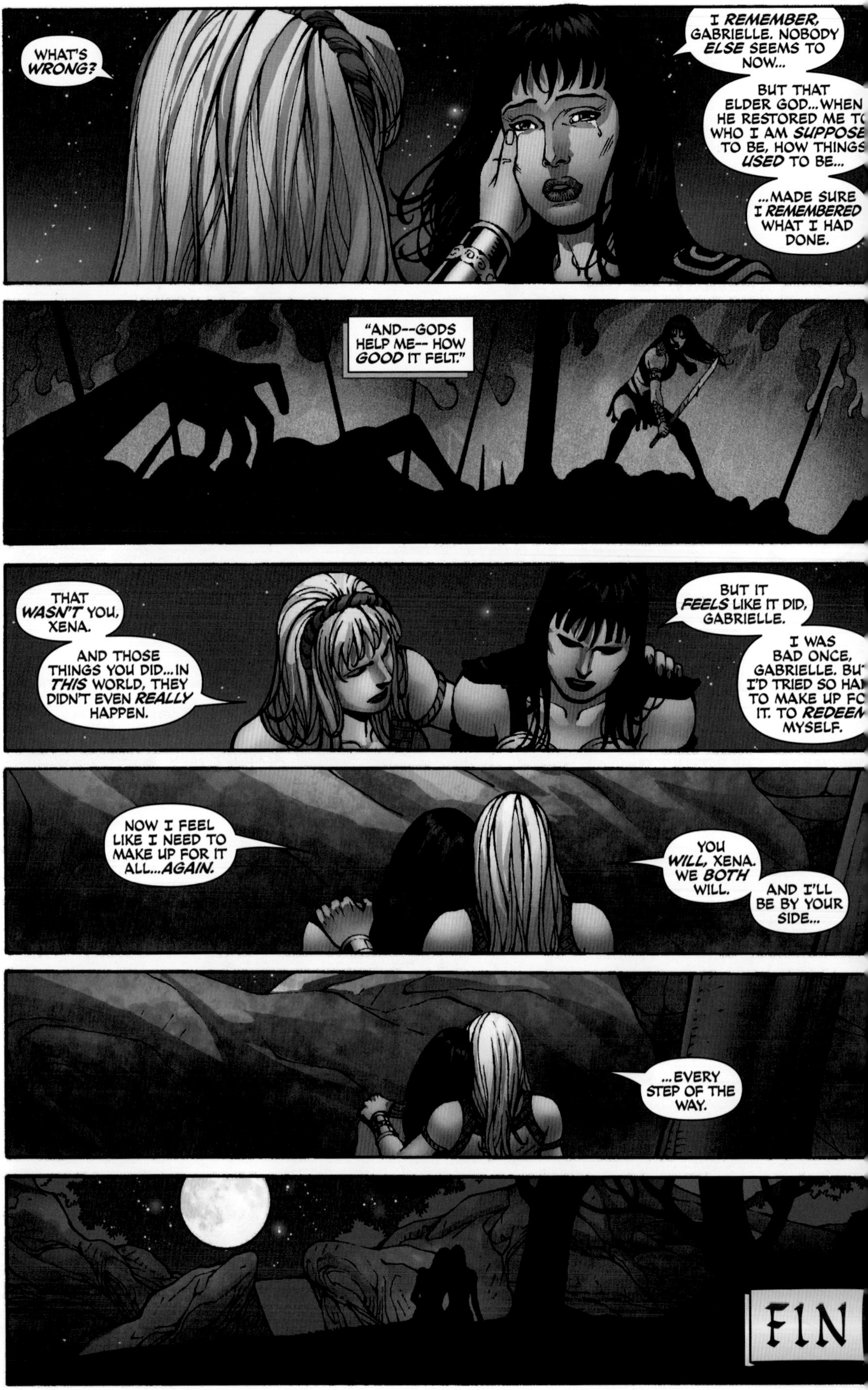
WHAT'S WRONG?
I REMEMBER, GABRIELLE. NOBODY ELSE SEEMS TO NOW...
BUT THAT ELDER GOD...WHEN HE RESTORED ME TO WHO I AM SUPPOSED TO BE, HOW THINGS USED TO BE...
...MADE SURE I REMEMBERED WHAT I HAD DONE.
"AND--GODS HELP ME-- HOW GOOD IT FELT."
THAT WASN'T YOU, XENA.
AND THOSE THINGS YOU DID...IN THIS WORLD, THEY DIDN'T EVEN REALLY HAPPEN.
BUT IT FEELS LIKE IT DID, GABRIELLE.
I WAS BAD ONCE, GABRIELLE. BUT I'D TRIED SO HARD TO MAKE UP FOR IT. TO REDEEM MYSELF.
NOW I FEEL LIKE I NEED TO MAKE UP FOR IT ALL...AGAIN.
YOU WILL, XENA. WE BOTH WILL.
AND I'LL BE BY YOUR SIDE...
...EVERY STEP OF THE WAY.
FIN

STRANGE VISITOR

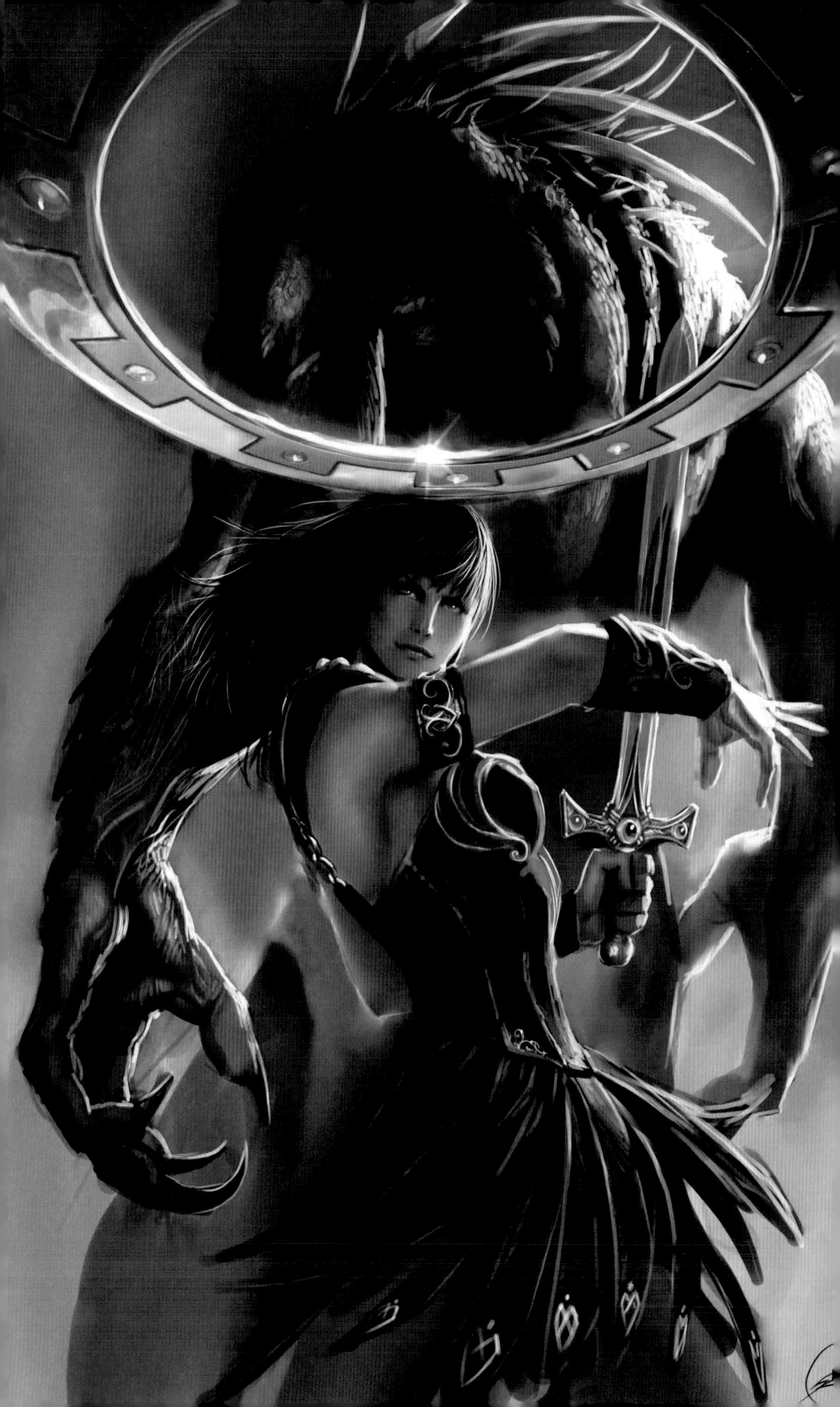

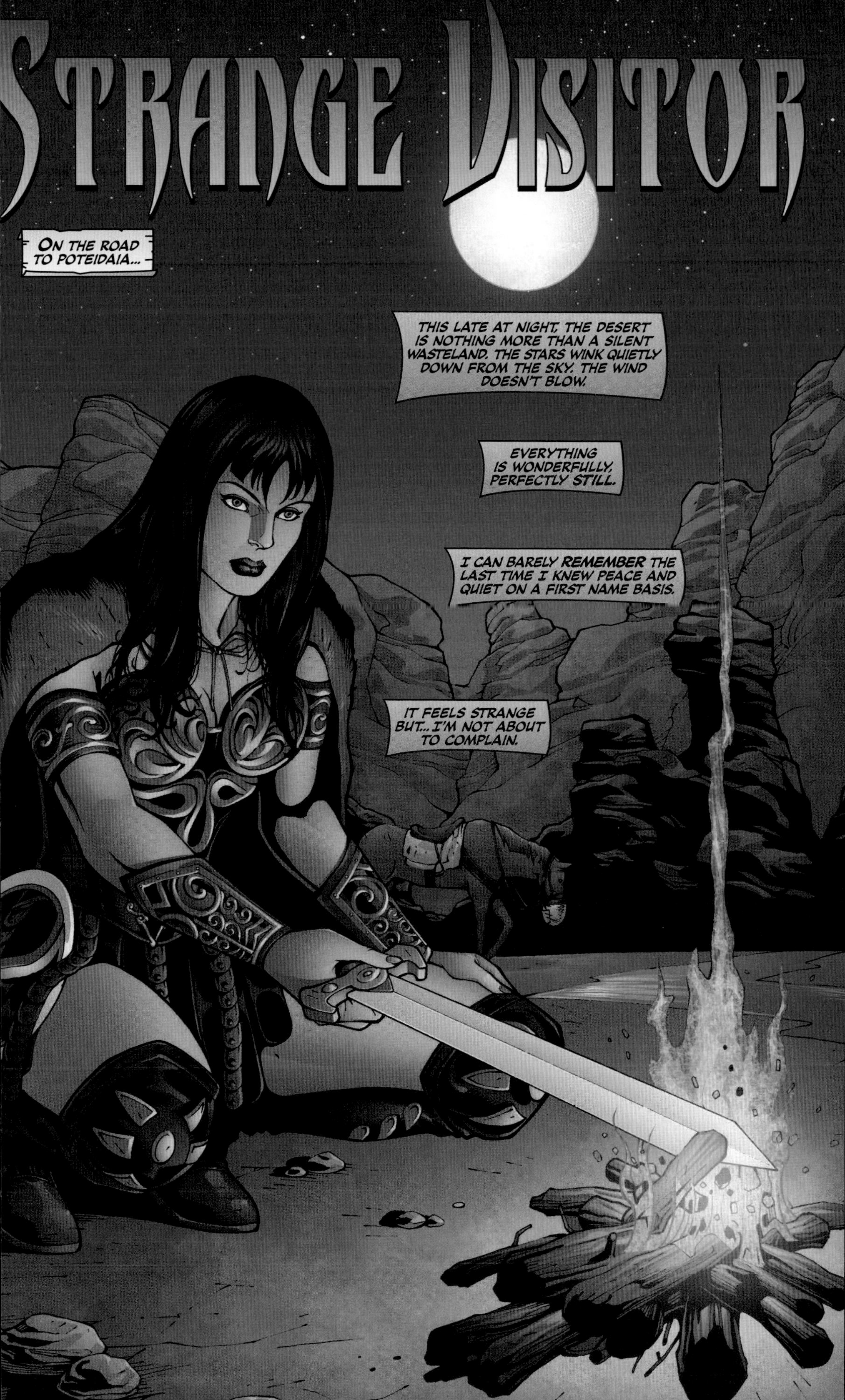
STRANGE VISITOR
ON THE ROAD TO POTEIDAIA...
THIS LATE AT NIGHT, THE DESERT IS NOTHING MORE THAN A SILENT WASTELAND. THE STARS WINK QUIETLY DOWN FROM THE SKY. THE WIND DOESN'T BLOW.
EVERYTHING IS WONDERFULLY, PERFECTLY STILL.
I CAN BARELY REMEMBER THE LAST TIME I KNEW PEACE AND QUIET ON A FIRST NAME BASIS.
IT FEELS STRANGE BUT... I'M NOT ABOUT TO COMPLAIN.

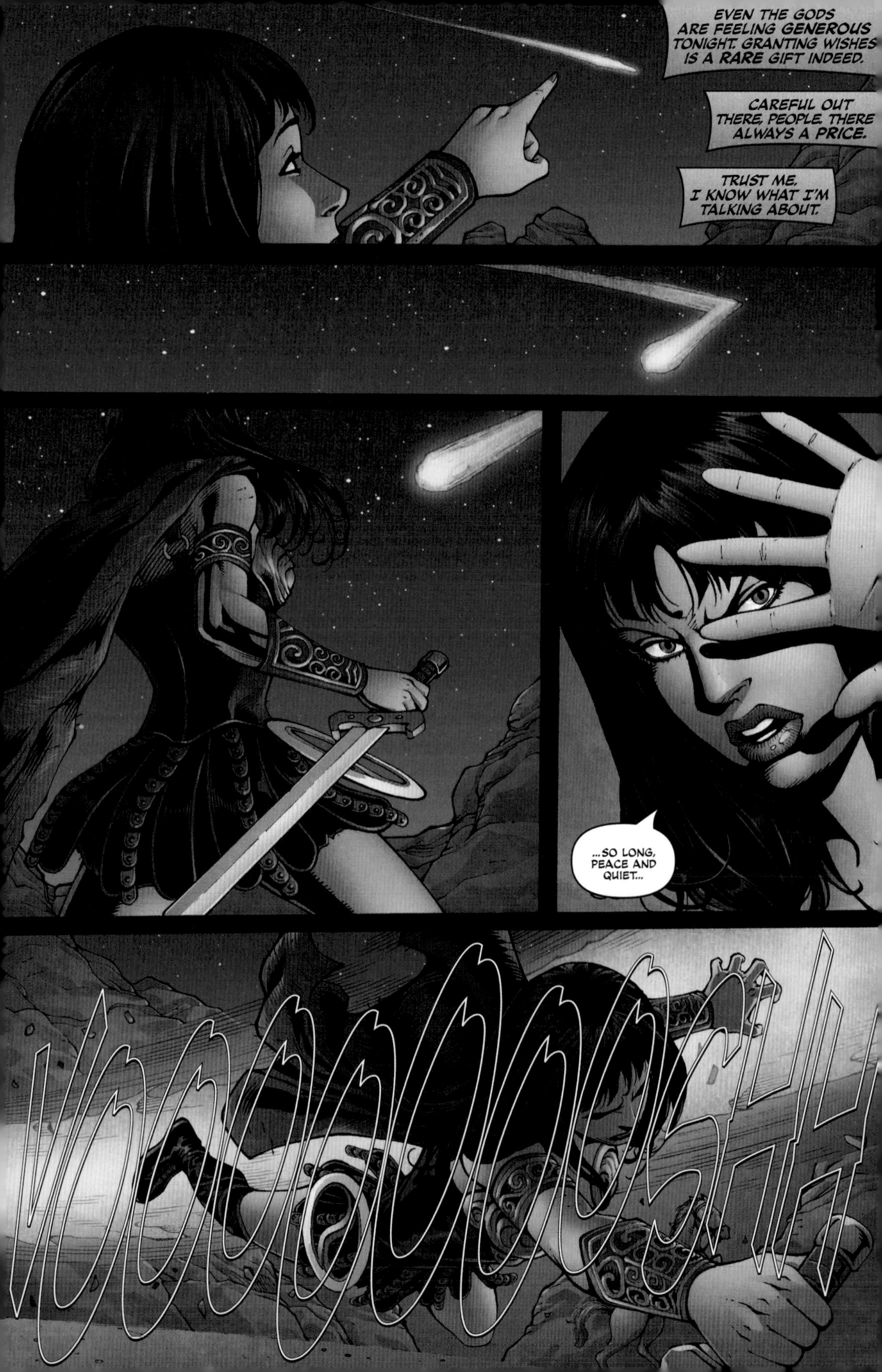
EVEN THE GODS ARE FEELING GENEROUS TONIGHT. GRANTING WISHES IS A RARE GIFT INDEED.
CAREFUL OUT THERE, PEOPLE. THERE ALWAYS A PRICE.
TRUST ME. I KNOW WHAT I'M TALKING ABOUT.
...SO LONG, PEACE AND QUIET...
VOOOOOOOOSHH

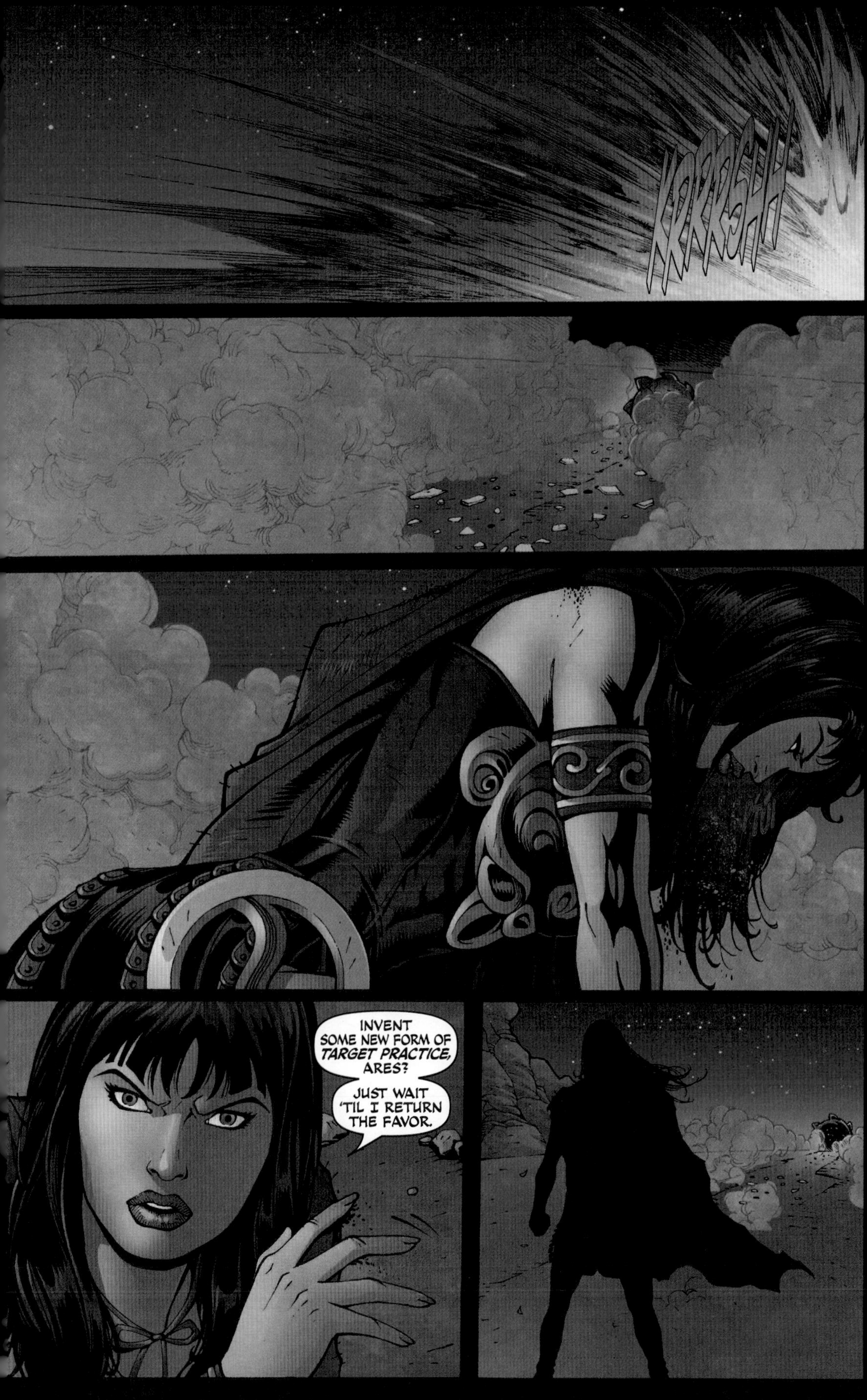
KRRRSHH
INVENT SOME NEW FORM OF *TARGET PRACTICE,* ARES?
JUST WAIT 'TIL I RETURN THE FAVOR.

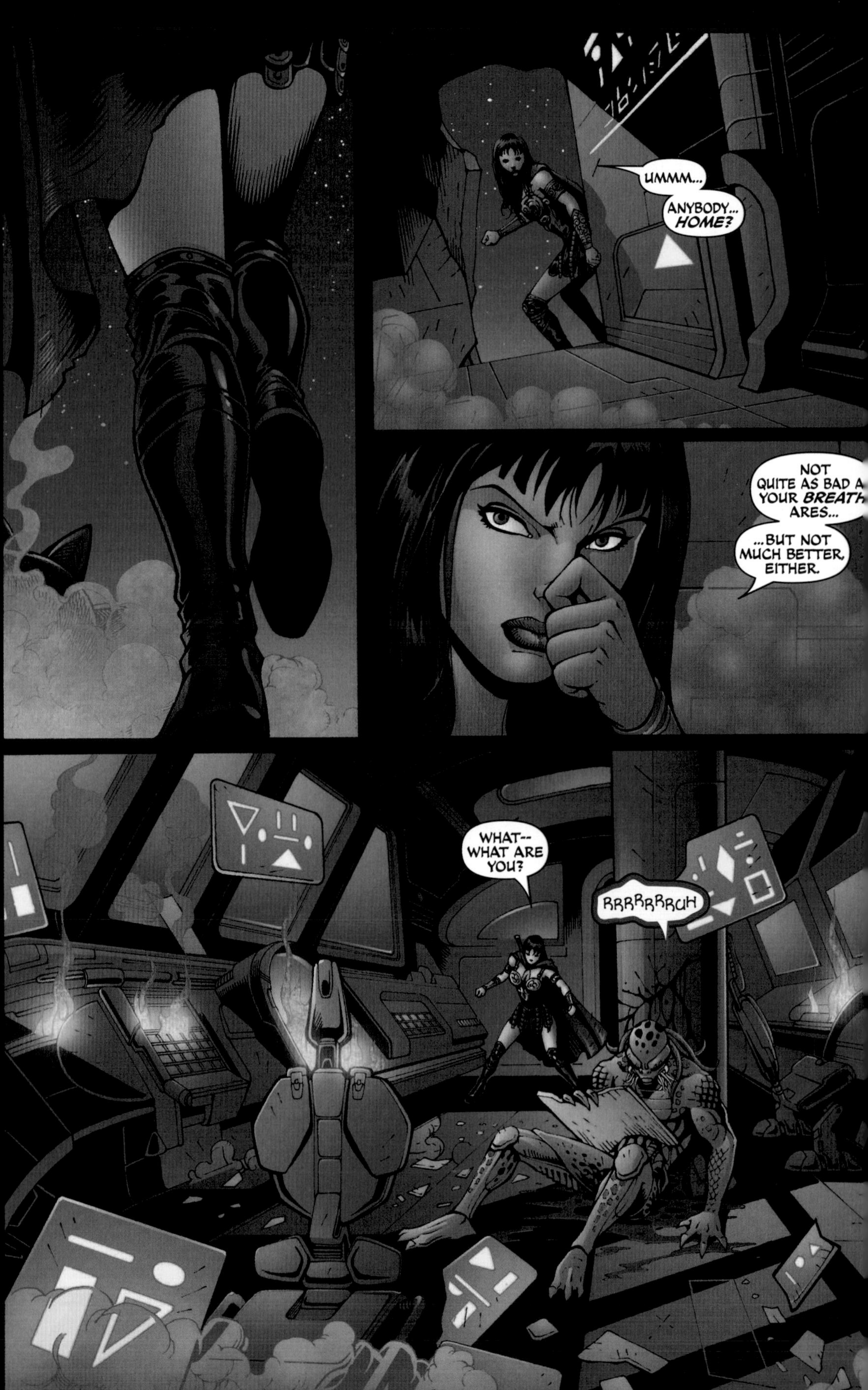

UMMM...
ANYBODY... HOME?
NOT QUITE AS BAD A YOUR BREATH ARES...
...BUT NOT MUCH BETTER, EITHER.
WHAT-- WHAT ARE YOU?
RRRRRRRUH

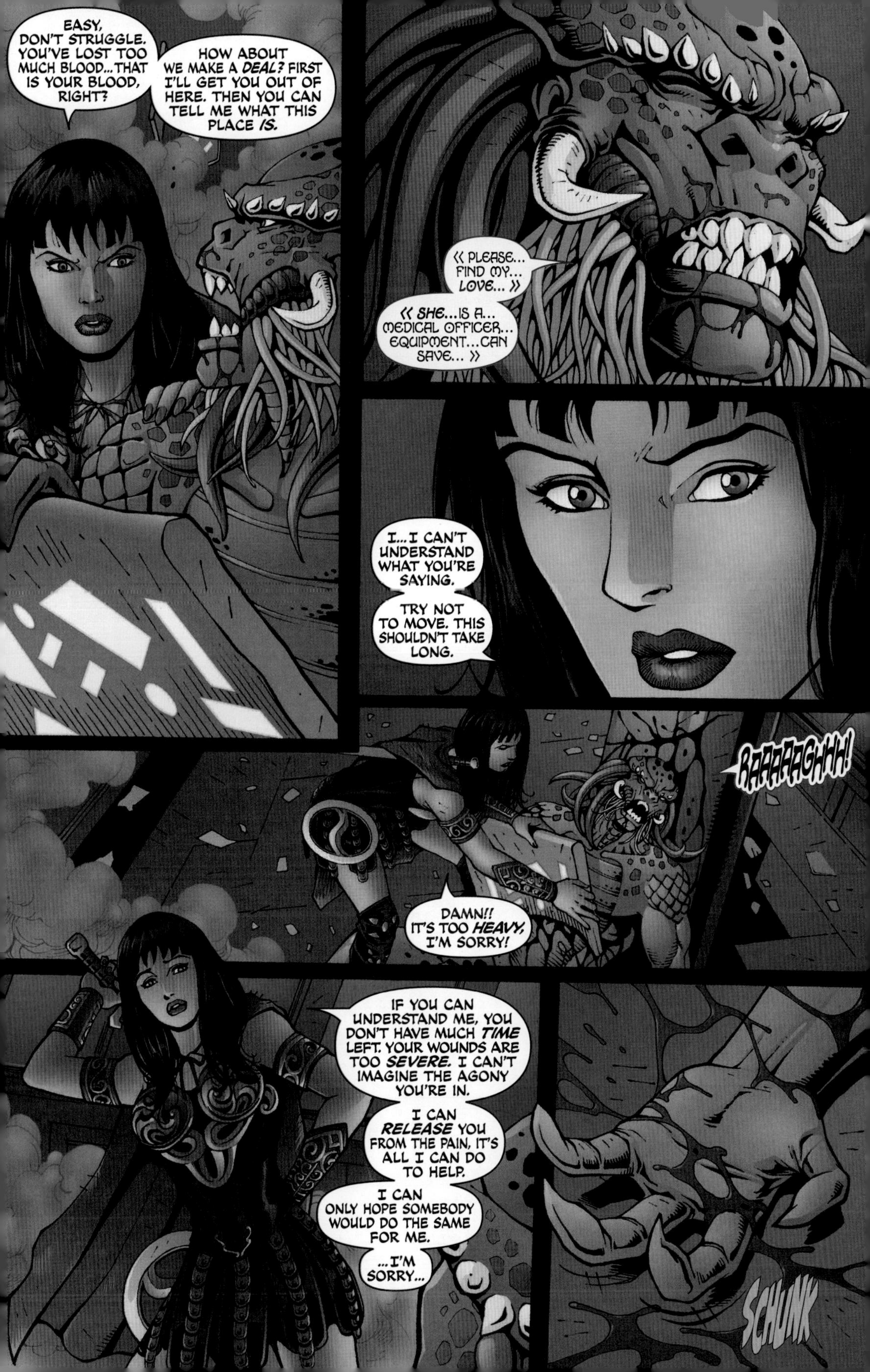
EASY, DON'T STRUGGLE. YOU'VE LOST TOO MUCH BLOOD...THAT IS YOUR BLOOD, RIGHT?
HOW ABOUT WE MAKE A *DEAL?* FIRST I'LL GET YOU OUT OF HERE. THEN YOU CAN TELL ME WHAT THIS PLACE *IS.*
« PLEASE... FIND MY... *LOVE...* »
« *SHE...*IS A... MEDICAL OFFICER... EQUIPMENT...CAN SAVE... »
I...I CAN'T UNDERSTAND WHAT YOU'RE SAYING.
TRY NOT TO MOVE. THIS SHOULDN'T TAKE LONG.
RAAAAAGHHH!
DAMN!! IT'S TOO *HEAVY,* I'M SORRY!
IF YOU CAN UNDERSTAND ME, YOU DON'T HAVE MUCH *TIME* LEFT. YOUR WOUNDS ARE TOO *SEVERE.* I CAN'T IMAGINE THE AGONY YOU'RE IN.
I CAN *RELEASE* YOU FROM THE PAIN, IT'S ALL I CAN DO TO HELP.
I CAN ONLY HOPE SOMEBODY WOULD DO THE SAME FOR ME.
...I'M SORRY...
SCHUNK

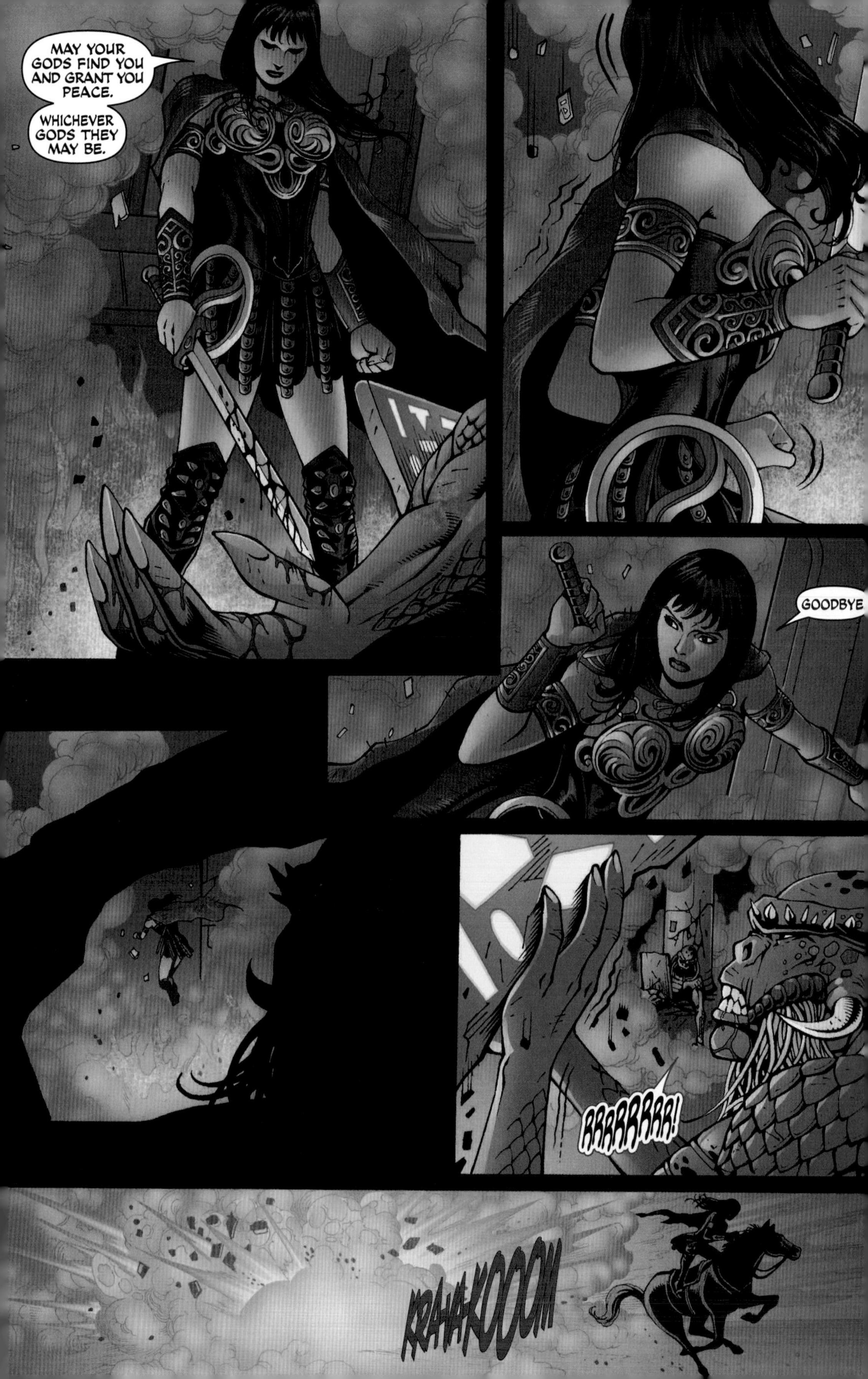
MAY YOUR GODS FIND YOU AND GRANT YOU PEACE.
WHICHEVER GODS THEY MAY BE.
GOODBYE
RRRRRRRR!
KRAVAKOOOM

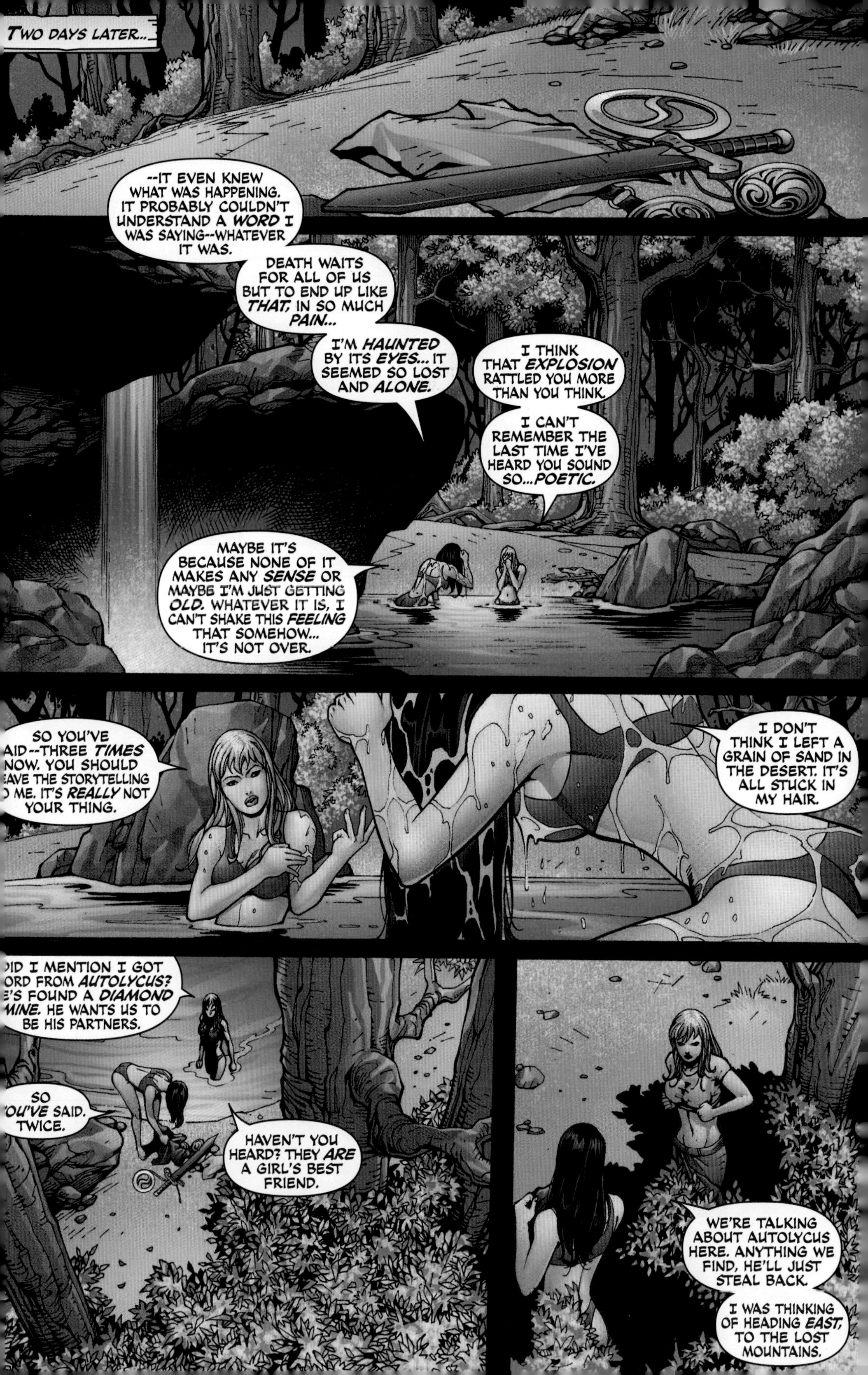
TWO DAYS LATER...
--IT EVEN KNEW WHAT WAS HAPPENING. IT PROBABLY COULDN'T UNDERSTAND A WORD I WAS SAYING--WHATEVER IT WAS.
DEATH WAITS FOR ALL OF US BUT TO END UP LIKE THAT, IN SO MUCH PAIN...
I'M HAUNTED BY ITS EYES... IT SEEMED SO LOST AND ALONE.
I THINK THAT EXPLOSION RATTLED YOU MORE THAN YOU THINK.
I CAN'T REMEMBER THE LAST TIME I'VE HEARD YOU SOUND SO...POETIC.
MAYBE IT'S BECAUSE NONE OF IT MAKES ANY SENSE OR MAYBE I'M JUST GETTING OLD. WHATEVER IT IS, I CAN'T SHAKE THIS FEELING THAT SOMEHOW... IT'S NOT OVER.
SO YOU'VE AID--THREE TIMES NOW. YOU SHOULD EAVE THE STORYTELLING O ME. IT'S REALLY NOT YOUR THING.
I DON'T THINK I LEFT A GRAIN OF SAND IN THE DESERT. IT'S ALL STUCK IN MY HAIR.
DID I MENTION I GOT ORD FROM AUTOLYCUS? E'S FOUND A DIAMOND MINE. HE WANTS US TO BE HIS PARTNERS.
SO OU'VE SAID. TWICE.
HAVEN'T YOU HEARD? THEY ARE A GIRL'S BEST FRIEND.
WE'RE TALKING ABOUT AUTOLYCUS HERE. ANYTHING WE FIND, HE'LL JUST STEAL BACK.
I WAS THINKING OF HEADING EAST, TO THE LOST MOUNTAINS.

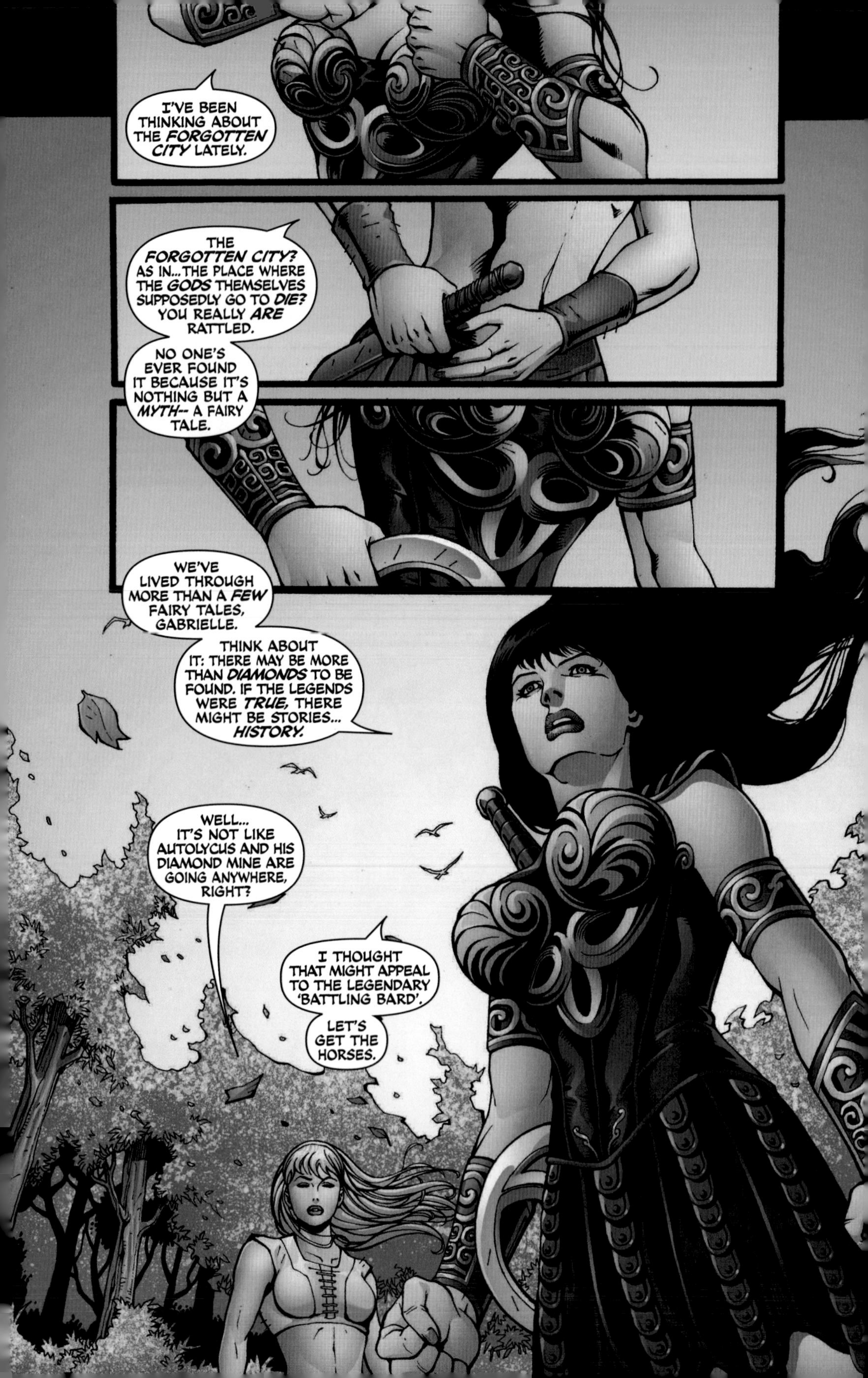

I'VE BEEN THINKING ABOUT THE *FORGOTTEN CITY* LATELY.
THE *FORGOTTEN CITY?* AS IN... THE PLACE WHERE THE *GODS* THEMSELVES SUPPOSEDLY GO TO *DIE?* YOU REALLY *ARE* RATTLED.
NO ONE'S EVER FOUND IT BECAUSE IT'S NOTHING BUT A *MYTH*-- A FAIRY TALE.
WE'VE LIVED THROUGH MORE THAN A *FEW* FAIRY TALES, GABRIELLE.
THINK ABOUT IT: THERE MAY BE MORE THAN *DIAMONDS* TO BE FOUND. IF THE LEGENDS WERE *TRUE,* THERE MIGHT BE STORIES... *HISTORY.*
WELL... IT'S NOT LIKE AUTOLYCUS AND HIS DIAMOND MINE ARE GOING ANYWHERE, RIGHT?
I THOUGHT THAT MIGHT APPEAL TO THE LEGENDARY 'BATTLING BARD'.
LET'S GET THE HORSES.

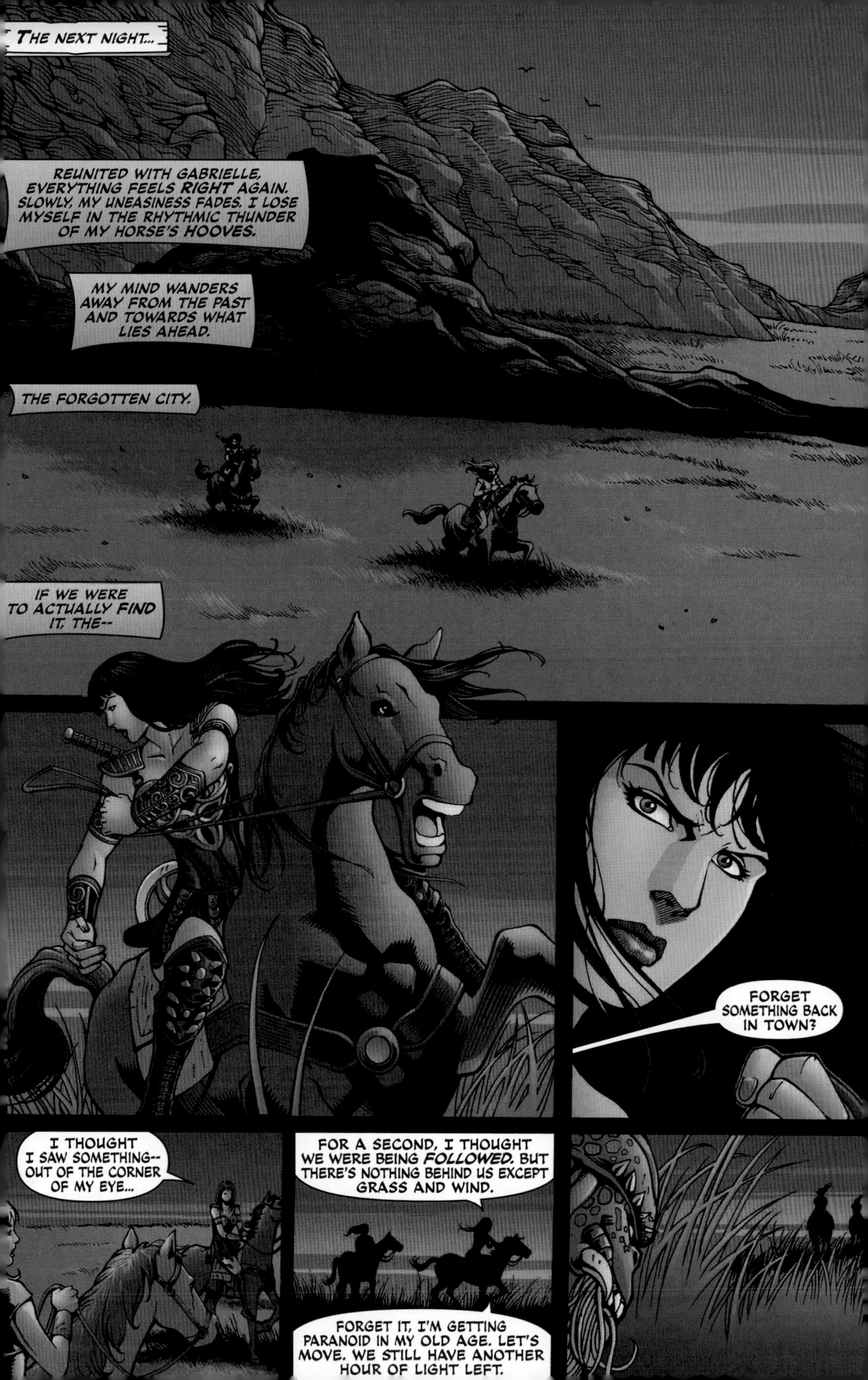
THE NEXT NIGHT...
REUNITED WITH GABRIELLE, EVERYTHING FEELS RIGHT AGAIN. SLOWLY, MY UNEASINESS FADES. I LOSE MYSELF IN THE RHYTHMIC THUNDER OF MY HORSE'S HOOVES.
MY MIND WANDERS AWAY FROM THE PAST AND TOWARDS WHAT LIES AHEAD.
THE FORGOTTEN CITY.
IF WE WERE TO ACTUALLY FIND IT, THE--
FORGET SOMETHING BACK IN TOWN?
I THOUGHT I SAW SOMETHING-- OUT OF THE CORNER OF MY EYE...
FOR A SECOND, I THOUGHT WE WERE BEING FOLLOWED. BUT THERE'S NOTHING BEHIND US EXCEPT GRASS AND WIND.
FORGET IT, I'M GETTING PARANOID IN MY OLD AGE. LET'S MOVE. WE STILL HAVE ANOTHER HOUR OF LIGHT LEFT.

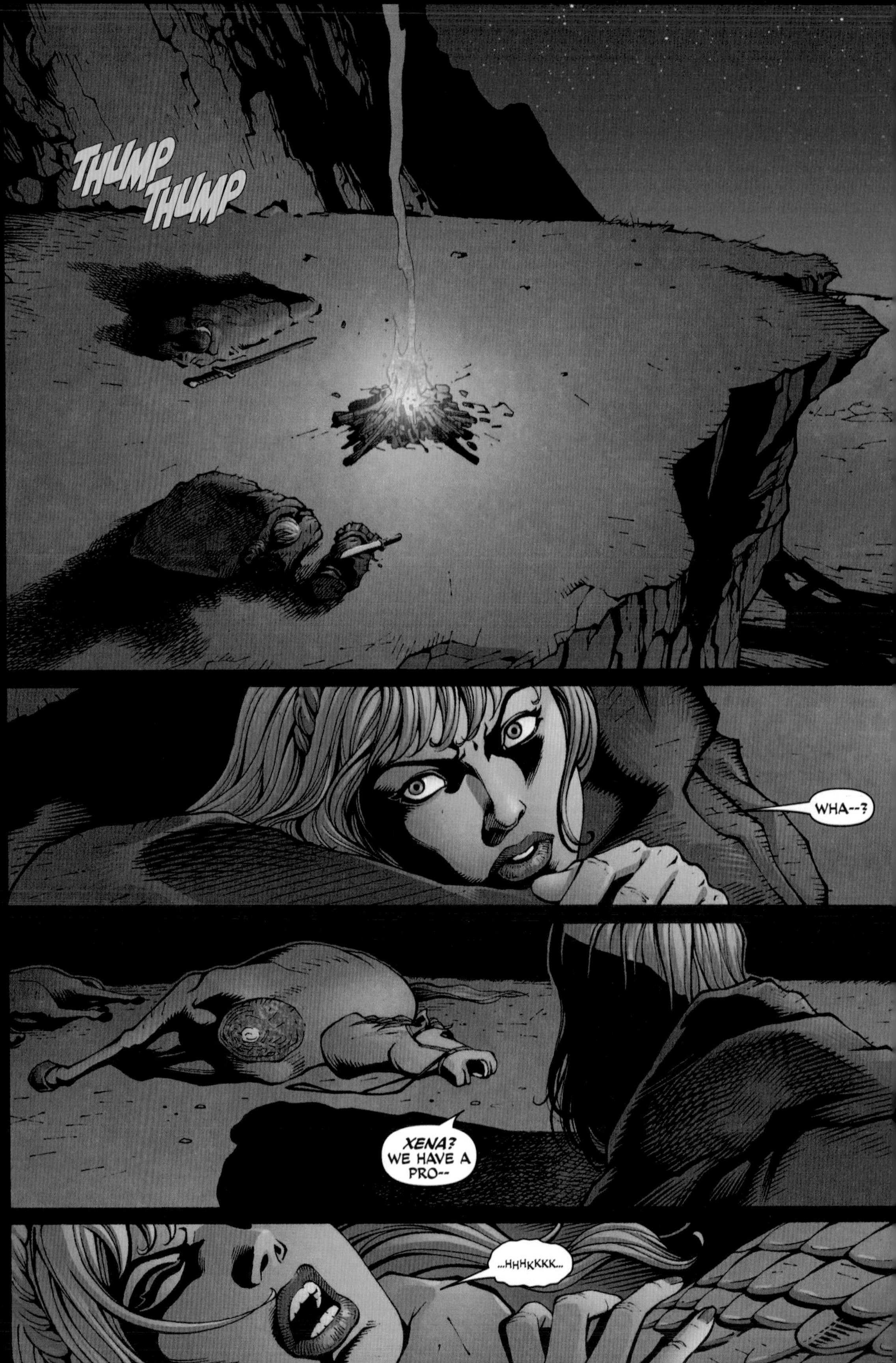
THUMP THUMP
WHA--?
XENA? WE HAVE A PRO--
...HHHKKKK...

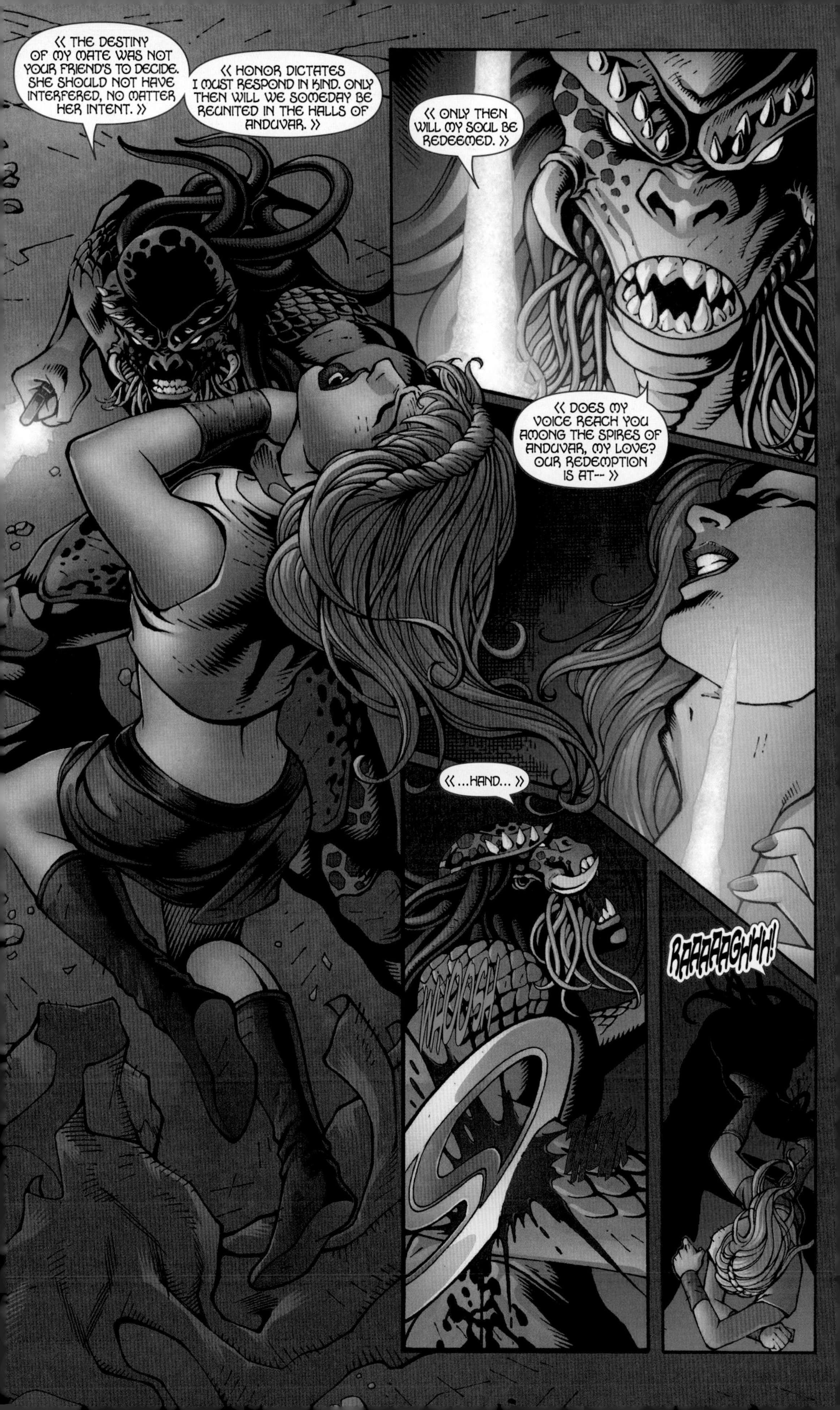

<< THE DESTINY OF MY MATE WAS NOT YOUR FRIEND'S TO DECIDE. SHE SHOULD NOT HAVE INTERFERED, NO MATTER HER INTENT. >>
<< HONOR DICTATES I MUST RESPOND IN KIND. ONLY THEN WILL WE SOMEDAY BE REUNITED IN THE HALLS OF ANDUVAR. >>
<< ONLY THEN WILL MY SOUL BE REDEEMED. >>
<< DOES MY VOICE REACH YOU AMONG THE SPIRES OF ANDUVAR, MY LOVE? OUR REDEMPTION IS AT-- >>
<< ...HAND... >>
WHOOSH
RAAAAAGHHH!

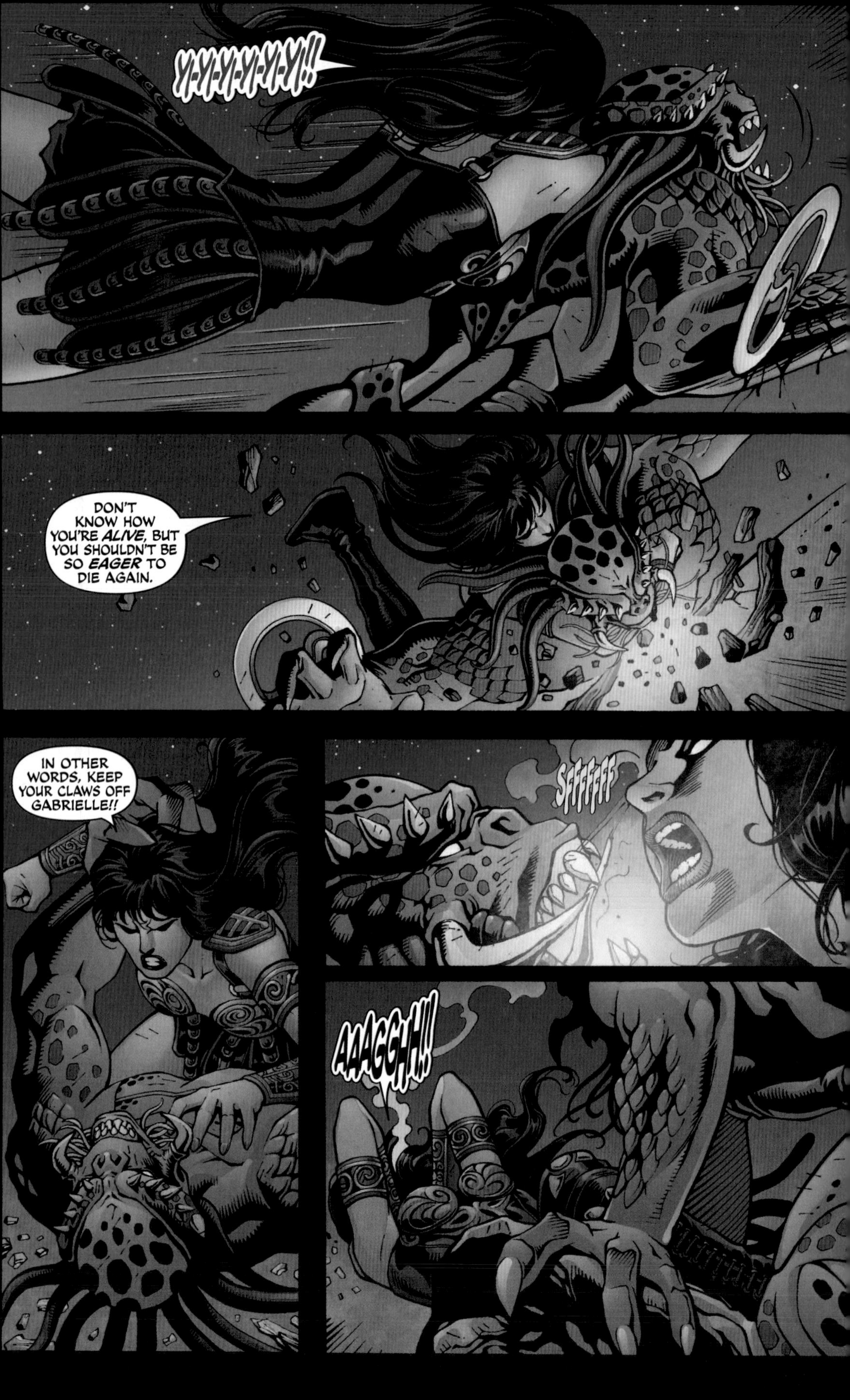
YI-YI-YI-YI-YI-YI!!
DON'T KNOW HOW YOU'RE ALIVE, BUT YOU SHOULDN'T BE SO EAGER TO DIE AGAIN.
IN OTHER WORDS, KEEP YOUR CLAWS OFF GABRIELLE!!
SFFFFFFF
AAAGGHH!!

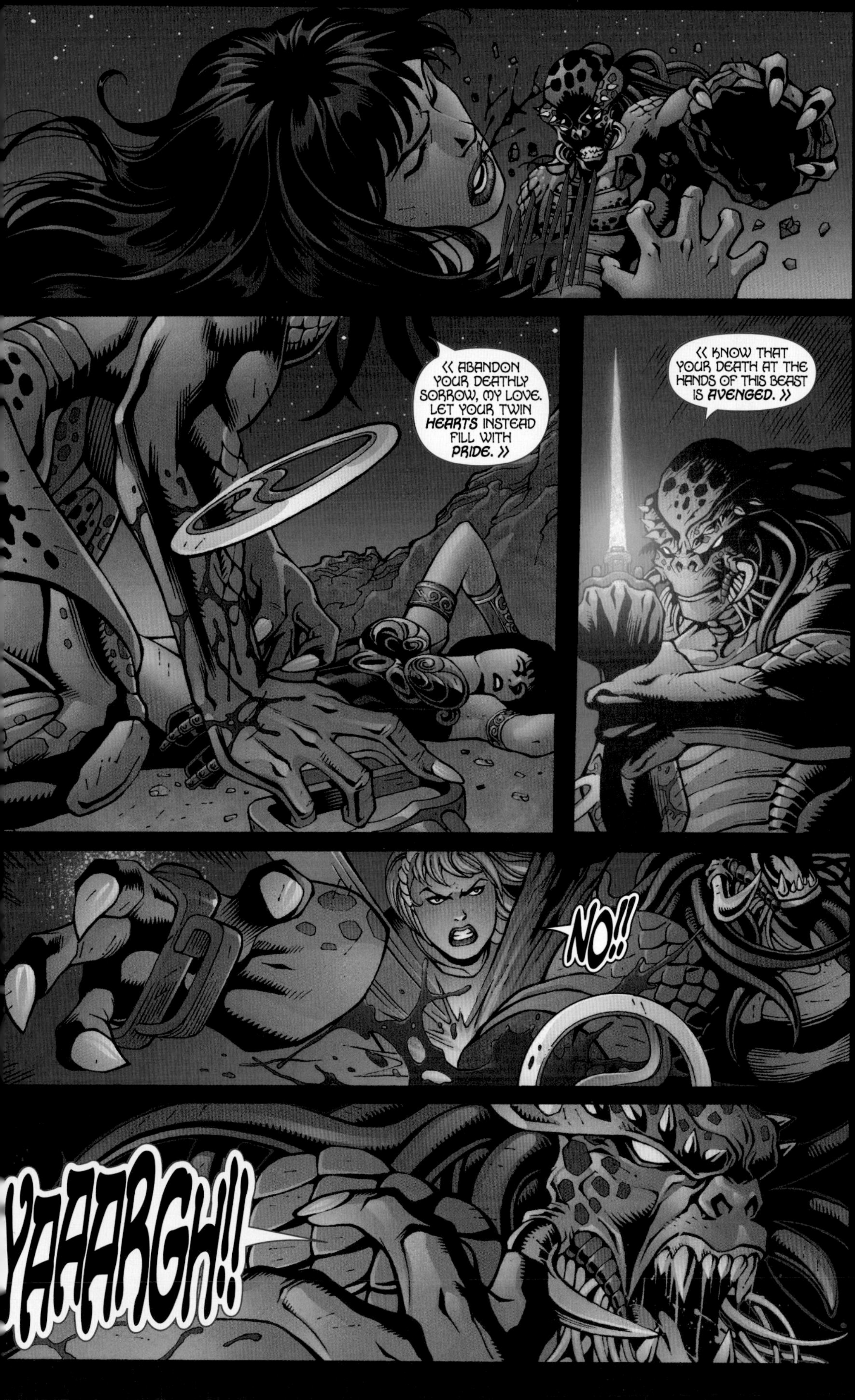
WHAH
<< ABANDON YOUR DEATHLY SORROW, MY LOVE. LET YOUR TWIN HEARTS INSTEAD FILL WITH PRIDE. >>
<< KNOW THAT YOUR DEATH AT THE HANDS OF THIS BEAST IS AVENGED. >>
NO!!
YAAARGH!!

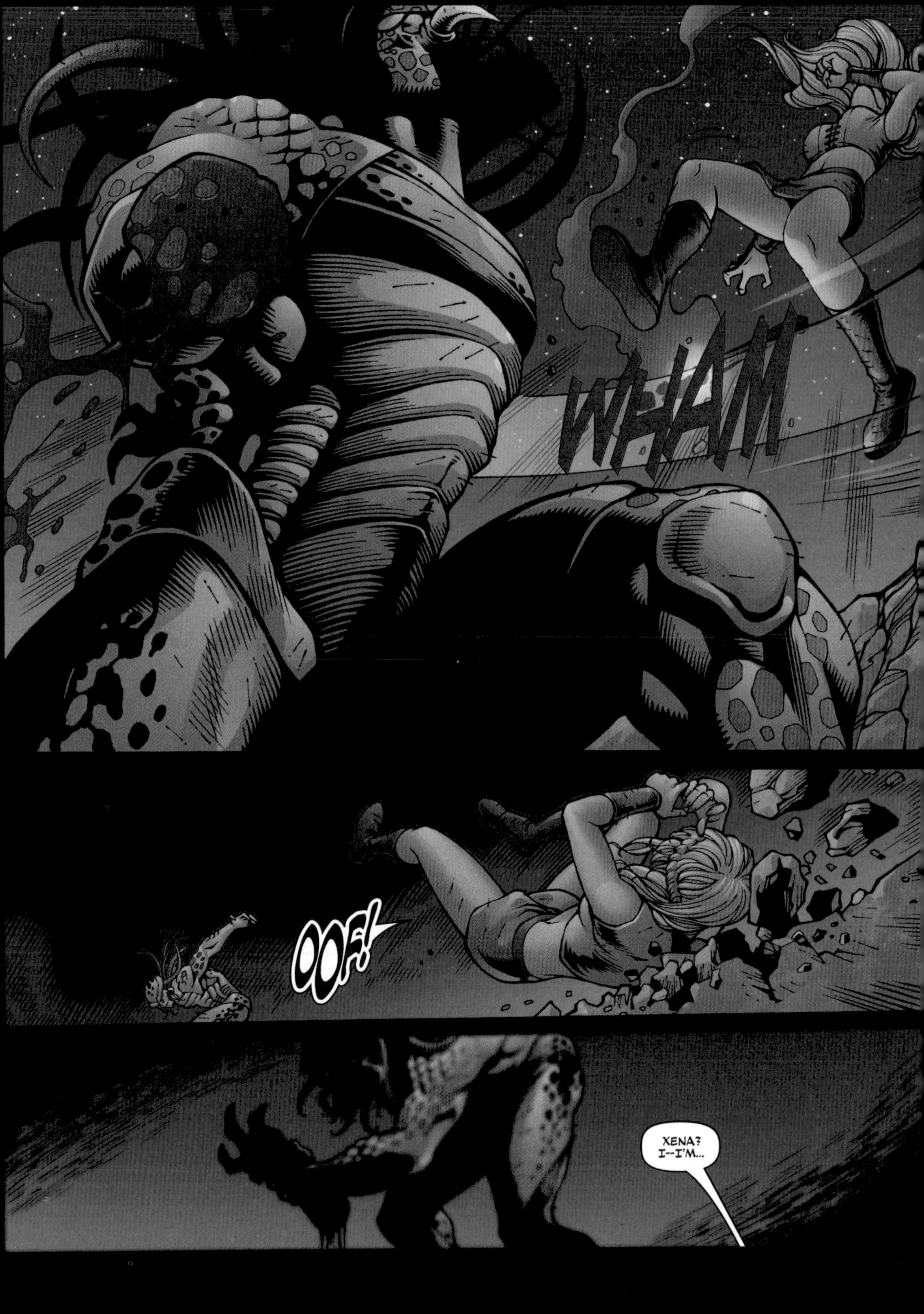
WHAM
OOF!
XENA? I--I'M...

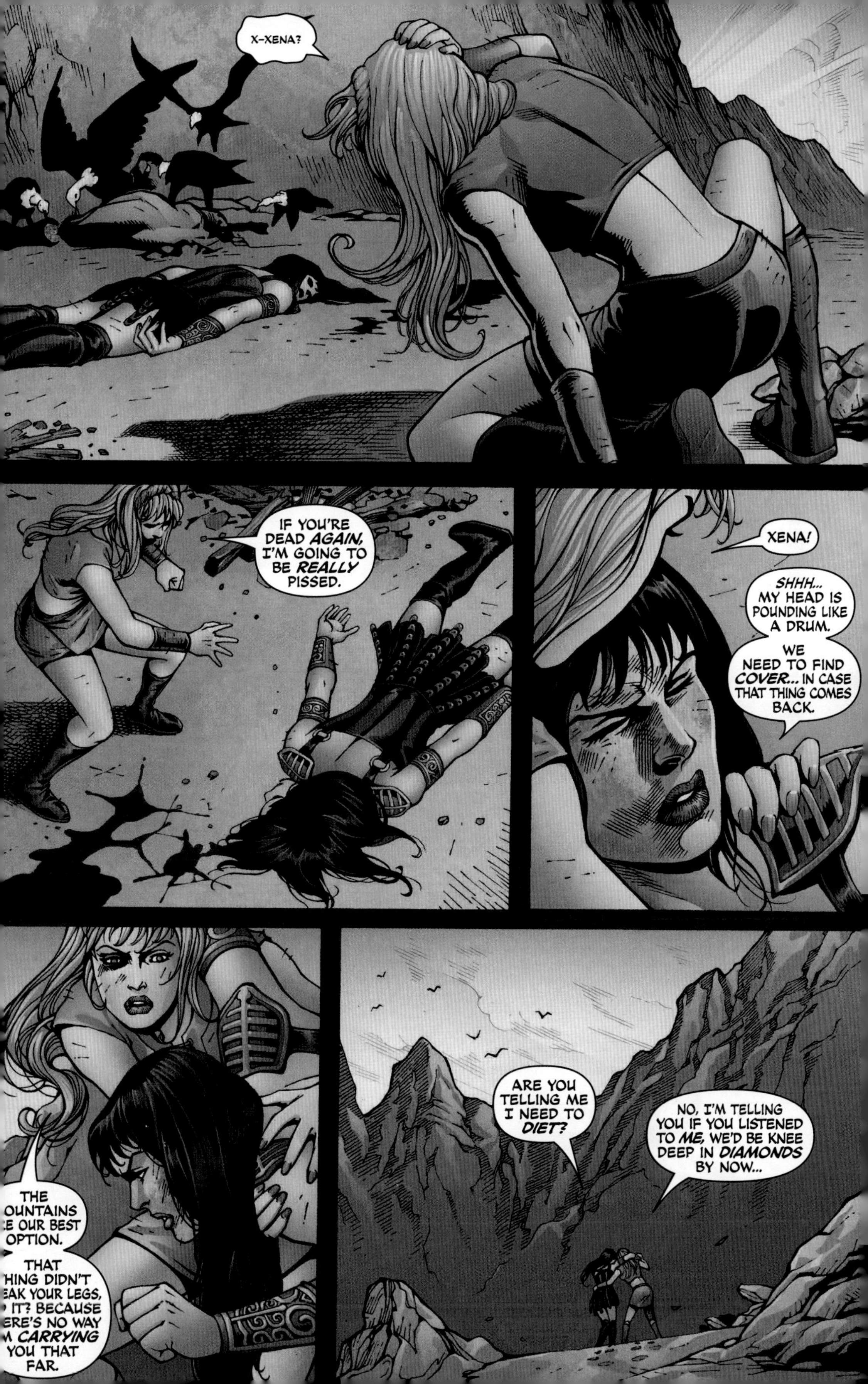
X-XENA?
IF YOU'RE DEAD AGAIN, I'M GOING TO BE REALLY PISSED.
XENA!
SHHH... MY HEAD IS POUNDING LIKE A DRUM.
WE NEED TO FIND COVER... IN CASE THAT THING COMES BACK.
THE OUNTAINS E OUR BEST OPTION.
THAT HING DIDN'T EAK YOUR LEGS, IT? BECAUSE ERE'S NO WAY M CARRYING YOU THAT FAR.
ARE YOU TELLING ME I NEED TO DIET?
NO, I'M TELLING YOU IF YOU LISTENED TO ME, WE'D BE KNEE DEEP IN DIAMONDS BY NOW...

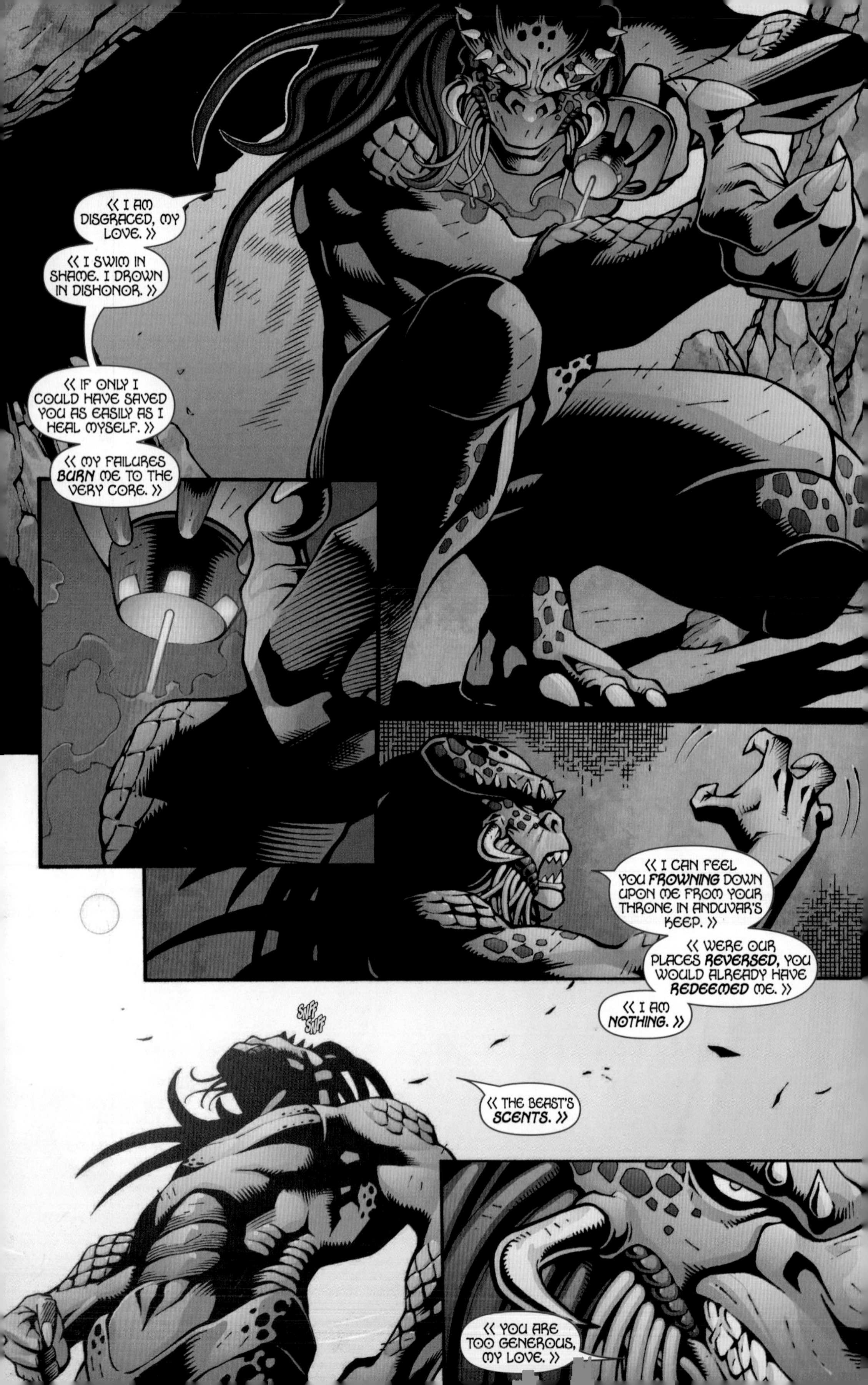

<< I AM DISGRACED, MY LOVE. >>
<< I SWIM IN SHAME. I DROWN IN DISHONOR. >>
<< IF ONLY I COULD HAVE SAVED YOU AS EASILY AS I HEAL MYSELF. >>
<< MY FAILURES **BURN** ME TO THE VERY CORE. >>
<< I CAN FEEL YOU **FROWNING** DOWN UPON ME FROM YOUR THRONE IN ANDUVAR'S KEEP. >>
<< WERE OUR PLACES **REVERSED,** YOU WOULD ALREADY HAVE **REDEEMED** ME. >>
<< I AM **NOTHING.** >>
SNIFF SNIFF
<< THE BEAST'S **SCENTS.** >>
<< YOU ARE TOO GENEROUS, MY LOVE. >>

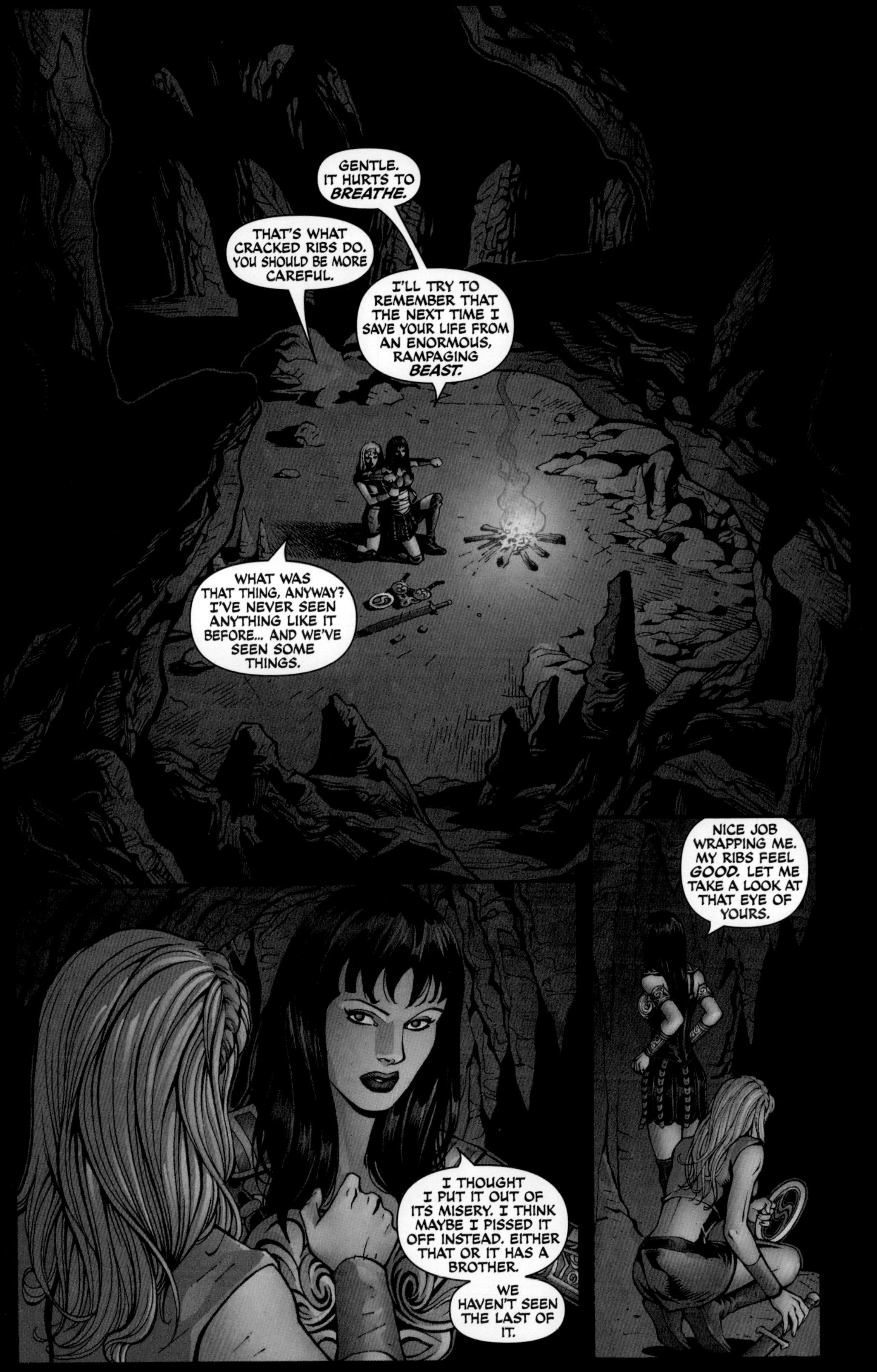
GENTLE. IT HURTS TO *BREATHE.*
THAT'S WHAT CRACKED RIBS DO. YOU SHOULD BE MORE CAREFUL.
I'LL TRY TO REMEMBER THAT THE NEXT TIME I SAVE YOUR LIFE FROM AN ENORMOUS, RAMPAGING *BEAST.*
WHAT WAS THAT THING, ANYWAY? I'VE NEVER SEEN ANYTHING LIKE IT BEFORE... AND WE'VE SEEN SOME THINGS.
I THOUGHT I PUT IT OUT OF ITS MISERY. I THINK MAYBE I PISSED IT OFF INSTEAD. EITHER THAT OR IT HAS A BROTHER.
WE HAVEN'T SEEN THE LAST OF IT.
NICE JOB WRAPPING ME. MY RIBS FEEL *GOOD.* LET ME TAKE A LOOK AT THAT EYE OF YOURS.

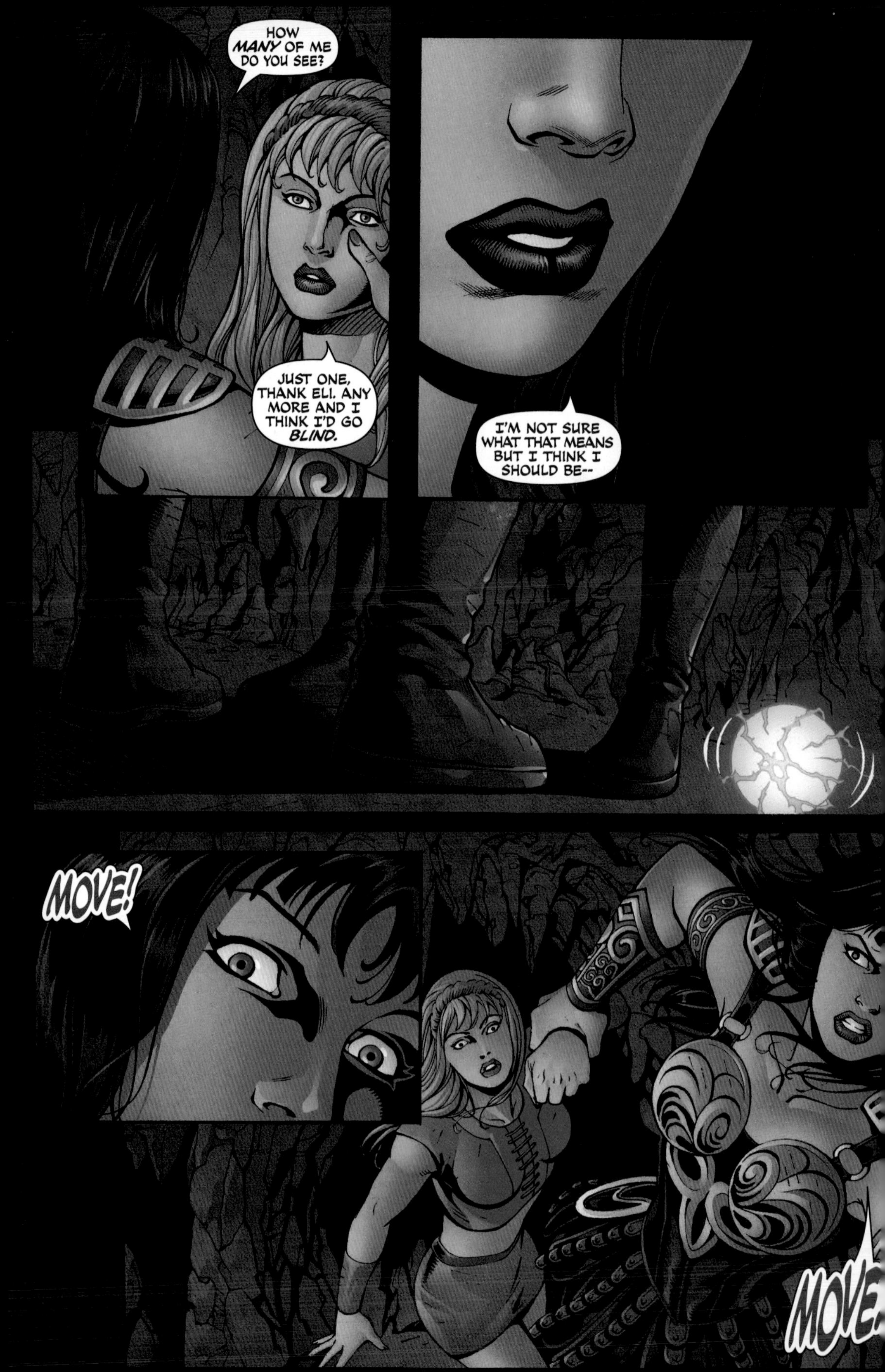

HOW MANY OF ME DO YOU SEE?
JUST ONE, THANK ELI. ANY MORE AND I THINK I'D GO BLIND.
I'M NOT SURE WHAT THAT MEANS BUT I THINK I SHOULD BE--
MOVE!

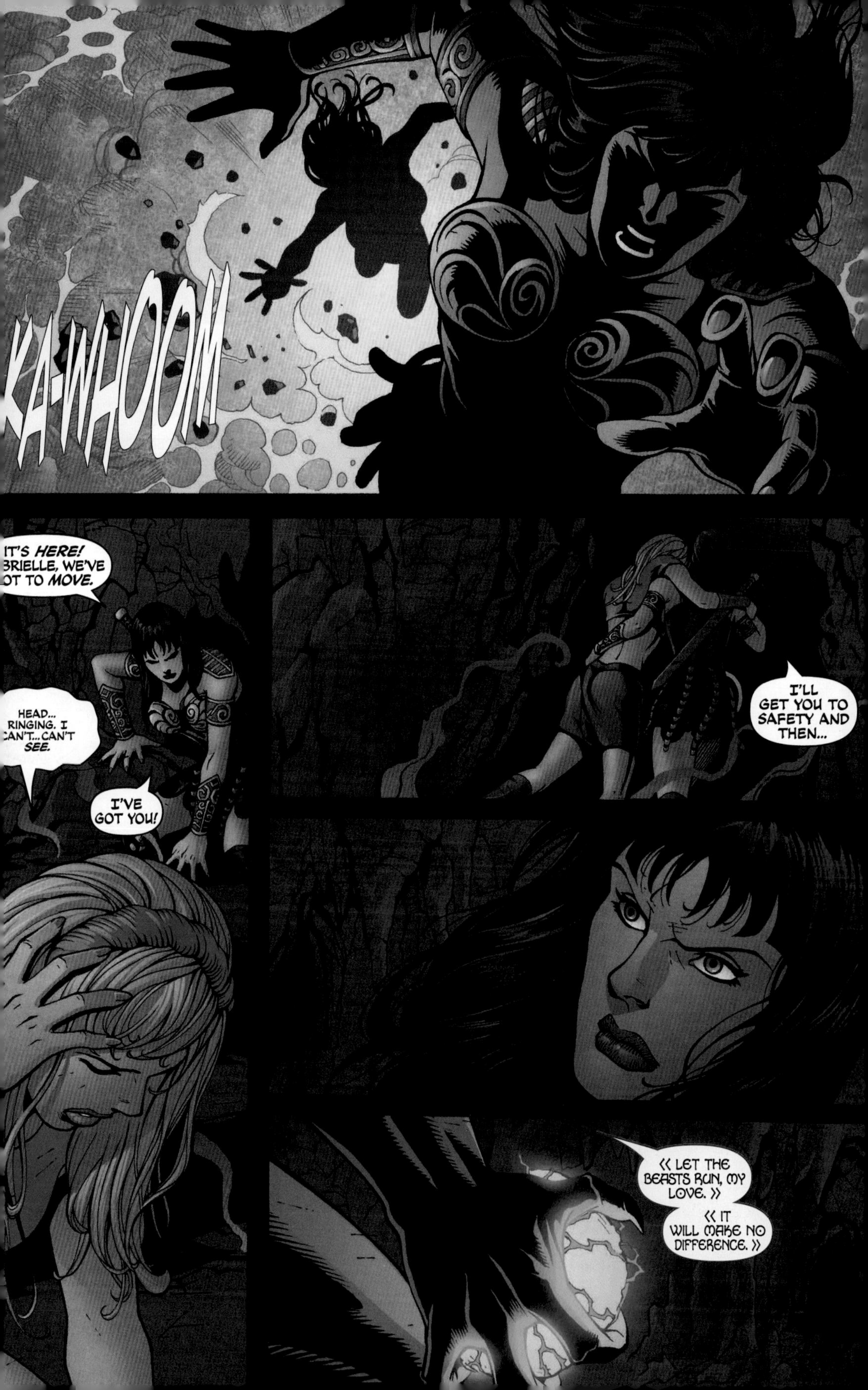
KA-WHOOM
IT'S HERE! BRIELLE, WE'VE OT TO MOVE.
HEAD... RINGING. I CAN'T...CAN'T SEE.
I'VE GOT YOU!
I'LL GET YOU TO SAFETY AND THEN...
« LET THE BEASTS RUN, MY LOVE. »
« IT WILL MAKE NO DIFFERENCE. »

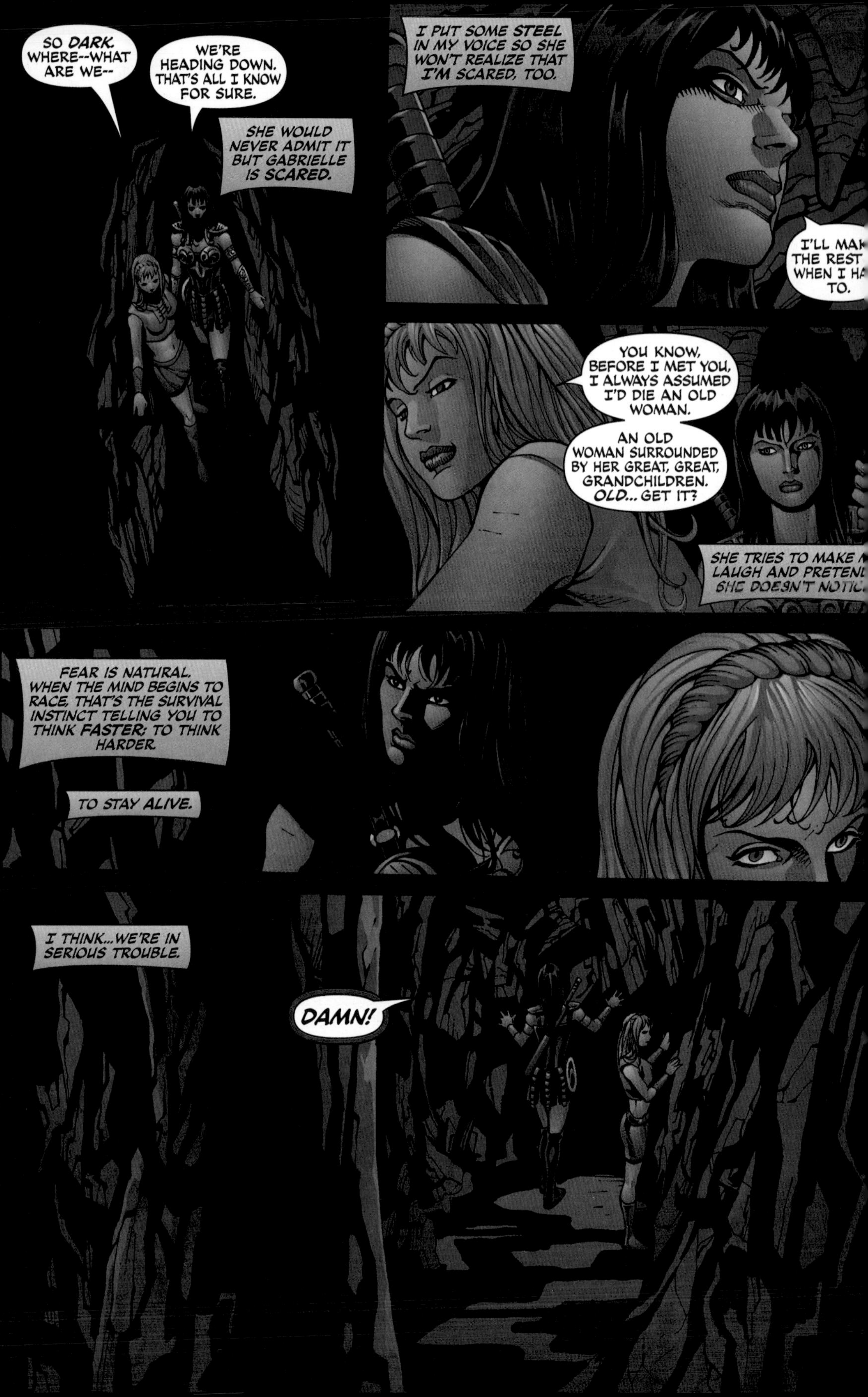
SO DARK. WHERE--WHAT ARE WE--
WE'RE HEADING DOWN. THAT'S ALL I KNOW FOR SURE.
SHE WOULD NEVER ADMIT IT BUT GABRIELLE IS SCARED.
I PUT SOME STEEL IN MY VOICE SO SHE WON'T REALIZE THAT I'M SCARED, TOO.
I'LL MAK THE REST WHEN I HA TO.
YOU KNOW, BEFORE I MET YOU, I ALWAYS ASSUMED I'D DIE AN OLD WOMAN.
AN OLD WOMAN SURROUNDED BY HER GREAT, GREAT, GRANDCHILDREN. OLD... GET IT?
SHE TRIES TO MAKE LAUGH AND PRETEN SHE DOESN'T NOTIC
FEAR IS NATURAL. WHEN THE MIND BEGINS TO RACE, THAT'S THE SURVIVAL INSTINCT TELLING YOU TO THINK FASTER: TO THINK HARDER.
TO STAY ALIVE.
I THINK...WE'RE IN SERIOUS TROUBLE.
DAMN!

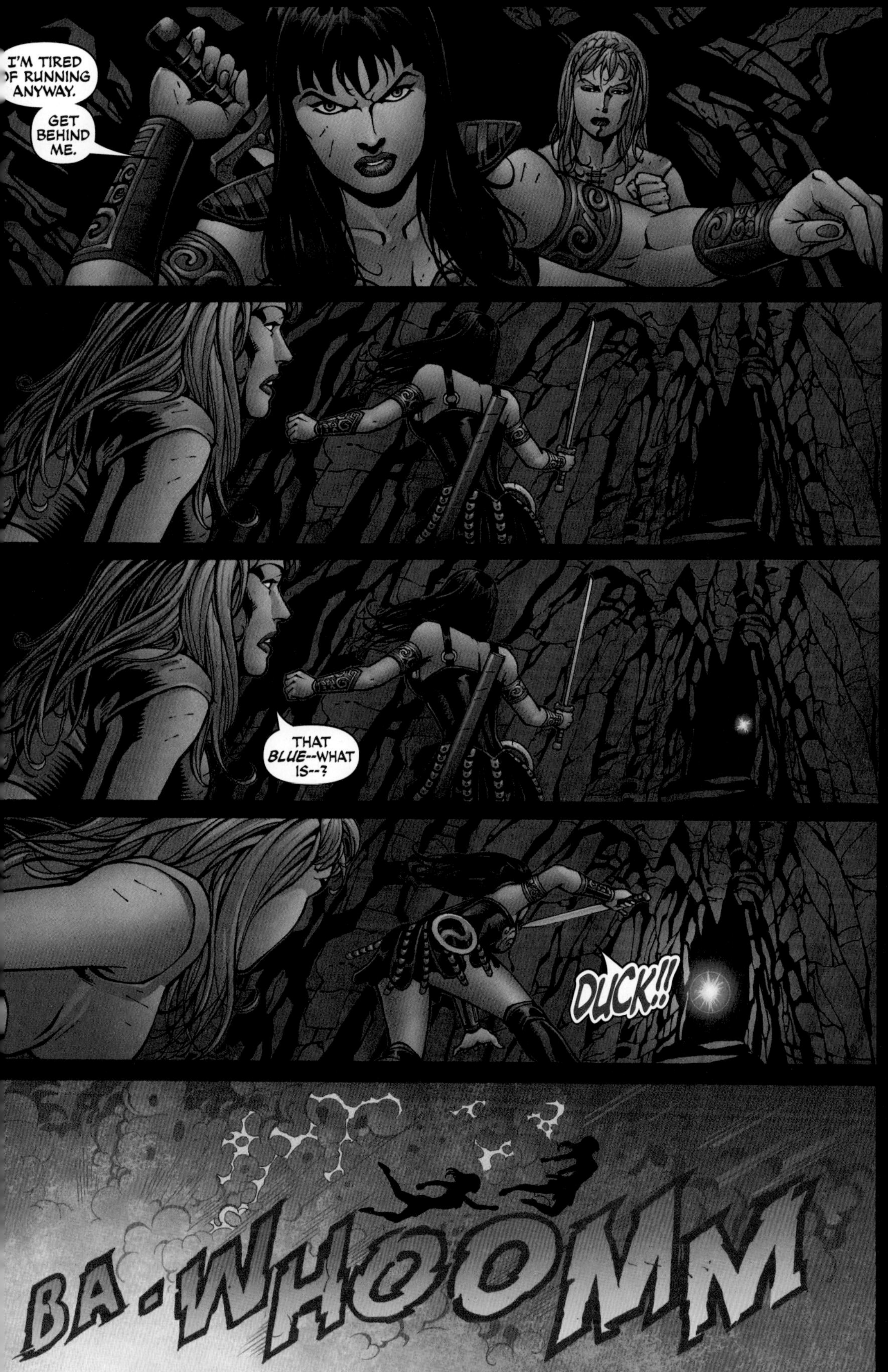

I'M TIRED OF RUNNING ANYWAY.
GET BEHIND ME.
THAT BLUE--WHAT IS--?
DUCK!!
BA-WHOOMM

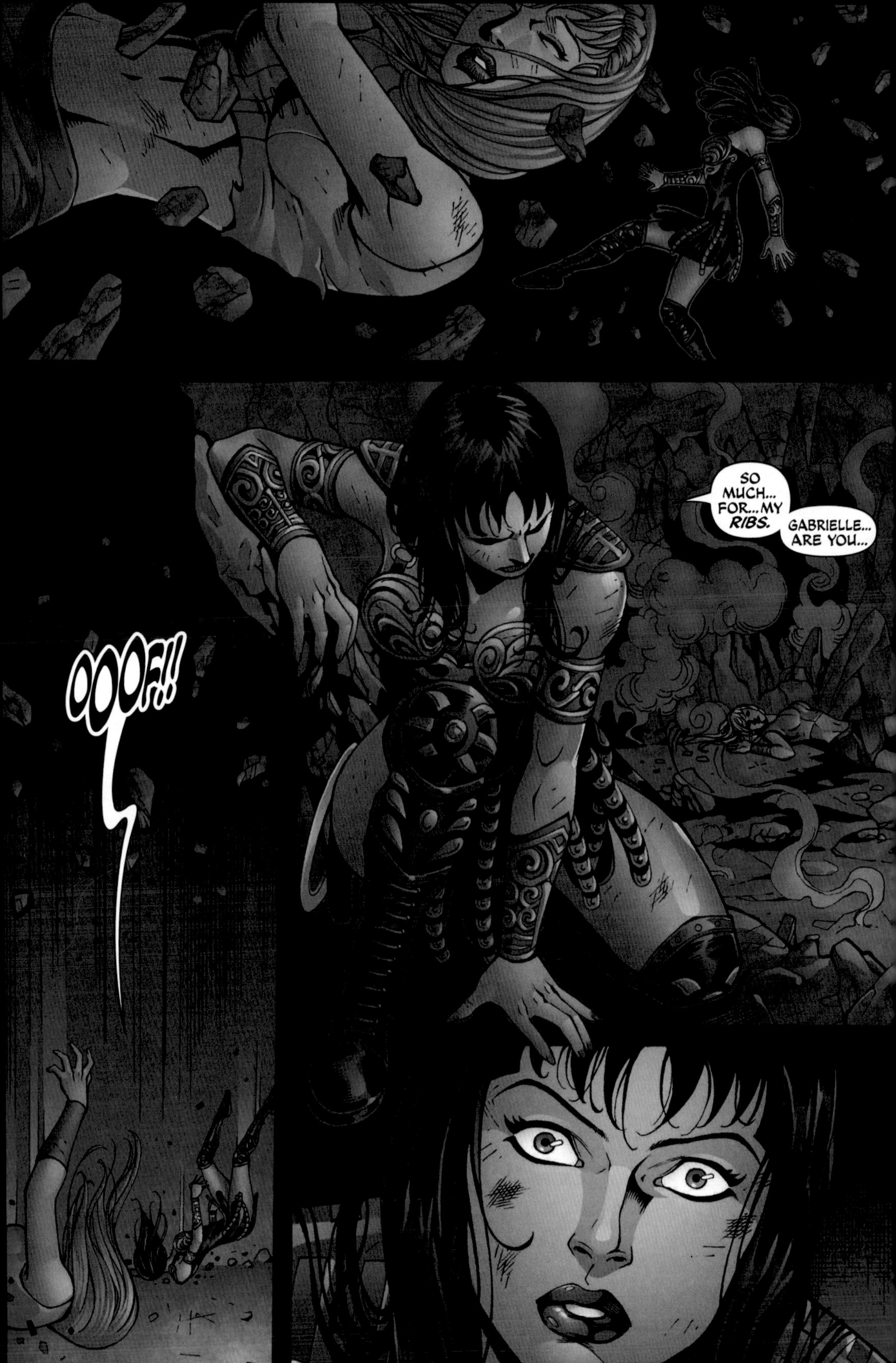
SO MUCH... FOR...MY RIBS.
GABRIELLE... ARE YOU...
OOOF!!

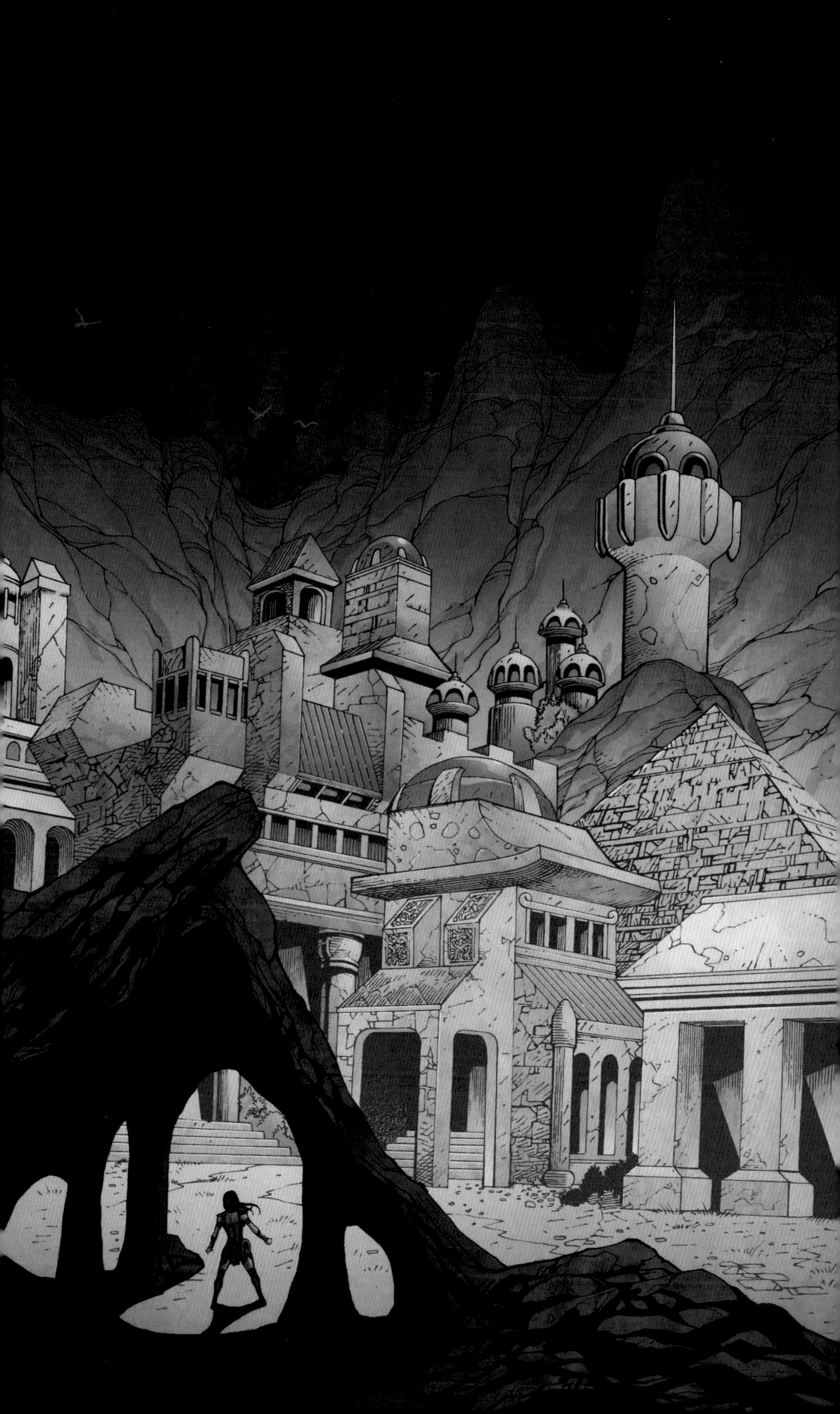

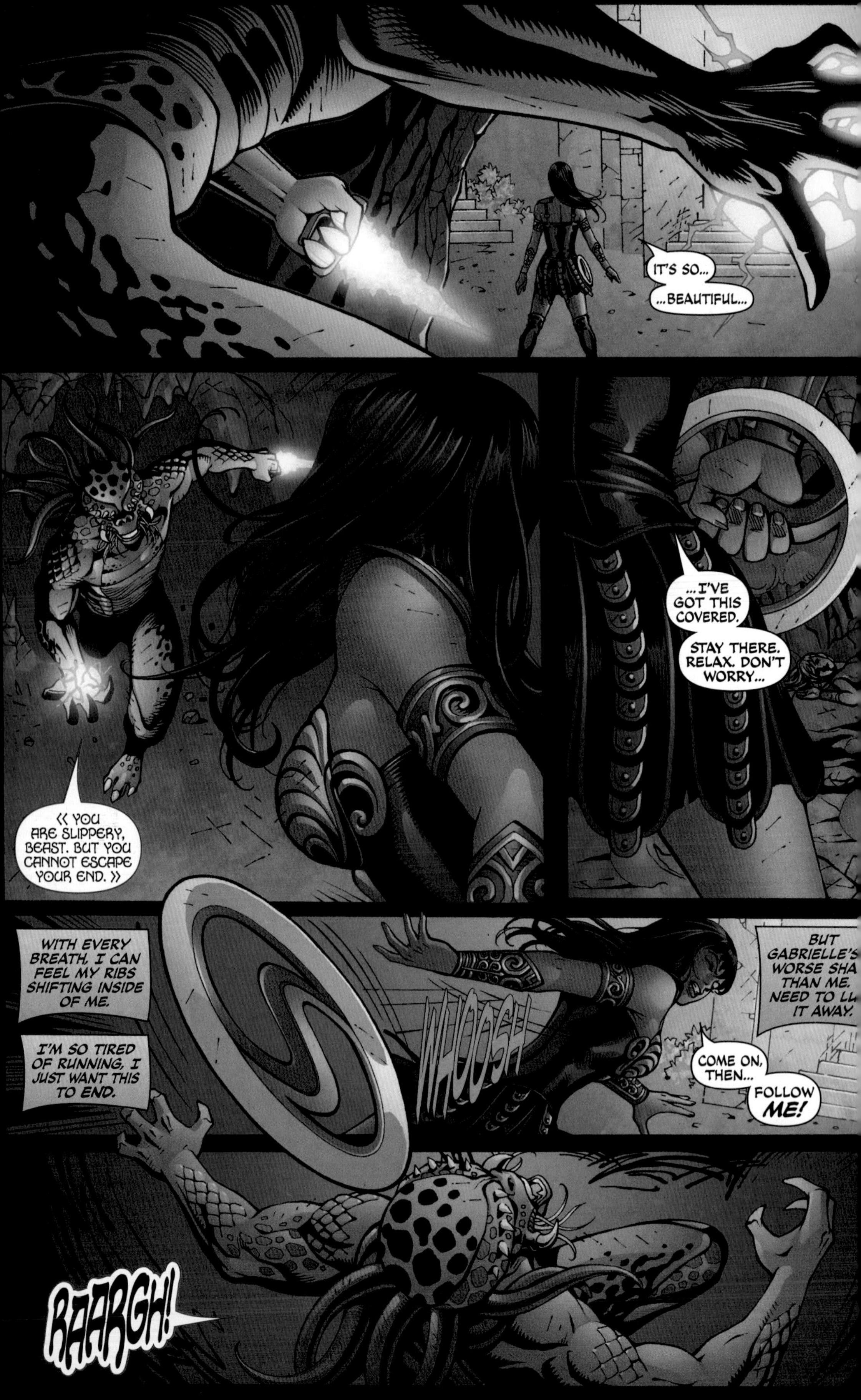
IT'S SO...
...BEAUTIFUL...
...I'VE GOT THIS COVERED.
STAY THERE. RELAX. DON'T WORRY...
<< YOU ARE SLIPPERY, BEAST. BUT YOU CANNOT ESCAPE YOUR END. >>
WITH EVERY BREATH, I CAN FEEL MY RIBS SHIFTING INSIDE OF ME.
I'M SO TIRED OF RUNNING, I JUST WANT THIS TO END.
WHOOSH
COME ON, THEN...
FOLLOW ME!
RAAARGH!

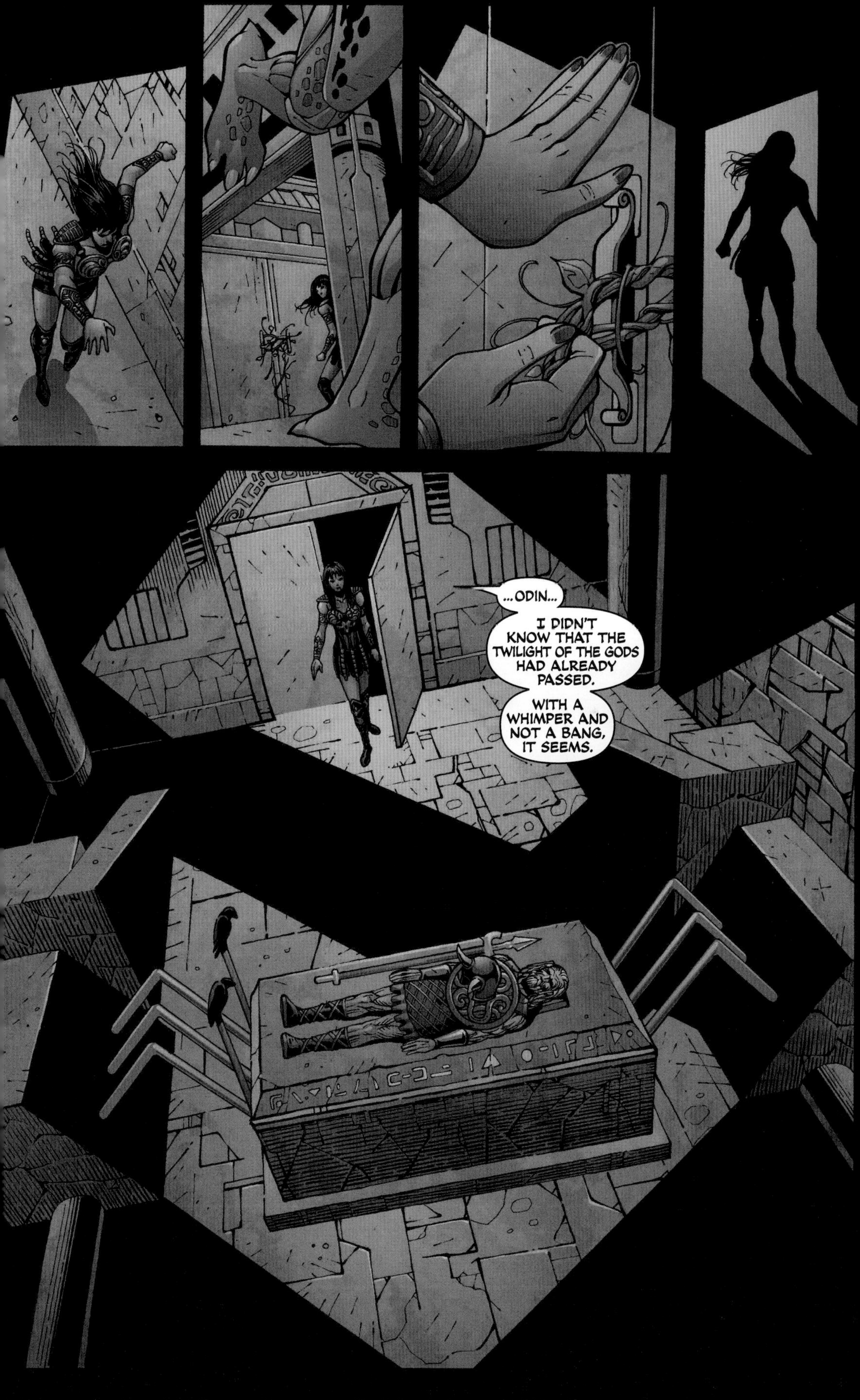
...ODIN...
I DIDN'T KNOW THAT THE TWILIGHT OF THE GODS HAD ALREADY PASSED.
WITH A WHIMPER AND NOT A BANG, IT SEEMS.

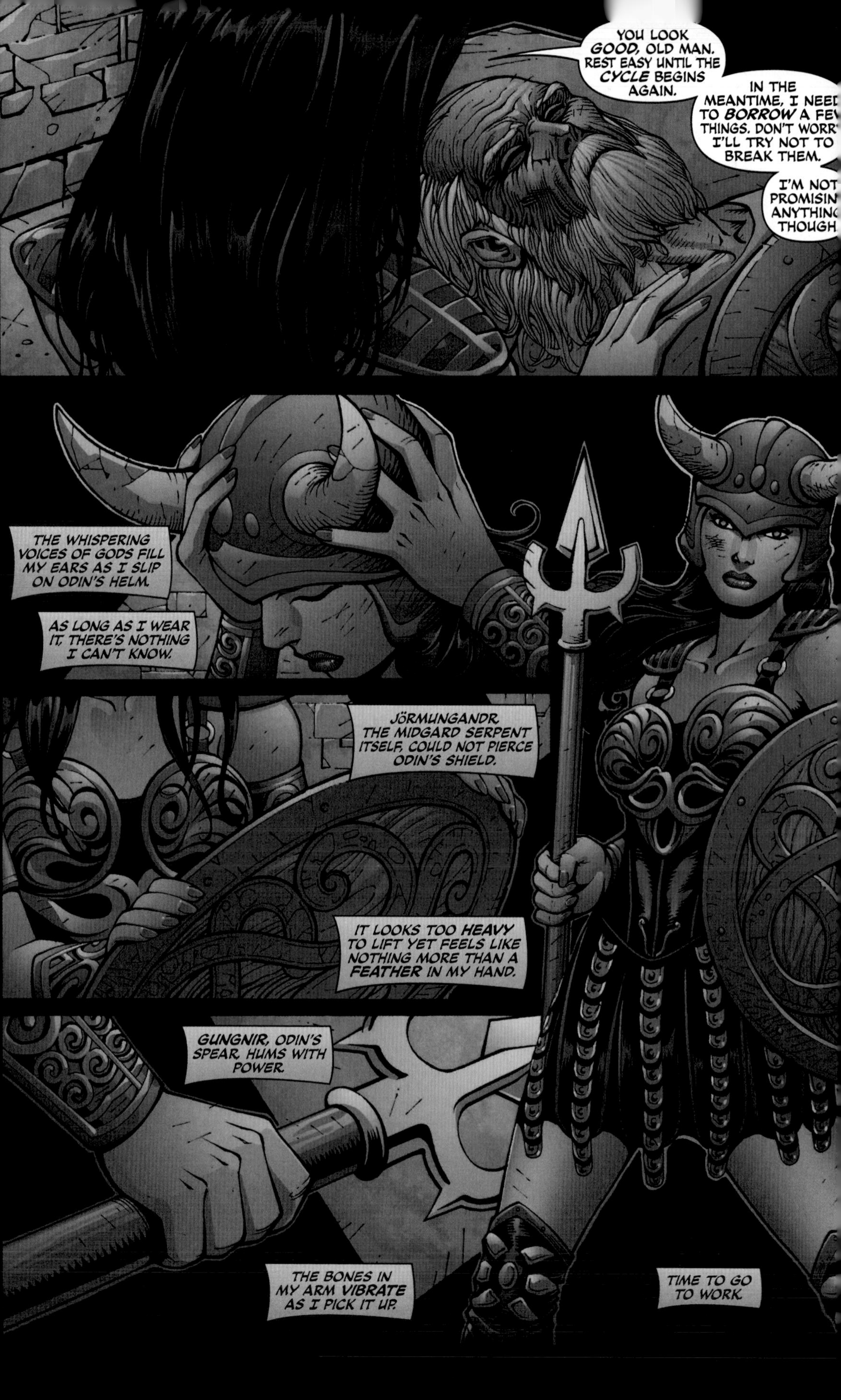
YOU LOOK GOOD, OLD MAN. REST EASY UNTIL THE CYCLE BEGINS AGAIN.
IN THE MEANTIME, I NEED TO BORROW A FEW THINGS. DON'T WORRY I'LL TRY NOT TO BREAK THEM.
I'M NOT PROMISING ANYTHING THOUGH
THE WHISPERING VOICES OF GODS FILL MY EARS AS I SLIP ON ODIN'S HELM.
AS LONG AS I WEAR IT, THERE'S NOTHING I CAN'T KNOW.
JÖRMUNGANDR, THE MIDGARD SERPENT ITSELF, COULD NOT PIERCE ODIN'S SHIELD.
IT LOOKS TOO HEAVY TO LIFT YET FEELS LIKE NOTHING MORE THAN A FEATHER IN MY HAND.
GUNGNIR, ODIN'S SPEAR, HUMS WITH POWER.
THE BONES IN MY ARM VIBRATE AS I PICK IT UP.
TIME TO GO TO WORK.

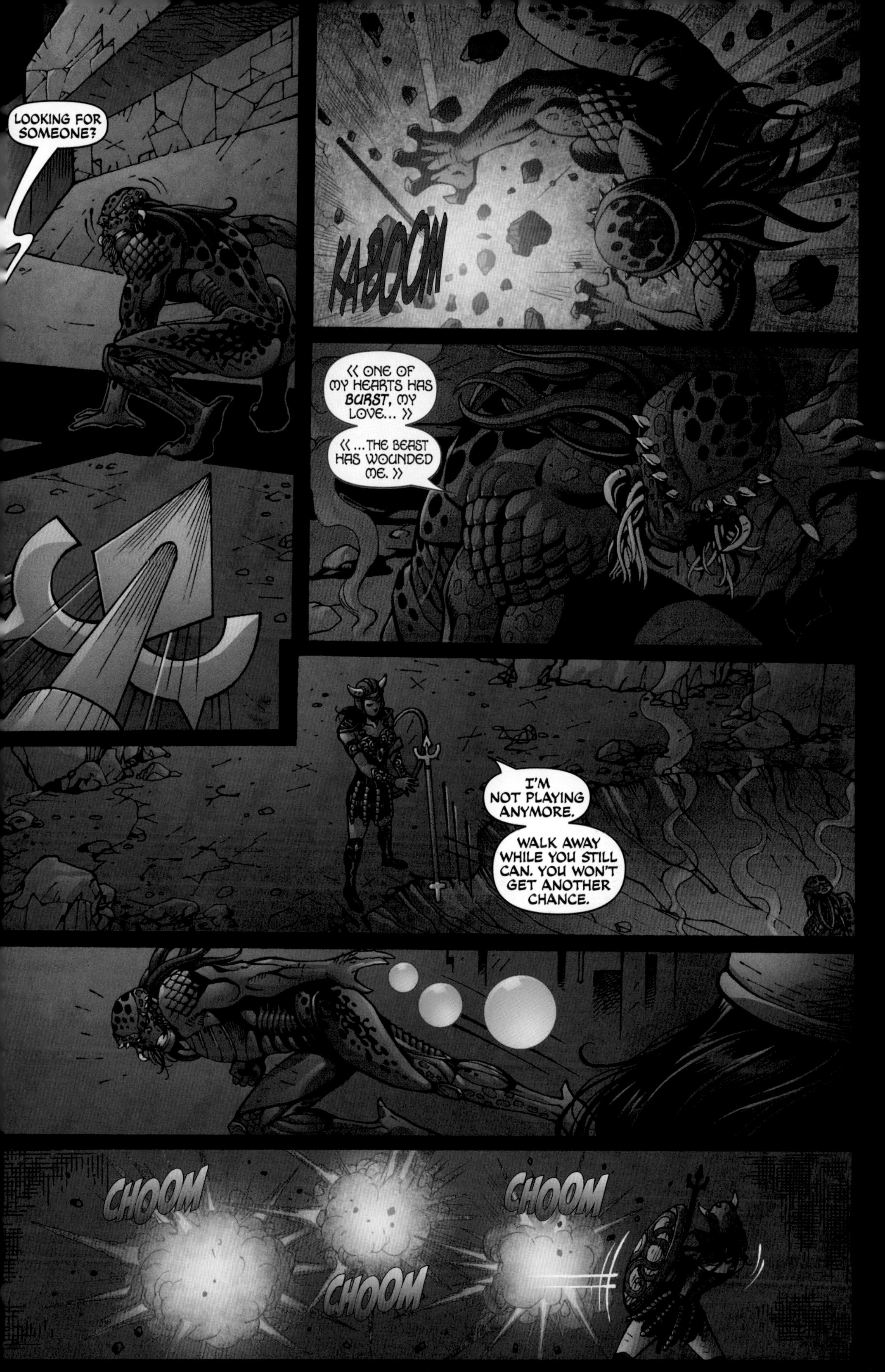
LOOKING FOR SOMEONE?
KABOOM
« ONE OF MY HEARTS HAS **BURST**, MY LOVE... »
« ...THE BEAST HAS WOUNDED ME. »
I'M NOT PLAYING ANYMORE.
WALK AWAY WHILE YOU STILL CAN. YOU WON'T GET ANOTHER CHANCE.
CHOOM
CHOOM
CHOOM

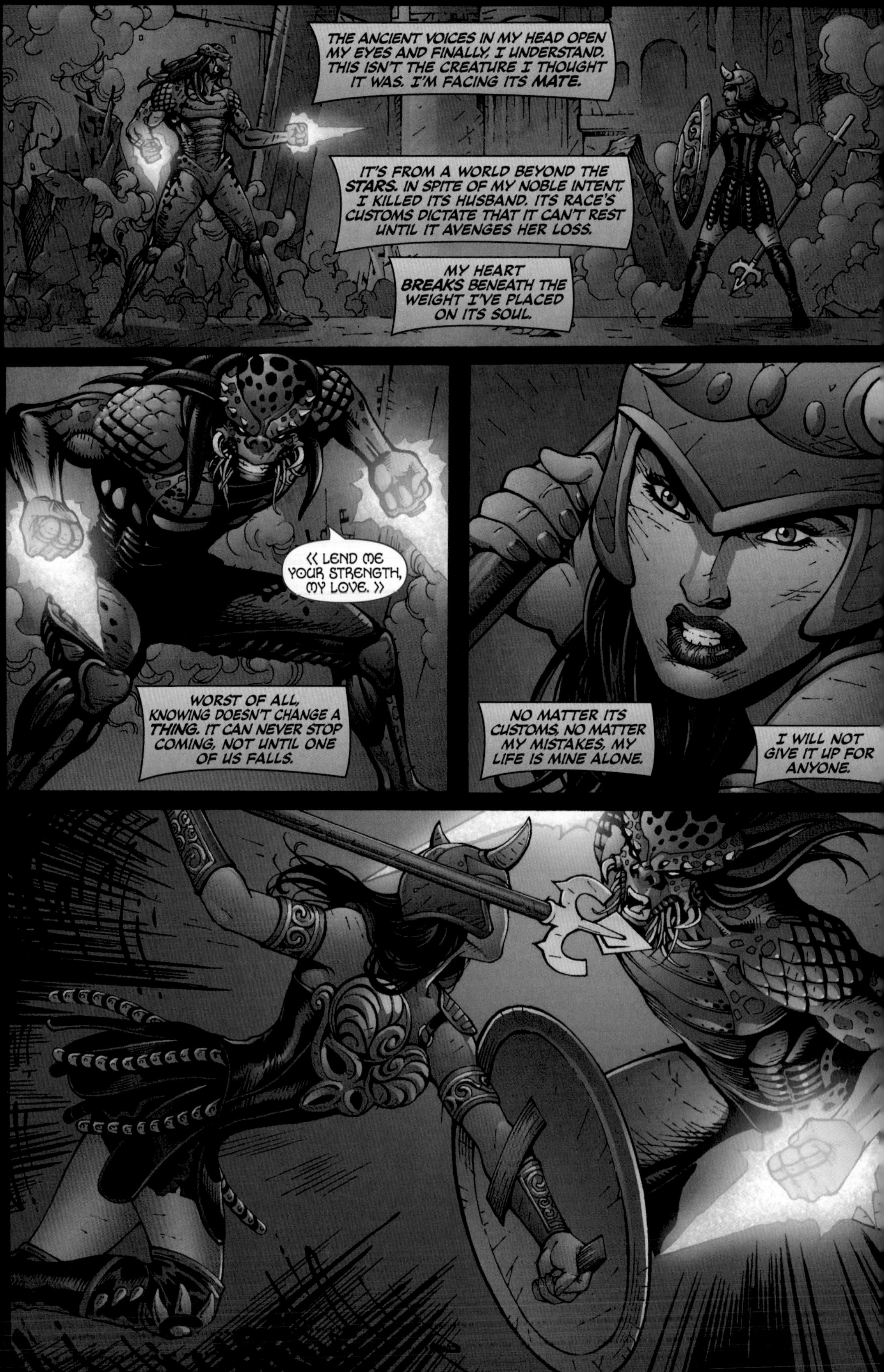
THE ANCIENT VOICES IN MY HEAD OPEN MY EYES AND FINALLY, I UNDERSTAND. THIS ISN'T THE CREATURE I THOUGHT IT WAS. I'M FACING ITS MATE.
IT'S FROM A WORLD BEYOND THE STARS. IN SPITE OF MY NOBLE INTENT, I KILLED ITS HUSBAND. ITS RACE'S CUSTOMS DICTATE THAT IT CAN'T REST UNTIL IT AVENGES HER LOSS.
MY HEART BREAKS BENEATH THE WEIGHT I'VE PLACED ON ITS SOUL.
«LEND ME YOUR STRENGTH, MY LOVE.»
WORST OF ALL, KNOWING DOESN'T CHANGE A THING. IT CAN NEVER STOP COMING, NOT UNTIL ONE OF US FALLS.
NO MATTER ITS CUSTOMS, NO MATTER MY MISTAKES, MY LIFE IS MINE ALONE.
I WILL NOT GIVE IT UP FOR ANYONE.

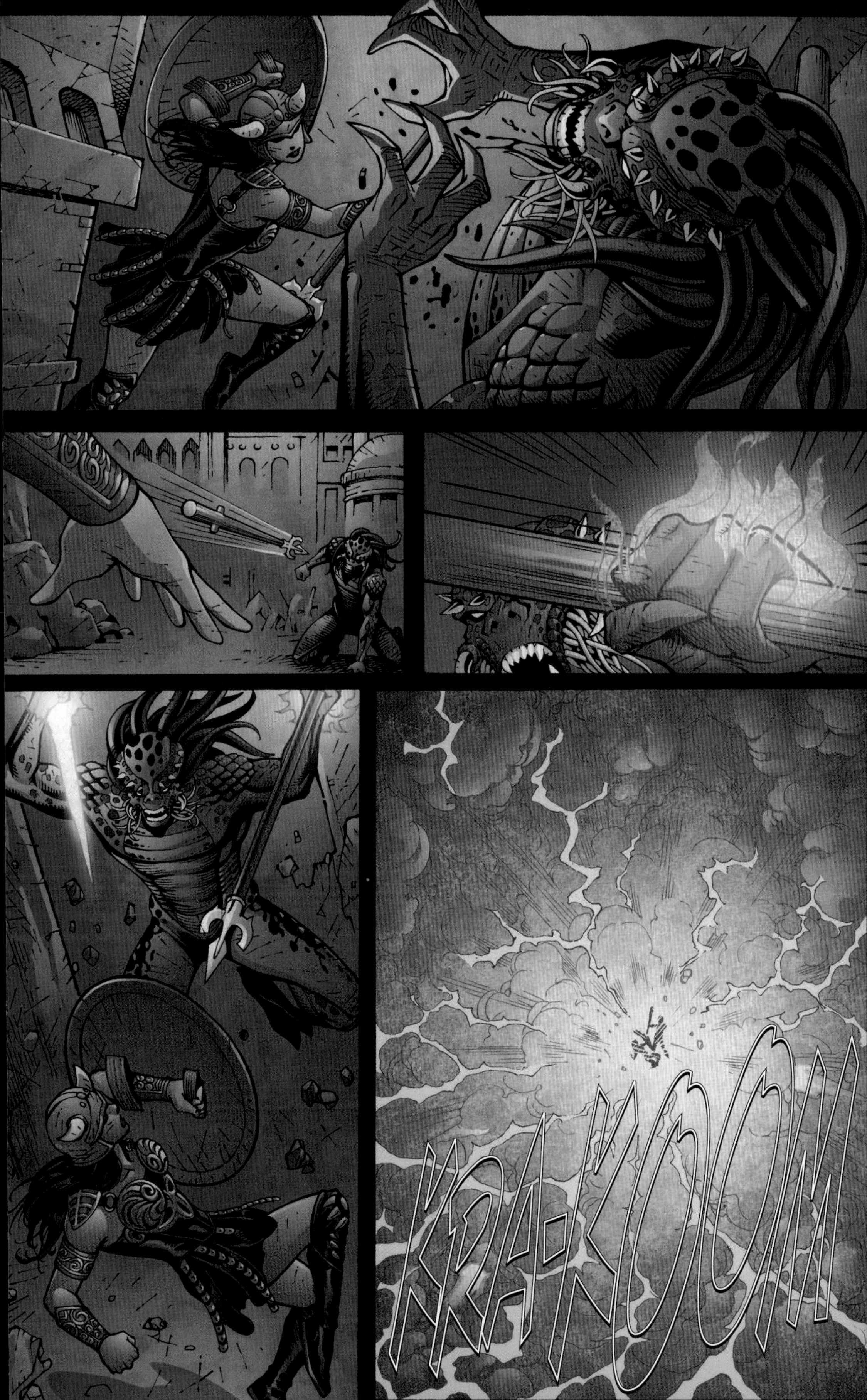
KRAKOOM

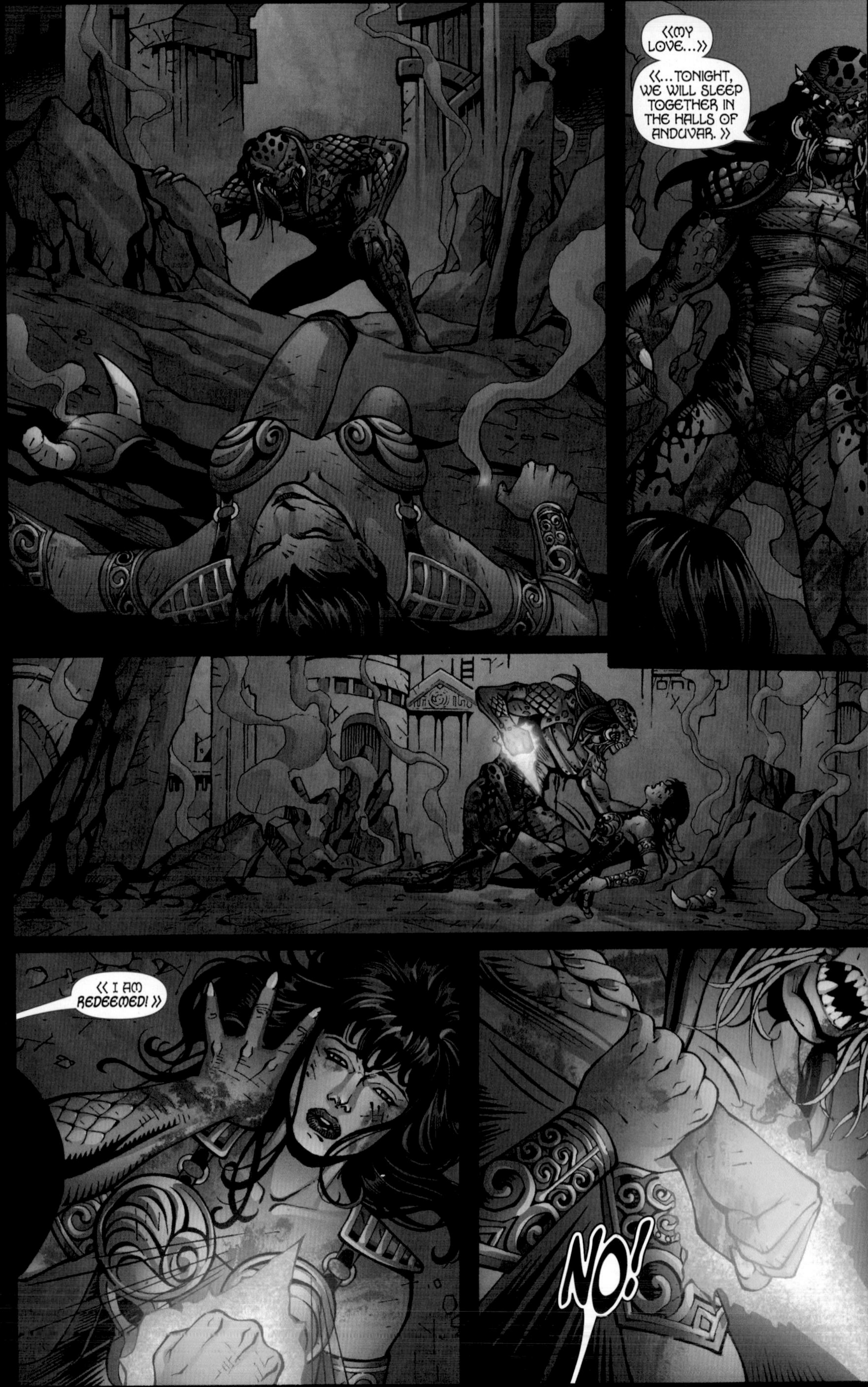

<<MY LOVE...>>
<<...TONIGHT, WE WILL SLEEP TOGETHER IN THE HALLS OF ANDUVAR.>>
<<I AM REDEEMED!>>
NO!

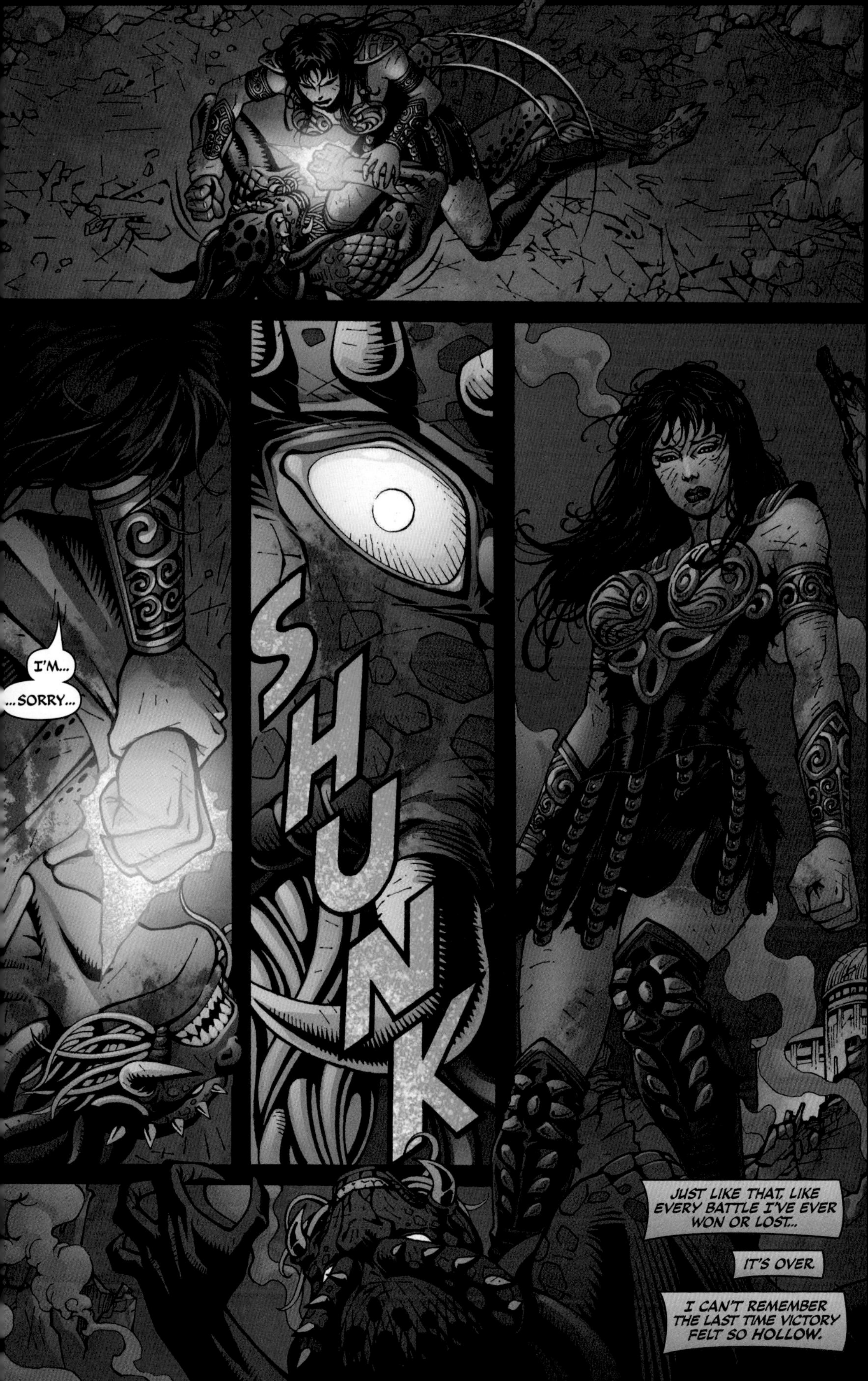
I'M...
...SORRY...
SHUNK
JUST LIKE THAT, LIKE EVERY BATTLE I'VE EVER WON OR LOST...
IT'S OVER.
I CAN'T REMEMBER THE LAST TIME VICTORY FELT SO HOLLOW.

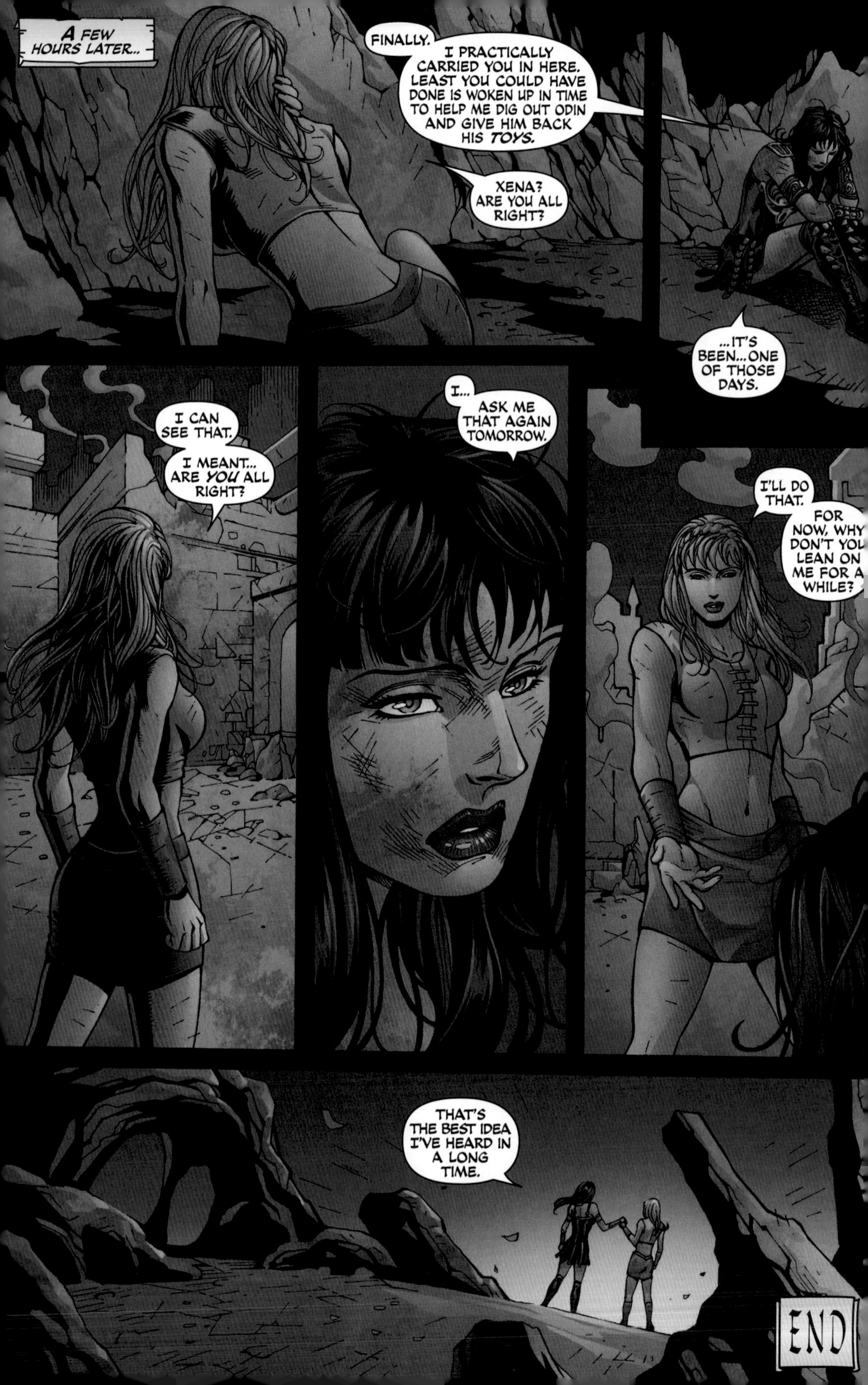
A FEW HOURS LATER...
FINALLY.
I PRACTICALLY CARRIED YOU IN HERE. LEAST YOU COULD HAVE DONE IS WOKEN UP IN TIME TO HELP ME DIG OUT ODIN AND GIVE HIM BACK HIS TOYS.
XENA? ARE YOU ALL RIGHT?
...IT'S BEEN...ONE OF THOSE DAYS.
I CAN SEE THAT.
I MEANT... ARE YOU ALL RIGHT?
I...
ASK ME THAT AGAIN TOMORROW.
I'LL DO THAT.
FOR NOW, WHY DON'T YOU LEAN ON ME FOR A WHILE?
THAT'S THE BEST IDEA I'VE HEARD IN A LONG TIME.
END

XENA

COVER GALLERY

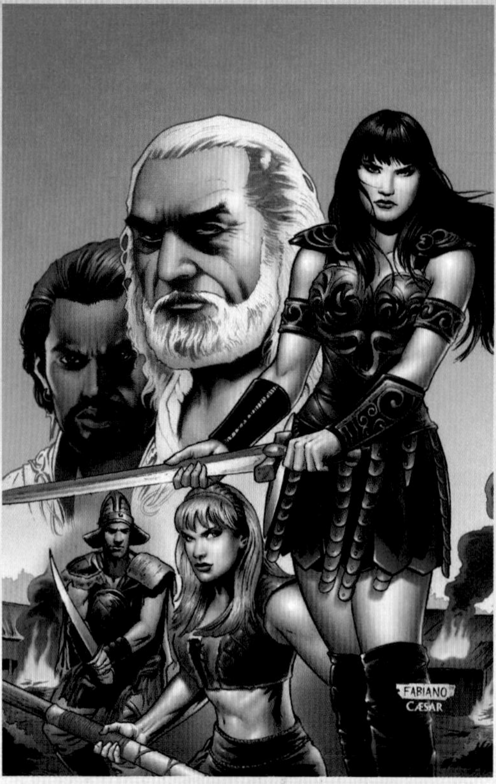
FABIANO
CÆSAR

CONTEST OF PANTHEONS, ISSUE ONE
Fabiano Neves

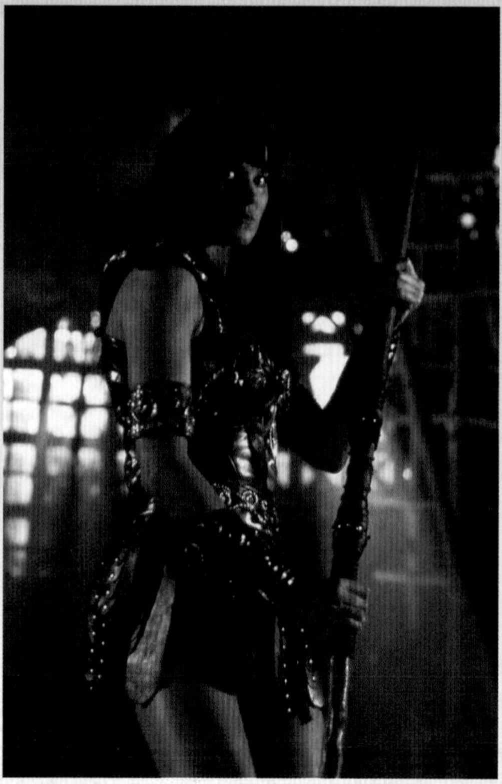

CONTEST OF PANTHEONS, ISSUE ONE
Photo Cover

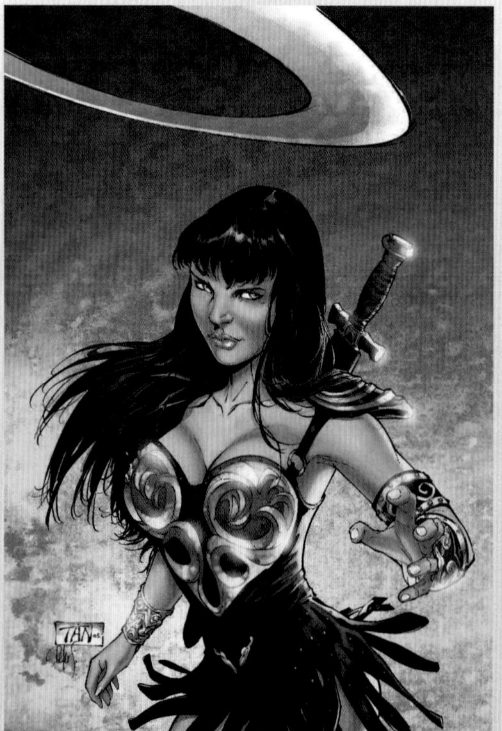

CONTEST OF PANTHEONS, ISSUE ONE
Billy Tan

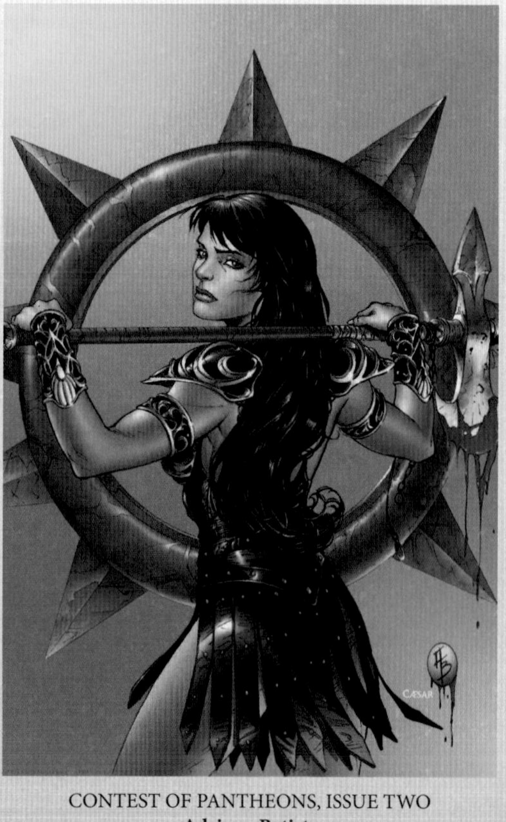
CÆSAR

CONTEST OF PANTHEONS, ISSUE TWO
Adriano Batista

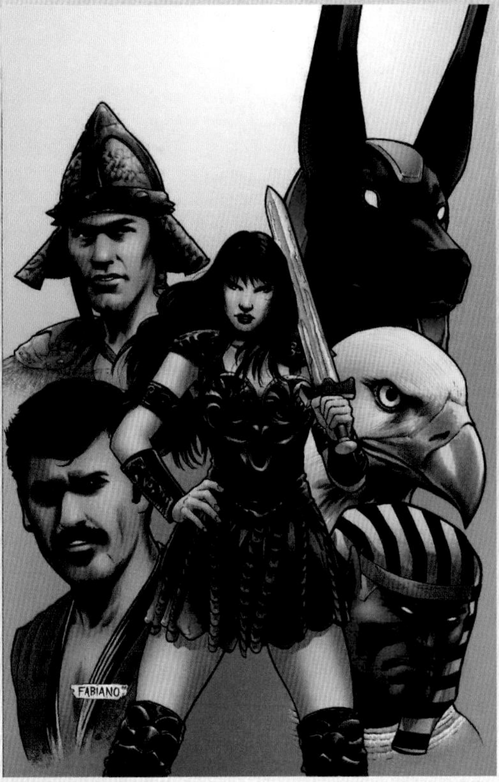
FABIANO

CONTEST OF PANTHEONS, ISSUE TWO
Fabiano Neves

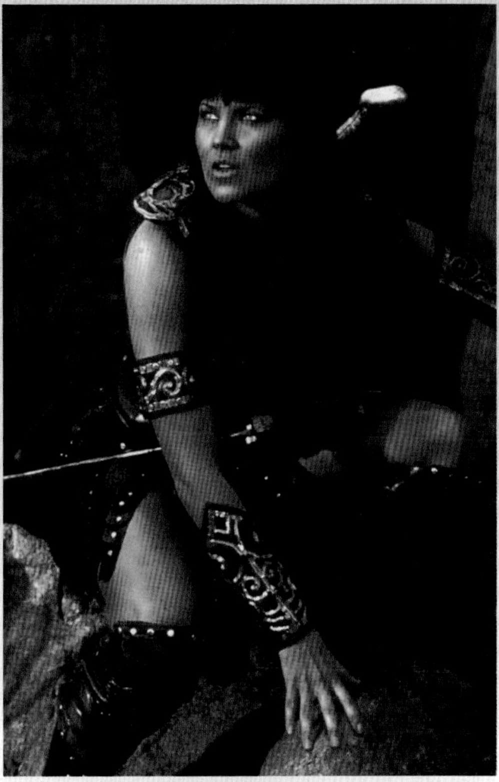

CONTEST OF PANTHEONS, ISSUE TWO
Photo Cover

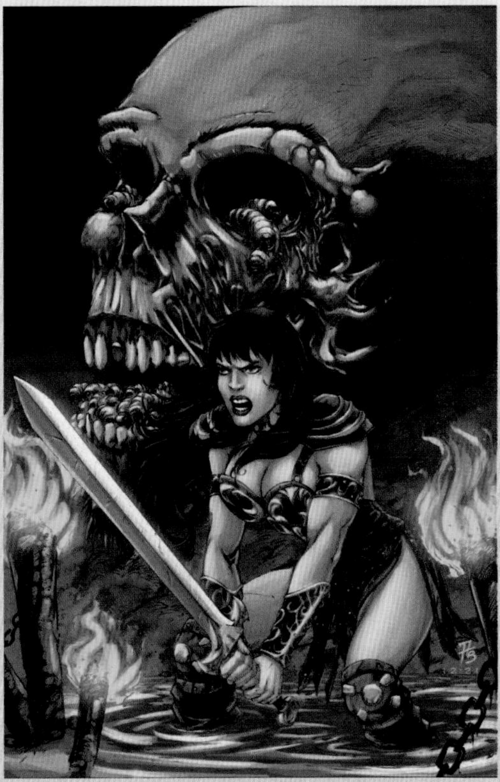

CONTEST OF PANTHEONS, ISSUE THREE
Adriano Batista

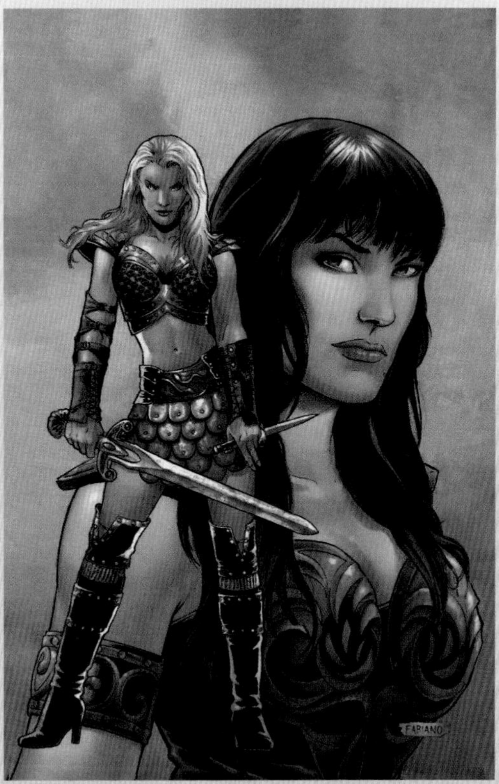
FABIANO

CONTEST OF PANTHEONS, ISSUE THREE
Fabiano Neves

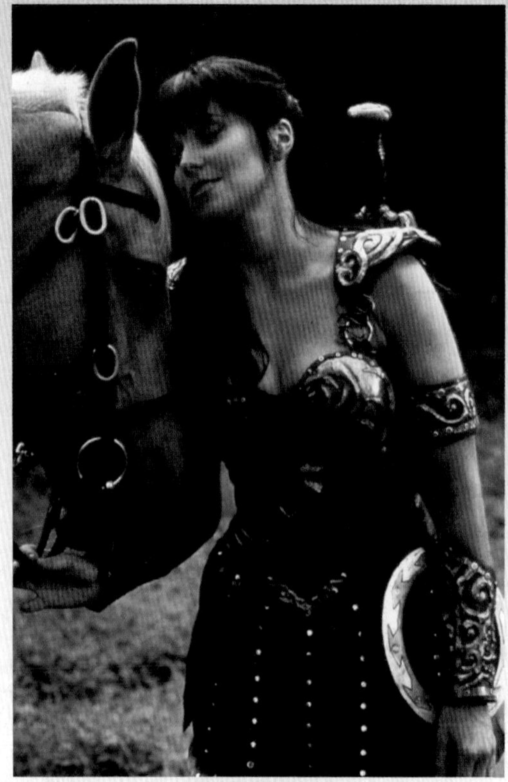

CONTEST OF PANTHEONS, ISSUE THREE
Photo Cover

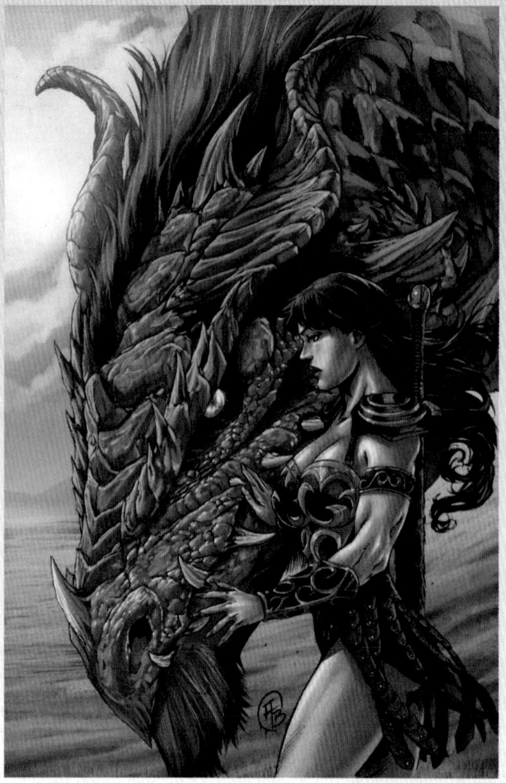

CONTEST OF PANTHEONS, ISSUE FOUR
Adriano Batista

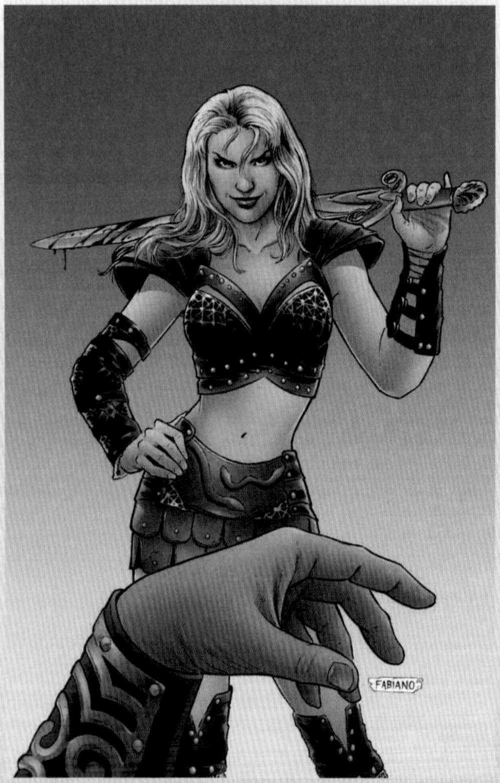
FABIANO

CONTEST OF PANTHEONS, ISSUE FOUR
Fabiano Neves

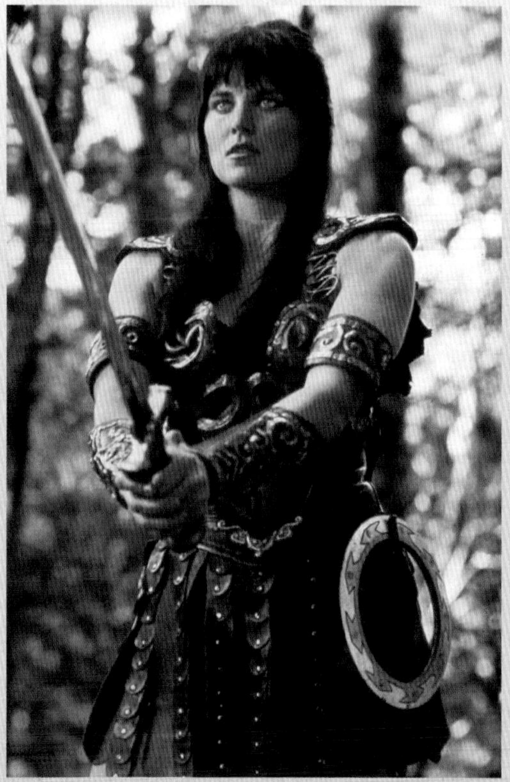

CONTEST OF PANTHEONS, ISSUE FOUR
Photo Cover

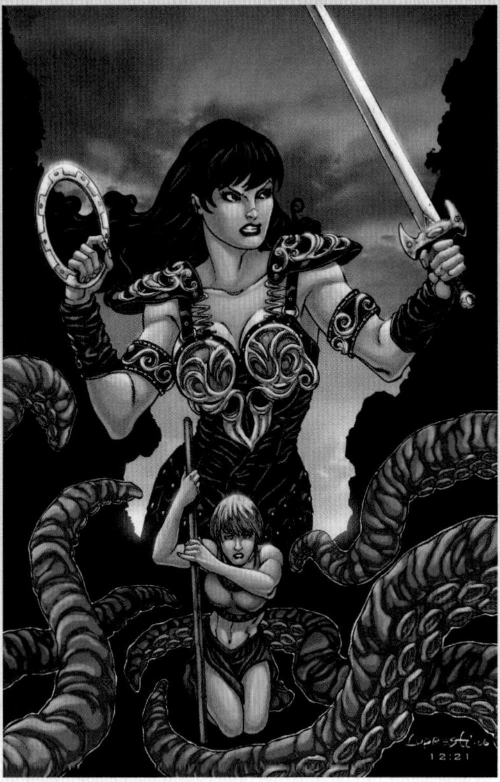
Lopresti 06
12:21

DARK XENA, ISSUE ONE
Aaron Lopresti

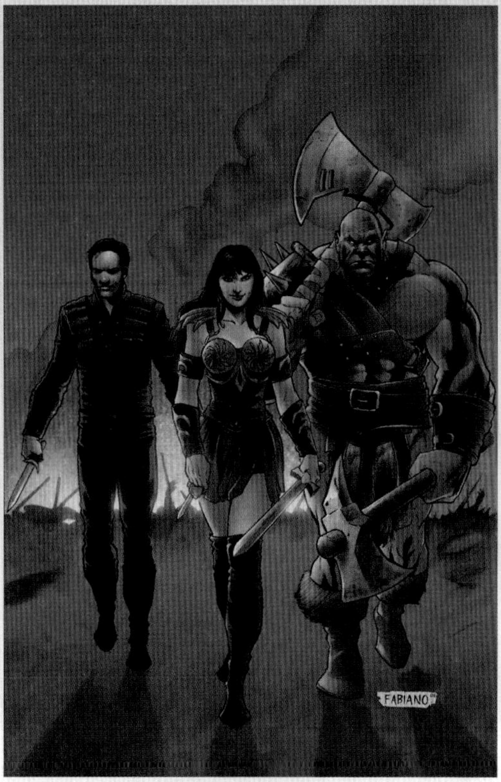
FABIANO

DARK XENA, ISSUE ONE
Fabiano Neves

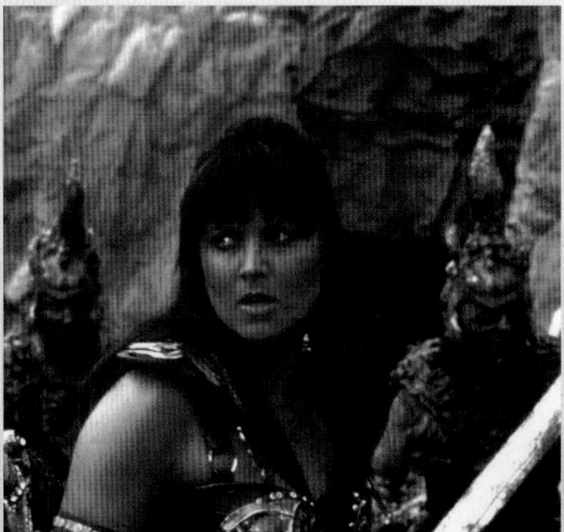

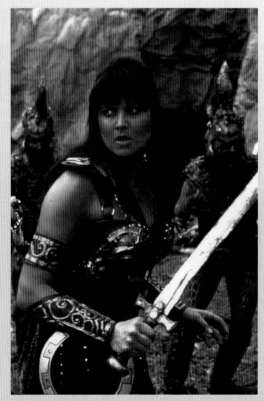

DARK XENA, ISSUE ONE
Photo Cover

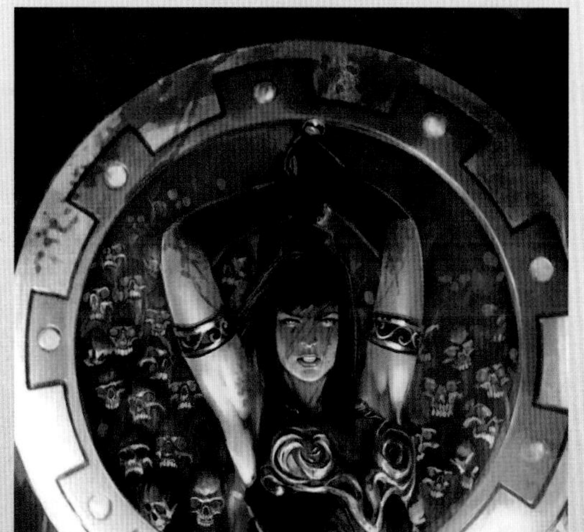

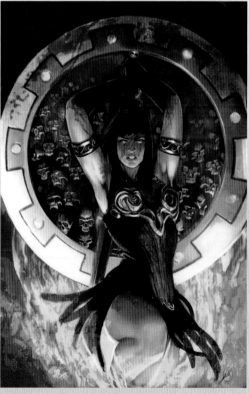

DARK XENA, ISSUE ONE
Stjepan Sejic

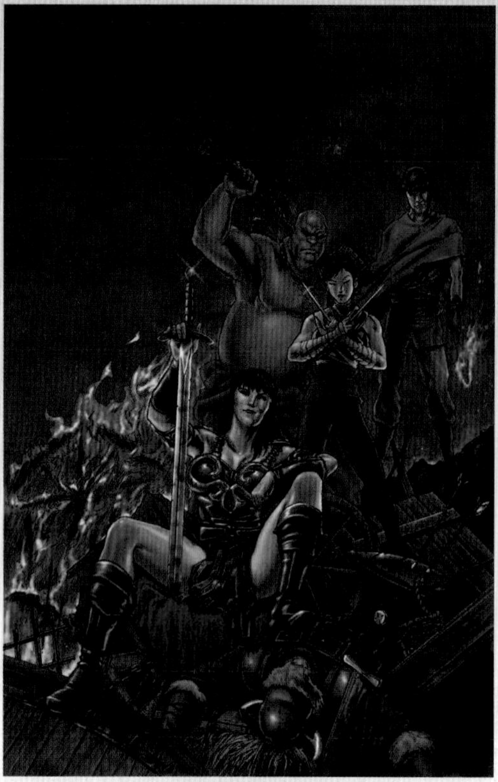

DARK XENA, ISSUE TWO
Jonathan Lau

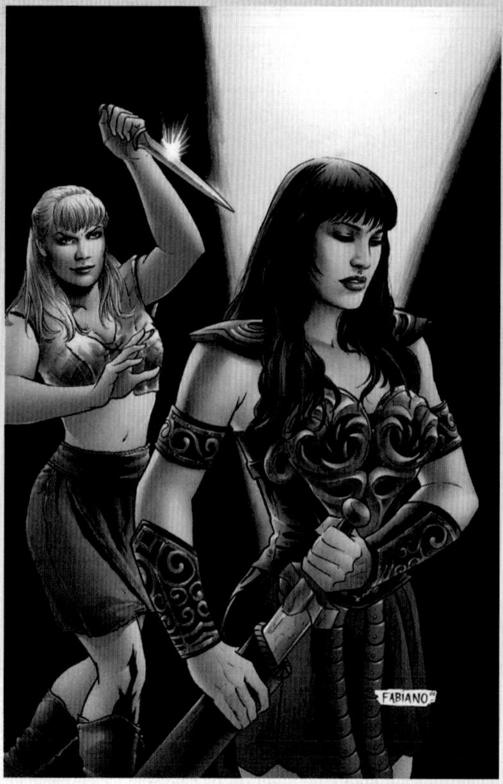
FABIANO

DARK XENA, ISSUE TWO
Fabiano Neves

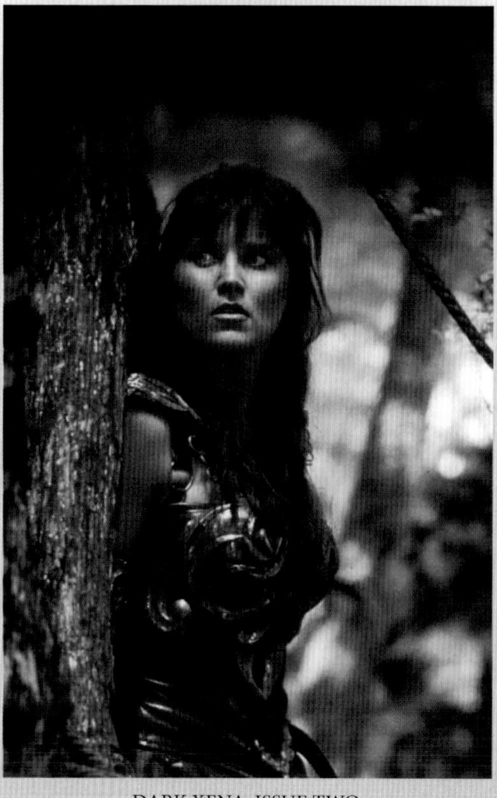

DARK XENA, ISSUE TWO
Photo Cover

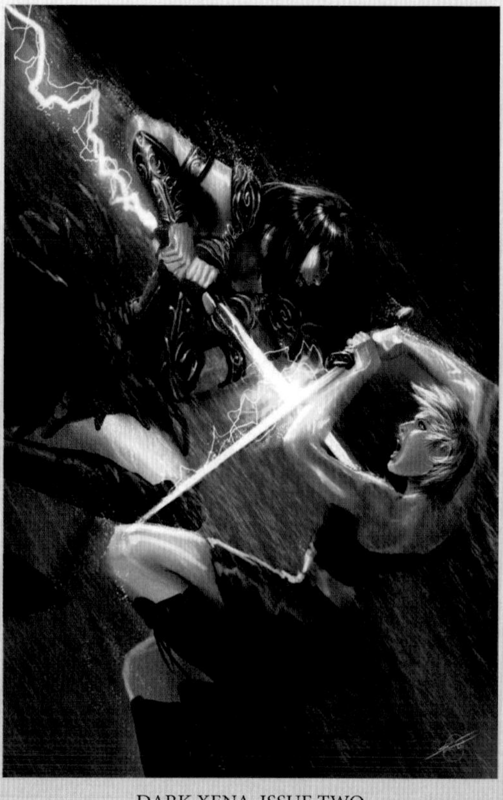

DARK XENA, ISSUE TWO
Stjepan Sejic

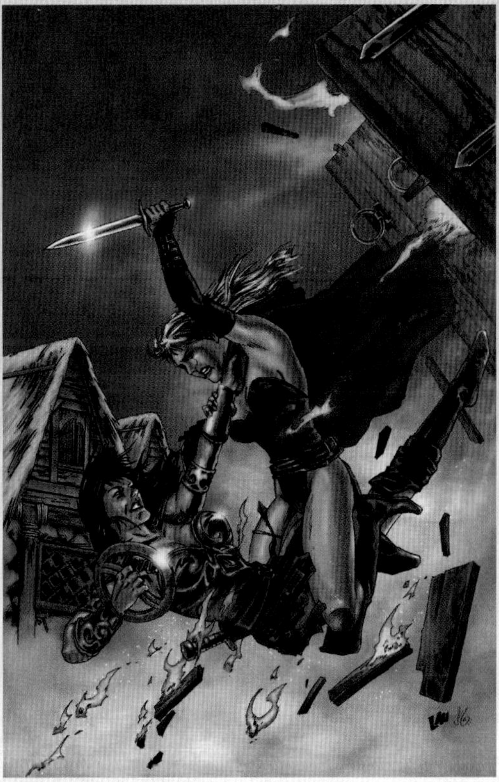

DARK XENA, ISSUE THREE
Jonathan Lau

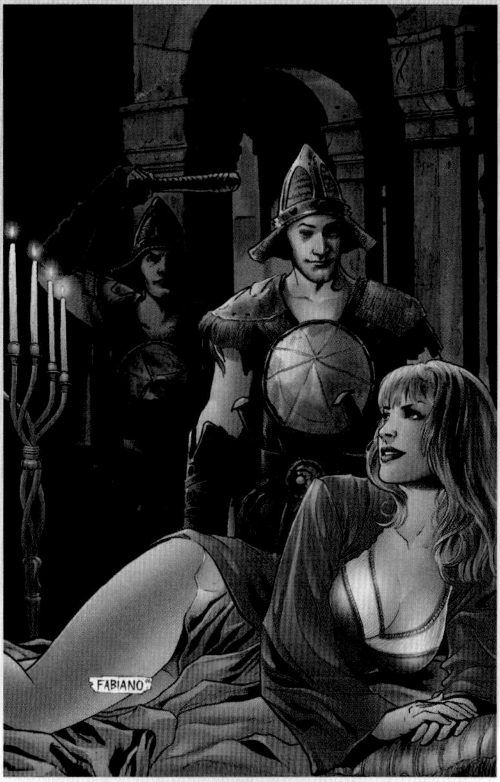
FABIANO

DARK XENA, ISSUE THREE
Fabiano Neves

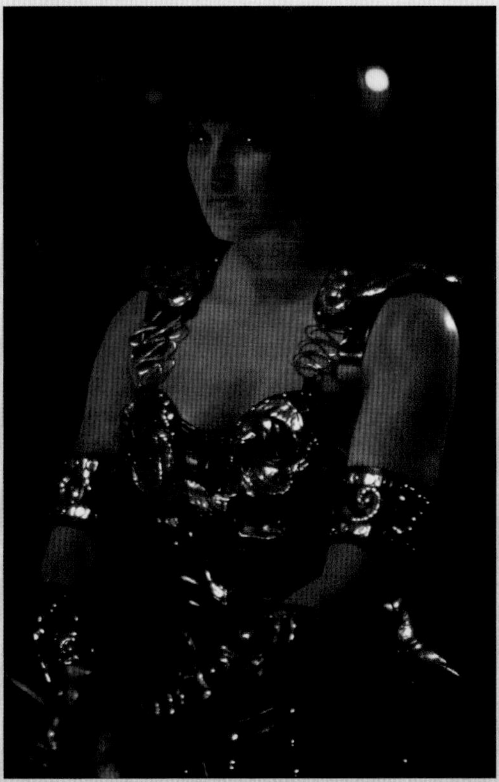

DARK XENA, ISSUE THREE
Photo Cover

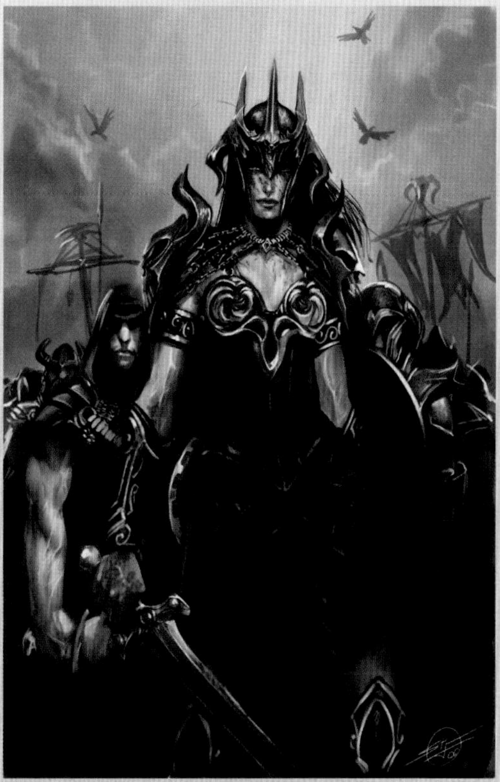

DARK XENA, ISSUE THREE
Stjepan Sejic

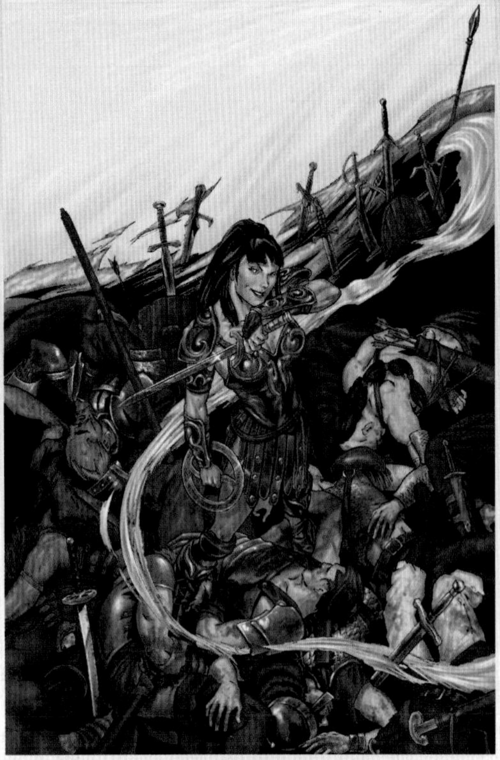

DARK XENA, ISSUE FOUR
Jonathan Lau

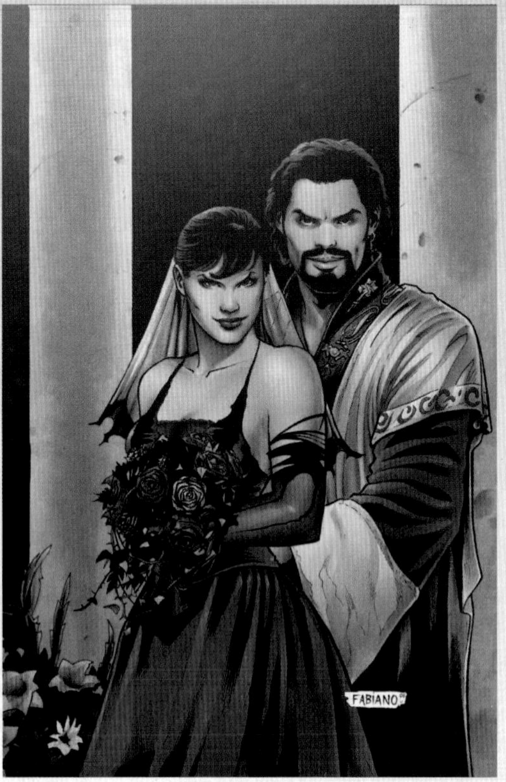
FABIANO

DARK XENA, ISSUE FOUR
Fabiano Neves

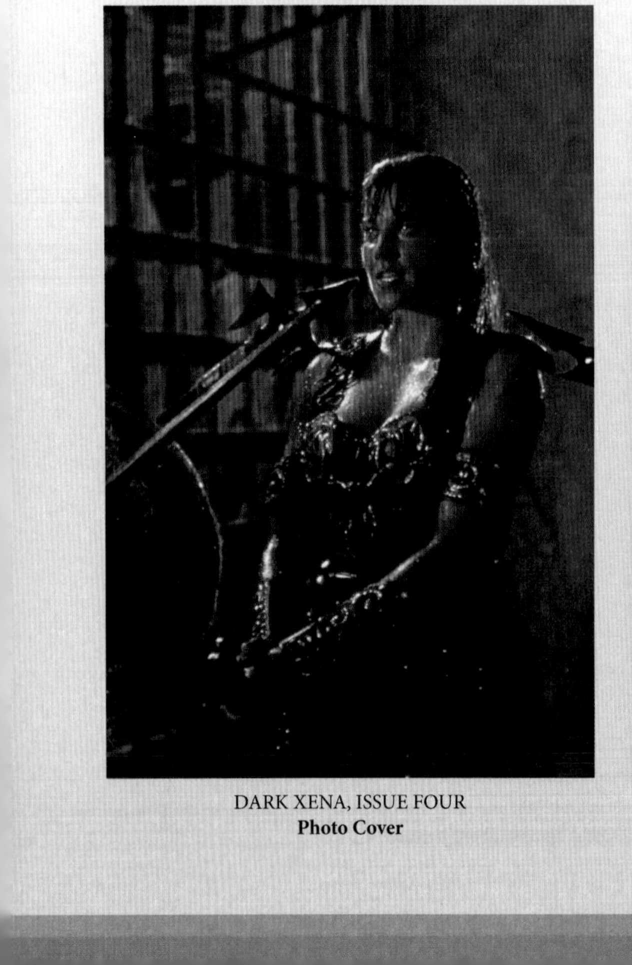

DARK XENA, ISSUE FOUR
Photo Cover

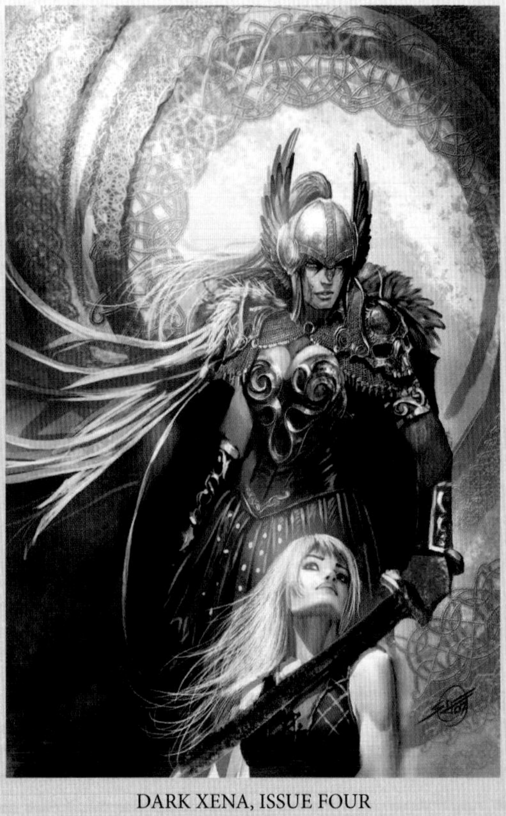

DARK XENA, ISSUE FOUR
Stjepan Sejic

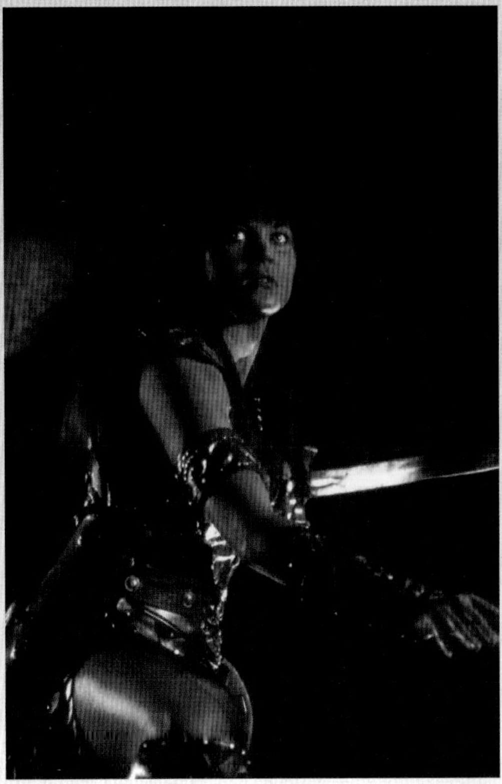

XENA ANNUAL
Photo Cover

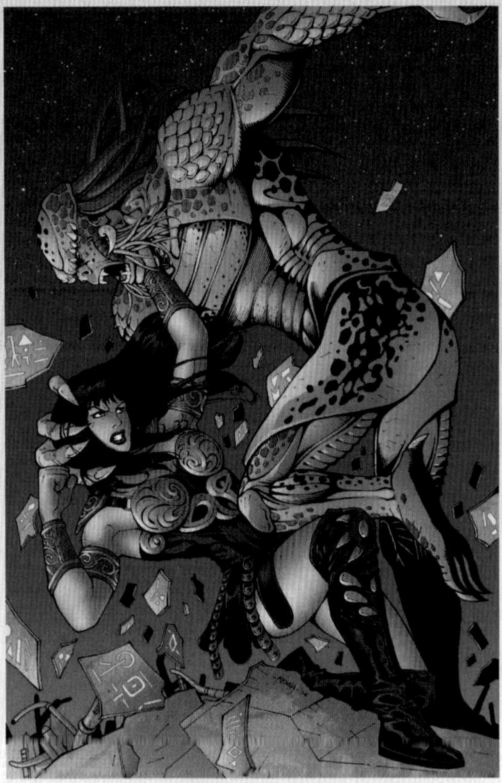

XENA ANNUAL
Noah Salonga

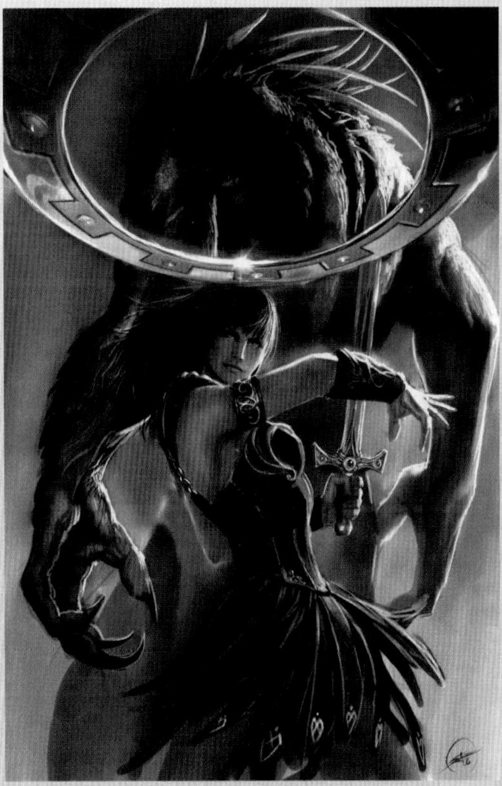

XENA ANNUAL
Stjepan Sejic

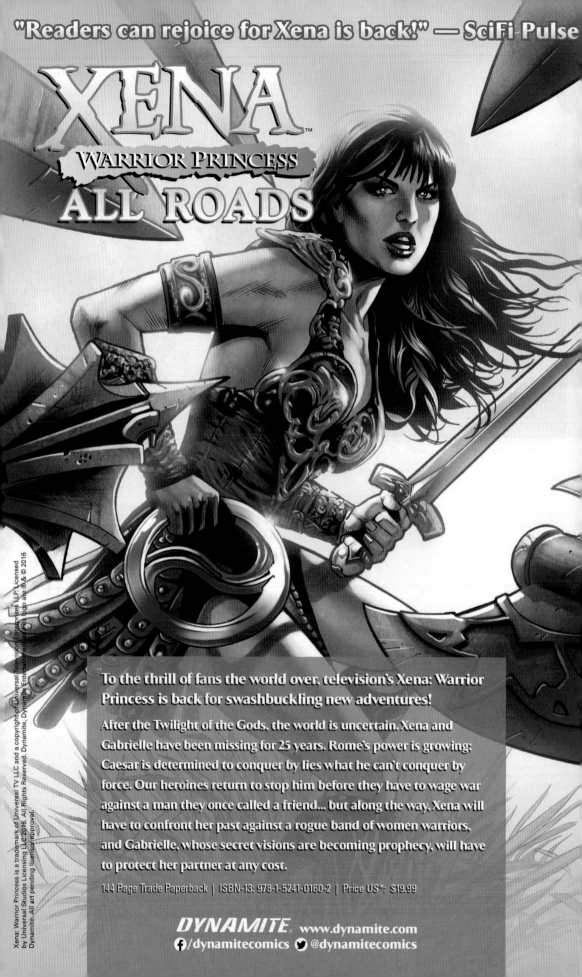